MW00532230

THE JEWISH WRITINGS

◆◆◆ THE ◆◆◆
JEWISH WRITINGS

Hannah Arendt

Edited by
Jerome Kohn and Ron H. Feldman

SCHOCKEN BOOKS, NEW YORK

Copyright © 2007 by The Literary Trust
of Hannah Arendt and Jerome Kohn
Introduction copyright © 2007 by Ron H. Feldman
Translation of "The Professional Reclassification of Youth," "A Guide for
Youth: Martin Buber," and "Some Young People Are Going Home" copyright ©
2007 by Catherine Temerson
Translation of "Against Private Circles," "Original Assimilation," and afterword
by Edna Brocke, " 'Big Hannah'—My Aunt," copyright © 2007 by James McFar-
land
Translation of "The Enlightenment and the Jewish Question," "The Gustloff
Trial," "The Jewish Question," "Antisemitism," "The Minority Question,"
"The Jewish War That Isn't Happening," "Between Silence and Speechlessness,"
"The Political Organization of the Jewish People," "Jewish Politics," "A Way
Toward the Reconciliation of Peoples," "The Crisis of Zionism," and "The
Eichmann Case and the Germans: A Conversation with Thilo Koch" by John E.
Woods, copyright © 2007 by Schocken Books, a division of Random House, Inc.

All rights reserved. Published in the United States by Schocken Books, a division
of Random House, Inc., New York, and in Canada by Random House of Canada
Limited, Toronto. Originally published in hardcover by Schocken Books, a division of Random House, Inc., New York, in 2007.

Schocken Books and colophon are registered trademarks of
Random House, Inc.

The afterword in this edition, " 'Big Hannah'—My Aunt," is translated from an
unpublished German essay by Edna Brocke, copyright © 2007 by Edna Brocke.
The essay "Stefan Zweig: Jews in the World of Yesterday," translated by Susannah Young-ah Gottlieb, is taken from *Hannah Arendt: Reflections on Art and Literature*, edited by Susannah Young-ah Gottlieb, copyright © 2007 by the Board of
Trustees of the Leland Stanford Jr. University, published by Stanford University
Press. All rights reserved.

Grateful acknowledgment is made to Peters Fraser & Dunlop Group Ltd. for permission to reprint an excerpt from "Where Are the War Poets?" from *The Complete Poems* by C. Day-Lewis. Copyright © 1992 by The Estate of C. Day-Lewis.
Reprinted by permission of Peters Fraser & Dunlop Group Ltd.
(www.pfd.co.uk) on behalf of the Estate of C. Day-Lewis.

Library of Congress Cataloging-in-Publication Data
Arendt, Hannah, 1906–1975.
    The Jewish writings / Hannah Arendt ; preface by Jerome Kohn;
introduction by Ron H. Feldman

    p. cm.
Includes bibliographical references and index.
ISBN 978-0-8052-1194-8
    1. Jews—History—1789–1945. 2. Jews—History—1945– .
3. Antisemitism. 4. Zionism. 5. Holocaust, Jewish (1939–1945)
I. Kohn, Jerome. II. Feldman, Ron H. III. Title.
DS125.A66 2007
305.892'4—dc22   2006044380
www.schocken.com

Book design by Peter A. Andersen
Printed in the United States of America
First Paperback Edition
2 4 6 8 9 7 5 3 1

CONTENTS

Contents

III

THE 1950s

Contents

IV
THE 1960s

PREFACE

A Jewish Life: 1906–1975

Jerome Kohn

"The human sense of reality demands that men actualize the sheer passive givenness of their being, not in order to change it but in order to make articulate and call into full existence what otherwise they would have to suffer passively anyhow."[1]

I deliberately begin with a quotation from *The Human Condition* (1958), unquestionably one of Hannah Arendt's most read, studied, and scrutinized works, and one in which there is hardly any mention of Jews, Jewish affairs, or Jewish history. Indeed, the only discussion that might be called "Jewish" takes place in the book's last chapter, "The *Vita Activa* and the Modern Age," in the penultimate section on "Life as the Highest Good." There Arendt shows a negative interest in the Decalogue: the way it "enumerates the offense of murder," she writes, "without any special emphasis, among a number of other transgressions," does *not* make "preservation of life the cornerstone of the legal system of the Jewish people." She goes on to distinguish "the Hebrew legal code" as occupying an "intermediary position . . . between pagan antiquity and all Christian or post-Christian legal systems," a position that "may be explicable by the Hebrew creed," she says, "which stresses the potential immortality of the people, as distinguished from the pagan immortality of the world on one side and the Christian immortality of individual life on the other."[2]

Although that important distinction is made in the only overtly "Jewish" passage in *The Human Condition*, I want to suggest that the sense of the first sentence I quoted from the same work—which makes the general claim that "the human sense of reality demands" all human beings to "actualize" the

"givenness of their being" lest "they . . . suffer [it] passively anyhow"—
cannot be fully grasped without recognizing its poignancy as originating in
Arendt's experience as a Jew living in the twentieth century. This is only one
example of how the "incidents of living experience," whether or not they are
stated explicitly,[3] lie at the root of Arendt's thinking and inform her writing
even at their most abstract level; yet it is an example with a certain priority,
since it deals with the human capacity for action, which initiated political theorizing in the first place, with Plato, and remains, at least for Arendt, its
essential or underlying subject (*subiectum*).

Hannah Arendt was born one hundred years ago in Hannover; when she
was three years old she moved with her family to Königsberg; at eighteen she
left home to study philosophy, Protestant theology, and Greek philology at
the universities of Marburg, Heidelberg, and Freiburg; four years later she
completed her formal studies with a dissertation on "The Concept of Love in
Augustine."[4] When still a child, however, she became aware of her Jewishness, not by having been told by her family that she was a Jew, but from the
antisemitic slurs of her schoolmates.[5] If her teachers made antisemitic
remarks she was instructed to stand up, leave the schoolroom, go home, and
report exactly what had been said, whereupon her mother would write a letter of complaint to the authorities in charge of such matters. On those occasions little Hannah had the rest of the day off from school, which, in her
words, "was marvellous!" On the other hand, she was not permitted even to
mention at home the slurs of children her own age, but was told to answer
them herself, unassisted. At an early age, and among her earliest Jewish
experiences, Arendt became versed in the ways of "paying back" the "striking blows"[6] of her peers by responding to them *as a Jew*, by asserting her
Jewishness. That act was first performed in childhood, and would be
repeated later in life, when it no longer had anything to do with the accustomed thoughtlessness of children.

From the beginning Arendt found being a Jew "special," but in no sense
"inferior." She "looked different" from her schoolmates, and, though a German national, she felt a part not of the German but of the Jewish people.
Almost half a century later, in a letter to Gershom Scholem included in this
volume, she wrote: "To be a Jew belongs for me to the indisputable facts of
my life, and I never wanted to change or disclaim anything about such facts."
Why? Not out of pride, or what Scholem had accused her of lacking,

namely, "love of the Jewish people," but out of "a basic gratitude for every-thing that is as it is; for what is *given* and not *made;* for what is *physei* [brought about naturally] and not *nomō* [brought about conventionally or legally]." Having been born a Jew was part of "the sheer passive givenness of [her] being," as was having been born a woman, and as was also, I suppose, the potentiality of her mind, the sheer capaciousness of her imagination. It was the latter that prompted her, at the age of fourteen, to take down from the shelves of the family library the works of Immanuel Kant. First she learned his philosophy, which influenced her tremendously, and later she followed his example by *daring* to think for herself.[7] It may be worthwhile to look at these three "givens" of Arendt's being, at their connections and disconnec-tions, in a little more detail.

The need to understand, probably the primary need of Arendt's life, can never be fulfilled by thinking alone. For the more the need "to understand whatever happens," as she once put it, "without doing anything"[8] is fed by thinking, the farther thinking reaches out for what is increasingly complex and difficult to understand, even for what defies thinking altogether.[9] In retro-spect it seems as if Arendt were bound one day to think about thinking itself, that is, to focus her thinking on the activity of the thinking ego, the condition sine qua non but not *per quam* of understanding. When she finally did so she found three things of vital concern to her: that the thinking ego withdraws from the world *in order* to think about what appears and happens in the world; that the activity of the thinking ego is an intense inner dialogue with itself, acting back upon itself; and that, in its pure activity, the thinking ego is "age-less, sexless, without qualities, and without a life story."[10] These three things imply three more things of particular concern to us: that the conditions of the activity of thinking—world-withdrawal and self-reflexivity—are utterly dis-tinct, indeed the opposite, from those of the modalities of active life (*vita activa*); that the thinking ego is not an identical *one* but a nonidentical *two*-in-one; and that the actualization of the power of the mind in the activity of thinking differs fundamentally from the actualization of the other "givens" of Arendt's being, that is, from becoming an identifiable woman, who is not "sexless" or "ageless" and has plenty of "qualities," and an identifiable Jew, whose "life story," as it turned out, is well worth telling and retelling.

But things are never simple with Hannah Arendt. Her womanhood may be said to have been first actualized, and also tested, when she fell in love—

literally into love—with Martin Heidegger. From her seat in the lecture hall in Marburg, she saw herself reflected in his eyes, not narcissistically as the object of his desire, but as the woman he had awakened, whom she had not encountered before. To her he wrote: "to be in love" *is* "to be pressed into one's own-most existence"; "*amo,*" he said, "means *volo ut sis* . . . I love you—I will you to be what you are." For him, in a more troubled vein, she wrote that their love "obliterated all reality, caused the present to shrivel," saying that "she felt as if everything were now slipping away, vanishing . . . with the hidden uncanniness of a shadow stealing across a path."[11] She was nineteen; Heidegger was thirty-six, married with two children, and embarked with his then friend Karl Jaspers on a revolution in philosophy. For Heidegger this meant following a path of thinking that sought to retrieve and bring to consciousness what had long been forgotten in the history of thought, in philosophy as well as the various branches of theoretical and practical knowledge. His thinking probed past thinking, going ever farther back through the history of thought in an effort to dislodge what was unthought at each of its stages. With the force of a magnet, Heidegger drew his students, none more than Arendt, to ask the first, last, and most fundamental question about the being of all entities, the source of thought itself, which the thinking ego in its ongoing, endless activity is not wont to ask—that is, not wont to risk silencing its own inner dialogue by hearkening to and heeding the call of being.

The "ontological difference" between entities and their being does not lead to an *understanding* of thinking's origin; on the contrary, it points beyond the subject-object distinction, beyond the separation of the entity that understands from anything that can be understood. The passion of Heidegger's teaching reveals no-thing, *no-thingness,* and caused his loving and most receptive student to experience the reality of the present, the world of existing things, the historical time in which strictly human events occur, and, it may be added, the biographical time in which human substance or character is formed,[12] as shadows disappearing across his paths of thinking. Three years later, in a work that no less than any other of her writings is embedded in her "living experience," Arendt attempted to understand the profound, never-to-be-forgotten, and in more ways than one vexed experience of loving a man whose life, as much as any man's has ever been, for better and worse, was spent in pursuit of one overriding thought, the meaning (as he first called it) or the truth (as he later called it) of being. This work is unique in Arendt's oeuvre, however, in that it is written from an artificially imposed distance, elaborately embroidered as an academic dissertation on Augustine, the philosopher who some fifteen hundred years earlier had distinguished forms of love: *appetitus* or craving, *cupiditas* or wrong desire, *caritas* or right desire, and neighborly love, love for those with whom one shares the world. As an analysis of Augustine's conception of love, Arendt's work is appropriately theological: all forms of human love lead to the love of God, for Augustine the eternal entity that alone can be enjoyed in and for itself (*frui*), and to attain which—to attain one's own future life—all temporal objects, including the world itself, are rightly to be used (*uti*). The work is also fraught with tensions, especially regarding neighborly love. How can one who is drawn out of the world by the love of God—let alone drawn beyond God by the thought of being—still live in the world and enjoy anything or love anyone within it? The Augustinian version of that question is tucked away at the end of a long scholarly footnote,[13] and is never answered; the fact that it is not answered, in my opinion, holds the key not only to Arendt's dissertation but also to the seeming paradox of her changed but lasting love for Martin Heidegger.

But what of her Jewishness? It is that which chiefly concerns us here. We have seen that Arendt considered her Jewishness, the way she appeared to others, a "given" of her being which she never wanted "to change or disclaim"; and also that she was called upon to defend her Jewishness as soon as she discovered, through a form of antisemitism, that she was a Jew. Perhaps defending herself as a Jew may be seen as an act inspired by "gratitude" for the very gift that others denigrated, or perverted, or attempted to rob her of altogether. Be that as it may, neither gift nor gratitude made her Jewishness "articulate," or called it "into full existence," in anything like the sense that her womanhood was articulated in the experience of love,[14] or that the potency of her mind fully existed in the activities of understanding—which for Arendt included impartial and communicative judging in addition to thinking. Although some Jews may "actualize" their Jewishness in their religious creed and beliefs, Arendt is not among them. Is there another dimension of human being, as real as love and understanding, but as distinct from them as from religious obervance? Is there a dimension of our existence in which we as plural beings are capable of spontaneously acting into the world, beginning something new and changing the world, and by the same token making manifest, in our absolute distinctness from every other human being, *who* we are? Of course we all know that for Arendt there is such a dimension, and that it is the dimension on which the entire realm of politics—of what she means by politics—and political life depends.

But knowing something is never the same as understanding it. There is, moreover, prior to political considerations, though in her case not unrelated to them, the question of what being a Jew means to Arendt. There are times when an anecdote or joke can illuminate a difficult question, if only by showing what its answer is not. Arendt once asked a student who did not look Jewish but had a decidedly Jewish surname about his "background." Assuming he knew what she was getting at, he responded, with a slight sense of embarrassment, that his father, whose family was Jewish, was raised as a Jew, but that his mother, whose family was French and Scottish, was raised as a Christian Protestant. As a result of his being "half Jewish," as he put it (if even that, in view of his non-Jewish mother), his religious education had been practically nil, gratuitously adding that, if anything, he had an aesthetic predilection for Roman Catholic masses. Arendt looked at her student for what seemed to him an interminable time—though it probably lasted less than twenty seconds—with numbing incredulity, before abruptly changing the subject. About six months later, when Rosh Hashanah came around, the student found himself again with Arendt. She asked him if he were going to celebrate the holiday, and when he said that he had no plans to do so, she said, "Well, anyway, I want to wish a happy New Year . . . to the Jewish half of you." They both laughed, he somewhat uneasily. But he never again referred to himself as "half Jewish." Arendt's joke opened his eyes to the fact that neither his mixed heritage, nor Christian mother, nor lack of a religious upbringing altered what it means to be, not half a Jew, but a Jew at all—a member, willy-nilly, of the Jewish people. She saw through her eyes, and the eyes of the world she knew, what all along he had been looking at narrowly and partially from the shelter of his own singular point of view. She judged his insularity, and communicated her judgment in a way that filled her student with a sense of being liberated from it.

As this volume bears ample if incomplete testimony,[15] Hannah Arendt probably wrote more about Jewish affairs in general than about any other topic. I want to share with readers the phenomenon that struck me when finally, after months stretching into years of searching out, sifting through, and compiling these writings, I was able to step back and reflect on the collection as a whole. What struck me then was the dramatic and in the end ironic—Socratically ironic—trajectory these essays and articles trace in the thought and life of a Jewish woman who was born in Germany in 1906 and died in America in 1975.

Arendt's experiences as a Jew may be said to have five principal phases. There is, first—while in her twenties, when blackening clouds of anti-semitism were gathering in the sky over Germany—Arendt's initial interest in the story of German Jewry. The word "story" seems preferable to "history" since Jewish history, either in its absence or presence, is the central concern of the first essay published here, "The Enlightenment and the Jewish Question." The term "Jewish question" in this context refers to the problematic situation of an identifiable people living in a land that is not their land but that of another people.[16] The story Arendt tells is of the status of Germany's Jews mainly from the seventeenth century on, of how that status changed from one of physical segregation to—in the wake of the French Revolution, the Declaration of the Rights of Man, and more proximately Prussia's defeat by Bonaparte in 1807 and the subsequent French occupation—one of civil emancipation. It is clear to Arendt that the Emancipation Edict of 1812 did not, and was never intended to, preserve the identity of the Jews as a people, and therefore did not introduce a new Jewish presence into German political life—such as it was. On the contrary, earlier Enlightenment thinkers—Gotthold Lessing on one side and his friend Moses Mendelssohn on the other—viewed the possibility of Jewish emancipation as the long-awaited opportunity for Jews to be recognized as human beings *like* other human beings. In other words, for the Enlightenment mentality the purpose of emancipating Jews was to grant them the human rights enjoyed by non-Jews, and to "improve" their lot by erasing their determinative history. Henceforth their "unfortunate" history of persecutions and pogroms as Christ killers, stretching back to the Middle Ages, would be submerged and forgotten in future history, which was envisioned as the irresistible progress of mankind.[17] What would be new was that Jews, as fully equal members of mankind, as rightful sharers in universal reason—the essence of humanity to the Enlightenment—would now be free to participate in that history-to-be.

J. G. Herder, whom Arendt sees as a proto-Romantic, was critical of the principles of the Enlightenment. For him the formation (*Bildung*) and hence the toleration of Jews depended on the restoration of their history; "the irrevocability of all that has happened" shows, first, that Jews are not the same as other peoples, and, second, that for Jews to understand their history—by which he meant thinking it through from its beginning—is the sole condition of their being liberated from it. First the emancipation and then the assimilation of Jews, their education and formation, their "humanization," will be the result of a political decision sharply to be distinguished from the Enlightenment principle of *Selbstdenken*, an independent thinking in what for Jews, without their history, Herder sees as a vacuum. That vacuum will be filled when Jews, understanding the uniqueness of their history and importing it into the present, become separated from their past. In the separation provided by their understanding, Jews will realize that the destruction of the Temple had already, two thousand years before, destroyed their historical continuity as a people. Jews are indeed a historical people, who by understanding their "exceptional" history will realize they are no longer God's "chosen people." Their "Palestine," and all that word may signify apart from a geographical territory, can then be theirs wherever they find themselves, dispersed, as they are, throughout the world. The formation of Herder's present-day liberated German Jew, in other words, is contingent on understanding that his past is "alien" to him. Herder deprives Jews not of their handed-down history but of their past, a distinction that will be of immense importance to Arendt later on. Here she already questions whether understanding their history at the price of the reality of their past means anything other than that Jews, once again, "stand face-to-face with nothing"—the very vacuum Herder's philosophy of history sought to fill.

In sum, the civil emancipation of Jews, which in any case was repealed less than a dozen years after it was proclaimed,[18] accomplished little more than to make their social assimilation, their integration into German "society," seem viable. Let us retain from the foregoing the segregation of Jews in the dark, worldless privacy of the ghetto, on the one hand, and the emergence of Jews not into the light of the public realm but into the respectability of society, on the other. And let us also retain Arendt's first encounter, via the Jewish question, with the rights of man, the supposedly "inalienable" rights of every human being.

"The Enlightenment and the Jewish Question" was published in 1932.

The following year, when Arendt was twenty-six, the Reichstag was burned and Adolf Hitler and the National Socialist Party rose to power. In July 1933 Arendt was arrested in Berlin for working, though she was not a Zionist, with a Zionist organization; upon her release (thanks to the good graces of a German policeman who was not a Jew) she promptly left Germany, illegally crossing the Czech border, and by way of Prague and Geneva reaching Paris, where she discovered friends and acquaintances who as Jews and/or Communists were in the same political situation of statelessness as herself.[19] The second phase of Arendt's Jewish experience was her political awakening to the fact that she was no longer a German national, which, as I see it, is as inseparable as the two sides of a coin from her growing awareness of the impending disaster of the failure of the social assimilation of German Jews.[20] The failure of the project of social assimilation would have entirely unpredictable political consequences,[21] notably the deprivation of Jews in Germany of the most "basic human rights, the right to work, the right to be useful, the right to found a home," and eventually of their right to live— Jews would be deprived even of the privation of their old segregated ghetto lives. As part of her politicization it is not surprising that during the Paris years, from 1933 to 1940, Arendt became as much of a Zionist as she would ever be. At least the Zionists, whose goal of establishing a Jewish nation-state she never shared, saw the urgency for Jews to take action against the dangers facing them.

In France Arendt wanted to do something that mattered: she found a job with Youth Aliyah, a Zionist organization that provided the means and training that enabled German and eastern European Jewish youths, from the ages of thirteen to seventeen, to quit Europe and emigrate to Palestine. Among the minor treasures in this volume is an article she wrote in French in 1935, "Some Young People Are Going Home" ("Des jeunes s'en vont chez eux"), in which the reader catches a rare glimpse of Arendt as a social worker and practical psychologist. One young man who came to her felt doubly isolated, from the community into which he had been born and by the "despair" of his parents, who had tried to escape to Palestine but had been refused entry. By speaking with Arendt he came to realize that what he perceived as the "shame" of his parents' "personal misfortune" was in fact "the misfortune of an entire people," and, more important, that as a newcomer, a member of a new generation, he was not a castaway in the world but, on the contrary, was needed by a different community from the one he had lost—that now there was a way open for him, if not for his parents, to join in solidarity with Jewish pioneers in the faraway land of Palestine, in Eretz Israel, his ancestral homeland. It is not known if this young man was among those Arendt brought to Palestine in 1935 and settled in kibbutzim, but one hopes so.

In 1936, in a letter to Heinrich Blücher, Arendt makes clear in words she would not have used to the youths in her care the reason she herself believes in Palestine as the Jewish homeland: "Palestine," she writes, "is not at the center of our national aspirations because 2,000 years ago some people lived there from whom in some sense or other we are supposed to be descended, but because for 2,000 years the craziest of peoples took pleasure in preserving the past in the present, because for them 'the ruins of Jerusalem are, you could say, rooted in the heart of time.'"[22] In the 1930s Arendt derives the right of Jews to a homeland neither from Zionist visions or ambitions, nor from the 1917 Balfour Delaration that largely acceded to them, but, as she put it some twenty years later, from "the potential immortality of the [Jewish] people."

Arendt later recalled that at this time, as it had not before, being a Jew "had become my own problem, and my own problem was political. Purely political!"[23] The role Blücher, who had been a strategist for the Sparticist Bund and a member of the German Communist Party, played in Arendt's political education has often been noted and can hardly be exaggerated. He was not a Jew but more than sympathetic to the Jewish cause insofar as he saw it as part of a greater cause. He writes to Arendt:

> Jews have to wage their national war on an international scale. However, the mass of this marvelous international dynamite must be protected so that it is not turned into shit in the chamber pot of a Parasitic Jewish International. . . . What we want is for [Jews] to come back to the East as the carriers of the flame finally returning from the West, with the ultimate word of freedom on their lips, with the slogan of liberation of all those exploited and oppressed, together with the great struggle of the only class that will remain revolutionary till the very end—the modern working class.[24]

Those are the words of an idealistic Marxist, whom Arendt salutes as her "beloved miracle-rabbi." But for her the realm of politics, which she first experienced in Jewish politics, is fundamentally not encompassed by ideals of any kind, any more than it is by strategies, regardless of their utility in achieving particular political goals. "If antisemitism is the ferment of racial hatred," says Blücher, "then this concrete question will be able to turn itself dialectically into one of the ferments of the world revolution."[25] Not so for Arendt, and not only because she was never a Marxist or Communist. Her increasing need at this time was to examine the ways that antisemitism had changed from a lingering social prejudice into an ideological worldview, and in so changing had become her own concrete political problem; and to comprehend how this had been possible in Germany, of all places, where Jewish emancipation had been "equated with the struggle for human freedom" for two hundred years, and where more Jews were absorbed, at least economically, into the fabric of society than in any other European country.

A major, previously unpublished essay in this book—edited from an undated and uncompleted German manuscript, which from interior and exterior evidence Arendt almost certainly was writing in France in the last years of the 1930s until, in 1940, she was interrupted by being interned in a camp for "enemy aliens" in southern France—points directly to Arendt's turn to, and original orientation in, the realm of politics. The essay is called "Antisemitism," and no doubt will bring to mind the first part of *The Origins of Totalitarianism*, which bears the same title. One difference between them is fully evident in the style of the earlier essay, which is far less censorious of Jewish public figures. Benjamin Disraeli, for example, appears in the essay in a single footnote, in a context that bears no relation to Arendt's scathing portrait of him in *Origins*. Another related difference is that when *Origins* was published in 1951 Arendt already knew that she had written a political rather than a historical book. She wrote it, as she said, to see an unprecedented form of government destroyed, namely totalitarianism, which is not mentioned in the essay. Though soon she would be writing to see antisemitism destroyed, here she is intent to understand the ground from which it later grew into Nazi policy. Antisemitism is one of Arendt's great topics, and her first deep probing of it is a detailed analysis of its development in modern German history. But what her probing unmistakably shows is that the twists and turns of German history, far from indicating a possible resolution to the problem of antisemitism, present it, from a political point of view, as an impasse.

"There have been numerous attempts," she writes, "to blur the fundamental difference and downplay the historical dissimilarities between the full scope of the medieval hatred of Jews on the one hand . . . and the scope of modern antisemitism on the other—in all its varying colors, from social hatred of 'piggish capitalism' to hatred of the race, from the antisemitism of the aristocracy to that of the petite bourgeoisie, from its first timid beginnings at the start of the nineteenth century to its fulfillment in the twentieth." She continues:

> What is thereby achieved is nothing less than once again to abstract the Jewish question out of the historical process and to destroy the common ground on which the fate of both Jews and non-Jews is decided. Both "medieval barbarism" and "everlasting antisemitism" leave us Jews without any hope. If medieval barbarism can erupt against us, then that would appear to be the most valid proof that we are not part of and have no home in modern history.

That is not, of course, her own opinion.[26] Arendt's point is rather that throughout modern German history Jews were pawns, more or less and *almost* necessarily willing pawns, in the game of power politics. They were used by the monarchy, the aristocracy, and the liberals, and discarded by each of those opposed factions when their usefulness, which was financial, was either used up or no longer deemed socially desirable. Jews were then seen neither as individuals nor as a distinct people, and less as a separate class than as a caste within German society, a caste that bore the brunt of a revived antisemitism "that feeds," as Arendt puts it, "upon the 'fear of ghosts.'" The "illusion" of assimilated Jews, that their being Jewish was a private and not a public matter, was in effect shattered, and it is out of this "poisoned social atmosphere" that antisemitism slowly emerged as a political ideology.

The manuscript of this essay—unfinished but well over one hundred pages in length—culminates in the conservative aristocracy's attack on the liberal values of the bourgeoisie, which came at a historical moment in the nineteenth century, between 1812 and 1823, when the absolute monarchy in Prussia, the power of the state, lacked the support of both the aristocracy and the bourgeoisie: the great Junkers, in the eyes of the monarchy, wanted to eat its power, and the bourgeoisie wanted a constitution to assure its primarily economic interests. The shared opposition to the monarchy of the aristocracy and the bourgeoisie, however, in no way united them, for the reactionary aristocrats' privileges were thought by them to come "from God" and to be rooted in hereditary property rather than wealth; the aristocrats disdained "the merchant 'who feels equally at home in all nations'"; the freedom of trade, dear to the bourgeois heart, was to the Junkers the opposite of German patriotism.

The attack of the aristocracy on the bourgeoisie, at least at first, was not aimed at the Jews. It was rather the liberal bourgeois citizens, shamed by the aristocrats' accusations that they were nouveaux riches, lacked roots, and were a disintegrative and destructive force within the German nation, who redirected the attack against the Jews. "For in the end the liberals' truly destructive self-hatred gave rise to a hatred of the Jews, that being the only means liberals had of distancing themselves from themselves, of shifting slander to others who, though they did not think of themselves as the 'bourgeoisie,' were forced to be its one hundred percent embodiment." At the end of the essay as we have it, Arendt writes that the "distorted and intentionally mendacious equation of profit with usury . . . [and] of usury with the bourgeoisie pointed, as if all by itself, to the Jews, who had once been usurers and who lived on as such in popular memory, pointed, that is, to the 'real' usurers—and distancing oneself from them would surely mean salvaging one's social position." But by then an incipient ideological antisemitism had passed into the hands of more "violent" classes that, like the Junkers but for different reasons and from an entirely different position on the social spectrum, despised the bourgeoisie. Stung in one way or another by the Junkers' feudal arguments, all classes of German society, from the aristocracy to the bourgeoisie to the peasantry, and not excluding the monarchy, which even in its independence from any social class was aware that its power would be vitiated if it lacked all popular support, were henceforth suspicious of the Jewish presence in Germany.

Let us retain three things from this phase of Arendt's Jewish experience: that German history revealed the Enlightenment's "inalienable" human rights as jeopardized by the social sphere in general and by its economic and financial interests in particular—the sphere, that is, into which most Jews in Germany were forced by one set of circumstances to assimilate and subsequently, by another set of circumstances, forced out of; that her first glimpse of a political realm, in which a diversity of people live *together* within the same borders, came as she saw it disappearing in Germany; and that the notion of a Jewish people, which previously had been taken for granted, was suddenly no longer self-evident. "Gouvernements passent, le peuple reste," but now the future and the very meaning of a Jewish people had become problematic to her.

In July 1940, when the opportunity presented itself, Arendt fled from the internment camp in Gurs, eventually reuniting with Blücher, whom she had married the previous January, in Montauban. In Marseilles they set about the complicated business of obtaining visas to leave France for America. Via Lisbon, they arrived in New York on May 22, 1941. The tumult of events preceding total war issued in a ten-year period, from 1941 through 1950, which was by far the most productive of Arendt's writings on Jewish politics,[27] incorporating the third and fourth, and anticipating the fifth, phases of her experience as a Jew. The first of the many articles Arendt wrote for the New York German-Jewish newspaper *Aufbau* was published on October 24, 1941. In it we hear for the first but certainly not the last time her outraged and indignant voice, here rejecting the demand that Jews *ought* to be grateful to those non-Jews, in this case the eminent French writer Jules Romains, who helped some of them escape Nazi persecution:

> What concerns us Jews . . . and what makes us blush again for the hundredth time is our despairing question: Is our alternative truly only between malevolent enemies and condescending friends? Are genuine allies nowhere to be found, allies who understand . . . [t]hat in this war our freedom and honor hang in the balance no less than the freedom and honor of the nation to which Jules Romains belongs?

The "freedom and honor" of Jews—if they are to constitute a distinct people, rather than a caste of unconscious pariahs, among the peoples of the world—sound and resound throughout the activist and at times militant pieces Arendt wrote for *Aufbau*. But it would be a mistake not to note that "Jewish Chances: Sparse Prospects, Divided Representation," published on April 20, 1945, concludes this series of articles on a note of disillusion that Jews "have not been honored with even a semblance of participation in the organization of victory and peace" following the war, and even more so that an internal "Jewish spat," as she puts it, will prevent a unified representation

of Jews at the upcoming conference in San Francisco. In only a few days'
time that conference was to be convened to consider matters vital to Jews as a
people, including the question of "the replacement of the [British] mandate
by an international trusteeship" in Palestine, and that of "the status of stateless persons," whose plight in Europe, though more desperate than hers in
America, Arendt readily imagined from her own ongoing experience of
statelessness.

In between the first and the last, these short and accessible newspaper
articles provide a unique Jewish perspective on the course of the Second
World War, a *political* perspective that as such is the concern of Jews and
non-Jews alike. In them she calls for the mobilization of Jews in *action*, the
formation of an international Jewish army to fight the Nazis under its own
flag. That flag will unfurl before the eyes of the world, making visible the
freedom of the Jewish people—"my" or "our" people, "our brethren," as
Arendt consistently refers to all Jews. It was as she was writing these articles
that she learned of the destruction of European Jewry at the hands of the
Nazis, which only intensifies her appeal to all living Jews for action, which
later, more abstractly, she describes as the highest human activity in active
life. At the same time she expresses nothing but admiration for the labor and
work—the two other activities of active life—of the generations of Jews in
Palestine, turning what was a desert into the oases of a potential Jewish
homeland. Though her political perspective is opposed to Herzlian Zionism,
insofar as the latter would use hatred of the Jewish "substance" as the means
for Jews to become "a people like all other peoples," Arendt recognizes that
Zionists operate within the realm of politics. She strongly contrasts political
Zionists with antipolitical Revisionists, who employ the means of terror to
intimidate or kill those they perceive as enemies, in effect saying, "If you
are not with us you are against us, and do not deserve to live in Palestine."
In these articles Arendt is well aware of Jewish disputatiousness—so many
Jews, so many opinions—but her regular *Aufbau* column, under the banner "This Means You," explicitly asks *individual* Jews to join together, not
only to form an army but also to sit down at a table and discuss their differences: not to disown their own opinions but to think about and seriously consider opinions other their own, and by speaking and listening to their peers
rise above their disagreements and participate in the formation of a genuine

Jewish plurality. The meaning of a Jewish people, a free people that acknowledges and respects the freedom of others, is manifest in the third phase of Arendt's experience as a Jew.

In "A Way toward the Reconciliation of Peoples" Arendt makes an interesting distinction between a people and a nation, which introduces the fourth phase of her Jewish experience. When Pétain signed the German-French armistice, which demanded that every refugee in France be handed over to the Nazis, Arendt says he "annihilated the French nation." The foundation of the French nation-state was shaken when it ceased to be a state of law, when the rights of its citizens were abrogated, when justice was no longer its principle, and when an ideology, namely antisemitism, became its policy. What was left was the French *people*, which does not mean every Frenchman but those who mobilized against the state, resisting its power, acting in freedom, and restoring justice. Freedom and justice are the leitmotifs of the journal kept by the French poet René Char when he fought with the French Resistance during the Second World War, a journal aptly titled "Hypnos Waking," and his words from it inform the last chapter, "The Revolutionary Tradition and Its Lost Treasure," of *On Revolution* (1963). Arendt speaks here of rebellion and not revolution, but it is difficult to doubt that the seeds that later grew into the more abstract work were experientially planted in this essay, whose primary subject is the rebellion of Jews against their Nazi oppressors. The goal of revolution is to found a new state, a new kind of state—not a return to the status quo ante—and this is precisely what Arendt sees as the goal of the Jewish people.

The writings that make up the greater part of the fourth phase of Arendt's Jewish experience are those reprinted in this volume from Ron H. Feldman's no longer available *Hannah Arendt, The Jew as Pariah: Jewish Identity and Politics in the Modern Age* (1978). These essays are identified in the bibliographical information in the publication history that follows, and are discussed in some detail in Ron Feldman's introduction following the publication history. Feldman's introduction speaks for itself and it is not my intention to repeat or anticipate it. My concern is rather with two matters important in the present context: first, the opportunity Arendt saw for Jews to become a nation, their opportunity, after all they had been through, to retrieve a fragment of their past and again become "a light unto the nations"; and second, the structure of the state that might embody their nationhood and its principal condition. Arendt's well-known and much debated notion of a "right to have rights" has, I believe, its source in these matters. If it were a civil right, it would be among the rights of persons deprived of such rights, as Jews were so often deprived in the past and more radically than ever by the Nazis. It would make no sense. A "right to have rights," as I see it, must be the right of a people to become a nation by founding a state whose institutions announce and guard the civil rights of its citizens. A "right to have rights" is not a civil but a political right, and politics is always for Arendt what goes on between a plurality of individuals speaking together about what concerns them in common, generating the power to do what they determine can be done by acting together. Founding a new state is a risky business, as we know from both ancient and modern history—hence Arendt's considerable interest in foundation *myths*—but *because* of what they suffered and endured, Arendt thought that Jews, her own people, had an opportunity to found a state whose power potential might be very great. The Jewish people, exercising their "right to have rights" and mindful of the role of justice in their past, could found a state that would require nothing beneath them to sustain its existence: they themselves would be their own foundation.[28]

The structure of a new state in Palestine, as Arendt saw it, should not be that of a European nation-state. The Jews are an island surrounded by a sea of Arabs, as she says, and alone, without the help of the United States and other states, could hardly survive if Arab peoples joined together to crush them. The aid in money and matériel the state of Israel receives has so far allowed it to survive, but peace has never appeared as the goal of the many wars and almost constant conflicts that have engaged it since it was carved out of the British Mandate in 1948; and the various "road maps" to peace, which have mainly been drawn not by Arabs and Jews together but by diplomats from outside states and organizations, have led almost nowhere. Already in 1948 Arendt foresaw what now perhaps has come to pass, that Israel would become a militaristic state behind closed but threatened borders, a "semi-sovereign" state from which Jewish culture would gradually vanish. In 1948 Folke Bernadotte, who in mediating between Arab and Jewish interests called for the right of hundreds of thousands of Palestinian Arabs to return to the homes from which Palestinian Jews had driven them—the right of Arabs and Jews to live as neighbors—was shot dead by the Revisionist Lehi group or Stern Gang. Bernadotte, a man of peace and judgment, was in

Arendt's words "the agent of nobody . . . murdered by the agents of war" ("The Failure of Reason: The Mission of Bernadotte").

The present state of Israel bears little resemblance to the binational Arab-Jewish state envisioned by Arendt, for whose realization in Palestine she worked with Judah Magnes ("Magnes, the Conscience of the Jewish People") and others. Its structure would be a council system of governing, a system that, one could say, is genuinely revolutionary. "Local self-governing and mixed Jewish-Arab municipal and rural councils, on a small scale and as numerous as possible, are the only realistic political measures that can eventually lead to the political emancipation of Palestine," as Arendt puts it. In this structure power would be generated by agreements handed up, not down, from level to level of councils, arising from the levels in which ordinary Jews and Arabs come together to deal with the common problems that lie between them and relate them. Politically speaking, there is no "other" to be excluded in the council system, and its power potential is immense: it could become, as Arendt suggests, a federation of Mediterranean peoples, which would not be a sovereign state but rather a new autonomous polity with its own large place in the world. The condition of the council system of governing does not entail loving one's neighbor but rather entering into political friendship with him. Political friendship, which Arendt later traces to Aristotle's *philia politikē*, is much the same as the public spirit in which promises are made to be kept; the rule of one people over another would be ruled out in a public-spirited polity of different peoples. After 1950, when her great hope for a binational state in Palestine was unfulfilled, Arendt's writings on Jewish affairs diminished in quantity. She entered a period of reflection on the meaning of human freedom and its complex relations to active life (*vita activa*), and while those relations, and their reversals, are embroidered in the philosophic-historical tapestry of *The Human Condition* (and seem more revelant today than ever), their depth cannot be fathomed apart from recognizing their source in Arendt's experience as a Jew.

The fifth phase of Arendt's Jewish experience came more than a decade later, when she reported, at her own request, on the trial of Adolf Eichmann in Jerusalem. It is the experience of the rejection, entirely unwarranted, of a Jew by her own people. The fundamental problem was and still is that her report *realizes* the need for a new way of understanding after the unprecedented evil of totalitarian crimes rendered traditional categories of philosophic and political thought, and with them traditional moral and religious standards of judgment, useless. By a new way of understanding Arendt does not mean inventing neologisms: it is, after all, the ancient problem of human evil that she faced in the countenance of a single man. Relying on no traditional categories or standards, she *judged* Eichmann not as a demoniac but as a banal bureaucrat, an "expert in the Jewish question" who efficiently arranged the murders of millions of Jews—men, women, and children—*against whom he harbored no "ill feelings."*[29] Eichmann reiterated his lack of ill feelings toward Jews both in his pretrial examinations and in his testimony during the trial, as if it ought to be comprehensible to those who heard it, whether or not they believed it. His defense held that Eichmann was merely a small cog in a vast machine, that he only obeyed the orders of his superiors, that Hitler's word was law, and so forth, but his lawyers never mentioned Eichmann's lack of enmity toward Jews. Not only was it unbelievable but also, so they thought, it had no legal bearing on what he had done. Unless he was insane, which clearly he was not, it could not possibly exculpate their client. In that they were right.

Arendt alone saw then what not many have seen since, that the evil Eichmann perpetrated defies the categories in which men and women have thought for centuries. The man had a conscience, which as the voice of God or *lumen naturale* is meant to distinguish right from wrong; he even believed he adhered to a version of Kant's categorical imperative, which, to the astonishment of the court, he recited more or less accurately. It was the thought-defyingness of Eichmann's evil that released, through the power of her imagination,[30] Arendt's judgment—the other and politically more potent ingredient in her ability to understand—condemning him to death.[31] By ceaselessly insisting that the evil Eichmann was responsible for cannot be thought *and* by judging it, Arendt wanted Jews to see the reality of the horror that had befallen them—that they were sent to their deaths en masse by someone who did not even dislike them. Had they done that, how could they ever deny Palestinians the rights Jews rightly claim for themselves? How could they ever, after their own experience, treat Palestinians as if they were superfluous?[32]

As she says here ("The Disappearance of Six Million"), the situation after the Holocaust requires a "reappraisal of our mental habits," a reappraisal that is "truly agonizing," indeed so agonizing that it threatens to make our humanity "irrelevant." Arendt's human refusal not to judge, which echoes Socrates' human refusal not to think, had the bitterly ironic result of her expulsion from Jewish communities in America, Europe, and Israel. That was more than difficult to bear, but she never willingly would have drunk Socrates' hemlock: too much was at stake for humanity in her judgment that the most extreme evil is committed without thought and without being able to be thought. The concept of the banality of evil struck Arendt in Jerusalem, and she attempted to communicate its meaning for the rest of her life.[33]

Who one is is always conditioned, and the primary condition of who Hannah Arendt was in her absolute distinctness is, I believe, the fact that she was born a Jew. That does not mean she was a Jew like other Jews, or that her life is an exemplary Jewish life, which it may or may not be—for by definition an example is what others emulate. These Jewish writings from more than thirty years are less exemplifications of Arendt's political ideas than the experiential ground from which those ideas grew and developed. It is in this sense that Arendt's identity as a Jew, or, as I would prefer to call it, her experience as a Jew, is literally the foundation of her thought: it supports her thinking even when she is not thinking about Jews or Jewish questions. Arendt's experience as a Jew was sometimes that of an eyewitness and sometimes that of an actor and sufferer of events, both of which run the risk of partiality; but it was also always that of a judge, which means that she looked at those events and, insofar as she was in them, at *herself* from the outside— an extraordinary mental feat. The enlarged mentality required of a judge usually reflects the experiences of others, experiences that are not immediately his own but are so generalized by his ability to reproduce them in imagination that his impartial judgment reveals their meaning. As a Jew Arendt reproduced her own experiences, which is the epitome of the reflexivity in reflective judgment, and in her case suggests that being a judge and a *conscious* pariah among her own people are virtually synonymous. Her awareness that she was a conscious pariah is probably the crucial factor that allowed her to see the political dimension in Kant's understanding of aesthetic reflective judgment.

To conclude I turn again to *The Human Condition*: "The life span of man running toward death would inevitably carry everything to ruin and destruction if it were not for the faculty of interrupting it and beginning something new, a faculty which is inherent in action like an ever-present reminder that men, though they must die, are not born in order to die but in order to begin."[34] Later she continues and enlarges that thought:

> . . . action and politics, among all the capabilities of human life, are the only things of which we could not even conceive without at least assuming that freedom exists. . . . Without [freedom] political life would be meaningless. The *raison d'être* of politics is freedom, and its field of experience is action. . . .[35]

And once she simply declares: "The meaning of politics is freedom."[36] These are all general statements, and like the one with which I began these remarks, I cannot but see them as grounded in Arendt's Jewish experience. In 1975, the year she died, she spoke of a voice that comes from behind the masks she wears to suit the occasions and the various roles the world offers her. That voice is *identical* to none of the masks, but she hopes it is *identifiable*, sounding through all of them.[37] Since her death, Arendt's voice has become ever more identifiable as the actualization of the "givens" of her being, as the voice of a Jewess, a Jewish woman, through whose imagination we see, so to speak, an X-ray of a common human world, a world that is different from and, in every sense that matters, appears more real than the one in which we live today. Hannah Arendt may have doubted that such a world will ever be achieved, but she was convinced that *striving* to achieve it is worth as much as anything else in our lives, provided only that we want to be free.

Notes

1. H. Arendt, *The Human Condition* (Chicago: University of Chicago Press, 1998), p. 208. In a footnote she adds: "This is the meaning" of Dante's *Nihil igitur agit nisi talens existens quale patiens fieri debet*, which, "though quite clear and simple in the Latin original, defies translation." This linguistic procedure, often repeated, is among Arendt's ways of making the past present.

2. Arendt, *The Human Condition*, p. 315.

3. Cf. H. Arendt, *Between Past and Future* (New York: Viking, 1968), p. 14.

4. An English translation of *Der Liebesbegriff bei Augustin: Versuch einer philosophischen Interpretation* was published, twenty-one years after Arendt's death, with the rather cinematic title *Love and St. Augustine* (Chicago: University of Chicago Press, 1996).

5. Arendt speaks openly about her childhood in "'What Remains? The Language Remains': A Conversation with Günter Gaus," in H. Arendt, *Essays in Understanding 1930–1954*, ed. J. Kohn (New York: Schocken Books, 2005), pp. 6–8.

6. Arendt, *The Human Condition*, p. 25 and n. 8.

7. Cf. the first paragraph of Kant's essay "An Answer to the Question: 'What Is Enlightenment?'"

8. "Hannah Arendt on Hannah Arendt," in *Hannah Arendt: The Recovery of the Public World*, ed. M. A. Hill (New York: St. Martin's, 1979), p. 303.

9. The latter has rarely been acknowledged by philosophers; nevertheless it was his thinking that led to Socrates' aporias, Kant's that issued in the antinomies of pure reason, and Arendt's that brought her face-to-face with "thought-defying" evil.

10. H. Arendt, *The Life of the Mind*, vol. 1, *Thinking* (New York: Harcourt Brace Jovanovich, 1978), p. 43.

11. *Hannah Arendt–Martin Heidegger Briefe 1925–1975*, ed. U. Ludz (Frankfurt Am Main: Vittorio Klostermann, 2002), pp. 31, 25. Arendt's words are taken from a sort of parable she wrote for Heidegger, called "Schatten," in which she refers to herself in the third person.

12. In 1969 Heidegger wrote to Arendt: "More than anyone, you have touched the inner movement of my thought and of my work as a teacher" (*Hannah Arendt–Martin Heidegger Briefe*, 193). In 1949 Arendt wrote to Karl Jaspers: "What you call impurity I would call lack of character—but in the sense that [Heidegger] literally has none and certainly not a particularly bad one. At the same time, he lives in depths and with a passionateness that one can't easily forget" (*Correspondence, Hannah Arendt–Karl Jaspers, 1926–1969*, ed. L. Kohler and H. Saner [New York: Harcourt Brace Jovanovich, 1992], p. 142).

13. H. Arendt, *Der Liebesbegriff bei Augustin: Versuch einer philosophischen Interpretation* (Berlin: J. Springer, 1929), p. 68 n. 2: "Wie kann ich als ein von Gott Ergriffener und von der Welt Abgetrennter dennoch in der Welt leben?" Arendt once remarked in conversation that if Heidegger were ever to write a theology the word "being" would not appear in it.

14. Ultimately with Heinrich Blücher, whom Arendt met in Paris in 1936, married in 1940, and lived with until his death in 1970. To him she wrote (with a not-so-veiled reference to Heidegger): "I always knew . . . that I can only truly exist in love [which] is why *I was so frightened that I might get lost.* . . . It still seems incredible to me that I managed to get both things, the 'love of my life' and a oneness with myself. And yet, I only got the one thing when I got the other" (*Within Four Walls: The Correspondence between Hannah Arendt and Heinrich Blücher, 1936–1968*, ed. Lotte Kohler [New York: Harcourt, 2000], pp. 40–41, emphasis added).

15. Her biography *Rahel Varnhagen: The Life of a Jewish Woman*, the entire first part and many other sections of *The Origins of Totalitarianism, Eichmann in Jerusalem: A Report on the Banality of Evil*, and numerous other relevant writings, all of which are in print, are not included here. Neither are certain documents in the Arendt archive, including an early essay on Adam Müller, a figure unlikely to be known to contemporary anglophone readers, a number of book reviews, and some rather sketchy memoranda for discussions with university students on the Eichmann "controversy," which may yet prove of interest to scholars and researchers. Many of Arendt's letters dealing with Jewish affairs have already been published in seven volumes of her individual correspondences, and more such letters will appear in the forthcoming edition of her general correspondence.

16. The figure of the Wandering Jew is the age-old symbol of Diaspora Jews, "a people without a land in search of a land without a people," which, as Arendt remarks, could be found only "on the moon" or in a "fairy tale."

17. Progress, as Kant might have put it, from an "age of enlightenment" toward an "enlightened age." Cf. "An Answer to the Question: 'What Is Enlightenment?'"

18. The Law for the Estates of the Provinces of 1823 restricted the right to vote to those "in communion with a Christian Church." The civil rights of German Jews were finally enacted into law in 1869.

19. Arendt remained stateless for eighteen years, from 1933, the year she left Germany, until 1951, when she became an American citizen.

20. The phases I speak of are experiential and not altogether chronological. Arendt had already done research on Jewish assimilation for several years, and her study of the life of Rahel Varnhagen—all of

which except the last chapter, or the last two chapters, was written before she left Germany—bears the fruit of that research, including the important distinction between Jews as "pariahs" and "parvenus." My coeditor Ron Feldman's extensive treatment of that distinction in his Introduction relieves me of the need to do so here. What interests me is Arendt's sense of frustration with her study of Rahel after her arrival in Paris: her "critique of assimilation," she said, had been "politically naive" and "had hardly anything to do with . . . genuine political antisemitism" (*Correspondence, Hannah Arendt–Karl Jaspers*, p. 197).

21. Some of these consequences were not so much foreseen as imagined by Franz Kafka as already present in his own society. See "The Jew as Pariah: A Hidden Tradition" in this volume, in particular Arendt's account of Kafka's *The Castle*, from which the following quotation is taken.

22. *Within Four Walls*, pp. 20–21. The interior quotation, which is also cited in "The Enlightenment and the Jewish Question," is from J. G. Herder.

23. Arendt, *Essays in Understanding*, p. 12.

24. *Within Four Walls*, pp. 16–17.

25. Ibid., pp. 19, 15.

26. Arendt's historically informed opinion, however, is sharply to be distinguised from other twentieth-century German-Jewish thinkers, including Franz Rosenzweig, Leo Strauss, and Gersholm Scholem. The latter, as he wrote to Arendt in 1946, did believe in "the 'eternity' of anitisemitism"; Rosenzweig's "new thinking" is antipolitical: "The charge of Jewish life is to announce peace to the nations, not through action but through inaction" (Peter Eli Gordon); and Strauss discerned, without seeking to resolve, "the theologico-political predicament" inherent in Judaism. See Gordon's soon-to-be-published paper, "The Concept of the Unpolitical: Critical Reflections on the Theological-Political Problem in German-Jewish Thought," delivered at a conference in honor of Arendt's centennial in Berlin, October 5–7, 2006.

27. In the presentation of these writings thematic considerations have sometimes prevailed over chronological order.

28. I am grateful to Jessica R. Restaino, who in a letter used some of the terminology in this sentence.

29. H. Arendt, *Eichmann in Jerusalem: A Report on the Banality of Evil* (New York: Viking, 1963), p. 30, emphasis added.

30. This is the power that Jaspers refers to when he writes to Arendt, well before the trial, that even if what she has "grasped" were put "into a logical structure that is simple and easy to teach, one will still always have to go back to the source in you to participate in that power that enables others to see" (*Correspondence, Hannah Arendt–Karl Jaspers*, p. 274).

31. Arendt agreed with the court that Eichmann should be hanged but not with the traditional standards of its judgment, that he had intended to do wrong or had acted from "base motives." Her judgment states that because Eichmann did not *want* "to share the earth with" all human beings, no human being "can be expected to want to share the earth with" him, which is the sole reason he should be executed. Arendt's full judgment appears in *Eichmann in Jerusalem*, pp. 277–79.

32. I am not suggesting that Palestinians are "innocent victims" but that they lacked and still lack the power of a state, which the state of Israel had and has, to settle its conflicts politically.

33. For example in "Some Questions of Moral Philosophy" (1965–66) and "Thinking and Moral Considerations" (1971), both in H. Arendt, *Responsibility and Judgment*, ed. J. Kohn (New York: Schocken Books, 2003), pp. 49–146 and 159–89 respectively; and throughout the posthumously published *The Life of the Mind*.

34. Arendt, *The Human Condition*, p. 246.

35. Arendt, *Between Past and Future*, p. 146.

36. H. Arendt, *The Promise of Politics*, ed. J. Kohn (New York: Schocken Books, 2005), p. 108.

37. Arendt, Cf. *Responsibility and Judgment*, pp. 12–14.

A NOTE ON THE TEXT

To begin with, the reason that the words "antisemitism" and "antisemitic" have been used throughout this volume, instead of the more common "anti-Semitism" and "anti-Semitic," is not simply because Hannah Arendt spelled them that way in the first part of *The Origins of Totalitarianism* and elsewhere. Rather, as she says here in the second footnote to the introduction to the long essay "Antisemitism," "Semitic," like "Indo-Germanic," was a "linguistic" term before it became an "anthropological and ethnic" one, and only in the last third of the nineteenth century was the ideological "catchword 'antisemitic'" coined and applied "to Jews in general." The point is that there never was an ideology or movement called "Semitism," which makes "anti-Semitism" and its cognates logical misnomers.

In the sense that it contains writings by Arendt in French as well as German and English, this volume is unique. In part, but only in part, the different languages reflect where Arendt was when she used them. There are many exceptions, including "The Gustloff Trial," "The Jewish Question," and "Antisemitism," all written in German after Arendt left Germany. "The Gustloff Trial," which is an account of the trial of David Frankfurter, the young Jew who in 1936 assassinated Wilhelm Gustloff, the leader of the Nazi contingent in Switzlerland, is signed "Helveticus." But from letters Arendt wrote in 1936 to Heinrich Blücher from Geneva and Zurich, we know that she went to Switzerland to help Frankfurter *and* that she wrote an article under a pseudonym. More important, the style and tone of this account, which presage the style and tone of her report on the trial of Adolf Eichmann in Jerusalem twenty-five years later, have convinced those most familiar with Arendt's German (Lotte Kohler foremost among them) that this article could not have been written by anyone other than Arendt. "The Jewish Question" is marked in Arendt's hand *Skizze* (sketch), and was apparently prepared for a speech delivered to German-speaking émigrés living in

Paris; "Antisemitism" was clearly intended as a major work on the history of German antisemitism, for which her native German was better suited than her adopted French.

Another exception is the more than fifty German pieces Arendt published in the newspaper *Aufbau* after she arrived in New York. Those pieces, of which this is the most complete collection in any language (a few have been omitted because they are repetitive of other articles included here) are divided into three categories: "The Jewish War That Isn't Happening" (October 1941–November 1942); "Between Silence and Speechlessness" (February 1943–March 1944); and "The Political Organization of the Jewish People" (April 1944–April 1945)—following the taxonomy of Marie Luise Knott's German edition, published in 2000. The title of that edition, *Vor Antisemitismus ist man nur noch auf dem Monde sicher* (*The Moon Is the Only Place Where We Can Still Be Safe from Antisemitism*), is a quotation from one of the pieces. The divisions, however, are not Arendt's but indicate, in a general way, her changing emphases during the course of the Second World War. The Crémieux Decree ("Why the Crémieux Decree Was Abrogated") may not be familiar to every reader. Due to the extraordinary efforts of Adolphe Crémieux, France's Jewish minister of justice, the decree granted French citizenship to all Algerian Jews in 1871. For the same reason, it may be appropriate to note here that Count Folke Bernadotte ("The Failure of Reason: The Mission of Bernadotte"), a grandson of King Oscar II of Sweden, was the United Nations Security Council mediator in the Arab-Jewish conflicts in Palestine in 1947–48, until he was murdered by Jewish terrorists.

Fourteen of the original eighteen entries in *The Jew as Pariah*, edited by Ron H. Feldman, the coeditor of this volume, and published in 1978, only three years after Arendt's death, are republished here. What has been left out are three pieces not written by Arendt and one, "Organized Guilt and Universal Responsibility," which is included in *Essays In Understanding 1930–1954* (Schocken Books, 2005). *The Jew as Pariah* has been out of print for many years and the essays reprinted here are essential in understanding the meaning to Arendt of being a pariah, her conception of how a new state in Palestine should be founded, and her reaction to the controversy provoked by her book on Adolf Eichmann. Some of these essays have been revised, and one has a different title. What appeared in *The Jew as Pariah* as "Portrait of a Period" is a review of Stefan Zweig's autobiograhy *The World of Yester-*

day. "Stefan Zweig: Juden in der Welt von gestern" ("Stefan Zweig: Jews in the World of Yesterday") is the title of Arendt's longer German review of the same book and is used here. Susanna Young-ah Gottlieb translated the German review, and when it was compared with the English one the decision was made to preserve the strengths of both by interweaving them in a single essay.

There follows a complete bibliographical list of the contents of *The Jewish Writings,* with the publications in which the essays originally appeared.

PUBLICATION HISTORY

The essays in *Jewish Writings* originally appeared in the following publications:

I THE 1930s

"The Enlightenment and the Jewish Question" was originally published as "Aufklärung und Judenfrage" in *Zeitschrift fur die Geschichte der Juden in Deutschland* 4 (1932).

"Against Private Circles" was originally published as "Gegen Privatzirkel" in *Jüdische Rundschau* 38 (1932).

"Original Assimilation: An Epilogue to the One Hundredth Anniversary of Rahel Varnhagen's Death" was originally published as "Originale Assimilation: Ein Nachwort zu Rahel Varnhagen 100 Todestag" in *Jüdische Rundschau* 38 (1932).

"The Professional Reclassification of Youth" was originally published as "Le Reclassement Professionel de la Jeunesse" in *Le Journal Juif* 12 (1935).

"A Guide for Youth: Martin Buber" was originally published as "Un Guide de la Jeunesse: Martin Buber" in *Le Journal Juif* 12, no. 17 (April 16, 1935).

"Some Young People Are Going Home" was originally published as "Des Jeunes s'en vont chez eux" in *Le Journal Juif* 12, no. 26 (June 28, 1935).

"The Gustloff Trial" was originally published as "Prozess Gustloff" in *Die neue Weltbühne* 33 (1936), p. 51.

"The Jewish Question" was previously unpublished.

"Antisemitism" was previously unpublished.

II THE 1940s

"The Minority Question" was previously unpublished.

"The Jewish War That Isn't Happening" was originally published in the *Aufbau* between October 1941 and November 1942.

"Between Silence and Speechlessness" was originally published in the *Aufbau* between February 1943 and March 1944.

"The Political Organization of the Jewish People" was originally published in the *Aufbau* between April 1944 and April 1945.

"Jewish Politics" was previously unpublished.

"Why the Crémieux Decree Was Abrogated" was originally published in *Contemporary Jewish Record* 6, no. 2 (April 1943).

"New Leaders Arise in Europe" was originally published in *New Currents: A Jewish Monthly* 2, no. 4 (1944).

"A Way toward the Reconciliation of Peoples" was originally published as "Ein Mittel zur Versöhnung der Völker" in *Porvenir* 3 (Buenos Aires, 1942).

"We Refugees" as originally published in the *Menorah Journal* (January 1943), pp. 69–77. Reprinted in *The Jew as Pariah*, ed. Ron H. Feldman (New York: Grove, 1978), pp. 55–66.

"The Jew as Pariah: A Hidden Tradition" was originally published in *Jewish Social Studies* 6, no. 2 (April 1944), pp. 99–122. Reprinted in *The Jew as Pariah*, ed. Ron H. Feldman (New York: Grove, 1978), pp. 67–90.

"Creating a Cultural Atmosphere" was originally published in *Commentary* 4 (1947). Reprinted in *The Jew as Pariah*, ed. Ron H. Feldman (New York: Grove, 1978), pp. 91–95.

"Jewish History, Revised" was originally published in *Jewish Frontier* (March 1948), pp. 34–48. Reprinted in *The Jew as Pariah*, ed. Ron H. Feldman (New York: Grove, 1978), pp. 96–105.

"The Moral of History" was excerpted from "Privileged Jews," *Jewish Social Studies* 8, no. 1 (January 1946), pp. 3–7. Reprinted in *The Jew as Pariah*, ed. Ron H. Feldman (New York: Grove, 1978), pp. 106–11.

"Stefan Zweig: Jews in the World of Yesterday," translated by Susanna Young-ah Gottlieb, was originally published as "Stefan Zweig: Juden in der Welt von gestern," in *Sechs Essays* (Heidelberg: Schneider,

1948), pp. 112–27; reprinted in *Die vorborgene Tradition: Acht Essays* (Frankfurt am Main: Suhrkamp, 1976), pp. 74–87. An earlier English version appeared under the title "Portrait of a Period" in the *Menorah Journal* 31 (1943), pp. 307–14; reprinted in *The Jew as Pariah*, ed. Ron H. Feldman (New York: Grove, 1978), pp. 112–21.

"The Crisis of Zionism" was previously unpublished.

"Herzl and Lazare" was excerpted from "From the Dreyfus Affair to France Today," *Jewish Social Studies* 4, no. 3 (July 1942), pp. 235–40. Reprinted in *The Jew as Pariah*, ed. Ron H. Feldman (New York: Grove, 1978), pp. 125–30.

"Zionism Reconsidered" was originally published in the *Menorah Journal* (October 1944), pp. 192–96. Reprinted in *The Jew as Pariah*, ed. Ron H. Feldman (New York: Grove, 1978), pp. 131–63.

"The Jewish State: Fifty Years After, Where Have Herzl's Politics Led?" was originally published in *Commentary* 1 (1945–46), p. 7. Reprinted in *The Jew as Pariah*, ed. Ron H. Feldman (New York: Grove, 1978), pp. 164–77.

"To Save the Jewish Homeland" was originally published in *Commentary* 5 (1948). Reprinted in *The Jew as Pariah*, ed. Ron H. Feldman (New York: Grove, 1978), pp. 178–92.

"The Assets of Personality: A Review of *Chaim Weizmann: Statesman, Scientist, Builder of the Jewish Commonwealth*" was originally published in *Contemporary Jewish Record* 8, no. 2 (April 1945), pp. 214–16.

"Single Track to Zion: A Review of *Trial and Error: The Autobiography of Chaim Weizmann*" was originally published in the *Saturday Review*, February 1949.

"The Failure of Reason: The Mission of Bernadotte" was originally published in the *New Leader* 31 (1948).

"About 'Collaboration'" was originally published in *Jewish Frontier* (October 1948), pp. 55–56. Reprinted in *The Jew as Pariah*, ed. Ron H. Feldman (New York: Grove, 1978), pp. 237–39.

"New Palestine Party" was originally published as a letter to the editor in the *New York Times*, December 4, 1948.

III THE 1950s

"Peace or Armistice in the Near East?" was originally published in the *Review of Politics* 12, no. 1 (January 1950), pp. 56–82. Reprinted in *The Jew as Pariah*, ed. Ron H. Feldman (New York: Grove, 1978), pp. 193–222.

"Magnes, the Conscience of the Jewish People" was originally published in *Jewish Newsletter* 8, no. 24 (November 24, 1952).

"The History of the Great Crime: A Review of *Bréviaire de la Haine: Le IIIe Reich et les Juifs (Breviary of Hate: The Third Reich and the Jews)*, by Léon Poliakov," was originally published in *Commentary*, March 1952.

IV THE 1960s

"The Eichmann Controversy: A Letter to Gershom Scholem" was originally published in *Encounter*, January 1964. Reprinted in *The Jew as Pariah*, ed. Ron H. Feldman (New York: Grove, 1978), pp. 245–51.

"Answers to Questions Submitted by Samuel Grafton" was previously unpublished.

"The Eichmann Trial and the Germans: A Conversation with Thilo Koch" was originally published as "Der Fall Eichmann und die Deutschen: Ein Gespräch mit Thilo Koch" in *Gespräche mit Hannah Arendt*, ed. A. Reif (Munich: Piper Verlag, 1976).

"The Destruction of Six Million" was originally published in *A Jewish World Symposium—The Jewish World*, September 1964.

" 'The Formidable Dr. Robinson': A Reply by Hannah Arendt" was originally published in the *New York Review of Books* (January 20, 1966), pp. 26–30. Reprinted in *The Jew as Pariah*, ed. Ron H. Feldman (New York: Grove, 1978), pp. 260–76.

INTRODUCTION

The Jew as Pariah: The Case of Hannah Arendt * *(1906–1975)*

Ron H. Feldman

I

> All vaunted Jewish qualities—the "Jewish heart,"
> humanity, humor, disinterested intelligence—are
> pariah qualities. All Jewish shortcomings—tact-
> lessness, political stupidity, inferiority complexes
> and money-grubbing—are characteristic of up-
> starts. There have always been Jews who did not
> think it worth while to change their humane atti-
> tude and their natural insight into reality for the
> narrowness of caste spirit or the essential unreal-
> ity of financial transactions.[1]

Hannah Arendt's life was played out during the "dark times" of the twentieth century. She was one of the most remarkable—as well as one of the
last—offspring of a German-Jewish milieu which produced more than its
share of great literary, scientific, and artistic figures. An outstanding political
and cultural critic, her purpose as a thinker was to help us understand the
meaning and direction of events in a world of deadly chaos.

Probably best known to the general public as the author of *Eichmann in
Jerusalem,* over which a great storm erupted in the Jewish community and
for which she was vehemently condemned in the Jewish press, Arendt's

---

*This essay appeared in a slightly different form in *The Jew as Pariah: Jewish Identity and Politics in the
Modern Age* (New York: Grove Press, 1978).

reputation as one of her generation's most gifted political thinkers rests on two other works: *The Origins of Totalitarianism* and *The Human Condition*.

When Hannah Arendt died, she was out of favor with the Jewish community as a consequence of *Eichmann in Jerusalem:* few of the eulogies which traditionally follow upon the death of such a prominent figure appeared in the Jewish press. Partly because she was subjected to a modern form of excommunication from the Jewish community and partly due to the power of her other writings, her Jewish writings were for the most part neglected and forgotten.[2]

This was most unfortunate, for it led to a less than complete understanding of both her political theory, for which she was renowned, and her view of modern Jewish history, for which she was castigated. In fact, there is an essential link between her conception of Jewish history and her political theory: her view of the modern Jewish condition serves as an introduction to her political theory, while her political theory illuminates her interpretation of Jewish history.

This collection not only serves to expand the public's knowledge of her work but, more importantly, when taken together these essays are of intrinsic importance because they present a coherent and powerful, albeit nonconformist, understanding of what it means to be a Jew in the modern world. Although many of the essays were written over fifty years ago, the issues they deal with continue to be of contemporary importance: the destruction of European Jewry by the Nazis, the relationship of world Jewry to the State of Israel, the relationship of Israel to the Arabs both within the borders of the Jewish State and without, and the peculiar historical position of Jews within modern Western society.

Fundamentally these essays show that Hannah Arendt chose the role of a "conscious pariah." In Arendt's view, the status of pariah—the social outcast—characterizes the position of the Jews in Western Europe following the Enlightenment and emancipation because they were never truly accepted by European society. "During the 150 years when Jews truly lived amidst, and not just in the neighborhood of, Western European peoples, they always had to pay with political misery for social glory and with social insult for political success."[3] This outsider status gave rise to two particular types: the *conscious pariahs* who were aware of it, and the *parvenus,* who tried to succeed in the world of the gentiles but could never escape their Jewish roots. For Arendt, the conscious pariahs were those who really did most for the spiritual dignity of their people, who were great enough to transcend the bounds of nationality and to weave the strands of their Jewish genius into the general texture of European life . . . those bold spirits who tried to make of the emancipation of the Jews that which it really should have been—an admission of Jews as *Jews* to the ranks of humanity, rather than a permit to ape the gentiles or an opportunity to play the parvenu.[4]

By affirming both their Jewish particularity and their right to a place in general European life, the conscious pariahs became marginal not only in relation to European society—as all Jews were—but to the Jewish community as well. They were neither parochially Jewish, like their Eastern European cousins, nor were they part of the wealthy Jewish upper class of bankers and merchants that controlled Jewish-gentile relations. According to Arendt, the conscious pariah is a hidden tradition: "hidden" because there are few links among the great but isolated individuals who have affirmed their pariah status—such as Heinrich Heine, Rahel Varnhagen, Bernard Lazare, Franz Kafka, and Walter Benjamin—nor ties between them and the rest of the Jewish community; a "tradition" because "for over a hundred years the same basic conditions have obtained and evoked the same basic reaction."[5]

The parvenus—the upstarts who try to make it in non-Jewish society—are the products of the same historical circumstances and are thus the pariahs' counterparts in Arendt's typology. While the pariahs use their minds and hearts, voluntarily spurning society's insidious gifts, the parvenus use their elbows to raise themselves above their fellow Jews into the "respectable" world of the gentiles. The parvenus are at best accepted only as "exceptions" to the stereotype of the uncouth, unworldly ghetto Jew—and those Jews who succeed with this ploy feel themselves superior to their fellow Jews. Those Jews who spurn social acceptance on the basis of this self-deceit have been few, but in exchange for their isolation from both Jewish and gentile society, these conscious pariahs gain the honesty that makes life worth living, a clear view of reality, and a place in both European and Jewish history.

Not only did Hannah Arendt formulate and celebrate the Jewish pariah as a human type, she epitomized it in her life and thought. As a conscious pariah who was committed to, yet critical of, both her Jewish and European inheritances, her intellectual project as a whole was founded in the problematic of Jewishness in the modern world. The transformation of Judaism into Jewishness in an increasingly secular world meant that, like Kafka, she had lost the Judaic heritage of her fathers without gaining a firmly rooted place in the European polity, which itself was in the process of collapse. As a pariah, her work is characterized by the dialectical tension between her Jewishness and modern Jewish experience, on the one side, and her European and generalized human experience in the modern age, on the other. The result was a unique outlook on both Jewish and European concerns in which the specifically Jewish and broadly European experiences constantly inform one another. Arendt's most lauded work, *The Origins of Totalitarianism,* is clearly the product of a conscious pariah, without equal as an intricate and beautiful pattern into which both Jewish and European concerns and history are intentionally woven together.

Not standing exclusively inside or outside either her Jewish or European heritage, Hannah Arendt uses both as platforms from which to gain a critical insight into the other. On the one hand, she consciously stands outside the Jewish tradition, subjecting the experience of the Jews in the modern world to the criticism of a German philosopher rooted in the European classics. Distinguishing between Jewishness—an existential given that one cannot escape—and Judaism—a system of beliefs which one can adopt or reject—she adamantly accepts the one and rejects the other. In doing so, she became a rebel among her own people. On the other hand, Arendt uses her experience as a Jew and her perspective as a conscious pariah standing outside the mainstream of Western society to analyze and gain an understanding of that society. By claiming that "[i]t is no mere accident that the catastrophic defeats of the peoples of Europe began with the catastrophe of the Jewish people,"[6] Arendt places the modern Jewish experience at the center of her critique of modern society.

This Jewish-European dialectic in her work has been a perpetual source of misunderstanding on the part of critics concerned with both her Jewish and non-Jewish work, for she falls within no established historical or philosophical perspective. Much like Kafka, with whom Arendt has a feeling of particular closeness and to whom she expresses a particular debt, the Jewish element is crucial though not exclusive: her Jewishness is not her sole concern nor the sole determinant of her work, but our understanding of her work is both diminished and seriously distorted if we overlook it. Arendt's own understanding of her peculiar perspective is best expressed in her letter to Scholem:

> What confuses you is that my arguments and my approach are different from what you are used to; in other words, the trouble is that I am independent. By this I mean, on the one hand, that I do not belong to any organisation and always speak only for myself, and on the other hand, that I have great confidence in Lessing's *selbstdenken* [thinking for oneself] for which, I think, no ideology, no public opinion, and no "convictions" can ever be a substitute. Whatever objections you may have to the results, you won't understand them unless you realize that they are really my own and nobody else's.[7]

II

> The enthusiastic Jewish intellectual dreaming of
> the paradise on earth, so certain of freedom from
> all national ties and prejudices, was in fact farther
> removed from political reality than his fathers,
> who had prayed for the coming of Messiah and
> the return of the people to Palestine.[8]

The twentieth century saw the most momentous changes in Jewish history since the destruction of the Second Temple in 70 C.E. The annihilation of European Jewry by the Nazis during World War II, and the founding of the Jewish State of Israel shortly thereafter, have radically changed the position of Jews in the world. The result has been a transformation of relations amongst Jews themselves and between them and the other peoples of the world. Though inextricably linked, the Holocaust and the Jewish State raise two different sets of questions. The Holocaust is the end of an era of Jewish existence and therefore raises questions about the past—how and why it happened. The Jewish State is the beginning of a new era and therefore raises questions about what it means to be a part of the Jewish people today and in the future. Of course, the answers to the second set of questions have been and must be influenced by the answers to the first, whether explicitly articulated in thought or implicitly contained in action. The task of trying to understand how and why the Holocaust happened and what has—or should be—changed as a result is the central task of Jewish thought in the post-Holocaust era.

The essays in this volume, particularly when read together with Arendt's other works in which Jewish history is discussed—*The Origins of Totalitarianism, Rahel Varnhagen, Men in Dark Times,* and *Eichmann in Jerusalem*—present Hannah Arendt's response to this challenge. Not only does she attempt to understand the sources of modern antisemitism by tracing the historical relationships of Jews and gentiles, but she also criticizes the modes of Jewish self-understanding and world-understanding that resulted in the Jewish responses of unbelief and passivity in the face of destruction.

Hannah Arendt's critical assessment of Jewish history is based on the fundamental political conviction that the world is what we make of it. There is no Hegelian "cunning of reason," but "rather does unreason begin to function automatically when reason has abdicated to it."[9] The Jews, by the very fact of their existence, are "one group of people among other groups, all of which are involved in the business of this world. And . . . [the Jews do] not simply cease to be coresponsible because . . . [they] became the victim of the world's injustice and cruelty."[10] Unlike both the "scapegoat" theory, which claims that the Jews were accidental victims, and the "eternal antisemitism" theory, which claims that the Jews are inevitable victims, Arendt tries to show that the catastrophic end to the history of the Jews in Europe was neither accidental nor inevitable. Rather, it was the result of the specific history of Jewish-gentile relationships. If the Jews were so politically blind that they did not understand the implications of their own actions and those of their opponents, it was the result of what Arendt considers the key feature of Jewish history in the modern period: the Jews' *worldlessness.*

Jewish history offers the extraordinary spectacle of a people, unique in this respect, which began its history with a well-defined concept of history and an almost conscious resolution to achieve a well-circumscribed plan on earth and then, without giving up this concept, avoided all political action for two thousand years. The result was that the political history of the Jewish people became even more dependent upon unforeseen, accidental factors than the history of other nations, so that the Jews stumbled from one role to the other and accepted responsibility for none.[11]

In Arendt's view, the continued existence of the Jewish people throughout the period of the Diaspora was until very recently much more the result of Jewish dissociation from the dominant Christian world than gentile dissociation from the Jews. It is only since the nineteenth century that antisemitism has had a significant effect on Jewish preservation. Given the conditions of the Diaspora, this dissociation was the only possible method of self-preservation and, Arendt claims, survival has been the single aim of Jewish political thought and action since the Babylonian exile. This traditional solution to the problem of survival was to help prepare the basis for the later dissolution of the Jewish people; for, by making dissociation the basis for their survival, the Jews came to conceive of their existence as almost totally separate and independent from the rest of the world. Consequently, the Jews became ignorant of conditions in the real world and incapable of recognizing new opportunities and new threats to their survival as they arose.

Until the end of the Middle Ages, by Arendt's account, the Jews "had been able to conduct their communal affairs by means of a politics that existed in the realm of imagination alone—the memory of a far-off past and the hope of a far-off future."[12] This conceptual framework was destroyed by an event that ushered in the beginning of the modern age for the Jews: the failure of the mystical messianic movement centered around Shabbatai Tzevi in 1666. The great historian of Shabbatai Tzevi is Gershom Scholem, and it is in "Jewish History, Revised," her review of Scholem's *Major Trends in Jewish Mysticism,* as well as "The Jewish State: Fifty Years After" that Hannah Arendt presents a unique political twist to the understanding of that event.

Shabbetai Tzevi's appearance on the scene was the culmination of a two-century period during which Jewish-gentile relations were at an all-time low and during which the mysticism of the Kabbalah had become popularized and extremely widespread. Because of their lack of involvement in and control over the political world in which they lived, the Jews were strongly attracted to mystical thought since "these speculations appeal to all who are actually excluded from action, prevented from altering a fate that appears to them unbearable and, feeling themselves helpless victims of incomprehensible forces, are naturally inclined to find some secret means for gaining power for participating in the 'drama of the World.'"[13]

The messianic fervor which gripped the entire Jewish world had no basis in particular events occurring in the non-Jewish world, but was the result of the internal dynamics created by accepting mysticism as a substitute for political action; the Kabbalah saw the events leading to the messianic perfection of the world as a matter exclusively concerning God and His people Israel. When acted upon, the yearning for political reality that was confined within mystical categories could only shatter those categories because they offered no basis for evaluating political realities. Thus, when Tzevi turned apostate in the face of the reality of the sultan's power and the popular messianic hope for a physical return to Zion was dashed, the traditional Jewish religious framework for understanding the world was dealt a severe blow.

But, according to Arendt, this confrontation with reality did not engender a more "realistic" understanding among the Jews; understanding can exist only when there is a framework within which to place events. In her view, the Shabbetai Tzevi catastrophe destroyed the traditional framework without replacing it with another. The result was an unprecedented worldlessness:

> In losing their faith in a divine beginning and ultimate culmination of history, the Jews lost their guide through the wilderness of bare facts; for when man is robbed of all means of interpreting events he is left with no sense whatsoever of reality. The present that confronted the Jews after the Shabbetai Tzevi debacle was the turmoil of a world whose course no longer made sense and in which, as a result, the Jews could no longer find a place.[14]

In Arendt's view, the Shabbetain movement was "a great political movement" of "real popular action" which let loose onto the public scene what she sees as Jewish mysticism's "exclusive concern with reality and action."[15] The result, however, was a catastrophe "greater for the Jewish people than all other persecutions had been, if we are to measure it by the only available yardstick, its far-reaching influence upon the future of the people. From now on, the Jewish body politic was dead and the people retired from the public scene of history."[16] The legacy of the period of Jewish estrangement from the non-Jewish world, played out in the subsequent history of Hasidism, the

Reform movement, attempted assimilation, and revolutionary utopianism, was that the Jews were "even less 'realistic'—that is, less capable than ever before of facing and understanding the real situation."[17]

The "real situation" was that by the seventeenth century the Jews were becoming involved in the world as a whole and moving into positions of potential political power. According to Arendt's analysis, presented in *The Origins of Totalitarianism,* the Jews, in the persons of the court Jews and the international bankers which followed them, were instrumental in the ascendence of the absolute monarchies and the subsequent development of the nation-state. Unlike the declining nobility and the privatistic bourgeoisie, "the Jews were the only part of the population willing to finance the state's beginnings and to tie their destinies to its further development."[18]

While being the state's financiers had great potential for political power, as the antisemites were quick to understand, the worldless mentality of the Jews was such that "they never allied themselves with any specific government, but rather with governments, with authority as such."[19] The wealthy Jews involved in "finance politics" were more concerned with continuing legal discrimination against the poor Jewish masses to preserve their privileged position of prestige and power within the Jewish community than in attaining power over the gentiles. As the practical rulers of the Jewish community, they were conscientious about their role as its protectors, but ignorant of their real potential among non-Jews. Their political concerns and perceptions never extended further than the pursuit of the only political goal the Jews ever had: survival. "The Jews, without knowledge of or interest in power, never thought of exercising more than mild pressure for minor purposes of self-defense."[20]

The Jews didn't realize that the modern state—a supposedly political entity ruling over class society—soon came into conflict with various classes which comprised that society. Their special services to and special protection from the political authorities prevented either the Jews' submersion in the class system or their emergence as a separate class. They were thus the only distinctive social group that owed its continued existence to the government, unconditionally supported the state as such, and, like the state, stood apart from society and its class distinctions. The result, Arendt observes, was that "each class of society which came into a conflict with the state as such became antisemitic because the only social group which seemed to represent the state were the Jews."[21]

Precisely because they were neither part of class society nor the state's politically active governing clique, the Jews were oblivious to the increasing tension between state and society at the same time that they were driven toward the center of the conflict because they stood between the two as part of neither. Politically naïve enough to believe that their true lack of interest in power would be seen and accepted for what it was, they were taken completely by surprise when twentieth-century political antisemitism rose to power on the basis of charges of a Jewish world conspiracy. This political myopia reflects

> the most serious paradox embodied in the curious political history of the Jews. Of all European peoples, the Jews had been the only one without a state of their own and had been, precisely for this reason, so eager and so suitable for alliances with governments and states as such, no matter what these governments or states might represent. On the other hand, the Jews had no political tradition or experience, and were as little aware of the tension between society and state as they were of the obvious risks and power-possibilities of their new role.[22]

Oblivious to the fact that they were instrumental in the development of the nation-state, the Jews were equally unconcerned with the maintenance of the nation-state system against the rise of the bourgeoisie's imperialist designs. Indeed, the Jews unwittingly helped the process along. Having "reached a saturation point in wealth and economic fortune . . . the sons of the well-to-do businessmen and, to a lesser extent, bankers, deserted their fathers' careers for the liberal professions or purely intellectual pursuits"[23] rather than fighting the growing influence of big business and industry that was causing a decay of their political position.

The great Jewish influx into the arts and sciences resulted in the development of a truly international society whose basis was the "radiant power of fame."[24] This phenomenon is extensively discussed in Arendt's essay, "Stefan Zweig: Jews in the World of Yesterday." For Arendt, this was yet another permutation of that quality of the Jewish condition that had made the Jews useful in the first place, their inter-European, nonnational character. The Jews entered into the cultural world and became the "outstanding reviewers, critics, collectors, and organizers of what was famous . . . the living tie binding famous individuals into a society of the renowned, an international society by definition, for spiritual achievement transcends national boundaries."[25]

Although assimilated Jews rarely recognized the fact, since within this international society their Jewish identity could effectively be lost, it was precisely those attributes—"kindness, freedom from prejudice, sensitiveness to injustice,"[26] "the 'Jewish heart,' humanity, humor, disinterested intelligence,"[27] and "fraternity"[28]—which were the privileges of the Jews as a pariah people that produced this particular kind of greatness. These gifts derived from "the great privilege of being unburdened by care for the world."[29] It is a privilege dearly bought, however, for the price is "real worldlessness. And worldlessness, alas, is always a form of barbarism."[30]

This barbarism was reflected in that Jewish unconcern with the political affairs of the world which developed to such an extent that the assimilated Jews "lost that measure of political responsibility which their origin implied and which the Jewish notables had still felt, albeit in the form of privilege and rulership."[31] They forgot the fact that in every Jew "there still remained something of the old-time pariah, who has no country, for whom human rights do not exist, and whom society would gladly exclude from its privileges."[32] Their activities brought them such social prominence that "Jews became the symbols of Society as such and the objects of hatred for all those whom society did not accept,"[33] while at the same time they lost interest in the "finance politics" that had brought them a modicum of protection from the state.

Arendt's critique concludes that Jewish worldlessness, which had its source in the Jews' attempt to preserve themselves by a radical and voluntary separation from the Christian world five hundred years earlier, culminated in the Jews' being more exposed to attack than ever before. More aware of theatrical appearance than political reality, the Jews had a blind faith in the state that had protected them since the emancipation; they forgot that this protection had rested on their performance of unique and necessary functions. The lack of involvement in the political world which had led religious Jews to single out divine providence as the key factor determining the Jews' political fate led secularized Jews to believe that Jewish history "takes place outside all usual historical laws."[34] What had appeared as God's unpredictable will—to which Jews responded with moralizing and penitential prayers—

was now viewed as accidental and drew the similarly unpolitical response of Jewish apologetics. Thus, when the Dreyfus Affair demonstrated a very real threat to the Jews' existence and its slogan of "Death to the Jews" became the rallying cry around which Nazism later grew by leaps and bounds, the Jews, who had become "an object of universal hatred because of [their] useless wealth, and of contempt because of [their] lack of power,"[35] were the last to grasp the political significance of events.

In Hannah Arendt's gloomy picture of Jewish political history there is, however, one positive response to the unreality and worldlessness of the pariah status. This is Zionism, "the only political answer Jews have ever found to antisemitism and the only ideology in which they have ever taken seriously a hostility that would place them in the center of world events."[36]

III

> From the "disgrace" of being a Jew there is but
> one escape—to fight for the honor of the Jewish
> people as a whole.[37]

The Zionist movement was founded by Theodor Herzl in August 1897, when the first Zionist Congress met and created the World Zionist Organization. Herzl had been a typically assimilated Jew until his Vienna newspaper sent him to cover the Dreyfus case. The impact of this event transformed him into an ardent Jewish nationalist. Herzl saw "the Jewish problem" of the antisemites as the political threat that it was and proposed a radical solution—the creation of a Jewish state. As the essays from the 1940s in this collection show, Hannah Arendt's view of the Herzlian brand of political Zionism which shaped the movement's perspective and policies is laudatory of its strengths, yet sharply critical of its shortcomings and potential dangers.

According to Arendt's understanding, Herzl viewed antisemitism as a natural conflict which arose from the fact that the Jews were a national entity separate and different from the nations amongst whom they lived. Because it was natural and inevitable, "Antisemitism was an overwhelming force and the Jews would have either to make use of it or to be swallowed up by it."[38] Necessarily flowing from the Jews' Diaspora existence, antisemitism was the almost eternal "'propelling force' responsible for all Jewish suffering since the destruction of the Temple and it would continue to make the Jews suffer until they learned how to use it for their own advantage."[39] Properly handled, it could lead the Jews to control over their destiny: Herzl believed that the antisemites were both rational and honest and that the Jewish problem was the most serious problem facing Europe. The "honest antisemites" would therefore help him implement his grand scheme to rid them of their Jews, gain Jewish independence, and solve the Jewish problem once and for all. Arendt commends Herzl, for his

> mere will to action was something so startlingly new, so utterly revolutionary in Jewish life, that it spread with the speed of wildfire. Herzl's lasting greatness lay in his very desire to do something about the Jewish question, his desire to act and to solve the problem in political terms.[40]

In Arendt's interpretation, Herzl's political Zionism was not the ideology of a mass revolutionary movement but was, rather, the creed of secularized Western European Jewish intellectuals. Zionism's great asset was that it answered the need that had existed among the Jews since the Sabbatian catastrophe had shattered the traditional Jewish framework of understanding and started the Jews on their perilous journey towards worldlessness: it offered a path back to reality. While its doctrine of eternal antisemitism is similar to other nineteenth-century ideologies which attempted to explain reality in terms of irresistible "laws" and history in terms of "keys," Zionism and the Zionist movement was unique, according to Arendt, because "the case of the Jews was and still remains different. What they needed was not only a guide to reality, but reality itself; not simply a key to history, but the experience itself of history."[41]

The great achievement of Herzl's Zionist theory is that it escapes the view which sees history as a totally fortuitous series of events understandable only in terms of providence and accident. Its great limitation is that Jewish history is reduced to mere surface manifestations of one unchanging law over which the Jews have no control and whose source is their mere existence as a nation. Thus, while Herzl and his followers were realistic enough to recognize the political actuality of antisemitism, the ideology of "natural" antisemitism meant that no political analysis of it was necessary. Their view, according to Arendt, presupposes the eternity of antisemitism in an eternal world of nations, and moreover, denies the Jewish part of responsibility for existing conditions. Thereby it not only cuts off Jewish history from European history and even from the rest of mankind; it ignores the role that European Jewry played in the construction and functioning of the national state; and thus it is reduced to the assumption, as arbitrary as it is absurd, that every gentile living with Jews must become a conscious or subconscious Jew-hater."[42]

Implicit in this notion of a natural and inevitable antisemitism was that political reality consisted of an unchanging and unchangeable structure whose main components were the Jews on one side and the nation-states on the other. For the political Zionists, "politics" therefore meant international relations, affairs of state. Herzl's political action consisted of attempts at high-level diplomacy with the great powers, all of which came to nothing. Zionist political policy became one of unrealistic *Realpolitik*. Rather than organizing a powerful popular movement of world Jewry, relying on their own power to achieve their aims, and allying themselves with the oppressed peoples of the Near East, Arendt believes that the Zionist movement "sold out at the very first moment to the powers that be."[43] Furthermore, the ideology of eternal antisemitism led the Zionists into another typical response of the persecuted Diaspora Jew: rather than fighting antisemitism on its own ground, the Zionist solution was to escape.

> The building up of Palestine is indeed a great accomplishment and could be made an important and even decisive argument for Jewish claims in Palestine. . . . But the upbuilding of Palestine has little to do with answering the antisemites; at most it has "answered" the secret self-hatred and lack of self-confidence on the part of those Jews who have themselves consciously or unconsciously succumbed to some parts of antisemitic propaganda.[44]

Another consequence of Herzl's static view of reality was a blind hatred of all revolutionary movements and his patronizing attitude toward the Jewish masses of Eastern Europe. The only political Zionist who ever proposed that the Zionist movement "organize the Jewish people in order to negotiate on the basis of a great revolutionary movement"[45]—what it should have been, according to Arendt—was Bernard Lazare, the French-Jewish author and lawyer who was the first to publicize the innocence of the accused Captain Dreyfus.

Remembering that Arendt is first and foremost a political thinker,[46] and that her aim is to present a political interpretation of Jewish history, it is understandable that Bernard Lazare stands out as a figure of singular importance and greatness in Arendt's account of Jewish history and Zionism. According to Arendt, Lazare was the first to translate the Jews' social status as a pariah people into terms of political significance by making it a tool for political analysis and the basis for political action.

> Living in the France of the Dreyfus affair, Lazare could appreciate at first hand the pariah quality of Jewish existence. But he knew where the solution lay: in contrast to his unemancipated brethren who accept their pariah status automatically and unconsciously, the emancipated Jew must awake to an awareness of his position and, conscious of it, become a rebel against it—the champion of an oppressed people. His fight for freedom is part and parcel of that which all the downtrodden of Europe must wage to achieve national and social liberation.[47]

Having become a conscious pariah as a result of the Dreyfus Affair, to whom "history is no longer a closed book . . . and politics is no longer the privilege of gentiles,"[48] Lazare perforce became a Zionist.

Lazare belonged to the official Zionist movement only briefly, however. Having attended the Second Zionist Congress in 1898, where he was immediately elected to the Actions Committee, Lazare resigned from the committee and separated himself from the Zionist Organization in 1899 because the committee was acting like "a sort of autocratic government [that] seeks to direct the Jewish masses as though they were ignorant children."[49] Lazare wanted to promote a revolution within Jewish life, to criticize the role Jewish finance played in internal affairs and the effects it had on the relation of the Jews to non-Jews. But, Arendt claims, there was no possibility for such radical views within "Herzl's essentially reactionary movement."[50]

> Herzl's solution of the Jewish problem was, in the final analysis, escape or deliverance in a homeland. In the light of the Dreyfus case the whole of the gentile world seemed to him hostile; there were only Jews and

antisemites. . . . To Lazare, on the other hand, the territorial question was secondary—a mere outcome of the primary demand that "the Jews should be emancipated as a people and in the form of a nation." What he sought was not an escape from antisemitism but a mobilization of the people against its foes.[51]

In terms of the perspective Arendt displays through the essays in this collection, the importance of Lazare as a model of what it means to be a political pariah is hard to overestimate. It is significant to note that Hannah Arendt edited the first collection of his essays that appeared in English, *Job's Dungheap* (1948), writing a short biography for that volume. Not only is his work the source from which Arendt derives many of her insights into both modern Jewish history and Zionism (it is from Lazare that Arendt borrows the terms "pariah" and "parvenu"), but his experience as an outspoken Jew cast out from the Jewish community because of his criticism closely parallels the experience of Arendt herself. Interestingly, in the 1940s, when Arendt wrote about Lazare's exclusion from Jewish circles due to his views on how the Dreyfus case should have been handled, she could not have anticipated what was to cause her a similar experience of modern excommunication: the trial of Adolf Eichmann. Although in the first case it was the Jews who were on trial and in the second it was antisemitism, both Lazare and Arendt based their criticism of the trials' conduct on the grounds that justice for the defendant must be the aim of legal proceedings, not political demagoguery and showmanship.

According to Arendt, the lesson of Lazare's experience as a Jewish political thinker and actor is that "[a]s soon as the pariah enters the arena of politics, and translates his status into political terms, he becomes perforce a rebel."[52] The social pariahs of the nineteenth century, such as Heine and Varnhagen, drew comfort from the world of dreams and fantasy, secure in the knowledge that as compared to nature, human concerns are pure vanity. In the twentieth century, however, Arendt believes that such a retreat is no longer possible: the pariah must become political. Thus, the first consequence of becoming conscious of one's pariah status is the demand that the Jewish people "come to grips with the world of men and women."[53] The duty of the conscious pariah is to waken one's fellow Jews to a similar consciousness so as to rebel against it. "[Lazare] saw that what was necessary was to rouse the Jewish pariah to fight against the Jewish *parvenu.* There was no other way to save him from the latter's own fate—inevitable destruction."[54] This call to action was founded on the conviction that

> [h]owever much the Jewish pariah might be, from the historical view-point, the product of an unjust dispensation . . . politically speaking, every pariah who refused to be a rebel was partly responsible for his own position and therewith for the blot on mankind which it repre-sented. From such shame there was no escape, either in art or in nature. For insofar as man is more than a mere creature of nature, more than a mere product of divine creativity, insofar will he be called to account for the things which men do to men in the world which they themselves condition.[55]

This responsibility for the human world, whether one is a victim or a vic-timizer, is at the core of Hannah Arendt's political philosophy, and it is the basis for her politically radical, self-critical analysis of the modern Jewish experience that leads to a Zionist conclusion. But Arendt's Zionism is not in the mainstream Herzlian tradition; it is, rather, in the dissident mold of Bernard Lazare, who wanted to be a revolutionary among his own people, not among others. It is well to keep this point in mind as we turn to Arendt's critical assessment of the founding of the Jewish State of Israel.

IV

> The real goal of the Jews in Palestine is the build-ing up of a Jewish homeland. This goal must never be sacrificed to the pseudo-sovereignty of a Jewish state.[56]

Hannah Arendt's essays on Zionism and the Jewish State were written prior to 1950, the most crucial period in the history of the Zionist movement. Her views were shared by only a very small minority of Zionists, most of whom were organized in the *Ihud,* the latest in a long line of small organizations of Palestinian Jews whose purposes were to promote Jewish-Arab understand-ing and cooperation. Never very large or effectual, the *Ihud* and its advocacy of a binational solution to the Jewish-Arab conflict was well known because it contained a large number of outstanding intellectual, cultural, and philanthropic leaders such as Rabbi Judah Magnes (president of the Hebrew University), Henrietta Szold (the organizer of Youth Aliyah and founder of Hadassah), and Martin Buber.

In the mid-1940s, however, the *Ihud*'s advocacy of binationalism was out of step with the mainstream of the Zionist movement. While for many years the Zionist majority was in favor of coexistence with the Arabs in a binational Palestine, by the end of World War II, in reaction to the genocide of European Jewry, the Zionist maximum—the establishment of a sovereign Jewish State—had become the Zionist minimum. This shift in the Zionist position is the crux of Arendt's criticism of official Zionist policy throughout this period, for she maintained—in 1945, when the Zionist movement demanded a Jewish State in all of Palestine, again in 1948, when they had accepted the principle of partition, and once again, in 1950, after Israel had been established by force of arms—that the creation of a Jewish State was out of touch with the realities of the situation in the Near East and the world at large.[57]

Arendt's criticism of Zionist politics is founded on a deep concern with the fate of the Jewish people following the Holocaust. The realization that millions of Jews had gone to their deaths without resistance resulted in a revolutionary change in Jewish consciousness. "Gone, probably forever, is that chief concern of the Jewish people for centuries: survival at any price. Instead, we find something essentially new among Jews, the desire for dignity at any price."[58] According to Arendt, this shift had the potential to become the basis for "an essentially sane Jewish political movement,"[59] for it indicated a desire to deal with reality and live freely in the world. The problem was that in their desire to overcome the centuries-long experience of worldlessness, the Jews grasped onto the unrealistic ideological framework of Herzlian Zionism and its doctrine of eternal antisemitism. The result was the famous "Masada complex" in which this newfound desire for dignity was transformed into a potentially suicidal attitude. The danger to the Jewish homeland, as Arendt saw it, was that "[t]here is nothing in Herzlian Zionism that could act as a check on this; on the contrary, the utopian and ideological elements with which he injected the new Jewish will to political action are only too likely to lead the Jews out of reality once more—and out of the sphere of political action."[60]

It was this dangerous course Arendt had in mind when she wrote that "at this moment and under present circumstances a Jewish State can only be erected at the price of the Jewish homeland."[61] Since the "Jewish homeland" has been virtually synonymous with the "Jewish State" since Israel's independence in 1948, it may be difficult to understand Arendt's distinction. In order to do so, we must piece together Arendt's own particular brand of Zionism.

Arendt observes that "Palestine and the building of a Jewish homeland constitute today the great hope and the great pride of Jews all over the world."[62] This deceptively simple sentence contains the essence of her conception of the Jewish homeland as a place that is a *center* and a place that is *built*. Arendt's Zionism is in many ways similar to the "cultural" Zionism of Bialik and Ahad Haam, but she arrives at it for reasons that in her view are highly political. The establishment of a Jewish cultural center in Palestine is a conscious act of creation on the part of the Jewish people; it is a positive response to the crises that have racked Jewish life since the time of Shabbetai Tzevi, for it is an attempt by the Jews to create a political realm, take control over their lives, and reenter history after the Diaspora with its accompanying worldlessness and powerlessness. The building of the Jewish homeland is a profoundly political act, for it means not only the fabrication of a "world" within which a truly human life can be lived but the fabrication of a specifically Jewish world. This cultural specificity is of great importance, "[f]or only within the framework of a people can a man live as a man among men."[63]

Many people have recognized that the *Yishuv* (the pre-state Jewish community in Palestine)—and, later, the State of Israel—was a highly artificial creation. This is usually understood to be a criticism of the Jewish homeland, for the whole point of the homeland in Herzl's ideology is to "normalize" and make "natural" the Jews' "unnatural" Diaspora existence. For Arendt, however, "precisely this artificiality gave the Jewish achievements in Palestine their human significance."[64] The greatness of the *Yishuv* was that it was the conscious product of the concerted will of the Jewish people and *not* the predestined product of any natural forces to which the Jewish people were subject. "The challenges were all there, but none of the responses was 'natural.'"[65] The economic development of the *Yishuv* bore little resemblance to the traditional colonial enterprise. Rather than the usual "original accumulation" in which native riches are exploited with the help and at the expense of native labor in order to enrich the colonial power, the riches of the *Yishuv* "are exclusively the product of Jewish labor."[66] The revival of the Hebrew language, the erection of the Hebrew University, the new modes of human organization and cooperation found in the *kibbutzim,* and the establishment of great health centers "can certainly not be explained by utilitarian reasons."[67]

Unlike those Zionists who considered the establishment of a state to be not only the goal but the ultimate sign of success of the Jewish people's effort to reestablish themselves in their ancient home, Arendt considers the *Yishuv* to already embody the aims of Zionism as she sees them. For Arendt, the Jewish homeland is a political space, a human world created by conscious human effort where a Jewish culture can come into being; this the *Yishuv* achieved, without political sovereignty and without being a majority in Palestine. Precisely because a Jewish community had been built where people could appear to each other, where there was an audience for works of literature and art, Jewish cultural genius no longer needed to either abandon its Jewish roots, in favor of "universal" European culture or else be relegated to the category of folklore. It was this political and cultural space of the "Jewish homeland" that Arendt felt was being sacrificed on the altar of the "Jewish state" by the unrealistic political demands of the Zionist movement.

In Arendt's opinion, the demand for a Jewish state simply ignored the fact that the majority of Palestine's population was Arab, and that Palestine itself was surrounded by millions of Arabs in the neighboring countries. The Zionist demand for a state left the Palestinian Arabs with only two choices: emigration or acceptance of their eventual minority status, both of which were unacceptable to a people striving for their independence. The inalterable fact of the Near East was that the Arabs were the Jews' neighbors. In order to preserve the Jewish homeland in Palestine once the British pulled out, the Jews had the choice of either working out an agreement with the Arabs or seeking the protection of one of the great imperial powers. By choosing the latter, the concept of a Jewish state would become farcical and even self-defeating insofar as that state would be a bastion of imperial interests in an area striving to liberate itself from colonialism. On the other hand, Arendt recognized that Arab policies were equally blind in not recognizing the needs and concrete achievements of the Zionists in Palestine.

The unrealistic approach to the Palestinian situation on the part of both the Jews and Arabs, Arendt observed, was the result of the British Mandate under which the British mediated between and separated the two communities from each other. This allowed Jews and Arabs to develop without any political regard or responsibility for each other and made it seem to each of them that the main political issue was how to deal with and ultimately get rid of the British, ignoring the permanent reality of the other's existence. The real issues at the heart of the conflict were "Jewish determination to keep and possibly extend national sovereignty without consideration for Arab interests, and Arab determination to expel the Jewish 'invaders' from Palestine without consideration for Jewish achievements there."[68] The Jewish and Arab claims were perfectly incompatible and mutually irrefutable, for both were the result of nationalistic policies reached within "the closed framework of one's own people and history."[69]

Arendt believed that cooperation between Jews and Arabs in the Near East could, by developing the area, be the basis for true sovereignty and independence. But the only way for this to occur was if both sides gave up their nationalistic and chauvinistic perspectives and claims. "Good relationships between Jews and Arabs will depend upon a changed attitude toward each other, upon a change in the atmosphere in Palestine and the Near East, not necessarily upon a formula."[70] Prophetically, she warned that "if this 'independent and sovereign' behavior . . . goes on unabated, then all independence and sovereignty will be lost."[71]

The inevitable war that would result from the spurious sovereignty upon which the Zionist movement had set its sights would almost certainly destroy those aspects of the Jewish homeland that in Arendt's view had made it "the great hope and the great pride of Jews all over the world." Prior to the *Yishuv*'s success during the War of Liberation (1948–49), the very survival of Israel was highly questionable. Like most Jewish observers then (and now), Arendt's prime concern was with the consequence for the Jewish people of a second catastrophe so soon after Hitler.

What would happen to Jews, individually and collectively, if this hope and this pride were to be extinguished in another catastrophe is almost beyond imagining. But it is certain that this would become the central fact of Jewish history and it is possible that it might become the beginning of the self-dissolution of the Jewish people. There is no Jew in the world whose whole outlook on life and the world would not be radically changed by such a tragedy.[72]

Today we know that such a tragedy did not occur; but unlike most observers of that period, Arendt asserted that "even if the Jews were to win the war, its end would find the unique possibilities and the unique achievements of Zionism in Palestine destroyed."[73] Without a peace agreement with the Arabs—and the Arabs were not prepared to accept a sovereign Jewish state in their midst—the internal nature of the *Yishuv* would be radically transformed. The result of an uneasy armistice with its neighbors, Arendt predicted, would be that concerns of military self-defense would come to dominate all other public interest and activities. "The growth of a Jewish culture would cease to be the concern of the whole people; social experiments would have to be discarded as impractical luxuries; political thought would center around military strategy; economic development would be determined exclusively by the needs of war."[74] With the constant threat from abroad, the country would have to be perpetually prepared for instantaneous mobilization; in order to sustain such a spirit of sacrifice, nationalism and chauvinism would quickly seep into the political and cultural atmosphere. Under these circumstances, a military dictatorship could easily result.

Arendt also felt that as a consequence of statehood the great achievements of the labor movement—particularly the *kibbutzim*—and of the cultural Zionists—particularly the Hebrew University—"would be the first victims of a long period of military insecurity and nationalistic aggressiveness."[75] They would become increasingly isolated as their "anti-nationalist" and "anti-chauvinist" Zionism did not fit the need for a statist ideology. But these would only be the first victims, "[f]or without the cultural and social *hinterland* of Jerusalem and the collective settlements, Tel Aviv could become a Levantine city overnight. Chauvinism . . . could use the religious concept of the chosen people and allow its meaning to degenerate into hopeless vulgarity."[76]

With its wars and *raison d'état*, Arendt asserted that statehood would make the Jewish homeland's relationship with the Diaspora problematic. While the cultural center of world Jewry would become a modern-day Sparta, its large expenditures on national defense would lead Israel to excessive financial dependence upon American Jewry. The consequences of this were potentially disastrous:

> Charity money can be mobilized in great quantities only in emergencies, such as the recent catastrophe in Europe or in the Arab-Jewish war; if the Israeli government cannot win its economic independence from such money it will soon find itself in the unenviable position of being forced to create emergencies, that is, forced into a policy of aggressiveness and expansion.[77]

As Arendt warned, Herzl's Jewish state did not solve "the Jewish problem"; the tragic result has been that antisemitism has been transformed into anti-Zionism. With sovereignty, the pariah people has not ceased to be a pariah—it has created a pariah state. As a small state located in a key area of superpower rivalry, Israel's destiny is almost as subject to uncontrollable and unforeseen accidental circumstances as the Jews' fate in the Diaspora. Arendt contends that the often-expressed Israeli belief that they can stand up against the whole world, if necessary, is just as politically unrealistic as the Diasporic unconcern with politics. She feared that it might lead to an equally tragic end.

V

> For the first time Jewish history is not separate but
> tied up with that of all other nations. The comity
> of European peoples went to pieces when, and
> because, it allowed its weakest member to be
> excluded and persecuted.[78]

In a complex and largely implicit manner, Hannah Arendt placed the Jews and "the Jewish condition" at the center of her critique of the modern age. By doing so she took one of Karl Marx's ideas and transformed it into part of her own system of thought. In the process she came up with both her own insights and a critique of Marx. A number of aspects of her political theory were arrived at in this fashion, but this case is special. The discovery was not of just one particular quality of modern society but concerns the central category of Arendt's and Marx's respective critiques of the modern age. As Arendt puts it, "(w)orld alienation, and not self-alienation as Marx thought, has been the hallmark of the modern age."[79]

It was Marx, in his essay "On the Jewish Question," who first put forward the thesis that the Jews, rather than being a backward people who had to be "civilized," were actually at the forefront of contemporary developments and embodied the true spirit of the modern age. According to Marx, the reason why "the Jewish question"—whether the Jews were fit for entrance into civil society—was being considered was not that the Jews had become similar to the Christians, but that society was becoming "Jewish":

> The Jew has emancipated himself in a Jewish manner, not only by acquiring the power of money, but also because *money* has become, through him and also apart from him, a world power, while the practical Jewish spirit has become the practical spirit of the Christian nations. The Jews have emancipated themselves in so far as the Christians have become Jews.[80]

It is among the Jews that Marx first discovers money as the "universal *antisocial* element of the *present time*" which is "the *supreme practical* expression of human self-estrangement" that causes "civil society [to] separate itself completely from the life of the state, [to] sever all the species-bonds of man, [and to] dissolve the human world into a world of atomistic, antagonistic individuals."[81] Marx later elaborates the antisocial element inherent in money as such into the social relationship defined by "commodity fetishism" and simultaneously shifts his focus from the Jews to the bourgeoisie. This is no accident, for the Jews were—at most—protocapitalists. As merchants, financiers, and moneylenders, more than any other group they had lived apart from the land and within the money economy during the medieval and early modern periods. It is thus among the Jews, according to Marx, that the real nature of capitalism—the alienation that results from the commodity fetishism inherent in money relations between people—first develops and reveals its inhumanity.

The Jews' social and economic existence within the moneyed sector of the economy in precapitalist society thus foreshadowed the direction in which modern society was moving. With the emergence of industrial capitalism— in Marx's view, the true basis of the modern social structure—Jewish merchant and finance capital became simply a parasitical sector of the capitalist class which received a portion of the surplus value expropriated from the laborer by the industrial bourgeoisie. Thus, while Marx first discovered what he considered to be the "secret" of capitalism by a consideration of the Jews and contended that historically it first developed among the Jews, he believed that the Jews did not have a unique place in the materialist dialectic of capitalist production which ground all people into either capitalists or workers. For Marx, the Jews had become unimportant in society and quickly ceased to figure in his analysis.

Avoiding Marx's misrepresentation of Judaism and his anti-Jewish rhetoric, more subtle and consistent in her analysis of Jews and "the Jewish question," Arendt never makes the facile assertion that modern society is becoming Jewish. Still, the Jews are at the center of her analysis. For Hannah Arendt, history is not made up of the mass of normal, everyday events. Rather, it is made up of the exceptional person and action that reveals the meaning of an historical period.[82] In the modern age, the experience of the Jews is the exception that illuminates the whole modern period, both in terms of the antisemitism that affected them from without and the worldless "Jewish condition" that affected them from within. Thus, while concurring with Marx's analysis that it is among the Jews that the characteristic phenomena of the modern age first appears, she also believes that, as the modern age develops, the dangerous effects of worldlessness are most clearly displayed in the history of the Jews. The very reason why Marx loses interest in the Jews—their marginal and unimportant status in terms of economic life—is precisely the reason why they are significant for Arendt. It is their very superfluousness, their separation from both state and society, that explains why "[i]t is no mere accident that the catastrophic defeats of the peoples of Europe began with the catastrophe of the Jewish people."[83]

In *The Human Condition*—which hardly refers to the Jews or Judaism—Arendt states that

> property, as distinguished from wealth and appropriation, indicates the privately owned share of a common world and therefore is the most elementary political condition for man's worldliness. By the same token, expropriation and world alienation coincide, and the modern age . . . began by alienating certain strata of the population from the world.[84]

In context it is clear that she is referring to the uprooting of peasants, but it is equally clear that among the Jews this lack of a "privately owned share of a common world" has been a condition of existence since the beginning of the Diaspora. The rootlessness of "the wandering Jew" antedates the rootlessness of the modern age, and more than any other factor was responsible for the worldless, unrealistic, and unpolitical perceptions Jews had of the world.

Until the Shabbetai Tzevi episode this worldlessness was kept within certain bounds. Although separated from the world around them, Arendt asserts that the Jews maintained an internal community whose cohesiveness and distinctiveness was expressed in the concept of exile, a fundamentally political notion which over the centuries had taken on religious form and become one of the central ideas of Judaism. Echoing Marx's analysis, the Jews lived within the market sector of the economy, a realm characterized by "the essential unreality of financial transactions."[85] But it wasn't the spread of the Jewish "god" of money that defined the modern age, as Marx would have it. Rather, the modern age was characterized by the cause which underlay the Jews' reliance on money wealth: the lack of any physical place to which people were rooted and from which they could orient themselves to the world, grasp reality, and experience history. The unique worldless situation of the Jews increasingly became the generalized condition of humankind. And, as the world within which they existed as a pariah people started to disintegrate, the Jews were at the forefront of the process because they had, as it were, a head start.

The atomization of communities into lonely individuals was a process most clearly visible among the assimilating Jews. On the one hand, assimilation spelled the end of the Jewish community. On the other hand, Jews were accepted into the ranks of high society only as exceptions. Thus, in order to become part of society, they had to escape from the Jewish community and become free-floating individuals. The road to assimilation by conforming to the standards laid down by high society was a precursor of the phenomenon of "conformism inherent in society."[86] What was demanded of the Jews was that they behave in an exceptional and peculiar but nevertheless recognizable—and hence stereotypic—"Jewish" way. The result of the ambiguous situation where they were supposed to both be—and not be—Jewish was that introspection characteristic of the "so-called complex psychology of the average Jew."[87]

In Arendt's analysis, the psychological conflict that derived from their unresolved social dilemma was that "Jews felt simultaneously the pariah's regret at not having become a parvenu and the parvenu's bad conscience at having betrayed his people and exchanged equal rights for personal privileges."[88] The result was that

> [i]nstead of being defined by nationality or religion, Jews were being transformed into a social group whose members shared certain psychological attributes and reactions, the sum total of which was supposed to constitute "Jewishness." In other words, Judaism became a psychological quality, and the Jewish question became an involved personal problem for every individual Jew.[89]

The Jews thus constituted the first large-scale example of what happens when political issues are dealt with on an individual, private level rather than a collective, public level. Thinking they were free from the given reality of their Jewish roots, Jews like Rahel Varnhagen tried to overcome their Jewishness by believing that "[e]verything depends on self-thinking."[90] Arendt, speaking from Rahel's point of view, comments that "[s]elf-thinking brings liberation from objects and their reality, creates a sphere of pure ideas and a world which is accessible to any rational being without benefit of knowledge or experience."[91] The result of this alienation from the real world was the breakup of the Jewish community into isolated, lonely individuals. "The terrible and bloody annihilation of individual Jews was preceded by the bloodless destruction of the Jewish people."[92]

For Arendt, the destruction of the Jewish community was only a predecessor to the destruction of communities throughout Europe. The subsequent result was the rise of ideologically based mass movements and the destruction of the nation-state. Despite its many problems and internal contradictions, Arendt does think that for a time prior to the economically inspired imperialism of the nineteenth century, the nation-state had provided a truly political form of human organization. The legal emancipation of the Jews was but one of its logical results. The destruction of the political organization of people in the nation-state and the class society upon which it rested was the first accomplishment of the Nazi movement's rise to power. By Arendt's account, class society was absorbed by mass society. The citizen, already turned into the bourgeois, now became the philistine: "the bourgeois isolated from his own class, the atomized individual who is produced by the breakdown of the bourgeois class itself."[93]

Citizenship, the foundation of politics, was now selectively denied to minorities—particularly Jews—on the basis of race. Stateless Jews, rightless people "thrown back into a peculiar state of nature,"[94] were among the first to discover that without the rights of the citizen there was no such thing as "the rights of man." The Jews, both pariahs and parvenus, found that once they became "outlaws" literally anything could be done with them, "that a man who is nothing but a man has lost the very qualities which make it possible for other people to treat him as a fellow-man."[95] Expelled from their homes and deprived of even the legal status of the criminal, nobody knew who they were or cared what happened to them. For the stateless, accident reigned supreme. They had absolutely no place on earth to go but internment and concentration camps. Statelessness was the ultimate manifestation of worldlessness, whose logical end is elimination from this world.

Precisely because of their worldless condition, the Jews became the first inhabitants of the laboratory of the concentration camp "in which the fundamental belief of totalitarianism that everything is possible is being verified."[96] It is here that worldlessness and atomization reach their ultimate form and people are reduced to nothing but their biological nature. Both individuality and community are systematically destroyed. The individuals shipped to the concentration camp are more effectively separated from the world of the living than if they were killed, for their very existence and memory are blotted out. World-alienation, a phenomenon which had made its earliest appearance in the modern age among the Jews, reached its climax with their destruction.

VI

Rahel had remained a Jewish woman and pariah.
Only because she clung to both identities did she
find a place in the history of European humanity.[97]

We are now in a position to briefly consider the bitter controversy which followed the publication of *Eichmann in Jerusalem*. What aroused her critics' ire more than anything else was her assertion that "[w]herever Jews lived, there were recognized Jewish leaders, and this leadership, almost without exception, cooperated in one way or another, for one reason or another, with the Nazis."[98] Gershom Scholem's reaction in his letter to Arendt was typical: "What perversity! We are asked, it appears, to confess that the Jews too had their 'share' in these acts of genocide."[99]

This criticism totally misses what Hannah Arendt is trying to show about the implications of total worldlessness, for which the "banality of evil" is a corollary. The horror is both that while Eichmann *never realized what he was doing,*[100] "the members of the Jewish Councils as a rule were *not* traitors or Gestapo agents, and *still* they became the tools of the Nazis."[101] It was no accident that the Jews were the first victims, and the utmost importance of considering the particularities of modern Jewish history is perhaps most succinctly summed up by Arendt in one of the most important passages in *Eichmann in Jerusalem:*

> It was when the Nazi regime declared that the German people not only were unwilling to have any Jews in Germany but wished to make the entire Jewish people disappear from the face of the earth that the new crime, the crime against humanity—in the sense of a crime "against the human status," or against the very nature of mankind—appeared. . . . The supreme crime it [the Israeli court trying Eichmann] was confronted with, the physical extermination of the Jewish people, was a crime against humanity, perpetrated upon the body of the Jewish people, and . . . only the choice of victims, not the nature of the crime, could be derived from the long history of Jew-hatred and anti-Semitism.[102]

For Hannah Arendt the destruction of the Jews is insolubly embedded in European history as a whole. It is only by recognizing the fact that the Jews *were* singled out by the Nazis that the crime against humanity appears, and it is precisely because of this particularity that the experience of the Jews *as* Jews is important for all humankind. It is no accident that the Jews were the first victims of the death factories which constitute the basis of totalitarianism; but they were just that, the *first* victims. Because it is exceptional, the Jews' fate sheds light on the history and experience of all people in the modern age.

As a conscious pariah, Arendt concerns herself with the Jews because she is both a Jew and a European, and she addresses herself to both the world as a whole and the Jews in particular. To the world she is saying that the Jews' condition is connected to everyone's condition, that what happened to the Jews is not an isolated instance but may happen to anybody because the crime itself is not uniquely Jewish, but was only perpetrated upon them. The lack of a political orientation to the world is what links the fate of the Jews to that of modern society as a whole.

Her experience as a Jewish refugee provided Hannah Arendt with the fundamental experience from which she derived worldliness as her standard of political judgment. Part of her impulse to search for paradigms of political thought and action in the experience of ancient Greece is that she wants to teach a sense of politics to a world in danger of doing what the Jews unwittingly did to themselves as well as what the Nazis did to the Jews. Arendt's great fear is that the condition of worldlessness which has characterized the Jews more than any other people in the modern age may become the generalized condition of our day.

To the Jews, Arendt is saying that part of the reason for the terrible end to their history in Europe is that they did not have a realistic political understanding of the world in which they lived. While Eichmann *"never realized what he was doing,"* the Jews never realized what was happening. In response to the Eichmann controversy, she reminds us that "[n]o State of Israel would ever have come into being if the Jewish people had not created and maintained its own specific in-between space throughout the long centuries of dispersion, that is, prior to the seizure of its old territory."[103] Her aim is to awaken Jews to the fact that whether or not they have been aware of it, they have been able to survive precisely because they have constituted a political community. To survive, they must break with the past in which accident reigned supreme and take conscious control of their destiny. The Zionist movement, and the *kibbutzim* in particular, are important phenomena not only for the Jews but for humankind as a whole because they demonstrate that *even* the Jews can establish a world through the power of collective action and that the so-called natural processes of society produce inevitable results only when human beings desert the realm of politics.

VII

Arendt's solution to her own "Jewish problem" was not to repudiate her Jewishness nor blindly affirm it, but to adopt the stance of a conscious pariah—an outsider among non-Jews, and a rebel among her own people. It was because of this marginal position that she was able to gain critical insights into both the Jewish and non-Jewish worlds. There are, of course, problems with both her version of modern Jewish history and her critique of modern society.[104] But, as is the case with truly original thinkers, the encounter with these problems is a valuable process for the reader.

The essays in this volume reveal the central importance of Arendt's experience as a Jew on both her life and work. The rising of Nazism pushed her from being a student of philosophy into political awareness and activism; her political education was as a Jew, and specifically as a Zionist. "I realized what I then expressed time and again in the sentence: If one is attacked as Jew, one must defend oneself as a Jew. Not as a German, not as a world-citizen, not as an upholder of the Rights of Man, or whatever. But: What can I specifically do as Jew? Second, it was now my clear intention to work with an organization. For the first time. To work with the Zionists. They were the only ones who were ready. It would have been pointless to join those who had assimilated."[105]

Arendt believed that the Jewish experience can only be understood by consideration of the complete context within which the Jews lived as a distinctive minority. Her focus was on the *interactions* between Jews and non-Jews. Issues concerning Jews were relevant beyond the borders of the Jewish community, and vice versa.

In the Jewish community Arendt's views—or, what have come to be seen as Arendt's views—continue to be subject of controversy;[106] no doubt this collection will add new fuel to that fire. Argument and criticism are intrinsic aspects of Jewish culture; criticism in itself is not self-hatred. Arendt may disapprove of the powers that be and specific policies they are practicing, but she was committed to the idea that there *is* a Jewish people and that Jews could and should participate *as Jews* in the politics of the Jewish community, and through it, in world politics. Her criticism of Zionist policies and leadership came from the perspective of someone whose allegiance was to the

Jewish people, of which the Zionist movement was only a part. In her words, "there can be no patriotism without permanent opposition."

Beyond the particular positions Arendt advocates, her stance is of lasting significance: she assumes the existence of a Jewish polity, one which is sufficiently strong, proud, and secure that all Jews have an inherent right to engage in vigorous political debate. One need not agree with all of Arendt's views to find this attitude to be a continuing model for Jewish political speech and advocacy.

Very few individuals have successfully balanced the reality of being both a Jew and a European, making of the emancipation what it should have been—the emancipation of Jews as Jews. Hannah Arendt provides a striking example of the potential fruitfulness of this combination. The threads of both heritages are woven together in such a way that to overlook or deny the influence of one or the other is to rip apart the very fabric of her life and thought. It is because she remained both a Jew and a European that she gained a place in history, and it is as both a Jew and a European that her life and work should be understood.

The Jewish experience of danger, trauma, and hope in the dark times of the twentieth century was one which Hannah Arendt shared. Very early in her life she took to heart the experience and final words of Rahel Varnhagen:

> The thing which all my life seemed to me the greatest shame, which was the misery and misfortune of my life—having been born a Jewess—this I should on no account now wish to have missed.[107]

Notes

1. "We Refugees," see p. 274.
2. The Spring 1977 issue of *Social Research* was devoted exclusively to Hannah Arendt, but not one of the eminent authors who contributed articles so much as mentioned her Jewish writings.
3. H. Arendt, *The Origins of Totalitarianism*, ed. J. Kohn (New York: Schocken Books, 2004), p. 76.
4. "The Jew as Pariah: A Hidden Tradition," see p. 275.
5. Ibid., p. 276.
6. "The Moral of History," see p. 314.
7. "The Eichmann Controversy," p. 470.
8. *The Origins of Totalitarianism*, p. 99.
9. "The Moral of History," see p. 314.

10. *The Origins of Totalitarianism*, p. 14.

11. Ibid., p. 17.

12. "The Jewish State: Fifty Years After," see pp. 377–78.

13. "Jewish History, Revised," see p. 306.

14. "The Jewish State: Fifty Years After," see p. 378.

15. "Jewish History, Revised," see p. 311. Those familiar with Hannah Arendt's other work will notice the affinity between this account and her discussion of the breakdown of tradition in the modern age presented in *Between Past and Future* (New York: Penguin Books, 2006), particularly the essays "Tradition and the Modern Age" and "What is Authority?"

16. Ibid., p. 311.

17. "The Jewish State: Fifty Years After," see p. 378.

18. *The Origins of Totalitarianism*, p. 29.

19. Ibid., pp. 37–38.

20. Ibid., p. 37.

21. Ibid., p. 38.

22. Ibid., pp. 35–36.

23. Ibid., p. 71.

24. "Stefan Zweig: Jews in the World of Yesterday," see p. 325.

25. *The Origins of Totalitarianism*, p. 72.

26. Ibid., p. 88.

27. "We Refugees," see p. 274.

28. "On Humanity in Dark Times: Thoughts About Lessing," *Men in Dark Times* (London: Cape, 1970), p. 13.

29. Ibid., p. 14.

30. Ibid., p. 13.

31. *The Origins of Totalitarianism*, p. 110.

32. Ibid., p. 151.

33. Ibid., p. 73.

34. Ibid., p. 309n.

35. Ibid., p. 26.

36. Ibid., p. 155.

37. "Stefan Zweig: Jews in the World of Yesterday," see p. 328.

38. "The Jewish State: Fifty Years After," see p. 377.

39. Ibid.

40. Ibid.

41. Ibid., p. 378.

42. "Zionism Reconsidered," see p. 358.

43. Ibid., p. 363.

44. "The Jewish State: Fifty Years After," see p. 383.

45. "Zionism Reconsidered," see p. 363.

46. It should be remembered that "politics" and "political thought" have special meanings and uncommon implications for Hannah Arendt. These are implicit throughout her work, but are particularly spelled out in *Between Past and Future* and *The Human Condition* (Chicago: University of Chicago Press, 1998).

47. "The Jew as Pariah: A Hidden Tradition," see p. 283.

48. "We Refugees," see p. 274.

49. Bernard Lazare, *Job's Dungheap* (New York, Schocken Books, 1948), p. 10.

50. "The Jewish State: Fifty Years After," see p. 381.

51. "Herzl and Lazare," see p. 339.

52. "The Jew as Pariah: A Hidden Tradition," see p. 284.

53. Ibid.

54. Ibid.

55. Ibid., pp. 284–85.

56. "To Save the Jewish Homeland," p. 401.

57. Foreshadowing the controversy over *Eichmann in Jerusalem*, the continued advocacy of binationalism by Arendt and the *Ihud* was strongly condemned by the mainstream Zionist establishment:

"Any program which denies these fundamental principles [the Biltmore Program, which called for the creation of a sovereign Jewish commonwealth], such as advanced by the *Ihud* or any other group, is unacceptable to the Zionist Organization of America and Hadassah, the Women's Zionist Organization of America." (Esco Foundation for Palestine, Inc., *Palestine: A Study of Jewish, Arab, and British Policies*, 2 vols., New Haven, Conn., Yale University Press, 1947, p. 1,087.)

Arendt responded to this criticism in "About 'Collaboration,'" see p. 414.

58. "The Jewish State: Fifty Years After," see p. 386.

59. Ibid.

60. Ibid., pp. 386–87. For Arendt there is an important distinction between ideology and politics: "an ideology differs from a single [political] opinion in that it claims to possess either the key to history, or the solution for all the 'riddles of the universe,' or the intimate knowledge of the hidden universal laws which are supposed to rule nature and man" (*The Origins of Totalitarianism*, p. 211). Ideology, with its certainty, is the pattern of thought characteristic of totalitarianism, while "common sense," with its element of doubt and opinion, characterizes a truly free political realm.

61. "To Save the Jewish Homeland," see p. 397.

62. Ibid., p. 394.

63. "The Jew as Pariah: A Hidden Tradition," see p. 297. The relationship between "fabrication" and "the world" is an important but complex one in Arendt's political theory. The interested reader should look at *The Human Condition*, especially the chapters on "Work" and "Action."

64. "Peace or Armistice in the Near East?," see p. 435.

65. Ibid., p. 436. The contrast between nature and its necessity on the one hand, and artifice and its freedom on the other, is treated in depth in *The Human Condition*.

66. Ibid., p. 435.

67. Ibid.

68. Ibid., p. 427.

69. Ibid., p. 430. The fundamental importance for politics of representative thinking, the ability to see things from another person's point of view, is discussed by Arendt in "Truth and Politics" in *Between Past and Future*.

70. Ibid., p. 427.

71. Ibid.

72. "To Save the Jewish Homeland," see pp. 394–95.

73. Ibid., p. 396.

74. Ibid.

75. "Peace or Armistice in the Near East?," see p. 450.

76. Ibid.

77. Ibid., pp. 449–50.

78. "We Refugees," see p. 274.

79. *The Human Condition*, p. 254. Other examples of Arendt's changing the focus of Marx's analysis are:

Introduction

(1) Marx believed that the establishment of the nation-state system was a result of the rise of the bourgeoisie, with imperialism the logical outcome of the expansion of capital. While Arendt agrees that imperialism was the result of the growth of capital and the bourgeoisie's involvement in politics, she asserts that the bourgeoisie's entrance into politics occurred only in the mid-nineteenth century and caused the imperialism which destroyed the nation-state.

(2) Arendt generally follows Marx's analysis in her discussion of the separation of people from the land and the development of modern society as a society of laborers "free" from the old "bonds" to land and community. For Marx the characteristic product of bourgeois society is the proletariat, and it is this class of wage laborers upon whom the capitalist mode of production is based that is the vanguard which is to make history. In contrast, Arendt thinks that the important result of laboring society is the creation of what Marx called the *lumpenproletariat*, which she expands to include the *déclassé* elements of all the classes that came to form the mob, for it was the mob that prepared the way for the mass movements and totalitarianism.

I think, in fact, that Arendt's view of the importance of political action and her notion of both action and freedom, the raison d'être of politics, are actually much closer to those of Marx than she thought. But this all depends upon which of the many interpretations of Marx one believes is accurate.

80. Karl Marx, "On the Jewish Question," Robert C. Tucker, ed., *The Marx-Engels Reader* (New York: W. W. Norton & Company, 1972), p. 47.

81. Ibid., pp. 47–50 *passim*.

82. Arendt's philosophy of history, including her critique of Marxist historiography, is most fully developed in her essay "The Concept of History: Ancient and Modern" in *Between Past and Future*.

83. "The Moral of History," see p. 314.

Arendt's attitude toward history has a certain affinity to that of her friend Walter Benjamin as expressed in his "Theses on the Philosophy of History," which he bequeathed to Arendt's guardianship shortly before his death in 1940. "*Thinking* involves not only the flow of thoughts, but their arrest as well. Where thinking suddenly stops in a configuration pregnant with tensions, it gives that configuration a shock, by which it *crystallizes* into a monad" (Walter Benjamin, *Illuminations* [New York: Schocken Books, 1969], pp. 262–63, emphasis added). By comparison, Arendt's overall intellectual project is perhaps most succinctly put in *The Human Condition* (p. 5), where she claims that her purpose "is nothing more than to *think* what we are doing" (emphasis added). This being the case, it is particularly revealing that in her reply to a critique of *The Origins of Totalitarianism* she states:

> I did not write a history of totalitarianism but an analysis in terms of history. . . . The book, therefore, does not really deal with the "origins" of totalitarianism—as its title unfortunately claims—but gives a historical account of the elements which *crystallized* into totalitarianism. ("A Reply to Eric Voegelin," in H. Arendt, *Essays in Understanding, 1930–1954,* ed. J. Kohn [New York: Schocken Books, 2005], p. 403, emphasis added.)

84. *The Human Condition*, p. 253.

85. "We Refugees," see p. 274.

86. *The Human Condition*, p. 41.

87. *The Origins of Totalitarianism*, p. 89.

88. Ibid.

89. Ibid., p. 88.

90. *Rahel Varnhagen: The Life of a Jewish Woman*, trans. Richard and Clara Winston (New York: Harcourt Brace Jovanovich, 1974) p. 9.

91. Ibid. I believe that it is from this experience of the assimilating Jews, in particular Rahel Varnhagen and Franz Kafka, that Arendt gained an insight into the phenomenon that she was later to describe as "the subjectivism of modern philosophy" which removed "the Archimedean point" out of the world

and into the mind of the human being. See especially the chapter titled "The *Vita Activa* and the Modern Age" in *The Human Condition*.

92. "The Moral of History," see p. 315.

93. *The Origins of Totalitarianism*, p. 448.

94. Ibid, p. 381.

95. Ibid.

96. Ibid, p. 565.

97. *Rahel Varnhagen*, p. 227.

98. H. Arendt, *Eichmann in Jerusalem: A Report on the Banality of Evil* (New York: Penguin Books, 2006), p. 125.

99. Gershom Scholem, "Exchange," *The Jew as Pariah*, p. 243.

100. *Eichmann in Jerusalem*, p. 287.

101. "'The Formidable Dr. Robinson': A Reply," see p. 497.

102. *Eichmann in Jerusalem*, pp. 268–69.

103. Ibid., p. 263.

104. For example, Arendt rarely discusses Eastern European Jewish history and ignores the attempts by Zionist and non-Zionist socialists to organize the Jews into "a great revolutionary movement." In her political theory she aestheticizes and sanitizes politics to such an extent that one often wonders what the exact content of "political action" really is. In a similar vein, her critique of Marx is not always based on a fair representation of his views. And, of course, the accuracy of the historical facts upon which she bases her interpretations of history has been widely questioned, most notably in the case of *Eichmann in Jerusalem*.

105. *Essays in Understanding*, pp. 11–12.

106. See, for example, Steven E. Aschheim, ed., *Hannah Arendt in Jerusalem* (Berkeley: University of California Press, 2001), the papers delivered at a 1997 conference of the same name.

107. *Rahel Varnhagen*, p. 3.

❖❖❖ I ❖❖❖

THE 1930s

THE ENLIGHTENMENT
AND THE JEWISH QUESTION

The modern Jewish question dates from the Enlightenment; it was the Enlightenment—that is, the non-Jewish world—that posed it. Its formulations and its answers have defined the behavior and the assimilation of Jews. Ever since Moses Mendelssohn's genuine assimilation and Christian Wilhelm Dohm's essay "On the Civic Improvement of Jews" (1781), the same arguments that found their chief representative in Lessing appear over and over in every discussion of Jewish emancipation. It is to Lessing that such discussions owe their propagation of tolerance and humanness, as well as the distinction between the truths of reason and those of history. This distinction is of such great importance because it can legitimate each accidental instance of assimilation that occurs within history and thus needs to appear merely as an ongoing insight into the truth and not as the adaptation and reception of a particular culture at a particular, and thus accidental, stage of its history.

For Lessing, reason, which all humans share in common, is the foundation of humanity. It is the most human connection that binds Saladin with Nathan and the Templar.* It alone is the genuine connection linking one person with another. The emphasis of humanness based on what is reasonable gives rise to the ideal of tolerance and to its promulgation. His notion that deep inside every human being—despite differences of dogmatic convictions, morals, and conduct—is the same human being, his reverence for all that bears a human countenance, can never be derived solely from the general validity of reason as a purely formal quality; rather, the idea of tolerance is intimately connected with Lessing's concept of truth, which for its part can be under-

*In Lessing's play *Nathan the Wise*.—Ed.

stood only within the context of his theological thought and his philosophy of history.

Truth gets lost in the Enlightenment—indeed, no one wants it anymore. More important than truth is man in his search for it. "Not the truth that someone has in his possession, but rather the honest effort he has made to get behind the truth is what defines human worth."[1] Man becomes more important than the truth, which is relativized for the benefit of "human worth." This human worth is discovered in tolerance. The universal rule of reason is the universal rule of what is human and humane. Because this humanness is more important than any "possession of the truth," the father in Lessing's fable gives each of his three sons a ring, but does not tell them which is the genuine ring, with the result that the genuine one is in fact lost. The German Enlightenment as represented by Lessing did not simply lose truth as religious revelation, but rather the loss is seen as something positive: the discovery of the purely human. In striving for what is genuine, man and his history—which is a history of searching—gain a meaning of their own. Man is no longer simply in charge of what is good, with his own meaning dependent on its possession; instead, by searching he can confirm this possession, which is neither objective nor salvatory. If the search for truth, the "expansion of one's energies," is regarded as the only substantial issue, then for the tolerant man—that is, for the truly human man—all religious faiths are in the end merely different names for the same man.

History has no power to prove anything to reason. The truths of history are accidental, the truths of reason are necessary, and accident is separated from necessity by a "nasty wide ditch," which to leap across would require a "μεταβασις εἰς ἀλλο γενος." The truths of history are simply not true, no matter how good the evidence, because both their factuality and their attestation are always accidental—the latter being likewise historical. The truths of history are "true"—that is, universally persuasive and binding—only to the extent that they confirm the truths of reason. So it is reason that must decide the necessity of revelation—and thus of history.[2] The accident of history can be ennobled by reason after the fact; reason decides subsequently that revealed history is identical with reason. Revealed history functions as humanity's educator. At the end of such an education, which we experience as history, will come the time of a "new eternal gospel" that will make further lessons superfluous. The end of history is its dissolution, when what is still relatively accidental is transformed into what is absolutely necessary. "Such an education provides man with nothing that he could not also have on his own"; it merely leads him to a perfection that in actuality already lies within him. Since reason is already included within revelation, history teaches reason to stand on its own. The goal of both divine revelation and human history is man's coming of age.

One consequence of history as educator is not entirely accessible to reason. Reason can only confirm history's "that," but must let go of its "how" as something outside its own purview. "But if a revelation can and must be a revelation, then it must be one more proof to reason of its own truth rather than an infringement on it, should reason find in revelation things beyond it." This statement does not imply a new acknowledgment of divine authority. It must be viewed in conjunction with Lessing's primary theological thesis: that religion is prior to and independent of Scripture. Truth as thesis, dogma, or as an objective and salvatory possession is not what is essential; religiosity is.

At first glance this seems nothing more than an enlightened version of Pietism. Lessing's *Fragments of an Unknown* can be confusing only to a theologian, not to a Christian, in the midst of whose faith Christ is unassailable, because such faith is pure internality. "Do this man's explanations, hypotheses, and proofs matter to the Christian? For him it's simply there, his Christian faith, which he feels to be so true, in which he feels so blessed." But underlying this emphasis on unassailable internality is the Enlightenment's mistrust of the Bible; pure internality is stressed because the objectivity of Scripture's revelation is no longer certain. The separation of religion and the Bible is the final futile attempt to salvage religion—futile because such a separation destroys the Bible's authority and, with it, God's visible and knowable authority on earth. "Religion is not true because the evangelists and apostles taught it, rather they taught it because it is true." If the truth of religion precedes the Bible, it is no longer objectively certain, but must be searched for. This enlightened acceptance of pietist religiosity simultaneously destroys Pietism. What is new is not the emphasis on internality, but rather that it is played off against objectivity.

History, then, appears in Lessing's work in two heterogeneous contexts.

First, history is the eternal search for truth; it begins with man's coming of age, but beyond that its horizon is limitless. Second, history is the educator of the human race, but it makes itself superfluous and ceases with man's coming of age. The first understanding of history allows man, once he has become aware of his reason, to begin anew and establish a history. This understanding is the only one that remains determinative in Mendelssohn's reception of Lessing's thought. But for Lessing this history that is to be founded anew is definitely anchored in the past. The past ruled by authority is, after all, an educator. Man has only just come of age—through an education God grants to man. Man's coming of age marks the beginning of a second history, which differs from the first in that, although it does not renounce every goal, it shifts any such goal to limitless time in general—truth is a goal reached only by approximation and in stages of increasing perfection. This theory of history has a fundamentally different structure from that presented in *The Education of the Human Race*. It is in no way a secularization of Christianity—and cannot be, since in it truth is reserved only for God[3]—but rather from the start it is directed solely toward man; it shifts truth as far into the future as possible, since truth is really not the concern of earthly man. Possession of the truth actually impedes the development of all of man's possibilities, inhibits the requisite patience, and turns his gaze away from what is human. Truth is of concern to God alone and is of no importance to man. This exclusive and unreserved affirmation of the eternally open-ended and fragmentary nature of all things human solely for the sake of humanity is shunted aside in *The Education of the Human Race*.

In Mendelssohn's reception of the Enlightenment, his "formation" (*Bildung*) still takes place within the context of an absolute allegiance to the Jewish religion. Defense of this allegiance—for instance against J. K. Lavater's attacks—was of great importance to him. Lessing's separation of the truths of reason and history provided him the means for his defense. But along with his apologia for Judaism he had to maintain the possibility of his own "formation"—and the absolute autonomy of reason asserted by the Enlightenment served his purpose. "Minds that think for themselves," Lessing says, "have the capacity to ignore the entire expanse of erudition and to realize that they must find their own path across that expanse the moment it is worth the effort to enter upon it."[4] This idea of being able to think for oneself is the foundation of

Mendelssohn's ideal of formation; true formation is not nourished by history and its facts, but instead makes them superfluous. The authority of reason prevails, and everyone can come to it alone and on his own. The thinking man lives in absolute isolation; independent of all others he finds the truth, which actually should be common to all. "Every man pursues his own path through life. . . . But it does not seem to me that it was the purpose of Providence for all humanity here below constantly to move forward and perfect itself over time." For Mendelssohn reason is even more independent of history, nor is it anchored in it. He expressly argues against Lessing's philosophy of history, against "the education of the human race, which my late friend Lessing fancied at the urging of some researcher of history or other."[5] A knowledge of history is not yet necessary for Mendelssohn's formation, which is simply liberation to think. He innately owes nothing to any object of the alien world of culture; he does not need to discover his "standing-in-nothing" within the dominant intellectual atmosphere.

In adopting the idea of autonomous reason, Mendelssohn had focused solely on the notion of thinking for oneself and remaining independent of all facts (whereas for Lessing, reason was a path for discovering what is human); so, too, the theory of the distinction between the truths of reason and history is given a new twist: Mendelssohn uses and dogmatizes it in his apologia for Judaism. For Mendelssohn the Jewish religion, and only it, is identical with what is reasonable, and that is because of its "eternal truths," which alone also entail religious obligations. The truths of Jewish history, Mendelssohn continues, were valid only as long as the Mosaic religion was the religion of a nation, which was no longer the case after the destruction of the Temple. Only "eternal truths" are independent of all Scripture and apprehensible in every age; they are the basis of the Jewish religion, and it is because of them that Jews are still bound to the religion of their fathers even today. If they were not to be found in the Old Testament, then neither the Law nor historical tradition would be of any validity. Because there is nothing in the Old Testament that "argues against reason,"[6] nothing counter to reason, the Jew is also bound to those obligations that stand outside of reason, but to which no non-Jew should ever be explicitly bound, since they separate men from one another. Eternal truths are the foundation of tolerance. "How happy the world in which we live would be, if all men were to accept and practice the truth that the best Christians and the best Jews have in common."[7] For Mendelssohn the truths of reason and history are different only in kind and are not ascribed to different stages in humanity's development. Reason is shared by all men, is equally accessible to all people in all ages. The paths to it, however, differ, and for Jews this includes not only acceptance of the Jewish religion, but also strict adherence to its Law.

Lessing made his distinction between reason and history in order to put an end to religion as dogma. Mendelssohn attempts to use it specifically to salvage the Jewish religion on the basis of some "eternal content" independent of its historical attestation. But the same theological interest that removes reason from history also removes the seeker of truth from history. All reality—the world around us, our fellow men, history—lacks the legitimation of reason. This elimination of reality is closely bound up with the factual position of the Jew in the world. The world mattered so little to him that it became the epitome of what was unalterable. This new freedom of reason, of formation, of thinking for oneself, does not change the world at all. The "educated" Jew continues to regard the historical world with the same indifference felt by the oppressed Jew in the ghetto.

This failure of Jews to appreciate history—based in their fate as a people without a history and nourished by an only partially understood and assimilated Enlightenment—is intersected at one point by Dohm's theory of emancipation, an argument that remained crucial for the decades that followed. For Dohm—the first writer in Germany to systematically take up their cause—Jews are never the "people of God" or even of the Old Testament. They are human beings like all other human beings, except that history has ruined these human beings.[8] But only Jews now take up this concept of history, since it provides them an explanation for their cultural inferiority, their lack of education and productivity, their deleterious effect on society. For them history becomes on principle the history of what is alien to them; it is the history of the prejudices that held sway over people prior to the Enlightenment. History is the history of a bad past or of a present still caught up in prejudice. Liberating the present from the burden and consequences of this history becomes the task of liberating and integrating Jews.

Such was the simple and relatively unproblematic situation of the first generation of assimilationist Jews. Mendelssohn was not just more or less in agreement on theoretical issues with champions of integration like Dohm

and Mirabeau; in their eyes and in the eyes of other Jews Mendelssohn likewise was and remained a guarantee that Jews were capable and worthy of
improvement, that the creation of a different social situation would suffice to
turn them into socially and culturally productive members of bourgeois
society. The second generation of assimilationists—represented by Mendelssohn's student David Friedländer—still clung to the Enlightenment's
theory of a ruined history.[9] No longer tied to religion as Mendelssohn had
been, they attempted to make use of this soil so favorable to their endeavors
by employing every means possible to enter society. They proved so adept at
assimilating the blind spots of the Enlightenment, which regarded Jews
solely as an oppressed people, that they denied their own history and
regarded everything particular about themselves as an impediment to their
integration, to their becoming full human beings.[10] In adopting Mendelssohn's and Lessing's distinction between reason and history, they decided in
favor of reason; indeed they went so far as to hone the idea to the point of
blasphemy, something that would never have occurred to Mendelssohn:
"And if someone wants to back a reflective, honest inquirer into a corner
with the objection that human reason is no match for divine reason. . . ?
That objection cannot discomfort him for a moment, since the very acknowledgment of the divinity of such a belief and such dutiful obedience belongs
before the court of human reason." For Friedländer the distinction between
reason and history no longer served to salvage the Jewish religion, but was
merely the means by which to be rid of it as quickly as possible. For
Mendelssohn freedom had still meant the freedom of formation and of the
possibility "to reflect upon oneself and one's religion." But now such reflection on the Jewish religion was merely a means for changing the Jews' "political condition." Mendelssohn's pupil openly contradicted his teacher, who
had advised: "Conform yourselves to the morals and conditions of the land
in which you have been placed, but hold steadfastly to the religion of your
fathers. Bear both burdens as best you can." Friedländer openly contradicted
such a statement when, appealing to the Enlightenment, reason, and a moral
sense that all men share equally, he recommended baptism as a means of
"public integration into society."

But by 1799 such a proposal came too late. The response of Provost
Teller, to whom it was offered, was cool. And Schleiermacher energetically
resisted such unwelcome guests. In characteristic fashion he assigned this

"epistle" to "the older school of our literature,"[11] and, in opposing an appeal to reason, emphasized that what is particular to Christianity is a moral sense that can only be watered down by such proselytes. Reason has nothing to do with Christianity. Schleiermacher wanted to protect what is peculiar to his own religion from what is necessarily different in the religion of foreigners. Reason provided the possibility of only a partial agreement—it applied to citizenship, not to religion. Schleiermacher favored integration as soon as possible. But integration would not be the beginning of total assimilation, although this is precisely what the Jews were proposing. "The Enlightenment fashion" that presumed all men to be originally equal and wished to restore that equality has become "contemptible." Schleiermacher demands that Jewish ceremonial law be subordinated to civil law and that the hope for a Messiah be abandoned. Friedländer agrees to both. He is not even aware that this might mean he is giving something up, for he wants to clear away everything that contradicts reason, which is the same for Christian and Jew alike—and he expressly demands the same of Christians. Twenty to thirty years earlier, when Lavater had demanded that Mendelssohn examine all evidence for and against Christianity and then make his decision "as Socrates would have," Friedländer's proposals would not have seemed so absurd as they now appeared to Schleiermacher and the rest of educated Germany.

A shift had taken place in Germany's awareness of history, one that finds its most characteristic expression in Johann Gottfried von Herder, who had initiated the critique of his own age, the age of Enlightenment. His essay "Auch eine Philosophie zur Geschichte der Bildung der Menschheit" [This too a philosophy for the formation of humanity] was published in 1774, that is, in the midst of the Enlightenment, and had no effect whatever on the older generation. But its influence on what was to become Romanticism was all the stronger and more crucial. It argues against the rule of reason alone, with its trite preachments of utility. It also argues against the rule of man alone, who "hates nothing more than what is wonderful and hidden." And finally it argues against a historiography that, following Voltaire and Hume, forgets reality in favor of those human abilities and possibilities that always remain the same.

We saw how, in adopting Lessing's ideas, Mendelssohn stressed above all else the isolation of each individual in being able to think for himself. Herder and the later Romantics (which is to say, the German tradition of greatest importance for the Jewish question) eliminated this notion and resumed the discovery of history that Lessing had initiated.

Herder objects to Lessing's statement that man receives nothing in his education that does not already lie within him: "Had man received everything out of himself and developed isolated from all external objects, it might then be possible to write a history of a man, but not of men, not of the entire race." Man lives instead in a "chain of individuals." "Tradition approaches him and shapes his mind and forms his limbs."[12] Pure reason, pure goodness, is "scattered" across the earth. No individual is capable any longer of comprehending it. It never exists as itself—just as there is no genuine ring for Lessing. It shifts, changes, is "apportioned in a thousand shapes . . . —an eternal Proteus." This constantly changed shape depends on realities that lie outside human powers, on "time, climate, need, world, fate." What is crucial is no longer—as it was for the Enlightenment—pure possibility but the reality of each human existence. The real differentiation among men is more important than their "virtual" sameness. "No doubt the most cowardly scoundrel still has some remote ability and possibility to become the most magnanimous of heroes; but between the latter and such a character's entire sense of being, of existence, lies—a chasm!"[13]

Consequently reason is not the judge of historical reality in man, but the result of the human race's total experience.[14] By its very nature this result is never at an end.[15] Herder accepts Lessing's notion of truth as "eternal search," but in a modified form. For though Lessing pushes the truth into some immeasurably distant future, reason as an inborn capacity remains for him untouched by such dynamics. But if reason, as the "result of experience," is itself historicized, man's place in the development of the human race is no longer clearly defined: "No history in the world stands a priori on abstract principles." Just as Lessing rejects truth as a possession that provides tranquillity for good and all, because such a possession would be inappropriate for man, so Herder refuses to recognize pure reason as the possibility of one truth. In opposition to both one single reason and one single truth stands the endlessness of history, and "why should I become a mind of pure reason when I wish only to be a man and, just as is the case with my existence, so, too, in my knowledge and belief to move as a wave upon the sea of history."

As a result, for Herder the relationship of reason and history are just the opposite: reason is subject to history, "for abstraction really has no laws governing history."

The rule of reason, of man who has come of age and is on his own, is about to end. History, what happens to man, has become opaque. "No philosopher can account for why they [peoples] exist, or why they have existed." In its opaqueness history becomes something impersonal and outside of man, but it does not become God. The transcendence of the divine has been lost for good and all; "religion should effect nothing but its goals through man and for man."

Parallel to this insight into the power of history over reason is a polemic against the sameness of all men. The deeper life is seized by history, the more differentiated it becomes. This differentiation has developed out of an original sameness. The older a people, the more it differs from every other people.[16] The consequences of historical events first give rise to differences among men and peoples. Difference does not lie in ability, talent, or character, but rather in the irrevocability of human events, so that there is a past that cannot be undone.

With this discovery of the irrevocability of all that has happened, Herder became one of the first great interpreters of history. It was through him that in Germany the history of the Jews first became visible as a history defined essentially by their possession of the Old Testament. This resulted in a change in the response to the Jewish question—by both Jews themselves and the larger world. This change was also influenced by new definitions that Herder provided for two concepts so crucial in this context: formation and tolerance.

Herder understands the history of the Jews in the same way that they interpret it, as the history of God's chosen people.[17] That they were then scattered is for him the beginning of and precondition for their effect on the human race.[18] He surveys their history down to the present and his attention is arrested by the Jews' unique sense of life, which holds to the past and tries to hold what is past within the present. To his mind both their mourning for a Jerusalem destroyed ages ago and their hope for a Messiah are tokens of the fact that "the ruins of Jerusalem . . . are rooted, so to speak, in the heart of time."[19] Their religion is neither a source of prejudice nor Mendelssohn's religion of reason, but the "inalienable heritage of their race." At the same time Herder recognizes that their history arises out of the Law of Moses and cannot be separated from it,[20] and therefore stands or falls with obedience to the Law. Their religion is moreover a religion of Palestine, and clinging to it means remaining a people of Palestine and thus "an Asian people foreign to our continent." He does not concede to them their sameness with other peoples—which for the Enlightenment is the only means of making them human beings—but instead emphasizes their foreignness. But that in no way means the abandonment of assimilation; in fact he is even more radical in his demands, but on another basis. Whereas for Dohm and Lessing discussion of the Jewish question arose primarily out of the question of religion and its toleration, for Herder assimilation is a question of emancipation and thus of politics. Precisely because Herder takes adherence to the "religion of one's fathers" seriously, he sees in it a symbol of national cohesion; a foreign religion becomes the religion of another nation. The task now is not to tolerate another religion—in the same way that one is forced to tolerate many prejudices—or to change a socially shameful situation, but rather to incorporate another nation within Germany.[21] Herder definitely sees the present state of affairs *sub specie praeteritatis*. The fact that the Jews have not perished despite all their oppression in a foreign world, but have sought to fit in, even if in a parasitical fashion—he understands even this as part of their history as a people.[22] What is important now is to make what is parasitical about the Jewish nation productive. To what extent such assimilation is possible even as the Law is still observed is a question of politics, to what extent it is possible at all is a question of education and formation, which for Herder means humanization.

Two concepts characterize humanity: formation and tolerance. Herder reserves his sharpest polemic for the Enlightenment's concept of formation—that is, thinking for oneself—which he castigates above all else for lacking any sense of reality. Such formation does not arise out of any experience or lead to "action," to its "application to life within a given sphere." It cannot form man, since it forgets the reality out of which he comes and in which he stands. The "backward step" of formation—of true formation which forms, re-forms, and continues to form—is governed by the past, "the silent, eternal power of precedence, of a series of precedents." The Enlightenment cannot preserve this past.

Education by formation as Herder defines it can have no interest in simply imitating these "precedents"; after all, Herder has just demonstrated the uniqueness of history, even of the greatest and most brilliant history. Formation attempts to discover what can be formative by understanding precedents. Such understanding (which is itself a truly new access to reality and is as remote from all polemics or any sort of allegorizing and interpreting of Scripture as it is from simple pious acceptance) contains within it, first, a summoning of reality—to accept it as it really was, without any covert purposes or thoughts—and, second, a distancing from the past—never to confuse the past and oneself, to take seriously and include in one's understanding the time that lies between the past and one's attempt to understand. In terms of its content, then, history is not binding on someone who understands it, because he understands it as unique and transient. Its formative function lies in the understanding per se. But what is past provides the basis for a new idea of tolerance. As with every human being, every historical epoch has its fate, whose uniqueness can be judged by no one; it is history itself that, in the remorselessness of its continuance, has taken over the role of judge. Tolerance, a "virtue of rare souls privileged by heaven," no longer discovers what is human per se, but understands it—understands it in all its guises and changes, understands its uniqueness and its transience. Tolerance corresponds to the understanding distance held by the educated person.

Thus in an oddly indirect way Herder gave the Jews back their history—a history that has become history understood. History is taken absolutely seriously as what has happened, yet without any direct belief in an original Director of what has happened. Secularization can no longer be undone. This indirect restitution of the actual content of the past totally destroys the past as Jews see it. If for Herder this past, like all pasts, was bound to a unique time that can never return, for Jews it was the very thing that had to be rescued again and again from its own transience. Herder does indeed give back to the assimilated Jew all that has happened as he interprets it, but what has happened has happened without God. Thus Herder robs the assimilated Jew of the freedom he had won in accepting the Enlightenment—even though it too stands *vis-à-vis de rien*—but places it under the power of fate and no longer under the power of God. The Enlightenment still had at least some direct link to the content of history in that it had dealt with it—whether by

rejecting, defending, or intentionally twisting it. Herder's understanding of
history, by giving priority to the events, is a final negation of binding obligations to any historical content whatsoever. For the Jews the destruction of
the content of history means the loss of all historical ties, for what is unique
about their history is that with the destruction of the Temple, history itself
had, in a certain sense, destroyed the "continuum of things" that Herder res-
cues from the "abyss." That is why Mendelssohn's defense of the Jewish religion and his attempt to salvage some "eternal content"—as naïve as it may
seem to us today—was not entirely pointless. It was still possible on the basis
of the Enlightenment; Jews were left with a last remnant of historical connection that has now been completely erased. Herder himself views this lack
of connection positively: "In his *Nathan the Wise* Lessing portrayed the
unprejudiced judgment of educated Jews, their more direct way of looking at things; and who would contradict him, since the Jew as such is relieved
of many political convictions that we can rid ourselves of only with great
effort, or not at all?" Herder stresses the lack of prejudice in educated Jews,
that is, of those who are not connected to any sort of historical content, to
which—despite "formation" and as a result of the continuum of time—the
non-Jewish world surrounding them remains subject. At the same time
Herder wants to place in a positive light those characteristics that the necessities of an unpleasant present—whether of a social nature or those of the
Diaspora in general—have caused them to display, forcing them to be doubly keen in business and biblical exposition.[23] Once the Jews are "formed" in
Herder's sense, they are restored to humanity, which according to their own
interpretation, however, now means that they have ceased to be the chosen
people.

> Having cast aside proud national prejudice, having abandoned customs
> that do not belong to our age and temperament, or even to our climate,
> they work not as slaves ... but indeed as cohabitants of educated
> peoples, assisting the building up the sciences and humanity's entire
> culture. . . . They are not to be led to honor and morality by ceding
> them mercantile privileges, they elevate themselves to these goals
> through purely human, scientific, and civil merits. Whereupon their
> Palestine is everywhere they live and work to noble effect.

And with that the Jews are once again put into a position of exceptionality that could still remain hidden during the Enlightenment, which had no fully developed understanding of history. Lessing's total equality demanded of Jews merely that they be human beings, something that ultimately, at least in Mendelssohn's interpretation, they could readily achieve. But here a special position is demanded of them—they are to be granted a special place within "humanity's entire culture" once "formation" and the distancing effect of understanding have destroyed all of the contents of history which formerly sustained them. Schleiermacher rejects Friedländer's proposals because he wants to see the special character of both Christianity and Judaism preserved. Thus Jews are expected to have an understanding of their own historical situation, an expectation they can hardly meet, inasmuch as their very existence in the non-Jewish world stands or falls with the essentially unhistorical argumentation of the Enlightenment. In their struggle for emancipation they are forced continually to perform a *salto mortali*, to attempt a leap into their own integration. They cannot put their trust in "letting nature take its course," in a "step-by-step" development,[24] for in an alien world they have no definite spot from which such a development can have its start.

Thus the Jews have become a people without a history within history. Herder's understanding of history deprives them of their past. Once again they stand face-to-face with nothing. From within a historical reality, from within a European secularized world, they are forced somehow to adopt themselves to this world, to form themselves. But for them formation is by necessity everything that is the non-Jewish world. Once they have been deprived of their own past, present reality begins to reveal its power. Formation is the only possible means they have to survive this present. If formation means above all understanding the past, then the "formed" Jew is dependent on an alien past. He comes to it by way of a present that he must understand because he participates in it. If the present is to be understood at all, then the past must be explicitly seized anew. Explicitly asserting the past is the positive expression of the distancing effect that Herder claims for the formed man—a distancing that Jews bring with them from the start. Thus out of the alienness of history, history emerges as a special and legitimate concern of the Jews.[25]

1932

Notes

1. G. E. Lessing, *Theologische Streitschriften* [Theological disputations], "Eine Duplik" ["A Rejoinder"].

2. Cf. Lessing, *Zur Geschichte und Literatur* [On history and literature], from the fourth article, "Ein Mehreres aus dem Papieren des Ungenannten, die Offenbarung betreffend" [Diverse items from the papers of an unknown man concerning revelation].

3. Cf. Lessing, *Theologische Streitschriften*, "Eine Duplik," p. i.

4. Lessing, *Theologische Streitschriften*, "Anti-Goeze" [Answer to Goeze], p. ix.

5. Moses Mendelssohn, *Jerusalem.*

6. Mendelssohn, *Correspondenz mit dem Erbprinzen von Braunschweig-Wolfenbüttel* [Correspondence with the hereditary prince of Braunschweig-Wolfenbüttel], 1776.

7. Mendelssohn in a letter to Bonnet, 1770; cf. Moses Mendelssohn, *Gesammelte Schriften* [Collected works], vol. 7, p. lxxxii ff.

8. Christian Wilhelm Dohm, *Ueber die Bürgerliche Verbesserung der Juden* [On the civic improvement of Jews] (1781), vol. 1, p. 45; vol. 2, p. 8.

That the Jews are human beings like all other human beings; that they should therefore be treated like all other men; that it is only barbarism and religious prejudice that has demeaned and ruined them; that only the opposite treatment commensurate with common sense and humaneness can make of them better men and citizens . . . these are such natural and simple truths that to understand them and concur with them are almost one and the same thing.

9. Cf. David Friedländer, "Sendschreiben einiger jüdischer Hausväter" [Open letter of several Jewish heads of household], p. 30 ff.

10. Ibid., p. 39.

The greatest advance of the Jews is surely also that their yearning for the Messiah and for Jerusalem grows ever more remote, just as reason is increasingly able to cast this expectation aside as a chimera. It is always possible that a few, living as hermits or otherwise distancing themselves from the world's affairs, still maintain such wishes in their hearts; but for the majority of Jews, at least in Germany, Holland, and France, such ideas no longer find any nourishment and ultimately their last traces will be eradicated.

11. Friedrich Schleiermacher, "Briefe bei Gelegenheit . . . des Sendeschreibens" [Letters on the occasion . . . of the open letter] (1799), *Werke* [Works], Part 1, vol. 5, p. 6 ff.

12. Johann Gottfried von Herder, *Ideen zur Geschichte der Menschheit* [Ideas on the history of man], Part 1, vol. 9, chs. 1 and 2.

13. Herder, *Auch eine Philosophie der Geschichte* (1774).

14. Herder, *Erläuterungen zum Neuen Testament* [Expositions on the New Testament], I, Book 3.

15. Herder, *Briefe das Studium der Theologie betreffend* [Letters concerning the study of theology], Part 2, letter 26.

16. Herder, *Ideen zur Geschichte*, Part 1, vol. 7, ch. 5, "Zusätze zu der ältesten Urkunde des Menschengeschlechts" [Addenda to the oldest record of the human race].

17. Ibid., Part 3, vol. 7, ch. 3, "Ebräer" [Hebrews]. "I am therefore not ashamed to take as my basis the history of the Hebrews as they themselves tell it."

18. Ibid. "And now they were dispersed through all the lands of the Roman world and from the time of this dispersion the Jews began to have an effect on the human race that it is difficult to imagine possible from their own narrow land. . . ."

19. Herder, "Die Denkmale der Vorwelt" [The monuments of the pre-world], Part 1.

20. Herder, *Brief das Studium der Theologie betreffend*, letter 4.

21. Herder, *Adrastea*. "To what extent this law and the modes of thought and life that arise from it may belong in our nations is no longer a religious dispute, but a simple question of state."

22. Cf. Herder, *Ideen zur Geschichte*, Part 3, vol. 12, ch. 6, "Weitere Ideen zur Philosophie der Menschengeschichte" [Further ideas about the philosophy of human history].

23. "Given tribulations such as have been inflicted upon this people for centuries, what other nation would have preserved the level of culture at which their momentous Book of Books, the collection of their Holy Scriptures, has kept alive among them the arts of writing and reckoning? Necessity and their trades have brought them to a keenness of eye that only a dull eye fails to perceive."

24. Wilhelm and Karoline von Humboldt, *Briefwechsel* [Correspondence], vol. 4, no. 236, p. 462.

25. This was first understood by the "Society for the Culture and Science of Jews" under the aegis of Leopold Zunz.

AGAINST PRIVATE CIRCLES

Until recently, our Jewish schools have served a vanishingly small percentage of Jewish youth. Where they were not rooted in Orthodox congregations, these schools have usually been attended by children whose parents wished to cultivate a specifically Jewish self-consciousness. They rested, that is, upon a particular attitude within Judaism. They were supported by their communities in only the most desultory way, because the communities sensed a danger in becoming "isolated" and alienated from the larger non-Jewish environment.

Beyond all differences of perspective, the contemporary situation demands *a Jewish school system built upon the very broadest basis*. Only in this way can such a system do justice to the facts that recent events have brought about; only in this way can the children emigrating from German schools today be not just *excluded* from one system but truly included into another.

Including these children is the most urgent task in the present circumstances. If the problem is left to solve itself, then *wealthy Jewish families* will band together into *private circles* and attempt to pass on some sort of a higher education. This would not only leave the current situation perniciously unaffected but would even legitimize its exclusionary policies. It would tear the children out of every social context, would place them in an artificial atmosphere alien to any reality, and would cultivate them neither into Germans nor into Jews. Even the most highly qualified teacher could do nothing to counter this fact, and above all could not prevent the children from becoming and from remaining essentially excluded people. Burdening a child with this fate is ultimately as unacceptable as exposing him to a hostile antisemitic environment.

Moreover, since such private initiatives are available only to the wealthy, they would threaten the very existence of Jewish *schools,* because they would draw away the *paying* children. We now confront the danger that someday we will have a fatally incapacitated Jewish school on the one hand and on the other myriad little circles.

It should not be objected that these private circles do not yet exist, that the demand for a Jewish grammar school [*Volksschule*] remains great, that things should simply be allowed to develop on their own. Private circles *will* arise; this is clear to anyone who is familiar with the mentality of German Jews. The demand for a grammar school is not evidence to the contrary. These private circles will claim to be providing a higher education. That is the actual danger. Once they have been set up, when countless Jewish teachers who are now without any income are employed in them, it will be extraordinarily difficult to gain control over them again. A *prophylactic propaganda* is necessary to enlighten parents to the danger threatening their children: the danger of an alienation from reality, the danger of a lack of character, the danger of a groundlessness within which the very reason for this groundlessness can no longer be perceived.

The Jewish schools will be the most important instrument available to Jews as a whole for influencing the coming generation. Viewed in a longer perspective, there is today hardly a question that has more existential ramifications and upon whose solution more depends. The more unified that solution proves to be, the smaller the differences between the individual schools and the more quickly all the children are included, the more that can be achieved. The coming generation must know the *history of Jewish assimilation* and of *antisemitism* as well as it knows the history of Judaism up until assimilation. Only in this way can they be provided with a basis from which to judge their environment and themselves in a genuinely *reasonable* way; only in this way can they lend substance to a self-consciousness which as a merely ethical command must always remain vacant.

The Jewish school should not commit itself to a principle of racial purity. It must from the start be prepared to accept half- or quarter-Jews, that is, everyone who has been forced into its arms by the political situation. For it is important to be clear on the fact that assimilation and its consequences cannot simply be revoked—whatever one may think of this assimilation. For the time being we are all still German Jews, which means "assimilated." Our children will not be able to grow up either in the ghetto or among the German public. This situation is something new in Jewish history. Only Jewish schools have a hope of confronting this unprecedented situation. And this only when they are led by people ready to view this situation without illusions.

Orthodox school system

In the context of our earlier discussion of the question of Jewish schools in Germany it has been brought to our attention that we ought to have mentioned what an impressive school system Orthodoxy in Germany has managed to construct, in particular the Adass Jisroel Congregation in Berlin. Orthodox Jewish congregations have already founded Jewish schools of higher education in Hamburg, Leipzig, Frankfurt, Berlin, and Cologne. Some of these have been established only in the last few years with great sacrifice and have acquitted themselves fully as educational institutions. It should be emphasized that these school systems owe their establishment to the efforts of both Orthodox and Zionist public figures.

1933

ORIGINAL ASSIMILATION

*An Epilogue to the One Hundredth Anniversary
of Rahel Varnhagen's Death*

I

Today in Germany it seems Jewish *assimilation* must declare its bankruptcy. The general social antisemitism and its official legitimation affects in the first instance assimilated Jews, who can no longer protect themselves through baptism or by emphasizing their differences from Eastern Judaism. The question of the success or failure of assimilation is more urgent than ever precisely for assimilated Jews. For assimilation is a fact, and only later, in the context of defensive struggle, does it become an ideology; an ideology one today knows cannot maintain itself because reality has refuted it more fully and unambiguously than ever before. Assimilation is the entrance of the Jews into the historical European world.

The role of the Jews in this world can be unambiguously determined neither sociologically nor in intellectual-historical terms. Specifically modern antisemitism, the antisemitism directed against assimilated Jews and which is as old as their assimilation itself, this form of antisemitism has always reproached the Jews with being bearers of the Enlightenment. That basically was the charge of Grattenauer's vulgar polemic of 1802 as well as Brentano's consummately witty satire reflecting the antisemitism of the late Romantics, of the German Christian Table Society [*Tischgesellschaft*]. This polemic is not accidental. It is true that at least at the beginning of the last century there was no unstructured assimilation. Assimilation always meant assimilation to *the Enlightenment*.

The Enlightenment promised the Jews emancipation and above all provided them with arguments for demanding equal human rights, hence almost all of them became Enlightenment advocates. But the *problem* of Jewish assimilation begins only *after* the Enlightenment, first in the generation that followed Mendelssohn. Mendelssohn could still believe himself in fundamental agreement with the Enlightenment avant-garde—which meant at the time the representatives of cultural Germany. But already his students found their appeals to reason and moral sentiment encountering resistance. Even Schleiermacher took the "Circular of Certain Jewish Household Fathers," written by David Friedländer, to be an example of "our earlier literary school." Initially the Jews could not understand the new historical consciousness that first emerged in Germany, because it provided them no further arguments for their demands.

That means: the Jews as a whole could no longer assimilate. Mendelssohn was still always able to speak in the name of "the" Jews, whom he wanted to enlighten and to free. He believed—like Dohm—that it was the Jews *as a whole* he would emancipate. The baptismal movement in the next generation shows that the Jewish question had become by then a problem for the *individual* Jew, had become the problem of somehow coming to terms with the world. That broad types of solutions can be discerned among what were in each case personal decisions does not refute the point. *The Jewish question becomes a problem of the individual Jew.*

II

Rahel, Henriette Herz, Dorothea Schlegel, and the Meyer sisters are examples of these "individuals." All they had in common was a desire to escape their Judaism, and all of them to some extent succeeded. Henriette Herz attempted it through scholarship. She mastered Latin, Greek, some Sanskrit, mathematics, and physics. The Christianity that Schleiermacher taught her became a self-evident cultural resource. She was respected, she was beautiful, she was much beloved. She developed a reputation for coldness because she remained untouched, nothing got through to her. With sound instincts she defended herself against every passion, against every serious engagement with the world. She believed one could study the world; she hoped that one could bribe it through virtue. And the world confirmed this by respecting her.

Dorothea Schlegel, Mendelssohn's youngest daughter, abandoned her husband, a respectable Jewish merchant, for Friedrich Schlegel. She did not encounter the world, she encountered Schlegel. She assimilated not to Romanticism but to Schlegel. She was not converted to Catholicism but to Schlegel's faith. She wanted to "build [him] a temple." Her love was entirely unreflected, merely the shining expression of her enthrallment. What remains is the fact that she really did succeed in surrendering herself, in devoting herself to someone else completely and being pulled through the world by him. The world was nothing but the transient foil for her feelings, for the whole excited passion of her inner being.

Marianne and Sarah Meyer came from a rich family that provided them with "an aristocratic education and cultured instruction." Their intelligence, their education, were identical to worldly sophistication. Marianne married Count Reuss and after his death bore the title of Lady von Eibenberg. Sarah lived many years in a happy marriage with the Livonian Baron Grotthus. Both of them resided in the great world, surrounded by recognition and flattery. They were taken up by society, even if here and there they were suddenly turned away, if certain houses would not receive them, if Gentz said their society was almost "mauvaise société," and if Prince Ligne's quip that Baron Arnstein was "le premier baron du vieux testament" made the rounds all through Vienna. These petty insults they had to be prepared to confront at any moment provoked immeasurable vanity in Frau von Grotthus, and in Frau von Eibenberg the "misanthropic knowledge of human character." It also gave rise to intelligence, attentiveness, and the art of making "even boredom entertaining."

These are simply a few individual cases that could be supplemented at will. It is characteristic of all these women that they understood how to erase the traces they left behind, that they were able to enter into the social world, that they had no need even to emphasize: "one must escape from Judaism" (Rahel).

III

In light of its risks and its necessity, to ask whether or not assimilation succeeded seems idle. Nor is it possible to determine if Rahel succeeded at it.

What is sure is that she never was able to erase the traces, to deny practically her origins, although it was she who made the angriest and bitterest remarks about her Jewishness. Nonetheless she never attempted to compensate for the groundlessness of her existence with surrogates, and she understood how to pursue every despair, even that over her heritage, with the utmost consequence. Thus she has become exemplary—less through what she said than through the course of her life itself—for a situation that was not hers alone.

Rahel studied nothing. She stressed to Veit, the friend of her youth, her "ignorance" and that she could not change it; "one must use it as it stands." No tradition had passed anything on to her, no history foresaw her existence. Purely independent, because born into no cultural world, without prejudice, because it seemed no one had judged before her, as if in the paradoxical situation of the first human being, she was compelled to appropriate everything as if she were meeting it for the first time. She was dependent on unprecedence. Herder once demanded explicitly an absence of prejudice from "cultured Jews." For Henriette Herz, the freedom from all content passed over into freedom for anything at all. Everything could be studied. Her independence became a senseless aptitude for everything. Since Rahel insisted upon her ignorance, she actually documented the generosity and indeterminacy of a particular historically given world; this was the source of her striking way of describing things, people, situations. Everything presented itself to her as if for the first time. She never had a memorized formula ready. Her wit, which was already feared when she was a young girl, was but this entirely unburdened manner of seeing. She lived in no particular order of the world, and refused to study any order of the world; her wit could unite the most incongruous things, in the most intimately unified things it could discern incongruities. This her friends praised as originality, while her enemies found in it an absence of style, a disorder, an unmotivated pleasure in paradoxes. And perhaps her manner of expression truly was without style, for she had no model, no tradition, and no precise consciousness of which words belonged together and which did not. But she was genuinely "original": she never obscured a thing with a familiar expression. Despite all her originality, all her rapacity for conquest, Rahel demonstrated not only the absence of prejudice but also the vacancy of someone entirely dependent upon experience, who must marshal an entire life behind each opinion.

Entertaining an opinion in the alien world is an essential aspect of assimilation.

For Rahel, this opinion derived from her life, depended upon the fact that human beings, destinies, occurrences did not leave her in the lurch, did not forget her, but met her. She could have escaped from this dependence upon her own life through senseless study or marriage. She attempted it once when she met Count Finckenstein, when he fell in love with her and she became his betrothed. She had enough influence over Finckenstein to have brought him to the altar. Even many years later it remained incomprehensible to her friends why she did not do so. The reason was quite simple: what could have been the history of her assimilation became her personal love story. She "surrendered to chance when she could have calculated everything." For only through chance could a world she found indeterminate meet her. She could have deceived herself into thinking that the chance that Finckenstein of all people was the first, *le premier qui a voulu que je l'aime*, made marriage necessary, and then she would have been sucked away like Dorothea Schlegel.

Having no social position that would render an orientation self-evident, the only possibility for Rahel to encounter the world was in her own life. That she relied on this life and its experiences was the precondition of her eventual success in breaking through to reality. But hardly more than the precondition. For in order to really enter an alien history, to live in a foreign world, she had to be able to communicate herself and her experiences.

IV

It is often remarked, doubtless correctly, that the most notable aspect of Rahel's assimilation, its test case, so to speak, was that she was among the very first truly to understand Goethe. But it must not be overlooked that this understanding was not a matter of any unusual cleverness or sensitivity but was rather the result of a predicament, the predicament of having to communicate and of needing for this communication a language. If her life was not to sink entirely into the void, she had to attempt somehow to transmit herself into history by communication. This attempt would have been completely hopeless and disoriented if she had not had in Goethe the "mediator" to whom she could attach herself and whom she could imitate.

Goethe was the great stroke of fortune in Rahel's life. "The poet accompanied me without fail throughout my life." "Powerful and hale, he brought together in me what unhappiness and happiness had divided in me and what I was not able to hold visibly together." He taught her the connection: that happiness and unhappiness do not simply fall on a creature from heaven, but that there is only happiness and unhappiness within a life, and that this life as such can be their coherence. Happiness and unhappiness are formative elements in *Wilhelm Meister*. In Meister's life the question of happiness or unhappiness hardly has any meaning; so much is it the case that everything that occurs has meaning that there is barely a site where something simply destructive could break in. Chance itself is here an "educated man" (Schlegel). Initially, Rahel's life had no history and was exposed to pure destructiveness; but the folly of this other life let her understand; it taught her that love, fear, hope, happiness, and unhappiness were not simply blind terrors, but when they were specifically situated, emerging from a determinate past and passing into a determinate future, that they were able to mean something which human beings could comprehend. Without Goethe she would have seen her life only from the outside, its ghostly contours. She could not have fashioned a connection between it and the world to whom she had to recount it. "I made company with his largess, he was eternally my most single and certain friend"; for he was the only person whom she had so truly to love that her life's "measure [was] found not in me but in him." He compelled her at length to acknowledge the world of objects, that is, to cease being disproportionately and pointlessly original. Because she understood him, and understood herself through him, he could become for her something like a succedaneum for tradition. She converted to him, joined forces with him, and so has a place now in German history.

Rahel did not acquire from Goethe the "art of existing" (Schlegel), but she did master to the point of virtuosity the art of communicating her own life, of presenting herself. That she could properly invoke Goethe's authority, that through the invocation of Goethe she could be not merely understood by others but in solidarity with them, this Rahel owes to a peculiar congruence between her own situation and the larger environment: whether her life succeeded or failed depended upon whether or not she could break through to the reality of the world. For totally different reasons the whole

generation, the generation of Humboldt, Schlegel, Gentz, and Schleiermacher, found itself in a similar circumstance.

V

The bearers of the Enlightenment, whose continuation is Romanticism, are
the citizens. Citizens no longer belong to any social rank, they no longer represent anything. The citizen can only offer "what he has," if he wants to
somehow "appear," then he is simply "laughable and tasteless." He cannot
"present" himself, he is not a "public person" (*Wilhelm Meister*) but merely
a private man. In representation such men had been visible. In the world of
the citizen, which has to do without representation, once the social ranks
have been dissolved there emerges the fear of not being seen, of having no
endorsement of one's own reality. Wilhelm Meister attempts through education to learn how to present himself. If he succeeds in this, he becomes a
"public person" and not just someone who "is only what he has." The people
who are capable of self-presentation meet together in salons. This presentation is their conversation.

The "salon" is Rahel's social opportunity and justification. She finds in it
the foundation upon which she can live, the space wherein she is socially recognized. The salon is her social reality. As long as this reality endures she has
no need of marriage or of baptism. Only when the salon disappears after the
unhappy war, or returns to the hands of those who had always belonged to
good society, is she forced to seek another possible existence, another possibility not to be passed over by history and forgotten. In 1811 she marries
Varnhagen and converts to Christianity. And Varnhagen devotes almost his
entire life to preserving her life, her letters, her person, and handing them
down to posterity.

1933

THE PROFESSIONAL
RECLASSIFICATION OF YOUTH

Their professional reclassification is of vital interest for all Jewish youth, whether right-wing or left-wing, religious or atheist, Zionist or assimilated. This is why we are listing below several key points and opening a discussion in which everyone is encouraged to take part.

1. One has always been aware that classifying Jews is abnormal, since neither being peasants nor workers is the basis of their social and economic existence. From the early days of their emancipation, the Jews began to preach reclassification as a universal panacea against antisemitism. Around 1900, when large numbers of people from Russia and Poland immigrated to America and Argentina, the Jewish charities started to reclassify these unfortunate individuals; this was how the large settlements in South America were born. Recently, Hitler made reclassification a political requirement for German Jews. Zionism, however, has given all these ventures a new meaning.

2. There are many reasons for reclassification. In some cases it permits a more effective assimilation; Jews, it is said, will be integrated into the population in a more balanced way, and no category will be overburdened with them. It is hoped this will lead to their being de-Judaized, but this overlooks the fact that *antisemitism arises wherever Jews create competition;* in Poland, for example, where a Jewish proletariat already exists, there is antisemitism among the workers.

3. Professional reclassification becomes urgent when the Jewish element is forced to abandon its position and prepare for a new emigration. Reclassification, in this case, must take into account specific regions where there is a real demand for a particular workforce; moreover, in-depth preparation is called for; dilettantism in this area can only ruin lives.

4. Reclassification is still prevalent in Zionism; there it is useful for the national construction and the social normalization of an entire people.

5. Professional reclassification based on charity is always suspect; of course, we are not calling into question the goodwill and genuine help of many great benefactors. *But charity is not solidarity; it usually helps only isolated individuals, with no overall plan; and that is why, in the end, it is not productive.* Charity divides a people into those who give and those who receive. The former, whether they like it or not, have a stake in the latter not jeopardizing their positions where they live, and hence in keeping them at a distance—which amounts to a sort of philanthropic antisemitism. Those who receive charity become undesirables, degraded and demoralized.

6. To sum up: *Professional reclassification must be in the hands of those who are determined to become a working people. It must not be done haphazardly and requires an overall plan if it is not to be social degradation but social rehabilitation. It is the striving for a normal state, by an entire people for an entire people.*

Lastly, we should be aware that professional reclassification is not the ultimate way to salvation, but just one of the ways. It must not lead to contempt for the spiritual. There was a time when every rabbi worked with his hands. It was a principle held by our ancestors, who combined the practical with the spiritual.

1935

A GUIDE FOR YOUTH:
MARTIN BUBER

When, almost two years ago, the German Jewish community, in its entirety, had to respond to the isolation imposed by the laws of exception, and the material and moral ruin of its collective existence, all Jews, whether they liked or not, had to become aware of themselves *as Jews*. At that decisive moment, anyone who knew the situation intimately was bound to feel anxious about the most difficult question: will one succeed in giving this new ghetto, imposed by the outside, a spiritual content? Will one succeed not just in organizing these Jews superficially, but also in linking them together by a *Judaic* bond, and making them into real Jews once again? Is there a man equal to this task? Does German Judaism have a guide in this area? Is there a leader who is more than a propagandist for Zionism, more than an eminent expert on Jewish problems, more than an excellent Judaic scholar and historian, and more than a living representation of Jewish culture—in short, someone who is all these things, and more?

In that sense, in our day, *Martin Buber* is German Judaism's incontestable guide. He is the official and actual head of all educational and cultural institutions. His personality is recognized by all parties and all groups. And furthermore he is the true leader of the youth.

He didn't just become a leader recently. For three decades, there hasn't been a young generation that hasn't felt his influence in a decisive way. For three decades, he has been staunchly opposed to both an exclusively political Zionism on the one hand, whose activity is often in danger of exhausting itself in negotiating and organizing, and to a fossilized Orthodoxy on the other that is in danger of hardening into traditional rites. A passionate Zionist from the time of his first publications at the beginning of the century, Buber has always known how to infuse Zionism with a distinctive spirit. He has an unparalleled way of combining the preservation of the past with the struggle for the future. Now and always, he has reiterated that the renaissance of the Jewish people can only come about through a radical return to its great past and its living religious values. This has won him the hearts and minds of all the young people who, in their journey to a forgotten Judaism, were desperately looking for the spiritual content of that Judaism from which they had become estranged.

What Ahad Haam had been for Eastern Europe, Buber became for Western Europe. What the young people were looking for but not finding, even in the best representatives of official Zionism, they discovered in this man and his work—a positive Judaism. Buber has presented and represented it for the last thirty years, ever youthful, ever renewed. Out of the "science of Judaism," which has sought for generations to bury a living people under the monument of exact philology and dead history, Martin Buber has created a "Jewish Science." This science seeks to make the most distant aspects of the biblical past alive and relevant to our present-day existence.

A great scholar who has played a major role in modern theological discussions in Germany, formerly professor at the University of Frankfurt, Buber has never been bogged down by his scholarship. He is always aware of how his knowledge can be useful in practical terms; he never shuts out the future in favor of the past. But he finds the seeds of the future in the past; the demands of the "Thou" of God toward the "I" of man—to use Buber's terminology—are found in Genesis and the Psalms, in the Prophets and the Book of Job. It is only by listening to these very ancient voices and learning to understand them that we will know how to fulfill the mission God gave to this, his people.

This updating of the past is at the heart of Buber's teaching, work, and influence. What has played an even greater role than his *Lectures on Judaism* is his splendid German translation of the Bible, undertaken many years ago in collaboration with Franz Rosenzweig. This translation has moved, fascinated, and influenced not only Jews, but all Germans interested in spiritual issues. No such endeavor had been attempted since Luther—to interpret the Bible poetically in another language, in accordance with its spirit. A hundred and fifty years ago, at the beginning of the emancipation, Moses Mendelssohn's German translation of the Bible in Hebrew letters enabled the Jewish youth of the ghetto to learn German and to enter, by this oddly circuitous path, into the German and European life of the period. Similarly, in our own day, Buber's marvelous undertaking is but a circuitous way of bringing the Jews back to Hebrew, the language of the Bible; a way of bringing them back to the Jewish past, its values and requirements. At both ends of German Jewish history, the beginning and the end, there stands a translation of the greatest Jewish possession—the Bible. And this fact expresses, perhaps better than anything else, the indissoluble link that exists between all of Jewish history—even the most modern—and its great beginning.

Whereas Buber's lectures and treatises, and above all his fundamental work *The Kingdom of God,* are aimed at a spiritual elite, his translation of the Bible, his rediscovery of Hasidism, and his new presentation of Jewish legends, are widely accessible and ensure him a broad sphere of influence. Today, these works should not be absent from any Jewish household. The fact that these Hasidic tales made such an impression on assimilated Jews clearly proves that Buber is right when he says, "Even in the most assimilated Jew there lives the knowledge and requirement of faith when one knows how to awaken his soul." He, Buber, succeeded in awakening the souls of these assimilated Jews. He succeeded because, with all his profound scholarship, he always remained a modern man in the best sense of the word. He was able to win over the youth because he didn't bury himself or Judaism under a great past, but knew how to rediscover the living roots of this past to build an even greater future.

I want to continue living, I want my future, I want a new, complete life; a life for myself, for the people within me, for myself in the people. For Judaism doesn't just have a past; on the contrary, for all that it has already created, I consider that Judaism has, above all, not a past but a future. Here is what I believe: Judaism, in truth, has not yet wrought its work, and the great forces that live inside the Jewish people, the most tragic and incomprehensible people of all, haven't yet made their vital contribution to the history of mankind.

1935

SOME YOUNG PEOPLE
ARE GOING HOME

Waifs!

Jews have been wandering around the world for two thousand years, taking in tow their belongings, their children, and their nostalgia for a homeland. They often lose their possessions in foreign countries. And what do they gain? The experience of sadness—the faculty of adapting and not letting themselves be annihilated. But children, not yet capable of fully understanding this destiny, lose everything: a stable household, a normal environment, their homeland, their friends, and their language. Not only are they uprooted, they are soon led astray . . .

The German emigration has brought us children, adolescents, and young people with no future, convinced that they are unlucky and will never amount to anything. Their parents, overburdened with worries, have no time to take care of them. Their lives are behind them; what they have accomplished or failed to accomplish is a settled matter. They barely think about the future and, focusing their concern only on the immediate present, forget the situation of their children. Besides, how can it be remedied? Children don't have the right to work, or to learn anything. They can only help in household chores and earn the few pennies that ward off starvation. Soon, though no one is at fault, children are exploited by their parents.

A Solution

It was under these circumstances that parents received a letter, a few months ago, from an organization still unknown to them: *Youth Aliyah*. The letter stated that additional certificates for Palestine are being granted to young people. Admittedly, not a great many. But the young people who have no papers, no possibility of learning anything in Europe, and are idling aimlessly in the streets, will be admitted into Eretz Israel. Today, our country is sufficiently large and sufficiently developed to take on the education of part of its youth. It is happy to do so. The Jewish settlements accept young immigrants for two years, and will provide them with schooling and practical training. They offer their farms as schools, their *Haverim* (comrades) as teachers.

That is what the letter said.

When they first receive the letter, parents are suspicious. Yet another rescue committee? More time and money wasted on the subway? The offer seems too good to be true; isn't there an ulterior motive?

The children, too, are skeptical. Every mother, of course, presents her child as the pearl of creation, but—paradoxically!—tries to silence the pearl and speak in its stead . . . The next day, however, the children, far from intimidated by the *shushes,* show up on their own at the Aliyah offices for a serious discussion of their future. And it is in the course of this interview that the real tragedy of these little Ahasueruses emerges.

The "Old Zionist"

One bright day, a father arrives with his son. Address: homeless shelter. He "just" ended up there.

First, he went directly from Germany to Palestine. He wasn't even allowed to disembark, but was sent on to Marseilles. From there, the Paris shelter was only "a step away." His fifteen-year-old son is with him. While the father is recounting their odyssey, the son is silent and unsociable. He is ashamed of their many misfortunes; he is annoyed by them; he behaves as if none of it concerned him, as if it were someone else's story and he were in the room by accident; he doesn't want to be identified with misfortune! On the other hand, he immediately proclaims that he is an "old Zionist." And the next day, he comes back alone, without his father. That's when we can talk to the reluctant young globetrotter without being disturbed. He shouldn't be ashamed of his misfortune! He shouldn't give it personal significance, for it isn't a personal misfortune; it is the misfortune of his entire people. Nothing is changed or improved by silence or hypocrisy. Yes, he will go to Palestine, not as a remedy to his own troubles, but as a member of an entire, large group, not because he is indigent, but because he is needed over there; he will build the country for himself and others, and for those who will come there after him. He will not be alone over there. And already here, he no longer has the right to feel alone, for he is showing a sense of solidarity with all those who share the same fate.

Time and again, the young people who come to Aliyah mention it to their friends and the friends also come by themselves, unaccompanied. This is the best propaganda. A young man of fourteen walks in. He wants to "get information." Where are his parents? "I would rather not worry them unnecessarily," he says, "before really making up my mind." He sees Palestine as "the only solution to the Jewish question," but wonders if he has the right to leave his father, for he handles all his French correspondence. Besides, can one leave before being an adult? The only answer to this question is: Youth Aliyah. As for the French correspondence, his thirteen-year-old sister will have to take care of it. Once everything is ready, he informs his parents, and two weeks later he is in the camp, where he begins to solve the Jewish question in a practical way by learning agriculture.

The Best Help!

Youth Aliyah is not a charitable institution. True, those who do not have money must be helped. But money alone does not solve the problem of these wanderers. Schools and professional training are a preparation for new migrations. And while the parents still have their doubts, young people are well aware of this! In every social milieu, there are young people who want to accomplish the *Haloutziouth* (the work of pioneers); this never fails to provoke more discussion among the representatives of the old generation and the new . . .

Most of the children are not yet damaged, but they are in despair. And even when they have been exposed to the worst, they change their ways very fast. The parents, alas, have learned to *schnor* in Paris; the children don't yet *schnor*, or if they do, they quickly learn not to when they are told that the extras they are wrongly demanding are taken from their own or their comrades' collective money.

Their ordeals in Germany, emigration, life in exile, have ruined the elders morally and made them too obsequious or too insolent. As for the children, as soon as they are put in a different atmosphere and given work, they quickly recover their natural dignity.

Several weeks of preparatory camp, with work and study, games and singing, reading and free discussion on all the issues they are interested in, restore their freedom and joy. Yes, it restores their lost youth.

This joy, this dignity, and this youth will be converted into strength and this strength will rebuild the country.

1935

THE GUSTLOFF TRIAL

As these lines are being written, the verdict in the trial of David Frankfurter has not been rendered. It is not all that important, either, whether the man who shot Gustloff will vanish behind the bars of the Graubünden Canton prison on the charge of murder or manslaughter. The trial's significance has been far greater than that.

Granted, it cannot be said that Frankfurter was any match for that significance. He is not a man of fixed purpose, nor a hothead—his is not a personality obsessed with ideas. No labor-union steward, no mediocre intellectual would have failed as badly as this defendant, would have missed so many chances to offer objections and present charges of his own. In the bourgeois patriarchal milieu of a Swiss courtroom—so very calm, so honorable, and so obviously all business—it may even have worked to his advantage that he was in fact the person the defense portrayed: a poor, sick student close to tears and trembling inside with agitation despite his external composure. It may also be that his lack of concentration when he gave his testimony, and his inability to fit the role fate had assigned to him, have encouraged the court to consider extenuating circumstances. In any case, Frankfurter is no hero of the age, but merely its victim—a victim who gave a loud scream. And because the shadows of the events in which he acted were so murky and vast, his scream was met with a worldwide echo. The shots fired by this desperate young Jew reverberated from the walls of Davos; the sound boomed out across Switzerland and struck at the heart of the world's conscience. That the world's conscience was allowed to speak—and at length—will be recorded on a page of honor in the history of Swiss justice.

And so it was only in the German press that Frankfurter was a central figure. For the rest of Europe it was the Third Reich that was sitting in the dock.

Berlin had seen this coming. In the days prior to the trial, the Hotel Steinbock was transformed into the headquarters of the German "delegation." Under the leadership of the expedition's general, the Bern diplomat von Bibra, all details had been planned and drilled: from the formal march out of the hotel to concerted demonstrations in the courtroom. One had to see for oneself just how meticulously it was all orchestrated, down to the distribution of carbon-copy instructions on how to react to the statement of charges and to various trial situations as they might be omitted or construed; or by the way the photographers they had brought along snapped shots of every journalist, of everyone listening in the courtroom; or how the "stenographers" (alias Gestapo agents) eavesdropped on every conversation during recesses. The Swiss police did their best, but for now they are far from being able to cope. The German contingent took up a third of the seats in the courtroom. The competition between those elderly press cripples Ullstein and Scherl and the younger Goebbels phalanx set the courtroom rattling. Commanding the battle were Drs. Grau, Grim, and Goebel; nevertheless, the victor in Chur was not their organization but an elderly gentleman of seventy-one, the counsel for the defense, Dr. Curti, who was very well prepared. He won because he summoned the truth. While spectators listened in stunned silence, the prisoners of German concentration camps—filthy, tortured, slain— passed by under the horrified eyes of the judges. Bathed in the sparkling sun- light reflected off snow-clad mountains, volumes of documents, photo albums, books, and sworn witnesses presented the hell where the lead of Frankfurter's bullets had been forged. And when the Swiss judges cast a glance at the accused Jew from Yugoslavia, they now saw him—despite the bias of locals against outsiders—in a different light. They understood his tears of rage and sorrow.

Overcome with emotion, Frankfurter wept as he recalled his pious father. This is what the *Angriff* wrote about those tears: "From time to time Frank- furter pulls out his handkerchief, blows the item he inherited from his father—a racially pure Jewish nose—and dabs at his drunken eyes as if try- ing to wipe away a few crocodile tears."

Well, Frankfurter's nose is straighter than Hitler's, and his eyes are not drunken but tear-stained—and yet it is all to the good that the German press wrote that. It provided the accompaniment to the guilelessly off-key aria sung by the much-photographed Dr. Grim, the canon they had brought along—though this time, in fact, it backfired on them. And as if on signal, the Swiss press, which had been waiting to hear the tone of the German press, now returned fire. It has been a long time since the local papers have written as much about the true state of affairs in the Third Reich as they have during this trial. They saw the Germans posing, protesting, carrying on as if they were the rulers of a *gau* (province) called Switzerland. "It was all the Germans could do not to put words to their outrage at such expert testimony," wrote the *Nachtausgabe*, which is all they could have done—at least in a foreign courtroom! Frankfurter's fate sank into the background, and during those four days it became clear to the Swiss public what dangers lay ahead if they were to yield to those voices that suggest clerical-fascist ideas and recommend a kind of assimilation with their neighbors to the north. Hitler lost this case.

But Frankfurter didn't win it either. In doing what he did, he was at the mercy of fate, and so too in his trial, whose central figure was Gustloff, the slain head of the Nazi foreign section in Switzerland, whom the Nazi press calls "the father of all Germans in Switzerland" and who had threatened to become the tyrant of Graubünden. And even though the *Berliner Zeitung* may call Frankfurter, a perfectly fine-looking man, a "criminal type," we will not make the physiognomy of the deceased—which resembled that of Streicher—the butt of our curses. We want to stick to the facts. And the fact is that for a good while not a single word, beyond an objective condemnation of his deed, was directed against Frankfurter—apart, that is, from what was said in a few newspapers that are fronts for unverifiable sources of money. Then the political situation grew more difficult, and with the rising tide of clerical-conservative-capitalist policies directed against the left, harder words about the prisoner in Chur began to wash up in the columns of the press. The atmosphere around Frankfurter turned gloomier, but the trial in Chur has brightened it again. The denunciation of true Nazi intentions, the accounts of espionage undertaken by the NSDAP's foreign section, the grisly principle of sadism as a weltanschauung—whose representative was the slain Nazi leader of Davos and a description of which set Swiss hearts trembling—these have all made the "Frankfurter murder trial" fade into the background. Instead, the case before the bar in this Graubünden Canton courtroom has been: *the Gustloff trial*. And that trial has been won—much to her own benefit—by Switzerland, which will not forget its lessons for a long time to come.

1936

THE JEWISH QUESTION

One of the essential hallmarks of the Jewish world's response to the Jewish question is a total lack of interest in dealing with antisemitism. After the catastrophe of 1933, the slogan heard in all Jewish camps was: *teshuva*, repentance, return to Judaism, let us take stock of ourselves—yes, even today in totally secularized Jewish circles one still hears it said that the call to return to the ghetto is *the* political slogan of the day.

In the meantime this slogan of "return" has born several remarkable and surely unexpected fruits. The *Jüdische Rundschau* admits an increasing lack of interest and a steadily declining membership in the Jewish Cultural Association and various *Lehrhäuser* [learning centers]—the very institutions to which until 1935 people made pilgrimages as if to a place of salvation. The Youth Association complains of a general growing disinterest in spiritual matters among the young. The collapse of 1933—which was a political, economic, and ideological collapse and at the same time the collapse of an entire spiritual world, including its values and what turned out to be only seemingly safe possessions—has led not to a new flourishing of Jewish life but to apathy and, in terms of the young, to a kind of rebarbarization.

And so in addressing our particular topic this evening, it is in this context that I shall offer a detailed account of what the slogans of 1933 actually mean.

The slogan of "return" is an admission of one's own guilt, both politically and, if you will, morally. This is already expressed in the word *teshuva*, or taking stock of oneself. From the very start, all segments of German Jewry surrendered the position or positions they held. The enemy was acknowledged to be an overwhelming power. And the ancient Jewish idea of a divine judgment shone through the statements of even the most enlightened German leaders. The refusal to analyze or deal with or indeed to confront antisemitism was tantamount to a political refusal to offer any defense whatever. For it said that one was not even interested in one's enemy, but merely submitted to his obviously overwhelming power. But there is no question that in politics knowing your enemy is at least as important as knowing yourself.

It seems to me that our political and spiritual leaders in these matters have abused and done almost irreparable damage to this concept of knowing yourself. Not because they should not know themselves and not because such self-knowledge and self-analysis might not have provided extraordinarily important and indispensable results, but by excluding everything else they have clouded our vision of the larger historical context in which we stand, whether we want to or not, and into which—despite utopian enthusiasts for the ghetto—we are dragged deeper day by day, that is, into which ever greater masses of our people are dragged every day. When one realizes that both Polish and Romanian antisemitism import their arguments from Germany, that even Franco, in a country where there are neither Jews nor a Jewish question, is battling the troops of the Spanish Republic while mouthing antisemitic slogans, and that we are now encountering German influence in Palestine, not to mention the countries of North Africa, then perhaps it becomes clear that in the interest of so-called world Jewry we cannot afford such slogans of "return" without endangering the Jews of every nation, including Palestine. And also that while our self-knowledge is quite commendable and thoroughly necessary and productive, it has been more or less *mal à propos*.

The deeper reason for this behavior is not—as one might easily, all too easily, be inclined to assume—cowardice. The historical reason is to be found, first, in the fragmentation and atomization and isolation of German Jewry from the Jewish people as such. One undeniably important result of this attempt at self-knowledge was the reconnection of German Jews with the Jewish people in general. The year 1933 struck nothing but isolated Jewish individuals, but not Jewry. This Jewry, granted by the grace of the Nazis, first had to be confirmed and constituted by us ourselves. The second reason was the realization that for our own history we are dreadfully dependent on the history of the world around us. The classic example of this has always been antisemitism. Out of this correct and very bitter realization arose the perfectly understandable illusion that simply by turning away, by "returning," by taking stock of ourselves, we could once again reconstitute a completely independent history and culture. It was an illusion for two reasons:

first, because another withdrawal from the European cultural community can only come at the cost of rebarbarization; and second, because one's own history can only be constituted as political history in the struggle against . . . and never in a vacuum.

It seems to me that there are two kinds of antisemitic countries: those where the Jewish question is genuine and those where it is not. Poland, for instance, is an example of a country with a genuine Jewish question, and the best example of an antisemitic country that has no Jewish question to solve is in those regions of present-day Spain that are in fascist hands. Spain is an obvious example of how the Jewish question can be artificially posed even where there cannot be any genuine interest in the question. Because Germany stands between those two extremes, it has perhaps become the classic land of antisemitism. German antisemitism today cannot be justified either socially or economically; moreover the steadily dwindling percentage of Jews in the German population makes the notion that this could be a major political problem look absolutely ridiculous.

Germany was once a country with a genuine Jewish question—that is, during the period of emancipation, which for all of Germany lasted less than eighty years. Until 1869 there was no total emancipation, but there was already complete assimilation, a complete infusion of Jews into all branches of the country's bourgeois economy—with known exceptions—a steadily expanding amalgamation of various segments of the population, and a recognition that Jews had equal rights, even though the factual reality of equal economic rights had not yet been given political or juridical legitimacy. The modern Jewish question arose out of the struggle for such legalization, and it was a genuine question, at least to the extent that it was a struggle about the acceptance of a people who until then had been a community closed completely in on itself, with other traditions and historical developments.

The Jewish question is a genuine question or a genuine problem—which means that there can be historical solutions—wherever truly large masses of people reside in the midst of another people from whom they are clearly set off by custom, wardrobe, the monopolization of certain professions, and historical development. This is the case, however, only in countries that are still more or less industrially underdeveloped, in which either the Jews are still a closed community—a caste originating in the Middle Ages—or for various reasons they have become the bearers of a certain progress, as for example in Poland where for a long time they have literally taken the place of an indigenous bourgeoisie, only to be thrown out now on the basis of what Schiller tells us happens to the Moor Othello once he has done his duty. In Poland, then, Jews are truly still recognizable in both instances, that is, as a "nation within a nation" and to a certain extent as a class set apart. In Poland there can be both hatred of Jews and a historical solution—that is, a solution that goes hand in hand with a particular historical development. An example of the former are pogroms of the sort that have marked the agenda of czarist Russia and present-day Poland; an example of the latter is total integration as is found in Soviet Russia.

In this sense there was no Jewish question in Germany in 1933. Which makes it all the more important to ask why in Germany of all places anti-semitic slogans held such promise of success and why of all places it was possible in Germany to remove Jews totally from the life of the German nation.

1937 or 1938

ANTISEMITISM

I Introduction

In 1781 Prussian court councilor Christian Wilhelm Dohm published his suggestions "On the Civic Improvement of Jews." Ten years later the National Convention of the French Revolution referred to its Declaration of Human Rights in proclaiming the emancipation of the Jews. Eighty-eight years later, in 1869, the German upper house rescinded "all previous restrictions of civil and legal rights based on differences of religious confession."[1] A mere two generations later, and the only persons in Germany who enjoy civil and legal rights are those who can prove that none of their grandparents was Jewish.

In 1701 Eisenmenger published his *Judaism Unmasked*, the ultimate compendium of all allegations raised against Jews in antiquity and the Middle Ages and a bountiful source even today for every sort of fabricated atrocity, from charges of ritual murder to tales of poisoned wells. A hundred years after Eisenmenger, only twenty years after Dohm's first proposals for reform, ten to fifteen years after the first tenuous proposals for assimilation, Grattenauer's *Against the Jews* places what sounds like a very modern version of antisemitism on the public agenda—and not just among semi-educated plebeians, but also among the Prussian capital's intellectual elite: Friedrich Gentz, Clemens von Brentano, Achim von Arnim, Adam Müller, Heinrich von Kleist. The entire circle of patriots that formed around the German Christian Table Society turns antisemitic. In 1869, the same year that full civil emancipation took effect in Germany, the first edition of Wilhelm Marr's *Victory of Judaism over Teutonism* is published. By the 1870s, the Jewish question is no longer a topic of discussion, but rather a point around which there crystallizes a political movement whose catchword is "antisemitism."[2] By 1933 all the proposals, one might say all the pipe dreams, of a

130-year-old movement are fulfilled—with the exception, that is, of the perennial suggestion for solving the Jewish question by slaying all the Jews.

The capitulation of the German Jews was swiftly followed by that of world Jewry, with all its attendant momentous consequences—for indeed all the protests, resolutions, and congresses merely cast sand in their own eyes, certainly not in the eyes of their foes. The burden of this capitulation has been primarily borne by Zionist circles, which though certainly not to blame for it, have indeed exploited it. This Zionism with a bad conscience was more or less an accidental preexistent asylum to which desperate people could flee for the sake of a bit of hope and some remnant of dignity.

The political failure of German Jews and of world Jewry in the face of the German catastrophe offers a fine basis for a thorough elucidation of the 150-year history of which it is the ignominious culmination, that is, for uncovering the true value of emancipation and clarifying its real historical significance. To the extent that the development that once drew us into German and European history and now expels us from it was not Jewish but foreign history, it inevitably presents itself to the same extent—and certainly most imperatively for us today—as the history of antisemitism.

It is of course also no accident that this catastrophe occurred in Germany—or that German fascism focused in its very nature and its program on antisemitism, or that its leadership came from splinters of old antisemitic parties and groups. Nor does it have anything whatever to do with the old "ventilation" theory—that a scapegoat has to be found for national discontent—or with the explanatory theory that traces it to the "notorious" Judaization of the press, theater, and freelance professions. Both theories are attempts to avoid taking fascism and antisemitism seriously. The first, the ventilation theory, is on the same level as the old joke that asks the question about who is to blame for everything, to which the answer is "the Jews and the bicyclists," followed by the astonished question, "Why the bicyclists?"—to which the answer is "Why the Jews?" Judaization, on the other hand, as the basis for antisemitism leaves all questions open, whether as an explanation originating with Jews themselves who demand more "discretion," or whether as an antisemitic phrase that regards Jews as a plague upon the land against which their far more powerful hosts cannot—for some extraordinary reason—defend themselves.

That the Jews are the source of antisemitism is the malicious and stupid insight of antisemites, who think that this vile tenet can account for hecatombs of human sacrifices and mountains of paper demanding murder, pillage, and arson. But Jews have made this same tenet their own, proving, as needed, either the timelessness of antisemitism or the timelessness of the Jewish mission in the world. And the eminently political importance our foes attach to these theories inversely makes them politically impotent the moment they arise among us, devoid of even the most wretched reflection—like rags pulled from the dusty storage bin of the nineteenth century to dress a persecuted, pogromized people and turn it into a fairy tale of princes and princesses.

Jewish history, which for two millennia has been made not by Jews but by those peoples that surround them, appears at first glance to be a monotonous chronicle of persecution and misfortune, of the brilliant rise and fall of a few individuals, atoned for by pogroms and expulsion of the masses. In consequence, when Jewish history is written by Jews, it has usually been a tacitly—rarely *expressis verbis*—conscious or unconscious attempt to come to terms with their foes or, better, with the history of their foes. But one must also clearly differentiate between history written from a nationalist perspective that attempted to defend the honor of the Jewish people by proving that they do indeed have a history of their own and the apologetics of a history written by assimilationists.

In the hands of the *assimilationists* Jewish history was turned into a *history of the injustice* inflicted on us, that lasted until the end of the eighteenth century, when—with no transition and by the grace of God and/or the French Revolution—it merged into *world history,* to whose "creeping pace," as Hermann Cohen put it, we have cheerfully entrusted ourselves. By contrast, enlightened Jews in the East attempted to write a Jewish *national history* in the spirit of the nineteenth century, which in our case meant following the traces of Jewish history against the backdrop of European history in order painstakingly to patch together an outline of the unified national development of a scattered nation. Ostensibly protected by equal civil rights, those in the West managed to smuggle the history of the Jewish people right out the back door and replace it with a history of the Jewish religion, whose purest and loftiest expression was without doubt the Reform synagogue—a methodology which, if rather theoretical, rid them of their embarrassing origins, allowing them in one single bound to plunge into a world history whose "creeping pace" temporarily made way for a paradoxical display of both fierce patriotism and slavish "gratitude."³ This lofty objectivity of Jews in the West, for whom being a Jew was now nothing but a religion in which they no longer believed and who in consequence attempted to make the entirety of Europe's historical past their own, quite apart from the fact that this history had once subjected them to pogroms and persecution—this indifference of the assimilationists was countered by the partisanship, which is its greatest merit, of the nationalist history of the East. Thus the latter succeeded in writing a "world history of the Jewish people," which apart from its value as a planned, cohesive collection of materials, proved one thing: that the Jews are a people. It is against this—and not against an obvious inability to understand certain historical connections—that assimilationist historians directed their outraged polemic. After all, their own preoccupation was to prove that Jews are all sorts of things—a religion, the salt of the earth, world citizens par excellence—but not a people.

Both types of Jewish historiography are characterized by their inability to come to terms with *antisemitism;* both attempt to reduce it to individual opinions about Jews. Nationalist historiography makes do with simply examining history for tendencies either friendly or hostile to Jews and, having evaluated these views, assembles them into a patchwork. Assimilationist historians, however, who have the advantage of at least taking antisemitism seriously, though only in its most innocuous forms, refute individual opinions—the misconceptions of great men, the lies of lesser men—in the belief that this is the best way to contribute to the progress of the age. To the antisemites' charge that Jews are unproductive, they call Moses and the Prophets, Maimonides, Spinoza, Heine, and Marx as witnesses to the contrary. One erroneous quotation from the Talmud is countered with another accurate one. By its very nature, the list of such arguments is endless and limited only by one's foes' talent for invention. Since it is *uncritical* in the literal sense of the word, such an approach never asks the question as to what makes antisemitism—and accusations that are, after all, believed—possible. It never asks about the actual conditions that are the basis for such "calumnies and misconceptions." This is especially true for the modern age. For those epochs prior to any proclamations of emancipation, there is a real recognition of and reckoning with those forces that have determined our history—but only because and to the extent that the distant past has already been condemned by the very milieu in which Jews happened to live. With emancipation, all Jewish-based critique of the non-Jewish milieu ceases entirely. For assimilationists the history of the Jews coincides with the history of those nations among whom they live. Jewish history degenerates into a chronicle of various urban communities of Jews—and even this is written as an apologia, as proof of the antiquity of the respective Jewish community, while antisemitism, whether as opinion or political movement, is excluded from such a positive history and henceforth categorized as "medieval barbarism" and "outmoded prejudice."

Whereas nationalist historiography is based on the uncritical assumption of a *distance on principle* between Jews and their host nation, assimilationist historians opt for an equally uncritical assumption of a 100 *percent correspondence* between Jews and their entire host nation. The advantage of the nationalist hypothesis over that of the assimilationists is a purely practical one: it does not lead to illusions that are quite so absurd. For example, in Germany there was a German working class and bourgeoisie; there were German storekeepers and farmers, Bavarians, Prussians, Swabians, and so forth; and there were also pure Germans per se: the Jews. Long before Hitler ever invented his *Volksgenosse* [ethnic comrade], this same abstraction had crept into the minds of half a million people. The Jews were Germans and nothing more. And since they were nothing but Germans, there could be no differences of interest between them and any given segment of the German people.

Zionist criticism is to be credited for finishing off this absurdity by demonstrating that these "nothing but Germans" were able to present themselves in such an excessively positive light only because—inasmuch as they were never truly assimilated anywhere—they did not in fact fully belong to any society. What is more, their own exaggerated patriotism allowed them to deceive themselves, but no one else, as to this fact.

But for Zionism—as for nationalist historiography—status as a "nation of foreigners" is just as undifferentiated as 100 percent correspondence is for the assimilationists. Instead of one abstraction—the German people—we now have what are more or less two opposing abstractions: the German people and the Jews. This likewise strips the relationship between Jews and their host nation of its historicity and reduces it to a play of forces (like those of attraction and repulsion) between two natural substances, an interaction that will be repeated everywhere Jews live. Thus Zionism remains rooted in its insight into the absurdity of assimilation and soars to heights of counter-assertions that are just as purely dogmatic. For Zionism, factual assimilation—that is, the fact of a complete transformation of the Western European Jews—is extraneous to a Jewish substance that is forever the same, opposed to which is the equally eternal substance of the host people. Relationships between the two are governed by a respect achieved through each keeping its appropriate distance. It is, of course, most lamentable that of late this respect is in fact rather one-sided—that is, tendered solely by Zionists, who, by way of compensation, do not shrink from demonstrating all due respect to the other substance even when it takes the form of antisemitism.[4] For Zionism the history of emancipation is the prelude to a catastrophe that had to attend the development of national awareness. According to this view, things went well for so long only because of liberal illusions and the individualistic biases of the Enlightenment.

Assimilationists were never able to explain how things could ever have turned out so badly, and for the Zionists there still remains the unresolved fact that things might have gone well. These are both the same shortcoming, and both arise out of a shared Jewish *fear of admitting that there are and always have been divergent interests between Jews and segments of the people among whom they live.* As a means to avoid having to acknowledge any true and specific foe, generalization and misinterpretation turn factual rapprochement into 100 percent correspondence and factual difference into substantial alienation. Jewish fear consigns the exploration of their own affairs to the transitory needs of antisemites. Only assimilation on an international scale, which would be tantamount to the disappearance of the Jews, or a social order that knows no opposing international interests could put an end to the fact that there are differences of interests. Only acknowledgment of this factor can serve as a benchmark as to whether people recognize the existence of the Jewish question or attempt to conceal it.

Such attempts at concealment tend to be most clearly enunciated in so-called *solutions to the Jewish question.* Of interest to us here are only those that are formulated by Jews for Jews. This means we shall exclude Soviet Russia, the only country where the civil rights of Jews are guaranteed by law in its constitution, which defines antisemitism as a crime within the context of the penal code and therefore as a threat not just to Jews but to society as a whole.

It also lies outside the scope of our observations simply because Russia's solution to the Jewish question solves nothing on an international scale, nor is that its programmatic intent.[5]

Complete assimilation and the Zionists' building up of Palestine have not remained at the stage of mere invention or proclamation, but still determine down to the present day almost everything that can halfway be called Jewish politics. Both theories have modern antisemitism as their essential cause and are therefore to be universally understood as argument, polemic, justification, or simply a way out.[6] The core conceptual charge leveled by our foes is—in general terms—that Jews are *foreigners*. Since Herder first defined Jews as "an Asian people foreign to our continent,"[7] his charge has moved in many directions. In every case, however, it was the only charge that simple, direct apologetics found difficult to answer. It is worth noting that the formulation of a regular theory was required in order to counter this definition—and it only. For in fact its direct consequence is to place in doubt the legitimacy of emancipation, which arose out of a foreign, non-Jewish historical constellation for which Jews had never struggled and that did not belong to the course of their history. That is at least how the matter looks at first glance. How it in fact came about, we shall discuss later.

Both theories, whether of the assimilationists or the Zionists, neither of whom are suicidal by profession, retain the charge of foreignness in a certain sense—the assimilationists by degrading it to a harmless difference of religion and thrusting every other difference into a past that, as everyone knows, corrupted the Jews by treating them badly. Everything other than a difference of religion is a remnant of an ugly history that is to fall away by itself in the process of assimilation. As for the difference in religion, Jews—since Moses Mendelssohn—have the advantage over Christian Europe of a pure monotheism, which the rest of humankind will likewise achieve at the end of time (this having become the messianic hope!). In all other points emancipated Jews are already participating in the history of humankind. No one answers the question as to what the history of humankind—apart from the national history of its peoples—consists of, unless it be evolution toward a pure monotheism.

This flight into the history of humankind cannot come to terms theoretically with the fact of the manifest happenstance that has turned Jews with a Jewish past into citizens of various countries with varied pasts. This embarrassment gives rise to the kind of comical patriotism that causes German Jews to date themselves back to Hermann the Cheruscan and French Jews to Vercingétorix.

All theories that see the Jews' salvation in *assimilation* are based on the premise of a host people who form a totally unified, undifferentiated organism. The goal is integration into this organism. Jews become German citizens of the Jewish faith. Any admission that one belongs to a certain class of people is avoided. Whoever dares to state this is labeled a Jewish antisemite. This leads to the most embarrassing and absurd practical situations. In order to assimilate and engage as many Jews as possible in the assimilation process—since as living proof of their shared foreign origins, every unassimilated Jew is a danger to all the others—organization is a prerequisite. Since the beginning of the nineteenth century, Jews in the countries of Western Europe have existed politically as Jews only in organizations whose purpose is to make them vanish—while, of course, making a not insubstantial contribution to the preservation of German Jewry. Since in their own minds Jews were in conformity with the vaguely defined general interest of the German people, and yet paradoxically were an organization of their own, they felt themselves compelled to affirm their particular trust in whatever government happened to be in power, which for them was always simply a coincidental expression of that ostensible general interest. On principle they are always—and cannot be anything but—loyal. Glorying in their loyalty, they let themselves be certified by successive governments—never noticing how untrustworthy this makes them appear in the eyes of each. The antisemitic charge of treason is pure fabrication, but belief in it has its basis in this tactic of assimilationist Jews. In that sense 1933 is simply the natural outcome of 100 percent Jewish conformity with the German people. Hitler, the true representative of *the* German people, used the Jews to lend both an ideological basis to his chimera of racial theory and a sentimental basis to the concept of the *Volksgenosse* [ethnic comrade]. All he needed was flat-out to declare the ever loyal Jews to be public enemy number one.

The reduction of Jewish foreignness to the threadbare cloak of religion was not enough to cover the nakedness of an entire class of people who no longer believed in defending themselves, who, being open to every sort of attack, regarded each with total incomprehension. Despite all protestations to the contrary, all economic statistics prove that German Jews belonged not to the German people, but at most to its bourgeoisie. And even this differen- tiation was not enough, as we shall see. Despite all such patriotism, inter- national Jewish unity is documented by a coerced solidarity with "brothers in faith" that follows every pogrom. While the cloak of religion becomes increasingly threadbare—fewer and fewer "brothers in faith" attend syna- gogue, fewer and fewer "Christians" go to church—the foreignness remains and grows stronger. And at the end of our tale what happens to this whole bundle of botched Jewish theorizing, which used religion to conceal other things but also continued to cling to religion as a way of preserving some remnant of autonomy—in the end and in service of a higher antisemitism, Jews are treated to the additional misfortune of being tossed into the same pot as the Christians, indeed of being considered identical with them.

For eight hundred years, ever since the crusades, Jews have been perse- cuted, beaten, mocked, and branded as heretics. And why? Because they were so obstinate as to remain Jews even though there was Chris- tianity in this world. And today, as Christianity loses prestige, what happens to us? Suddenly laudable Christianity is contemptible Judaism, Europe's Christianity is itself a Judaization that has deprived the Germans of their splendid religion. (Moritz Goldstein)

Long before the actual catastrophe, these obvious contradictions—and the still more evident ineffectiveness and uselessness of desperation's brain- children—could have led an honest, unbiased man unversed in the history of this cauldron of woe to draw the following conclusion: "We could easily demonstrate our foes' absurdity and show them that their hostility is unfounded. But what would be gained? Proof that their hatred is genuine. When all calumnies have been refuted, when all false judgments have been thwarted, their aversion toward us remains irrefutable. There is no helping anyone who doesn't understand that."[8]

This "insight"—actually the description of a phenomenon and the admis- sion of a fiasco—is the Western European point of departure for Herzl's *Zionism*. Hatred of others becomes a generalized fixation and then is dis- placed upon a false objective: the Jewish substance. This Jewish substance takes the form of Jews in an anomalous situation and can therefore be expressed anomalously. The ultimate goal of Jewish politics is the normal- ization of the conditions for the development of the Jewish substance. To become a people like all other peoples—that is the goal, but always with the specific provision: *like all other peoples*. Compared to this foreignness of substance and the aversion arising from it, all individual charges and calumnies are mere symptoms, and as such can neither be cured nor taken seriously. There is, of course, agreement with individual points of the assimilationist apologia, but disagreement as to its efficacy. Whereas assimilationist apologetics resolved antisemitism into the errors and calumnies of individuals, Zionism presumes and finds something *behind* personal opinions—not, however, certain verifiable facts, but rather the eternal struggle of substances foreign to one another, thereby absolving antisemitism anew of any historical analysis of relationships. In this regard, too—in the complete lack of a historical viewpoint—Zionists certainly accept the inheritance handed down by the assimilationists, but turn it upside down. Where the latter imagined they had become *like* the German people, the former respond: No, as antisemitism proves, we are totally *foreign* to and despised by that other people on the basis of its inalterable substance. Such a schematic generalization appears to conform perfectly to the National Socialists who crystallize their worldview of a *Volksgemeinschaft* [ethnic community] in antisemitism. How this is possible is, of course, the fundamental question for any historical examination of antisemitism today.

German Zionism increasingly led the way in Western Europe, just as did German antisemitism. The Zionist substance theory appeared to be a perfect match for conditions in Germany. This gave the movement its theoretical élan but there was an initial moral impulse as well. Protest against a life that in any case must be paid for with a broken back provides a good start for descriptions of such phenomena, but remains mired in mere description. Since Zionism is based in an utterly unhistorical theory, it proves incapable of any real analysis. From the outset it is overrun and falsified by others with real interests of their own—be it the masses of Jews in the East or the Jews in the West, the vast majority of whom remain in their fatherlands. In the interest of the latter, Zionism must maintain a double patriotism in order to prove as loyal as the assimilationists had always been. Even Zionism does not dare represent specific Jewish interests within a given fatherland, but must project an ideal outside its borders, as if Jewish interests exist only in Palestine. And since it is dependent on the help of wealthy Jews—who, when it comes to material questions, don't do very well with ideals—it must appeal to *their* interests and keep the "brothers in faith" in the East at a good distance from *their* fatherlands—which ultimately means appealing to the worst element, to those who are most clearly in conflict with the interests of Jews as a whole.

That is why Herzl's initial attempt to base Zionism on real analysis—beginning with the so-called "overproduction of the middle class"—was never developed, but led only to piles of statistics. Far more significant in terms of theory has been Buber's Zionism, which attempts to explain Jewish "substance" by way of pseudophilosophical profundity. Fixating foreignness in something substantial gives rise to a mad urge to define Jewry, Jew, Jewish, and so forth. The answers are both varied and contradictory, and it would be quite foolish to discuss them in detail—since all of them take their cue from whatever the "zeitgeist" may prompt their authors to say, each may be passé by tomorrow. In any case, simply posing such questions also puts theoretical Zionism in permanent and highly dangerous proximity to the worst partisan interests and antisemitic theorems. If definitions are indeed called for, those based on race would appear to be the most tried and true, even though the doctrine of race grows out of a very different context and only secondarily out of any need to define what a Jew is.

In every regard Zionism is the legitimate heir to assimilation. It arose as assimilation foundered and is the consequence of an abandoned and failed emancipation. It draws its legitimation out of the misfortune and sorrow into which the illusionary policies of the assimilationists have plunged all of Western Europe. It has more to show for itself than all such policies together—and that is the building up of Palestine, which is after all both a fact and a factor of Jewish politics that can no longer be excluded from our thinking or our speech. But with that reality, with Palestine, Zionists are at their wits' end. Although they long ago had to admit that Palestine is not *the* solution to the Jewish question, they have focused purely on Palestine and lost interest in the most vital questions of the Jewish Diaspora. Drawing upon the assimilationist illusion of a unified people, Zionism has substituted the illusion of a unified, eternal substance. Although Zionism counters undifferentiated loyalty with the principle of foreignness, it has also adopted a blindness for any differentiation between friend and foe, all of whom are equally foreign.

Zionists are incapable of representing Jewish interests on a global scale. They never come to terms with the equality of rights granted Jews in the

Soviet constitution, but are willing to negotiate with openly antisemitic governments. By defending the interests of an ostensibly unified world Jewry, they betray the immediate interests of the Jewish masses in Eastern Europe—see, for example, the Palestine Transfer Agreement with the German government, which paves the way for all antisemitic governments to increase exports and augment foreign exchange. But since all so-called reason—which for these heirs of assimilation is represented solely in assimilationist apologetics—has now foundered on the power of others, Zionists are prepared at any time to abandon resistance and recognize might as right. Every forfeiture of national dignity is justified by the assertion of the primacy of Palestinian interests and the renaissance of Jewish "substance."

Thus ends the story of the reawakeners of Jewish self-awareness and national dignity. The Don Quixotes, who on the basis of pure ideals and pure moral protest believed they were protesting and acting with benevolence, have become practitioners of realpolitik, blind devotees of temporary power relationships. For fear of a few Jewish capitalist interests, they hold congresses that do not even risk protesting the persecution of Jews. Zionism as a political movement is being ground down between interests dedicated to building up Palestine and those advocated by large segments of Jewry. It has never had the great masses behind it, but has lived on credit as the avantgarde of the Jewish people. Today the fronts have hardened and its credit has been exhausted.[9] For the sake of Palestine it has abandoned Jewish politics on a global scale. It represents only people still waiting for certification so that Zionism may help them flee their oppressors and the more progressive segment of the Western European Jewish bourgeoisie, which, trembling for its own existence, hopes that Zionism—like all emigration organizations—will provide some relief.

Zionism's lack of interest in its political foe, its programmatic blindness to both friend and foe, contains within it—viewed *à la longue*—the dangerous illusion of the possibility of *autonomous Jewish politics*. This idea was first formulated clearly and programmatically in the brochure "Auto-emancipation," published by Pinsker in 1882. Pinsker already presents bourgeois assimilation as a failure and attempts to find a new answer for the hatred of Jews, for this eternal "fear of ghosts" among the nations. In contrast to emancipation in Western Europe, "auto-emancipation" is not to be a "gift" or a pact that can be terminated by the powerful whenever and wherever they please, but rather a kind of national rebirth, a *self*-liberation from the ghetto—and its guarantee lies in the struggle to obtain it. In this context Palestine was and is regarded as the territory where self-emancipation can be accomplished. The building up of Palestine and the autonomous Jewish politics that accompany it—it is with this that Zionism stands or falls as an idea down to the present day. And that is why the current Zionist organization holds fast to it despite all its obvious contradictions and every conceivable sophistry—almost as if it wanted to demonstrate *ad oculus* the impossibility of such politics.

In principle Zionism as a political movement directs its appeal to all Jews. It bases its appeal on the thesis that the status of Jews around the world will depend on Palestine's being built up, that only this can guarantee them a better political position. For this it needs at least the appearance of independent policies that are based on and exclusively serve Jewish interests. In its propaganda it maintains its polemic—though with steadily dwindling intensity—against all those who want to turn Palestine into a mere "asylum for the night."

In reality what we are witnessing is how with each passing day Zionism is being forced into a vassal relationship with Britain, a status it must accept to avoid being punished with the loss of what has already been achieved. This indictment is an old one. Ever since the Balfour Declaration, Jews have been called the "pacemakers of British imperialism." Zionism's response speaks of "coordinated interests." Things have come to a point where there is no longer any doubt that Jewish interests are subordinate to those of the British. "Without the Jews there would be no Palestine," a British politician said recently. Certainly *for England* there would be no Palestine without the Jews. Once again we are the receivers of our emancipation, this time not in the name of "human rights," but rather as national rights presented to us as a "gift"; and even a "Jewish state"—which we have not dared mention for decades now, even in our own propaganda, just as in his day Mendelssohn did not dare in his own name to demand emancipation—is offered to us as addendum to foreign interests and as part of a foreign history, that of the British Empire.

Since the days when Polish nobles invited Jews into their country to act as tax collectors, buffering them from the peasants they hoped to suck dry, there has never been such an ideal coordination of interests, such ideal cooperation. In those days, too, Jews arrived rejoicing in the convergence of so many interests and unaware of their future role. They knew no more about Polish farmers than Zionist officials did about Arabs prior to the Balfour Declaration. In those days the Jews of Central Europe were fleeing from the pogroms of the late Middle Ages to an Eastern paradise of converging interests, and we are still feeling the consequences of that today. Even back then we were neither great villains nor paid agents—but were simply paying the price of barely staying alive.

The bankruptcy of the Zionist movement caused by the reality of Palestine is at the same time the bankruptcy of the illusion of autonomous, isolated Jewish politics. Having been put to the test, the catchword of auto-emancipation has become an empty phrase—though, granted, the most foolish and misleading phrase of modern history. Every dreamer of the dream of autonomy who accepts this gift—given by the accident of political constellations—from allies whom he must then idealize for the sake of autonomy, may one day discover that his ally is his enemy. Whoever imagines that there is an eternally abiding Jewish "substance" that lies far above the daily struggle of various interests, will one day see his finest ideals betrayed into the hands of the worst of interests.

Zionist slogans have become empty phrases. Concealed behind them are the interests of a petite bourgeoisie pursued by pogroms and reduced to poverty in the East and of a highly imperiled bourgeoisie in the West, which must nevertheless attempt to stop the flood of emigration out of their own countries. The former are sent on their way, financed by the latter—just as was the case in the system of charity of well-placed Jews against which Zionism once staged its lovely rebellion. Both "parties" are prepared to make any political concession, prepared to accept the support of antisemitic governments or to become troops guarding British imperialism, prepared, that is, to renounce Jewish politics in general. The successor to the failure of bourgeois assimilation is a failed bourgeois nationalist movement.

"How poorly defended Israel is! False friends stand guard outside its gates, while its guards within are foolishness and fear" (Heine, "The Rabbi of Bacharach").

II *The Classic Land of Antisemitism*

No nation in recent world history has inflicted on the Jews as much misfortune as Germany. No pogrom in Poland or the Ukraine was ever as devastating as the triumph of National Socialism, with its establishment of a theoretical antisemitic worldview.

No nation in recent world history has meant as much to the Jews as Germany. Nowhere was greater service rendered to the liberation of Jews than in this same Prussia, where, from Lessing to Wilhelm von Humboldt, the Jewish question and Jewish emancipation were equated with the struggle for human freedom and universal justice.

Just as for us the year 1933 marked the beginning of the disenfranchisement of Jews—including those of Poland and Romania, to name just the two countries with the largest Jewish populations—so, too, Lessing's *Nathan the Wise* and Dohm's essay once spread word of the Declaration of the Rights of Man for Jews as proclaimed by the French Revolution. But so, too, the first great pogroms of modern times—in Russia during the 1880s—were "predicted" and justified in the eyes of an enlightened urban population and of progressive Europe as a whole by means of an antisemitic work translated from the German[1]—a wretched but often repeated attempt to harmonize modern antisemitic trends with the butchery decreed and tolerated by insufferable feudal conditions and to present the result as the peak of modernity and progress.[2] So, too, laws regulating the Jews of Romania—which suited the seventeenth or eighteenth centuries, but certainly not the nineteenth or twentieth, and which the Treaty of Versailles abrogated for only a brief two decades—drew breath from that same German antisemitism and its cry: "Romania for the Romanians." So, too, even England's liberals had to ease their consciences with the help of Marr and Treitschke during the anti-Jewish campaign of the Eastern Crisis of 1877–78.[3]

What appears at first glance to be the absurdity of coupling hypermodern slogans with extreme backward conditions loses its significance when one disregards for a moment the purely ideological armor of such movements and realizes that the modern mass migration of Jews began with the Russian pogroms of the 1880s. From 1800 to 1880, on average only three thousand Jews moved each year from East to West. In the wake of the Russian pogroms, 50,000 Jews emigrated annually during the last two decades of the nineteenth century—an increasingly smaller percentage of whom have remained in Europe, while a majority have moved to America. Prior to the World War 135,000 Jews were on the move each year. Due to restrictive immigration laws in almost all countries and to an abating need among Russian Jews to emigrate, the number of migrating Jews has fallen to 65,000 annually, and has never again attained its prewar records.[4] With Hitler's seizure of power the need to emigrate achieved a previously unknown intensity; but because of the generalized persecution of Jews that is a consequence of German antisemitism, Jewish emigration has again come to a standstill. The Jewish masses are not being admitted into any country in the world. The history of the Jewish people is again becoming unified. The era that divided them into Eastern Jews and assimilated Jews was followed by the era of migration, which in turn has come to an end with the generalization of antisemitism and the rekindling of the Jewish question in almost every country in the world. Any differentiation between "progressive" bourgeois and backward feudal nations has become untenable. With the help of more progressive nations, backward countries are lending their barbarism very modern, fascist forms, and progressive nations are reverting to barbaric methods as the most effective means of adding ferment to their rule.

Even as the first modern pogroms were raging in Russia, the first international congresses of antisemites were being held in Germany. German antisemitism had already invented a kind of common theoretical basis for the various, contradictory tendencies found among Europeans hostile to Jews. In most of the countries of Europe Jews had not yet been granted emancipation.[5] While Jews everywhere were still fighting their fight using arguments that came also from Prussian history—for ever since Adolphe Thierry and Mirabeau, no struggle for Jewish liberation in Europe had failed to borrow its pathos from Lessing and its arguments from Dohm[6]—the modern war to destroy Jews, under the aegis of German intellectual ascendancy, was being heralded in many of those same countries.

From Lessing's *Nathan the Wise* to Rosenberg's *Myth of the Twentieth Century,* every liberation and every catastrophe that has befallen the Jews of Europe has been able to borrow its theoretical foundation and its pathos from Germany—and always long before some practical application came due in Germany itself. A good hundred years lie between Lessing and emancipation;

it did not take even sixty-five years to move from Marr, the founder of modern antisemitism as a political movement, to Hitler's victory. It was not until the total victory of antisemitism that Germany gained its genuine "classic" status as regards the Jewish question; it was not until the Third Reich that the radicalness of theory found itself no longer contradicted by any sort of practical compromise. The brief era of equal rights was never able to boast of such a claim.

It is as puzzling as it is understandable that Jews were the ones who put their trust most uncritically in the country to which they theoretically owed the most. By the end of the eighteenth century in Prussia, the Jewish question was posed as part of what at the time were the most pressing political questions of European history. Repression of Jews became a symbol of the social conditions of the age. The struggle to emancipate Jews was not about the Jews, not about an oppressed people; what was *theoretically* demanded was a visible symbol of human liberation, of progress, of the abandonment of prejudices.

This proved the source of a great deal of mischief. From the start, the Jew became *the* Jew, individuals became a principle. Nathan the Wise is not some noble man of Jewish ancestry, but rather a poetic example, poetic proof that the Jew *can* be noble—much as Moses Mendelssohn was turned into a living example, into living proof of this possibility. Liberation was to be extended not to Jews one might know or not know, not to the humble peddler or to the lender of large sums of money, but to "the Jew in general" as he *can* be and was found in Mendelssohn, his new representative; and he, in turn, not as a Jew but as a human being. Even the Jew is a human being—the most improbable thing of all. And so the Jew became the principle of what it means to be human, his liberation a symbol of man's liberation. Such discussions of the Jewish question always remained on a theoretical level and were about the rights of man, not about achieving equal rights for a fellow citizen of a faith different from that of the Christian state and world around him.

Jews were to be the example, the test case for human rights, to provide proof as to what extent "human nature which is universally the same is capable of the most accomplished cultivation and the most unfortunate degeneration." The Jews are merely the example by which such degeneration and cultivation are to be shown. Dohm's purpose is "not to write an apologia either for Jewry or the Jews, he merely presents the cause of humanity and defends its rights. How fortunate for *us* when that cause becomes *ours* as well, when one cannot urge the rights of man without advocating ours at the same time."[7] With these words Mendelssohn is simply summarizing the *theoretical* basis from which Lessing and Dohm posed the Jewish question.

The great opportunity, despite all its drawbacks, that Germany gave the Jews was that there was no way to sever this linkage with the cause of the Jews—neither by non-Jews, who as antisemites were suspicious of men of the Enlightenment in any case, nor by Jews, who later would gladly have secured their emancipation quite apart from all political struggles. After all, if we want to fight for our rights today, we must fall back on these first beginnings, for only on this basis do we have any prospect of finding allies and of joining in the struggle for freedom in all its political forms. Ever since the German Enlightenment posited the theoretical equation of the cause of the Jews with that of human rights, ever since the French Revolution put that linkage in practice, the pattern that our history would follow has been irrevocably traced.

The excellent advantage that grew out of posing the Jewish question in this fundamental way became a significant disadvantage when economic assimilation—which in Germany was denied its political legitimacy for almost eighty years—turned an oppressed and persecuted people into bankers, merchants, and academics. Such abstract thinking very quickly took its revenge on us when "friends" became foes once they were forced to observe that living Jews were not universally oppressed. During this process, by which an oppressed people with certain limited privileges and functions became citizens without political rights, the Jews lost their best political friends: the heirs of the Enlightenment, who had insisted on emancipating the Jews along with the rest of humanity and now accused the Jews of turning emancipation into a privilege that they demanded for themselves and not for all oppressed peoples. These former friends finally became antisemites themselves, because in one way or another they continued to be troubled by the old messianic chimera of a "chosen people" who enjoy some special position. They no longer hoped for the Christianization of all mankind that would follow upon the "conversion of the Jews," but they did hope for mankind's liberation, of which the emancipation of the Jews was but a symbol. "The Jew, if he views the matter correctly, should not propose

or hope for elimination of his particular affliction or abrogation of his particular bondage, but rather for the overthrow of a principle."[8]

It is no accident that when the Jewish question is posed in this fundamental
way, the Jews are turned into little more than an example, almost a mere pretext, that they are seen by their "friends" in particular as nothing but a principle within a process, and that never once in the sad course of history over
the last 150 years have they been regarded by others as living human beings.
Dohm explicitly stated what the position of the friends of the Jews would be
if they ever ceased for a single moment to regard Jews as a principle,
example, or pretext. "Certainly it would be better," our great *friend* Dohm
says, "if the Jews, along with their prejudices, did not exist—but since they
do exist, do we really still have a choice from among the following: to wipe
them off the face of the earth (presuming such a thing can even be conceived
of in our day) all at once or by taking measures that gradually achieve that
goal; or to let them remain in perpetuity the same unwholesome members of
society that they have been thus far; or to make them better citizens of the
world?"[9]

Jews in all their concrete noxiousness are to be overlooked for the sake of
the Jew, whose oppression is a disgrace to mankind. The issue was turned
into such an abstraction, because there was such unanimity as to Jewish noxiousness. Modern antisemitism, which knows that Jews are not universally
"noxious," turns this abstraction on its head by overlooking "decent" Jews
with whom one may be personally acquainted ("there are decent Jews as
well") in favor of *the* Jew, who has at last been discovered to be the evil principle of history. *The classic form in which the Jewish question was posed in the
Enlightenment provides classic antisemitism its theoretical basis.*

To transform the Jew from a living individual into a principle, into an
agglomeration of characteristics that are universally "evil" and, although
observable in other people as well, are always called "Jewish" (whereas any
others have been "Judaized"), in short, to transform the Jew into *the* Jew and
then to conjure up all the things that are *Jewish* about him—all of these are
tendencies found throughout modern antisemitism, which in its essence can
be distinguished from the medieval hatred of Jews precisely because of its
abstractness. Racial antisemitism, although it attempts to concretize *the* Jew
by means of definition, cannot get along without the concept of "Judaization" and/or the "white Jew." Germany did not become the classic land of

antisemitism because of Hitler or even because a few Jews have been beaten to death—in the East no one even concerned himself about such minor matters. But rather because, long before putting any of this to practical use, Germany—with what might be called total disinterest—expounded modern abstract antisemitism most radically and consistently. Germany could serve as a model to the whole world because (1) it turned away most sharply from hatred of Jews as practiced before the era of emancipation, and (2) managed to discover in *the* Jew a principle with which to transform the world.

III *Antisemitism and Hatred of the Jews*

It goes without saying that modern antisemitism is heir to medieval antecedents and thus to the ancient hatred of the Jews as well. One must also admit that so close a tie with the Middle Ages is found almost nowhere else in modern intellectual history—nowhere are so many specific assertions, statements, and views so directly adopted. Eisenmenger's *Judaism Unmasked* (1701) in its numerous editions has been their transmitter, and there are scarcely any medieval accusations—from ritual murder to usury—that cannot be found verbatim in some modern piece of filthy literary trash. The more backward the nation—Poland, Russia, Romania—the more any tendencies to a general worldview are lost in a heavy overgrowth of realistically detailed superstition and primitive fear of spooks. Nor can modern antisemitism exist without appealing to fears whose origins lie in an inability to understand historical contexts—such as the ancient, deeply rooted dread of the Wandering Jew (and the more primitive—that is, the more unversed in history the level of society is—the deeper the roots), of Ahasuerus, of these "lateborn children of death" (Clemens von Brentano), of the incomprehensible phenomenon of an ancient people who have survived so many European catastrophes without land or soil, that is, apparently without any earthly ties, who do not live in an earthly fashion and who cannot die as other peoples do, who like a ghost have rescued themselves out of times long past, in order to feed themselves like vampires upon the blood of the living.[1]

Antisemitic agitators have known how to make good, steady use of this inherited fear of ghosts so frequently reactivated in modern times. But no more than that. Antisemitism became politically effective only after it moved past telling horror stories and on to a theory that could both be linked to many more modern, indeed always burning issues and cater to certain tendencies of political struggles that originally and for the most part had little to do with Jews. Propaganda that exploited superstitions dragged in from the Middle Ages—especially when directed at peasant populations—had twofold value: first, it gained adherents for the movement even in regions and among social classes where there were no Jews at all; and second, the universality of the evil principle that the "Jew is everywhere and nowhere" that had to be presented to an "enlightened" population found its correspondence in an omnipresent ghost for classes incapable of either a worldview or any other view from which to draw abstractions. In the jargon of antisemitism, this ancient phobia of Jews is called "the healthy instincts of the common people."[2]

For the Jews another consequence of this primitive campaign of lies proved more important than the direct effect of such agitation. Tracts appealing to "the healthy instincts of the common people" appeared to discredit antisemitism in the eyes of educated classes.[3] Because this agitation appeared in such crude, indeed, obviously absurd forms, it offered a very opportune pretext for getting rid of the whole issue by means of pure apologetics. That sort of literature was really nothing but "trash and filth" or "medieval barbarism"; equating it with antisemitism removed the sting from the political struggle.

There have been numerous attempts to blur the fundamental difference and downplay the historical dissimilarities between the full scope of the medieval hatred of Jews on the one hand (which from the Crusades down to Luther assumes a fairly unified form) and the scope of modern antisemitism on the other—in all its varying colors, from social hatred of "piggish capitalism" to hatred of the race, from the antisemitism of the aristocracy to that of the petite bourgeoisie, from its first timid beginnings at the start of the nineteenth century down to its fulfillment in the twentieth. What is thereby achieved is nothing less than once again to abstract the Jewish question out of the historical process and to destroy the common ground on which the fate of both Jews and non-Jews is decided. Both "medieval barbarism" and "everlasting antisemitism" leave us Jews without any hope. If medieval barbarism can erupt against us, then that would appear to be the most valid proof that we are not part of and have no home in modern history. And talk about "everlasting antisemitism" simply goes one step further and casts us out of human history entirely.

Neither hypothesis can be proved. In terms of barbarism, the modern world has far outdone the medieval world. And as for equation of hatred of Jews with antisemitism, the antisemites have, despite all inherited ideas, consistently and very explicitly distanced themselves from the Middle Ages. "I hereby unconditionally offer to protect the Jews from persecution for religious reasons," Marr remarks—the same man who bears the lion's share of responsibility for all modern German antisemitism. Antisemitism does not come from hatred of the Jews, but instead, as he explains, it is the other way round: hatred of Jews is an early form of antisemitism, an antisemitism trapped in religious forms. "And so God and religion had to foot the bill for all persecutions of the Jews, when in fact these were nothing more than the struggles of peoples and their instincts against a very real Judaization of society, a struggle for existence."[4] It is hard to decide which is more absurd: to speak of a "Judaization of (feudal) society" or to find so-called medieval barbarism lurking within its modern form. Ultimately they both amount to the same thing, which is, as Marr maintained, secularization of the ancient hatred of the Jews. But that leaves us with the same desperate question that the young Börne asked as early as 1819: "It was once thought that the Jews would not go to heaven, and so they were not to be tolerated here on earth either. But now that we have granted them heaven, why then should anyone want to drive them from the earth?"[5]

Christian hatred of Jews regards Jews as the people that gave birth to Christ and crucified him, that were once chosen, but cursed ever since. Opinions about the Jews and the hate directed against them are uniformly derived from the church, in whose plan of salvation and mission the conversion of the Jews plays an important, indeed central role. A baptized Jew is no longer a Jew, but a Christian. The entirety of anti-Jewish literature in the Middle Ages was either written by Jews or quotes them as authorities.

Christians and Jews were bound together by the Old Testament, separated from one another by the New Testament and the Talmud. As Christians see it, a member of the chosen people is visible in each member of the cursed people, and for the church each Jew's misfortune is necessary because he is a "living witness for Christian truth," whom the Christian "should not eradicate for fear that he may thereby lose knowledge of God's laws" (Innocent III, who introduced the "yellow patch" in 1215).[6] Death at the hands of the Inquisition or at the stake is thus a more or less successful conversion. The conversion of all Jews will ultimately coincide with the Kingdom of God on earth. The countless persecutions of Jews in our own time are therefore not at all comparable with those of the late Middle Ages, of the sixteenth and seventeenth centuries, which by then are true campaigns of extermination. This new kind of pogrom had already found its justification in Luther, who stands at the turning point between the medieval and the modern and whose hatred of Jews displays the first modern elements.

In his social life the Jew is universally subjected to exceptional laws that segregate him, but also allow him certain privileges in his dealings with Christians, certain marginal rights, first as a merchant, then as a pawnbroker, and finally as a moneylender. Jews are tolerated as part of general economic life only as long as their financial functions exist on the periphery. The more important, the more crucial these functions become for the rest of society, the more quickly the Jews are segregated from it. First they are driven out of commerce, then out of the pawnbroker business, and finally out of larger credit transactions. Driven out of one country, Jews are lured to another by certain privileges. The peripheral economic rights granted by such privileges are often as necessary for an economy as their religious existence is for Christianity and their presence as witnesses to Christian truth is for the church.

The *unadulteratable historical basis for the hatred of Jews* in the Middle Ages lies in the "stiff necked" opposition of the Jews to Christ and to all of Christian culture; and its equally unadulteratable *social* basis lies in the role Jews played in commerce and banking. The medieval association of the Jew with the usurer has only very little to do with modern associations, which are random by nature and say little about the actual role of Jews in an economy, but are instead ever-changing character traits, character masks forced upon them, whose arbitrariness is restrained by, and can only be understood on the basis of, specific needs.

Such modern arbitrariness begins with the definition of the Jew. Since the Jew no longer has an indisputable identity in Western European nations, one of the antisemite's most urgent needs is to define him. Whether the Jews are a religion or a nation, a people or a race, a state or a tribe, depends on the specific opinion non-Jews—in whose midst Jews live—have about themselves, but it certainly has no connection whatever with any germinal knowledge about the Jews. As the peoples of Europe became nations, the Jews became "a nation within the nation"; as the Germans began to see in the state something more than their political representation, that is, as their fundamental "essence," the Jews became a state within a state. As the word "international" began to bounce around inside people's heads, Jews came to represent the "international of gold," and a bit later, by an ingenious combination of state and international, to advance—in the form of the "elders of Zion"—to an international state. And since the end of the last century, when the Germans transformed themselves at last into Aryans, we have been wandering through world history as Semites; just as it is to the arrogance of the Anglo-Saxon "white man" over against colonial peoples that we owe the epithet "white nigger."

In comparison to such nonsensical foolishness, even medieval definitions—despite their most superstitious lies and bloodiest fairy tales—were closer to the reality of Jews of the period. Ritual murder was a lie, but the religious hatred that lay behind it was genuine. It was a lie that all Jews are usurers—they vanished amid the masses of impoverished craftsmen and peddlers. But to the extent that the Jews came into social contact with the population or parts of the population around them, they made their appearance as moneylenders. Until the sixteenth century Christians were forbidden to lend money at interest.[7] Being a Jew meant being relegated to a certain social status just as was everyone else, although that of the Jew was the lowest and most ostracized; but it had one privilege, even if it was no more than the right to lend money. Even the term for a Christian usurer, "baptized Jew,"[8] did not have the connotation of the modern term "white Jew," but meant that his Christian baptism was merely external, that he was pursuing a "Jewish" trade. A Jew, on the other hand, who had himself baptized was not a "baptized Jew," but a Christian.

The Jew held status in this society only as a usurer, just as in its culture he was only an enemy of Christ. In the feudal Christian world, status indicated profession. For the Jew, to the extent that he took any part in that world, both his status and profession were predetermined by his religion. Only in that way could religious hatred become amalgamated with social hatred; both

together resulted in the fanaticism of medieval pogroms. In contrast to practically all Jewish historians, Bruno Bauer, as a young Hegelian, explicitly
notes and emphasizes that it was precisely their active hostility to the Christian culture that made the Jews part of the history of Europe. "The Jews
were oppressed because . . . they had tried to stop the wheel of history. Had
the Jews not been part of the workings of the law of causality, their role
would have been purely passive . . . which would have meant there was no
bond tying them to history. . . . Theirs would have been an utterly lost
cause." There is a clear point to the polemic directed against Jews and their
friends who, ever since Dohm, have never ceased to bewail Jews because of
the awful way they are treated. It is the modern shaping of the Jewish question, it is compassion—and the disdain of the antisemites that followed hot
on its heels—that first attempted to cast the Jews out of history.

Every modern form of antisemitism, quite apart from its historical development or differentiating hallmarks, lacks the basis that underlay the hatred
of Jews: the concrete knowledge of Jews that served as the foundation for all
distortions. The history of the hatred of Jews was *about* Jews, and not much
more than that. The history of antisemitism always conceals many other tendencies in which Jews do not play the crucial role. One could discuss its history as a history of associations—quite random associations that contain
only a minimum of reality when it comes to Jews, but very necessary associations when viewed from amid the struggles of the period.

IV *Usurers, Pariahs, Parasites*

The disappearance of Jew-hatred and the rise of modern antisemitism in the
nineteenth and twentieth centuries were preceded by a crucial change in the
relationship between Jews and their host peoples in Central and Western
Europe. This change began in the seventeenth century and continued
throughout the eighteenth, until in the middle of the nineteenth it was given
legal and political form as assimilation.

Prior to this period the Jews came into contact with other peoples only
during catastrophes and expulsions. Economic life in the ghetto was limited
to minor craftwork and peddling. These communities were headed by a few,
very wealthy individuals, who acted as intermediaries in contacts with the

outside world and essentially earned their money by lending money to that world. The usurer had, as it were, a monopoly on the ghetto's foreign commerce. For both Jews and non-Jews alike he was the representative of his people—for the latter because he was the only Jew with whom they came in contact, for the former because, given the extraordinary density of ghetto populations, an entire community often depended on his charity. But communities relied not only economically but also politically on such benefactors, who as financial agents for princely courts maintained the relationships necessary for the community's protection. Thus very early on there arose that fateful personal union—which has not been done away with even today—that embraces prominence, philanthropy, and political representation.

Over the next centuries the Jewish usurer rose first from court Jew to creditor of absolutist states, and finally as a nineteenth- and twentieth-century banker he achieved, if not the peak of his power, then of his social and communal prestige. Despite such changes in position and function, his role within Jewry remained the same, that is, if he did not renounce it altogether and abandon the Jewish community. The total picture has, however, shifted somewhat. Just as entire communities once lived off the philanthropy of a few moneylenders and toward the end of the nineteenth century entire districts of the Russian settlement area lived off the millions of Baron Hirsch, today large segments of Polish Jewry live off dollars that American Jews collect to send back home. Within the Jewish community itself, no class division has taken place so far. The rich Jew, standing in the midst of the capitalist economic system, has not as yet appeared to the poor as their "exploiter," nor have the poor been regarded by the wealthy as mere "labor power." To the extent that the two ever do meet—which occurs only during catastrophes—to the poor the rich man is still his benefactor, and to the rich the poor man is a freeloader.

When—in the eighteenth century—these few wealthy court Jews first escaped the strictures of laws applying to Jews, and when the larger class of prosperous Jews made known their own claims to emancipation, the masses of the people began to receive civil rights from the hands of the same benefactors who, as supplicants and petitioners, had previously provided the ghetto its meager protection. But for Jews there was a difference, emancipation was linked to a tacit and over time self-evident condition: they must become like those who had first been granted civil rights directly and by way of exception. If one wanted to be emancipated and still remain a Jew, there was and is within the world of Jewish life only the old alternative: philanthropist or freeloader. All those who exempted themselves from this alternative were lost from the Jewish world.

The Jews of the court and finance, the usurers and tax collectors, were the first Jews to escape the walls of the ghetto;[1] the first court Jews to enjoy full civil rights were those attached to Frederick the Great in Prussia. Their names were Itzig and Ephraim, to whom Frederick chartered the mint and who were rewarded for highly dubious maneuvers that brought in six million thalers annually during the last few years of the Seven Years' War.[2] In them we see before us the first emancipated Jews. The honor granted them should be ranked all the higher inasmuch as under the same king and only with great effort and difficulty, the most famous Jew of the day, Moses Mendelssohn, managed to attain extraordinary status as a protected Jew, though this did not even apply to his children. All enlightened intercession demanding Jewish emancipation and citing Mendelssohn's example was thus of no benefit to him, let alone to the Jewish people, though Itzig and Ephraim were silently rewarded this very prize for their accomplishments, making them models and pioneers for their people as this fact came to be widely known. Thus if we really want to understand emancipation—both the conditions under which it was granted and the path that Jews had to follow to achieve it—we need to have a passing acquaintance with what it was that the first emancipated Jews achieved on the way to becoming our "liberators"—much to our misfortune.

During the twelfth and thirteenth centuries, as commerce was passing from the hands of Jews into those of a new and growing urban bourgeoisie, *usury*, the lending of money, began to gain significance for Jews. For two hundred years usury remained tied to *pawnbroking* and was thus still a form of commerce. In our eyes the usurer appears to be a cross between the traditional accumulator of wealth and a modern department store owner, who, being bound to no particular trade, turns every object into a commodity. It was not until the fifteenth century, when the church established its own pawnbrokeries (*montes pietatis*), that Jews were forced to become pure moneylenders, who fully deserved to be called usurers because of the enormously high interest they charged to make up for the incalculable risks a usurer takes when neither collateral nor law secures his investment. At the time usury played no more important role in terms of the major commerce of the period than it does today.[3] Theirs was small-scale credit advanced to spendthrift nobles or to farmers whose crops had failed, or to craftsmen driven into poverty and want by some unforeseen misfortune. Money lent to the indigent and the extravagant served only consumption, and the interest was purely a premium charged for risk; it did not increase production, but could at most reduce it, whether by excessive increase in the spendthrift's consumption or by the indebted craftsman's or farmer's forfeiture of tools or seed corn. Thus usury was one of the signs of the disintegration of feudal society, not of the beginning of a capitalist economy.[4]

The usurer was extraordinarily limited in his range of actions. The risk appeared acceptable only for the smallest sums of money. He could satisfy solely individual needs—whether as a result of someone's extravagance or misfortune. He in no way entered into the productive economy of his country.[5] He could gain a more general significance only in a very indirect sense: ruling princes began very early on to use Jewish usurers as agents for extorting additional money from their subjects—illegal taxes as it were—only to turn on them, expelling them and confiscating their wealth. In fact when in need of extra profits, they would even bring Jews into their realms for that very purpose.[6]

Usury linked to such highly individualized circumstances offered Jews neither civil nor political advantages. If usury had been the only basis of contacts with their surroundings on into the mid-eighteenth century, they would never have been emancipated. Their civil status would never have advanced by means of individual protection extended by some prince or other—a protection that carried no legal or political guarantees and that from one day to the next might be abrogated and end in expulsion.

Proceeding from more or less antisemitic biases, all modern definitions of Jews as a people—with the one exception of definition by race—have their historical basis in medieval and late medieval conditions. The Jews as *parasites*, as a nation of *pariahs*, as a *caste*—all that, with the exception of a few, but very crucial remnants, was eliminated economically in the course of the eighteenth and nineteenth centuries, while at the same time, by means of a kind of political (antisemitic) countermovement, Jews were actually redefined as a caste of pariahs and parasites.

The *parasites* were Jewish usurers—parasites of the disintegration and destruction of the feudal social order. Their corresponding needs were born out of a dying world that assigned them the fateful role of supplying usurious capital, which served consumption, but had only a destructive influence on production. The Jews were *pariahs* as long as they remained politically powerless. This corresponded to the "sponge policy" of the princes, the intent of which was to prevent the wealth that Jews were amassing from becoming "primary accumulation of capital" and thus a first step toward capitalism itself. Jewish capital was constantly being decimated and dispersed by pogroms, expulsion, and confiscation.[7] Living in uncertainty and depending on "illegal and irrational sources of income as war-profiteers, hired tax collectors, and officials paid on a percent of the moneys raised, etc." (Max Weber), the Jews were the pariahs of developing European capitalism.[8]

The Jews were a *caste* ever since they lived segregated from and unincorporated in the history and economic life of the world around them, existing on their own or at best parasitically on others—in short, insofar as their existence was not conditioned and defined by other layers, castes, or classes of society. Since their sole allies were those segments of feudal society in decline, above all the nobility, which as it declined closed ranks ever more tightly to form its own caste, the Jews almost inevitably became a complementary phenomenon to the symptoms of a nobility in decline—to the luxury and extravagance that they were financing. Traces of this Jewish past have lingered down into recent times everywhere. It is from them that modern antisemitism pieces together the bits of reality that it requires but which grow scanter every day.

German Jews were pariahs until 1869. For more than fifty years—between the failure to enact the Emancipation Edict of 1812 and the repeal of restrictions on Jews in Prussia in 1869—Jews lived without legal or civil status. Since their civil rights were intentionally never written into law, both their economic position and cultural assimilation had to appear illegal. Living outside the law and yet fully integrated into the economic life of the world around them, the Jews' special position within the German nation was so difficult and controversial that they retained characteristics of a caste even though they had long since ceased to be one. Once emancipation had been proclaimed, such characteristics lived on wherever Jews were socially ostracized.

The life of Jews remained parasitic only in those rare instances where popular revolution did not touch them and they still continued to gnaw at the vestiges of feudalism. In Germany this was true of Hessia, where usurious loans to farmers were primarily in Jewish hands, a fact that ever since has provided a rich resource for antisemitic propaganda, a deep well of examples that never runs dry.[9] Other remnants include Jewish pawnbrokers in the poorer neighborhoods of some cities.

An antisemitism dependent on random associations has known how to use precisely such instances for defaming Jews, and it has equated them with one of the social, political, and economic forms they assumed in the past. But this antisemitism has its basis neither in the broader context of reality provided by the past nor in a more narrow context—still just broad enough to provide examples—passed down into the present. The foundations of antisemitism are found in developments that have very little to do with Jews. Yet it is typical of the whole spectrum of antisemitism that it has constantly tried to reach back to old, traditional forms of Jewish life and conceal present forms. Characteristic of this persistently repeated methodology is the way it accuses Jews, for example, of being parasites at precisely the point when they have ceased to be parasites, or the way it begins weaving fables of a monstrous, diabolic, and secret power at the very point when they are losing power—which never was diabolic or very secret. Thus the actual disenfranchisement of Jews in Germany did not occur at the high point of their influence, but rather when collectively they had already lost every trace of political power.

The tragedy of the history of the Jewish people has assumed different forms and been played out in many acts, one of which has just come to an end. In some countries the entry of Jews into modern bourgeois history and their participation in the economic development of the countries where they live have been reversed. The lies of antisemitism have finally lied the truth: they have lied the Jews—who in reality are cruelly powerless—back into a dislocated reality long since past. German Jews once again have neither rights nor a country, are citizens of no nation—*pariahs*. Cast up on the shores of strange lands, chased into the cracks and crevices of strange economies that have not exactly awaited their arrival, they are once again *parasites*. Wrenched from the context of class relationships in their own country—neither bourgeoisie nor proletariat, neither petite bourgeoisie nor farmers—they exist only in relationship to themselves, a society outside of society, a *caste*.

V *Court Jews and Human Rights*

The history of the emancipation of the Jews began in the seventeenth and eighteenth centuries in all the countries of Europe in which absolutist states and their landed nobility stood in conflict with the guilds of the cities. In the course of the eighteenth century a few Jews in fact managed to become very wealthy and—even more significantly—to remain so. In their wake a whole segment of the ghetto population achieved respectable prosperity. The decisive factor, however, was that their prosperity and wealth arose from a very different source than previously—not out of poverty and extravagance, but out of the needs of the state.

We can no longer discuss eighteenth-century history without the Jews— whether as *suppliers to the army* and *creditors of the state* in German-speaking areas, or as *hired tax collectors* in Poland and pre-Revolutionary France. In addition, princes sucked their populations dry by regularly contracting Jewish usurers to doggedly extract the taxes normally levied by the state in cash. The usurer, who joined forces with the tax collector by advancing the obligatory sums, often hired himself out later as a tax collector as well. The transformation of usurer into tax collector was above all the determinative factor for the economic advancement of French and Polish Jews.

A *hired tax collector* already has a very close relationship to the government of a country for whose taxes he is the guarantor. His use to the state as an additional resource for sucking the populace dry is no longer "accidental," but has its basis in a contract with the force of law. The state itself integrates the Jewish tax collector into at least one segment of the nation's economy and assigns him a place within its system of political control. In all its aspects his position is therefore far superior to that of the usurer. Although his profit is only that of a middleman and not integrated into the normal economic life of the country, it is nevertheless regularized and independent of the fate of individuals, of their poverty or extravagance. The state itself has taken over the usury business and monopolized it in the form of taxes, and thus for the hired tax collector usury becomes an irrelevant supplementary source of income.

Even under this changed set of circumstances Jews were sometimes expelled. But whereas only a hundred years before expulsions were staged in order to rob Jews of their acquired wealth, they now took on the purely political character of shifting people's rage at being sucked dry to the middleman in the process. Confiscations of wealth by means of expulsion became ever rarer. The wealth of hired Jewish tax collectors was partially protected—but not their lives or their right to settle permanently.

It was not until the eighteenth century, when the Jew became an *agent of the court,* that he was granted protection of his person—a first step leading directly to emancipation. He differs on principle from his medieval predecessor, the *court Jew,* who since the eleventh and twelfth centuries—having first been driven as a large-scale lender from Italy, and then later from England and France as well—had served as a financial adviser who managed princely wealth.[1] But the relationship of such court Jews to princes and nobles remained private and had no larger economic or political consequences. Their significance lies in the fact that they were forerunners to agents of the court, whose connections to the state of an absolute monarch were founded on such princely relationships.

The reason it is so difficult to pinpoint exactly when the financial adviser and manager of the private property of princes became the creditor to the state itself is that until the last third of the eighteenth century the finances of the monarchy were identical with those of the monarch. Only toward the end of the century did the methods for financing a modern state replace those used for financing the court of an absolute monarch, which in turn were linked to the loans and pawnbroking deals offered to a moribund feudal aristocracy. As late as the first third of the eighteenth century, "Austria's creditors were in fact the emperor's creditors." Which meant that the debt of the entire nation was in the hands of his court Jew.[2]

Agents of the court owed their unprecedented advancement, by which they became pioneers of emancipation, to two factors. The first was the Thirty Years' War, which had been less hard on the Jewish population and had turned cash into a highly coveted rarity throughout the impoverished land. The second was that states simultaneously began to find themselves in dire need of funds and yet had no way to secure a regular flow of tax moneys. A further factor smoothing the way for Jews to enter into a state's financial affairs was the general uncertainty and disorder then common in a state's general economy. Only Jews were prepared to accept almost any business deal—a fact that need not be explained by some strong compelling instinct for commerce. It arises quite naturally out of what was—already by that time—the unusual and rather atavistic economic mind-set of Jews, for whom interest had long been nothing more than a reward for risk, while the people around them were already calculating profit in rationalistic capitalist terms. It was only natural that Jews were inclined to take on any risk if the reward was commensurate.

Over the course of the century the disparity between state finances and normal capitalist production became increasingly more pronounced. Budgets for armies in the eighteenth century were huge (and were unproductive expenses),[3] but so too were both the profits to be made from them and the possible losses that had to be risked. Only when all other possibilities had been exhausted were Jews brought in as creditors.[4] As this proved to be increasingly necessary, princes learned the advantages of borrowing from Jews, who were the first bankers with international connections. Jew Y could pay and deliver to armies fighting far from home what Jew X had promised back in their homeland.

The *delivery of war supplies* was therefore of importance for Jews in general, since by its very nature it had to involve relatively large segments of the population. Only a few Jews dealt directly with the state, but a great many people scattered across provinces and countries provided the materials— cloth, animal feed, grain—to those explicitly appointed as agents of the court. In consequence, divisions began to emerge between, first, those who continued to live their old life cut off from the world, that is, the poor; second, those who participated in the "export monopoly" of notable Jews and thereby achieved a moderate prosperity; and third, the court agents themselves, the wealthy men who became the prominent members of Jewish communities. It was not until this point that the growth in the authority of such notables began to define their role within the ghetto itself, even though economically they no longer enjoyed the independence usurers had had in previous centuries; but the close business ties of the middle class that they had lifted up with them produced a more solid foundation of common interests than any philanthropy extended to the very poor, which also continued, though on a smaller scale. The Jewish community native to Germany and Austria grew out of this aforementioned moderately prosperous group— suppliers of war goods and small-scale money changers—and so quite naturally it could never extricate itself from the political influence of "court Jews," of the notables to whom it owed its own rise.

A few decades later the prosperity of a still relatively small middle class provided the social basis for emancipation, but had almost no political consequences during the eighteenth century itself. Although only a very few of those who had grown rich in the business of war found themselves in a position to act as creditors to the state, the immense debts of eighteenth-century absolutist states proved extraordinarily helpful in paving the way for Jews to engage in high finance.[5] Between 1695 and 1739 the emperor of Austria borrowed 35 million guldens from thirteen Jews residing in his country.[6] Even in Bavaria, where Jews played a relatively minor role, they lent the state a fifth of its debt. Such large debts arose out of the absolutist state's needs to finance an army and to install a new professional bureaucracy to counter both the aristocracy and bourgeoisie. Only those princes who accomplished this could maintain themselves against both the aristocracy and this new class and, in doing so, destroy the feudal order. Jewish moneylenders played a leading role in the further development of this state apparatus.[7] When we look back now, we can speak of Jews holding a powerful position only in this transitional period—power that they never had before and would never have again. For to the same degree that the bourgeoisie learned to make good use of the newly instituted apparatuses of the state and its bureaucracy, the power that Jews had over the affairs of state declined proportionately until it was as good as entirely eliminated. Ultimately it was simply a sign of the backwardness of the German bourgeoisie and of the obsolescence of its political system that Jews could still play a certain role—albeit a very limited and second-class one—under Wilhelm II.

It is difficult to say who was the first agent of court in this new style. We know many names from the late seventeenth century on into the final third of the eighteenth—in Bavaria, Austria, Württemberg, and Prussia. The most powerful were the Rothschilds, who transformed themselves from direct creditors and moneylenders to the state into the investment bankers behind the loans made to almost all European states and who, thanks to Metternich's reactionary regime, with which they were closely allied, held a unique position of power until well into the nineteenth century. And among the last of them was Bleichröder, whose power in Prussia arose out of Bismarck's clashes with parliament and the bourgeoisie.

Prior to the Rothschilds, no court Jew had stood out as a man of unusual wealth. Each depended upon his own credit among other Jews, although within a much smaller circle than did the suppliers of war goods. Only the sum of all Jewish wealth made his dealings possible. At the height of their wealth members of the Rothschild family were the first to be independent of such intra-Jewish credit. Up until that point what had differentiated court Jews in principle from usurers, each of whom went about his business separately, was their interconnection, their dependence upon one another.

If we take the Rothschilds during the period of the Napoleonic wars, when almost half of Britain's loans to the Allies—some 20 million pounds[8]—passed through their hands, as the high point of this development, and then take the world of petty usurers lending money to aristocrats and village farmers as its beginning, it is the court Jews of the eighteenth century who occupy the middle point. They were still lending money to princes—no longer for personal expenses, but rather to the state through them. Their relationship to the state, however, was not yet so close, their influence not yet so large, their own fortunes not so immense that they could underwrite and finance such loans in their own names.[9]

In regard to the protection of his own person, the distance between our court Jew and the Rothschilds or other wealthy Jews of the nineteenth century is minimal, but the progress he achieved in comparison to the lack of any personal rights in the seventeenth century is very great. The court Jew in an absolutist state cannot be robbed of his assets or expelled. His credit is as good as the money that he in fact provides. And since his credit depends on his person, the finances of the state are endangered if he has no personal rights. His protection can no longer be at the discretion of cities or minor principalities. The Jewish question becomes a question of state. The court Jew is the Jew who protects the state itself. The state guarantees the personal safety of "its" Jews, that is, the credit of its Jews, just as the court Jew is the guarantor of the state's finances and obligations.

The fact that court Jews cease to have no rights does not mean, however, that they are accepted into the society, let alone the bourgeois society, of their day. Because their moneys are not invested in budding capitalist production, they remain at the threshold of bourgeois society, but have hardly any contact with it. In those days the war economy that they helped to finance was anything but an affair of society or of the people as a whole. Something that served the nation or helped it to win a war was certainly not considered to be in the interest of the people. Frederick II might be able to pursue his Seven Years' War with the help of the tricks of Ephraim, the Jew he had put in charge of the mint, but the people did not hate Ephraim any less for it. Mercenary troops hired by one's own state were as feared as enemy armies. The most desirable goal during a war—according to Frederick II, who surely ought to have known—was for "the peace-loving citizen not even to notice the nation had struck a blow." And Clausewitz calls the typical army of the eighteenth century "a state within a state" and its wars "merely an affair of government alienated from the interest of the people."[10]

The Jews were part of the "state within a state" and its war and army economy. Thus from the outset they are separated from all other classes, and find themselves to be the exception. To be sure, since they deal with all those agencies that are involved with the state's income, they are now in closer contact with the economies of their nations than previously. But that does not result in social contact with levels of society of roughly comparable wealth. Moreover, the state's income consists in fact of nothing more than direct or indirect—and often excessively high—taxes, receipts secured by Jews in their function as tax collectors and owed them as creditors of the state. As such, these receipts and revenues are from the start viewed with hostility by the entire population. Standing at the threshold of bourgeois society, the Jews help the state build an administration appropriate to a bourgeois era—a fact about which the bourgeoisie still has no idea. What remains from this era is simply popular hatred of the middlemen in the state's exploitative system. For Jews this means they have no possibility of influencing or even becoming involved in what the era produces. The failure of the eighteenth century to establish such a connection was only minimally corrected in the nineteenth, when Jews were finally granted a position within pure bank capitalism. But capitalist production was undergoing immense growth and the state was becoming increasingly less dependent on private moneylenders, so that, having gained such a position, Jews now lost influence. But they still retained the hatred of the people, who believed that the clearest explanation for capitalist robbery could be found in banking capital.

Once the usurer had been transformed into a banker for the state, once usury and pawnbroking had turned into the credit business and the position of hired tax collector had immunized some Jews from persecution, governments—particularly those in Prussia and Austria—began to work out the details of new regulations for Jews. Of course this was not emancipation, but it was the preliminary step that led directly to it. Protection was granted by the highest political agency, the monarchs themselves—the king of Prussia, the emperor of Austria. This meant that the regulation of Jews, as well as later emancipation, was a matter of high-level policy quite independent of local authorities. Wherever local administrations still made such decisions, for example in so-called free cities, everything remained—even beyond the eighteenth century—just as it had been before. The history of political emancipation clearly shows that only the modern state—and by no means modern society— has evidenced any interest in protecting and emancipating Jews. Thus at the Congress of Vienna the cities of Frankfurt, Hamburg, Bremen, and Lübeck demanded that Napoleonic emancipation be rescinded, with the result that emancipation in Germany was delayed for another fifty years. To counter this, Metternich supported a resolution which amounted to a guarantee of all civil rights that Jews had gained up to that point—not because he was in personal debt to the banking house of Arnheim in Vienna, and not because of a sudden surge of libertarian tendencies, but because he was a "reactionary" and represented the interest of an absolutist state and its financial policies.[11]

Thus we see that well into the nineteenth century Jews were most stubbornly denied human rights wherever the bourgeoisie held power. Some of the most important of these rights were slowly granted them, little by little, by states and monarchies that half patronized, half suppressed the bourgeoisie in their claims to power. Such was the situation in Prussia and Austria, where for a long time it remained undecided which social classes would lose, retain, or achieve power. The behavior of "free cities," which were governed by the bourgeoisie, is so characteristic precisely because, after the brief period of Napoleonic rule, the majority of Jews must surely be counted as part of the bourgeoisie.[12]

The position of the German bourgeoisie will be discussed elsewhere. But several points need to be anticipated here in order to qualify the almost universally accepted thesis that Jewish emancipation was directly dependent on the rise of the bourgeoisie. As true as it is to say that Western Jews owed their prosperity to capitalist development in Europe, it must also be said that the class underpinning this development, the bourgeoisie, delayed the day of proclamation of human rights for Jews wherever it could—with the sole exceptions of the first Revolutionary vanguard in France[13] and a few of those involved in Germany's revolution of 1848. In Britain, the most bourgeois country in Europe, the Jews were not emancipated until 1868; in Switzerland, which has as good as always been ruled exclusively by the bourgeoisie, emancipation waged an especially hard struggle.

Absolutist states were thus most likely to be inclined to legalize the economic functions of Jews, which is to say, to pay the corresponding political price for their achievements. The regulation of Jews in Prussia under Frederick II showed a tendency to grant Jews certain protections and a field of action for their specifically "Jewish" economic activities, while keeping them in their place as Jews. There were no pretenses whatever of assimilation—in contrast to the Austrian Edict of Toleration issued under Joseph II.[14] An urban Jewry was promoted, but agriculture and ownership of land continued to be forbidden and the path to most crafts blocked. Only those professions of direct use to the state were promoted—that is, suppliers of war goods, bankers, and exporters of the wares of state-run factories. Jewish communities were expressly declared responsible for the debts of individual bankrupt Jews, a provision that guaranteed that the poor were efficiently excluded and other undesirable elements kept at a distance. In this way the interests of the state became the interests of the Jewish community itself—Jews were turned into a pillar of the state. Since right of residence was based on wealth, especially in Berlin and Vienna, and since within a family marriage was taxed, with the occasional exception of the eldest son, at a decreasing rate for each additional marriage, Berlin's three thousand Jews were soon among the most well-to-do residents of the Prussian capital. The state had never shown such consideration and scrupulousness for the welfare of its Christian subjects.

But for the masses of poor and backward Jews that the Prussian state had inherited with the division of Poland and the occupation of Silesia, the old lack of any rights remained in place. The broader class of prosperous Jews were granted statutory protection, whereas a certain few who could show that they had performed some service necessary for the state's existence were granted *exceptional* civil rights, in the form of "general privileges." In between these two there was only a statute for the "extraordinarily" protected Jew, that is, someone who personally enjoyed a protected status—right of residence, right to earn a living—but could not pass these rights, this "dignity," on to his children.

Protected and encouraged by the state, the class of prosperous, urban Jews grew larger and larger. Ascendant court Jews pulled ever growing circles of people up with them. In the last third of the eighteenth century, there were already three thousand Jews in Berlin alone—all of them, of course, well-to-do, since their right of residence was linked to their wealth. At the same time more and more Jews became economically dependent on the fortunes of their guest country. Those who had achieved such status were still only a very small percentage of the Jewish people and had lost sight of those masses of people whose lives remained untouched by their rise. Prussian policy toward the Jews split them geographically—the poor remained in Posen, the rich lived in Berlin and provincial capitals. Within the borders of Western European countries—since all this holds true, *mutatis mutandis*, for Austria and France as well—the dichotomy of rich and poor, of craftsmen and lenders of money to the outside world, which had defined life in the ghetto, becomes the dichotomy of *Western and Eastern Jews.*

And with that, the social transformation of modern Judaism so crucial for the entire century was inaugurated. To the extent that Prussian, Austrian, and within certain limits French policy in regard to the Jews does away with the ghetto, it turns the social disparity familiar to the ghetto, that of rich and poor, into a geographical dichotomy. By favoring one large class of Jews and leading them to the threshold of modern economic life, such a policy transforms a people's social differences into a historical dichotomy, which is to say one between Jews who continue to live as they have for one or two centuries and others who, for the good of the state, have ceased to lead the isolated life of a caste. But even these privileged Jews are a long way from showing even the rudiments of a budding bourgeoisie—they do not use poor Jews as a workforce, if for no other reason than that they are geographically separated from them. They do not enter into private capitalist production because it is not directly encouraged by the state and because they have no labor at their disposal. The poverty of the Jewish people is completely pointless, since it serves no productive purpose. For those businesses in which Jews remain active they need neither Jewish nor non-Jewish labor. Only where the geographical separation of rich and poor did not occur—as for instance in Poland—could the rudiments of Jewish enterprise develop, although it attained no great significance since it was constantly hampered by the backwardness of the country.

The laws guaranteeing *protection of residence, person, and property*—that is, human rights as understood by the eighteenth century—were *paid for* by prosperous Jews in the form of special taxes and achievements. Total civil rights—the general privileges which made the Jewish businessman the equal of the Christian—were awarded to Itzig and Ephraim for outstanding achievements. Human rights were ranked according to one's ability to pay. General privileges, tantamount to emancipation, were not a "gift," but rather an exact compensation in the form of a *reward*. They did not become a *gift* until such compensatory protection was granted to the modest stream of impoverished Jews—who, despite all measures taken by the state to prevent it, were effectively supported by the Jewish community. To be sure, this was not the gift of a government—as antisemitic historians have always tried to present it—but rather one given *to poor Jews by rich Jews,* who ultimately answered for the former's debts in the form of collective liability. Compensation first became a gracious gift within the Jewish world itself—a present given with conditions, however. The rich had already fulfilled those conditions. The Jewish notables—one of those who headed the Jewish community in Berlin was the "generally privileged" Itzig—have until this day never ceased to demand the respect due them for their gift of protection and, later, of "freedom." After all, they were assuring both the state and the world around them of the usefulness of their entire tribe. Their attitude toward "Eastern Jews" and "freeloaders" demonstrates that they have never forgotten who actually paid for their emancipation and for whom it was originally intended.

On the threshold of emancipation, it was the court Jew and the "mint Jew" who were granted civil rights as a reward. The freedom of a few demonstrates clearly and without any pretty turns of phrase—first to many and later to all too many—the price exacted for human rights.

VI *Exceptional Jews*

Two models defined and guided the Prussian Jews' "struggle for liberation": political and legal liberation granted by the state to generally privileged "mint Jews" and the recognition by cultivated society of the achievements of Moses Mendelssohn. Education and commerce continued to be the focus of life for all of assimilated German Jewry until catastrophe struck.

Like the generally privileged Itzig and Ephraim, Mendelssohn was an exception, was "exceptional," and all three were recognized as such by the world around them—although very different worlds were involved. One could hope to advance only if one rose above the Jewish masses by proving oneself to be very different from them, whether in terms of intellectual qualities or economic achievements for the state. The division of Jews into "East and West," rich and poor, educated and uneducated, offered German Jews an opportunity: it prevented ruthless ambition—following a pattern set by history and rewarded anew each day—from ending in a war of each against all and gave rise to a new sense of solidarity, however paltry that might look in individual cases. Only legal separation by the state could put in the place of the old ghetto community more than a group of desperate parvenus; it created two new geographically and economically divergent entities. The relatively small number of Frederick's protected Jews rose *collectively* above the masses of poor Jews from Posen and West Prussia. The following century's policy of Jewish assimilation was based far less on the well-known "atomization" of the Jews than on this concept of *collective exception*.

By geographically separating rich and poor Jews, Frederick's regulations for Jews provided a firm foundation for supporting an exceptional Jewry. In 1803 Prussia's protected Jews constituted only about 20 percent of the country's total Jewish population. Unfortunately no statistics for this period record economic differentiation. But the census of 1834 reveals just how drastic the situation was. The wealthy bourgeoisie of Prussia (wholesalers, bankers, and persons of independent means) was six times larger than that of Posen; the middle class (self-employed professionals and retailers) comprised more than half the Jewish population of Prussia, but in Posen barely a third; almost 60 percent of the Posener Jews (peddlers, craftsmen, day laborers) had no property worth mentioning, whereas in Prussia only 37 percent were without property; more than a fifth of the population of Posen lived in abject poverty and were a burden on an already poor community; in the much more prosperous Prussian communities such charity cases made up only 6.5 percent.[1]

Eastern Jews as a social backdrop proved advantageous in promoting the self-awareness of both Prussia's protected Jews and its "educated society," but they were equally disadvantageous for regularizing Jewish statutes in terms of improved civil rights. For the Prussian state *emancipation* meant—and could only mean—a *generalization of general privileges,* which were expressly not intended to apply to Jewish peddlers and day laborers. It was only after a disastrous war that cost Prussia those provinces most heavily populated with Jews that the situation changed for protected Jews, who in one fell swoop now comprised 90 percent of the entire Jewish population.[2] By 1808 they had been granted rights of the city. The Emancipation Edict of 1812 was intended for them. Since they were all held to be exceptional Jews, there was a readiness to emancipate them as a whole, as Jewry.

The restitution of old borders that followed the War of Liberation necessarily worked against efforts aimed at emancipation. Retraction of a series of rights once again robbed what was now a mere 53 percent of protected Jews of their equality, and what rights were left to them were changed back into privileges. Once again they are seen as privileged over against the Jews of Posen, who formed almost half of all the Jews and until the last third of the nineteenth century must be regarded as Prussia's real "Eastern" Jews. Until 1848 the Poseners were unable to gain even basic civil rights within the Prussian state. Their incorporation into the body of what was once Prussia's protected Jewry, that is, into the community of "exceptional" Jews, likewise occurred "by way of exception." Whether they had the same civil "maturity"—that is, the same economic position—as their favored brethren had enjoyed for a century was decided on an individual-case basis. They were absorbed into privileged Jewry only very slowly; in 1848 they comprised more than a third, that is, 37 percent, of the Jewish population.[3]

It is a paradox of the history of German Jewry that social *assimilation* in the sense of full recognition by non-Jewish society was granted them only so long as emancipation was blocked by the very backdrop which put them in such a favorable light. It is quite understandable how even down to the present day all assimilated Jews find it very difficult to leave behind this awareness of themselves as the "exception," for that is what has always been behind all their talk about "Eastern" and "Western" Jews. For never again, despite whatever guarantees of equality the state might grant them, would things go as well for them socially as they did under Prussia's flag. The closer emancipation drew near—which had been under serious discussion since the eighteenth century and for which the way had been paved by the granting of rights of the city in 1808—the more hostile the surrounding world became. Those brief twenty-five years before the turn of the century, until the outbreak of war in 1806–7, represented for a very small group of wealthy and educated Jews the realization of a dream that in face of all contrary realities would continue to be dreamed for a good hundred years. In that window of time the old hatred of Jews had been laid aside and the new antisemitism was hardly born yet. Until it perished, assimilated Jewry held fast to a phrase that was in fact true for only a few decades: enmity toward Jews was unworthy of an educated man.[4] To be sure, Jewish influence at the end of the nineteenth century and during the Weimar Republic was more visible and—with the help of the press and cultural institutions—more powerful as well. But never again would it be so open, so undisguised, so certain of its cause. The belief that their own cause was the cause of humanity is what lent women in Jewish salons their candor, lent the Jews of the time their singular freedom and clear conscience in dealing with the Jewish question and Jew-hatred.

In their pursuit of education and wealth, Berlin's exceptional Jews had good luck for three decades. The *Jewish salon,* the idyllic mixed society that was the object of so many dreams, realized under often highly disagreeable concessions, was the product of a chance constellation of factors in a period of social change. Jews were a stopgap solution between one declining form of social interaction and another that had not yet established itself. There in Jewish homes, the *aristocracy* and *actors*—both, like the Jews, standing outside of bourgeois society, both accustomed to playing a role, to representing, expressing, and portraying "what one is" and not, like the bourgeoisie, "what one has" (to borrow a phrase from *Wilhelm Meister*)—provided a foothold for homeless bourgeois *intellectuals* and a resonance they could not hope to find elsewhere. Given the looser structures of convention of the time, Jews became socially acceptable in the same way that actors were, and the aristocracy attested to their, very provisional, "presentability at court."[5]

At that period the economically backward and politically servile Prussian bourgeoisie could not even imagine a more liberal form of social interaction, which of course always involves social presentability. Although it took barely one hundred years—from Lessing and Klopstock to the deaths of Goethe and Hegel—to create the great store of German bourgeois culture and knowledge, bourgeois society of the period was itself completely incapable of assuring a person an education in the sense of a core that would form and train him for presentability in public life.[6] There is no more decisive example of this than the classic novel of education, Goethe's *Wilhelm Meister,* whose hero is "educated" by aristocrats and actors, his education consisting of being "raised up from a bourgeois to an aristocrat" (to use Victor Hehn's telling phrase).[7] There is likewise no more decisive proof of the isolation of the German intellectual and his capitulation before the aristocracy, which in return helped him earn, at best, a very limited bourgeois livelihood, but never a new social homeland. For there was nothing real, either economically or intellectually, about his being raised up "from a bourgeois to an aristocrat." It merely meant that Prussian Junkers, who were concerned with almost everything but education,[8] hired bourgeois tutors for their sons—those brilliant, starving fellows for whom a desperately constricted German bourgeois world apparently had no other place.

Jewish salons were thus no more anchored in any class of society than German education was, even though centers of educated social interaction were taken as a sign of Jews' having found some anchor in society. In fact the opposite was the case—precisely because Jews stood outside of society, they became, for a time, a kind of neutral meeting ground for the "educated." In the same way that Jewish influence on the state faded as soon as the bourgeoisie exercised the influence for which it was, so to speak, preordained by the course of history, so, too, but much earlier, the Jewish element was eliminated from society at the first sign of social interaction among the educated bourgeoisie.[9]

When, therefore, the idyll of a mixed social interaction collapsed, perishing in the catastrophe of 1807, not all that much actually happened. That idyll owed its existence solely to its political inconsequence and fell apart so quickly and totally for that very reason. But in view of the fact that for the Jews such good times would never return and that from then on they would have to pay for social recognition with broken backs and concomitant bad consciences, it is a sign of foresight when someone looking back from the second decade of the nineteenth century regards the year 1806–7 as far more crucial than the disappointments of the Congress of Vienna or the reactionary storm of 1819. "Where are the days when we were all together! They went under in 1806,* went under like a ship, carrying life's loveliest treasures, life's greatest joys" (Rahel Varnhagen).[10]

But what are we actually holding in our hands when we think back to

---

*The year Napoleon entered Berlin, which marked the end of the old order, that is, of the Holy Roman Empire.—Ed.

those "happy days"? As long as the German bourgeoisie let itself be represented socially by actors and aristocrats, the Jews were included. And who else recognized them socially? As for the nobility, their position vis-à-vis the Jews had long since diverged somewhat from that of other people. They had long since excepted their "own" Jews to tend their bodies, land, and cattle. In their eyes such exceptional Jews included all of Berlin's Jewry—at least all those with whom they associated.

It is, however, characteristic of how things proceeded that neither Dohm's theory nor Lessing's position—both of whom concluded from the fact of Mendelssohn's "exception" that such dignity could belong to his entire people, and thus to all people—proved decisive in the social and political liberation of the Jews. What happened instead was nothing more than the extension of state practice and the expansion of the social concept of exceptional Jews, both of which were prepared to include ever larger circles of Jews. Ultimately Berlin's exceptional Jews were no more and no less *assimilated,* that is, recognized by society, than their fathers, the Jews who had been emancipated by the Grand Edict as protected Jews, that is, recognized by the state. The former were the true image of the latter and had little in common with the pathos of Lessing's Enlightenment and the French Revolution's struggle for freedom. The Enlightenment and the Revolution had melted in their hands into a social idyll.

VII *Society and State Abolish Exceptional Jews*

Prussia's surrender in 1807 of its eastern provinces with their large Jewish populations meant that protected Jews still within its borders were deprived of their useful backdrop. As if overnight, and very much to the surprise of the patriotically inclined Jews of Berlin, Jewish salons were deserted, Jews isolated, the illusion of exceptional Jews eliminated from society. By tacit understanding—with hardly a sound, with almost no ugliness—the assimilation that had only just begun was reversed.

This social change to the detriment of Jews was noticed at the time by only a few individuals,[1] and has barely been acknowledged by historians. For them the preparations made for the Emancipation Edict of 1812 eclipsed all stirrings of antisemitism, leading them to label the period prior to the War of

Liberation as cordial toward Jews. The state and society at the time, how-ever, were so far from being identical that it cannot be said that any class of society actually stood behind the state, let alone behind its measures on behalf of the Jews. The absolute monarchy was still "absolutely" separated from the people even when it undertook reforms on their behalf. Thus social antisemitism remained for the time being just as ineffective as political philosemitism and tendencies toward assimilation had been in the preceding decades.

The loss of this backdrop, which marked the social death of the Jews, was also their sole political chance: liberation from all those elements that did not "maintain" and were not directly useful to the state. It was the first, but not the last time, in the eerie history of Western Jews that they were forced to exchange social prominence and political misery for social misery and a very feeble ray of political hope.

The defeat of 1807 became the turning point in the history of Prussia's Jews, because of the two crucial political points at which the special interests of Jews stood out clearly. The entire anti-Jewish mood of the time was con-centrated, first, on the state's protection of Jews and, second, on the political advantages that Jews enjoyed under French occupation. The state's interest in those protected Jews still remaining within Prussia revealed very clearly that this was not a matter of individual exceptions but of a collective that was perforce bound up very closely with the interests of the absolute monarchy. In addition, however Prussian and patriotic the Jews' inclinations might be, no one could be certain that they might not sympathize with Napoleon, who had liberated them in all territories he occupied. Both factors made Jews sus-pect. Educated society in Berlin had discovered its patriotism via Napoleon and had simultaneously found its focus in its opposition to an absolute state. Leading the battle against Napoleon were the "patriots," who were recruited from the bourgeois intelligentsia and had also always been loyal to the aris-tocracy. Leading the battle against the state was the aristocracy, who set the tone in society and had been extremely embittered by the state's reforms, one of which was the plan for emancipation.

This initial social antisemitism had not yet taken on a truly aggressive quality. Granted, one already regarded Jews as the representatives—which in fact they were not—of certain ideas, but at least not yet as *the* representa-tives. At any rate they were already identified with enlightenment, bourgeois (philistine) attitudes, and sympathies with the French, whereas in fact they had come to be the most loyal of loyalist citizens. During the idyllic social conditions of the previous decades they had lost all sense of political and intellectual reality. They neither sympathized with Napoleon, nor had they found a way to join the bourgeoisie. Rich Jews, with the house of Rothschild in the forefront, financed the wars of legitimate ruling houses against Napoleon, all the while looking for ways by which to gain noble titles and Christian orders and honors.[2] But in fact there was little chance of their ever achieving a social connection with the small circle of liberals who were behind the reform movement. Here Jews were compromised by aristocratic assimilation. Reformists thought that behind those social connections they could see the old usurious support given to their ancient predatory enemy.

The century-long connection between Jewish usurers and aristocratic spendthrifts was slowly falling apart, but it was during those same years that aristocrats had made Berlin's Jews "acceptable at court." Jewish loans to aristocrats had meanwhile been supplanted by credit given to the houses of absolute monarchs. Loans extended to individual debt-ridden court flunkeys were now just bribes and a means for securing a sphere of influence with the state.[3] The partiality of aristocratic society toward Jews quickly came to an end due to political and economic conflicts of interest, which first emerged after 1807 and centered on the issues of the increasing influence of Jews on the state and their growing lack of interest in the aristocracy. All the same, this aristocratic swan song dedicated to the past unfortunately sufficed as a quick reminder to others of something that in fact no longer existed, and soon resulted in the creation of bourgeois *liberal* arguments against the Jews based on a reality that had been withering away for a long period of time and whose social luster was already growing dim.

At precisely the same moment in history (1807) that saw the aristocracy become antisemitic, first in its behavior and then in its arguments, the bourgeois liberal author Buchholz leveled his accusations against *Jews and aristocrats*.[4] In order to be rid of the aristocracy, one must first be rid of the Jews, because "the aristocracy is so closely bound to the Jews that it cannot continue without them; both exist by way of mutual support and complement, the aristocracy assisting the Jews with force, the Jews the aristocracy with cunning and fraud." This and nothing else is the consequence of this first "assimilation": the bourgeois citizen's resentment, his outrage at the social arrogance of the Junkers and at a newfangled mode of social interaction that included everyone but himself. Members of the intelligentsia (that is, those born to the bourgeoisie) who frequented Jewish salons were as out of place as Lessing had once been in the bourgeois society of his day. This outrage was of course aimed primarily at those exceptional Jews who were received more quickly than anyone else into "good society." Such obvious rancor toyed with the idea of equating aristocracy and Jewry, though little of that found its way into the new German antisemitism. What remained was the rancor.

How strong that resentment must have already been can be seen in the fact that Grattenauer's *Wider die Juden* [Against the Jews], the first antisemitic tract for the rabble, achieved a circulation of 13,000 copies when it was published in 1803.[5] To Grattenauer, a down-on-his-luck and debt-ridden lawyer, goes the incontestable glory of having been the first to introduce into antisemitic literature the rabble-rousing, vulgar German that it has never ceased to employ since. It says a great deal about the mood of a wide circle of people that this piece of rubbish—while explicitly scraping and bowing before the aristocracy[6]—reveals a hostile attitude toward aristocrats as part of its polemic against Jews.[7] Grattenauer no longer wants to hear about "this or that Jew, about any Jewish individual," and is the first to use the happy phrase "the Jew in general, the Jew everywhere and nowhere," the meaning of which was no clearer to him than to his contemporary readers. What is clear in every regard is the rancor that he shares with so many about connections that none of them have. This inspires him to provide a very graphic description in which Jewish social situations are nothing but a swindle, inasmuch as they have no legal basis and are based solely on connections,[8] on, so to speak, an excessive standard of living that is a daily slap in the face of the law.[9] From all of which he then deduces the requisite illegality of the tribe, its "revolutionary tendency," and a "spirit that puts bourgeois society in serious danger."

Grattenauer was not a lucky man. He was a few years ahead of his time, and despite great momentary success remained without influence, indeed was personally severely compromised. It was not yet time for an antisemitism of either the rabble or the bourgeoisie; it could prevail neither in the witty form of a Buchholz nor in the vulgar form of a Grattenauer. Both lacked that narrow basis of reality that is more useful than any rancor, which itself never needs to be expressed and yet lends antisemitic arguments their bewildering effectiveness. Both lacked the backing that can be provided only by society itself—by a certain rank or class that knows how to make use of now heavier, now lighter ammunition. Over time the most trenchant phrase in Grattenauer's brochure, "the Jew everywhere and nowhere," remained misunderstood in an era when the exception and only the exception was assimilated.

The state's dilatory handling of the Jewish question had made social assimilation possible. Exceptional Jews, who stood out against the dark masses of Jewry, emerged as real individuals who could be assimilated individually. They could nevertheless remain Jews, which then easily became a very personal matter, something that made them personally "interesting" and yet was not unwelcome on a private level. The biographies of important Jews of the period—whose youth was spent in the 1780s or at the latest toward the turn of the century—reveal, strangely enough, how all of them, despite the personal uncertainty of youth and the indifference of adulthood, returned to Judaism in old age.[10] The same phenomenon is evident from a decline in the number of Jewish baptisms and mixed marriages after 1815.[11] The flight from Judaism—into baptism or personal uncertainty—becomes impossible as soon as the Jewish question is posed collectively, at which point being Jewish is an inescapable fact for the individual as well.

The state, in wanting to eliminate its exceptional, its protected Jews, by way of emancipation and to mix them into the population, created for them a paradoxical social situation. To the same extent that the state desired their dissolution as a nation, which it sought to legalize through emancipation, it also created for them, as a collective to be emancipated, a special position. They existed socially once again as Jews, precisely because they were to be emancipated as Jews. Over the next few decades, the purely formal act of emancipation assumed an ever more concrete form because of the state's delaying tactics, until it finally became an eminently political factor. Despite its formality, this paradox at once became a social reality because the Jews' new special political position corresponded to their special economic position within the state's economy.

The emancipation of French Jewry, which the Revolution emancipated *along with* the bourgeoisie, had at one time offered a political opportunity for escaping this paradox. Napoleon's policy toward the Jews, which ended in the *décret infâme* of 1808 that specified special treatment of Alsatian Jews, provides the clearest evidence of how the old special position of Jews in terms of economics prevented this opportunity from achieving its full potential.

In Germany, however, which never had a bourgeois revolution and thus no *explicit* liberation of the bourgeoisie as a class, Jews appeared to be the only people in need of emancipation or the only emancipated, and thus privileged, segment of society. The longer the country continued without an explicitly bourgeois emancipation, the firmer the conviction had to grow among the bourgeoisie that Jews enjoyed a special position—meaning that the argument that Jewish emancipation was proof of a collective, be it national or economic, connection became all the more persuasive. After all, the Jews were the only group that had achieved, even if haltingly and incompletely, a change in their political status, which, as others saw it, made it a "gift," if not indeed a privilege.

Only Wilhelm von Humboldt—who, as is well known, exerted a major influence on the Edict of 1812—appears to have seen that Jewish emancipation carried with it the danger of achieving just the opposite of its intent. He wanted to let liberation occur without any attention being called to it and sharply criticized a "*gradual* repeal" of restrictions, since that would "only confirm in all those points not repealed the very segregation it wishes to abolish," and "by this same new and greater freedom double the attention paid to any remaining restrictions and thus work against itself." And what Humboldt feared is exactly what happened: emancipation remained in force for only a few years and a "gradual repeal of remaining restrictions" became the principle underpinning the state's Jewish policy.[12]

Humboldt believed in the omnipotence of the state, that it was able simply to dictate to society the emancipation of the Jews. The protracted delay in emancipation, especially the negative effect it had on society before its enactment, made this unhappy course of events inevitable and suggests the impossibility of political liberation when society and the state are already in conflict.

Sharing Humboldt's desire for reform and his illusions were other well-known Prussian statesmen, the most important of whom was Hardenberg, himself a Jew. They truly believed that with emancipation Jews in general could be assimilated so completely that the problem would disappear, and were blind to the social consequences of their actions. That was the natural mode of thought for officials of the state, which had never paid any attention to assimilation, to the changed social position of "its" Jews. It was aware of its exceptional Jews, but not as individuals, only as protected Jews in general; it viewed them collectively as a group with definite achievements and definite economic possibilities. It had already awarded general privileges to those who were particularly capable and was now in the process of extending such privileges to all Jews. The state argued—as did those who, much to our detriment, would later call themselves philosemites—from the individual to the general, except that its example was not a philosopher but a court or "mint" Jew. Without even knowing it, the state turned its individual Jews into a communal entity, a specifically marked segment of society—without knowing it, but also consciously profiting from it later on. But this same semiambiguous collectivity served the interest of nineteenth-century Jews—an interest totally dependent, however, on the state. Here was a segment of society ostracized by society that was always loyal to and ready to pursue the interests of the state.

Those who responded most quickly to the situation created by the state's Emancipation Edict were the Jews themselves. They established associations for educating and improving Jews who were not exceptional Jews, who had not yet ascended to the high level of exceptional people apparently indistinguishable from the world around them. The effect of such associations, whose sole purpose was the dissolution of Jewry, was the organized preservation of German, and assimilated, Jewry.

Given this state of affairs, emancipation provided antisemitism its first basis for differentiating between Jews as individuals and Jews in general—"the Jew everywhere and nowhere." Antisemites immediately sensed what the state would not say and what the advocates of emancipation did not know: individual achievements of court Jews and rewards granted to a few Jews by way of exception were now to serve as the basis for treating achievement collectively and for granting more general rewards, all in order to provide a fundamental support for the state. A few, apparently chance instances of good fortune were to be turned into a privileged economic class, a few exceptional cases were to become a principle anchored in the state. In short—to use the language of an antisemitism that feeds upon the "fear of ghosts"—the Jew as an individual, who had by now almost been assimilated, was to become the Jew in general, "everywhere and nowhere," who never again would be accepted with an open heart by society.

This is one of the most important wellsprings of modern antisemitism, which was a social reaction to an action taken by the state. It could find fertile soil only among those classes who stood in open opposition to the state. Both the elegant standoffishness of liberals and the vulgar pogrom-happy antisemitism of those who had made a failure of their own bourgeois lives continued to have no effect as long as society and all its classes viewed the state more or less with indifference. Thirteen thousand copies of Grattenauer's tract did scarcely any harm to the Jews of Berlin, which proves that even widespread antipathy toward Jews becomes dangerous only when it can link itself with other political trends. Such was the case when patriots, who hated the state for having more or less betrayed their country to Napoleon, began to form a nationalist movement of bourgeois intellectuals hostile to the state and allied themselves with an aristocracy infuriated by the reforms of that same state.

The social expression of this alliance, which barely survived the War of 1813–14, was the German Christian Table Society, a patriotic society that was hostile to the government and whose chief target was Hardenberg.[13] At the same time it was Germany's first programmatically antisemitic organization. Its rules stated that "Jews, Frenchmen, and philistines" would not be accepted as members. The antisemitism of the period was more effective the more closely it tied itself to this group. A scurrilous piece of scant wit by Clemens von Brentano ("The Philistine before, in, and after History") was read aloud there and proved far more dangerous than any caterwauling. For it spread not hatred of Jews, but antipathy toward Jews in precisely the same circles on which Jews were socially dependent, thus preparing the ground for the more massive attacks that first became a pressing issue after the Congress of Vienna. Intellectuals, who in any case had recognized Jews socially only at the bidding of aristocrats, quickly abandoned them once the aristocracy lost interest. And they even provided the aristocracy with arguments for its own retreat.

True, exceptional Jews did not in fact cease to exist in one fell swoop. All these antisemites could be seen in the homes of Jews—Clemens von Brentano as well as Achim von Arnim, even Kleist and Adam Müller. But such contacts were now limited to only a few individuals. When talk turned to *the* Jews, no one argued any more using the example of some exceptional Jew he might know. Once the "Eastern Jews" had vanished along with Prussia's surrendered provinces, society created a new backdrop: the Jews in general—against which an individual might stand out if he happened to prove of some personal use or was prepared to show an extraordinary lack of character.

As a new intelligentsia hostile to Jews—a generation called "political Romantics"—saw itself compelled to take sides in the conflict now openly erupting between the state and the Junkers, it had already opted socially for the aristocrats and needed only to offer them the additional sacrifice of its own freedom. This same state of affairs was only poorly disguised by Romantic converts who offered the church the sacrifice of an intellect that—as proved by history from Kant to Hegel—could function only in a bourgeois context. And yet these intellectuals remained homeless and tended as before to look for some ground to stand on by joining the civil service. For the aristocracy, then, they were dubious allies who had to be prone to treachery the moment the bourgeoisie took hold of the apparatus of the state and ceased to see in it a charitable nursery for its own unemployed intelligentsia. But that did not happen in Germany until 1918, when the aristocracy, finding itself betrayed and sold out by all sides, suddenly saw its loyal "educated friends" in the camp of "upstanding" republicans and democrats.

Until then, and especially in the early nineteenth century, the aforementioned dubiousness of the relationship proved very useful to the aristocracy and very harmful to the Jews. It served in fact—and that is the real historical significance of political Romanticism—to reconcile the absolute state and the Junkers. Out of these ideological nuptials Adam Müller and Joseph Görres bring forth a total state based on class status or estate. They helped set the Junkers, who were not exactly brilliant theorists, back on their feet and taught them how to vilify the bourgeoisie as unpatriotic because it was caught up in "venery with gold"; as unreliable because it was not a living totality, but "ragged and splintered" in both its public and private life; and thus place it beyond the reach of the state, which as *the* totality can lay claim to the total life of its subjects. The worship of an ideal Christian state, in which the aristocracy was once again to be the "first estate," has its correspondence in a ruthless attack on the government of the time, on Stein and Hardenberg, who dared to infringe upon the interests of the Junkers and who were therefore said to be replacing the aristocracy with a "new aristocracy of mammon, whose princes are Jewish by blood." The "living totality"— the state—should be cleansed of inorganic and poisonous elements, that is, of all those who cannot claim legitimacy through their heritage and descent by birth. Descent by birth is divinely decreed—this being the source of the state's designation as Christian—and stands in opposition to the "human arbitrariness" of the parvenu. Organic philosophy of history oscillates between two opposite extremes: the aristocracy, to each member of which a family chronicle awards the highest active legitimation, in the image, as it were, of divine decree; and the Jews, whose origin is anyhow defamatory and who have wormed their way into the organism of the *Volk*, in the image of human arbitrariness. The *Volk* lives between these two extremes, organically subservient to the "princes of blood" and ruled over by the "living totality" of the state. Both disdained and idolized, the *Volk* excludes itself from history in order to serve as its dark foundation, and is always ready for every appeal to its instincts, which in their animal brutality proceed to become divine judgments.[14]

Romantic theories of the state are the fertile soil of all antisemitic ideology. The Jews have no place in "organic history." Only "human arbitrariness"— that is, the actual course of history—has made Europeans of the Jews. They have achieved their social position *despite* their descent by birth. In the years that followed, no one would need to use the differentiation between "public and private life"—however ambiguous it might be—more than assimilated Jews, who hoped to avoid all conflict by declaring themselves to be Germans in public and Jews in private. They lived in the illusion that being Jewish was a private matter and any mention of it indiscreet.

Since the age of political Romanticism, no one has shown less discretion in this matter than "educated" Germans. Their "tact" finally became so shabby that it looked very much like an insult. Not even the great masses of Eastern Jews, whether inside or outside of Germany's borders, did more to help a poor band of assimilated Jews to develop a sense of themselves as a collective exception. From now on each one of them had to prove that although he was a Jew, he was not a "Jew." And in so doing he had to betray not just a portion of those "brothers in faith left behind," but also his entire people, including himself.

VIII *The Aristocracy Turns Antisemitic*

As long as antisemitism cannot establish a basic link with the great political struggles of the time and as long as it is not supported by at least one unified level of society, it remains without political significance and poses no threat to Jews. Social antisemitism, which so painfully impeded the assimilation of "exceptional Jews," appears to exist in this less harmful form only to poison the atmosphere and to prepare both parties, Jews and non-Jews alike, for what lies ahead. Indeed Jewish assimilation, to the extent that it was merely one chapter in the history of the secularization of the Jewish people, could not be undone. Those Jews who were protégés of the state could not be hindered in their passionate desire to acquire a European education, nor even in their attempt to become Germans after their own fashion. But even a relatively harmless social antisemitism could at any point manage to make this small group of people—who, moreover, with some justification thought of themselves as having cast aside their Jewishness—socially homeless. It created a closed, castelike level of social pariahs, who in return deceived themselves about their situation and whose circles or salons became a caricature of "good society." As external pressure, social antisemitism hindered and impeded the necessary political differentiation prescribed by economic conditions and—as long as it was itself politically impotent and thus malicious, ambiguous, and insidious—led Jews to display an equally malicious and ambiguous solidarity, which, although it has long since become totally pointless, still governs a good deal of our political life today and helps create the political ineffectiveness that clings to all our gestures and actions.

Political antisemitism emerged only very slowly out of the fog of a poisoned social atmosphere. Its contours, however, can be traced even during the period when its efficacy was purely social. One should not be deceived by the fact that for many decades these beginnings—inasmuch as they could boast of no actual political effects—kept getting lost in the fog of the imponderable factors of social life. For in due time they would once again, and without any significant transformation, become a more intensely efficient political factor with a much nastier face. The entire nineteenth century is permeated with instances of antisemitism's being transformed back into a purely social and ostensibly harmless phenomenon. Antisemites enjoyed the advantage of being able to sink back into the social class to which they belonged and to continue working and increasing there. This proved to be the principal disadvantage to the Jews and their great protector, the absolute monarchy—that is, it left them incapable of finding some sort of social home, of providing a social foundation for their political successes, so that they were forced to stand aside and watch as each political failure of the anti-semites turned into a social success, poisoning the atmosphere anew and preparing fertile soil.

Assimilated Jews everywhere are quite rightly afraid of this devilish machinery—they are always afraid of their own success. It is a machinery that breaks their backs and robs them of their ability to judge, to be able to tell friend from foe. A mechanism that transforms political arguments into the imponderable factors of social life or insidiously glosses them over, or at any rate makes use of every official failure to establish a social basis, creates total confusion among its victims, for whom, until the eve of catastrophe, their own history remains in desperate darkness, populated by arbitrary, illu-sionary phantasmagoria.

Social antisemitism ceases to be relatively harmless when it no longer focuses solely on Jews, when it abandons the lofty detachment with which the well-born treat the parvenu—which the Jew in fact is—and in one way or another draws Jews into the political battles of the day. We already saw hints of this in the Jewish antipathy of the German Christian Table Society, which linked Jews with the bourgeoisie and the French. The source of such links was the aristocracy's political argument with both the bourgeoisie and the modern state. From the start, antisemitic arguments were interjected into both fronts of this two-front war that Prussia's Junkers kept on waging with various degrees of fierceness well into the twentieth century. This is the point around which, over the course of many decades, the most disparate elements crystallized, joining together to form a unified structure again and again, despite the numerous occasions when its political core split apart.

The absolute monarchy in Prussia, which between 1807 and 1813 accom-plished, though always from the top down, several necessary reforms for the protection of both farmers and the bourgeoisie, was equally detested by Junkers and liberals. In the eyes of liberals the few reforms that were accomplished—and even those dealt very gently with the aristocracy—were offset by an absolute rule based on no constitution. On the other hand, and with some justification, the aristocracy saw in these reforms—which robbed them of their status as landlords with jurisdiction over farmers and made it possible to buy and sell landed property—an attack on their monopoly over political power.

Within this context there was good reason for the aristocracy's hatred of the Jews. To curse "honorable old Brandenburg-Prussia" as a "newfangled Jewish state" was certainly "unseemly," as Hardenberg put it, but to do so was not entirely without its reasons.[1] We have already seen to what extent court Jews contributed to the financial underpinning of the modern state. The modern transformation of court Jews into the state's creditors and bankers was an accommodation to the modern needs of an absolute monarchy. Though on a different basis, the financing itself remained the same, and the role prominent Jews played was only slightly changed. Lacking any other financially powerful class that was loyal to the monarch and had an interest in the state, the state fell back on the Jews for almost every loan.

The purpose of these royal reforms was to enhance the power of the state and to make the entire apparatus of civil servants as independent of Junker interests as possible.[2] The commercial bourgeoisie was strengthened by freedom of trade, the peasantry was liberated, the aristocracy was deprived of special tax privileges, large tracts of land could be bought and sold—in short, the feudal "order" was destroyed and indeed class warfare was unleashed between the bourgeoisie and the Junkers, between commercial capital and landed interests. All of which was meant to strengthen the power of the monarchy[3] and remove the king from the class of landowners, of which, as the largest landowner in Prussia, he had until then been the *primus inter pares*. This end was served above all by the sale of royal domains in 1809, which acted as an alarm signal for the aristocracy.

After 1815 the Junkers regained much of their influence on the apparatus of the state; in no other country were aristocrats able to profit so splendidly from the monarchy's fear of constitutions and parliaments. They loyally helped the Prussian, and later German, state throttle the bourgeoisie, turning its nationalism into Byzantinism, and with their lackey mentality obstructing intellectual and scientific development. But when, at the end of their glorious indirect rule, they once again attempted to make the head of state identical with themselves, to turn a pensioner of the state into a Junker by installing Hindenberg in Neudeck, their apparent success—given the obdurate silence of the republic and of the entire civil service—functioned as an alarm signal for very different "heirs" than themselves.

There was one thing, however, that the Junkers always knew: that the notion of an absolute monarchy, in the sense of an absolutely independent authority, standing above all classes, dispensing perfect justice, and representing only national interests, was the fantasy of these professional bureaucrats who would later be called "social monarchists."[4] That is why the Junkers simultaneously opposed both the state, which was encroaching upon their interests, and the bourgeoisie, upon whom they appeared for a brief moment—until 1815—to rely.[5] But this was truly no more than an appearance. The avant-garde of the bourgeoisie, the liberals, knew well enough that reforms from on high offered no political guarantees, and so demanded nothing less than a constitution. The absolute power of the monarchy consisted on the one hand in an irresolute, very shaky determination neither to be eaten by the great Junkers nor to toss the entire nation to them for meat, and on the other in a very definite determination not to give the bourgeoisie any share of political power by consenting to a constitution.

Caught between Scylla and Charybdis, a frightened, "independent" monarchy found only one financially powerful segment of society that was both loyal and demanded no political price, or only a very small one, in return for its financial support—the protected Jews. The price, the Emancipation Edict of 1812, was paid at the very moment when the "absoluteness" of the monarchy had attained its point of perfection—that is, when it could no longer depend upon sympathy from any segment of the population. The Emancipation Edict was made possible because the monarchy or, better, the state, had temporarily severed its ties with the Junkers and at the same time felt, likewise temporarily, no pressure from the bourgeoisie.

The monarchy's ephemeral and shaky independence from all levels of society offered it the remarkable and singular opportunity to draw within its circle of influence the best minds and freest spirits of Germany at the time. Among the most significant, and for Jews the most important, was Wilhelm von Humboldt, whose famous "Opinion on Emancipation from 1809"[6] proved to be of no small help in deceiving Jewish intellectuals as to the real motives behind emancipation. Nothing perhaps provides more striking proof of German humanism's lack of political sophistication than its fantasy that its core political idea—instruction and education—could be realized through a reformist state. According to Humboldt, the purpose of emancipation was "not so much to teach respect for Jews, as to put an end to an inhumane and prejudiced mode of thinking that does not judge a person by his unique characteristics, that is, as an individual, but rather sees him as a member of a race who by necessity, as it were, shares certain of its characteristics." It is true that the state did attempt to exert an influence on society for a while (as long as Hardenberg was chancellor—that is, until 1819) and to force it to assimilate the Jews—by forbidding inflammatory antisemitic tracts and the like; but of course it could in no way prevent whatever classes of society were in the ascendancy at the moment from declaring which remnants of emancipation were still acceptable. Official policy revealed not a trace of humanistic arguments or support from politicians, who in their hostility to the government later became part of revolutionary Young Germany.

All attempts by the state to unite emancipation with some sort of assimilation foundered on the open conflict that had broken out between the monarchy and the aristocracy, as well as on the state's latent conflict with the bourgeoisie. The state's efforts on behalf of the Jews placed them in the foreground of every conflict that arose. Cordiality toward the Jews was shown at most by a segment of the civil service, with Hardenberg in the lead—who, by the way, for that very reason was held to be corrupt. The civil service, however, at best only secondarily consisted of men from bourgeois circles and was inclined first and foremost to defend the interests of absolutism—which also explains why it became such a bitter foe of the aristocracy and such a devoted friend of the Jews.[7] Precisely during the years of emancipation, the state had no social base other than its paid functionaries—and emancipation at their hands was hardly a thing to be recommended.

Perhaps the emancipated Jews of Prussia would have had a somewhat better chance for assimilation in the sense of acceptance by the world around them had the Prussian state of the period at least given some thought to using the bourgeoisie as a new basis for its authority. The state, however, did not really take the matter seriously, as is evident from its so-called liberation of the peasants, which indeed did away with their status as serfs under the jurisprudence of their landlords, only to place them under the authority of the state and to make of them a new type of soldier. Not only had they not been freed economically, but they were also more enslaved than before.[8] Reforms under Stein helped the aristocracy enlarge its estates enormously,[9] which resulted more in a modernization of landed property than in a liberation of the peasantry. What had been planned and promoted as an expropriation of the Junkers ended up creating a landless peasantry. The estates of aristocrats—and not of peasants—were subjected to forced reforms, extracted from obsolete structures of authority and property, and made to conform to a modern concept of capital. The true high point of the peasant "liberation" came with the clearly reactionary Compensation Act of 1821, which awarded the aristocracy almost 2.5 million acres of land, 18 million thalers in cash, 1.5 million thalers in annual rents, and an annual emolument of a quarter million bushels of grain.[10] The Prussian state had pulled off the feat of making capitalists of its Junkers without declaring them to be part of the bourgeoisie—or having to burden them with the odium of being seen as capitalists. Following an indirect route laid out by the state, the aristocracy had been given a basis for economic livelihood without having to forfeit all that many political prerogatives.

An important historical by-product of this weakening of the Prussian peasantry was the further separation of farmers from the urban bourgeoisie. These ill-fated reforms—decried, moreover, by the aristocracy as bourgeois—had made the peasantry suspicious and then, with a single blow, reactionary, sending them running back under the wing of the Junkers. Thus the bourgeoisie, which until well into the middle of the nineteenth century was relatively small in number, was robbed of its natural basis of masses living on the land, without whose help it cannot—as the history of the last few centuries teaches—accomplish its own revolutions.

The absolute monarchy emerged from its reforms stronger than before. Granted, it never succeeded in radically eliminating the political influence of the Junkers; but it had in any case decisively defeated its far more dangerous enemy, the liberal bourgeoisie. The course of later history shows that on the whole this resulted in an extraordinary prolongation of its rule.

In its two-front war to prevent the bourgeoisie from gaining economic power and to win back lost political positions, the aristocracy denounced the Jews as the sole group within society that supported its enemy the state and saw them as an important factor in the state's economy. Both assertions corresponded more or less with reality, but since they really referred to Jews only in terms of economic relationships, they lacked the antisemitic barb so dangerous to Jews. It was not until people began to equate the emancipation of the Jews with ostensible bourgeois reform and to characterize them as the real beneficiaries of more open trade laws, including the buying and selling of landed property, that simple hostility toward Jews among a rather limited segment of the population gained its antisemitic sting: that is, linkage with a reactionary political movement that would define the entire century.

Both bourgeois reform and Jewish emancipation were seen as useful to the absolute state. But that is the only tie that bound them together.[11] By stamping the bourgeoisie with the stigma of being Jewish, the aristocracy's antisemitic propaganda found that narrow basis of reality that has to underlie all antisemitic slander. In this regard 1809 is significant, for during that year the bourgeoisie was given the right to administer cities and Jews were granted local citizenship, including the right to elect and be elected as town councilors. And even after the Congress of Vienna, triumphant reactionaries were unable to revoke the rights of urban Jews—yet another sign that emancipation was about the privileged group of Jews already protected by the state and not about Jewry as a whole. In all of this the bourgeoisie remained thoroughly passive. Believing it could coerce assimilation, the state decreed Jews to be members of this class of society, though of course they belonged to it neither economically nor, in any real sense, socially. All the same this is the first indication of a development that would unfold over time.[12]

As propaganda, the antisemitic and false linkage of freedom of trade with Jewish emancipation had one great advantage: the urban guilds were against both. Since time out of mind they had been hostile to Jews, whom, in their role as suppliers to the court and promoters of manufacturing, they saw as representatives of the state; they also suspected—and quite rightly so—that freedom of trade would strike a lethal blow to their ancient guild privileges. By introducing antisemitic polemics, the aristocracy was able to turn an old archenemy into an ally. It was not until the end of the century that Jews first became aware of the danger of this alliance when—in Engels's words—"the petty aristocracy, the Junkers, who had been taking in ten thousand marks and paying out twenty thousand and had thus fallen into the hands of usurers, joined the cause of antisemitism and screamed in chorus along with guild members, shopkeepers, and a petite bourgeoisie ruined by competition with capitalist tycoons."[13] All of which had long since begun. To the same extent that the progressive bourgeoisie had lost its mass base in the peasantry out in the country, the aristocracy gained a new base for its political propaganda in the cities—a base that it could infect with its ideology and lead wherever it chose.

Whereas in their war with the apparatus of the absolute state the Junkers had employed antisemitic arguments from the start, their war against the bourgeoisie was at first entirely free of them. There is no clearer proof that Jews belonged to the state's narrow economic segment than the fact that they are not even mentioned by Ludwig von der Marwitz in his polemic against freedom of trade—and this from a man who in another context had called Brandenburg a "newfangled Jewish state."[14] The less these polemics have to say about the Jews in the context of freedom of trade, the more clearly and unambiguously they reveal their original antibourgeois tendencies. Bourgeois reform is the "revolutionizing of the Fatherland,"

> the war of those who have no property against those who do, of industry against agriculture, of buying and selling against stability, of crass materialism against God's established order, of vain profit against the law, of the present moment against the past and the future, of the individual against the family, of speculators and counting houses against fields and trades, of bureaucracy against conditions that have arisen out of the nation's history, of acquired learning and vain talent against virtue and honorable character.[15]

It is amazing how quickly and with what a sure hand the Junkers set to work building their chorus of all backward-looking or necessarily apprehensive strata, especially the guilds and farmers. But what is also astonishing is the total correlation between the description of the nascent capitalism of commercial banks and entrepreneurs with later antisemitic tracts. There is hardly a single argument or characterization that would not later be applied to Jews in absolute terms: the bourgeoisie is unpatriotic, crassly materialistic, revolutionary;[16] it lives only for the moment, has no sense of history, lacks any connection with the nation; it is deceitful and wants to earn its money by speculation rather than by honest work.

Concepts that would later become increasingly abstract are still based on very visible evidence: people who work for their living are materialistic, as opposed to people of property who can no longer be observed earning their living.[17] A person is patriotic if he owns large parts of the fatherland, and unpatriotic if he owns none of it. The "perpetuity" of landed property is "stable," buying and selling it is flat-out "destructive." What in part characterizes the social being of humanity's nonaristocrat is his "original" lack of property, which he can only purchase, so that whatever he has is "external," whereas for the aristocrat being and having coalesce as historical property.[18] The bourgeoisie is deceitful because the way it earns its living is illegal; the parvenu uses his wealth to disguise his "inborn" lack of property. The bourgeois man is bound to the moment, that is, to the present, to which he owes his living; he is berated as "egoistic and individualistic" because he has himself, and not his family kinship, to thank for what he has and is. The aristocrats, however, whose privileges came from God and eternity itself and who were in full possession of the fatherland and all virtue, found it expedient— in a time of bourgeois patriotism—to corner love of the fatherland for themselves by disdainfully pointing to that unpatriotic fellow, the merchant "who feels equally at home in all nations"[19] and makes not even the slightest mention of the battle of Jena and the capitulations that followed.

This malicious description of the bourgeoisie is the historical wellspring of almost all antisemitic arguments. The only thing lacking here is for Marwitz to apply it to the Jews. This proved relatively easy to do and was originally merely intended as the ultimate defamation: the bourgeois man is in truth no different from the Jew. For this, one needed only to declare that earning a living by profit and interest was the same as usury: the bourgeois citizen was nothing but a Jew and a usurer. The only people with a right to an income free of labor are those who already possess wealth. The "wild ambition" unleashed by freedom of trade produces nothing but social parvenus[20]— and no one rises from greater social depths than the Jew. Just as one fears a future Rothschild in every peddler, one also despises every Rothschild for the lawlessness he shares with the peddler.

The Jews of Prussia—suppliers to the court, creditors of the state, buyers and exporters of porcelain manufactured by the state, dealers in coins and jewels, small money changers, and even smaller peddlers—were anything but integrated into the very limited ranks of those merchants and entrepreneurs who made up the avant-garde of the bourgeoisie. Only in an aristocrat's eyes was one parvenu as good as another, which is why aristocrats were those least inclined toward patent social antisemitism. The Jew, as parvenu, offered a caricature of the bourgeois citizen. For a bourgeoisie lacking in self-confidence, no wound cut deeper than to hear its traits called Jewish.

The bourgeoisie understood that antisemitism was the way to cast off this odium. In the end all that is left of bourgeois traits is that they are "Jewish." In the end only Jews are crassly materialistic, unpatriotic, revolutionary, destructive, speculative, and deceitful, living only for the moment and lacking any historical ties to the nation.

Thus what proved so dangerous to the Jews was not the aristocracy's historically determined hatred of the financiers of the modern state, but rather that arguments and characteristics trimmed and tailored for totally different people ended up attached to them. All antisemitic arguments are feudal in origin. Hardly any better evidence of the vast and literally overwhelming influence that, until only recently, the Junkers and their accomplices had on politics, society, and ideas can be found than in the monotonous history of antisemitic argumentation. Even now vulgar sophists and claimants to narrow worldviews are perfectly happy to rummage around in the endless dichotomies—each easily extendable by random association—of eternal and transient, stable and disintegrative, deeply rooted and uprooted, constructive and destructive, positive and negative. That the Prussian aristocracy succeeded in drilling these categories and value judgments into the head of the German bourgeois citizen until he was ashamed to be one—that is the real and, as it were, "ideological" misfortune of German Jewry. For in the end the liberals' truly destructive self-hatred gave rise to a hatred of the Jews, that being the only means liberals had of distancing themselves from themselves, of shifting slander to others who, though they did not think of themselves as the "bourgeoisie," were forced to be its 100 percent embodiment.

The origins of German antisemitism, the defamation of the bourgeoisie by the aristocracy, continued to strongly determine the history of modern Jewry. The more closely antisemitic argumentation was linked with old feudal polemics, the better it was suited for export to countries with feudal or semifeudal conditions—that is, to countries to the East with their great masses of Jews. This is why the Jewish question is so crucially important for the Jewish people as a whole, despite the relatively small number of German Jews. German antisemitism conquered the world under the banner of the Prussian Junkers. Aristocratic arguments against Jews and the bourgeoisie turned out to be a terrible weapon—not when wielded by the aristocracy itself, but when once placed in the hands of a suppressed and self-doubting bourgeoisie.

Not when wielded by the aristocracy, which after 1815 was content with simply postponing the bourgeois emancipation of the Jew *sine die*. The aristocracy had once again become the first estate in the state—with the tacit consent of a bourgeois, lower-level bureaucracy. It once again felt so closely bound to emperor and throne that for many decades it kept its antisemitism within the limits dictated by the state. Following the byway of the monarchy, it found a road back to its old bankers. The Jews no longer made loans to aristocrats but simply paid their debts—a gratuity regularly demanded of Jews for access to high society and intercession with the monarch for those charters of nobility they so longed for. The no-interest loans, the gifts, and the cordial invitations to participate in business deals that accompanied the ascent of the Rothschilds wherever they were active all speak an eloquent language.[21]

As insignificant as these novel, "disinterested" dealings were, they nevertheless managed to compromise the cause of the Jews. Their protectors were growing ever more reactionary—men to whom they owed nothing more than the rise of a very few, and nothing less than the denial of human rights to them all. And as retainers of their protectors, Jewish mediators and notables became more reactionary themselves:[22] "The rich among us . . . being privy to the councils of despots, were open to the suggestion that if the people were to gain power they would only bind the Jews in tighter chains" (Börne).[23] As the successor to Humboldt and Hardenberg, Metternich became the defender of the Jews (opposing the citizens of Frankfurt at the Congress of Vienna); he became the great protector of and creditor to the Rothschilds, and put his novel approach to use most effectively in preventing emancipation in Austria. Which in no way alters the fact that he was wisely prescient and completely right in saying to Salomon Rothschild: "When the devil comes to fetch me, he'll fetch you too."

The more the aristocracy regained its influence on the state and the more it once again set the tone for society, the more its aggressive antisemitism reverted to the imponderable factors of social life. The Jews had already been robbed of the only social home they had known at the beginning of the century. Now only as aristocrats did they have entry into aristocratic society, only as baptized Christians into circles loyal to the state and the civil service upon which the Christian state was based. The aristocracy quickly realized that Christianity was still its best ally against the Jews. Religion allowed them to forgo the aggressiveness that the state found inopportune, to disregard the present, and, to whatever extent feasible, to focus instead on the medieval reality of the Jews. Antisemitic measures in their Christian form were also acceptable to the monarchy. This opened the way for the official abrogation of human rights and the repeal of emancipation in 1823.[24]

Meanwhile the weapon of antisemitic argumentation was passed into the hands of other classes of society, was inherited by more powerful and violent successors. A class that for its own social purposes had every reason to distance itself from the bourgeois manner in which it earned its living—without actually being able to abandon it—took over the task of defaming the bourgeoisie, essentially by means of the distorted equation of profit with usury. The distorted and intentionally mendacious equation of usury with the bourgeoisie pointed, as if all by itself, to the Jews, who had once been usurers and who lived on as such in popular memory; pointed, that is, to the "real" usurers—and distancing oneself from them would surely mean salvaging one's social position.

In the next chapter we shall see how developments in the Jewish economy made it especially easy to posit such an equation, as well as how the bourgeoisie put aristocratic arguments to good use and at what historical moment.*

(circa 1938–39)

Notes

I INTRODUCTION

1. Text of the law as signed by Wilhelm I and Bismarck, quoted in Dubnow, *Weltgeschichte des jüdischen Volkes* [History of the Jews in Russia and Poland], vol. 9, p. 340.

2. At the turn of the nineteenth century "Semitic" and "Indo-Germanic," as used by Schlegel and Eichhorn, were purely linguistic terms. They were first used as anthropological and ethnic terms by Christian Lassen in his *Indische Altertumskunde* [Ancient India] (1847). Lassen characterizes Indo-Germanic peoples as the most gifted and productive, that is, as "good," and Semitic peoples as egoistic, greedy, and unproductive—in short, as "bad." Cf. W. ten Boom, *Entstehung des modernen Rassenantisemitismus* [Formation of modern racial antisemitism] (1928), p. 11 ff. Boom quotes Lassen at length and rightly observes: "It is certainly no accident that this statement comes from a man who represents a science that was in fact born out of the spirit of Romanticism."

*At this point the manuscript breaks off. If more was written it apparently has not survived.—Ed.

The political transformation of the word "Semitic" into the catchword "antisemitic" as well as its application to Jews in general comes from Wilhelm Maar, circa 1870.

3. Hermann Cohen, *Jüdische Schriften* [Jewish writings], vol. 2, *Emanzipation* (1912), p. 223. "We feel that we have become persons of culture (following the Emancipation Edict of 1812). What sense of *gratitude* can have deeper roots than that which lifts us up to become a moral personality. . . . All the injustice we must endure should not mislead us into doubting *progress over time.* . . ." (p. 224). "Let us make confident use here as well of *world history* and its creeping pace. . . . One consequence that arises for us . . . out of this edict is that our *patriotism* is deeper than before and still not exhausted." Truly: "World history follows meandering paths" (p. 227). [Italics in the original.]

4. The *Jüdische Rundschau* [Jewish panorama] has been offering constant proof of this ever since 1933. Especially in the first years, it was prepared to go to any and all lengths. Of course there are Zionists who think differently about the issue and display somewhat more national dignity. But they are not typical, because "respect" is a direct consequence of the Zionist "substance" theory—linked to inherited loyalty. Otherwise it could not have been set into practice so quickly as a matter of general agreement.

5. The Russian Revolution of 1917 has resulted in nothing more and nothing less than what was promised in the Revolution of 1789—total bourgeois emancipation. Jews will no longer be discriminated against only when every act of antisemitism is considered an attack on society as a whole. Which is not to say that *the* Jewish question is now to be solved by imitation of the Russian model. Indeed one cannot even tell whether the Jewish question has been solved in Russia. Insofar as the emancipation of Russian Jews is simply total bourgeois emancipation, the question can be "solved" only at the cost of the continued existence of the Jews of Russia. Granted, the Russian Revolution has done away with this very framework by recognizing Jews as a nation or "nationality." But this expanded emancipation has as such had no real effect on the Jewish question, since it has occurred hand in hand with the complete severance of Russian Jews from other Jews around the globe. Isolated from all other Jews, Russian Jews cannot maintain themselves as a nation, since the Jewish nation is determined and defined by its international attachments.

6. This holds true as well, of course, for nationalist movements among Eastern Jews, even though the forms are less blatant and somewhat camouflaged—popular renaissance, auto-emancipation, etc.

7. "In Europe as well, this people is and will remain an Asian people foreign to our continent, bound to the ancient law given to them. To what extent this law and the modes of thought and life that arise from it may belong in our nations is no longer a religious dispute, but a simple question of state." Herder, *Adrastea.*

8. Moritz Goldstein, "Deutsch-jüdischer Parnass" [German-Jewish Parnassus], in *Kunstwart,* Annual 25, no. 11 (1912).

9. This is apparent not just in a general stagnation of the number of Congress voters, but also in an actual decrease of votes, as in Poland in 1935, when there was a 25 percent decline over against the previous Congress. The movement's decline has recently been openly admitted by a functionary of its National Fund, who surely ought to know. Cf. Nathan Bistritsky, "Le Sionisme dans les pays de la diaspora," in *La Revue Juive de Genève,* no. 50 (July 1937).

II THE CLASSIC LAND OF ANTISEMITISM

1. Wilhelm Marr, *Der Sieg des Judentum über des Germanentum* [The Victory of Judaism over Teutonism] (1st ed., 1869); for the translation cf. Dubnow, *Weltgeschichte des jüdischen Volkes,* vol. 10, p. 120.

2. Likewise symptomatic of the medieval character of the pogroms in Russia is the role that a baptized Jew named Brafmann and his *Kahalbuch* (1869) played in domestic Russian propaganda and/or prefatory agitation. (Cf. Dubnow, *Weltgeschichte,* vol. 9, p. 416). At the same time, in its attempt to explain itself to

Europe, the Russian government made use of the "ideology of exploitation"—a very modern term, but quite nonsensical given Russian conditions. (Cf. Dubnow, *Weltgeschichte*, vol. 10, p. 136 ff.)

3. Cf. I. G. Tolemacke, *In Defense of Russia*. The liberals' antisemitic campaign was aimed at Lord Beaconsfield, Benjamin Disraeli, a Jew who took a pro-Turkish stance in the Turkish-Russian conflict. The struggle between Russia and Turkey was interpreted as the collision of Christianity and the Semitic world.

4. Cf. Arthur Ruppin, *Les juifs dans le monde moderne* (Paris, 1934), p. 52.

5. Jews achieved political emancipation in Great Britain in 1866, in Austria-Hungary in 1867, in Germany in 1869, in Italy in 1870, in Switzerland in 1874, and in Russia in 1917, but not until 1919 in Poland, Romania, and the Baltic states, where it took the form of laws governing minorities.

6. Four years after the publication of Dohm's work, the Royal Academy of Sciences and Arts announced an essay competition, whose topic is itself characteristic: "Are there means by which to make the Jews of France more useful and happy?" Of the three prize-winning submissions, that by the lawyer Thierry is most obviously influenced by Dohm. Far more effective was a pamphlet published by Mirabeau in 1787, *Sur Moses Mendelssohn et sur la réforme politique des juifs*—both a review and in part a verbatim translation of Dohm's work.

7. Moses Mendelssohn, "Vorrede zur Übersetzung von Manasseh ben Israel, *Rettung der Juden*" [Preface to the translation of Manasseh ben Israel, *Vindication of the Jews*]. This preface appears separately as an appendix to the 2d edition of Dohm's work (1782).

8. Bruno Baner, *Die Judenfrage* [The Jewish Question] (1843), p. 87.

9. Christian Wilhelm Dohm, *Über die Bürgerliche Verbesserung der Juden* [On the Civic Improvement of Jews] (1781).

III ANTISEMITISM AND HATRED OF THE JEWS

1. What a great temptation it is to describe the survival of the Jewish people as a ghostly phenomenon becomes especially clear when Jews themselves make use of such images and metaphors. Thus Börne describes the "misfortune of the Jews" as follows: "It appears to arise out of a dark, unexplained horror that flows into Jewry, which like a specter, like the mocking and menacing ghost of a slain mother, accompanies Christianity from its cradle onward." *Für die Juden* [For the Jews], Part 1, 1839.

2. The interpretation of antisemitism as a *phobia of Jews* has become the official theory of Zionism. It was first introduced theoretically by Pinsker as a fear of ghosts ("Auto-emanzipation," 1st ed., 1882). Pinsker's error is very understandable. He saw before him the first signs of the failure of Western assimilation, which he was wise enough to interpret correctly. He tried to explain it, however, as coming from the hatred of Jews that he was familiar with in Russia.

3. That only a limited number of educated people would discredit themselves by being antisemites should have been apparent from the fact that in Germany it was the "educated" people who were the first antisemites and boasted about the healthy instincts of the common people—cf. Joseph Görres and Fries, a professor of philosophy in Berlin. Tracts presented the same material in a form understandable to everyone.

4. Wilhelm Marr, *Der Sieg des Judentums über das Germanentum*, p. 8 ff.

5. Ludwig Börne, *Für die Juden*, Part 1.

6. Quoted from H. Coudenhove, *Das Wesen des Antisemitismus* [Antisemitism throughout the Ages] (1901), p. 167.

7. In his appeal "To Pastors, That They May Preach against the Usurer" (1540), Luther shows his modern point of view insofar as he no longer mentions Jews as usurers, but speaks of how the lending of money was in fact praised as a Christian institution of "service and benefit."

8. Cf. Bernard of Clairvaux, 1146: "Petus judaizare dolemus Christianos foenerstores si tamen Christianos et non magis baptizatos Judaeos convenit appellare." Quoted in Coudenhove, *Das Wesen des Antisemitismus.*

IV USURERS, PARIAHS, PARASITES

1. Bavaria granted its court Jews special status in the early eighteenth century, at the very point in time when the operative regulations for Jews proved to be an impediment to these court Jews' new commercial activities. Cf. Paul Sundheimer, "Die jüdische Hochfinanz und der bayrische Staat im 18. Jahrhundert" [Jewish High Finance and the Bavarian State in the Eighteenth Century] (*Finanz-Archiv*, 41. Jahrgang, vol. 1 u. 2, 1924). The first liberated Jew in Bavaria was Noe Samuel Isaak. "For as long as he held a claim against debt owed him by the prince elector's house, he was not subject to the first article of the fifth book of state and police regulations. This meant that Noe was exempted from the rule that all commerce between a Bavarian subject and a Jew was invalid and punishable by confiscation" (p. 6). This provides clear evidence of how the way was opened for the first dealings between Jews and non-Jews in order to benefit the *state* and its immediate interests.

2. The reason the Prussian state owed such great gratitude to these two Jews to whom the mint was chartered is very amusingly described by R. Lewinsohn in *Les profits de la guerre:*

> En 1757 Frédéric II afferme les ateliers de la Monnaie de Dresde et de Leipzig aux banquiers Veitel Ephraim Fils et Daniel Itzig et autorise ces derniers à fabriquer 20 thalers avec la quantité d'argent qu'on employait jusqu'alors pour en frapper 14. . . . Au cours des années des guerres suivantes, ce système prend un nouveau développement. La Monnaie de Brandenbourg est également affermée aux banquiers Ephraim et Itzig qui sont autorisés à frapper des pièces contenant à peine 50% de la teneur antérieure en argent. Or, il ne s'agit pas seulement de mettre cette monnaie . . . en circulation à l'intérieur du pays, mais surtout de la répandre à l'étranger. . . . Le fait est que ce trafic . . . rapporte à l'état prusse pendant la dernière période de la guerre 6 millions de thalers par an.

3. Jews were seldom involved in commercial transactions in which credit was extended to merchants, and then usually only if the risk was so great that normal credit was not available. Thus in *The Merchant of Venice*, for example, a merchant borrows money from Shylock because his entire wealth is tied up in goods being shipped on dangerous sea routes.

4. Werner Sombart's demagogic, bogus theory that capital earned from Jewish usury was attendant at the birth of later capitalism (cf. *Die Juden und die Wirtschaft* [Jews and Modern Capitalism]) has been countered by F. Rachfahl in "Das Judentum und die Genesis des modernen Kapitalismus" [Jewry and the Genesis of Modern Capitalism] (*Preuss. Jhb.*, vol. 147, 1912) and Herman Waetjen in "Das Judentum und der Anfang der modernen Kolonisation" [Jewry and the Beginnings of Modern Colonization] (*Vierteljahrsschrift für Sozial- u. Wirtschaftsgeschichte*, vol. 11).

5. For the difference between usurious and capitalist credit, cf. F. W. Newman, *Lectures on Political Economy* (1851). "The banker differs from the usurer in that he lends money to the rich, but seldom or never to the poor. He lends at less risk and can thus offer better terms. For both these reasons he does not encounter the popular hatred directed against the usurer." Gilbert, *History and Principles of Banking* (1837), shows that usury was marginal to a feudal, that is, primarily agricultural society. "For someone in an agricultural society, a situation in which he needs to borrow money seldom arises unless he has been reduced to poverty and misery." He goes on to define the difference between the roles usury and credit play by noting that "in our day the rate of profit regulates the rate of interest, in those days the rate of interest regulated the rate of profit." This means that from the start capitalist production—far

from having arisen out of capital raised through usury—stood in open opposition to usury. Cf. Karl Marx, *Theorien über Mehrwert* [Theories of Added Valued], vol. 3, ch. 7, Appendix. "Capitalist production initially had to fight against usury to the extent that the usurer himself produced nothing." That the Jewish usurer did *not* produce anything is a characteristic of Jewish economic history during assimilation.

6. Cf. Max Weber, *Wirtschaftsgeschichte [General Economic History]*, ch. 3, sec. 8, "Der Zins in der vorkapitalistischen Epoche" [Interest in the precapitalist era], p. 287. What characterizes Jewish credit is

that it gave the state the opportunity to institute policies with a spongelike quality—exploitation of the population by Jewish rates of interest, followed at irregular intervals of confiscating the profits and outstanding loans, while at the same time expelling Jewish creditors. In this way Jews were hounded from town to town, from country to country; princes literally formed cartels for the purpose of robbing Jews, such as the one arranged by the bishop of Bamberg with the Hohenzollern burggrave of Nuremberg, by which they shared the booty whenever Jews had to flee from their respective areas of control.

7. Accumulation of large amounts of capital took place in England and Holland and in colonial trading companies. Waetjen, "Das Judentum und der Anfang der modernen Kolonisation," proves that Jews had little or nothing to do with this process.

8. Max Weber, *Wirtschaftsgeschichte*, p. 313. Cf. also Weber's *Religionssoziologie* [Sociology of Religion], vol. 1, p. 181 ff., where he differentiates Jewish capitalism, which he calls "speculative pariah capitalism," from its puritan form, which he calls "bourgeois organization of labor," and goes on to show that the latter has been the determinative factor in the development of modern capitalism.

9. The first antisemitic member of the Reichstag, Otto Boeckel, represented the farmers of Hessia. He owed his election solely to speeches inveighing against the Jewish usurers who lent to farmers and proclaiming his opposition to conservatives and large landholders. In the Reichstag he voted with the Free-Thinking Party and the Social Democrats. Cf. Kurt Wawrzinek, "Die Entstehung der deutschen Antisemitenparteien" [The Rise of German Antisemitic Parties], *Historische Studien*, H. 168, 1927.

V COURT JEWS AND HUMAN RIGHTS

1. Cf. the article "Finanz- und Bankwesen" [Finance and Banking] in the *Encyclopaedia Judaica*.

2. Cf. M. Grunwald, *Samuel Oppenheimer und sein Kreis* [Samuel Oppenheimer and His Circle] (1913). "After Oppenheimer's death (1703) it became apparent that his personal debts were closely intertwined with Austria's debt. A property tax of 5 million florins had been levied against him. His failure to pay had precipitated a very serious economic crisis. . . . His death (and his debt) was also an economic crisis for the state. Austria's creditors were in fact the emperor's creditors." Paul Sundheimer ("Die jüdische Hochfinanz und der bayrische Staat im 18. Jahrhundert" [Jewish High Finance and the Bavarian State in the Eighteenth Century] (*Finanz-Archiv*, 41. Jahrgang, vol. 1 u. 2, 1924, p. 13) describes the same state of affairs in Bavaria, where the elector prince himself had "urgently advised the representative assembly to pay moneys owed Noe when due, otherwise the Jew's own credit would be compromised, which would prove disadvantageous to the princely house."

3. The following figures help to illustrate the sums involved. They represent the percentages of a state's budget allotted to its armed forces during the period discussed here. They are taken from W. Sombart, *Studien zur Entwicklungsgeschichte des modernen Kapitalismus* [Studies in the History of the Development of Modern Capitalism], vol. 2, p. 51 ff.

Expenditures for the armed forces

Country	Year	Percentage
Switzerland	1639	60
	1680	74
France	1784	66
Brandenburg under the Great Elector Frederick Wilhelm I	1640–88	66
Prussia under Frederick I	1701–13	55
Prussia under Frederick II	1740–86	86
Prussia under Frederick Wilhelm III	1797–98	71
	1805–06	75

4. Paul Sundheimer ("Die Jüdische Hochfinanz," vol. 2, pp. 8–9): "Without doubt the Jews were always called in when there was no better way out. This fact is apparent both when Jews acted as moneylenders and when they were suppliers to the army."

5. In Bavaria, for example, "the state debt had grown to 20 million florins when the Jews Noe and Wertheimer were called upon for the purpose of supplying credit." Sundheimer, "Die Jüdische Hochfinanz," vol. 2, p. 43.

6. Cf. Grunwald, *Samuel Oppenheimer*, p. 168.

7. Alfred Philipp, *Die Juden und das Wirtschaftsleben. Eine antikritische-bibliographische Studie zu W. Sombart, Die Juden und das Wirtschaftsleben* [Jews and Modern Capitalism: An Anticritical-Bibliographic Study of W. Sombart, the Jews and Economic Life] (Strasbourg, 1929):

> In Prussia and probably other states as well, court Jews were very helpful in strengthening the absolutist rule of the prince over against the cities, estates, and the nobility directly attached to the Reich. Absolute monarchs deliberately used Jews for just this purpose. They were as important an instrument for building the modern state as the creation of a civil service loyal to the prince. In the struggle against the guilds for the purpose of advancing the principle of mercantile manufacture, the prince was happy to pit the Jews against the guilds.

8. Cf. R. Lewinsohn, *Les profits de la guerre*, p. 58 ff.

9. Sombart's sham history of how evil capitalism arose out of the evil capital of Jewish usury has long since been scientifically refuted. (Cf. p. 77, note 4.) An especially egregious example will have to suffice here. In his *Studien* Sombart contrasts the Fugger and Rothschild families, both of whom "owe their wealth to war," and then remarks that "they represent the two forms by which such wealth can be amassed; one could contrast them as the *German* and the *Jewish* forms, the direct advancement of a loan vs. the floating of a loan on the stock market. The one: *eye-to-eye personal credit*. The other: *impersonal credit behind the public's back*" (author's italics). In point of fact, of course, the same difference exists between all loans made in the nineteenth century over against those of the previous century—for example between those made by the Rothschilds and those made by court Jews. In the eyes of a German professor, if he is an antisemite, the *three hundred years* between the Fuggers and the Rothschilds are as but a day.

10. Quoted here from Franz Mehring, *Die Lessing Legende* [The Lessing Legend] (Stuttgart, 1906), p. 195.

11. Cf. Dubnow, *Weltgeschichte*, vol. 9, p. 3. It is a well-known fact that Napoleon's campaigns brought emancipation to the countries he conquered and that this was reversed by the Congress of Vienna at the express urging of the cities, especially of Frankfurt am Main. No sooner had Jews been "liberated" there than they were disenfranchised again. The same thing occurred in Hamburg, and in Lübeck there was an out-and-out expulsion of Jews. During the congress the cities declared that the *disenfranchisement of Jews* was their *right* by law and proved this in a brief prepared by the University of Berlin's legal faculty, which at the time was headed by Savigny, the founder of the historical school of jurisprudence; these reactionary findings carried no weight, however, in the Prussian capital itself.

12. According to Unna, *Statisik der Frankfurter Juden bis 1866* [Statistics for the Jews of Frankfurt until 1866], there were 939 employed Jews in 1824, and 547 self-employed businessmen, of whom 192 were involved in finance, 149 in the textile industry.

13. French policy toward Jews before the Revolution differentiated between Spanish and Portuguese (Sephardic) Jews and Alsatian (Ashkenazic) Jews. The former were hired tax collectors to whom the state was obligated, much as in Austria, Prussia, and other Central European countries. Prior to the Revolution, Alsatian Jews had a monopoly on peddling and usurious loans to farmers. The Declaration of 1791, which proclaimed the same human rights for all people, was followed in 1808 by the *décret infâme,* which reverted to the old distinction and introduced special conditions for Alsatian Jews, thereby allowing special privileges for the Jews of Bordeaux. The *décret infâme* corresponds exactly with the policy toward Jews pursued by other European states—with the one difference that, given the faster rate at which developments took place in France, the reestablishment of equal rights was achieved somewhat sooner.

14. The Austrian Tolerance Edict of Joseph II in 1787 opens all "Christian" trades to Jews, provides an economic bonus for baptism, even allows agriculture, and puts an end to the autonomy of Jewish communities. In practice, however, both forms of regulating Jews amounted to much the same thing, especially since in Vienna only "prosperous" Jews were tolerated and the prohibition against Jews settling there remained in effect.

VI EXCEPTIONAL JEWS

1. Cf. Heinrich Silbergleit, *Die Bevolkerungsverhältnisse der Juden im Deutschen Reich* [Population Ratios of Jews in the German Reich] (1930), Table 29, which singles out the year 1834 to compare Posen with all other regions of Prussia and provides percentages of Jewish families who earned their livings as:

	in Prussia	in Poland
1. Wholesalers, bankers, manufacturers	4.3%	0.9%
2. People of independent means	4.3%	0.9%
3. Independent professionals	4.3%	3.0%
4. Retailers, commissioned agents, innkeepers	49.3%	34.8%
5. Farmers	0.4%	0.4%
6. Peddlers	10.6%	7.9%
7. Craftsmen	10.0%	23.0%
8. Day laborers and menials	10.3%	7.3%
9. Charity cases without a profession	6.5%	21.3%

Categories 1 and 2 are classified here as the bourgeoisie, 3 and 4 as the middle class, 6, 7, 8, and 9 as persons without property. The very small category 5, of farmers, is distinct.

In the period before 1812 these differences were surely even more marked, since after 1816 there was a steady stream of Jews moving from West Prussia and Poland to other Prussian provinces. Between 1825 and 1834 all Prussian provinces excluding West Prussia and Posen showed an 18 percent increase in their Jewish populations, Posen and West Prussia an increase of only 11 percent—a difference definitely not due to a lower birth rate. An indication of this migration is the tenfold increase in the number of "foreigners" among the Jews of Berlin between 1816 and 1883, from 0.8 percent to 11 percent. Cf. Silbergleit, Table 9. The census of 1834 in Prussia does not distinguish between "native" Jews and "Eastern" Jews. One can surely assume, however, that a larger percentage of those Jews without property were not among the exceptional Jews of Prussia, but were instead part of those "Eastern Jews" who were assimilating only very slowly. In reality the professional and economic differences between Eastern and Western Jews must therefore have been far greater than the statistics for 1834 show.

2. Cf. Silbergleit, Tables 4, 5, and 9. For 1803 we are counting as "exceptional Jews" all those who

lived in areas that remained part of Prussia in 1808 and were therefore included in the Emancipation Edict of 1812. The 80 percent of "Eastern Jews" were to be found primarily in either West Prussia or Posen. According to the census of 1811, exceptional Jews make up circa 90 percent of the Jewish population in what was left of the state of Prussia, while 10 percent were Jewish "foreigners," that is, ordinary Jews without exceptional status or Eastern Jews. For the years 1816 and 1843 (and/or 1846), we can use the simple differentiation between Jews with or without rights of the city—that is, between those who were included in the Emancipation Edict and could claim an "exceptional" position, over against the Eastern Jews of the newly acquired provinces.

3. The tacit equation here of Eastern Jews, Jews without rights of the city, and Jews from the Posen region can be adequately justified by the fact that the latter accounted for an overwhelming percentage of "foreign Jews." In 1816 eight out of nine Jews were denied rights of the city, and by 1846 their number had "sunk" to four out of five.

4. The extent to which such tolerance had spread in educated circles is splendidly illustrated by a little anecdote from 1788. A Berlin production of *The Merchant of Venice* included a brief apologetic prologue addressed to "discerning Berlin," which "is beginning to have a higher regard for the brethren in faith of the wise Moses Mendelssohn."

5. Thus the salon of Henriette Herz was created by Count Dohna, and that of Rahel Levin was given its social stamp of approval by Prince Louis Ferdinand. One can also mention in this connection the very high number of marriages between Jews and aristocrats, which, unlike in later decades, had social consequences for their fellow Jews whom they left behind. The correspondence of the period shows that those who had newly arrived in such brilliant circles did not break off all Jewish connections.

6. This explains the explicit distaste with which the bourgeoisie of the period regarded all social presentation. The liberal writer Buchholz calls it a mere "sham." Friedrich Buchholz, *Untersuchungen über den Geburtsadel* [Observations on noble birth] (1807), p. 51 ff.

7. Viktor Hehn, *Gedanken über Goethe* [Thoughts on Goethe] (2d ed., 1888), p. 260 ff., where a "common citizen," an unbridled antisemite, raised to the nobility by the czar provides a very amusing—because it is so unthinkably disrespectful—example of how Goethe "worked his way up out of the petite bourgeoisie and suffered unutterably in cleansing himself of the dross."

8. Buchholz (*Untersuchungen über den Geburtsadel*), p. 151, notes with satisfaction that "whenever the urge for art or science awakened in the nobleman, he found it necessary to descend to the level of the common citizen."

9. This is to be taken with a grain of salt. When after 1807 the Jewish salons were deserted almost from one day to the next, new social gathering places formed, by way of transition, primarily in the homes of aristocrats, for instance of Countess Voss and Prince Radziwill. To that extent the salon of Privy State Councilor Stägemann was the exception. But it proved to be considerably more viable than all the others. Moreover, the nature of the attendees changed almost immediately. The bourgeois element predominated; those aristocrats who attended came from the military and civil service, that is, from the lower ranks of the nobility. Actors and Jews were excluded. Cf. H. Arendt, "Berlin Salon" (Berliner Salon, *Deutscher Almanach*, 1932), in H. Arendt, *Essays in Understanding*, ed. J. Kohn (New York: Schocken Books, 2005), pp. 57–65.

10. From an unpublished letter (1819) from Rahel Varnhagen to Pauline Wiesel, who at one time was the mistress of Louis Ferdinand. Varnhagen Archive of the Berliner Staatsbibliothek.

VII SOCIETY AND STATE ABOLISH EXCEPTIONAL JEWS

1. Cf. Wilhelm von Humboldt, letters to his wife, 1808.

2. Cf. Egon Caesar Conte Corti, *Der Aufstieg des Hauses Rothschild* [The Rise of the House of Rothschild], pp. 120 ff., 189 ff. The story of the Rothschild coat of arms is both very revealing and amusing.

The design that the brothers presented to the Austrian emperor for his approval contained a whole collection of heraldic insignia, lots of animals, and a crown. The Austrian inspector for heraldic designs said that "the Israelite nation was not familiar enough with the merits of the eagle," and brutally removed all the animals and the crown. The Rothschilds were left with only two half-eagles.

3. The story of the house of Rothschild offers an excellent example of this development. Old Meyer Amschel (late eighteenth century) still concluded regular credit transactions with private persons. His sons earned enormous sums by lending to states, especially to Austria, but often lent money at no interest to private persons for the sole purpose of securing their social position. The third generation would have nothing to do with such private loans, and simply paid bribes. Cf. Conti, *Der Aufstieg des Hauses Rothschild,* vols. 1 and 2.

4. Friedrich Buchholz, *Untersuchungen über den Geburtsadel,* p. 167 ff.

5. Grattenauer made use of a recently published work in Latin, *De civitate Judaeorum,* by criminal councilor Paalzow, which provided convoluted and boring proof of the civic immaturity of Jews.

6. Indicative of Grattenauer's subservience and lack of character is a statement from 1803, when the aristocracy still dared to show some liberal tendencies. "The education of the human race since the reestablishment of the sciences has been directly and indirectly generated, advanced, and disseminated by the aristocracy."

7. "It is quite absurd for the Jewish *gens*—which to demonstrate their culture walk about the Tiergarten on stilts, publicly gorge themselves on bacon on the Shabbat, memorize aloud Kiessewetter's *Logic* or sing arias from *Herodes* while strolling our promenades—to think they dare demand exceptions be made to general strictures of the law."

8. "To my mind it remains an inexplicable contradiction how someone can believe he has a perfect right to demand my regard and trust in private life, and yet is capable of enduring public discrimination, whereby I may regard his testimony in court as only conditionally valid and his oath as only conditionally sacred."

9. "The conversation begins with an apostrophe to the enlightened age . . . which is followed by some boring tale concerning the person they have just taken their leave of, how interesting the topic of conversation had been, to what grand persons of rank they must now speed upon their way in posthaste haste. . . ."

10. As was the case with Heinrich Heine and Rahel Varnhagen.

11. Only in Hungary—as a result of especially backward conditions and the total absence of a native bourgeoisie—did assimilation into the aristocracy continue into recent times. Which explains why Hungary has the highest percentage of Jewish baptisms and mixed marriages, three times as many, for example, as Vienna, which also ranks at the top.

12. Cf. Wilhelm von Humboldt, "Gutachten zur Emanzipation von 1809" [Opinion on Emancipation from 1809], in Freund, *Judenemancipation* (1912), vol. 2, p. 270 ff.

13. Cf. Reinhold Steig, *Kleists Berliner Kämpfe* [Kleist's Battles in Berlin].

14. Cf. Adam Müller, *Elemente der Staatskunst, Vorlesungen gehalten* 1808–9 [Elements of Statecraft, Lectures Held in 1808–9]; and Joseph Görres, "Fall der Religion und ihre Wiedergeburt" [The Fall of Religion and Its Rebirth] (1810), in *Politische Schriften* [Political Writings], vol. 1, p. 132 ff.

VIII THE ARISTOCRACY TURNS ANTISEMITIC

1. Cf. "Letzte Vorstellung der Stänter der Lebusischen Kreises" [Most recent remonstrance of the estates of Lebus province] from 1811 with marginal notes by Hardenberg for the king. The author of this especially sharply worded petition by the Junkers is presumably Ludwig von der Marwitz, the most gifted spokesman for the Prussian aristocracy at the time. The "Vorstellung" together with marginal glosses was published in Meusel, *Ludwig von der Marwitz* (Berlin: 1908), vol. 2.

2. This is revealed with special clarity in Hardenberg's direct report to the king on June 23, 1811, where, among other things, he says: "They [the feudal interests] present themselves as coregents and if one were to allow them their interpretation which cedes to them obsolete positions and agreements, there would be few remaining instances where their concurrence would not first be required in the exercise of princely rights . . . and royal decisions."

3. It is clear even from the presentation of a Delbrück, who was loyal to the Hohenzollerns, that the so-called citizen or liberal reforms had very little to do with freedom, and with the bourgeoisie only to the extent that the sole means of securing the apparatus of the absolute state over against the aristocracy was via the circuitous route of those few reforms. He writes: "The rebuilding of the state was accomplished not with a mind to freedom, but by means of a much more rigorous centralization with a view to increasing bureaucratic absolutism." Delbrück-Molinski, *Weltgeschichte* [World History], vol. 2, p. 273 ff.

4. The "most recent remonstrance" quoted above predicts in great detail the dangers the king would encounter if he found himself all alone and confronted by the masses of the people, and in no position to risk "arousing discontent." There could be no security for the king unless the aristocracy continued to be a kind of "middle estate" between him and the people.

5. Hardenberg was the most determined—though personally very hesitant—representative of the attempt to curb the Junkers. Thus, in opposition to the Junkers, he remarked that "the middle estate described here will form on its own." But the price would have been no less and no more than a constitution, just as the bourgeoisie, in their fierce fight for "throne and altar," later proved to the constitutional monarchy.

6. Cf. Ismael Freund, *Judenemanzipation* [Jewish emancipation] (1812), vol. 2, *Urkunden* [Documents].

7. Just as "Prussian reform was something that came from the top down and not the bottom up" and was initiated "by the will of the king" and not coerced by the people or the citizens (Delbrück, *Weltgeschichte*, vol. 2, p. 274), so, too, Prussian reformers were not simply representatives of the bourgeoisie, but primarily civil servants of the Prussian state. Stein had followed a career in the civil service since 1780 and Hardenberg since 1792. They "quite rightly saw themselves as . . . carrying on the mission of the absolute monarchy, and did so by representing the fundamental ideas of the modern state over against privileged feudal interests" (Meusel, in his introduction to Marwitz's collected writings, p. xxxviii). This—and not bourgeois motives—was the source of the bitter hostility toward feudal interests, just as it, and not the French Revolution or the German Enlightenment, was the source of cordial attitudes toward the Jews.

8. Stein's reforms required that upon being "liberated," peasants cede at least one-third of their land to their landlord, and indeed, if the latter had a claim on them by inheritance, half of it.

9. The buying and selling of landed property and the ceding of large portions of peasant lands left the landlords in the position of being able to buy out the peasants entirely, and of thus enlarging their landed holdings—something Marwitz had predicted by the way.

10. Cf. Franz Mehring, *Zur preussischen Geschichte* [On Prussian History], p. 131 ff.

11. The almost accidental equation of pro-Jewish and pro-bourgeois polemics can be found in Clemens von Brentano's foolish pamphlet, "Der Philister vor, in und nach der Geschichte" [The Philistine Before, In, and After History], which in part equated Jews with philistines, but also presented the two as opposite poles of the same issue: the Enlightenment. Also interesting in this context is the very nasty portrayal of Hardenberg as the representative of a "major trait of all philistines": "statecraft bound with scurrility."

12. Commerce in metals, the garment industry, dealing in grain, and banking—economic activities that furnished the most important positions held by Jews in almost all countries—had all arisen during the eighteenth century out of the business of supplying war materials or out of financial dealings with

the state and/or state manufactures. In the economy of the nineteenth century the Jews merely expanded upon positions that they had already assumed in a different economic context.

13. Letter of Friedrich Engels from 1890, in S. V. Adler, *Reden und Briefe* [Speeches and letters] (1929), vol. 1.

14. Ludwig von der Marwitz, "Letzte Vorstellung der Stände der Lebusischen Kreises."

15. Meusel, *Ludwig von der Marwitz*, vol. 1, p. 402.

16. Joseph Görres, *Politische Schriften*, vol. 1, p. 163.

17. According to von der Marwitz, "genuine noble families" do not have charters: "their power and prestige arose early and was handed down before there was any such thing as a charter."

18. Cf. Lorzen von Stein, *Geschichte der sozialen Bewegungen* [History of the Social Movement], vol. 1, p. 157 ff. Stein still defines the landed property of the aristocracy as "historical property whose original acquisition cannot be traced in thousands of cases. Feudal property is the opposite of "capital" or bourgeois property, which, because it has "resulted from labor," is called "acquired property."

19. Ludwig von der Marwitz, "Letzte Vorstellung der Stände der Lebusischen Kreises."

20. "The son of every peasant wants to be a craftsman, every craftsman's son wants to be a scribe, the son of every scribe would be a president, of every schoolmaster a scholar, of every merchant or scholar a great lord." Meusel, *Ludwig von der Marwitz*, vol. 2, p. 270.

21. Cf. Corti, *Aufstieg und Blütezeit des Hauses Rothschild*. On the occasion of shares being floated by France's Northern Railway, Heinrich Heine described what participation in Rothschild shares meant:

Every share that this house grants to any individual is a favor—or to put it in no uncertain terms—a monetary gift granted by Herr von Rothschild to his friends. Even before they are traded, such shares . . . are worth several hundred francs above face value and anyone who begs Baron James de Rothschild for such shares at face value is a beggar in the truest sense of the word. But all the world is now a beggar before him, beggars' letters rain down upon him, and since the elegant world has set the dignified example, there is no longer any shame in begging. (*Lutezia*, Part 2, lvii)

Heine has often been accused of being such a "participant" himself, who, boasting "of an eagerness worthy of a publicist of manifold influence," maintained that he saw in Rothschild "a kind of natural confederate" and without a trace of false shame laid "claim to a subsidy from an allied power." Cf. the relationship between Heine and Rothschild in Friedrich Hirth, "Heine und Rothschild," *Deutsche Rundschau*, January/March and October/December 1915.

22. Within the Jewish community, the notables, especially the Rothschilds, took the side of the Orthodox against the Jewish Reform movement. In the 1830s the Orthodox faction of Frankfurt petitioned the Federal Council in opposition to a Reform rabbi who was the choice of the majority of the community. When the rabbi was nevertheless installed by Frankfurt's Jewry, the Rothschilds withdrew their gift of a synagogue. Even before Gabriel Riesser, Reform Jews were almost as disreputable in the eyes of the notables as openly revolutionary Jews.

23. Ludwig Börne, *Briefe aus Paris* [Letters from Paris], p. 78, letter of March 1832.

24. At issue is the Law for the Estates of the Provinces of 1823, in which for the first time the government officially linked the right to elect and be elected to a person's being "in communion with a Christian church." This was an open revocation of the Edict of 1812.

❖❖❖ II ❖❖❖

THE 1940s

THE MINORITY QUESTION

(Copied from a letter to Erich Cohn-Bendit, summer 1940)

I

The Jewish question was represented by two parties at the peace conference of 1918–20: first, by Zionists, who prior to the negotiations already had come to a special agreement with Britain (the Balfour Declaration, 1917)—that is, with one of the great powers; and second, by representatives of the masses of Jews in those Eastern European states that were about to be established. Both parties claimed to be a kind of solution to the Jewish question and both placed themselves under the League of Nations as their juridical and political guarantor. Nevertheless the Zionists did organize their own political arm in the form of what would later become the Jewish Agency, whereas Le Comité des Délégations Juives, the parallel body for Jewish minorities, was never defined as a political agent, but functioned simply as a complaint office that reported to the League and supplied delegates to minority congresses—that is, functioned as its own unpaid lawyer. This initial difference, which proved to be of advantage to the Zionists, was no accident. The Zionists after all had things to do: colonize, bring people to their country, raise money, and so forth; whereas the Jewish minorities were thought of as something inert and lacking all initiative, as if created by God merely so that they could be protected from pogroms.

Both these Jewish delegations acted and spoke without actually being rooted in the Jewish people. This again was less the case for the Zionists than for the delegates of the Jewish minorities, who had no organization whatever behind them. Jews from countries where emancipation had occurred—which meant essentially from those countries that would be making the decisions in these negotiations—did not want any kind of political representation, since they viewed themselves as simply a religious minority that as such was sufficiently protected—not as Jews, however, but as French-men, Britons, Germans, and so forth. This had two consequences. First, from the start, legislation concerning minorities had, for the Jews, a provisional, temporary quality. It was an expedient solution until actual emancipation, and/or until Polish, Romanian, and other Jews had been granted sufficient protection as Poles and Romanians, and/or until such states had achieved a level of civil maturity that there could be no question of their providing such protection. Second, it meant that the delegates for Jewish minorities were regarded as provincial representatives of certain geographically defined Jewries who were in no way connected with the rest of the Jewish people.

The goal of all legislation concerning minorities was to depoliticize minorities—for which cultural autonomy seemed the appropriate instrument. It has often been said that the Jews are the minority par excellence because they lack a motherland—a statement that is true at least to the extent that they were the only existing minority that could be completely depoliticized because they lacked the one political factor that, regardless of all legislated definitions, inevitably politicizes a minority: a motherland.

If then, for the purposes of critical analysis, one places oneself within the context of those negotiations, one has to say that the task of the Jewish delegates was to create a substitute for their motherland, and to do so quite independently of the issue of protection. Given the state of the question of nationality at the time, even without Hitler, the minorities would, for lack of political air, have suffocated in the vapors of their schools and synagogues.

A substitute for a motherland could have been provided both by Palestine—indeed by the mere idea of Palestine—and by so-called world Jewry. For various reasons the latter did not in fact exist and manifested itself only insofar as it denied a national quality to these newly created minorities—in order to extinguish their breath of life. Even back then, Zionism had no political solution for the Diaspora—which will perish for that same reason. Although all or almost all Jewish minority politicians (with the exception of Dubnow) were Zionists, it occurred to none of them to make use of the World Zionist Organization—the sole Jewish political organ, one recognized moreover by one of the great powers—or even to connect the two questions with one another. That would not have been impossible. What might have been said was: We, who have been granted the right to a national homeland in Palestine, demand the rights of a national minority in all the other countries of the world. These minorities will be protected by an organization of our own making (an elected body, and thus something more than a Comité des Délégations Juives); on the other hand we demand that you help us in Palestine (by importing Palestinian products, by tax policies—after the fashion of the Karen Hayesod, which would then never have sunk from a national institution to a farcical association, etc.). It then would have been clear to everyone that whoever strikes at Palestine is also at the very least striking at those Jews who have been recognized as minorities; and whoever strikes at the *golah* strikes at Palestine. This inescapable connection exists de facto in any case, but has failed to penetrate the conscious political thought of either group. And this was in the interest of the notables, whose claim of authority would have been badly shaken in the event of such a confederacy.

(All the factors leading to the failure of Jewish national politics can be demonstrated from the history of Zionism. That would presumably be more productive—and more could be learned from the mistakes that were made—than from any criticism of notables. For whereas notables are constantly sabotaging things for the sake of their own easily understood interests and their sabotage represents a genuine segment within the Jewish people, the Zionists sabotage their own movement. But more about that in another context.)

II

All politics dealing with minorities, and not just with the Jews, have foundered on the existent and abiding fact of state sovereignty. The League of Nations turned out to be a club that one could resign from whenever one wanted. Since by the end of the war significant minorities existed only in the newly created states, it was absurd that the rights of minorities—that is, a diminishment of state sovereignty—were forced upon the states that were constituted *against* Germany, while Germany itself was exempted. It was clear from this that in the future as well only the great nations could be counted on.

The fact of these arrangements, that is, the lack of minorities in these states, fundamentally changed as early as the Russian mass emigrations—at the latest by 1923–24. At this time we can observe the emergence of a new class of people in Europe, the *stateless*. If one regards European history as the development of the European nation-state, or as the development of European peoples into nation-states, then these people, the stateless, are the most important product of recent history. Since 1920 almost all European states have sheltered great masses of people who have no right of residence or consular protection of any sort—modern pariahs. That minority rights could not apply to them was an immediate hallmark of the failure of such rights—they foundered on this most modern of phenomena.

The inability to absorb these masses of people clearly demonstrates that the fact of assimilation has lost its crucial significance. There is no longer any such thing as assimilation in Europe—nation-states have grown too developed and too old. There is no longer any assimilation for Jews either. The chance of assimilation during the nineteenth century—actually, the late eighteenth century—was based in a reorganization of peoples that arose out of the French Revolution and in their development as nations. This process has now come to an end. No one else can be included. In fact, we now have the process in reverse: the addition of great masses of people and their degradation to pariahs.

Although they are Europeans, these pariahs are isolated from all specifically national interests. They are the first to have an interest in pan-European politics and, despite their various origins, such politics do bind, or could bind them together. But such politics can provide them no way of losing their original nationalities—even though that loss is their only chance. If everything were to play out very well, they might be the forerunners of a new Europe.

III

But let us simply disregard for now the very necessary critique of minority rights as they existed and functioned before the present war. There was something absurd about the issue in and of itself. Even in an ideal situation minorities can demand no more than cultural autonomy. Culture without politics—that is, without history and a national context—becomes vapid folkloristics and *Volk*-barbarism. The danger exists not only in Palestine; it was also clearly evident after the war in the degeneration of Jewish youth groups in both Poland and Germany. The intention was to establish modern minority rights on an exclusively juridical basis, but there was no change whatever in the underlying state of affairs. Only politics could have changed that; a people can be a minority somewhere only if they are a majority elsewhere. That fact cannot be dismissed with tricks like declaring the Jews a minority par excellence. That simply means they are not a minority at all.

I do not need to discuss at any length the most modern solution of the minority question, which consists of reimportation—much to the relief of states that have watched as minorities, genuine minorities, have been forced by their own majority to act politically and become a state within a state. Satisfying such minorities by gaining their agreement—cf. South Tyrol—clearly demonstrates that under current circumstances there appears to be no real solution to the question of nationality. As for the Jews, these newest methods are especially dangerous for them because they cannot be reimported to any motherland, to a state where they are a majority. For them it can only be a matter of deportation. Projects of this sort existed before the war and have multiplied since the Evian Conference. It is a very bad sign that the Zionist Organization has never protested such projects and that Jewish participation in this nonsense has included large segments of the territorialist movement—and all former notables tend to be territorialists. One should never sign one's own death warrant.

IV

From what has been said so far, it is obvious that my own inclination as regards this whole question is to throw the baby out with the bathwater. I simply do not believe in any improvement in the minority rights of Jews and to me it seems absurd to demand "better guarantees."

No European people is suffering as much as we are under these new circumstances. Not the Poles, not the Czechs. Our only chance—indeed the only chance of all small peoples—lies in a new European federal system. Our fate need not and dare not be bound up with our status as a minority.

That would leave us devoid of all hope. Our fate can only be bound up with that of other small European peoples. The notion that nations are constituted by settlement within borders and are protected by their territory is undergoing a crucial correction. Spaces that can truly be maintained economically and politically are constantly expanding. There may soon come a time when the idea of belonging to a territory is replaced by the idea of belonging to a commonwealth of nations whose politics are determined solely by the commonwealth as a whole. That means European politics—while at the same time all nationalities are maintained. Folkloristics would no longer be a danger within such a comprehensive arrangement. Until we have reached that stage, it makes no sense for us to return to the issue of minority arrangements—if only to prove that nationality does not perish when separated from soil.

The nineteenth century bestowed upon us the amalgamation of nation and state. Since Jews everywhere were loyal to the state—you do recall, don't you?—they had to attempt to shed their nationality, they had to assimilate. The twentieth century has shown us the ultimate consequences of nationalism, as evidenced by horrible relocations of peoples and various massacres, beginning with the Armenians and Ukrainian pogroms. The British Commonwealth reveals—in a distorted form, as is often, indeed usually the case—the rudiments of a new arrangement. Someone who is part of the British Empire does not therefore cease to be an Indian or a Canadian. That is another reason why this war—and the existence of England, the last bulwark against the new barbarism—is so important for us. Belief in a single homogeneous European nation is belief in a utopia—and not a pretty one at that. Such a belief could originate only in America—and then only on the basis of a United Europe. But I do not think it is utopian to hope for the possibility of a commonwealth of European nations with a parliament of its own.

As for us at least, this would be our sole salvation. And only because it has a chance—a real chance, in my opinion, though a small one—is there any point in wracking one's brains over it. Within such a commonwealth we could be recognized as a nation and be represented in a European parliament. For this "solution" of the Jewish question, the conundrum of a people without land in search of a land without people—practically speaking, the moon, or a folktale free from politics—would finally have become meaningless. It is in this framework that I see the "organized units" that are called for. To be sure, the very existence of the Jewish people would then depend on them.

The first prerequisite for such organizing is for us to be rid of all those Jews who do not want to be Jews. I assume that the already evident trend to be baptized will soon take on greater dimensions. We can only be glad of that. Even under the best circumstances the times will remain far too grave for us to continue to afford the luxury of assuming before the whole world moral and political responsibility for people who do not want to be part of us and are virtual traitors, inasmuch as they consider no means too awful, no path too degrading, if it leads to their individual escape hatch.

Recognition of the Jewish people by representation in a European parliament can only accelerate this process. But as I have already said, I likewise consider utterly passé any fears of complete assimilation, which could only be avoided by concentrating our numbers within a given territory. To the extent that assimilation is the process of making Europeans out of the masses of Eastern Jews, it is—God willing—already irreversible. There is no longer any need to attach moral ambiguity and dishonor to that process. Assimilation in the old style, however, leads irreversibly to baptism and to its own absurdity. Naturalization is actually already pointless as well. Since it takes three generations for people to truly become Frenchmen, Britons, or whatever, it cannot in fact be done at any less a cost. (The case is different with America!) And one can wait out those three generations only if by improbable good luck naturalizations bestowed by one government are not then later revoked by another. Three generations are simply not a starting point. If the pariah once had a chance of becoming a parvenu, it is now our chance politically to show that individual escape hatches—the Foreign Legion and so on—no longer exist for the individual but only for the masses, making them, of course, all the shabbier. Which means that all potential parvenus, who necessarily envision "individual" solutions, are grouped into masses and are on their way to being organized. And that will, with God's help, also change their attitudes.

V

In contrast to arrangements for minorities—which were always valid for only one country and implied that there were no Jews outside of the country in question—the organization itself must above all preserve a context of solidarity for the people as a whole. This means that, under certain circumstances, Palestine might regain its importance—although I find this territorial experiment increasingly problematic. In any case without an all-inclusive Jewish organization in both Europe and America that will take up the cause of Palestine as a region of settlement, it will be impossible to hold on to Palestine much longer—if only because the entire Near East will foot the bill only over against a united Europe.

What such a national alliance stretching across all of Europe would look like in juridical terms—that is, what concrete shape it would take—is still fairly enigmatic to my mind, though I pin great hopes on it. I previously thought in terms of professional organizations—the monopolization of certain chains of productions from their incipiency to their marketing—on the basis of a well-thought-out redeployment. But I am no longer certain about that idea either. In any case, the most important precondition for this to occur—our having been forced out of the intermediary professions—is already a reality. And that opens up the possibility of our depending in the future on workers and other productive elements.

Our worst political, and indeed factual, handicap will doubtless arise within our own ranks, among American Jews, who in total "naïveté" have inherited the role of the notables. One must admit, however, that they are also paying for it. American Jewry will doubtless assume it has the right to decide our fate and attempt to eliminate our own right to self-determination— like the directors of European origin on the American Jewish Joint Distribution Committee.

VI

To summarize: If even prior to the experiences of the last few years, solidarity on the part of the Jews with other minorities was extremely problematic, it has now proved to be harmful. All that remains of minority politics is the attempt to force us into the position of a minority in Palestine. On the other hand there is much to be said for the idea that solidarity with the other small European nations, whose territorial existence can no longer be assured, is increasingly becoming more meaningful and promising. Perhaps as a member of a European commonwealth and as part of a European state, the Jewish people can also look for a region to settle or actually hold on to Palestine. Any area of settlement outside of such a commonwealth and lacking its guarantees can be only a chimera or end in deportation to forced labor.

1940

THE JEWISH WAR
THAT ISN'T HAPPENING
Articles from Aufbau, *October 1941–November 1942*

The House of Judah's Gratitude?

Open Letter to Jules Romains
[1885–1972, French writer, president of PEN, 1941]

October 24, 1941

Dear Jules Romains,

Far be it from me to interfere in the quarrels of various PEN clubs or in the differences that some members of that organization appear to have with one another. But in your open letter to Mr. Ferdinand Bruckner (*Aufbau*, October 17) you turn, strangely enough, to a topic that makes this quarrel among high priests a matter of great interest to the purely lay circles of Jewish refugees. You complain in fact very loudly and articulately about the ingratitude of Jews for whom you have done so much. We Jews, as you yourself suggest several times, are not much liked in this world, and it will certainly sadden many of us to lose yet another protector or at least to have angered him. But there will also be a few among us who in reading your letter do not respond with sadness in our hearts, but with a blush of shame. I would be very pleased if the following considerations could show you that everything depends upon these latter few—even at the risk of your never again assisting a Jewish colleague to obtain a visa to flee or be granted release from a concentration camp by the Ministry of the Interior.

Let me begin then with what you believe you have done for the Jews. First there is the scandalous affair at the Prague Congress, where, as you tell it, Wells [H. G. Wells, 1866–1946] refused to agree to a resolution against antisemitism, and you pushed the resolution through and thereby, as you see it, saved the honor of PEN. For what should one actually be grateful? Without doubt you took this political step neither for the sake of persecuted Jews in Germany, whom this resolution could neither benefit nor harm, nor for the Jewish members of PEN, but rather solely because you were of the opinion that antisemitism is an unjust, cruel, and ignoble policy that poisons the political life of nations—that is, for the sake of your own honor and the reputation of the organization you represent. At that point the Jewish members of the German delegation were presumably still of the opinion—which in the meantime has proved false—that they were representatives of the antifascist cause in German letters rather than officially protected Jews, and that they could regard you as an ally and comrade-in-arms, rather than as a benefactor.

The same holds true, *mutatis mutandis,* for those Jews whom you helped to acquire French visas or to gain a short-lived release from French concentration camps. I happened to know one of these fortunate people very well. We often spoke of how the example you provided was a good sign that the French spirit was alive and well, that French writers could demonstrate collegiality despite all political differences and present dangers. For that very reason Europe appeared not yet to have died in France. In our conversations neither he nor I would have dreamed that there could be any mention of gratitude.

It does not speak against these Jews, but rather *for* them, for their *courage,* not for their *cowardice,* that as pariahs everywhere in this world they dared to stand in opposition to or at least not on the side of their benefactors when they no longer agreed with the latter's politics. Whatever one may think of a "policy of suffocation," the chief witnesses that you offer in your cause can only impress those who know nothing of French political conditions. It is true that one should never kick a dead lion, but one should also never forget that it was Daladier's [1884–1970, French politician] close friend and later propaganda minister Giraudoux [1882–1944, French writer] who with his *Pleins Pouvoirs* made antisemitism socially acceptable again for the first time since the Dreyfus affair; and that it is to Sarraut's [1872–1962, French politician] cynical, candid, and creative antisemitic genius that we can attribute the fact that thousands of young Jews are currently perishing in the Sahara, all under the terrible magic formula: *libéré sous condition d'engagement dans la Légion Etrangère* [released on condition of joining the Foreign Legion].

What concerns us Jews in all this and what makes us blush again for the hundredth time is our despairing question: Is our alternative truly only between malevolent enemies and condescending friends? Are genuine allies nowhere to be found, allies who understand, not out of either sympathy or bribery, that we were merely the first European nation on whom Hitler declared war? That in this war our freedom and our honor hang in the balance no less than the freedom and honor of the nation to which Jules Romains belongs? And that condescending gestures like the arrogant demand for gratitude from a protector cuts deeper than the open hostility of antisemites?

An answer to these questions would exceed the bounds of this letter and scarcely be of any interest to you. But in closing, might I—in order to avoid any misunderstanding—remind you of Clemenceau's [1841–1929, French politician] stance in the Dreyfus affair? Of Clemenceau, the only person who—throughout that odious tale of social scandal, which, as Halévy [1872–1962, social and cultural historian] put it, was an argument between two lies—in taking the side of the condemned Jew, was fighting for the survival of his own cause, the Third Republic, and who never expected gratitude from those Jews whose cowardice he despised and denounced countless times. He, you see, understood that in a political battle there are only enemies and friends, but no benefactors and protégés. "Un des ennuis de ceux qui luttent pour la justice c'est d'avoir contre eux avec la haine des oppresseurs, l'ignorance, la faiblesse et trop souvent le lâche coeur des opprimés" [What lames those who struggle for a just cause is that, along with the hatred of the oppressors, they must also do battle with the ignorance, weakness, and all too frequent cowardly hearts of the oppressed].

The Jewish Army—The Beginning of Jewish Politics?

November 14, 1941

Prompted by the anniversary of the Balfour Declaration [1917], America's Zionist organizations have openly demanded a Jewish army for the defense of Palestine. The demands and resolutions of a political avant-garde that do not express the immediate will of the whole can result in creative policies only if those demands successfully mobilize wider circles of the people. If that does not happen, the best of programs, the most correct of decisions, end up in history's wastepaper basket of failed and fumbled possibilities.

What is still today the isolated demand of Palestinian Jewry and its representatives outside of Palestine must tomorrow become the living will of a majority of the Jewish people to join the battle against Hitler as Jews, in Jewish battle formations under a Jewish flag. *The defense of Palestine is part of the struggle for the freedom of the Jewish people.* Only if the Jewish people are prepared to give their all for this struggle will they also be able to defend Palestine.

The Jewish will to live is both famous and infamous. Famous, because it spans a relatively long period in the history of European peoples. Infamous, because over the last two hundred years it has threatened to degenerate into something totally negative: the will to survive at any price. Our national misery begins with the collapse of the Shabbetai Tzevi movement [Shabbetai Tzevi, 1626–76, Jewish messianic pretender]. Ever since then we have proclaimed our existence per se—without any national or usually any religious content—as a thing of value. The Jewish nation has begun to resemble an old man who at eighty wagers with himself that he can make it to 120, and with the help of an overrefined diet and the avoidance of all activity, renounces life and dedicates himself to survival; he lives from one birthday to the next and rejoices in that one day of the year on which he can proclaim to relatives who are not entirely well-wishers, You see, I've done it again. At present Hitler is busy trying to snuff out that old man's life. What we all hope is that he is wrong, that he's dealing not with old men, but with the men and women of a nation.

A Jewish army is not utopian if the Jews of all countries demand it and are prepared to volunteer for it. But what is utopian is the notion that we could profit in some way from Hitler's defeat, if we do not also contribute to it. Only the real war of the Jewish people against Hitler will put an end—and an honorable end—to all fantastical talk about a Jewish war. An old and very contemporary Zionist proverb says that freedom is no gift. *Freedom is also not a prize for suffering endured.*

One truth that is unfamiliar to the Jewish people, though they are beginning to learn it, is that *you can only defend yourself as the person you are attacked as.* A person attacked as a Jew cannot defend himself as an Englishman or Frenchman. The world would only conclude that he is simply not defending himself. Perhaps this precept of political battle has now been learned by those tens of thousands of French Jews who feared a "Jewish war" and thought they had to defend themselves as Frenchmen, only to end up separated from their French fellow warriors and interned in Jewish prison camps in Germany. And certainly it has been learned by those hosts of Jewish volunteers who as French Legionnaires of various sorts believed that their own battle against Hitler would lead to naturalization, and who are now sitting in French internment camps or busy building the Sahara Railway. They can speak of their good luck if they have not been deployed in direct battle against Britain and Russia.

Just as in life friendship is distorted and ruined by fixation on a person, so too in politics the unconditional identification of one's own cause with the cause of another distorts and ruins an alliance. The Jews in Palestine know that, as evidenced by their refusal to let their own cause vanish into the British cause—and yet they have no more fervent wish than truly to help the British. They know that they can help neither themselves nor the British if they do not take up arms for themselves—as Jews, in Jewish battle formations under a Jewish flag, henceforth visible to all as the allies of Britain.

Jews today are obsessed with the fixed idea of their own meaninglessness. Some of them hope this means they can exit the political stage yet once again, and some are in honest despair at belonging to a powerless and evidently completely depoliticized group. We too have not been untouched by the sickness that has befallen the nations of Europe: despair, cynical disappointment, and imagined helplessness.

The storm that will be unleashed in our own ranks by the formation of a Jewish army with volunteers from around the world will make clear to those in honest despair that we're no different from anyone else, that we too engage in politics, even if you usually have to extract it painfully from the murky code of the petitions of Jewish notables and charitable organizations, and despite the fact that our politics has been especially adept at alienating itself from the Jewish people. We are, however, hardly the only people who have been led to the rim of the abyss of destruction by a plutocratic regime. War is too serious a matter, Clemenceau said, to be left to the generals. Well, *the existence of a people is definitely too serious a matter to be left to the rich.*

The question of the formation of a Jewish army will not be decided by statesmen in secret discussions or by petitions signed by influential Jews. We will never get that army if the Jewish people do not demand it and are not prepared by the hundreds of thousands with weapons in hand to fight for their freedom and the right to live as a people. Only the people themselves, young and old, poor and rich, men and women, can reshape public opinion, which today is against us. *For only the people themselves are strong enough for a true alliance.*

Active Patience

November 28, 1941

The British government has once again rejected the formation of a Jewish army. Which is to say that Britain is not yet ready to make the cause of freedom entirely its own. And—like the Indians—we shall once more have to be patient.

If it is true that politics can be compared to drilling very slowly into a very hard board (Max Weber), then patience in politics means to continue drilling steadily—and not apathetically waiting for a miracle. Miracles don't happen in this world, but even very hard boards can be drilled all the way through.

All the same, this rejection forces upon us a pause that we should patiently use for better and more fundamental preparation. And for that it can be useful to engage in some theoretical reflections whose immediate purpose is *to strengthen Jewish self-awareness and weaken Jewish arrogance.* Jewish feelings of inferiority—what can we do, we're a very minor factor in the current struggle—would never feel so free to express themselves if it were not for the Jewish arrogance that stands behind them: nothing can happen to us, the world cannot live without Israel.

When at the end of the last war the statesmen of Europe believed that their treaties dealing with minorities had solved the question of nationality for good and all, the first wave of refugees was already streaming across Europe, and since then it has dragged into its vortex the populations of all European nations. Stateless refugees of Russian origin were followed by stateless refugees from Hungary; then came those from Italy; after a short pause it was Germany's and Austria's turn; and today—except for Britain—there is no European nation that has not robbed a larger or smaller number of its citizens of their citizenship, driving them into exile, leaving them to the goodwill or bad will of other countries, without consular or legal protection of any kind.

Future historians will perhaps be able to note that the sovereignty of the nation-state ended in absurdity when it began to decide who was a citizen and who was not; when it no longer sent individual politicians into exile, but left hundreds of thousands of its citizens to the sovereign and arbitrary decisions of other nations. No international guidelines have been able to deal with the problem of stateless persons, a problem that is unsolvable in a world of sovereign nations. The treaties of 1920 dealing with minorities were already obsolete when they were enacted, because no provision was made for people without a homeland.

Stateless people are the latest phenomenon in recent history. None of the categories, none of the legal arrangements that arose out of the spirit of the nineteenth century applies to them. They have been excluded both from the national life of their countries and from the class struggle of their societies. They are neither minorities nor proletarians. They stand outside all law. No form of naturalization can any longer gloss over this fundamental lack of civil rights in Europe. There were always too many naturalized citizens, and no reasonable person could fail to see that the least change in government could suffice to undo naturalizations enacted by a previous government. Naturalized or not naturalized, concentration camps were always standing at the ready. Rich or poor, one belonged to the ever-growing ranks of European pariahs.

The nineteenth century knew no legal pariahs: "The law in its majestic equality forbids both rich and poor to sleep under bridges and to steal bread" (Anatole France). The social pariahs of the nineteenth century were Jews, who no longer had any standing and for whom no provision was made in any social class. But for individuals there was, as has often been discussed, a way out of this pariah existence: you could become a parvenu. The social parvenu is a typical phenomenon of the nineteenth century, just as the political pariah has become one of the central figures of the twentieth. There is no longer any way out of this political fate for individuals. Whether someone wished to remain a social pariah—even if in the form of the rebel—was still more or less left to the decision of the individual. It was up to him whether he wanted to exchange the original humanity and rationality of someone who is forced to endure life directly, without prejudice or ambition, for the wretchedness and stupidity of someone who must expressly renounce all naturalness, all human solidarity, and every unbiased insight into human relationships. It was up to him whether he wanted to offer his awareness of reality, schooled in the most primitive and thus important matters of existence, in payment for the speculative insanity of someone who is cut off from all natural connections, who lives only for himself in the unreal world of financial transactions and within the confines of a world of social caste.

Historically, the misfortune of the Jewish people—since the days of general privilege granted the court Jew and of emancipation of the exceptional Jew—has been that the parvenu has been more important than the pariah; that Rothschild was more representative than Heine; that the Jews themselves were prouder of a Jewish prime minister than of Kafka or Chaplin. Only in the rarest instances did the pariah rebel against the parvenu as his own caricature. Donning the mask of the philanthropist, the parvenu poisoned all Jews, forcing his ideals upon them. The philanthropist turned the poor man into a freeloader and the pariah into a future parvenu.

The events of the last few years have brought the figure of the pariah to the political forefront. As for the Jews, the parvenus have again become pariahs, and this development is final: "On ne parvient pas deux fois" [One is never a parvenu twice] (Balzac). It has turned out, moreover, that one cannot place a European people outside civil and political law without consequences. Just as over the last few centuries the Russian solution has been followed by all European nations, with one emigration following on the heels of another, so too the Jewish people were merely the first to be declared a pariah people in Europe. Today all European peoples are without rights. That is why refugees from every nation, driven as they are from country to country, have become the avant-garde of their own people. The world citizens of the nineteenth century have, quite against their will, become the world travelers of the twentieth. We should keep this tradition ever in mind. For the sense of inferiority that we have developed stands in diametric opposition to our political significance.

Never in the history of the last hundred years have the Jewish people had so great an opportunity to be free and to advance into the ranks of the nations of humanity. All European nations have become pariah peoples, all are forced to take up the battle anew for freedom and equality. For the first time our fate has turned out to be no special fate, for the first time our struggle is identical with Europe's struggle for freedom. As Jews we want to fight for the freedom

of the Jewish people, because "If I am not for me—who is for me?" As Europeans we want to fight for the freedom of Europe, because "If I am only for
me—who am I?" (Hillel) [first century A.D. Jewish sage].

Ceterum Censeo . . .*

December 26, 1941

Jews are fighting today on all the world's battlefronts: British Jews in the
British army, Palestinian Jews in the Libyan expeditionary corps, Russian
Jews in the Red Army, and finally American Jews in both army and navy.
But, as reported by the JTA [Jewish Telegraphic Agency], when Palestinian
Jews, returning from a hard-won battle, dared to raise a little Jewish flag, it
was removed at once. And in the same way, once this war is over, our delegations will be removed from the congress halls of the mighty, of nations both
large and small. And we shall not be able to complain: it will have been our
own fault.

Ever since the birth of political antisemitism at the end of the last century,
Jewish theoreticians of the most varied colors have been preparing the Jewish people for this defeatism. Some tell them that they don't even exist, that
they are only an invention of antisemites; others say that antisemitism is
merely the "superstructure" of a necessary economic process, by which Jews
will of necessity lose their current economic position and likewise of necessity cease to exist; and finally a third group says that antisemitism is a necessity of nature, the irrational and thus uncombatable expression of the
repulsive forces that arise between alien nationalities, from which therefore
you can only take flight. Just as significant as Zionism's moral effect on individuals, just as tremendous as the conquest of Palestine by hard work, is the
catastrophic effect of no one's having ever found a political answer that
addresses what for Jews is the principal political movement of our time: antisemitism.

Jews today respond to the great struggle for their existence according to
these same schemata. Some are convinced by "how good it is that no one
knows Rumpelstiltskin's name." Others are happy in the knowledge that in

---

*The words with which Cato the Elder concluded his speeches, regardless of their topic, in the Roman
Senate: "For the rest I declare that Carthage must be destroyed." For Arendt it is antisemitism that must
be destroyed. —Ed.

being exterminated they personify the zeitgeist. And the third group has but one anxious concern: to defend nothing more and to demand nothing more than Jewish territory in Palestine as a safeguard for a *yishuv* [Hebrew: people] of 500,000 souls, as that little piece of earth where one hopes to be safe from antisemitism. But the moon is the only place where we can still be safe from antisemitism; and Weizmann's [Dr. Chaim Weizmann, 1874–1952; chemist and politician] famous statement that the answer to antisemitism is to build up Palestine has proved to be dangerous lunacy.

We can do battle against antisemitism only if we battle Hitler with weapons in our hands. But this battle must in turn be waged on the basis of certain theoretical insights whose consequences we wish to make a reality. The first of these insights is that we enter this war as a European people, who have contributed as much to the glory and misery of Europe as any other of its peoples. This means that we must do battle with all those in our own ranks who claim that we are and have always been nothing but the victims and targets of history. *It is not true that we have always and everywhere been the persecuted innocents. But if it were true, it would be dreadful indeed—it would in fact remove us far more completely from human history than any actual persecution ever could.* The second insight is that because "Zionism is Europe's gift to the Jews" (Kurt Blumenfeld) [1884–1963; general secretary of the World Zionist Organization, 1911–14; president of the Zionist Union for Germany, 1924–33], Palestine can be regarded solely as an area of settlement for European Jews. In other words, that Palestine's politics are to be derived from the larger politics of European Jewry and not vice versa, whereby Palestinian politics cannot determine Jewish politics as a whole. For, third, the solution to the Jewish question is not to be found in one country, not even in Palestine. For Jews in America, Palestine can become the European motherland that, unlike all the other peoples of America, they have thus far had to do without. For Jews in Europe, Palestine can form an area of settlement as one of the crystallization points of Jewish politics on an international scale, as well as the core of its national organization.

Political movements do not arise in a vacuum. We have only one truly political organization: the Zionist Organization. Within it—while working against the apathy of an apparatus that is as bureaucratic, given to compromise, and removed from reality as any other political apparatus nowadays—we must return to the original national, revolutionary slogans of the movement and, as best we can, transform them into concrete demands. The first of these slogans concerns the struggle within the Jewish community: *against* an international of freeloaders and philanthropists, and *for* a national recuperation of the Jewish people. The second is the old slogan about self-emancipation: the equality for which the "generally privileged" moneyed and court Jews had to pay in cash was regarded by the Jewish masses as a gift from the hands of its notables. Self-emancipation means: equal rights for a people who by the work of their own hands make this earth richer and more beautiful; freedom for a people who in their struggle have proved that they prefer death to slavery.

In this connection the most important event of the last week was the Washington Conference of the "Committee for a Jewish Army," about which *Aufbau* reported in its most recent issue. The conference had two positive results. First, it proved that *non-Jewish public opinion* recognizes and accepts a Jewish army as a perfectly natural demand. Second, and more importantly, it moved the B'nai B'rith Hillel Foundation, with student organizations in sixty-two American cities, to institute a "national panel discussion" on the topic: "Should a Jewish army be organized for service to the Allied cause to fight alongside of the Polish, Czech, Norwegian, and other similar legions?"

Despite these events, and although we should greet every step taken in this direction, we have two objections against the conference and its committee. There is always a danger whenever Jewish politics first lets its demands be certified by non-Jewish circles, and hardly a single Jew spoke at this conference. That bears a nasty resemblance to the methods of the politics of petition practiced by our notables, to whom one could always have put the question: In whose name are you speaking? Moreover, these non-Jewish friends of ours have in part doubtless spoken in the name of people whom they barely know from hearsay, the Revisionists. And second, as for the Revisionists themselves, we shall not put aside our mistrust until and unless they declare straight out that their policy of terror in Palestine during the period of unrest was a disastrous mistake and that they are prepared not only to come to terms with the working class but also to recognize that our rights in Palestine can be represented only by the workers. *For if the Jews are to live in Palestine by right and not by sufferance, it will only be by the right they have earned and continue to earn every day with their labor.*

A First Step

January 30, 1942

The strong and pure echo heard a few days ago at the New World Club in response to Kurt Blumenfeld's remarks on the question of a Jewish army proves that people can be mobilized when they are addressed by someone who wants to be nothing more than "one of the people." The language that the people listen to is not just simple (which gets confused these days with monumental) and not just inspiring (which gets confused these days with demagogic), but is also the language of reason. Blumenfeld's success was due precisely to the fact that he spoke not as a demagogue but "simply" as a man of reason. Only a few individuals find the language of the people, and do so only when they know that they are allied with the people—whereas all demagogues, who think of themselves as leaders or members of an elite, are fluent masters of the language of the mob.

Blumenfeld demonstrated his legitimacy in this regard by pointing out, at the very start of his address, that he was a stranger here and "not living among his people." With that he made it clear that he spoke as a representative of the Jewish people in Palestine. He derived the demand for a Jewish army from the right to take up the sword, which can be denied to no one who has put his hand to the plow or trowel. An army in our sense can be mustered only from working men who reach for weapons only if they are forced to in extreme emergency. Militarists and people who find value in battle and war per se have no place in such an army. Modern soldiers are "civilians in uniform" and can justify their being given the right to kill—which always is and always will be a burden on the conscience of anyone who is not a pervert—only because they are forced to do so in order to defend the fruits of their labor and the meaning of their civilian life.

War demands not only a horrible readiness to kill, but also the readiness to die. But you can be ready to die only when you know for certain why you are fighting, and only when you are a full-fledged citizen of the community that embodies that "why." Palestinian Jews know what they are defending: their fields and trees, their houses and factories, their children and wives. And without any doubt they belong to a community, for we are there "by rights and not just out of sufferance." The question is different for us stateless Jews from Europe, who, because we are refugees, live everywhere only out of sufferance and nowhere by rights. Since Blumenfeld is of the opinion that today only Palestine represents the unifying bond of world Jewry, he therefore calls upon stateless Jews around the world to volunteer for service in the Jewish army in Palestine—and thereby to utilize the only possible form that all Jews have in this war for proclaiming their rights and responsibilities to and for Palestine.

What lies behind such formulations is the old Zionist idea that Palestine and Palestine *alone* is already the solution to the Jewish question. For some of us it might appear that the events of the last years have shown with sufficient urgency that we are not safe from our foes even in Palestine and that even Palestine can help us only if Jews throughout the world are prepared to defend themselves against their enemies. There are no longer any anti-semites whom we might convince by building up Palestine or mollify by emigrating from the countries of the Diaspora.

On the other hand there are hundreds of thousands of Jewish refugees from Europe who need to take up the cause of those brothers who have been left behind. They know of course that only the area of settlement in Palestine can guarantee them their rights in the future; but they have also learned that the security of Palestine will depend on them and their status in a liberated Europe.

In politics failures provide a smooth path for comfortably sliding straight downhill. The path of success, however, is one sown with thorns and along it we make only tedious progress. With the help of Kurt Blumenfeld's speech, we have taken a short step along it. Nothing whatever guarantees us that the seven-mile boots of failure won't swiftly undo that step—nothing except our will to stand up for what we believe is right in the cause of freedom and necessary for the cause of the Jewish people.

Who Is the "Committee for a Jewish Army"?
Letter to the Editor

March 6, 1942

It is indeed true that Jews are a people like every other people. Had we needed further proof of this truism, the fascist movement, which is so busy trying to distort the face of the Jewish liberation movement called Zionism, would have provided it for us.

Nothing succeeds like success. That fascist politics was first successful in a few large nations turned heads among some groups in all small nations. But in their excessive zeal to be modern, our Jewish fascists had no time to take a closer look at the structure and politics of their big brothers. They have understood neither what a racist state is nor why all these quislings cannot help being antisemitic.

For months now the Committee for a Jewish Army—whose initiators are members of the Palestinian fascist organization Irgun, and who make no effort to disguise this fact—have been allowed to propagandize openly in this country for a Jewish army. But now at last the official voice of the Jewish Agency in America, the Emergency Committee for Zionist Affairs, has decided—quite late, to be sure—to distance itself from these gentlemen, who for years now have not only employed terrorist methods in their fight against Arabs in Palestine, but have also shot and killed Zionists as well. I quote:

> There is no connection whatever between Zionist bodies in this country and the Committee for a Jewish Army. A number of people are associated with the Committee for a Jewish Army who at one time [!] belonged to an extremist wing of the Revisionist Organization. The American Emergency Committee for Zionist Affairs is against the fund-raising campaign being led by the Committee for a Jewish Army.

Indeed, this comes quite late and sounds quite tame. The background to this story is revealed very clearly in remarks found in the February issue of [the Emergency Committee's] *News Letter*, the implications of which are as follows. While the Zionists were sleeping, the Revisionists grabbed the initiative. They collected some money and collected some names that added glitter when they appeared in print as the members of the Committee for a Jewish Army. It is clear that a considerable number of the freedom-loving names that appear there are those of people who do not know that the committee is a Revisionist organization and presumably assume that it represents official and legitimate bodies that they would be glad to assist. One can surely assume that people like Hallet Abend, Melvyn Douglas, Max Lerner, Kenneth Leslie, Ludwig Lore, Reinhold Niebuhr, and Harry A. Overstreet would wish to protect their names from any fascist stain. The blame lies with the official Zionists: their retreat and inability to educate the public has resulted in embarrassing some of their friends, who will presumably be hesitant about lending their aid in the future.

The Committee lists Pierre von Passen as its national chairman and Alfred A. Strelsin as chairman of its executive board. Both are well known as liberal pro-Zionists, and both would presumably feel better among friends—if only the official Zionists had bothered to seize the initiative.

But such assumptions cannot be made for several other members of the Committee. Y. Ben-Ami is an extreme right-winger in Palestine, Ben Eliezzer is a well-known Revisionist, as is Meir Grossman. Eri Jabotinsky, the son of the Revisionist Vladimir Jabotinsky, is also on the list. And this much can be learned just from published documents.

The public has not, however, learned of several ongoing events. For months now, negotiations have been in process between the Committee for a Jewish Army (the Revisionists) and a subcommittee of the Emergency Committee for Zionist Affairs (the official umbrella organization for all Zionist groups with the exception of the Revisionists). These negotiations have dragged on and on—which reveals that within the American Zionist leadership no clear majority exists in opposition to the Revisionists.

The Revisionists have been able to dupe the official Zionists because, however misplaced their goals may be, they at least clearly and obviously know what they want. And the initiative belongs to such people.

The Revisionists have no right to speak for Palestine. Since 1927 they have sought in vain to create a base in the masses there: as anti-British nationalists, as anti-Arab terrorists, and as strikebreakers. . . . If such well-known fascists presume to claim a leadership role for "free Jews," that is no more a trump card than King Carol's offer to move to the head of the "free Romania" movement, just because it has as yet proved impossible to expose him publicly at home.

The Revisionists' main goal is not to build an army, but is merely another attempt to gain influence within the Zionist Organization by the back door. They hope to accomplish this with the help of reactionary Zionists or non-Jews who think that these Revisionists represent Zionism.

Why have the Zionists neither engaged in a broad propaganda campaign for the Jewish army nor opposed the Revisionists? One of the external reasons for the Emergency Committee's inaction is the fact that the man charged with the execution of its decision is himself a man of the right wing: Emanuel Neumann [1893–1980, twice president of the Zionist Organization of America]. But more importantly, a large portion of the leadership of the

Haddasah and the Zionist Organization are foes of labor and sympathize, at least in part, with the Revisionists. And finally, the leaders of Zionist labor have not been effective enough in promoting their antireactionary principles. In 1935, the Mapai (Labor Party) hesitated when the issue was the exclusion of the Revisionists from the World Zionist Organization. They have repeatedly attempted to make peace with strikebreaking Revisionists.

Weizmann, the president of the World Zionist Organization, will be in this country within a few weeks. It is well known that he is a steadfast advocate of a Jewish army and an equally steadfast opponent of the Revisionists. What he will find here among official Zionist bodies is an uncertain and precarious situation. The inaction of the Zionists and the action of the Revisionists will doubtless make Weizmann's work for a Jewish army more difficult than it would have been in any case.

Moses or Washington

(This Means You)*

March 27, 1942

It is a dreadfully long time now since Moses led the children of Israel up out of the land of Egypt, out of the house of bondage. Even the renowned memory of the Jews, the memory of an ancient people that holds to this myth of its foundation, is beginning to deteriorate. Even ancient peoples forget the deeds of their patriarchs when they can no longer make sense of the deeds of their grandfathers, fathers, and sons.

When Reform rabbis took control of our national feasts a hundred years ago and let them vanish into a religion that no one believed in any longer, they did not in fact succeed in dissolving the Jewish people into a "Mosaic confession." But they did achieve one thing: they destroyed the legends of its founding. Ever since, we are no longer an ancient people but a very modern one, simply burdened or blessed with an especially long national history.

This "reform," which ruthlessly and nonchalantly removed all national, all political meaning from the tradition, did not reform that tradition—it has

---

*This is the first article of a biweekly column that Hannah Arendt was assigned to write for an insert, "Jewish World," included in the *Aufbau*. The columns were written in German, but the words "This Means You" are in English.

in fact proved to be its most powerful preserver—it merely robbed it of its living meaning.

As long as the Passover story does not teach the difference between freedom and slavery, as long as the Moses legend does not call to mind the eternal rebellion of the heart and mind against slavery, the "oldest document of human history" will remain dead and mute to no one more than the very people who once wrote it. And while all of Christian humanity has appropriated our history for itself, reclaiming our heroes as humanity's heroes, there is paradoxically a growing number of those who believe they must replace Moses and David with Washington or Napoleon. Ultimately this attempt to forget our own past and to find youth again at the expense of strangers will fail—simply because Washington's and Napoleon's heroes were named Moses and David.

The history of humanity is not a hotel where someone can rent a room whenever it suits him; nor is it a vehicle which we board or get out of at random. Our past will be for us a burden beneath which we can only collapse for as long as we refuse to understand the present and fight for a better future. Only then—but from that moment on—will the burden become a blessing, that is, a weapon in the battle for freedom.

Cui Bono?
Case Against the *Saturday Evening Post*
(with Joseph Maier)

April 3, 1942

When trying to explain someone's convictions, one has the right to invoke a *cui bono*—whom does it benefit?—only as a last resort, that is, only when the reason of a reasonable and insightful person is no longer of any help. Milton Mayer has brought us to that desperate point. What we cannot understand is his appeal—apparently that of a secularized Jew—to the Prophets, to the chosen people of God, and to the Orthodox Jews of Poland. Not that we do not understand this sort of Judaism. We know the position taken by his old Jew, well protected and segregated behind the "barrier of the law," perhaps better than he does, and we recognize that it has very little to do with a banal awareness of leading an upright life and a great deal with a belief in the vengeful God of Israel. But it would never occur to this same old Jew to make such clever and in many regards accurate remarks in the *Saturday Evening Post*: He would not accuse non-Jews of not being Christians, nor heathens of not being humane. Since Mayer's critique cannot come from a pious Jew, but on the other hand does not come from an unbelieving Jew, we have embarked upon our search to discover the extraordinary nut inside this nutshell.

It was not long ago that Milton Mayer (in his *Saturday Evening Post* article, "I'll Sit This One Out") openly declared himself on the side of those who are uninterested in the struggle against fascism. For a Jew that means more than a mere acknowledgment of indifference toward this war for justice and freedom. Because, first, isolationism and the ideology of the America First Committee are not a matter of isolated individuals, but of a party with very specific political demands supported by specific political groups. Not only does Mr. Mayer think it unnecessary to do anything for that Polish Jew he so admires, but he also takes no offense at having to sit at the same table with antisemites and fascists: with men great and small, with a certain kind of congressman, senator, and record-setting pilot. Did he—in order to spare the Jews any accusation of warmongering—feel "called upon" (as Jerome Frank did in the first phase of his development) to serve the Jewish cause by wanting to sell all America into slavery? By that logic, Father Coughlin could play the role of savior of the Jews. But the ways of the assimilated are mysterious. Even to themselves, they elude all theological understanding.

It is also not unknown that Milton Mayer moves in certain Catholic circles. One is tempted to think that this might have some influence on his position on the Jewish question. For the Catholic Church, Jews are both God's chosen and, after the crucifixion of Christ, cursed people. According to their plan of salvation—as one can read in the Epistle to the Romans, chapter 2— God and suffering humanity are waiting for the promised return of the Lord upon the conversion of the Jews. Until that happens, the Jews must remain true to their Law, while preserved from destruction by the *ordo christianus*, and live as meek and indigent witnesses to the truth of the salvation history revealed in the crucified and resurrected Christ. If the Jews were to be untrue to their own Law, without becoming Christians, or if—as Zionism demands—they were to become a people like all other peoples, the plan of salvation is undone.

That is why clerical antisemitism—apart from a few excesses—has always been against the rich (or to use Mayer's term, materialistic) Jew, because his existence contradicts the theological demand that he be meek, and against the secularized, unbelieving Jew, because his existence contradicts the theological demand of his being chosen and different on principle. It is from this position that modern Catholicism has very often been critical of an assimilated Jewry, a position that has seemed strangely close to Jewish-Zionist self-criticism.

But you must have a certain legitimacy if you are to criticize the Jewish people today, in a time of their greatest need. To attain such legitimacy it does not suffice simply never to have sat at the table with the enemies of your people. It can only grow out of passionate involvement on behalf of the future of your people, for whom more is at stake than the saved souls of isolated individuals. Self-criticism is not self-hatred. The criticism the Jewish patriot offers his own people is intended to prepare them better for the struggle. Rebellion of this sort can never do harm. Milton Mayer's dubious courage to speak half-truths benefits only the impudent lies of antisemites. Anyone who, like him, wants to chase us back into the ghetto, dressed as always in patched rags from the dusty closet of theology, has excluded himself from the ranks of those whom we, the people, are prepared to listen to.

Paper and Reality

(This Means You)

April 10, 1942

A strange silence has fallen over the issue of a Jewish army. Every conceivable organization has written resolutions in its favor, the "protest rabbis" have remained in a minority, much to the honor of their guild, and a few hastily assembled masses have had the chance to show their sympathy with applause. That is very little, when you consider that the Jews of Palestine are still unarmed; that the Jews of Europe, if they do succeed in escaping their enemies, are sent to their death by their friends; that more than a third of the Jewish people are sitting behind barbed wire; and that these resolutions and this applause (which could have had political significance only if it had been preceded by organized protest) have proved only one thing: that the people have to be organized for battle today. Covert defeatism is to be found not in the people, but in functionaries who think that a fund-raising campaign is more important than agitation for a just cause, and that there is more promise in pursuing relationships with the mighty upon the earth than in organizing the people.

While we have been busy making sure that the demand for a Jewish army remains on paper, we can console ourselves that four institutions have, with scientific meticulousness, been busy preparing us for peace: the Institute of Jewish Affairs (which is affiliated with the American Jewish Congress) and the institutions of the American Jewish Committee, the Jewish Labor Committee, and Agudath Israel. In order to exploit fully the chance of coming to the most divergent results on the same issues and of maintaining the greatest "neutrality," these four peace teams work in total isolation from one another. And since especially the first two of the aforementioned institutions have known how to secure the cooperation of renowned Jewish scholars, the inevitable upshot has of course been the publication of articles and valuable collections of materials (above all, the study on Jews in the Soviet Union commissioned by the Institute of Jewish Affairs and the collection of emancipation edicts provided by the American Jewish Committee).

Scholars are remarkable people, and we have had some very sad experiences with them in recent years. At some point, when they fell prey to the dominance of positivism, they became "unpolitical"; for the sake of pure correctness they forgot what truth is, and frivolously separated themselves from the cause of freedom and justice. Ever since, they have been prepared to offer a helping hand to every political system. Their objectivity can be put to the service of any subject. And indeed there has been no lack of subjects either.

And so we too are being prepared "unpolitically" for peace. It is true that a discussion about the goals of peace always tends to arise during a war—and so far it has always turned out that the only goals of peace that are realized are those already implemented in war and the way in which it is fought. But so far no people has ever come up with the idea of trying to replace participation in a war with *dreaming* in advance about participation in a peace conference. This is a scholarly idea, and we like to hope that our scholars will not succeed in turning a "people of the book" into a people of papers.

Because as long as a Jewish army remains on paper, the best collections of materials in the world are just stacks of dead paper. If we do not manage to achieve what has finally been granted to the Indians—a place in the midst of the United Nations*—there will be no peace for us all that soon. This war is not about how big or small a people is, it is about freedom for all peoples. And the struggle of the United Nations will remain incomplete as long as those nations are not prepared to sit at a table with the pariah of all peoples and to include it in the ranks of those on the battlefront.

All Israel Takes Care of Israel

(This Means You)

April 24, 1942

The world in which we live is full of sorcery, magic, and ordinary hocus-pocus. Rising like irregular boulders out of the chaos of ancient and hyper-modern superstitions—brewed by despair and spread like advertising around the world by machine guns—are yesterday's truths, almost sunk in the mire. And a few of those truths have also been included in sorcery's great book of despair disguised as science. Except that they have been able to convince the masses in direct proportion to their loss of political effectiveness.

Among the distorted truths with a real capacity for duping even reasonable people is the old adage, *All Israel takes care of Israel.* For who in this most devastated of worlds does not wish to hear the call of solidarity with an open heart, and who does not wish to belong to some sort of mutual insurance society? In the period before emancipation, when there was still an autonomous Jewish congregation, the whole congregation took care of paying to the state or the prince the taxes and debts of each of its individual members. The ghetto was one great mutual insurance company.

Over the course of the seventeenth and eighteenth centuries, court Jews assumed this task, inasmuch as their power in the congregation was based on wealth and relationships with princes, and their position at court was based on their belonging to world Jewry and to international connections arising from that fact. Out of the democratic organization of a pariah people there grew the plutocratic regime of a doubly powerful class of parvenus. They assumed responsibility for those to whom, and to no one else, they owed

*At the time the term "United Nations" was used for the coalition of the Allies at war with the Axis powers. The world organization known by that same name was not founded until 1945.

their wealth, power, and what, for the time, were unlimited opportunities. And the people willingly let themselves be ruled by them, for the people owed them their security, their chances of rising in society, and a new self-awareness. For if antisemites still smell a Rothschild in every door-to-door salesman, one ought not forget that for more than a hundred years every door-to-door salesman thought of himself as a future Rothschild. *All Israel took care of Israel.*

At the height of their power—in the wake of the failed revolution of 1848 and under the rule of Napoleon III—after the founding of the Alliance Israélite Universelle,* Western Europe's Jewry dared to claim this adage as its own motto. They lived in the proud illusion of a people who were united and governed by it and to whom it would guarantee, on the basis of international monetary transactions between nations, security and upward mobility. They believed themselves powerful enough for all Jews, because they were rich enough to assume the responsibility of taking financial care of all Jews. It was a splendid time, when businessmen still dreamed of national unity and monetary transactions still provided them with a sense of political power.

Reality, however, very quickly began to look a bit more shabby. All Israel took care of each other's tickets to the borders of their own land and guaranteed governments that uninvited guests, whose money no longer protected them in their own country, would vanish without further ado or expense; and if this did not happen voluntarily out of concern for their own security, those same governments adopted very unpleasant practices to remind Israel of its chosen motto and to interpret it in new ways. Until finally the Nazis used barbed wire to turn their version of Jewish solidarity into reality—into ghettos that made no distinction between rich and poor, between Western and Eastern European Jews.

Let us not be taken in by magic charms. The All Israel Insurance Company has gone bankrupt. Jewish solidarity would be a fine thing if it were backed up by the people's awareness that it is their responsibility to take their political fate into their own hands. You can use the catchword of solidarity to induce a people to complain of its rags or to establish a "blood brotherhood."

---

*A representative organization founded in Paris on a nonreligious basis in 1860. It was the forerunner of the Jewish World Congress.

Solidarity does not arise simply out of a common enemy, because there is no such thing as a solidarity of fear; one cannot depend, you see, on frightened people. The Jewish solidarity of our fathers had much in common with the peaceful and profitable practice of keeping sheep in a herd; the wolf likes to scatter the herd, not keep it together. A common enemy can only *awaken* solidarity—and in the exact same measure as it awakens the desire to join together in defense, instead of running and scattering.

The Devil's Rhetoric

(This Means You)

May 8, 1942

Hitler has once again spoken and presented in detail his opinions about both the role of the Jews in this war and the role of *the* Jew in world history. Journalists and politicians have once again offered detailed interpretations of the ins and outs of this speech, examined it for its obvious and deeply hidden intentions—without ever considering it necessary to speak one syllable about the Jews. There is no doubt that this persistent "oversight" often occurs with the best intentions. There is no doubt that it already has had and will continue to have the most awful consequences.

For while people search for what is not and what cannot be included in such a speech—that is, the hidden objectives of the next German offensive—they allow the patent propaganda of its weltanschauung, which "explains" all political riddles in the simplest terms and the effects of which truly ought to have been tested enough by now, to be spoken openly and without any interpretation. The conspiracy of silence about the fate of the Jews is not merely the bitterest experience of this war for us; it is also at the same time—given that propaganda is an effective weapon in this war—one of the Allies' greatest handicaps.

Hitler has a formulaic explanation that is overwhelming in its simplicity: by adopting the differentiation between a people and its government, which is of such great importance for the Allies, he claims that in fact only two peoples are engaged in the life-and-death struggle of this war—the Jews and the Germans. All other peoples have merely been driven into this war by their governments. Both Germans and Jews are the only peoples validly represented by their governments, which are identical with them; except that the

Germans have an open government, the Jews a secret one. All peoples, except the Germans, are governed by the Jews. This war, the war between the supernaturally good Germans and the supernaturally evil Jews, has caused so much suffering to other good peoples because the Jews don't want to fight and instead make use of other peoples' governments in order to secure, ah yes, "world domination."

What makes this propaganda so terribly dangerous is that it is based on no facts whatsoever—yes, openly and brazenly flies in the face of all facts. It is based solely on the idea of a fundamental inequality among peoples. A supernaturally good people and a supernaturally evil people are merely the framework into which all other peoples are forced, as if into a straitjacket, and by which they are then dominated.

The idea of a fundamental, natural inequality of peoples, which is the form that injustice has taken in our time, can only be defeated by the idea of an original and inalienable equality among all who bear a human countenance. Only a justice that creates just relationships can vie with an injustice that creates unjust relationships. And since—for various reasons, all of which one may indeed deplore—the idea of injustice has been imputed to and exemplified by the Jewish people, those who must fight for equality and justice have no choice but to lay aside their remarkable skittishness and openly speak the name of the Jewish people in order to grant them their share of justice when they justly demand national freedom and to assure them their equality as an equally valued ally. This is the only sort of propaganda for which the "devil's rhetoric" is no match.

The "So-called Jewish Army"

(This Means You)

May 22, 1942

At the Extraordinary Zionist Conference, about which the most recent issue of the *Aufbau* reported in detail, something truly extraordinary did happen: the official burial of the Jewish army. The eulogists spoke of a "so-called" Jewish army, of "pretentious words," of "fantasy numbers," and of the constructive plan to permit a "few Jewish regiments" to fly their own flag. Now it is possible that the Colonial Office, out of the same great political wisdom that it has demonstrated with such thoroughness in the Far East, does not wish to arm "natives" in their own formations or give the Jewish Agency the right to mobilize. Why, one asks in amazement, can we not then allow the Colonial Office the honor of leaving the unarmed Jewish *yishuv* in Palestine to its enemies or the protection of God? Since when is the response to defeat an audible sigh of relief?

The only person who can pose such questions is someone who still has not grasped just how deeply in love with reality the man who practices realpolitik is. The mere fact that some issue actually exists arouses in him such enthusiasm that he can no longer ask whether what exists is for or against him. Moreover, since realities closest at hand are those that one feels most strongly, a person who thinks realistically only reckons with what is directly before his nose. Chamberlain, who, as a devotee of the most realist politics that modern history has known, *sacrificed* distant Czechoslovakia, and the French, who realistically mocked the idea of "dying for Danzig or Prague," have proved that realpolitik can lead directly to a politics of adventurism and foolish gambles, if only one pursues it with sufficient rigor. What is considered ultimate political wisdom in London nowadays can turn out to be a highly dangerous gamble in Jerusalem tomorrow, a gamble against the same Providence in which practitioners of realpolitik are not even in the habit of believing. To leave almost 600,000 people (whom one proposes *urbi et orbi* as the core of the Jewish nation) unarmed, without any possibility of defending their own soil, not to give them even a chance of entering the fight—that may look very realistic in the environs of the Colonial Office in London; everywhere else and especially in Palestine it looks like suicide, like the destruction of one's own reality.

But the man who practices realpolitik often has more than just reality against him. He must take into account an immediate and still more unpleasant fact: ordinary people don't understand him. For example, they don't understand his distaste for "grand words," especially when they sense that they are living in dangerous times. Those men whom we Jews call "men of the people" are such fools that they cannot shake off the presumption that ideas lie behind certain words. For the practitioner of realpolitik, however, ideas have the suspect quality of being able to move people to change reality. And to what could a man who practices realpolitik actually cling if that were possible, if the "firm foundation of fact" began to tremble beneath his feet? But when the status quo is as awful as the White Paper, when facts are as lethal as the *Struma* and the *Patria,* as Mauritius and Atlit,* then one would do better not to speak of them. For such facts bear the carrion smell of politics, of that most demagogic of all arts, which wants to try to create new realities.

The term "Jewish army" also belongs to that category of unpleasant grand words. Having sprung from the facts, there clings to it—twist and turn it however you like—the idea of freedom. And indeed we know that in this war there are armies fighting for freedom.

But these, let us call them "so-called armies," or let us speak of "so-called oppressed nations," were created by people who are happy to talk big. That is because they have spooking about in their brains such fantastical ideas as "war is merely the continuation of politics by other means," and that implies they must therefore take part in the pursuance of this war if they are not to be automatically excluded from politics in general. It is also because an unprecedented oppression has broken through the heart's customary inertia and yet has not broken their hearts. And ever since, these fools at least are no longer prepared to act upon the foundation of facts created by the enemies of their people, but are of such a utopian turn of mind as to want to fight their way to a new foundation.

What if our politics, the politics of a people of whom a third are very close to extermination, were to be led not by very wise practitioners of realpolitik but by those utopian fools that we Jews call men of the people— what might happen then? Fools would assume that no Colonial Office in the world ought to be able to forbid a people to defend its soil with weapons in hand; and that no protectorate power in the world can assume this heavy and bloody work for another people. They would point to Burma and Singapore, and note that unpredictable things can happen in a war, even to the British army. They would on the other hand point to "protected Jews" and note that protection can sometimes guarantee physical survival, but never political freedom. These fools could not therefore be placated with either "a few regiments" or "so-called armies." They would come forward with fantastic arguments such as how all the nations in this war have between 8 and 15 percent of

---

*The *Struma* and *Patria* were ships filled with Jews trying to flee to Palestine in November 1940. The British refused them entry. The *Struma* struck a mine on its return trip; the *Patria* blew up in the harbor before it was to take its passengers, on British orders, from an internment camp at Atlit, near Haifa, to one on the island of Mauritius.

their population under arms, and suggest that the *yishuv,* numbering almost 600,000 people and given its especially favorable age range, can and must be able to mobilize more than a few regiments—the 12,000 men (approximately six regiments) perhaps who are already serving as British colonial soldiers?— which count as a mere 2 percent of its population. They would therefore seriously consider the astronomical number of 100,000 men, who, as 16 percent of the Jewish population, would only slightly exceed the percentage of the British mobilization.

If these fools had their army, they would no longer busy themselves so much with statistics concerning how many European Jews will have *had* to die by such and such a date. They would find it enough to mourn those who have already died and to fear total extermination, something statistics do not calculate but which nonetheless is not just a matter of numbers on paper. They would instead try to take a few thousand German soldiers prisoner, in the justified hope that this might improve the rations supplied to the Warsaw ghetto. They would, as is only proper, at least *attempt* to replace the rules of extermination and the rules of flight with the rules of battle.

Yes, if there were such a thing as miracles, if one could defeat one's enemies without fighting, if the millions of Jews in concentration camps and in ghettos were dying simply according to the rules of statistics, if we had the miraculous guarantee that Palestine might one day be located not on the Mediterranean, but on the moon, far removed from every attack, if the dead aboard the *Struma* could be brought back to life—in short, if my grandmother had wheels and was an omnibus, we fools and men of the people would perhaps begin to take an interest in whether that omnibus were about to make a left- or right-hand turn.

A Christian Word about the Jewish Question
(This Means You)

June 5, 1942

Perhaps the time has now come for those great discussions of Western civilization—such as the discussion between Jews and Christians or between believers and unbelievers—without which it is hard to imagine a future for the world we share. The skeptic at any rate, that amiable gentleman who tyrannized public opinion for so many decades, has died with hardly anyone's noticing; he can no longer prevent us from talking about serious matters and seeing comical matters like his famous article of faith—"the opposite is equally true"—from their humorous side.

Rather more unpleasant is how in the meantime the evil seed he sowed shortly before his demise—perhaps in revenge for the fact that people had finally begun to see the ugly grimace of heartlessness behind his mask of tolerance—has sprouted, leaving us surrounded now by whole swarms of those upside-down skeptics we call fanatics. Amidst the clamor of tirelessly bickering sectarians, the voice of reason and humanity is as easily lost as it was until recently amidst the subdued murmurings of professional doubters.

For those of us who—whether religious or unbelieving—have not yet sold our souls to the devil of idolatry, I would urgently like to recommend Jacques Maritain's book, *Ransoming the Time* (Scribner's, New York, 1941), in which he initiates the discussion between Christians and Jews. I hope they will begin by reading the chapter on "neighbors" and accept Maritain's suggestion that tolerance be replaced by fellowship or, still better, by "civic friendship." Just as certainly as all can be lost in such discussions if we gloss over the differences that divide us, so too we will never even enter into conversation if we are incapable of assuming the basic premise of our humanity. It is reason's great prerogative to "understand more languages than it speaks," and it is man's great prerogative to be more than a "model of pure ideas" (p. 118). In that reasonableness and in that humanity lies the philosophical guarantee for a political concept of humankind.

On the other hand, for those of us who do not keep the 613 commandments and prohibitions and do not pray for the coming of the Messiah—and we make up the majority of our people—I would like to suggest we not follow Maritain's pronouncements on the chosen status of Israel, which he identifies as meaning all the Jewish people, "do what they will" (p. 175). The fact that Jesus of Nazareth, whom Christians call the anointed one, was a Jew can function for both us and Christian peoples as a symbol of the Greco-Judeo-Christian cultural world. Israel may assume this or that place in Christian theology; it is not up to Jews to form an opinion about that. But as part of the communal life of nations and within the history of humankind, we do have the right to be "a people like all peoples" and human beings among our fellow human beings.

For in this human and political context, the great law that governs all truly human affairs is the law of *normality*. In this earthly world in which we live any exception to that law is a monstrosity that turns something supernatural into something unnatural. Those Jews who no longer believe in their God in a traditional way but continue to consider themselves "chosen" in some fashion or other, can mean by it nothing other than that by nature they are better or wiser or more rebellious or the salt of the earth. And that would be, twist and turn it as you like, nothing other than a version of racist superstition.

Christians of the Protestant or Catholic faith, men like Paul Tillich and Jacques Maritain, know that the Jewish question is one of the touchstones of Christianity today and that the struggle against antisemitism concerns far more than a theological dispute. Which is why in this matter, as in others, we for whom being Jewish primarily involves the fact that we belong together politically and nationally should not leave our representation solely to rabbis.

"Not One Kaddish Will Be Said"
(This Means You)

June 19, 1942

In the National Socialist weekly *Das Reich*, Goebbels has explained that the extermination of the Jews of Europe "and perhaps outside of Europe" is about to begin. The murder of five thousand Jews in each of the cities of Berlin, Vienna, and Prague is to mark the start of this mass slaughter, the initial response to the monstrous fact that all peoples in and outside of Europe have shown their resolve to put an end to Nazi domination at any price. The deed preceded the announcement: On May 28, immediately after the assassination of Heydrich, three hundred Jews were snatched from the streets of Berlin and shot; their wives and children were transported to concentration camps. The laws of the devil are, sad to say, more reliable than statistics. While we are busy reckoning according to the laws of probability how many Jews will survive this war and immigrate to Palestine or other countries, the fear of those few who believe that reality depends not on those laws, but rather on men and sometimes on devils, is on the verge of being proved most horribly justified.

Ever since the devil seized power, ever since he invented the machinery of terror, that most efficient of modern instruments of propaganda, so that he could turn his doctrine of "right is what works" into reality, he has used Jews for all practical demonstrations of that terror. For what now seems an eternity, but is not even ten years, the fate of the Jews has made it increasingly clear where this train is headed—except that the span of time between experiment and total implementation has grown shorter and shorter. It took years before not just Jews but also Czechs, Norwegians, Dutchmen, and Frenchmen were attacked. Months passed before it was not just Jews who were open game in occupied countries. For weeks one heard only of the deportation of Jews; now the French and the Poles have followed and there is already a plan under consideration for driving three million Dutch from their homes. And finally within only a few days the men of Lidice followed three hundred Jews in Berlin to their deaths, and Czech women and children were sent to concentration camps like the Jewish women and children before them. If I were not a Jew, but belonged to some other European people, my hair would stand on end in fear the moment a single hair on the head of a Jew was touched.

There was once a happy time when men could choose freely: better dead than a slave, better to die standing than on your knees. And there was once a wicked time when intellectuals grew feebleminded and declared life to be the highest good. But now the dreadful time has come when every day proves that death begins his reign of terror precisely when life becomes the highest good; that he who prefers to *live* on his knees will *die* on his knees; that no one is more easily murdered than a slave. We who are alive have to learn that you can't even live on your knees, that you don't become immortal by chasing after life, and that if you are no longer willing to die for anything, you will die for having done nothing.

"Not one mass will now be sung, not one Kaddish will be said." These dead leave no written wills behind, hardly so much as a name; we cannot pay them our final respects, we cannot comfort their widows and orphans. They are victims, in a way that there have been no victims since Carthage and its Moloch were destroyed. We can only dream their dreams to an end.

The inheritance of these dead will fall to those who mourn enough to be resolved, are shocked enough to stand firm, have imagination enough to overcome great distances, are human enough to weep in solidarity for the dead of all peoples, and are terrified enough to emigrate from utopias, from those inhospitable lands we Jews so love to inhabit. The issue of a Jewish army is only in small part a matter for diplomats. It is the issue of these heirs, who will demand it in the name of the living and in the name of the dead.

With Our Backs to the Wall
(This Means You)

July 3, 1942

Since the outbreak of war Jews and non-Jews, Zionists and even non-Zionists, anglophile Americans and even the British, have been trying to make it clear to the Colonial Office and to those in charge of the British war effort that in the Near East—in sad contrast to other parts of the empire—a reliable ally is already in place, who, relative to conditions prevailing there, has a considerable reserve of men and no greater desire than to put them, under honorable conditions, at England's disposal. One can assume that by now the Colonial Office has been made aware of this fact. It is even probable that there are no longer any illusions about another fact of importance to the British war effort—that is, about the position of the Arabs, particularly since last week saw the invasion of Egypt, but no declaration of war on the Axis by the Egyptians as previously pledged.

But there is a hitch to the matter, and it grows increasingly clear that there is only this one hitch: the people there who would be such loyal allies are Jews. And there is no hiding this fact because these particular Jews, in shocking contrast to their "wiser" brethren throughout the world, have taken it into their heads to live as Jews, just as other peoples live, the way God made them and without covering their nakedness with the fig leaf of a different nationality. Public discussion of this vexing issue is difficult. But the Jews should have some understanding for the difficult situation their stubbornness puts their friends in. After all, they really must know—or so one hears every day—that this war is an ideological war, and that one cannot, after all, lend credibility to Hitler's claim that it is being waged on behalf of the Jews. It is bad enough that no one can deny that Jews have a certain interest in its outcome; an alliance with the Jews—that would be grist for Hitler's propaganda mills! (Common sense says that *only* when Jews fight as Jews will poppycock about others fighting *for* them vanish—but thus far common sense has never been able to disrupt the speculations of practitioners of realpolitik.) The

Jews should therefore understand and be grateful to be offered the coat of a British colonial soldier and allowed to die for the British Empire instead of for their land, their wives and children, and the honor of their people.

Jewish politicians have done all they can to undermine the Jewish people's interest in Jewish politics. What is left are a few cries of alarm by the Committee for a Jewish Army, a few people in Zionist leadership positions who know and publicly state that "he who is not in this war, is also not in its peace" (Nahum Goldmann [1895–1982, president of the World Jewish Congress]). For even if one disregards for a moment the threat to Palestine—which grows greater every day—the Jewish army is the most important and, until it is realized, the sole mission of Jewish politics. But the Jewish people are busy with optimistic or pessimistic judgments about events; the optimists worry about the coming peace, the pessimists about the imminent extinction of the Jews. Well versed in fear and hope, we live out our days in despair and unconcern.

It is not all that easy to make individuals or whole peoples apathetic, but we appear to have managed it. For two hundred years we have left it to plutocrats and philanthropists to govern us and represent us in the world. For two hundred years we have let ourselves be convinced that the surest way to survive is to play dead. And with such success that even among ourselves we are often not sure whether we are among the living or the dead; with such success that we move about in a make-believe world where everything is upsidedown. If we find ourselves in danger, we hope for a miracle, and if we are feeling relatively safe, we're afraid of our own shadows; we consider political movements like antisemitism to be a law of nature, but assume that the rules of battle, which if not natural are at least human, are figments of the imagination; raising money is for us a deed, but organizing ourselves as a people is demagogic nonsense; if the enemy is at the gate, we make constructive plans for the future—and forget about the coming day. When you realize what all is at stake here, it could make your skin crawl.

If You Don't Resist the Lesser Evil

(This Means You)

July 17, 1942

There has been a small change in what has become the almost monotone question-and-answer game between the Jewish Agency and the British government concerning the formation of a Jewish army and a Jewish home guard for Palestine: the voice of the Jewish Agency is softer, that of the British opponents of a Jewish Palestine louder and more self-assured, while the voices of our friends in the British populace, Parliament, and press have as good as fallen silent. You cannot make demands that contradict your actions and get away with it. There comes a day when the whole world sees those demands as empty words. Our policy in Palestine has consisted of demanding a Jewish army in our words and meanwhile as good as setting up recruiting stations for the British army. In times as bloodily serious as ours, people very quickly learn that when it comes to politics you do best to watch each other's hands and not just mouths.

The immediate consequences of this ambiguity are bad enough. It is over-whelmingly probable that we will not get a Jewish army and not even get those few Jewish regiments that Weizmann still considered quite probable at the Zionist conference last May. Moreover we hear how Jews who have fled to Palestine prefer the legions of their old homeland to the British army. The danger of damage to the *yishuv* is obvious, and the Jewish Agency protests in desperation. But the response of these refugees is only too understandable: if they cannot fight as Jews, if they're told that the lesser evil is to fight for a foreign army, then they will prefer formations in which, along with the same military rights, they also have the same political rights and, at least theoreti-cally, the same citizenship as their comrades and commanding officers. Block someone's escape route, and you can never predict where he will find his best chance for an exit.

And the indirect consequences are even more serious: the purpose for which we could be fighting positively in this war, the national liberation of the Jewish people, is lost without a Jewish army, without positive participa-tion in the war. All that is left for us to win in this war is something purely negative: perhaps other nations can be prevented from exterminating us.

The politics of the lesser evil has always had a nasty tendency to hold on to the great old evil and thus to prepare the way for even greater new evils. When out of fear you twist the lesser evil into the lie that it is something good, you eventually rob people of the capacity to differentiate between good and evil. But you can't pursue politics with people who are accustomed to accepting evil instead of resisting it—even if that is under the pretense of avoiding a greater evil. And so the Germans voted for the lesser evil of Hindenburg and then didn't find Hitler all that bad. And so we Jews sat there, quite peaceful and unpolitical, in French internment camps and consoled ourselves with how much worse Dachau was. And so Jews spoke up for Italian fascism because they were convinced that the best way to cast out the devil Hitler was with the Beelzebub Mussolini. But just as it was certain that Beelzebub would ultimately come to terms and ally himself with the top devil, we can be equally certain that in being tossed from one rock of lesser evil to the next rock, we can only end up in the abyss of catastrophe. And the best English friends and the best armies in the world will not save us from this fate for which we ourselves are to blame.

The line between the least achievable good, something to which demands have to be reduced under some political circumstances (and in this case that would be a Jewish home guard) and the least evil that must be accepted (and in our case that would be integration into the British army and the disappearance of Palestinian Jews as a factor in Jewish politics)—that line is a thin one, thin as a hair. Sometimes it is hard to discern, but it can be found if politicians are resolved on principle to resist evil in every form, which means people who can prove that they have never made a pact with it. To the extent that one can speak of Jewish politics at all, it clings to the basic evils of liberalism with a determination that might be of value in a better cause. Its strategy is to yield to "force" without a fight, and its tactic is mindlessly to sniff out the path of least resistance.

Pro Paul Tillich*

July 31, 1942

An argument concerning a very serious and important issue has broken out among émigrés. It began with something quite banal: a well-known writer,

---

*The émigré writer Emil Ludwig (1881–1948) gave a Fourth of July speech that was reprinted in the *New York Times* on July 6, 1942. In it Ludwig suggested that Hitler was a real expression of who the German people truly are and advised a draconian postwar policy of a protectorate that would forever deny them political power. On July 17, 1942, the theologian Paul Tillich (1886–1965) countered in the *Aufbau* with an article that accused Ludwig of a racism not unlike antisemitism, and asked German Jews in America to distance themselves from him.

who in the last world war wore the very German colors of the German imperialism of the day, and who in the thirties wore the fascist colors of Italian imperialism, is trying his hand with a new great power by encouraging the American people to adopt an imperialism, which, thank God, is thus far nonexistent. Although not even thirty years ago he was convinced that the "world should be mended by the German spirit," and not even ten years ago was thrilled by the superiority of Italian bombs dropped on the tribes of Ethiopia, this same man, since he is a Jew, now finds he has no choice but to award the palm of superior wisdom to Anglo-Saxon peoples. And since one is always happy to participate when superiority takes command, our writer already sees himself as the teacher of superior morality, marching through the Brandenburg Gate beside the future victors.

In the name of German refugees, Paul Tillich, who has always been a bitter enemy of racist madness and fascism of every shape and color, raised a vigorous protest here. And he added, quite rightly, that Jews were the last people to have any reason for spreading a way of thinking that has demanded such awful sacrifices of them.

The beginnings, then, are banal, but significant: the idolization of the victor; the adoration of "great men"; the disdain for the average American citizen, whose fight, as the Gallup Poll has shown, is not with the German people, but instead, and thus all the more bitter, with German fascism; and a mistrust of freedom, justice, and the people's political will. All this is, whether covertly or openly, the familiar nihilism of those intellectuals who for more than sixty years have proved so very helpful in preparing the way for the National Socialist mentality and have therefore in all countries—and more easily than any other class of people—accepted fascist regimes and their racist theories. The conflict is so serious because of all peoples only we Jews never had the possibility to truly "get in step"; and because only Jews, without exception, have been forced into emigration. But it would be both foolish to assume therefore that Jews alone are immune to this terrible sickness unto death, which has infected half the world, and unjust to be especially offended if they engage in racist madness.

It is very difficult to be a friend of an oppressed people. It is doubly difficult when one has never been one of the oppressed. It is very sad to learn that every slave has a tendency to dream of owning slaves and that the oppressed masses—however passionately their sufferings plead the cause of freedom—

learn the language of freedom only slowly and with difficulty. The language of slaves, however, that mixture of abasement and secret arrogance, of fear and hope, of ignorance and self-important smugness, is hard to bear. The friend of the oppressed will always need that great confidence in our fellow men which teaches us to laugh, the calm courage that makes untiring protest easy, and a casual detachment from those baneful, bloody alternatives that always seem so appropriate wherever there are oppressors and oppressed. Only then, when he has resisted the heartlessness and cruelty of the oppressor, will he summon the energy needed to endure the "cowardly hearts of the oppressed," who always wait for the battle to be won before "hastening to aid in victory" (Clemenceau).

Friends of the oppressed will always end up in conflict with the oppressed themselves. Every great friend of the Jews has had trouble with the Jews— and it is in these very conflicts that the Jewish people have been able to tell their genuine friends from false patrons. But just as surely as Clemenceau first truly took up the cause of the oppressed Jewish people (in the form of Captain Dreyfus) when he openly and undauntedly denounced the actions of French Jews, so too, in protesting against these German Jews, Tillich has surely done a greater service to the Jewish cause than all those patrons who think they have done enough if they give some Jewish organization the appearance of parity by lending it their non-Jewish name, who magnanimously acknowledge our great men or some sort of achievement, or who think they are helping Jewish friends by declaring that there are no Jews and no Jewish question.

We Jewish patriots, who have been forced for so long to do battle against both slave owners and a slave mentality, will greet that person as our friend and ally who directly or indirectly helps us to eradicate the madness of racial superiority and to restore the humanity, the solidarity of the human race.

Confusion

(This Means You)

August 14, 1942

The hopeless confusion and dangerous ambiguity of almost all modern national liberation movements are not likely to shed much light in our already so very murky world. What all can be done with the word "liberation" in this world of ours without fear of consequences was nicely proved by the Arab national movement, when a few years ago, during the period of Palestinian unrest, it sold itself to German and Italian imperialism in the hope of feathering its own nest by playing one side off against the other. Something similar has apparently happened with certain parts of the Indian national movement. A not insignificant number of their leaders are now sitting in Berlin and Tokyo. It remains to be seen whether it was wise simply to incarcerate its remaining leaders, who have not—or not yet—thrown themselves into the arms of the Axis powers. Gandhi threatened to negotiate with Japan, and for his part another Indian (at the very moment when the people of Europe are about to disabuse themselves of arrogant poppycock about the "white man's burden") quickly pointed out, in that unctuous tone we have come to know only too well, all that the West has yet to "learn" about Asia: both were almost equally heavy blows inflicted on the cause of oppressed peoples.

The actions of the British Colonial Office and the latest declaration by Amery [British colonial secretary in Palestine prior to 1929] show that England is determined to rely upon India's Muslims. This in turn can result only in further attempts to placate the thoroughly fascist-infiltrated Arab national movement in the Near East and lure them to the British side with even greater promises. (The speech in Parliament by Lord Moyne [deputy minister of state in the colonial administration of Egypt], in which he proposed that Jews be removed from Palestine and resettled elsewhere, is unfortunately only too characteristic of these recent tendencies.) Anyone who knows the situation in the Near East may indeed be rather skeptical of these attempts at placation, which can only come at the expense of the Jews. But it is clear that in the face of open hostility to the Jews in the Arab world, and among its Muslim allies, we Jews suffered a serious defeat on the day that the British Colonial Office declared war on the Indian Congress Party.

The ambiguous politics of oppressed peoples—the nasty tendency to barter for privileges instead of fighting for freedom; the narrow-mindedness that hopes to find "redemption" in every change; the tendency, only too common in history, to play the oppressor as soon as one is liberated—this is all an old worry familiar to democratic politicians. (And the Jewish national movement of Zionism is in no way the white sheep among all these more or less black ones; we all know how many Zionists have dreamed of profiting from British imperial interests in the Near East.) Still worse is the fact that such ambiguities have forced many of our contemporaries, and indeed often not the worst of them, into a fateful indifference, indeed hostility, toward all movements of national liberation. They saw only the abuses and forgot that all political movements are subject to them. And fascists all around the world have made the finest use of their indifference.

It is a somewhat different matter with those Jewish snobs who—because they are unwilling to risk anything for public causes—loftily declare themselves above ties to their nation. These peculiar heroes of freedom, who fight for freedom first by deserting the cause of their own oppressed people and then by going looking for security and protection in some other great nation, now tell us, the Jewish patriots, that we are not "progressive." Well, treason has never yet put an end to the existence of an entire people; and just as "emancipated" women have had little success in saving the world by removing the difference between male and female, our "emancipated" Jews will not succeed in arguing themselves and us out of this world.

Few things are as important for our current politics as to keep oppressed people's struggles for liberation free from the plague of fascism. This war will be won only if in its course all peoples are liberated, and that means transforming all "races" into peoples. The politics of an oppressed people is, as the Indian example shows, the most difficult of all. As long as democracy does not govern the world, such politics will balance on the razor's edge. The narrow line of justice runs between the Scylla of blind revenge and the Charybdis of impotent cowardice.

The Return of Russian Jewry

(This Means You)

August 28 (I) and September 11 (II), 1942

I

Beyond the struggle for a Jewish army, there is one other political issue of crucial importance for the future existence of our people: it is the renewed connection with the Jews of the Soviet Union. More than a year has passed since Russian Jews took the first steps out of their isolation, and each of these steps is important and telling. The first thing we heard after a silence of twenty-five years was an appeal to "world Jewry" to unite in the struggle against Hitler and fascism. Then came a call to those Jews living in the safety and prosperity of democratic countries to supply the Red Army with five hundred tanks and one thousand airplanes and to give these weapons names taken from the great army of dead Jewish warriors. The final and in some regards most noteworthy fact is the statement by the Moscow congregation that they had joined in the day of fasting proclaimed by American rabbis.

During the last twenty-three years Russian Jewry has been declared dead so often and with such peculiar obstinacy that no one should actually be amazed that, suddenly very much alive again, it is attempting to participate in the politics of the Jewish people. For in history, the death of peoples and institutions tends to go unnoticed by their contemporaries, and a great deal of commotion in that regard is often the direct result of a lot of smoke and not much fire. When a segment of our politicians (and statisticians) decided to become scholars and offered us proof in black and white that one of the most important and valuable parts of our people was dead, there was a political reason behind it, and the source of their science was in political ideologies and interests that had very little to do with preparing for the future, and a great deal to do with trying to cling to the past.

The end of Russian Jewry has been predicted by the entire world of philanthropy, which is neither able nor willing to imagine that Jews can also exist without charitable enterprises. That world took its refuge in religion, the one factor, as we all know, that is allowed to constitute the Jewish people, and now that same world has to hear that after twenty-five years of a Soviet regime not even the Jewish religion has let itself be wiped out. Russian Jewry has taught the philanthropists a truly awful lesson—it has proved to them that if worse comes to worst we can also live and even pray without them.

Those lost Russian Jews were, moreover, the most powerful argument of the remarkable nationalists who believed a people exists only thanks to its enemies and thus expected the end of antisemitism could only result in the end of the Jewish people. They were supported in this, strangely enough, by their political archenemies, Communist Jews, who have spoken so often, rightly or wrongly, in the name of the Soviet Union and babbled on about the "end of the Jewish people" only because both the ancient fear of the pogrom and the fortunately not quite so old pushiness of assimilated Jews still sat deep in their bones. The events of this last year have at any rate brought an equally happy and drastic end to the eerie theory that secularized Jews need antisemitism to remain Jews.

If our prophets both here and there had not been so busy tracking down general and necessary—that is, inhuman—developmental tendencies, they would perhaps have come up with the banal but more human idea of asking our Jews what they would actually like to be: White Russians or Georgians or Kirghiz or Mongols or maybe Jews. And they would have received the hardly astonishing answer that in a land where neither assimilation nor being a Jew brings with it the least advantage, three million people, that is, approximately 90 percent of Jews living in the Soviet Union (see the study on Jews in the USSR published by the Institute of Jewish Affairs), declared themselves to be of Jewish nationality. In other words: antisemitism encourages Jewish suicidal tendencies; the end of official and social discrimination promotes Jewish national awareness. Jews are human beings, not professional actors who constantly have to change identities in order to be happy. And only under inhuman conditions do human beings attempt to change the color of their skin or the shape of their noses or the number of letters in their names. If you leave them in peace, they don't even think of dabbling in God's work.

Whether these last years of total isolation from the world's Jews have helped or harmed Russian Jewry is something for history professors to determine precisely in fifty years or so. More important for us is that we establish a connection with a part of our people that no longer knows the twofold bondage of antisemitism and philanthropic domination.

And even if Russian Jews are as politically unfree as all other citizens of the Soviet Union, they are nevertheless the first Jews in the world to be legally and socially "emancipated," that is, recognized and liberated as a nationality.

II

There are no human institutions and revolutions, however radical, that can secure human freedom over the long term. There are likewise no laws and arrangements, however radical, that can guarantee the security of the Jewish people over the long term. That is one of the reasons why it is so useless to quibble over the "solution" to the so-called Jewish question, and why it is so useful for us to criticize actual Jewish politics, which has now survived its own bankruptcy, and to think about laying a future foundation for our people's politics.

To the extent that security is at all possible in these times and to the extent that Jews can be made secure on the local level, then Jews in the Soviet Union are protected. To the extent an emancipation from above, without any direct political action by Jews, can have meaning, then Russian Jews are emancipated. In pursuing its policy of nationalities, the Russian Revolution has carried the emancipation begun with the French Revolution to its logical conclusion; it is anchored today in the constitution of the Union, which equates antisemitism with an attack on one of the nationalities of the USSR and pursues and punishes it as a crime against society, like theft or murder. If the Soviet Union were on another planet and the fate of Russian Jews truly independent of world Jewry and vice versa, we still would have been able to speak of a national liberation of Russian Jews—because they are the first Jews to be emancipated as a nationality and not as individuals, the first who did not have to pay for their civil rights by giving up their status as a nation.

To the extent that there can be a social normality without a territory for Jewish settlement, then social conditions for Russian Jews are normal. Fortunately there is in fact no absolute equality in their standard of living, but neither is there the excessive and thus inhuman poverty, nor the excessive and thus inhuman wealth, that have demoralized our people for two hundred years. No freeloader can hope to set up the connections that will make him as rich as Rothschild; no philanthropist needs to fear the misfortune of ending up as poor as those living on Rothschild's charity. This social normalization is politically more important than occupational normalization, the full attainment of which has no more proved possible in Russia than in Palestine over the past few decades. Certainly the thousands-of-years-old separation of the Jewish people from cultivation of the soil is bad, even inhuman (and the greatest achievement of the Palestinian *yishuv* is to have reversed this separation); but the hundreds-of-years-old separation of Jewish poverty from Jewish wealth, including the dubious relationships between them, was worse and more inhuman.

What has always made these achievements of Russian Jewry questionable in our eyes was their isolation from the rest of the world's Jews. How sad and embarrassing that it evidently took this war to make it clear to Jews that there can be neither a locally restricted antisemitism nor a locally restricted Jewish paradise, that if one persecutes Jews in Warsaw and Berlin and Paris, the Jews of Moscow and Jerusalem are directly threatened. But one cannot truly claim that this isolationist illusion has been a monopoly of Russian Jews. Nothing differentiates these Jews less from the average mentality of world Jewry than the delusion that it is possible to free Jews or to secure their rights in just one country. We know only too well that—apart from the voluntary philanthropy of American and the often coerced charity of European Jews—Jews in all countries were under the delusion that they were isolated from what was happening to Jews in neighboring countries. We know that even segments of the Palestinian *yishuv* and prominent Zionist politicians believed that building up Palestine was independent of world politics and that the fate of the *yishuv* could be separated from that of world Jewry.

Events have forced Russian Jewry, along with the Soviet Union itself, out of its isolation. For Jewish politics this can be as crucial a factor as having the workers of Palestine join the ranks of Jewish people. Behind that first concrete proposal of Russian Jews to supply them one thousand airplanes and five hundred tanks for the battle against Hitler—a proposal that came to naught because of technical stipulations of the Lend-Lease Act—there at least lay a political conception. Tanks with Jewish names and driven into battle by Jews, and airplanes, paid for by American or South African Jews and piloted by Russian Jews—that would have offered a real opportunity for the Jewish people to participate visibly in this war, a patent manifestation of that people.

Because they are poor and because they are engaged in the battle, because they likewise no longer have any fear of antisemites or are in awe of philanthropists, Russian Jews appear to have awakened to political life. Should that turn out to be the case, we shall truly have made another step forward in the battle against Hitler.

What Is Happening in France?

(This Means You)

September 25, 1942

It has often been said that Germany was the first country to be conquered by Hitler; and that claim is correct if one also adds that the conquest took place to the applause of a large part of the German people, and amidst the indifference of a still larger part. Hitler in any case began his drive across Europe by liquidating the existence of the German nation (and replacing it with the Reich and race). It perished in the infamy of Dachau and Sonnenberg, in the infamy of torture cellars, in the infamy of the Nuremberg Laws, in the infamy of a war against women, old men, and children. And if Germany's descent into blood and race taught the world what horror and outrage are, the demise of the French nation—simply because with its Revolution it became the European nation par excellence—threatens to end in nihilistic despair for the whole of European history.

The sudden burst of outrage among the French people—so effectively reinforced by the French clergy—against the planned mass deportation of Jews out of Vichy France has taught both "realistic" collaborationists and despairing nihilists an unexpected and astounding lesson. For who could have expected that now of all times, when the unhappy, poor, hungry French people are fully caught up in their own cares, that same people would rebel over the very measure that could rid them of several thousands of those with whom they are forced to share hunger rations, of those whom the mob despised for so long as Jews and foreigners. Who expected this rage from this people, after their national catastrophe appeared to have left behind only individuals and the mob. From Yugoslavia to Norway and from France to Czechoslovakia, the Nazis are having increasingly to deal with people awakening amid the ruins of their fallen nations. But what characterizes the events in France this time is that they are not simply symptoms of angry self-defense, but an expression of a sense of human responsibility for others, and that means an expression of political will. These events are also not an expression of sympathy, as frequently repeated phrases like "these poor unfortunates" might lead you to believe. For given the powers of imagination common to all, given the horrors of this war—far exceeding the general human capacity for sympathy—there is hardly any room left in the hearts of those directly involved, among whom the French must surely be counted. They have "merely" become sensitive to shame and do not want to have the same thing happen on French soil that has happened in Germany, Poland, Romania, and Hungary. And these are precisely the first signs of a reawakening national awareness.

These events bring us Jews into a political constellation for which there is no precedent in modern history. Since the creation of nation-states we have been protected by a series of changing governments and more or less rejected by society. Over the last fifty years ever-increasing classes of people have, as a result of conflict with their own states, become antisemitic, leading finally, with the demise of the nation-state governed by law, to the current persecution of Jews. For a society to attempt to protect us against measures taken by the state, for a people to revolt against its government for the sake of foreign Jews, is so new to Jewish history that one can be certain it will take at least twenty years before this new reality makes its way in the heads of our practitioners of realpolitik.

But Jewish men of the people would do well to pay more attention to these first signs of future things on the European continent than to the grand plans proposed by our various institutes for a peace conference. In this European catastrophe, not only the old nation-states have perished but also those conflicts and differences between those peoples who have achieved nation-statehood and those who were "merely" peoples—all of them have become simply peoples. Until Hitler the Jewish question was one of the countless unsolved nationality questions that have poisoned European history. To whatever extent all peoples will recover from this catastrophe they will feel united in solidarity against those who claim racial superiority and the right to dominate—united in solidarity one with the other, even with Jews. Only in such a context of solidarity do we Jews have our great opportunity for national emancipation.

The Crisis of Zionism

(This Means You)

October 22 (I), November 6 (II), and November 20 (III), 1942

I

Characteristic of this year's national meeting of the American Zionist Congress was the great gulf between a series of political speeches on the one hand, which—in contrast to the extraordinary meeting last May—did not come from the movement's dusty archives, but were truly contemporary; and on the other, a resolution that, with the exception of a hard-fought rejection of the Ihud party,* is so vague and pointless that it could be signed by everyone and needed to be signed by no one.

Upon closer inspection, the reason for this crucial weakness in our politics is only too clear. During this war there is for us only one single goal in our program that must be achieved if all Jewish politics is not to fail: participation in the war with full and equal rights, that is, a Jewish army. Since this goal was not made the central focus of the entire conference, the best political speakers had no choice but to delineate, whether in fear or hope, the future peace conference; this meant that practically all the problems of current Jewish politics were at least touched upon, which is a great deal more than one can say for usual Zionist Congress meetings. But the basic mood of the meeting was expressed in the frequently repeated declaration that Zionist leadership ought not to commit itself one way or the other—which is definitely less an expression of political wisdom than the admission of our own weakness and lack of political will.

An exception to this was found in the speech of Nahum Goldmann [1895–1982, president of the World Jewish Congress], who, by consciously revisiting Herzl's conception of the Jewish question as an issue of transport, tried to enter into the grand political fray. It is no accident that it was a lead-

---

*The Ihud (Unity) party, whose goal was to establish an autonomous Arab-Jewish state in Palestine, was founded by Judah L. Magnes in response to the "Jewish commonwealth" resolution of the Biltmore Conference.

ing American Zionist, Stephen S. Wise [1874–1949, first president of the American Jewish Congress], who immediately heard in this the similarity in sound between the words "transportation" and "deportation" and emphasized the right of European Jews to exercise free choice. The days when one could engage in "top-down" politics (Herzl), the days of being able to enter into the great game of realpolitik by firmly established powers, are long past. Those politics died a shameful death in Munich in the autumn of 1938. Since then the grand imperialist game is being played only by fascists—by the Hitlers and Mussolinis, the Lavals and Francos, whose machinery of terror directed at their own people is indistinguishable from the machinery of war directed against foreign peoples. You cannot join in any sort of game with peoples who are fighting for their existence, battling for their freedom—you must join in their battle.

The founding of the Ihud party made the Arab question one of the central issues addressed. American Zionists have doubtless realized that this very unpolitical party of reconciliation could arise only because our politicians have been in hopeless confusion for decades now. The most accurate analysis of the Arab anti-Jewish movement came from Emanuel Neumann, who emphasized the imperialist nature (shared with every pan-movement) of pan-Arabism and called the idea of an Arab federation an "invention of British power politics." This suggests that we all should be interested in emphasizing as sharply as possible that no questions of nationality and no conflicts can be solved within the framework of a colonial system, no matter what form it takes. On the other hand it seems to me that we can accomplish nothing before any tribunal in this world on the basis of Goldmann's standpoint of a higher justice to which smaller local injustices should conform. This Hegelian historical dialectic is as outworn and passé as Herzl's dream of transforming politics into organization. We live in a time when all those many little injustices with which we have been only too happy to reconcile ourselves have become one single organized injustice, the rule of the devil on earth. The catastrophe is in fact that there is no longer any gray, only black; which of course does not mean that we have all miraculously turned snow-white. But in the course of this war there is not much else that we can do. And that in turn is the great opportunity—an opportunity greater than the catastrophe.

For the time being all peoples, and the Jewish people especially, are stuck in the middle of this catastrophe. To the extent that this disaster threatens to exceed the human heart's capacity for suffering and sympathy, to that extent all our hearts can be turned to stone. The merit of Goldmann's speech was that it was not heartless and that even his call for "smaller injustices" remained human. As long as a politician is capable of saying, "It is the tragedy of our generation that while one half is being slaughtered the other half must stand by watching helplessly," he has a right to his errors and mistakes.

But this does not undo the fact that the real crisis of Zionism is that Herzl's conception of it is urgently in need of revision; that we stand before the task of reformulating our right to Palestine; that our relation with Britain must be put on a new basis; that our impotently clinging to the Balfour Declaration and a mandate system that no longer exists leads to fruitless politics; and that we have not even learned to stutter in the language of the common man, to which, according to the frequently quoted speech of Henry Wallace, the future is said to belong.

II

Until less than twenty years ago, the Zionist movement in America was essentially an extension of Eastern European Zionism. The overwhelming majority of its members were recruited among newcomers of the first, at most the second, generation. American Zionism itself is still very young; its practical political responsibility, however, is already very large and the world in which it is supposed to take political action is so radically changed that all the tenets and tactics of its tradition are more likely to burden and encumber it than to promote and inspire it.

Zionism has never been a true popular movement. It has indeed spoken and acted in the name of the Jewish people, but it has shown relatively little concern whether the masses of that people truly stand behind it or not. From the time of Herzl's negotiations with the ministers of czarist Russia or of imperial Germany until the memorable letter that one English lord, Lord Balfour, wrote to another English lord, Lord Rothschild, addressing the subject of the fate of the Jewish people, Zionist leaders have been able—

without any great support from the Jewish people—to negotiate with statesmen who likewise acted *for* their people and not as representatives *of* their people. These paradisal days of "statesmanly wisdom" are now past in Europe, and in America they never existed. Efforts on behalf of a Jewish army reveal most clearly that sympathies and negotiations with "influential personages" do not even get us to the point of being taken seriously. Until a real popular movement arises out of our various committees and political bodies, we do not stand a chance of that.

If it wants to hold its own in the world, American Zionism—which has an amazingly clear idea of the universal and revolutionary meaning of this war—must meet the task of politicizing the Jewish people and clarifying for them just how significant Palestine is for their own political existence. Certain philanthropic elements within its own ranks, whose influence has grown greatly since the founding of the Jewish Agency, present the main obstacle to that task: first, because the Jewish people, which can boast a long experience with its philanthropists, will not be rid of their own mistrust of the Palestinian experiment as long as it is presented to them in first-class hotels by elegantly dressed ladies and gentlemen as a gigantically expanded shelter for the homeless; and second, because it also appears doubtful to the whole world, including the Jews themselves, whether there will really be so many homeless after this war is over.

The fundamental conflict between the Jewish national movement and Jewish plutocrats, the conflict between a revolutionary popular movement and a traditional apparatus of power and control, was never fought out in Europe; the conflict has instead been suffocated in endless academic discussions between assimilationists and Zionists about the purely ideological issue of whether Jews are a people or not. Evidently no one saw the forest for the trees. Precisely because everyone in this land, thank God—from the president on down to the last Jewish or non-Jewish worker—is united in the belief that there is a "Jewish people of America," a belief that has no room for purely ideological differences between Zionists and non-Zionists, those political conflicts are clearly exposed to the light of day. They will have to be fought within and outside of our organizations. American Zionists have the great advantage of having learned their politics in a land with a democratic tradition. Their insights, however, will only begin to bear fruit if they apply them to the Jewish people and radically democratize the movement.

American Zionism has on the whole a healthy aversion to overusing the antisemitism argument, which was part of the arsenal of Zionist propaganda. Herzl's thesis, according to which antisemitism is an unavoidable evil that can be healed by the evacuation of the Jews, has turned out to be wrong. Antisemitism has become a much more terrible weapon than Herzl could ever have dreamed. Today it is the most dreadful weapon of the most dreadful imperialism the world has ever known. There is no longer any spot on this earth to which Jews could be evacuated that is safe from it.

On the other hand, in the course of a single generation antisemitism has simply been eliminated in a country that fifty years ago was held to be at least as incurably antisemitic as Germany is today, and it was done in connection with a just and very modern solution to the nationality question. The current effect of these political experiences in a faraway land is greater than any social antisemitism closer to home, and every Jew that we want to turn into a Zionist with the help of the antisemitism argument knows instinctively or expressly that he is not safe from antisemites even in Palestine, that antisemitism is not a natural phenomenon but a political one, to be tackled with political means, and that it is always better to defend yourself against your enemies than to run from them.

This means, however, that Zionist propaganda must finally put itself on solid footing instead of standing on ground our enemies prepare for us, that it must base its argument on the realities we have created in Palestine and on the determination of its people to be free, and not on declarations by an English lord or on the sufferings our people have endured.

III

A specter is trying to creep out onto the killing fields of this world. As a hope it haunts the minds of some "statesmen"; as a fear it crouches in the hearts of our best men—as in the words of the young British poet:

> It is the logic of our time,
> No subject for immortal verse,

> That we who lived by honest dreams
> Defend the bad against the worse*

The political name of this specter is: *status quo,* and it is the great fear of the common man, whose expectations were given such grand expression in Henry Wallace's most recent speech. The status quo, the ghost haunting the old house of the European continent, is capable of turning it into unsafe quarters for the armies of the Allies.

If it were not so sad and so serious, there could be no more absurd spectacle than to watch Jewish and Zionist politicians, of all people, stubbornly holding on to the status quo. All their postwar plans assume that Hitler's bestial antisemitism will yield to a milder form, such as that represented by prominent members of the Polish government in exile, the result of which would be a forced mass evacuation of Jews out of Europe. All their political demands are based on a mandate that was granted by a now defunct body and guaranteed by a series of no longer existent states. Even when they still existed, neither that body nor those states gave the holder of the mandate any serious problems on our behalf. They were all still very much alive when the British White Paper blocked immigration and the purchase of land, thereby silently abolishing the Balfour Declaration at the very time of greatest Jewish need. Responsible politicians in executive positions, moreover, never fail to assure us that they are not among "those people" who believe the British Empire in its current form will no longer be viable. All this is, to be sure, not enough to satisfy our opponents in the British Colonial Office; but it is more than enough to preclude new friendships and natural sympathies.

No people has less cause to long for the status quo than the Jewish people. For us the status quo means that—with a few exceptions—the world is divided into those countries that want us to leave and those countries in which we are not allowed entry. In the ranks of the latter, Palestine has already achieved a very prominent position, especially when one thinks—apart from everything else—of the *Struma,* the *Patria,* and Mauritius. It lies in the logic of this development that Lord Moyne, for example, is already trying to secure Palestine an honorable position in the ranks of that first group of nations.

---

*"Where Are the War Poets?" (1943), by the Anglo-Irish poet and critic C. Day-Lewis (1904–72).

Zionist politicians have the great advantage of having climbed down off the tightrope on which Jewish politicians have done their balancing act high above the ground. But the shock was probably too great; for instead of landing on the earth, where normal mortals are usually found, they are sunk up to their necks in the soil of Palestine, which unfortunately badly limits their field of vision. That can be the only reason why they do not understand that the status quo in Europe and in the world would inevitably also mean the status quo in Palestine; that if antisemitism is not defeated and millions of Jews are forced to evacuate, that will not make British colonial policy any more friendly toward Jews, leaving these millions standing before barred gates in Palestine.

It is correct that a number of American Zionists do not share this short-sighted view; but they have no representatives in executive positions and no program of their own. Certainly the status quo lies within the realm of possibilities after this war, but it is equally certain that every program that takes the status quo into account also helps to realize it. But those who do not want to be signatories to the defeat of the Jewish people before it has occurred will sooner or later have to unite on the basis of a few fundamental demands:

They will have to say goodbye to old notions that say the past per se bestows rights or that one can buy a land with money or that in their noble-mindedness noble lords can give a land away. They will declare instead that the right of the Jewish people in Palestine is the same right every human being has to the fruits of his work; that the Arabs had 1,500 years to turn a stony desert into fertile land, whereas the Jews have had not even forty, and that the difference is quite remarkable. They will very eagerly take up the differentiation that Willkie recently made between the British Commonwealth and the British colonial empire, because that Commonwealth is one of the most promising of organizational forms for nations and no one can know if one day it will not prove strong enough to accept peoples of non-British heritage into its ranks. This would give them a real basis for uniting their struggle against colonial administration with positive policies on the part of Britain.

On the other hand they will support all efforts for a federated Europe, because within such a union of nationalities the Jewish question is solvable and guarantees can be given to Palestine as an area for Jewish settlement. But they will also demand an identical political status today for all of Europe's Jews, which includes the recognition of Jewish nationality and makes anti-semitism punishable under the law as a crime against society. Once Jewish politics is established in this spirit, it will not only make life worth living, but also make each of us glad to come into this world as a Jew.

BETWEEN SILENCE
AND SPEECHLESSNESS
Articles from Aufbau, *February 1943–March 1944*

French Political Literature in Exile
February 26 (I) and March 26 (II), 1943

I

The French émigré community may be said to be at least as divided and socially at least as disparate as the German. From members of the Croix de Feu, who with as yet still unexplained abruptness rediscovered their patriotism and hastened to join de Gaulle, via bourgeois parties of all shades and made up of Jewish and non-Jewish businessmen, to representatives of the Front Populaire, the Ligue des Droits de l'Homme, and the Socialist Party—they are all represented. And now that a large segment of the diplomatic corps has also decided it was wiser to side with Darlan and to distance themselves from Laval, the Third Republic is almost totally back together and reconstituted.* (For the latest developments and the various factions in the French camp, see Yves R. Simon, "France and the United Nations," in *Review of Politics*, January 1943.)

Just as most certainly nothing better demonstrates the Weimar Republic's inability to govern or even stay alive than the helplessness and lack of political productivity of its politicians in exile, so too the end of the Third Republic is most easily inferred from the chaos that it has brought as its inheritance into emigration. There is of course no lack of hopes and dreams of restora-

---

*Jean François Darlan (1881–1942), vice premier in the Vichy government in 1940, concluded an armistice with the Allies in 1942 but was assassinated a month later. Pierre Laval (1883–1945), prime minister in the Vichy government, pursued a policy of deportation of Jews.

tion. But it is the representatives of those dreams themselves who are best at seeing to it that their dreams will never fructify. There is scarcely any need to criticize their books, because they criticize themselves simply by the fatal boredom they provoke in the reader.

The overhasty and insolent pessimism of the Western world's intellectuals not only equated the collapse of the Third Republic with the end of France, but also believed that it provided proof of the "end of Western civilization." Although it is surely especially difficult for the politicians and former dignitaries of the Third Republic not to consider the Third Republic an eternal and indispensable institution, Pierre Cot, its former minister for air, wrote an article on democracy for *Free World* a few months ago that is certainly one of the best examples of current journalism. But sadly, apart from this one exception, it must be said that all the actual revolutionary and in the best sense modern books are by men who, judging by their past, belonged more to the opposition on the right. And that those good journalists whom we were accustomed to see as more on the left have turned out to be strangely "reactionary." Julien Benda's [1867–1956] *La grande épreuve des démocraties* (Edition de la Maison Française, New York, 1942) is the best proof of this. Armed with great knowledge from the treasure house of the European tradition, he in fact arrives at no other conclusion than that there are "moral races," at no other position than the same antiquated chauvinism that has demonstrated its bankruptcy in this war. Such absurd blundering into racist theory is no accident; it threatens everyone who has not found his way out of the positivist world. Benda holds fast to the positivist claim that the state exists to secure human happiness. It is an old truism that at the end of this dead-end road stands despotism. Even Hobbes was an advocate of despotism because he was too concerned about the private welfare and security of *Leviathan*'s subjects; and Kant also warned us not to confuse justice and freedom with the welfare of citizens, since the latter is presumably better secured by despotism than by any other form of government. Which only goes to prove yet again that all the truly important problems of our time, which are being settled in such a horribly bloody fashion, are not modern, but very old. But the more bloodily the sins of our fathers are visited upon us, the more impatient and intolerant we shall become with those who cannot cease to commit them again and again.

Nothing more clearly illustrates the inner collapse of the European party system than the fact that the strongest indictment of fascism comes from a man who has been a royalist all his life and who held the grandest illusions about the Spanish Falange. Georges Bernanos's [1888–1948] *Les grands cimetières sous la lune* (his book on the Spanish Civil War) will provide future historians with more information about fascist barbarism than most of those thick tomes that come with a pedantic apparatus of notes. Bernanos's new book, written in exile, *Lettre aux Anglais* (Atlantica Editoria, Rio de Janeiro, 1942), has been penned not by an orator, although France's grand rhetorical tradition is very much alive in him, but by a man who speaks about what has filled his heart and mind to overflowing for a long time now, and he speaks endlessly, because for him everything is interconnected and because for a great writer all this no longer has anything to do with artistic principles, but only with truly saying it all. The book's content is a great eulogy for and diatribe against the French bourgeoisie. From it there speaks the author's great disgust for those who drove the best men of the war generation into political ineffectuality, his great despair at what was not done, and great anger at being deceived. The book's greatness lies in the fact that this disgust for the postwar period does not end up as disgust for mankind in general—and that must have been extraordinarily difficult for a man whose ability to provide ordered and reasoned explanations are in no way commensurate with his artistic hypersensitivity and observational gifts. Instead, his disgust is what spurs him on to wage a chivalrous war for "the honor of man—not the honor of a party, or a system, or even of a fatherland."

Bernanos's example makes clear how much has already been gained, how much can be achieved, if someone simply has his heart in the right place. For his head is still full of erroneous and dangerous notions—like that of "race"; full of abstruse and dangerous prejudices, like his antipathy for Italians and Jews. But it would be petty and pointless to dwell on these, because they are hardly of any consequence in comparison to some very splendid realizations: for instance, that fascism, which babbles on so much about youth, slays childhood and has turned children into vicious dwarves; that human beings, who once practiced idolatry out of ignorance, have returned to the idols of despair for no other reason; and that the world has been cast into its present delirium tremens by the very same people who believed in nothing but *bon sens,* realities, philistine moderation, and conventional wisdom—a delirium tremens that exceeds not just the predictions of the fantasist, but also the poet's powers of imagination.

II

If we can declare with certainty that Bernanos is the strongest writer among French émigrés, then Yves Simon [1903–61, French philosopher, student of Jacques Maritain] is perhaps the most politically astute and productive of their theoreticians. His first book, *The Road to Vichy* (Sheed and Ward, 1942), is among the best written so far about the events that led to a collapse already in preparation from 1918 on. His new book *La marche à la délivrance* (Edition de la Maison Française, New York, 1942), in English translation as *The March to Liberation* (Milwaukee Tower Press), tackles the difficult task of discovering fundamental political principles for our future actions. If Simon wrote his first book as a Frenchman and as a historian whose best understandings are informed by sorrow and political passion, his second book is written by a European, by a politician for whom observation of the past has become nothing but preparation for tomorrow's action.

The best credentials this professor of philosophy has to offer for venturing into "foreign territory" is his declaration of shared responsibility and shared guilt in past catastrophe. He sees such shared guilt both in the indifference of his generation toward politics, including their arrogant attack on public life, and, more concretely, in the peculiar blindness that prevented the French, of all people—because they had espoused the cause of reconciliation with the Weimar Republic—from seeing that the condition of such a reconciliation would have been to crush Hitler. They were still living in the nationalist delusion that Germany equals Germany, just as their opponents, the French chauvinists with their babbling about "eternal Germany" prepared the way for an accommodation with Hitler—it really made no difference to them what government they concluded a peace with.

Since Simon is not one of those people who write thick books or make long speeches in order to prove the impossible—that is, that they are always right—he manages in just one thin volume to pose many of the questions of our time and to shed some light on them. It is difficult to prepare for a future without being utopian—and that means, as Simon also notes, without embracing methods that inevitably lead back to the total state: "Utopia gives birth to absolutism because it can only become history by means of absolute force." This is related to the fact that utopian thinking always attempts to anticipate the future in all its details. Genuine political thought avoids as best it can anything too concrete and is content with proposing and implementing general ideas. The kind of generality—sometimes verging on vagueness— with which Simon discusses the most recent issues of our time is hard to avoid, but it is all the more proof of the living force of his ideas.

In his discussion Simon proceeds from a few fundamental observations. The first says: "The Germans would never be in Paris if this war were not an international civil war." This in turn is for him proof that we are at the end of national wars and that the French catastrophe is only the clearest evidence that we are watching the end of the nation-state as it has existed until now, of the nation that was the first to organize as a nation-state and that brought forth the ideas of the French Revolution. A second such fundamental observation is that we—in contrast to the intelligentsia of the past few decades— have found new and productive access to the old, grand formulas of the French Revolution. In other words, that the intellectual content of the French Revolution, having long since been declared dead, has begun to awaken from its state of suspended animation. Third, Simon discusses how all the political questions of our day exist essentially throughout the world, that there is no escape: "One escapes from a curved surface only by climbing down into a ditch or up to heaven." And since there no longer exists any way out of the great crisis of our time, every moment of despair becomes a kind of cosmic catastrophe and every hope grows until it is "as big as the world."

A brief glance at the rest of the book is all that can be offered here. The best is without doubt found on those pages where Simon proves that the usual alternatives before which our politicians are always so happy to set us and that poison all our political thought—authority versus freedom or liberal economics versus totally planned economies, and so on—serve no one except our foes, that they are nothing other than the product of the failed imaginations of those "thinkers" who are accustomed to equate "the history of mankind with that of a small privileged minority" or to confuse "the golden age of liberalism with the golden age of freedom." One of those errors to which, among other things, we owe the fact that we have come this far so splendidly.

The least satisfying parts of the book are those where a monarchy for France is discussed in excessive detail. And a more serious problem, though rather inconsequential for Simon's essential insights, is his uncritical acceptance of Sorel's concept of an elite.

The Real Reasons for Theresienstadt
Letter to the Editor

September 3, 1943

. . . moreover I do not agree with the depiction that your newspaper gives of Theresienstadt. Theresienstadt was among the first camps and thus cannot have been planned as an "alibi."* Since 1940 I have been very closely following all deportations and measures taken in the camps and believe that a consistent political agenda lies behind them all, despite occasional local variations.

1. Jews are tolerated and sometimes shown favors wherever there is a chance of stirring up antisemitism among the population. Example: Until 1941 the sale of supplies of French goods to German soldiers was arranged to pass through Jewish hands and people had the impression that German soldiers were being expressly encouraged to buy in Jewish quarters. The result was that Jews in the area of Toulouse, to which those Polish Jews living in France had fled, returned to Paris in great numbers. After a few months these Jews were then arrested and sent to concentration camps—the populace was supposed to be left with the impression that they were being protected from Jews.

2. Jews are deported from areas where the population is not antisemitic— for example, Holland—to those places where local antisemitism can be counted on—for example, Poland. When the Poles began to pull back a bit from their antisemitism and even showed some sympathy for Jews, the latter were either transported farther to the east or exterminated.

3. Jews are transported out of areas where their mere presence might lead to centers of resistance—for example, Germany. When Frau Müller sees

---

*In the *Aufbau* of August 27, an article titled "Theresienstadt as Model Ghetto" described the conditions in the camp as an "alibi," a false façade, for what was really going on.

that Frau Schmidt next door is nice to Frau Cohn, Frau Schmidt knows she no longer needs to fear Frau Müller and that perhaps she can even discuss things with her. In this sense deportations from Germany, with which the whole horrible mess began, were actually planned as preventive measures with a view to domestic politics.

4. The Nazis have repeatedly calmed the population, especially in Czechoslovakia and Germany, by declaring that their intent is not the extermination of the Jews but their segregation. And that is the purpose of Theresienstadt, which after all lies in the middle of the protectorate—that is, in a region that can be watched over by local civilians and thus can no longer be considered antisemitic.

5. Mass executions occur only in areas that are either uninhabited, like the Russian steppes, or where it is quite likely that at least a part of the local population can be persuaded to participate more or less actively, as in Poland and Romania. Exterminations become total only when expressions of sympathy become too obvious.

6. As you know, Jewish attempts to emigrate, even in France, were encouraged only where the issue was primarily one of political refugees. In the past few months the Nazis, by way of the Bulgarian and Romanian governments, have offered to allow very large numbers of Jews to leave. Such magnanimity would very clearly change if the Allies would actually declare themselves ready to accept these Jews. As long as they do not, the Nazis can declare to other peoples: You see how Jews are viewed in foreign countries, where they are free and equal. Only you are so foolish as to be carried away by some "unpolitical" sense of sympathy for these vermin. —I do not know whether this propaganda is still effective today.

7. How very hard the Nazis try to accommodate autochthonous antisemitic tendencies is evident from the fact that recently in France only foreign or newly naturalized (which for the French is the same thing) Jews were deported—under the pretense of repatriation, which doubtless met with the approval of considerable segments of the public.

I am writing to you about these observations in response to your Theresienstadt article since I have long been of the opinion that our kind of reporting is often met with incredulity precisely because it usually neglects to explain the connection between the persecution of Jews and the Nazi apparatus of total control.

Can the Jewish-Arab Question Be Solved?

December 17 (I) and December 31 (II), 1943

I

Ibn Saud [1880–1969, king of Saudi Arabia] recently issued an absolutely hostile statement about Jewish claims to Palestine, thereby dealing yet another heavy blow to the Zionist movement. What we have here is the first statement in which this utterly independent personage in the Arab world indicates there is to be a new politics—that is, he shows his desire to play an active role in the so-called Arab national movement, after having previously kept his distance from its corrupt politics of intrigue. And that makes his position all the more significant today. He would hardly have broken his silence if plans for an Arab federation were not taking shape at this moment. Although the position of the United States in regard to the situation in the Near East has not yet been made public, there is hardly any doubt that the policy of the British Empire is directed toward a fairly loose federation that would include Iraq, Syria, Palestine, Transjordan, Egypt, and presumably Saudi Arabia as well. There have been more than enough signs to suggest that this policy will pay no regard whatever to Zionist protests. This is all the more blatant, since hostility toward a Jewish national homeland is the strongest link binding the various Arab countries, the one point about which they all agree.

In the open game of power politics the Jews, who after all occupy no position of power, can be regarded as *une quantité négligeable*. This has become especially true ever since Zionist leadership gave up on a Jewish army for reasons of realpolitik, when in fact a Jewish army would offer a certain guarantee for a Jewish future in Palestine. Instead we have been presented with two mutually exclusive Zionist programs concerning the future constitutional status of Palestine. One of the two advocates the formation of a Jewish commonwealth in Palestine and by making extreme demands is evidently trying to compensate for the lack of any basis for negotiation. Proposed is an autonomous state based on the idea that tomorrow's majority will concede minority rights to today's majority, which indeed would be something brand-new in the history of nation-states.

A Binational State?

The alternative proposal of Dr. Magnes [Judah Leon Magnes, 1876–1948, founder of the Ihud party] envisions a binational state in Palestine, integrated into an Arab federation and affiliated with an Anglo-American union. Precisely the utopian character of this program for a Jewish state has won for it a larger number of adherents than might normally be expected for a plan by a university professor who holds no position in the world of politics. At least we must grant this much: this second program takes into consideration the real factors that play a role, and it appears to fit admirably into the concept of a revitalized British Empire. There is, however, a hitch, for Dr. Magnes's binational state would leave the Jews in the position of a permanent minority within a larger Arab empire that would exist under the weaker or stronger protectorate of a third party, either under the aegis of the British Empire or the United States or under protection shared by both powers. In which case we definitely cannot exclude the possibility that after the war Palestine might become the worst Diaspora problem of all, instead of being a place for Jewish national emancipation to develop.

Apart from the fact that these two "programs" are mutually exclusive, they both use the same mode of political thinking. Both hold to the discredited notion that national conflicts can be solved on the basis of guaranteeing minority rights. The advocates of the Jewish commonwealth or state want a Jewish majority and are prepared to guarantee the Arabs their rights as a minority, whereas the existence of a binational state within an Arab federation would mean instead that it would be the Jews who have minority status. Both proposals, moreover, cling to the idea of a sovereign state or empire whose majority people is identical with the state.

The attempt to solve national conflicts by first creating sovereign states, and then guaranteeing minority rights within state structures made up of various nationalities, has suffered such a spectacular defeat in recent times that one would expect no one would even presume to think of following that path again.

We need only recall postwar history in most of the nations of Eastern and Central Europe, for the failure to grant minorities the justice due them was surpassed only by the fact that these minorities enjoyed, at least theoretically, the most splendid legal protection. Since the peace treaty of 1918 history can offer an onerous number of arguments against this traditional solution for national conflicts. There is no reason to hope that the national problem, which is what we are dealing with in Palestine, can be solved in terms of national politics, and it makes no difference whether one seeks that solution in a small sovereign Jewish state or in a huge Arab empire.

The truth is, to speak in sweeping generalities, that Palestine can be saved as the national homeland of Jews only if (like other small countries and nationalities) it is integrated into a federation. Federative arrangements hold out good chances for the future because they promise the greatest chance for success in solving national conflicts and can thus be the basis for a political life that offers peoples the possibility of reorganizing themselves politically. Precisely because of the strong appeal that this new idea exerts on the hopes and wishes of many European nations, it has become rather fashionable to use the term "federation" for almost any combination of nation-states— from the old alliances to the new systems of national blocs that are now being called regional federations. But whether one plans nation-states as isolated structures or in some combination with other states, the conflict between majority and minority, such as we have in Palestine, lives on.

And as with this conflict, so too with the old alternative between minority rights (as in the proposal of the American Jewish Conference) and the slogan of "population transfers" (as suggested by Revisionists), though the latter will never work without fascist organizations.

If "regional federations" of sovereign states are nothing more than a new system of alliances, then the so-called Arab federation is merely a cover for a grand empire. For the advocates of the British Empire this "federation" is tantamount to a loose union of the various Arab states, where the usually fierce quarrels among the ruling families will create sufficient space for the British to exercise their influence in the Near East. On the other hand, for the ruling Arab families this federation means a purely Arab realm, within which each individual clan struggles with the others to gain control of a large and enduring Arab empire that consists of an Arab majority and many small minorities. In both cases the term "federation" is an intentional misnomer. A genuine federation is made up of different, clearly identifiable nationalities or other political elements that together form the state. National conflicts can be solved within such a federation only because the unsolvable minority-majority problem has ceased to exist.

The first such federation realized was in the United States of America. In this union no individual state has any dominion whatever over any other, and all the states together govern the country. The Soviet Union solved its nationality problem in a different way; it dissolved the czarist empire and created a union of nationalities, each with equal rights regardless of size. The British Commonwealth of Nations—in contradistinction to the British Empire—could be yet another valid possibility for a federation. A great majority of both the British populace and members of Parliament approve of this transformation of empire into commonwealth. Yet at present the two systems exist concurrently: the Commonwealth, a free union of Anglo-Saxon nations, and the Empire, in which the members of the Commonwealth govern vast colonial regions inhabited by peoples of non-Anglo-Saxon origin.

As soon as these peoples are granted the status of a dominion, as is already the case for India, the transformation of the empire into a commonwealth and a genuine federation will have been achieved. Given the importance of the Near East as the gateway to India there is no reason why Palestine might not also be included within this framework.

II

So far, however, Palestine is tied to the British Empire. The status of its population, both Jewish and Arab, is clearly that of natives. No one knows whether the so-called Arab federation will remain part of the British Empire or will be allowed to develop into an independent Arab empire. But one thing is certain: As far as the Jews are concerned, they would probably be treated equally badly in both instances.

If, however, the Near East were to be granted a place within a new British Commonwealth that included peoples of non-British origin, then there would no longer be a Jewish problem in its current form.

The Jewish people could then achieve political status as a *people* with equal rights within all regions belonging to the British Commonwealth. The same holds true for Arabs. In Palestine both Jews and Arabs would enjoy equal rights as members of a larger system that ensures the national interests of each. And the question of who should rule over whom would then have become meaningless. Without requiring a national state of their own, the Jews would have the same political status as all other members of the Commonwealth, whereby Palestine would be given special status as a Jewish homeland.

A further possibility for a reasonable solution of the Palestine question would be *a kind of Mediterranean federation.* In a model of this sort the Arabs would be strongly represented and yet not in a position to dominate all others. Insofar as it is generally recognized that neither Spain, nor Italy, nor France can exist economically without their possessions in North Africa, this sort of federation would provide for these three countries a fair and just solution to the colonial question. For Jews it would mean the restoration of both their dignity and their place among the nations of the Mediterranean, to the cultural glory of which region they have contributed so much. But in this case as well one would have to insist that those Jews living within the boundaries of this federation be granted a status that enjoys equal political rights and that special weight be given to Palestine as the Jewish homeland.

This political framework can of course be expanded until it includes a larger federation of European countries. It is clear that both the Near East and North Africa would have to belong to such a system. This would be more advantageous for the Jews, for it would mean that they would be recognized as members of the European community of peoples, that they would have an intra-European status, that Palestine would receive guarantees that it would be the homeland of European and world Jewry, and that favorable conditions would be created for the radical elimination of antisemitism.

Under such roughly sketched plans, the Arabs would be brought into union with European peoples. And surely this ought to frighten no one who is aware of the great and lasting achievements that the Arab people once passed on to Western civilization. If they are given the opportunity to overcome feudal, backward conditions and terrible poverty, then there is really no reason why they cannot be in that same situation again. Such an opportunity is preferable to placation or, worse, encouragement of pan-Arabism, which sooner or later, like all pan-movements, will inevitably degenerate into imperialist power politics and end in destructive conflicts among peoples that have to live together one way or the other.

The Jewish people have the right and the duty to say in what kind of world they want to live. This much is certain: without their active participation there is no way to put an end to the tragic Jewish problem or to the alarming reality of antisemitism as a political weapon. In the face of utopian demands and "realistic" attempts at placation, both of which have arisen out of justified despair, we must develop constructive ideas about the future of the Jewish people—ideas that remove the artificial isolation of both the Jewish and Palestinian problem. Both will be solved only within a political framework that also guarantees a solution to national conflicts and problems among the other peoples of Europe.

THE POLITICAL ORGANIZATION
OF THE JEWISH PEOPLE
Articles from Aufbau, *April 1944–April 1945*

For the Honor and Glory of the Jewish People
April 21, 1944

April 19 marked the anniversary of the beginning of the armed uprising by the Jews of the Warsaw ghetto. What the Nazis thought would be a matter of a few hours turned into a great battle that lasted several weeks. What we in our timidity were at first inclined to consider a local outburst of despair quickly turned out to be the beginning of a series of armed revolts in concentration camps and ghettos, followed shortly thereafter by the organization of Jewish guerrilla bands with their own Jewish flag. Something for which Jews around the world, and especially Jews in the Palestinian *yishuv* had petitioned for years—the formation of a Jewish army—was suddenly created by those from whom we would have least expected such deeds, people broken in body and spirit, the future inhabitants of asylums and sanatoriums, objects of worldwide Jewish charity. Those who a year before were still screaming to be saved, helpless victims of bloodthirsty murderers, people who at best would end their lives one day as recipients of foreign charity, suddenly came to the overnight decision to help themselves if possible, and to help the Jewish people no matter what. If they themselves could not be saved, they wanted at least, as they said in their own words, to salvage "the honor and glory of the Jewish people." And in doing so they ended the pariah existence of the Jewish people in Europe and, by claiming equal rights, joined the ranks of other European peoples in the struggle for freedom.

Honor and glory are new words in the political vocabulary of our people. We would perhaps have to go back to the days of the Maccabees to hear such language. This is not how martyrs speak, who know only the glory of God, nor is it the language of those in despair who know only the sad courage of suicide. Rather here speaks a people's momentary avant-garde, those who intend to lay claim to its political leadership tomorrow. Just as the new face of Europe is being prepared in underground movements in all countries, so the new status of the Jewish people among the peoples of Europe is being prepared in the Jewish underground movement.

A Jewish underground movement can only become a reality where European antisemitism is dwindling as a mass phenomenon. That should be clear to anyone who for even one moment pictures the conditions under which an illegal body of troops must operate in the midst of other peoples. A Jewish civilian population that could protect Jewish guerrillas and supply them with food no longer exists. They are absolutely dependent on the solidarity of not just other underground movements but also of the non-Jewish civilian population. This is also one of the prime reasons why there was such a delay in the formation of bands of Jewish guerrillas, why all of Europe first had to seethe with unrest before they could enter the fray. Antisemitism first had to be destroyed within the bloody school of Nazi terror, for the courage of despair, which drives individuals to suicide, can never organize a people. A people finds the courage to fight only if there is even the smallest chance of success. No one can defend himself against a whole world of enemies. The Nazi policy of wiping out entire populations has made blind obedience more dangerous than open rebellion. It is not only better, it is safer to belong to a guerrilla troop than to be sitting in a concentration camp or to be dragged off to forced labor. This helps mobilize not just the elites within all European peoples, it also defines the entire situation politically and militarily. Nazi deportation orders are direct orders for the underground to mobilize. This holds true for all European peoples, but it holds true to a far greater extent for the Jews.

We know very little about the politics of these fighting Jews. All the same, what little has found its way to us allows a few conclusions about their political aspirations. Above all there is the fact that they fight under their own flag—and that means that they intend to battle *as Jews* for the freedom of Jews. There is moreover the fact that on some occasions they have raised the Polish flag alongside their Jewish banner. And that means they are acting in friendship and solidarity with the Polish people, but without identifying themselves as such. We can assume that many of them may want to immigrate to Palestine. But they are not about to be evacuated, and they cannot be terrified by hatred toward Jews. If they do immigrate, then it will only be because they learned in battle to demand more than individual protection and personal security. They will go because they demand freedom and equal rights as a nation and security as a people.

But even those who may want to remain—and most will presumably have to remain for a good while in any case—could scarcely be offered the restoration of the status quo. In the Jewish underground movement there is no longer any difference between Western and Eastern Jews, between assimilated and unassimilated, and the old system of security whereby the Jewish masses were protected by their "well-to-do brethren" in other countries has proved to be a dangerous illusion. Only the same status throughout Europe for those of Jewish nationality, a status linked to legal sanctions against antisemitism in all countries, only the recognition of equal rights for a people and not just for an individual, can bring to fruition the integration of the Jewish people into the future community of European peoples, the road to which is being paved today by a Jewish community working in solidarity with other underground movements in Europe.

U.S.A.—Oil—Palestine

May 5, 1944

The failure of the Wagner-Taft resolution to be passed in Congress is one of the worst disappointments inflicted so far on Zionists and the Jews in Palestine.* The United States, which after the previous war tried in vain to play a role in the political reorganization of the countries of the former Ottoman Empire, appeared determined this time not to let itself be outmaneuvered in that part of the world. This aroused justified hopes among Palestinian Jews. They were counting on the repeated sympathy expressed by both Congress and the administration for building a Jewish national homeland, counting on the strength of American Zionism and the traditional help that the U.S.

---

*In 1944 the five-year pause in immigration to Palestine stipulated by the British White Paper was to end. Senators Robert A. Taft and Robert F. Wagner introduced a resolution in the U.S. Senate that made it clear that the United States intended to leave the door to immigration open to millions of surviving Jewish refugees.

government has tended to give to those countries and peoples around the world who are represented by strong national splinter groups in the New World. These hopes have been shattered, at least for now.

The *yishuv* in Palestine has thus far had no chance to stand on its own two political feet. Its disappointment is all the greater, since for over a decade its trust in Britain has been badly undermined. It has come to feel, in every respect, the repercussions of the sudden turnaround by the British Colonial Office in the 1930s, which during the postwar period had appeared more inclined to increase tensions among Arab states and to look at least in part to Jewish support, but was now working to secure agreements among the Arabs. But since the ruling Arab family dynasties could agree on nothing except an anti-Jewish policy in Palestine, such a policy of "reconciliation" could hardly end up as anything but a crystallization of anti-Zionism. It is understandable enough—if not all that reasonable—that the greater part of the Zionist movement began some time ago to look around for another protector. And while a certain segment of Revisionism seemed to be betting on Russia, others, especially in Palestine, put their hope in America.

The significance of the Near East for Britain and America can be expressed nowadays in a single word: oil. The question of America's own current oil reserves and their eventual supplementation by still-inexhaustible regions of Saudi Arabia plays a relatively subordinate role here. The control of both air and sea lanes will in the future depend on oil hubs around the world. And for both—and that means for future world commerce—the Near East has assumed a key position. If the assumption is correct that after the war about half of the entire world's shipping will be in the hands of the United States, that fact alone will force American foreign policy to secure its own oil hubs.

Which also means that the laying of an oil pipeline from the Persian Gulf to the Mediterranean, as planned by the American government, will become one of the most important factors in postwar politics. Since it has evidently been determined that Arabian oil is to cover much of the needs of European countries, America's future influence on intra-European matters will depend to a large extent on this pipeline. A clause was already included in the proposed contract between the oil companies and the government stating that the sale of oil to foreign countries can never run counter to American interests. Another clause spoke of America's active participation in the peace, welfare, and political integrity of the governments of oil-producing countries. And with that the American government is unequivocally expressing its will to energetically pursue its foreign political interests in the Near East.

The Arabs, who have had such brilliant success blackmailing Britain in all sorts of ways, immediately decided that they needed to exploit this plan in order to squelch any expressions of friendship for Jews. No sooner had they succeeded in that, than they put the entire project in jeopardy. After the White Paper had finally become operative, King Ibn Saud tried first to play the British off against the Americans. For that purpose he called to mind the original concessionary treaty from 1933 in which he had given preference to American oil companies over their competition, because the former were independent of their government. He declared to the American representative in Saudi Arabia that if the American government itself were to become involved he would favor closer oil relationships with Britain, and he called in an adviser on oil issues from England, under the pretext that the American experts were incompetent. Almost at the same time it was announced that King Farouk of Egypt was introducing a new export duty on oil—which at the very least jeopardized Alexandria as the endpoint of the planned pipeline, since American oil would hardly be competitive on the European market with British oil that could be shipped free of duties from Haifa. Finally it turned out that construction at Haifa—the second-best possibility after Alexandria—could not possibly be considered, since under the League of Nations mandate no foreign power except the power holding that mandate had the right to buy or lease land in Palestine.

There is no question that because of its legitimate global economic interests America has been compelled to join the political game in the Near East. The only question is whether America chooses to be master of these future necessities by employing yesterday's outdated colonial methods. This is even less desirable since the Arabs are evidently brilliant masters of the rules of *divide et impera,* by which today the Arabs, but possibly tomorrow the Jews, can be assigned the task of guarding oil hubs. America's great chance indeed lies in the fact that it does not have a colonial tradition or imperialist ambitions. The greatest proactive bastion of its foreign policy is not that it possesses oil, but rather the trust that the peoples of the world have placed in the foundations of this great republic from its inception.

The Balfour Declaration and the Palestine Mandate
May 19, 1944

Those who announced the Balfour Declaration have often been accused of giving away a country that did not even belong to them. Anti-Zionist Jews, too, who as members of the Jewish plutocracy have not been in the habit of displaying exaggerated scruples when it comes to imperialist practices, could seem very thin-skinned when it came to the issue of Palestine. The Zionists saw the international basis for the Balfour Declaration in the Palestine mandate guaranteed by the League of Nations, whereas the Arabs claimed that the precise wording of mandates expressly requires the mandate holder to develop independent, sovereign governments in the area under its control, that this has already taken place in Iraq and has at least been promised to Syria, and that only the Jews, and/or the Balfour Declaration, have hindered a similar happy solution to the Palestine question.

The mandate system was, after all, never more than a legal fiction that seemed useful for camouflaging political reality. In the words of one of the British members of the Permanent Mandate Commission of the League of Nations, it was thought of as a compromise between declarations the Allies had made during the previous war to the effect that they did not want to annex territory and their contradictory desire at the end of the war to annex parts of the Turkish Empire and former German colonies. Politically the mandate system was already abolished by the end of the 1920s, that is, when Iraq was released from its mandate status. On that occasion (1) the League of Nations, as guarantor of the entire system, was informed only belatedly; (2) Iraq was bound to Britain in a treaty that several members of the Permanent Mandate Commission regarded as a shift from mandate status to a protectorate; and (3) the question of minority rights in Iraq (one of the serious reasons for mandate control in all these areas) was to be "solved" in such a way that the League of Nations was prevented from supervising it, and the Kurds were told that they would do best "to throw in their lot with the Arabs." The termination of the French mandate in Syria was expressly supposed to follow the Iraq model.

It is true that an end to the Palestinian mandate has always been rejected by referring to the Balfour Declaration, which is quoted in the mandate. In point of fact Palestine has always been viewed by the people of the Indian

Office as the most important country in the Near East. During negotiations preceding the Treaty of Versailles, Lord Curzon [1869–1925, Balfour's successor as the British foreign minister] pointed out that above all Palestine was of crucially strategic importance for protecting the Suez Canal and thus for securing the route to India; and he insisted that at the conference itself Britain would reject any international administration of Palestine. It would certainly serve the cause of a politics free of illusion, if for our part we could come to see the Balfour Declaration in light of Indian Office politics. For even if the Declaration was indeed not dictated solely by selfish motives and the concerns of colonial policy, nevertheless over the longer term—that is, for as long as British policy in the Near East is essentially determined by British control over India—it can serve to implement only such interests and concerns. Protection of the Jewish national homeland by the Palestine mandate is not improved by the fact that the League of Nations—which had already shown itself impotent in the case of Iraq—no longer exists.

Differences concerning foreign policy within Zionism itself tend nowadays to concentrate on the question of whether it is better to have Britain or America or Russia as the holder of the mandate in Jerusalem. The principle of uncertainty would not thereby be improved in any way. Each of these powers can assume such an office only in pursuit of its own foreign policy and therefore its inclination will always have to be to concede only as much to domestic political forces as is compatible with control of the foreign policy of the region in question. This was already clear twenty-five years ago when Lord Milner [1854–1925, colonial minister] wrote to Lloyd George [1863–1945, prime minister] that the independence of the Arabs was, to be sure, one of the principles of British policy, but that independent Arab rulers should not be permitted to make treaties with any foreign powers except Britain. The transformation of the Iraq mandate into a treaty, by which the country is fully autonomous in its domestic politics but remains absolutely subject to British control of its foreign policy, has made it perfectly clear which clauses of the mandate treaty Britain truly intends to observe in an emergency.

The White Paper is a further, if not quite so momentous, step in the same direction, and must therefore—even beyond the issue of its wording—be a cause of very great concern. Yet it would be a big mistake to assume that the fundamental uncertainty concerning the political status in Palestine would be lifted by a change in the holder of the mandate or by additional protection offered by other very distant powers. The only realistic position would be a policy of alliances with other Mediterranean peoples, which would strengthen the Jewish status in Palestine and secure the active sympathies of our neighbors. Legal considerations and appeals to the mandate itself—such as those we read and hear daily in protest against the White Paper—are at least, given the seriousness of our situation, hopelessly inadequate.

The End of a Rumor

June 2, 1944

The doors behind which the five prime ministers of the British Commonwealth convened in London were not quite so hermetically sealed as has usually been the case with these public-secret negotiations that have become the fashion during this war. And although public-secret meetings have the disadvantage of giving rise to rumors in the realm of public opinion, the Empire Conference in London had the great advantage of shedding light on the future foundations of the British Commonwealth and of thereby putting an end to a whole series of rumors. And among these now dead rumors is the hope, which has reemerged over and over for years now, that a Jewish Palestine would have the status of a dominion.

The British Commonwealth, which is often confused with the British Empire, is the organization through which the British motherland is connected to all those countries of the world that were settled by Britons. Only together with these dominions do the British Isles form the British nation. Determined foes of the politics of empire, so-called Little Englanders, have often ignored this fact, much to their own detriment; their criticism never took into account the real necessity of British politics to pursue world politics for the sake of the nation. It must be said, however, by way of excuse, that only a few decades ago it was very difficult to make any correct judgments about the special organizational form of the Commonwealth (the name comes out of the previous war), and that only in the course of this war, in the give-and-take of contradictory proposals, has it developed in full clarity. The results of the Empire Conference present a provisional stopping point along that route.

The first important result of the conference was the rejection of a proposal made by the Australian prime minister to create a permanent Secretariat of the Commonwealth in London. Until now in fact only one part of the British nation, the motherland, has also been an imperial power, whose global political interests are oriented less toward its dominions than toward its control of India. Had the Australian proposal been adopted, this would have meant that the foreign policy of British countries strewn around the world would be uniformly directed from London and that for their part the dominions would assume shared responsibility for the motherland's colonial possessions. This would have bound the entire British Commonwealth to imperial politics. It is surely not by chance that the proposal failed primarily due to objections of the American dominion, Canada.

Evidently the second failed proposal is one that has been debated since last December concerning changes to the British Commonwealth first suggested in a speech by Jan Smuts. The South African prime minister wanted, as is well known, to include Western European nations in the British union, which would give Britain a firm foothold on the continent and thus put an end for good and all to the immediate danger to the British Isles that has always come from that direction in time of war. This would have meant transforming the British Commonwealth, which is simply a partnership within a single nation, into a true Commonwealth of Nations—in Smuts's proposal, then, a small-scale League of Nations, a model for banding together that other nations could then follow in the future.

Smuts's proposal is evidently the result of considerations that come from the early stages of the current war; from the period when Churchill, in confronting the German danger, offered the French a common government and common citizenship, and when, somewhat later, Cripps [Sir Stafford Cripps, 1889–1952, socialist, minister of aircraft production in Churchill's cabinet], in order to confront the Japanese danger, promised the Indians dominion status. That in both cases the reply was a rejection probably did not encourage the British to make any further such attempts. And Smuts's South African homeland, where Boers and English live together under dominion status, is hardly a suitable model to be followed. For ultimately it is not to the Boers but to the English element that the Boer Jan Smuts owes the small majority that, thanks to his own strong personality, he was able to put together, enabling him to lead the South African Union into war on the side of Britain. Although the extraordinarily loose connection between dominion and motherland stood the test in this time of extreme emergency, it proved unsatisfactory as soon as the reliability of non-British nationals entered into the equation.

The most important example in this connection is, of course, Ireland, which does not belong to the Commonwealth and did not even send a representative to the Empire Conference. This clearly shows how very much the organization of dominions is based on the national British element, and, in contrast, how unimportant geographic and even military factors are. For while Ireland's independence can only be protected by Britain, it has turned out that only America was in a position to defend Australia. This altered nothing: Australia belongs to the Commonwealth; Ireland does not.

It may be an open question whether the war has strengthened or weakened the British Empire, whether it will leave behind some or no changes in British colonial methods. The British Commonwealth at any rate has been strengthened by this test and will emerge clearly as the organization of the British (but only the British) nation. No one can predict whether, and if so for how long, India, and with it Palestine, will belong to the British Empire. It appears as good as out of the question that in the foreseeable future they will belong to the British Commonwealth.

Philistine Dynamite

June 16, 1944

For more than three years now the official Zionist organizations have tried in vain to deal with a group of "young people" who, with the "irresponsibility" of "charlatans," have established one "paper organization" after the other, although they enjoy none of the authority of any existing organization.* How it is that a half dozen "adventurers" could achieve, without any official help, such success in terms of both money and prestige, remains quite wisely unmentioned. For the truth is, of course, that the attraction of the group lay in its unsullied newness, which allowed it at least to hint at the vacuum created by the activity and inactivity of those organizations, so that, had their

---

*Arendt is speaking here of the Revisionists, especially the Bergson group, which on May 7, 1943, had taken out a full-page ad in *Aufbau*, calling for the rescue of all Jews under Nazi rule, their immediate transport to Palestine or other asylums, and the formation of a Jewish army with "suicide" commandos and squadrons of airplanes to bombard cities deep inside Germany, thereby bringing hope to Hitler's victims.

intentions been honest, their lack of bureaucratic status in any existing superannuated organization would have worked to their advantage.

But their intentions were evidently not honest. They did indeed found a Committee for a Jewish Army once they got wind that it was the will of the Jewish people to have a Jewish army; and they founded a Committee to Save the Jews from Europe once they saw that no one was paying serious attention to the passionate anguish of Jews and non-Jews over the fate of European Jewry. Both committees did a lot of advertising and presumably raised even more money. With the result that we have not yet heard of a single Palestinian or stateless Jew who was encouraged to register as a volunteer just in case a Jewish army ever was approved; nor is anything known about Jews they have rescued from Europe. This, and not the presumption of authority, is the genuine deception. For given the constitutions of our Jewish organizations— which are not all that democratic in any case—authority is, so to speak, there for the taking.

The activities of the Bergson group are very closely tied to Palestinian terrorist organizations. Their admission that they are connected to Irgun has doubtless enhanced their prestige. Their acknowledgment that they use terrorist methods has won them a certain sympathy in those Russian Jewish circles that have learned nothing since 1905 and for which the word "terror" comes with a halo of the heroism of Soviet revolutionaries. They do not know that the only thing old idealists have in common with the modern terrorists we are dealing with in Palestine is a word. With the former one could have argued whether in extreme instances ends justify means. But such an argument would be pointless with these people, because at the bottom of their hearts they believe not only that ends justify means but also that only an end that can be achieved by terror is worth their effort. Our modern nihilists no longer bother with a weltanschauung, but instead actively attempt to establish nothing. They do not care about something so "bourgeois" as differences between the guilty and the innocent, between true political representatives and minor civil servants just doing their jobs. They think it is all right to murder anyone who can be murdered—an innocent English Tommy or a harmless Arab in the market of Haifa.

Such a dedicated affinity to destruction easily takes on the look of genuine passion. It is of course more than questionable whether the Bergson group ever gave serious thought to a Jewish army. But one thing has definitely fired their imaginations: the possibility of creating suicide battalions, which they were proposing for a while. The fascist "master race" debased soldiers by turning them into murderers, and now the only idea that the fascists of a small oppressed people can come up with is to debase heroes by having them commit suicide. In both cases they could be quite confident of the applause of philistines sitting comfortably in their armchairs, from where the whole world simply looks like some sublime drama.

For what differentiates the philistine from the citizen is his absolute disregard for the public's welfare and ruthless pursuit of his own. The fascists have made a great impression on philistines around the world, because they have given their own irresponsibility the halo of heroism and by their active malevolence have rescued the philistines from their own passive malevolence. It was just one step from this morbid admiration for pillage and murder in politics to the "total" mobilization that—whether for the sake of a career or one's own life or one's family—swept away the Ten Commandments more quickly and efficiently than any nihilist theoretician could ever have dreamed.

But our modern terrorists have a chance only when the malevolent boredom of the philistine is joined by the grave despair of some citizens, who see their justified political demands simply passed over by official agencies. In this sense so-called *responsible* organizations truly and always share responsibility. Their justified pillorying of the Bergson group and Irgun would surely instill far more solid confidence had it been accompanied by a declaration of and explanation for their own mistakes and sins of omission.

This recent omission is made up for in part by the fact that these hyperradical "young people" were so imprudent that they left the sure foundation of activist propaganda in order to favor us with a piece of their own political doctrine. By differentiating between the Hebrew nation in Palestine and Europe and the Jewish religious community in other countries, they awakened familiar memories of those long ago times when Zionism provided an excellent asylum for persecuted Eastern Jews, relieving more fortunate assimilated Jews of responsibility for their people as a whole or of seeing to it that Jews could immigrate to their own countries as well. From the ranks of the people these youths heard the message that there was a will to form a Jewish army and a passionate desire to rescue Jews of Europe. The Hebrew nation was their very own invention. And so the nihilistic and now savage philistine of today has returned to the ideological house of his fathers—those peaceful, philistine Jews of yesteryear whose concern was their own security.

Guests from No-Man's-Land

June 30, 1944

If the thousand human beings to whom the American government granted temporary refuge in the United States had been individuals expelled from their native lands on account of their religious and political convictions, then this policy would have great significance. It would mean that one of the oldest and most sacred duties of Western states and one of the oldest and most sacred rights of Western man, the right of asylum, was once again being honored.

But the thousand we await here in America are not exiles in the ancient and holy sense. They have not been persecuted as individuals but rather as members of a race. No one asked about their religious confession or political persuasion. What they will find here, just as in the great refugee camps of the Middle East, is security and mercy. But this is a far cry from the ancient right of asylum.

For this right has disappeared, since the freedom and human dignity of the individual is no longer at stake, but the bare existence of human beings; as when particular persons no longer go into exile, but great masses of human beings living together in peace must flee their homes. In the entire codex of national or international law which governs the inner life and coexistence of nations, there is nothing that anticipates this grotesque case—the attempt to exterminate an entire people. Thus the Jews who have been driven from Germany since 1933 and Europe since 1940 live outside the law in the most literal sense. There is no precedent for their situation, and it is just a matter of luck when they encounter, as they do in this land, a tradition of immigration in which they are able to participate.

But nowhere are they gladly received—except in Palestine, where the law of the land anticipates their arrival. Everywhere the word "exile," which once had an undertone of almost sacred awe, now provokes the idea of something simultaneously suspicious and unfortunate. Even when a mere thousand of them are expected in a large country, there is always at least one parliamentarian asking in baffled tones just how far one intends to go trading "fine young Americans for refugees," and at least one widely read journalist ready to discredit them with the platitude that "not all refugees have been ennobled by their sufferings."

The unpopularity of refugees has little to do with their behavior and much to do with the ambiguous legal status under which Jews, and not only Jews, suffer. These new refugees emerge from a no-man's-land, from which they can neither be legally expelled nor deported. No mutual treaties that would hold between nations during wartime protect them or the land to which they come. Because they exist outside of the laws of nation-states, which recognize statelessness only as a limiting case and exception, they imperil the normal legal order of any land that admits them. No one really knows what to do with them once compassion has asserted its just claim and reached its inevitable end.

They are stateless, but can only be classified as hostile aliens—as if a no-man's-land could declare war on a nation. They are permitted to serve in the British army, while simultaneously their eventual repatriation is discussed—in the country of their common enemy. Tens and likely hundreds of thousands of them are active in all the European underground movements, as individual comilitants or in Jewish units; but no government in exile has yet thought to say what they plan to do with the foreign or stateless Jews who have helped them liberate their homelands. As Jews they are attacked, banished, murdered, but they cannot fight back as Jews, and often they do not even want to belong to these peoples. Since they obviously do not belong to any other people, they create the uncanny impression, in their complete dependence upon the compassion of others, in their naked mere-humanity, of something utterly inhuman.

For as much as the eternal insufficiency of law relegates man to the compassion of his fellow men, all the less can one demand of him that he replace the law with compassion. The appalling callousness of the Evian and Bermuda Conferences was only the all-too-human response to a superhuman demand. The precipitous pragmatists, who thought that one could save people first and only afterward determine their legal and political status, have shown themselves to be impractical and unrealistic. Only when European Jewry is recognized as a people alongside the other Allied powers will the question of guests from no-man's-land and the problem of the rescue of European Jews come a step closer to resolution.

The New Face of an Old People

July 14, 1944

Minsk and Vilna are in the hands of the Soviet army, the roads to Bialystok and Warsaw have been opened. The liberation of the Jews in Eastern Europe has begun, and the general who is in the special position of liberating old Jewish communities and who "will most probably be the first to lead his troops onto German soil is a very distinguished Jew," and, what is more, the youngest general in his army, Ivan D. Chernyakhovsky.

This fact has not only deeply touched and delighted the British minister Brendan Bracken, it will live on in the memory of many peoples because it embodies an almost preternatural justice that with a precision bordering on irony is directing the course of these events. It will live on in the memory of the Jewish people because we find in it an expression and confirmation of a people's just need for retribution, in contrast to which hysterical cries for revenge by a few Jewish literati seem like some grotesque perversion.

Historians know that history sometimes allows peoples to live on unchanged and marked by the same characteristics for centuries, only to be suddenly dumped, so to speak, out of the tin can of a dead time and into the dynamism of the present, in which they change more decisively within a decade or a quarter century than in all the preceding five hundred years. For suddenly it seems as if events have joined in conspiracy, as if the most contradictory realities cannot help leading to identical results. In our own time history apparently decided to perform this old trick—which always amazes historians—on the Jewish people.

After all, what does the Russian Revolution, which gave the Jews of the Soviet Union the gift of true emancipation as a people, have to do with the great movement by which the Jewish people liberated itself as a people in Palestine? Nothing, except that they both are centered on freedom. And when we observe the final results, that is, the change in the character of our people, that freedom appears to be more important than the long, bitter debates among the proponents of our various isms. A people that had been

pronounced politically dead and that without a doubt had ancient and stubborn prejudices against military virtues, suddenly gave rise to troops who are
among the best in the Allied armies and who showed military talents that
must be counted among the most admirable in this war.

History, however, is evidently not satisfied with proving the similarity
between hostile brothers. It paradoxically let the same result arise out of the
most horrible persecution and enslavement as out of these beginnings of
freedom. For the Jewish units of the Palestinian army and the Jewish nationality in the Soviet Union find themselves standing worthily side by side with
the heroes of the Jewish underground movement, the fighters in the ghettos
of Warsaw and Bialystok, the Jewish groups in Tito's army, the thousands of
Jewish guerrillas in France, and those partisans who before the fall of Minsk
opened the battle within the city itself, the majority of whom were presumably Jews.

What may appear to historians as a paradoxically profound spectacle, whose
threads only the gods know how to knot and unravel, appears to the politician
like the new face of an old people, who, having been slowly taught by a series
of catastrophes, awaken to new life with great suddenness. For him the deeds
of that Soviet Jewish general and the battles of European Jewish partisans
and the achievements of Palestinian Jewish units are stages and aspects of the
same great struggle—the Jewish people's struggle for freedom.

Days of Change

July 28, 1944

For us this war is already in its twelfth year, and our enemies, surrounded on
all sides, have begun to put the knife to each other. That is the beginning of
the end, even if no one knows how long the end will take. This is the "German doom," just as Hitler promised it, and no one knows if or how the German people will survive the doom of the organized "Aryan" race.

The Jewish people, however, will survive this war. It would be foolish to
believe that peace will be easier for us than a war in which, right to the end,
we fought as allies but were never recognized as one of the Allied nations. It
is difficult, in view of millions of slaughtered helpless victims, not to become
bitter. After so many empty promises, after so many disappointed hopes, it is
difficult not to harden your heart.

When peace comes we dare not lose our moment out of fear and hope, the two archenemies of Jewish politics. In order to understand European Jews—who have gone through so many hells that no one else can still instill fear in them and who have been fooled by so many vain hopes that they will not be duped by anyone else—we must keep in mind and before our eyes the precise details of the battle in the Warsaw ghetto. (This is only now possible thanks to the masterly report by Shlomo Mendelsohn in the most recent issue of the *Menorah Journal* [March 1944].) For in the streets of Warsaw, European Jewry, as if called to learn a final lesson, passed through and, as it were, repeated all previous stages of typical Jewish political behavior—until the achievement that changed the face of the Jewish people.

It began on July 22, 1942. It was on that day that the chairman of the "Jewish Council," the engineer Czerniakow, committed suicide because the Gestapo had demanded that he supply six to ten thousand people a day for deportation. There were a half million Jews in the ghetto, and the Gestapo was afraid of armed or passive resistance. Nothing of the sort happened. Twenty to forty thousand Jews volunteered for deportation, ignoring flyers distributed by the Polish underground movement warning against it. The population was "caught between fear and feverish hope." Some hoped that "evacuation" meant only resettlement, others that such measures would not affect them. Some feared that resistance would mean certain death; others feared that resistance would be followed by a mass execution of the ghetto; and since Jewish opinion in general was against resistance and preferred illusions, the few who wanted to fight shied away from assuming that responsibility.

The Germans made meticulous use of both hope and fear. They divided the Jewish population into categories: They gave papers to those who were working in German factories, and the workers felt safe. They established a Jewish police troop, which—together with Ukrainians, Lithuanians, and Latvians—carried out the deportations. And a part of the population turned traitor. They cut off two districts of the ghetto, in one of which there lived about six thousand Jewish workers, in the other something like 40,000 people, thereby preventing a sense of solidarity within the entire ghetto. Each person had his own special reasons for fear and hope.

A few weeks later the inhabitants of the ghetto abandoned hope. The truth about the deportees' destination had leaked out, and every illusion about "resettlement" was destroyed. But this did not result in resistance either. Fear abruptly took the place of hope. "Pale shades roamed the streets of Warsaw, their eyes vacant and terrified. They wandered from street to street in the delusion that perhaps the danger would not be so great in the next street," the Polish reporter says. At this point the Germans could relax—no resistance, active or passive, was to be feared from these people.

The Polish population, which had been informed about the final fate of the deportees, did not understand "why the Jews offered no resistance, why the Jewish police were so eager and the survivors so apathetic. Something like fatalism descended over the Jews despite all their fears, a sense of no escape that was reinforced by the fact that the civilized world showed practically no reaction." So the report of a Polish underground newspaper.

At the end of August a group of workers and intellectuals realized that ultimately armed resistance was the only moral and political way out. But evidently assuming that they still had the majority of the population behind them, "conservative circles in the ghetto categorically rejected every thought of struggle." By December the only people still living in the ghetto were young and relatively healthy—all others had been "resettled." Under the leadership of Zionists and socialist Bundists, a Jewish fighting organization had been formed and received its first weapons in late December, early January.

After a brief respite deportations were resumed in January 1943. Of the half million Jews whom the Gestapo had feared would offer resistance in July 1942, only about 40,000 were still alive; and the Gestapo had no fear of them. "On January 18 well-armed divisions of SS, supported by German and Latvian police, marched into the ghetto. They were met with something they never expected. A few Jews had barricaded themselves inside apartment buildings. A heavy battle ensued. The fighters' organization had amassed guns and ammunition. The battle lasted several days. On January 23 tanks rolled into the ghetto" (report from a Polish underground newspaper).

This first brief battle was fought exclusively by the Jewish underground, the general population took no part in it. An appeal directed to American Jews reads: "Only you can save us. You bear the responsibility before the judgment of history." The expected help from outside did not come, and in the following months the organized fighters organized the ghetto population, preparing them for what the Polish government's reporter rightly called the

"Jewish-German war." From the Jewish side this war was a *levée en masse*: everyone had worked together fortifying streets and buildings, everyone had a weapon, everyone had a specified task. Everyone knew that the coming war could end only in military defeat and would lead to physical annihilation. Everyone knew—in the words of the Polish underground newspaper— "that the passive death of Jews had created no new values; it had been meaningless; but that death with weapons in hand can bring new values into the life of the Jewish people." A final attempt by the Nazi commandant to reawaken illusions and hope in the ghetto found no response. Fear and hope had left the ghetto.

On April 19 the battle began. SS divisions, heavily armed with machine guns and tanks, marched into the ghetto. The Jewish defense was brilliantly organized. An out-and-out battle was fought for a week, with the Germans taking heavy losses in both men and matériel. They were driven out beyond the ghetto walls several times. After that they abandoned the military rules of war and shifted to tactics that combined cruelty with cowardice and that cost them the prestige of "Aryan military efficiency" in the eyes of the Poles. Proceeding from building to building, the SS attacked with flamethrowers and dynamite. The procedure lasted at least five weeks. At the end of June the underground newspapers were still reporting guerrilla skirmishes in the ghetto streets. To this day, this "victory" has remained the Nazis' last.

There was no one left to be deported from the ruins of the battlefield. Many had fallen with weapons in their hands. A few managed to save themselves and, with weapons in their hands, organized those dozens of Jewish battle units that have since been roaming the fields and forests of Poland and fighting for peace, for *our* peace.

A Lesson in Six Shots

August 11, 1944

"Young Jewish girls, submachine guns over their shoulders and grenades at their belts, march proudly through the streets of Vilna, for whose liberation they have fought for three years." According to the AP this comes from the report of a Moscow correspondent named Mikhailov. One of the girls, a seventeen-year-old named Betty, told her story to the correspondent in the following words: "A German came and took my family to the ghetto. That's how defenseless and docile we were in 1941. But the German regime taught us a lesson. Those who lived in the ghetto became the real avengers. I killed only six Germans, but there are Jews in our unit who have killed dozens."

The lesson is a very simple one, and in just a few sentences Betty summarized its essence. She is ashamed even to think of how one single German could with impunity lead sixty Jews into slavery and presumably death. With six shots she expunged the shame of those victims, those defenseless and docile victims. She did not give her last name to the correspondent for fear of being unduly praised.

I am greatly afraid that peace will teach Betty a second cruel lesson. She will learn how unfounded her fear of great fame was. She does not yet know that we actually glory only in being victims, innocent victims, and that we celebrate her and those like her not as heroes but as martyrs. She does not yet know this new, almost unconscious, almost automatic "conspiracy of silence," which with loud, far too loud, laments drowns out her voice and the voices of those like her.

Although her voice is loud enough. For people of goodwill it rings out daily in little—fragmentary and scattered—reports in the newspapers. It brings us the good news that for once and for us of all people the ancient laws of war (which slays the best—"our Patrocles lies there in death and Thersites has returned" [Friedrich Schiller, "The Victory Feast"]) have been reversed; that in the awful slaughter the Nazis have wrought, the survivors are to be counted among the best. Because certain death awaited the defenseless and docile.

But those of us who know the larger Jewish world somewhat better than Betty does, know how difficult it is for a people living a normal life to bridge the great gap that separates returning soldiers and civilians who stayed at home; how long it takes for a people to understand the essential lessons of its avant-garde; how slow our people in particular are at learning political lessons—and for us the real question is about the future of Betty and those like her. For without the help, the active, enthusiastic help of the entire Jewish people, neither she nor those like her in the countries of Europe will be allowed to bring in the harvest and enjoy its hard-won fruits.

We know what those Jewish fighters do not yet know—or will have forgotten in the fire of recent years—we know that the "philanthropic machine" that in Herzl's words has worked to "suffocate the desperate cries" of the oppressed may very well be put to use tomorrow to suffocate the political demands of those who have freed themselves. It is only too natural that the representatives of European Jewry in exile are separated from their people in the same way that other governments in exile are from theirs. Except that for us this can lead to far worse consequences, because our resistance movement is not a unified organization, is not limited to one territory, but is made up of scattered units who will not have a chance to come to agreement among themselves and with the representatives of world Jewry until the moment of armistice. Compared with the resistance movements of other European peoples, who have been making political preparations and had representatives abroad for years now, this is very late. It means that Betty and those like her will find it more difficult than their comrades among other peoples to establish the new reality that they and only they have the right to speak about.

But I would like to ask those among us who are of goodwill—who know that Hitler's fall cannot mean an automatic solution to the Jewish question, who are willing to prepare for the hard tasks of a Jewish future—not to forget Betty's six shots and as often as possible, as if in some old religious exercise, to recapitulate the stages of the battle for the Warsaw ghetto.

New Proposals for a Jewish-Arab Understanding

August 25, 1944

Opportunistic politics, which tries somehow to muddle through from day to day, usually leaves behind it a chaos of contradictory interests and apparently hopeless conflicts. Zionist politics of the last twenty-five years vis-à-vis the Arabs could go down in history as a model of opportunism. One of the Arab leaders from before the First World War rightly recognized the true core of Zionist failure when he called out to his Jewish partners in negotiation: "Gardez-vous bien, Messieurs les Sionistes, un gouvernement passe, mais un peuple reste" [Be very careful, Zionist gentlemen, governments come and go, but a people remains].

In the meantime the Turkish government vanished and was replaced by the British. This reinforced the Zionist leadership in its stance of negotiating with governments instead of with peoples. Until the unrest of 1936 that leadership did everything it could to minimize the Arab question. Only when, as a consequence of the unrest, the British government moved to show Arabs preferential treatment at the cost of Jews, did the Zionist Organization begin seriously to rack its brains about this question. And ever since, what we hear is talk either of a voluntary Arab immigration to Syria or Iraq or of a "tragic conflict" between two peoples that can only be decided internationally by the great powers—whereby a relatively small injustice (inflicted on Palestinian Arabs) has to be accepted as part of a "higher justice" for the Jews, who, in contradistinction to the Arabs, have no other country open to them but Palestine.

The sham of both these solutions to an unsolvable problem is obvious. Palestine is surrounded by Arab countries, and even a Jewish state in Palestine with an overwhelming Jewish majority, yes, even a purely Jewish Palestine, would be a very precarious structure without a prior agreement with all the Arab peoples on all its borders.

Parallel with the efforts of the Zionist Organization—for whom the impossibility of an honest agreement has evidently become axiomatic—there have been attempts for years now in Palestine itself to come to an agreement locally. The most recent of such attempts is that of the Palestinian League for Jewish-Arab Understanding and Cooperation, which has its basis in groups of workers and intellectuals, but is not to be confused with the suicidal proposals of the Magnes group, which is financed in part by plantation owners. The league demands *mass immigration and the building of Palestine as a Jewish homeland on the basis of a "permanent mutual understanding" between both peoples, a binational local administration, and*—once Jewish rights in Palestine have been secured—*Palestine's eventual entry into a federation with neighboring countries.*

The league has made considerable progress recently. By founding the newspaper *Mishmar,* it has managed to break through the policy of deadly silence practiced by the Hebrew press, and it has found active support among all left-wing worker groups, the most important of which is the Hashomer Haza'ir and its kibbutz organization. This close relationship with Jewish workers and farmers guarantees a revitalization of the local cooperation that has been attempted again and again by individual Jewish worker groups, but was all but totally destroyed in the unrest of 1936.

The latest stage in this development is the founding of an American branch, the Council on Jewish-Arab Cooperation, by several young American Zionists, who have just published the first issue of a new bulletin, an informational newsletter with editorial comment. Using material from Palestine's Hebrew and Arab press as it basis, the newsletter offers information otherwise difficult to come by here; the editorial part deals programmatically with poppycock about a "tragic conflict," provides an essentially correct analysis of class conditions in Palestine, and warns of the very real possibility of an agreement between the semifeudal Arab landowners and the capitalist, industrialized Jewish large landowners, both of whom are interested in cheap Arab labor, the preservation of the fellahin [Arab peasantry], and a very limited Jewish immigration.

The political core of this new intra-Zionist opposition is both the realization of the fatal, utopian hyperbole of the demand for a Jewish commonwealth and a rejection of the idea of making all Jewish politics in Palestine dependent on the protection of great powers. We can hope that in the course of these new groups' development they will not lose themselves in the endless thickets of sociological research—as has been the fate of so many opposition groups in the labor movement of our time. Over the long term, economic interests, whether those of workers or capitalists, are no substitute for politics, although one can use them politically. That is why it is right that an indigenous understanding between Jews and Arabs must first begin at the base, for it would be fatal to forget how often such efforts have been thwarted and rendered useless by political decisions made at the top.

It appears that the league in Palestine has understood this, for it declares the first of its tasks to be the struggle within Zionism itself. It is our assumption that the council will likewise avoid the danger of economic argument for its own sake. Since there is no work to be done at the base here, its task can only be that of a truly political organization and of a truly irreproachable news service. Should it succeed at that, it will have provided an important service for the sake of the Jewish people in Palestine.

Jewish Partisans in the European Uprising

September 8, 1944

The victorious advance of the Allied armies, the liberation of France, and the continuing disintegration of Germany's military and terror machine have once again revealed the original structure of this war to be that of a European civil war. It is amazing how much its end looks like its beginning—just with pluses and minuses reversed. Both back then and today the rapid drive forward of regular armies is made possible by the existence of a "fifth column." Both back then and today, for the European peoples themselves this war has unfolded in the form of a civil war. With just one difference—that the Nazis' fifth columns were recruited from members of the ruling classes, whose names were known worldwide and whose positions endowed them with a halo of respectability; whereas the Allies' fifth columns are made up of the masses, who have reached for their weapons and whose representatives are, with few exceptions, unknown. They have been fighting for years against all Nazis, of whatever nationality, and even as they celebrate their liberation by Allied armies, they understand that their own actions began and shaped it.

Given the nature of the war in Europe, the existence of a Nazi-controlled fifth column among Jews—details of which have often been reported in the columns of this newspaper—should come as no surprise. The "natural laws" of a special Jewish destiny have always lost their validity whenever Jews have refused to accept that destiny as their fate. In our time this has taken the form of betrayal by a small minority of Jewish millionaires and scoundrels—for example, in Italy, Poland, and Romania—and of open struggle by what appears to be a very considerable percentage of the people. Ever since Jews, after the battle of the Warsaw ghetto, took to organizing themselves as partisans just like everyone else, the fate and the character of their struggle have come to look more and more like those of their European neighbors. A telling point in this regard is that the battle of the Warsaw ghetto began—just as did the struggle of the French Maquis—with a rebellion against the enemy within, against the dreaded Jewish police, with the assassination of the commandant of those troops and with the not very cordial action of extorting a million zlotys from the Nazi-controlled Jewish council in order to buy weapons.

According to a report by Elieser Kaplan [1891–1952; treasurer of the Jewish Agency for Palestine], who consulted in Turkey with leaders of the Jewish underground, the number of Jewish partisans is approaching 100,000. All those in Poland are evidently fighting under the blue-and-white flag. But in other countries as well, where Jews have previously fought as part of non-Jewish units, there is a clear trend to organize Jewish units that then cooperate with other partisan groups. It has been reported from Lithuania that after years of mixed battalions, three independent Jewish units have been formed under the leadership of Shlome Brandt, Chone Magid, and Aba Kovner. In Carpatho-Russia, a troop of 1,400 Jews fought with the very Hungarians from whose concentration camps they had escaped. The most amazing news comes from France, from the last days of the Vichy regime, telling of how Jewish underground fighters, allegedly ten thousand in all, who until recently had been organized within the ranks of the Maquis, have set themselves up independently. If one can trust the reliability of these reports, this new, independent guerrilla force is the work of veterans of the battle of the Warsaw ghetto, who came to France to share with the Maquis their experience in fighting urban warfare. This is certainly a possibility, and it would be compatible with countless reports about the connections among various European underground movements.

The most detailed reports in recent weeks have come to us from Poland. In the streets of Warsaw, members of the Berek-Yeselevitch unit under the leadership of Aaron Kaplan are fighting "in the tradition of the heroes and martyrs of the Warsaw ghetto." For months now the Bar-Kochba unit has been fighting in close cooperation with the Red Army and turning over any enemy they capture to the Russians. After the liberation of Lublin they held a ceremony in memory of the dead of the battle of the Warsaw ghetto. The "Maccabees" are still operating in the forests around Radom, Kielce, and Miechow. Their specialty is sorties against concentration camps, from which they then recruit their troops. Over the last few weeks, in their attempt to skirt German lines and come to the aid of their comrades in Warsaw, they have suffered major losses. The Germans countered by putting a bounty of one hundred zloty on the head of every Jewish guerrilla—and it turned out that there are still a sufficient number of Endekes [Polish nationalist and anti-semitic party] left in Poland for the Gestapo to run an effective campaign of denunciation.

It is obvious: If you do not accept something that assumes the form of "destiny," you not only change its "natural laws" but also the laws of the enemy playing the role of fate. In Warsaw the Nazis tried to negotiate with the Jews and, evidently ignoring their own race laws, offered them the status of prisoners of war if only they would lay down their arms. The Jews refused of course. In Paris the Nazis tried to negotiate a prisoner exchange with French partisans. When they declared that "of course" Jewish prisoners could not be included in any agreement, the partisans immediately broke off negotiations. Even considerations of expediency could not bring these Frenchmen to recognize a "special destiny" for Jews.

On the "Salt of the Earth": Waldo Frank's "Jewish Interpretation"

September 22, 1944

No critique can demolish an ideology more utterly than its complete enactment. In the fullness of its flowering, the ideology reaches such an apex of absurdity that its credibility sinks to nothing. Precisely when it presents itself most purely, untroubled by any historical fact or any ideal truth out of which it once emerged, just then the ground crumbles from beneath its feet, because it has continued to interpret itself on its own authority alone.

It seems that an old and at one time widespread Jewish ideology is reaching this final stage of corruption. This false doctrine probably arose from the collapse of the Shabetai Tzevi movement and the loss of its messianic hopes, and was lovingly cultivated all through the nineteenth century, particularly in the emancipated countries. The doctrine secularizes the religious pretension of Israel to being the chosen people, frees that status from all observance of the Law and all hope for the Messiah, renders it absolute, and so equates Judaism with whatever fashion dictates is good and beautiful and admired by the age.

What occasioned this ideology was the need to justify the Jewish Diaspora, something that had been suffered as an affliction for millennia, since despair over the false Messiah had swept away the ancient hopes for redemption and a return to Palestine. This element of justifying the Diaspora and rendering it permanent was particularly convenient for the nineteenth century. For here an authentic possibility presented itself of making every country in Europe home without at the same time surrendering Jewish identity. What resulted from this much-varied theorem was a doctrine that takes the Jews to be "the salt of the earth," a sort of incarnation of humanity, and in which all the persecution they suffer becomes a symbol of the sinfulness of the non-Jewish peoples or an expression of their unpreparedness for the actual vocation of mankind.

Depending on the accidental worldview of the author, Judaism could be identified either with progress or with resistance to corrosive change, either with Enlightenment or with the preservation of religious piety. Jews could be understood as born proletarians, as natural allies of the bourgeoisie, or as the oldest Western aristocracy. Wherever convenient they could appear as the incarnation of justice or the incarnation of free competition of forces or the incarnation of nobility itself. In each case Jews were these incarnations and not mere mortals.

Naturally, Jewish nationalism is not essentially different from other sorts of nationalism. It is always the same story: general human qualities, general human tasks are claimed as the monopoly of a particular people by maintaining that this particular people has been exclusively chosen to administer these general values. The crucial point is always that—in the terms of the latest Jewish nationalists—"the idea becomes flesh," and so the determinate people are principally, that is, ideally, separated from all other people. Jewish nationalism differs from other sorts of nationalism only in having the added absurdity of being primarily propagated by those "liberal" and "radical" Jews who not only deny being nationalists but even make antinationalism a Jewish monopoly. Certainly an amusing difference, but one that alters nothing in principle or method.

The singular oddity about the most recent version of this ideology as it is presented in Waldo Frank's *The Jew in Our Day* (Duell, Sloan and Pearce, New York, 1944, p. 199) is that this time it comes bound with its own quite devastating refutation in the form of a preface by Reinhold Niebuhr. To Frank's claim that the Jews have been persecuted because it is their vocation to be better than other peoples, and to his criticism of a Jewish people who have adapted so successfully to the evil world around them that there should by rights no longer be a reason for that persecution, Niebuhr responds that "most Jews suffer neither because they are better than we are (as Frank would like to believe) nor because they are worse (as their slanderers maintain); but simply because they are a nation dispersed among other nations."

With that the problem is again returned to natural human foundations, upon which it is neither "shameful" nor honorable to be a Jew "simply because one was born a Jew" any more than it is to be an "Englishman or Frenchman or German" by birth. What Niebuhr does not say—whether out of civility or for other reasons—is that only a German or English or French or Jewish nationalist can claim that his birth already bestows an honor upon him and imposes upon him a duty. Only a German nationalist will claim that a German is unworthy of his Germanness unless he is better than an Englishman or a Frenchman. Although Niebuhr does not draw the ultimate polemical conclusions from his own argument, he does eventually endorse the Palestinian solution—perhaps without being fully aware that it was in fact the demand of Zionism that Jews become "a people like every other people," which largely demolished the Jewish nationalist nonsense of their being "the salt of the earth."

The second curious aspect of Frank's book is its quite extraordinary distortion of historical fact. All ideologies, of course, are liable to mendacious interpretations that twist reality into unrecognizable forms. But the claims in Frank's book go beyond even the limits of the usual ideological falsifications of history. We learn for instance that democracy was invented more than two thousand years ago by the Jews; that the Law of the Jews is the Law of Life; that in medieval times the Jews were allies of the rising bourgeois class against feudal nobility; that an eighteenth-century Galician Jew lived in an agrarian world unchanged since Amos and Isaiah—the business of a ban on purchasing land, the schnapps trade, and hucksterism was all dreamed up, it seems; that the whole Middle Ages was ruled by "soldiers and landowners, later demagogues and millionaires"—the pope, the king, and the emperor apparently being mere hallucinations of an antisemitic world; that only the Jewish fidelity to God taught medieval Christians that a God was immanent in the world—though for just this heresy the Jews pronounced the anathema over Spinoza; and—last but not least—that European culture foundered on the "superstition" [*sic*!] of an immortal soul.

Naturally this is a fantastic but nonetheless consistent exaggeration, though it is unlikely anyone has dared assert it in quite so naïve a fashion before. An exaggeration both in terms of the Jewish nationalist monopolization of all the author's cherished values (from which other peoples have apparently derived the entirety of their cultural treasures for the last two thousand years), and an exaggeration of the ignorance that always, if not always so obviously, underlies such historical rubbish.

From Army to Brigade
A Small Fulfillment of a Demand, but at Least a Fulfillment

October 6, 1944

Five years ago, with the outbreak of war, the Jewish Agency began negotiating with the British government about the formation of a Jewish army. Four years ago, during months of great defeats, the British broke off negotiations. Three years ago, during the period of German success in Africa, the Nazis began their systematic campaign of deporting and exterminating Jews. It was then that the Jewish masses first began to be politically active. In countless mass meetings and petitions—in North and South America, in Palestine and South Africa and England—they demanded the immediate formation of a Jewish army recruited from stateless and Palestinian Jews. The point was not committees of assistance or days of fasting or even protest, but of Jews joining the ranks of the United Nations in order to save our brethren in Nazi Europe and to defend our people under attack around the world. A vague longing in the hearts of individuals and a political demand by those representing Zionism grew into a mighty movement of an entire people.

This movement actually remained without leaders. For the Zionist Organization the demand for a Jewish army was one demand among many. For the people it became *the* demand. Frightened by the sudden fierceness of such agitation, especially in America, the British government reacted by being even a shade more dismissive than before. Until the spring of 1942, Weizmann, in his famous speech to the American Zionist Conference about the "so-called Jewish army," abruptly put an end to the entire movement.

And now, in the sixth year of this war, after the genuine, politically productive excitement of masses of people had long since dwindled to helpless grief and ineffective protest, the British war ministry has announced the formation of a Jewish Brigade. This is held to be Weizmann's diplomatic success, but sounds more like an inexplicably belated reply to the demands of the Jewish Agency in 1939 and has little to do with the popular movement that has since fizzled to nothing.

A Jewish army in 1942 would have meant that, according to the law of retaliation valid in time of war, the Nazis would have been forced to grant European Jews the status of enemy aliens, which would have been tantamount to saving them.* It would also have meant that Jewish partisans in Europe would not have had to bleed so dreadfully, but could have demanded the minimum of help the Allies gave to all other peoples fighting this war. A Jewish army at that point would have helped deter the "conspiracy of silence" that accompanied years of Jewish extermination and would never have let it come to the unbearable humiliation of the Jewish people, who felt that the whole world had damned them to the degrading role of victimhood. It is too late for all that now. And even hope of participation in the peace conference, which was such an effective argument in the agitation of the time, has died. The conference has long since begun, and it is highly unlikely that any of the "smaller peoples" will be granted a voice in it. That of course makes the formation of a Jewish army and the recognition of the Jewish people as one of the warring nations much less dangerous.

In granting the Jewish Agency the right to form a Jewish brigade, the British government has put an end to the long period of noncooperation that has in fact characterized Jewish-British relations since the announcement of the White Paper. This is its diplomatic significance. It is consciously thought of as a concession to the Jewish Agency, presumably in order to get Jewish institutions to accept partition plans for Palestine. It can only be viewed as a success credited to Weizmann and will perhaps once again strengthen his influence within the Organization. This would of course be important for any sort of partition plan, since Weizmann is an old supporter of partition, whereas Ben-Gurion, whose influence has grown in Palestine, is its bitter opponent.

The real, that is, political significance of the Jewish Brigade lies in Europe itself. There it may well become a first-rate centralizing force for existing scattered units of Jewish partisans. Jewish refugees in liberated areas could volunteer to join, which would perhaps give them a last chance finally to avoid the absurdity of having to identify themselves with other peoples whose nationality they formally share. This recognition of a Jewish nationality on the basis of a Jewish Brigade that is not limited just to Palestinians may under certain circumstances be the only thing that can save German Jews from losing their stateless status and being automatically made "Ger-

---

*Arendt is presuming that the Nazis still recognized the Hague Conventions, which, for example, would have meant that they could not allow Jews to starve.

mans" again once race laws are rescinded. It might also spare them and Jewish refugees of other nationalities from the awful possibility of being transported back to their former places of residence, and instead open the gates of Palestine to them. Above all it would give them the satisfaction of not being rescued by the agents of charity but of being freed by the soldiers of their own people.

In Memoriam: Adolph S. Oko

October 13, 1944

This man's benevolence was matched only by his intelligence. His nature was so nobly fashioned that benevolence and intelligence seemed but two aspects of the same essence animated by that most basic of all passions for the beautiful, the true, and the good. From this passion grew such an affinity for all the essential things of life and the world that he was utterly at home anywhere in the realm of spirit. In a republic of minds (and not of pedants) he could have best resided. Instead of that he confronted the barbarity of the age in the hectic ambition of all sorts of careerists, in the petty maliciousness—which he called the "extreme vulgarity"—of professionals of any kind, and it all provoked in him that dangerous disgust that substitutes in noble natures for hatred, and so easily tempts them into tedium vitae. Too clever not to know that (in his words) "politics is the destiny of the age," too good to retreat from the misery of his people into erudition, he had to engage the world without in any sense belonging to any part of it.

He was a great librarian and *his oeuvre is the Library of Hebrew Union College in Cincinnati.* He was the last of the great Spinoza scholars, leaving behind the most complete Spinoza collection of the day. And he would have led the Spinoza edition of the Heidelberg Academy of Science to its conclusion after the death of Carl Gebhardt, had German "scholars" not discovered in the meantime that Spinoza, like Oko, was Jewish. And finally, the *Contemporary Jewish Record,* whose director he was in his last years, became more and more his personal work. His great knowledge, paired with a rare sensibility and an unerring instinct for quality, and his passion for politics, newly awakened by the events of the 1930s, might have made the *Record* a genuine center of contemporary Jewish productivity.

Oko leaves behind three unfinished books: a Spinoza bibliography, a study of British and American Spinozism, and a Spinoza anthology he selected and translated. Everything he wrote turned beneath his pen into fragments—in part because he felt himself bound by the example of his subject to an ideal of absolute perfection, in part because in the face of the barbarity of the age words failed him. In the few sketches he published, above all in the few sentences with which he summarized the meaning of historical figures under the rubric of "Cedars of Lebanon" (in the *Contemporary Jewish Record*), is found such a precious, concentrated stylistic talent, such a mastery of succinctness and significance, that one asks oneself whether those whom the barbarity of the age strikes dumb are precisely those with the most to say.

"Free and Democratic"

November 3, 1944

Zionist congresses have always displayed an odd mixture of parliamentary debate and propagandistic agitation. The parliamentary debates tended to end with decisions voted by the majority, usually opposed by a minority. The propagandistic agitation found expression in the grand speeches about the general state of the Jewish people and was directed primarily to the Jewish world itself.

All this has fundamentally changed. The intra-Jewish agitation has vanished, presumably because it is considered superfluous. And one can scarcely even speak of parliamentary debates now. Resolutions are accepted unanimously, the only explanation for which is that they are meant as propaganda for the non-Jewish world. Dissenting factions have bowed to this; they no longer register a minority vote—even when they represent a relatively strong minority—but at most abstain from voting. As a result, at the most recent national conference of the American Zionist Organization a resolution was passed unanimously demanding that all Palestine, "undivided and undiminished," be made a Jewish commonwealth—all without even mentioning the existence of Palestinian Arabs. At the Jewish World Congress conference in November, the delegates of Hashomer Haza'ir and the Aliyah Hadashah,* showing their dissent only by abstention, voluntarily accepted

---

*Founded in 1942 by Central European Jews in Palestine out of protest over the policies adopted at the Biltmore conference, the Aliyah Hadashah (Hebrew, "new immigration") sought Jewish-Arab cooperation.

the instructions of the Vaad Leumi,* stipulating that the Palestinian delegation could vote only en bloc and prohibiting delegates from engaging in any
political activity outside of the dictated vote.

And if the basis of the unanimity with which all Zionist bodies pass resolutions these days is not a true uniformity of opinion—which as we all know
would be the end of any democracy—neither can it be explained solely
because opinion is being subjected to intra-Zionist terror tactics, which also
do exist. These minorities are evidently only too happy to be made part of
the majority, not because they believe that a maximalist program advocated
by the *yishuv* under the leadership of Ben-Gurion and by the Zionist Organization of America can actually be realized, but probably because they think
that unanimity is the best thing for propaganda and propaganda the best
thing for politics. Presumably they are also secretly of the opinion that a
maximalist program, which in terms of foreign policy can no longer be differentiated from the plans of the Revisionists, offers a basis for future negotiations and compromises. For the only difference that now exists between
Revisionists and Zionists is that the Zionists are prepared to compromise as
partners in negotiation, whereas the Revisionists, at least in their more
extreme groups, consider other methods more expedient.

Whether this position of apparent intransigence is very wise remains to be
seen. The façade of unanimity is at any rate only an exterior wall, behind
which are hidden differences that will not grow any smaller by not being
publicly discussed. And so in contrast to the unanimous rejection of any partition of Palestine displayed to the outside world, within the Organization
the opposite view is taken by the circle around Weizmann and the new group
of the Aliyah Hadashah, who believe that in partition and cantonization of
the land they have found a way out of the Jewish-Arab conflict. And so
within the Organization, the unanimously adopted "undiminished sovereignty" of a Jewish state displayed to the outside world is opposed, under the
leadership of the numerically strong Hashomer Haza'ir, by those who have
never even accepted the formula of a Jewish commonwealth, but have
always demanded a binational state.

Less well known, but no less crucial differences exist concerning the
question of Palestine's future foreign relations. Whereas the smaller circle

*Vaad Leumi, the Jewish National Council in Palestine during the period of the British Mandate.

around Weizmann, supported by the Aliyah Hadashah, demands, as it has all along, unconditional orientation toward Britain, sizable segments of the working class are hoping the Soviet Union will show active support of a Jewish Palestine. And still other circles close to Ben-Gurion see such great promise for the future in the United States and its strong Zionist Organization that they are no longer inclined simply to accept British demands or solutions as an *ultima ratio*.

Characteristic of these intra-Zionist differences is the fact that evidently all parties involved already view the division of the world by the great powers into spheres of interest as a reality, so that they don't even think about what lies closest at hand—that is, the relationship of their new state to its neighbors, to the peoples of the Mediterranean—as an independent factor, but argue only about which great power would better provide protection for their state to flourish.

In any case, the first evidence of the success of the "free and democratic Jewish commonwealth" is the suppression of all free and democratic discussion. Since the adoption of the Biltmore Program none of the political parties believes it can persuade its intra-Zionist opponents or even be given a hearing by them. Each hopes for a fait accompli handed to them by the great powers; each honestly believes that only a fait accompli will carry the power of persuasion. They are happy to be majoritized because, despite all the radical words and decisions, they scarcely believe any longer in the possibility of their own politics. The result of this sort of executive leadership, which judges political resolutions only by their immediate propaganda value, is the thorough obstruction of any normal way for a people to build political opinion; it means that fanatical and fanaticizing slogans become fixed in the minds of the masses, that all Jewish politics becomes the monopoly of professional politicians who behave like Führers, and finally it means the hardly happy transformation—but one so characteristic of our times—of a people into more or less fanaticized bands of "believers."

The Disenfranchised and Disgraced
December 15, 1944

Stateless people are the latest new phenomenon of recent history. Arising out of the vast migrations of refugees that have been changing the demographic maps of Europe ever since the Russian Revolution, they are, at least for the present, the most obvious product of thirty years of European wars and civil wars. Whether voluntarily or involuntarily, they have broken out of the old trinity of people-state-territory, which formed the solid foundation of the nation-state, and have thereby expanded over all of Europe the belt of peoples settled in a mixed hodgepodge that made Eastern Europe so unstable and the new nation-states formed by the Versailles Treaty so unviable. They confront the statesmen of this war and of the future peace with a similar but even more difficult problem than that presented by ethnic minorities at the end of the previous war; for they find themselves—politically, socially, and legally—in a constantly expanding vacuum, inside of which the laws of nations have no influence and which, if left outside the reach of the law, will set the very structure of the national state wobbling.

Neither the right of asylum, which was always intended for individuals and cannot easily take into account migrations of whole peoples, nor naturalization, which for countries not founded on immigration can only be offered as a self-limiting exception, can bring their numbers under control. All the solemn invocations of human rights, which are aimed only at protecting individuals from excesses of public force, cannot effectively protect them or create positive rights for them. For they arrive not as individuals but as compact ethnic groups, and they are attacked and persecuted not as individuals but as members of a people or a splinter group of a people lacking the protection of a state.

In recent times James G. McDonald, former high commissioner for refugees for the League of Nations—together with all the experts in the field, a great many social workers, and various Jewish organizations—has warned in vain that international conferences cannot simply ignore the refugee problem. For now everyone seems determined to avoid any general solution and to leave the treatment of refugees, the question of their present and future status, to each of the European governments now being formed. And although for now very little has been decided about the fate of these refugees, certain trends are already apparent that indicate that the end of the war will most certainly not automatically end the limbo of no laws and no justice in which many thousands have been vegetating for more than twenty years, others for more than ten, and in the case of the remnants of the regular Spanish army, for example, for more than six years.

The greatest danger they face is, paradoxically, normalization; for during the war against German fascism they found their place in the closed ranks of partisans; amid such universal illegality they were legal and could share the fate and glory of those engaged in the general struggle against fascism. But no sooner had de Gaulle publicly honored the Spanish Maquis at a huge rally in Toulouse and decorated them for their contribution to the liberation of France, than the French army ordered these same Spaniards—who enjoy no consular protection and are viewed as stateless—either to join the Foreign Legion or to be conscripted for forced labor. The resistance movement in France with its sense of honor and solidarity is still too strong for this order to have been carried out. But the hundreds of thousands of foreign Jews who fought for the liberation of France under their own blue-and-white flag were forbidden to march under it in the armistice parade of November 11.

The trend of international negotiations simply to ignore the existence of refugees has so far meant that the United Nations War Crimes Commission does not recognize as war crimes those crimes committed against Jews of non-Allied nationality. That means that the murder of German, Hungarian, Romanian, Austrian, and other Jews will go unpunished, that even in death these Jews find their status as free game reconfirmed. It required difficult and lengthy negotiations to make UNRRA [United Nations Relief and Rehabilitation Administration, founded in 1943] responsible for Jews of enemy nationality; and even this decision is merely a compromise between those who negotiated in good faith and the still unaltered principle of regarding Jews as citizens of those countries which have only recently tried to exterminate them. The Belgian government has already stamped the identity papers of German Jewish refugees who live in its territory, but were in fact legally expatriated, with the words "German nationality." The International Migration Service is focused above all on repatriation and has expressly stated that among its most difficult tasks will be that of "convincing people afraid to return to countries where they suffered so much that they will be safe there." And the only thing that the International Committee of Refugee Professional Workers could suggest to the Swiss government by way of solving its refugee problem was the request to give refugees a grace period during which they can prepare for a return to their professions in their former homelands, which most of them left ten and more years ago.

Given the nature of current international agreements, all attempts to solve the question of statelessness end up in making it possible to deport refugees again. This is the true reason why until now, despite the efforts of Jewish organizations and the goodwill of Allied governments, there has been no success at implementing an intra-European recognition of the Jewish people. Any such recognition that disregarded previous assignment of nationality would make it possible for Jews to be deported with no protection of nationality whatever. It would almost automatically exclude the possibility of deporting foreign Jews, or at least—if one were to consider Palestine as a "country of deportation"—make it far more difficult.

The real obstacle to solving the problem of refugees and statelessness lies in the fact that it is simply unsolvable as long as peoples are organized within the old system of nation-states. Instead, those who are stateless reveal more clearly than anything else the crisis of the nation-state. And we shall not master this crisis by heaping one injustice upon another merely so that we can reestablish an order that does not correspond either to a modern sense of justice or to modern conditions under which peoples actually live together.

Achieving Agreement between Peoples in the Near East— a Basis for Jewish Politics

March 16, 1945

It has been reported from Jerusalem that the foreign ministers of the Arab states have suggested as a compromise solution to the Palestine conflict the immediate immigration of 300,000 Jews, which would bring the total number of Jews to one million, establishing parity between Jews and Arabs. It was reported at the same time that, conditional upon a Jewish-Arab agreement, Britain would be prepared to devolve its mandate upon the United Nations.

A home that my neighbor does not recognize and respect is not a home. A Jewish national home that is not recognized and not respected by its neighboring people is no home but an illusion—until it becomes a battlefield. This simple statement of fact—the fact that the Arabs have thus far neither recognized nor respected the Jewish national homeland—could not, of course, be resolved by any declarations of distant powers or by any legalistic interpretations of international agreements. It is evidence of the illusionist, utopian, and unpolitical element that has so often clung to Jewish politics in Palestine, and which first expressed itself in an overestimation of what was practical and opportune and then in a radicalness of political demands.

This is the first time that representatives of the Arab people have offered an endorsement of Jewish immigration. And with a single blow that changes the situation of both the Jewish and Arab peoples. Jewish rights to Palestine, earned and founded on Jewish labor, are being recognized by the only partner who actually counts when it comes to recognition, because that partner is our neighbor. Zionism is relieved of the odium (which was also attached to the Balfour Declaration and the Palestine Mandate) of being the beneficiary and agent of foreign interests. Arab rights to their own politics are recognized, and the Arab national movement is relieved of the odium also attached to it, that it could unite behind nothing except hostility toward the Jewish national home.

It goes without saying that this Arab endorsement did not rain down upon us from the heaven of Arab goodwill like some unexpected blessing, but is the result of negotiations based on realpolitik. It goes without saying that Roosevelt also negotiated with the leaders of the Arab world, because important American interests are at stake in the Near East. But the decisive factor is that the results of these negotiations are aimed at bringing about a genuine agreement, instead of going over the heads of all participants and coercing decisions that no one can feel bound by and that therefore can lead only to the perpetuation of conflicts. It goes without saying that only a great power like America can secure the agreement of smaller nations to such decisions. The decisive factor is that it appears to be in the interest of American foreign policy that a new road is to be prepared for solving conflicts between peoples, its aim being the use of its own power to prepare the groundwork for smaller nations to be able to continue pursuing politics in relative independence.

This form of power politics, this realpolitik, differs from imperialist power politics in that its purpose is not to use the basis of present power to accumulate more and more unlimited power. One hallmark of imperialism is that in all conflicts it plays one partner off against the other in order to secure for itself permanent domination as the perennial referee and to play the charade of "tragic conflicts" as a way of keeping the peoples in question in a state of political sterility and permanent immaturity. The solution for which Roosevelt has evidently tried to pave the way in the Palestinian conflict attempts to lift it out of the tragic hell of the impasse that results from even the most measured imperialism and into the sphere of humanity, where sometimes better and sometimes worse and usually compromise solutions are to be found.

For it goes without saying that this solution is a compromise. Not because it does justice either to the radical demands of the Arabs or to the equally radical demands of the Jews; the demands of both sides were so unjust (on the part of the Arabs) or so utopian (on the part of the Jews) that they excluded the possibility of solutions on principle. But the Jews run the great risk of becoming a permanent minority in Palestine. This risk is presumably not too high a price for the huge benefit of achieving the Arab world's endorsement of Jewish immigration, because this recognition of Jewish rights offers on principle a basis for further negotiations. Once you have such a foundation under your feet, you can in fact afford to be "opportunistic"—which means trusting in the natural flow of time, in the natural changes in political constellations, and in the growth of one's own energies, all of which are guaranteed to occur.

Far more serious than contemplation of some distant future is that so far we have not achieved any recognition for our contribution to the war and therefore no representation in the negotiations of the United Nations. This will now be of crucial importance, because if the Palestine Mandate devolves upon the United Nations, the Arabs will be represented among those nations, but the Jews will not. This is a handicap that can lead directly to certain practical consequences in which we dare not acquiesce under any circumstances. The most important demand of Jewish politics—once the question of immigration is settled and Jewish-Arab agreement is established—is a fully accredited international representation of Jewish Palestine that enjoys equal rights with all others.

Over the last few years the Jewish people have had to grow so accustomed to the fact that all news is bad news for Jews that it will be very difficult for them to realize that what we have here is truly extraordinarily good and very promising news. The consequence of bad news was that Zionists have grown accustomed to formulating their demands in a vacuum and to dismissing out of hand every real political opportunity that did not promise immediate fulfillment of their demands. There is some fear that as a result of this politics of despair every offer that does not correspond to the Jewish people's own program—which definitely resembles a castle in the air—will be denounced as Chamberlainism, as appeasement, imperialism, and betrayal, which means that they will not understand that they are dealing here with something better in spirit than the Balfour Declaration.

However that may be—and we shall hope that the Zionist reaction will be different—one thing is certain: what happens from now on in the Palestinian question will depend in part, indeed in large part, on us. We have proved in Palestine that Jews can help themselves both economically and socially, if only they are left to do so. Now we have our chance to help ourselves politically as well—or to ruin ourselves. This is only just, and it is the sole justice that politics offers.

Jewish Chances: Sparse Prospects, Divided Representation
April 20, 1945

The Jewish people is not represented among the forty-four nations whose delegates will gather in San Francisco on April 25. However we may judge the real meaning of this conference—and a series of states, including some Arab states, have at least considered it important enough to declare war at five minutes to twelve—the refusal of the victorious powers to allow us a seat at the conference table is a serious loss of prestige for the Jewish people.

It is bad enough that we have not been honored with even a semblance of participation in the organization of victory and peace; still worse is that this neglect on principle forces us once again into our old role of official advisers, into our old methods of exerting unofficial influence. For as the whole world knows, it is only natural that we—not as individuals, not as American adherents of the Jewish religion, but as a people—have special interests and demands that we must represent one way or another. This is a dangerous omen of a restoration of the status quo that all European peoples greatly fear; and we Jews have cause to fear it more than all the others together.

In place of a representative of the Jewish people in San Francisco there will be—along with countless unofficial guests, who in the name of their organizations will attempt to gain the ear of one politician or another and the representatives of forty-two other organizations to act as advisers to the American delegation—two delegates from American Jewish organizations invited by the State Department. The American Jewish Conference and the

American Jewish Committee have been summoned to appear alongside Protestant and Catholic groups; they will all send a staff of assistants and experts; the Conference's representative is Henry Monsky, the Committee's is its president, Judge Proskauer.

In this case, in defiance of all the rules of arithmetic, *two Jewish advisers are less than one.* For this doubling up is simply the result of a fierce, unresolved argument between these two organizations as to who should be the sole representative. Since in this argument the non-Zionist Committee finds itself in the position of a hopeless minority, a few weeks ago it called upon the Conference, the Jewish Labor Committee, and the American Jewish Congress to unite, as it were, under its leadership and to agree upon a minimal program. Which of course was rejected. Whereupon the Committee managed, by means of connections and the argument that the Conference represents only the Zionist portion of American Jewry, to get itself admitted as an adviser.

As understandable as this intra-Jewish spat is to anyone familiar with the state of Jewish politics, it will surely appear incomprehensible to outsiders who gather in San Francisco and who will come to know both parties only by their memoranda. For their demands are in all essential points as good as identical: adoption of an international bill of rights; settlement of the problem of statelessness; restoration of Jewish rights and Jewish property; punishment for all war crimes committed against Jews. Finally, on the disputed question of Palestine, both parties are quite united in their sharp and principled opposition to the White Paper, just as both take a positive position as regards a possible transformation of the mandate into an international trusteeship. In making a further demand for a Jewish commonwealth, the American Jewish Conference is under no illusions about its chances at a gathering in San Francisco where Arabs sit with full and equal rights, while the Jewish Agency can only hope to gain a hearing during certain negotiations. Quite apart from this fact, there is Churchill's statement of a few weeks ago that the *Palestinian question will first be discussed after the war.*

The peculiarity of all the other demands is that they have little practical political significance. The international bill of rights has a fine chance of being honored with solemn approval. This would mean about as much as the solemn acceptance of the resolution at the Inter-American Democratic Conference in Mexico in 1944, which, as submitted by the Mexican delegation, renounced every form of discrimination in issues of immigration, where-upon the Mexican government closed its country's gates to almost all immigrants who did not come from Spain or the Western Hemisphere.

As for *restoration of Jewish rights,* it is already clear that there will no longer be any treaties dealing with minorities (which were the essential basis for the rights of all of Eastern European Jewry). And that leaves the restoration of Jewish property. The only remarkable thing in that regard is that thus far no Jewish body has found the courage to speak out against individual reparations—with which we have had the worst of experiences everywhere—and for a collective restitution, for which Jewish communities would appear as the plaintiffs and national states as the agents of restitution.

The real difference between these two Jewish advisers lies not so much in their practical demands as in the political background of their organizations. The American Jewish Committee truly represents only American Jewry, or better, a small part of it. The Conference, however, has immediately attempted to turn its invitation, which was extended only to American Jews, into a kind of representation for world Jewry. Together with the World Jewish Congress as the representative of all European Jewish organizations and the Board of Deputies of British Jews, it has formed a Joint Committee that has sent invitations to the Jews of South Africa and Soviet Russia.

In all questions regarding Palestine, provisions have been made for the *closest cooperation with the Jewish Agency,* which presumably will be represented by Nahum Goldmann and Elieser Kaplan, who will attend as observers. This alliance is to be welcomed because it thus avoids any appearance of American Jews' having assumed leadership of world Jewry in an undemocratic and patronizing fashion.

This, then, is the Jewish history that predates the San Francisco conference. Without any doubt questions of great interest to Jews will be discussed there—the most important of which will be the replacement of the mandate by an international trusteeship and the status of stateless persons. It is more than questionable, however, whether the Jewish advisers to the American delegation will be able to exert real influence on the form these vital issues will take.

JEWISH POLITICS

If the horrible catastrophe of European Jewry and the difficult, sad struggle to form a Jewish army and to gain recognition of the Jews as an ally of the United Nations result in our finally realizing that despite our millionaires and philanthropists we Jews are among the oppressed peoples of this earth, and that our Rothschilds have a better chance of becoming beggars or peddlers than our beggars and peddlers of becoming Rothschilds—if in other words this war politicizes us and pounds it into our heads that the struggle for freedom is tantamount to the struggle for existence, then and only then will our grandchildren be able to remember and mourn the dead and to live without shame.

Those peoples who do not make history, but simply suffer it, tend to see themselves as the victims of meaningless, overpowering, inhuman events, tend to lay their hands in their laps and wait for miracles that never happen. If in the course of this war we do not awaken from this apathy, there will be no place for us in tomorrow's world—perhaps our enemies will not have succeeded in annihilating us totally, but those of us who are left will be little more than living corpses.

The only political ideals an oppressed people can have are freedom and justice. Democracy can be their only form of organization. One of the most serious impediments to Jewish—and not just Jewish—politics is the fact that in our current intellectual world those ideals and that form of organization have been corrupted and dragged through the mud by an uprooted bohemianism. For almost fifty years now one generation after the next has declared their disdain for "abstract" ideas and their admiration for bestiality. Freedom and justice are considered concepts for feeble old men. The French Revolution's *égalité*, *liberté*, and *fraternité* are taken as signs of impotence, of an anemic will to power, and at best a pretext for better deals to be made. The so-called young generation—which ranges in age from twenty to seventy—

demands cunning of their politicians but not character, opportunism but not principles, propaganda but not policies. It is a generation that has fallen into the habit of constructing its weltanschauung out of a vague trust in great men, out of blood and soil and horoscopes.

The politics that grows out of this mentality is called realpolitik. Its central figures are the businessman who winds up being a politician convinced that politics is just a huge oversized business deal with huge oversized wins and losses, and the gangster who declares, "When I hear the word culture I reach for my revolver." Once "abstract" ideas had been replaced by "concrete" stock market speculation, it was easy for abstract justice to give way before concrete revolvers. What looked like a rebellion against all moral values has led to a kind of collective idiocy: anyone who can see farther than the tip of his own nose is said to live in a fantasy world. What looked like a rebellion against intellect has led to organized turpitude—might makes right.

Disdain for democracy and the worship of dictatorial forms of organization are especially fatal for small, oppressed peoples, who depend on the firm commitment of each individual. They least of all can forgo a democratic frame of mind, by which, as Clemenceau put it during the Dreyfus affair, the affairs of each individual are the affairs of all. In a dictatorship the individual has no political meaning—no matter how many of them wear uniforms— because the individual no longer has any sense of responsibility for anything beyond staying alive himself. Once the order from "higher up" is given, any number of SA men marching in ranks can be shot on the spot without bringing the parade to a halt. Each man is ready and willing to step over the corpse of his neighbor and march on. And once the businessman's opportunism has suffocated peoples and nations by atomizing them in a politics of cliques and clans, despotism takes this atomization to its logical conclusion, until finally sons denounce their own fathers, neighbors and friends denounce one another, for the sake of their careers or personal security.

Almost across the board, Jewish politics, to the extent that it exists at all, is run by people who have likewise grown up—without ever growing powerful!—worshipping power and opportunistic success. Their abhorrence for principles, their fear of betting on the wrong horse, their admiration of those who hold power on this earth, and their reluctance to mobilize the energies of their own people have cost us the deployment of a Jewish army. In the midst of the monstrous turmoil the world now finds itself in, those who are unwilling to take any risks are certain to lose everything. The time for compromises is past. Those who think they can live on their knees will learn that it is better to live and die standing up. We do not need any opportunistic practitioners of realpolitik, but we certainly do not need any "Führers" either. The trouble is, first, that a great many organizations and bureaucracies are working to prevent radical democrats from speaking to our people; and, second, that our people—those who are not yet behind barbed wire—are so demoralized by having been ruled by philanthropists for 150 years that they find it very difficult to begin to relearn the language of freedom and justice.

1942

WHY THE CRÉMIEUX DECREE
WAS ABROGATED

Four months and seven days after American troops landed in North Africa, Gen. Henri Giraud, French high commissioner, declared null and void all Vichy legislation affecting the country. The step followed months of strong public protest in Britain and America, and appeared to be taken with some reluctance after much explanation for the delay. General Giraud's declaration was made in an international broadcast on Sunday, March 14, but it was not until the next day that the British and American public learned with considerable indignation that they had been misled.

Easily overlooked among Giraud's pledges of adherence to the democratic principles of republican France was a brief sentence repealing a time-honored law of the French republic. "With the same desire to eliminate all racial discrimination," General Giraud had said, "the Crémieux decree of 1870 instituting distinctions between Mohammedan and Jewish inhabitants is abrogated." Stripped of its diplomatic verbiage this sentence meant, as the American press was quick to explain, that Algerian Jews were being deprived of their citizenship in order to appease the allegedly disgruntled Algerian Mohammedans. It completely ignored the fact that French citizenship has been available to Muslims for over seventy years. With one stroke it relegated the entire Algerian Jewish population to the status quo 1865! The real reasons for this measure in the midst of a war for the freedom of all peoples lie not in General Giraud's explanation but rather in the traditional power-seeking of French colonial and military groups.

—THE EDITORS, *Contemporary Jewish Record*

The colonial policy of France since the days of Jean Baptiste Colbert—and contrary to the colonial policy of other European nations—had favored complete assimilation of the natives in its possessions. They were to be "called to a community of life with the French . . . so that they may ultimately make with those of us who migrate unto Canada, one and the same nation." Such were the instructions given by Colbert in the seventeenth century to the French governor of New France, or Canada. The overseas colonies were to become French provinces, their inhabitants French citizens.

In spite of all the revolutionary changes in France during the last two centuries, there rarely was a government that departed from the general line of the principles laid down by Colbert and strongly supported by the Declaration of the Rights of Men. Algeria, however, was the first French colony which was close enough to be directly incorporated into the body politic of France, to become an integral part of the mother country.

Previously, in 1865, the French government had laid down the principles for the treatment of the native population in Algeria regarding their citizenship and their relation to the mother country, principles that as far as the Muslims were concerned went unchanged until 1919, when they were altered slightly.

The first article of the so-called *Senatus-consulte* of 1865, of special importance since the abrogation of the Crémieux decree, reads as follows:

> The native Muslim is a Frenchman; nevertheless, he will continue to be ruled by Muslim law. He can be admitted to the army and the navy. He can be appointed to civil posts in Algeria. He can, upon request, be admitted to French citizenship; but in this event he must be governed by the civil and political laws of France.

The second article provides the same benefits for Jewish subjects.

Neither native Jews nor native Muslims, however, showed themselves very eager to ask for French citizenship. Nevertheless, Napoleon III's government planned to naturalize the Jews "en bloc" in 1868. Two years later the French provisional government, the "Gouvernement de la Défense Nationale," with Adolphe Crémieux as minister of justice, executed the plans of the Second Empire by decreeing:

> The native Jews of the departments of Algeria are declared French citizens. Therefore, dating from the promulgation of the present decree,

their real status and personal status will be governed by French law; all rights acquired up to this day remain inviolable. . . .

The naturalization of Algerian Jewry, which generally is regarded—by friends and foes alike—as the work of Crémieux alone, had been prompted by two reasons. One was the defeat of France in the Franco-German War, which left French rule in North Africa seriously endangered. The decree (signed in Tours) was issued in the midst of a national crisis—the emperor had abdicated and part of the government had abandoned Paris—and served as an indication that the Jews were regarded as the only trustworthy part of the Algerian population. Indeed, a Muslim revolt did break out in 1871. It was, therefore, of no small importance to the government to have about 38,000 loyal Frenchmen in the colony at a time when trouble obviously lay ahead.

The second reason lay in the fact that Jews, unlike the Muslim natives, were closely linked to the mother country through their French brethren. Their "personal status," not very different from the customs of their Arab surroundings, did not appear to the French as typical of the Jewish people but rather as bad habits of a small portion of that people, somehow led astray—habits that could easily be corrected by the majority of the same people. French Jewry, represented by the Consistoire Central, could assume the responsibility of overruling native rabbis and could even give some guarantee for the rapid assimilation of Algerian Jewry. Accordingly, when the decree was issued, the Parisian Consistoire was given legal power to appoint all Algerian rabbis. Through the Crémieux decree, Algerian Jewry gave up its personal status and became subject to French law. The schools of the Alliance Israélite Universelle, together with the active policy of the Consistoire, assimilated the native Arabic-speaking Jews in a relatively short time and changed them into loyal French citizens.

But enemies of the Crémieux decree soon appeared. The first to oppose it formally was M. Lambert, the minister of the interior of the new French republic. His attitude, inspired by military circles, was in line with the opposition of the French colonial administration and French colonial officers. Their resistance to the Crémieux decree grew largely out of the fact that the new status given Algeria deprived them of much of their power.

Algeria had been ruled by a military governor-general who answered only to the Ministry of War and who was responsible for civil life and military security alike. In no other part of France was military influence so preponderant; the *préfets*, the whole of the civil administration, were subject to the authority of generals. The constitution of the country was a kind of military dictatorship. All this was changed in 1871, when a civil governor-general was appointed by the government and placed under the authority of the Ministry of the Interior. Thereby, the French army lost the only stronghold it possessed, where it controlled civil life and civilians.

Admiral Gueydon, who had been governor-general of Algeria from 1871 to 1873, was one of the first to blame the riots of 1871 on the Crémieux decree; he was closely followed by General Ducrot. Both gentlemen obviously had chosen to forget the earlier outbreaks in 1864. Colonial administrators like du Bouzet and Autun soon joined this opposition. They spoke in the name of the French colonials in North Africa, men who had never shared the views of the home government regarding colonial politics. During their stay in Algeria they had acquired a feeling of racial superiority that never had been known in France itself, and they felt their economic and political position at stake if French citizenship were granted to Algerian natives.

These French colonials became the major source of antisemitism in Algeria. They were antinative in general but became anti-Jewish when equality was given to native Jews. Through their influence and control, almost the entire Algerian press in the 1880s took an anti-Jewish stand and fought against the Crémieux decree. Street signs declared in 1882 that "all methods are good and should be used for the extermination of the Jews by Europeans." Edouard Drumont, a leading agitator, expressed the hope that a campaign of French antisemitism would start in Algeria, and he was not disappointed; during the Dreyfus affair the worst pogroms took place in Algiers (1898), and Drumont, who could not get enough votes in the mother country, found enough Frenchmen in Algiers to elect him to Parliament.

Meanwhile, the French Parliament continued to seek a formula that would permit the assimilation and naturalization of the other natives. Between 1887 and 1897 numerous bills were introduced, all of them proposing progressive naturalization of Algerian Muslims. In 1915, Georges Clemenceau introduced a bill that would have granted the Muslims citizenship without asking them to abandon their personal status. In 1919, when Clemenceau was premier, an amendment to the old *Senatus-consulte* was passed which provided some minor reforms but which still insisted on individual naturalization.

The reasons for the failure of the traditional policy of assimilation in a country that more than any other had been organized on the model of France are twofold. It is true that the natives did not want to renounce their personal status (which permitted polygamy and the denial of all rights to women) and that France could hardly grant them citizenship under this circumstance. French civil law and the French penal code have their bases in the equality of sexes, and the Islamic concept of paternal authority is in fundamental conflict with this principle of individual liberty. If the natives, especially the fellahin, oppressed by their "native aristocracy which rules and exploits them unscrupulously," have not abandoned polygamy it is also partly because the woman is the main source of "manpower" for the fellah, in fact the only one he can afford to "hire." Among the laborers and the intellectuals in the towns, however, polygamy has almost disappeared.

Far more important than these customs and even more important than the influence of the native aristocracy was the attitude of the French colonials, which was described by the great French colonial politician and statesman Jules Ferry in the following words: "It is difficult to make the European colonist understand that there exist other rights than his own in an Arab country and that the native is not to be molded according to his desires."

These French colonials, mostly large landowners whose prosperity depended upon cheap native labor and sympathetic government officials, lived in perpetual conflict with the governors-general appointed by the national government in Paris. The colonists, and not the governor, wielded the real power in Algerian affairs, for they could act through the administration. Moreover, through the deputies and senators of the French Parliament, they could even influence the government at home, as they did in 1924 when they forced the Chautemps government to ban Arab emigration from Algeria to France in order to keep their cheap manpower reservoir untouched.

This antinative rule by the French colonials is possible because of the inferior political status of the natives. Key political positions can be held only by French citizens, while the native Muslim population is limited to local self-administration. According to the law of 1884 (*Loi sur l'organisation munici-*

pale), natives only have the right to vote and to be elected to the Municipal Councils of the communities. Each of the three Algerian departments is represented by a Conseil Général, only one-fourth of whose members are natives, the remainder being French citizens. The three Conseils Généraux together form a kind of local parliament. The third important political body is the so-called Délégations Financières, which decides on the budget and taxes. This body is composed of twenty-four representatives of the French colonists (i.e., large landowners), twenty-four representatives of all other French citizens, and twenty-one natives who are appointed by the governor-general and usually selected from the rich Arab landowners. The members of the Conseils Généraux and the Délégations Financières together with the Conseil du Gouverneur (a council selected and appointed by the governor from his officials) form the Conseil Supérieur.

While the national government sought the naturalization of the Arabs and regarded the Crémieux decree as a beginning and a way to attract the Arabs by the privileges it gave to its citizens, its intentions have been frustrated during the last seventy years by the colonials, who used their legal power to prevent naturalization of the natives. They never recognized the naturalized native as a French citizen and did not allow him to share in the rule of the country. Furthermore, the local administration has proved to be much stronger than the national government in Paris. The governor-general, its only representative, wields little real power, as was most emphatically illustrated by the almost tragic case of Maurice Viollette (1925–27), one of the best governors Algeria ever had. Viollette was almost ousted by his administration because he tried to enforce the policy of the home government.

The few citizens of Arab origin were worse off than their nonnaturalized brethren, for—in the words of their spokesman, S. Faci—they were "repulsed by the natives and held in contempt by the French." In other words, the native Muslim who applies for French citizenship is confronted with the contempt of his own people, who call him a *m'tourni* (turncoat), and the hatred and discrimination of French society and administration. Moreover, applications for citizenship have to be filed through various administrative channels, beginning with the justice of peace. Since the documents needed, such as a birth certificate, are obtainable only from the administration or from the Muslim Municipal Councils, which are hostile to any naturalization, the total number of naturalizations granted up to 1934 was 1,359.

After 1919, there was hardly a year in which a new bill was not introduced in Parliament to normalize the status of Algerian natives, and between 1927 and 1937, nine such bills were discussed. Among them, we can distinguish three types of reforms. One called for special and separate representation for the natives within the French Parliament, notably in such bills as those presented by Moutet, a Socialist deputy. The second type of bill proposed naturalization without renunciation of personal status. It is best represented by the proposal Viollette made in 1931, which was also supported in 1936 by the Blum government. The third type is represented by the proposal of Cuttoli (1935), who wanted to naturalize the natives en bloc but with renunciation of personal status. Under this proposal natives would have the right to reject French citizenship if they wished to retain their personal status. However, none of these plans materialized. The only proposal ever backed by the government, the Viollette-Blum plan, was so violently attacked by the Algerian colonials and their representatives in Parliament that it had to be abandoned.

Since the days of the Dreyfus affair, antisemitic propaganda in Algeria has never subsided. Sporadic but bloody riots occurred in Algiers in 1898, in Oran in 1925, and in Constantine in 1934. They were not only tolerated by the administration and the police, but the whole atmosphere had been carefully prepared. Governor-general Viollette, speaking about Oran, declared: "The politics of M. Molle has been exclusively a politics of antisemitism." And in 1935, Viollette flatly told the Senate: "If there is antisemitism in Algeria, be sure that it is Europeans who fan it."

After 1934, Nazi propaganda also made itself strongly felt in all North African countries. Pan-Islamic committees, organized in Syria, Egypt, Tunis, and Algeria, were directed by a central committee in Berlin which, according to the French Senate, had at its disposal a fund of 20 million marks. Cries of "Vive Hitler" were common in Algerian movies, and considerable propaganda was circulated among the natives. There is no doubt that these activities were supported by the French colonials, who admired Hitler's racial policy and who were only too glad to see the violent feelings of the economically depressed and politically underprivileged population directed against Jews rather than themselves.

The 1936 elections to the French Parliament, the last before the collapse, already showed that the right wing in Algeria was much stronger than in France proper, although the Republicans still won a majority. But this majority was held principally because of the votes of Jews and a number of civil servants, who subsequently were ousted by the Vichy regime. However, it should be remembered that prewar party labels no longer reflected a candidate's true political allegiance and that sympathizers with Hitler, who later became collaborationists, could be found in all parties, from right to left. (Laval was a Radical-Socialist, and Fauré was a former colleague of Blum.) Therefore one need not be surprised to learn that, although out of ten Algerian deputies elected in 1936 only one openly belonged to an anti-Republican party, no more than two deputies protested against the Vichy decrees. And they belonged to two small center parties.

In Algeria, at the present time, out of a total population of 7,234,084 there are 987,252 Europeans, of whom 853,209 are or were French citizens. Of the latter, about 100,000 are Jews. (Since the separation of state and church, no special census is available for French countries.) The Jews, now deprived of their citizenship, revert to the status of natives: they have become French subjects.

Muslims today are judged by French laws and French courts in all matters other than those covered by their personal status (marriage and divorce, majority and minority, succession and paternal authority), over which Muslim law takes precedence. As French subjects (natives), however, they enjoy the same civil rights as French citizens; thus, since 1864 and in spite of personal status, natives can even become lawyers and practice this profession under exactly the same conditions as in France. They may represent natives or French citizens (though different civil codes are applied, and they may appear before any legal court in Algeria, either Muslim or French, for "it is the privilege of a lawyer to plead in all courts"). But the Algerian administrative system gives the natives little representation in the decisive political bodies of the country and deprives them of such rights as, for example, a voice in taxation.

The position of the Jews in this respect will be even worse: they will not be reinstated to the seats they formerly held in the Conseils Généraux of which the Vichy laws had already deprived them, for they had been appointed or elected to them as French citizens and not as native subjects.

Thus, in the matter of taxation, for instance, they will be entirely dependent upon a governmental body that not only cannot represent them but as a matter of fact will even prove hostile to their interests. And General Giraud has already declared that new elections are not to be expected.

Theoretically speaking, Jews, like other subjects, can apply for individual naturalization. Practically, however, their applications will be made impossible by an administration that is even more anti-Jewish than antinative and that has blocked naturalization of natives for the last seventy years. Theoretically, abrogation of the Crémieux decree will have but little effect upon the general economic life of the Jews. Indeed, the only serious handicap—the permit necessary to enter France, which during recent years was rarely granted to natives—does not play a role for the time being. Practically, abrogation of the Crémieux decree means that Jews will have no representation at all in the various political bodies of the country and that they will be in a worse position than the Muslims: they will not be represented at all!

Since Jews had no personal status but were entirely subject to French law, they were French citizens not by privilege but by right. General Giraud's abrogation of the Crémieux decree introduces into Algeria a new criterion for French citizenship and creates a distinction between natives and citizens that is in flagrant contradiction to all French laws, to all French institutions, and to the whole of French colonial policy. This distinction, abandoning as it does the basis of French law, language, and civilization, cannot be based upon anything else than racial origin.

If General Giraud, instead of abolishing the Crémieux decree, had extended French citizenship to all natives prepared to accept French civil law and to renounce personal status (as was proposed by Cuttoli in 1935), it might have been dubious whether under the present circumstances he had any legal right to make such a constitutional change. But at least he would have acted according to the standards of traditional French colonial policies, and he would have put into effect a law which had been discussed time and again before the Parliament. The possibility of repealing the Crémieux decree, however, had not been mentioned in Parliament for more than forty years.

General Giraud pretends to have nullified the Crémieux decree because it caused inequality among the natives and gave a privileged position to the

Jews. Actually, he has acted as an agent of those French colonials who always wanted to bring under their "dictatorship" the only part of the Algerian population that so far had escaped their arbitrary and selfish rule. The French colonials, in other words, took advantage of France's defeat and of their freedom from the control of the mother country to introduce into Algeria a measure which they would never have been able to obtain through legal channels.

APRIL 1943

NEW LEADERS ARISE IN EUROPE

The Jews have been the first victims of the Nazi regime and they have been the last to achieve a militant underground movement. It took them almost ten years to overcome the traditional Jewish aversion against military organization and to win the indispensable active cooperation of the other antifascist forces in Europe. Today, however, a Jewish underground army is an established fact. Ever since the glorious battle in the ghetto of Warsaw, it has grown in size, spread to new areas, and inspired ever more frequent uprisings in concentration camps. Ironically, though, while some Jews busied themselves to depict our brethren as helpless victims and pitiful objects of eventual rescue and relief, they have been strong and ingenious enough to organize themselves into Jewish fighting units.

Fighting units under their own flag, uprisings in concentration camps, cooperation with other underground movements all over Europe—these are more tangible and politically more significant facts than the rather dubious statistical data asserting that next to nothing may be expected from European Jewry in the near future. Sad as it may be, it is these fighting Jews and not tears over the countless numbers of those who perished in the great slaughterhouse that will help to shape the destiny of the Jews.

No technical inventions and no new weapons have so decisively determined the physiognomy of this war as the part played in it by the underground organizations. Dangerous as their lives may be, they guarantee at least as much safety for the individual member as the order of terror with which the fascist police gangs "protect" the unorganized "law-abiding" citizens. When we hear that less than 4 percent of those Frenchmen who receive the orders to report for forced labor actually comply with them, we realize that the deportation orders of the Nazis have become the recruiting orders for the European underground. There is no escape from the alternative (for Jews even less than for anybody else) of either fighting against the Nazis, and thus gaining a chance for life, or dying with almost mathematical certainty. In the end, we may find out that the morally strongest who risked their lives for the common cause of freedom have survived, whereas the weaker elements of the people who could not resist will have perished.

While nobody can possibly foretell how many Jews will be there to welcome the armies of liberation, it requires but little imagination to predict that these guerrilla fighters will present us with an entirely new type of Jewish mentality and with an entirely new set of problems. There is, of course, the great danger that organized Jewish charity, as little disposed to part with the old methods and practices as any bureaucracy, will try to deal with the people in the old manner. They might want to dispatch to them their "experienced" officials, whom nobody has ever prepared to meet proud, self-respecting, and thoroughly politically minded "victims." There is the great danger that we will lose the peace when we lose those men and women who are well trained for new Jewish leadership, but who hardly have learned how to behave when forced onto the grounds of charity. All our so-called and more or less self-appointed spokesmen of European Jewry will prove as little representative of the Jewish people in Nazi Europe as, say, the Greek or Yugoslav governments in exile represent their respective peoples. The only reason that we have not yet the same rifts and problems of those governments in exile is that we are more isolated from our underground movement than the others.

The very silence with which the official Jewish organizations veil the accomplishments of our underground—the somewhat perfunctory tribute to their heroism is constantly tempered by wailings over "the little energy left in Nazi victims"—is proof enough not only of our lack of imagination but of our conscious or unconscious desire to belittle the political importance of those fighters for the cause of Jewish freedom. It is true, every other day we are presented with new plans for postwar reconstruction which, according to the political convictions of their authors, range from complete evacuation of Jews from Europe to complete restoration of the Jewish communities. But neither party, as a rule, is ready to concede the decisive say to the politically minded "victims." This may well cause the disgust of people who certainly will feel that they have at least contributed as much to their own liberation as the Jews of other countries, and it may finally result in the disintegration of the forces that today are strong and well organized. The paramount question is not what to do with those who have somehow managed to stay alive in the concentration camps, but how to cooperate with those who have lived a free if extremely dangerous life.

This danger of losing the best elements of the Jewish people will be gravely accentuated by another trend which has been noted by one lonely preacher in the wilderness—William Zukerman: the fast disappearance of antisemitism all over the European continent. Were it not for this, a Jewish underground movement, Jewish fighting units, and so forth would never have come into existence. Here, for the first time in their recent history, Jews are not protected by any government and here for the first time they find themselves solely dependent upon the solidarity of their neighbors. This is not a question of such sentimental stories about the gentile who was nice enough to give a piece of bread to a Jew or decent enough to refuse to murder him. There has been a very definite change in the relationship between Jews and non-Jews, but that does not mean that the Jewish question will be solved automatically. For while a gang of clever murderers has certainly succeeded in making life a real hell, nobody ever will succeed in making it a paradise. In other words, mere decency or kindness will never solve the existing Jewish problems. That is the job of conscious political action on the part of the Jewish people, in cooperation with the other peoples of Europe.

However, the problem itself has changed because the whole structure of the people has undergone a violent transformation. The big Jews, once the absolute masters of Jewish politics, are conspicuous by their absence. French and German and Italian Jews are herded together with their Eastern brethren or fighters side by side. There is no longer the ghost of "the Jew everywhere and nowhere" whose identity no one quite knows: a member of a "national minority" or of a religious community or of the most powerful international organization or the personification of the "hidden forces behind the scene." Jews and non-Jews alike are pretty well aware by now that Jews suffer and fight because they are Jews—and not because of their religion or their being a minority; that the legendary international organization does not exist and that, in any case, they certainly are not the hidden forces behind the scene as depicted by Hitler. To the extent that *the* Jew is disappearing, Jews have come to life: organizing, fighting, proud of their flag and their deeds, suffering and hoping for a better future—a nationality like the other nationalities who sprang from the fostering soil of Western history.

Perhaps these Jews will want to go to Palestine. It would be logical enough—though not for the reasons usually cited, that is, because of mistrust and fear of further persecutions. Palestine does not lie on the moon and racial antisemitism as a weapon of imperialistic politics does not stop before the gates of the homeland. Antisemitism, if not obliterated everywhere, will threaten Jews anywhere. The opportunities for complete integration, on the other hand, may well be very great in the period after the war.

If they should choose to remain in Europe—and a majority of the people will have to, at least for a long transitional period—no one will be able to persuade them that simple restoration of the status quo ante, simple reintegration, would be either possible or desirable. And again, not because of Jew-hatred, not because of any hostile reactions of the non-Jewish peoples, but because of the organization of the Jews itself. For good or for evil, individual Jews no longer exist in any considerable number. If we plan to restore Jewish prewar life, we must realize that we shall have to destroy the present forms of Jewish organization, and this in all probability we could do only against the will of the Jewish people of Europe. For these have learned by the most bitter experiences that neither individual equality nor mere national segregation without active national life (under the name of minority rights) guarantees the existence of a people. For them a return to the "golden age of security" has become a mockery and protection by third powers—be they governments or high-placed brethren in other countries—a dangerous illusion. Whether they decide to take an active part in the upbuilding of Palestine or to become part of the comity of European nations, they certainly will insist on a new political status for Jews as *Jews*. Today as part of the European underground, they are organized and recognized as a distinct entity. Even as they raised the blue-and-white flag, they have manifested their political will. They have raised the banner of the Jewish people as a whole. Even as the other European undergrounds cooperate with this flag, they, too, have indicated the direction of the solution of the Jewish problem. It will do no good to ignore these voices in silence or in pity. We had better prepare ourselves for a new Jewish leadership which will arise from the ranks of the Jewish underground—as it will arise from the underground movements of all European peoples.

1944

A WAY TOWARD THE
RECONCILIATION OF PEOPLES

I

It has often been claimed that Germany was the first country that Hitler conquered. But that is only correct if one does not forget to add that the conquest was supported by a large portion of the German population and met with the passive toleration or even the tacit approval of still larger portions. In any case Hitler began his murderous advance across Europe and his destruction of the European world of nations with the annihilation of the German nation, which has perished in the infamy of Dachau and Buchenwald, in the infamy of torture chambers and the Nuremberg Laws, in the infamy of campaigns of extermination waged against women, old people, and children. The bloody phantom of the German race has arisen out of the ruins of the German nation. What is left is the German people, about one million of whom are sitting in Hitler's concentration camps.

On that day in Compiègne, when Pétain put his signature to the infamous paragraphs of the German-French armistice, which demanded that every refugee in France be handed over to the Nazis, even those who had fought under the French flag—on that memorable day Pétain tore the tricolor to shreds and annihilated the French nation. This annihilation likewise met with the approval of a sizable portion of the French population and the tacit toleration of an even larger portion. It was well known after all that the majority of refugees at issue were Jews. The Vichy government could depend on the same indifference with which the French had tolerated the infamy of Spanish concentration camps, the infamy of the Third Republic's treatment of refugees, and the infamy of a defeat without a struggle. It could depend even more on France's homegrown antisemitic tradition, which the French proudly kept in mind as they turned concentration camps for refugees into concentration—and deportation—camps for Jews. The French nation perished; what is left is the French people battling against their physical extermination with bombs and sabotage.

Born out of the French Revolution and founded by Napoleon's triumphant armies, the world of European nations has never been fully realized. Prevented by larger nations from developing fully in political and economic terms, it was always smaller peoples who fashioned the famous dynamite that set off the First World War. The Jewish question was part of these unsolved national problems in Europe. The Jews, the only European people who had never even been able to establish their own area of settlement, were ultimately the minority par excellence—a minority everywhere, a majority nowhere. Far from being alien or irrelevant to European politics, the Jewish question became a symbol for all of Europe's unresolved national questions.

European nations looked on with indifference as the weakest member of the family, the perennial stepchild, was first cheated out of its national claims to Palestine and then threatened with the loss of its physical existence in the Diaspora. They have paid very dearly for their lack of concern, because antisemitism has turned out to be the agent of destructive fermentation for the entire European world. At least for now, the price for their antisemitism is the loss of their existence as nations. One after the other they let the murderous hordes cross their borders almost without a fight, because they imagined that it was "only" a matter of Jews. At the forefront were the Germans, who for a long time believed that the Gestapo and its torture chambers were invented only for Jews. Until finally France decided to join in the dance of death by more or less welcoming the "smart ranks" of the Nazi army, firmly convinced that the only necks at risk were those of Jews and other "disagreeable foreigners." Not to mention Poland and Romania, who hoped to stifle their own misery right away with pogroms of their own making.

But by now the tables have been turned. The Nazis, who thought they had discovered that terror is the most effective means of propaganda, have managed, very much against their own will, to teach these peoples anew—at a tempo previously unknown in history—the concepts on which all politics are based: freedom and justice. Unrest is growing throughout Europe. Nordic peoples, with weapons in hand, refuse to be included in the "master race." The French clergy, who at one point had hoped to win people back to the church with antisemitism and on whose support Pétain had therefore so firmly counted, have discovered that they can fill churches by preaching *for* the Jews and demanding that believers protect Jews from the police. Right under the nose of the German army of occupation, the bishop of Paris strolled about wearing a yellow star, teaching practical Christianity in a most palpable way. In Yugoslavia Mikhailovitch's troops are liberating Jews from concentration camps, arming them, and fighting alongside them in the great battle of liberation. In Holland, in Belgium, in Denmark—the picture is the same everywhere: the rebellion is being sparked at precisely the same point where moral defeat began before the ensuing military defeat: the issue of how Jews are treated.

The Nazis are desperately trying to remove Jews from all areas where their mere presence provides a focal point for rebellion among the local population. They deport them to regions that can still be considered antisemitic and thus firmly on the side of the Nazis. But they are only pouring oil on the fire and have been forced to learn that under certain circumstances people have a good memory, that under certain circumstances the missing and the dead speak a louder, clearer language than those who are alive and nearby.

II

These events cast us Jews into a political constellation for which there is no precedent in modern history. Since the formation of the nation-state we have been more or less effectively protected (and sometimes privileged) by various governments and more or less fiercely rejected (and sometimes persecuted) by society. In conflict with their own governments, more and more segments of society became antisemitic over the last fifty years, until finally, with the collapse of the nation-state as a state of law, persecutions of Jews for reasons of state began to take place. That a society would attempt to protect us from measures taken by the state—as has happened among the French and Dutch, who have rebelled against their governments on behalf of their own and even foreign Jews—is such a new fact in Jewish history that it will definitely take at least twenty years for the practitioners of realpolitik among us to get this new reality through their heads.

Jews would be well advised to pay close attention to these first signs of things to come. The catastrophe in Europe has meant the end not only of nation-states but also of the conflicts and disputes between those peoples who had managed to form a nation and those who, like the Jews, had remained simply a people. It is hard to say which proved more effective in this regard, Hitler's armies or each nation's sense of its own shame. In any case each is once again simply a people awaiting national liberation—a liberation that can presumably be realized this time only in a federated Europe along the lines of what Napoleon once had in mind. The French Revolution, which brought human rights to the Jews at the price of their national emancipation, is about to take its second great step.

Amid the most awful persecutions in Jewish history, Jews have suffered horrible losses over these last few years, but the chances are now very great for a new orientation of Jewish national politics. For the first time in recent history we can appeal directly to other peoples in regard to our just claims to national emancipation—that is, to Palestine. For the first time since the end of the eighteenth century and at precisely the moment when there is no such thing as Jewish influence upon the mighty of this earth, other peoples have declared their solidarity with us. It should be apparent to every insightful person and to every democrat that we can expect more from this solidarity than from any protections granted us in the past.

This war is a war of "the common man," as Henry Wallace, the American vice president, has put it. We will have to assert our claims to Palestine among newly awakening peoples, will have to direct our words to the common man, to the average citizen of democratically organized nations. It is he who during the course of this war—and surely even more so after it—will come to understand the problems of the Jewish people better than all the civil servants in all the colonial administrations of this world. He will realize for his own sake that there is no solution to national problems without a national soil, and for the sake of his own national honor will be forced to practice justice. And he will understand this all the better the deeper he has fallen into the abyss of national shame, into which fundamental injustice has flung him.

Justice for a people, however, can only mean national justice. One of the inalienable human rights of Jews is the right to live and if need be to die as a Jew. A human being can defend himself only as the person he is attacked as. A Jew can preserve his human dignity only if he can be human as a Jew. For a

Jew—in a time when his people are persecuted and the scraps of desert land that he has turned into fertile fields through the work of his own hands are threatened—that means fighting for the freedom of his people and the security of his land. As surely as humankind is disgraced by every persecuted Jew, it is equally certain that the few Jews who have been graciously permitted to take part in this war as British colonial soldiers can never offset such disgrace. A people that no longer defends itself against its enemies is not a people but a living corpse. A people whom others will not allow to defend itself against its enemies is condemned to a fate that is perhaps humanly quite lofty but politically completely unworthy: a victim of world history.

III

Of all the peoples of Europe none has a greater objective interest than the Germans in seeing a real Jewish army take to the battlefield. Greater than the outrage of having unleashed this war is the infamy of waging war against the defenseless. The blood of murdered victims will cry to heaven far more loudly than the blood of slain enemies. It is one of the laws of life in the human community that every victim—but not every conquered enemy— cries for vengeance. That was understood by a certain German Protestant— who could truly not be suspected of being a philosemite—when in April 1933 he said: "The blood of these Jews will be upon our children and children's children." Only a struggle in which all the victims take part—and in which ultimately the Nazis of all countries are isolated and conquered by the people they now rule over—can anticipate this vengeance and eliminate it.

Today many people of German heritage are ashamed of what the Nazis have done in the name of their people. Many of them believe they have done enough if they declare themselves philosemites, express their sympathy to Jewish friends, give a Jewish association the look of parity by adding their names to a list, or go so far as to declare that for them there are no Jews. Well, we can understand these people's motive—and we know only too well how often it is Jews who force them to take these absurd personal positions. But that does not prevent such attitudes from being at best politically meaningless, and usually harmful. One need only imagine the democracies so bitterly slandered by Hitler defending themselves by declaring that they really do not exist—that would amount to the same sort of wisdom as advocating sui-cide as a way to avoid being murdered. As surely as Hitler is determined to exterminate Jews or democrats on a global scale, it is equally certain that he can be prevented from carrying out his intentions only if those under threat are determined to confirm their existence by defending themselves with their own hands. And just as a man who is threatened with murder should not trust a friend who suggests suicide as a way out of his predicament, Jews should not trust friends who try to convince them that collective suicide is the best way to ensure their collective security.

What we demand of the United Nations is nothing more than that it show the same solidarity with us that many European peoples under the pressure of the Nazis' terror machine have already shown us. We do not want prom-ises that our sufferings will be "avenged," we want to fight; we do not want mercy, but justice. "Il faut toujours rendre justice avant d'exercer la charité" (Malebranche), which might be translated as: He who does not practice jus-tice has no right to mercy. Mercy without justice is one of the devil's most powerful accomplices—it calms outrage and sanctions the structures that the devil has created. Freedom, however, is not a reward for sufferings endured and one does not accept justice as if it were crumbs from the table of the rich.

Over the past year a large number of Americans of German heritage have declared their sympathy for the movement to create a Jewish army. Some have gone even further and taken an active part in this most important aspect of the Jewish people's struggle for their rights. They alone are the real repre-sentatives of those one million Germans whom Hitler has imprisoned in con-centration camps. By their support for the just participation of Jews in this war—which truly is their war—they have contributed more than all those Jewish or non-Jewish antifascists who believe they are doing something to benefit the Jews by debating them out of existence.

The United Nations will not be complete as long as they are unwilling to sit at the same table with the pariah among the world's peoples. Just as the fate of the Jews today has become the symbol of what appears to be the rule of the devil on earth, so, too, the real criterion for the justice of this war will be seen in the degree to which other nations are prepared to fight their, our, and humanity's battle shoulder to shoulder with Jews.

1942

WE REFUGEES

In the first place, we don't like to be called "refugees." We ourselves call each other "newcomers" or "immigrants." Our newspapers are papers for "Americans of German language"; and, as far as I know, there is not and never was any club founded by Hitler-persecuted people whose name indicated that its members were refugees.

A refugee used to be a person driven to seek refuge because of some act committed or some political opinion held. Well, it is true we have had to seek refuge; but we committed no acts and most of us never dreamt of having any radical political opinion. With us the meaning of the term "refugee" has changed. Now "refugees" are those of us who have been so unfortunate as to arrive in a new country without means and have to be helped by refugee committees.

Before this war broke out we were even more sensitive about being called refugees. We did our best to prove to other people that we were just ordinary immigrants. We declared that we had departed of our own free will to countries of our choice, and we denied that our situation had anything to do with "so-called Jewish problems." Yes, we were "immigrants" or "newcomers" who had left our country because, one fine day, it no longer suited us to stay, or for purely economic reasons. We wanted to rebuild our lives, that was all. In order to rebuild one's life one has to be strong and an optimist. So we are very optimistic.

Our optimism, indeed, is admirable, even if we say so ourselves. The story of our struggle has finally become known. We lost our home, which means the familiarity of daily life. We lost our occupation, which means the confidence that we are of some use in this world. We lost our language, which means the naturalness of reactions, the simplicity of gestures, the unaffected expression of feelings. We left our relatives in the Polish ghettos and our best friends have been killed in concentration camps, and that means the rupture of our private lives.

Nevertheless, as soon as we were saved—and most of us had to be saved several times—we started our new lives and tried to follow as closely as possible all the good advice our saviors passed on to us. We were told to forget; and we forgot quicker than anybody ever could imagine. In a friendly way we were reminded that the new country would become a new home; and after four weeks in France or six weeks in America, we pretended to be Frenchmen or Americans. The more optimistic among us would even add that their whole former life had been passed in a kind of unconscious exile and only their new country now taught them what a home really looks like. It is true we sometimes raise objections when we are told to forget about our former work; and our former ideals are usually hard to throw over if our social standard is at stake. With the language, however, we find no difficulties: after a single year optimists are convinced they speak English as well as their mother tongue; and after two years they swear solemnly that they speak English better than any other language—their German is a language they hardly remember.

In order to forget more efficiently we rather avoid any allusion to concentration or internment camps we experienced in nearly all European countries— it might be interpreted as pessimism or lack of confidence in the new homeland. Besides, how often have we been told that nobody likes to listen to all that; hell is no longer a religious belief or a fantasy, but something as real as houses and stones and trees. Apparently nobody wants to know that contemporary history has created a new kind of human beings—the kind that are put in concentration camps by their foes and in internment camps by their friends.

Even among ourselves we don't speak about this past. Instead, we have found our own way of mastering an uncertain future. Since everybody plans and wishes and hopes, so do we. Apart from these general human attitudes, however, we try to clear up the future more scientifically. After so much bad luck we want a course as sure as a gun. Therefore, we leave the earth with all its uncertainties behind and we cast our eyes up to the sky. The stars tell us— rather than the newspapers—when Hitler will be defeated and when we shall become American citizens. We think the stars more reliable advisers than all our friends; we learn from the stars when we should have lunch with our benefactors and on what day we have the best chances of filling out one of these countless questionnaires which accompany our present lives. Sometimes we don't rely even on the stars but rather on the lines of our hand or the signs of our handwriting. Thus we learn less about political events but more about our own dear selves, even though somehow psychoanalysis has gone out of fashion. Those happier times are past when bored ladies and gentlemen of high society conversed about the genial misdemeanors of their early childhood. They don't want ghost stories any more; it is real experiences that make their flesh creep. There is no longer any need of bewitching the past; it is spellbound enough in reality. Thus, in spite of our outspoken optimism, we use all sorts of magical tricks to conjure up the spirits of the future.

I don't know which memories and which thoughts nightly dwell in our dreams. I dare not ask for information, since I, too, had rather be an optimist. But sometimes I imagine that at least nightly we think of our dead or we remember the poems we once loved. I could even understand how our friends of the West Coast, during the curfew, should have had such curious notions as to believe that we are not only "prospective citizens" but present "enemy aliens." In daylight, of course, we become only "technically" enemy aliens— all refugees know this. But when technical reasons prevented you from leaving your home during the dark hours, it certainly was not easy to avoid some dark speculations about the relation between technicality and reality.

No, there is something wrong with our optimism. There are those odd optimists among us who, having made a lot of optimistic speeches, go home and turn on the gas or make use of a skyscraper in quite an unexpected way. They seem to prove that our proclaimed cheerfulness is based on a dangerous readiness for death. Brought up in the conviction that life is the highest good and death the greatest dismay, we became witnesses and victims of worse terrors than death—without having been able to discover a higher ideal than life. Thus, although death lost its horror for us, we became neither willing nor able to risk our lives for a cause. Instead of fighting—or thinking about how to become able to fight back—refugees have got used to wishing death to friends or relatives; if somebody dies, we cheerfully imagine all the trouble he has been saved. Finally many of us end by wishing that we, too, could be saved some trouble, and act accordingly.

Since 1938—since Hitler's invasion of Austria—we have seen how quickly eloquent optimism could change to speechless pessimism. As time went on, we got worse—even more optimistic and even more inclined to suicide. Austrian Jews under Schuschnigg were such a cheerful people—all impartial observers admired them. It was quite wonderful how deeply convinced they were that nothing could happen to them. But when German troops invaded the country and gentile neighbors started riots at Jewish homes, Austrian Jews began to commit suicide.

Unlike other suicides, our friends leave no explanation of their deed, no indictment, no charge against a world that had forced a desperate man to talk and to behave cheerfully to his very last day. Letters left by them are conventional, meaningless documents. Thus, funeral orations we make at their open graves are brief, embarrassed, and very hopeful. Nobody cares about motives; they seem to be clear to all of us.

I speak of unpopular facts; and it makes things worse that in order to prove my point I do not even dispose of the sole arguments which impress modern people—figures. Even those Jews who furiously deny the existence of the Jewish people give us a fair chance of survival as far as figures are concerned—how else could they prove that only a few Jews are criminals and that many Jews are being killed as good patriots in wartime? Through their effort to save the statistical life of the Jewish people we know that Jews had the lowest suicide rate among all civilized nations. I am quite sure those figures are no longer correct, but I cannot prove it with new figures, though I can certainly with new experiences. This might be sufficient for those skeptical souls who never were quite convinced that the measure of one's skull gives the exact idea of its content, or that statistics of crime show the exact level of national ethics. Anyhow, wherever European Jews are living today, they no longer behave according to statistical laws. Suicides occur not only among the panic-stricken people in Berlin and Vienna, in Bucharest or Paris, but in New York and Los Angeles, in Buenos Aires and Montevideo.

On the other hand, there has been little reported about suicides in the ghettos and concentration camps themselves. True, we had very few reports at all from Poland, but we have been fairly well informed about German and French concentration camps.

At the camp of Gurs, for instance, where I had the opportunity of spending some time, I heard only once about suicide, and that was the suggestion of a collective action, apparently a kind of protest in order to vex the French. When some of us remarked that we had been shipped there *"pour crever"* in any case, the general mood turned suddenly into a violent courage to live. The general opinion held that one had to be abnormally asocial and unconcerned about general events if one was still able to interpret the whole accident as personal and individual bad luck and, accordingly, ended one's life personally and individually. But the same people, as soon as they returned to their own individual lives, being faced with seemingly individual problems, changed once more to this insane optimism which is next door to despair.

We are the first nonreligious Jews persecuted—and we are the first ones who, not only in extremis, answer with suicide. Perhaps the philosophers are right who teach that suicide is the best and supreme guarantee of human freedom: not being free to create our lives or the world in which we live, we nevertheless are free to throw life away and to leave the world. Pious Jews, certainly, cannot realize this negative liberty; they perceive murder in suicide, that is, destruction of what man never is able to make, interference with the rights of the Creator. *Adonai nathan veadonai lakach* ("The Lord hath given and the Lord hath taken away"); and they would add: *baruch shem adonai* ("blessed be the name of the Lord"). For them suicide, like murder, means a blasphemous attack on creation as a whole. The man who kills himself asserts that life is not worth living and the world not worth sheltering him.

Yet our suicides are no mad rebels who hurl defiance at life and the world, who try to kill in themselves the whole universe. Theirs is a quiet and modest way of vanishing; they seem to apologize for the violent solution they have found for their personal problems. In their opinion, generally, political events had nothing to do with their individual fate; in good or bad times they would believe solely in their personality. Now they find some mysterious shortcomings in themselves which prevent them from getting along. Having felt entitled from their earliest childhood to a certain social standard, they are failures in their own eyes if this standard cannot be kept any longer. Their optimism is the vain attempt to keep head above water. Behind this front of cheerfulness, they constantly struggle with despair of themselves. Finally, they die of a kind of selfishness.

If we are saved we feel humiliated, and if we are helped we feel degraded.

We fight like madmen for private existences with individual destinies, since we are afraid of becoming part of that miserable lot of *schnorrers* whom we, many of us former philanthropists, remember only too well. Just as once we failed to understand that the so-called *schnorrer* was a symbol of Jewish destiny and not a schlemiel, so today we don't feel entitled to Jewish solidarity; we cannot realize that we by ourselves are not so much concerned as the whole Jewish people. Sometimes this lack of comprehension has been strongly supported by our protectors. Thus, I remember a director of a great charity concern in Paris who, whenever he received the card of a German-Jewish intellectual with the inevitable "Dr." on it, used to exclaim at the top of his voice, "Herr Doktor, Herr Doktor, Herr Schnorrer, Herr Schnorrer!"

The conclusion we drew from such unpleasant experiences was simple enough. To be a doctor of philosophy no longer satisfied us; and we learned that in order to build a new life, one has first to improve on the old one. A nice little fairy tale has been invented to describe our behavior; a forlorn émigré dachshund, in his grief, begins to speak: "Once, when I was a St. Bernard . . ."

Our new friends, rather overwhelmed by so many stars and famous men, hardly understand that at the basis of all our descriptions of past splendors lies one human truth: once we were somebodies about whom people cared, we were loved by friends, and even known by landlords as paying our rent regularly. Once we could buy our food and ride on the subway without being told we were undesirable. We have become a little hysterical since newspapermen started detecting us and telling us publicly to stop being disagreeable when shopping for milk and bread. We wonder how it can be done; we already are so damnably careful in every moment of our daily lives to avoid anybody guessing who we are, what kind of passport we have, where our birth certificates were filled out—and that Hitler didn't like us. We try the best we can to fit into a world where you have to be sort of politically minded when you buy your food.

Under such circumstances, the St. Bernard grows bigger and bigger. I never can forget that young man who, when expected to accept a certain kind of work, sighed out, "You don't know to whom you speak; I was Section-manager in Karstadt's [a great department store in Berlin]." But there is also the deep despair of that middle-aged man who, going through countless shifts of different committees in order to be saved, finally exclaimed, "And nobody here knows who I am!" Since nobody would treat him as a dignified human being, he began sending cables to great personalities and his big relations. He learned quickly that in this mad world it is much easier to be accepted as a "great man" than as a human being.

The less we are free to decide who we are or to live as we like, the more we try to put up a front, to hide the facts, and to play roles. We were expelled from Germany because we were Jews. But having hardly crossed the French borderline, we were changed into *boches*. We were even told that we had to accept this designation if we really were against Hitler's racial theories. During seven years we played the ridiculous role of trying to be Frenchmen—at least, prospective citizens; but at the beginning of the war we were interned as *boches* all the same. In the meantime, however, most of us had indeed become such loyal Frenchmen that we could not even criticize a French governmental order; thus we declared it was all right to be interned. We were the first *prisonniers volontaires* history has ever seen. After the Germans invaded the country, the French government had only to change the name of the firm; having been jailed because we were Germans, we were not freed because we were Jews.

It is the same story all over the world, repeated again and again. In Europe the Nazis confiscated our property; but in Brazil we have to pay 30 percent of our wealth, like the most loyal member of the *Bund der Auslandsdeutschen*. In Paris we could not leave our homes after eight o'clock because we were Jews; but in Los Angeles we are restricted because we are "enemy aliens." Our identity is changed so frequently that nobody can find out who we actually are.

Unfortunately, things don't look any better when we meet with Jews. French Jewry was absolutely convinced that all Jews coming from beyond the Rhine were what they called *Polaks*—what German Jewry called *Ostjuden*. But those Jews who really came from Eastern Europe could not agree with their French brethren and called us *Jaeckes*. The sons of these *Jaecke*-haters—the second generation born in France and already duly assimilated—shared the opinion of the French Jewish upper classes. Thus, in the very same family, you could be called a *Jaecke* by the father and a *Polak* by the son.

Since the outbreak of the war and the catastrophe that has befallen European Jewry, the mere fact of being a refugee has prevented our mingling with native Jewish society, some exceptions only proving the rule. These unwritten social laws, though never publicly admitted, have the great force of public opinion. And such a silent opinion and practice is more important for our daily lives than all official proclamations of hospitality and goodwill.

Man is a social animal and life is not easy for him when social ties are cut off. Moral standards are much easier kept in the texture of a society. Very few individuals have the strength to conserve their own integrity if their social, political, and legal status is completely confused. Lacking the courage to fight for a change of our social and legal status, we have decided instead, so many of us, to try a change of identity. And this curious behavior makes matters much worse. The confusion in which we live is partly our own work.

Some day somebody will write the true story of this Jewish emigration from Germany; and he will have to start with a description of that Mr. Cohn from Berlin, who had always been a 150 percent German, a German superpatriot. In 1933 that Mr. Cohn found refuge in Prague and very quickly became a convinced Czech patriot—as true and as loyal a Czech patriot as he had been a German one. Time went on and about 1937 the Czech government, already under some Nazi pressure, began to expel its Jewish refugees, disregarding the fact that they felt so strongly as prospective Czech citizens. Our Mr. Cohn then went to Vienna; to adjust oneself there a definite Austrian patriotism was required. The German invasion forced Mr. Cohn out of that country. He arrived in Paris at a bad moment and he never did receive a regular residence permit. Having already acquired a great skill in wishful thinking, he refused to take mere administrative measures seriously, convinced that he would spend his future life in France. Therefore, he prepared his adjustment to the French nation by identifying himself with "our" ancestor Vercingétorix. I think I had better not dilate on the further adventures of Mr. Cohn. As long as Mr. Cohn can't make up his mind to be what he actually is, a Jew, nobody can foretell all the mad changes he will still have to go through.

A man who wants to lose his self discovers, indeed, the possibilities of human existence, which are infinite, as infinite as is creation. But the recovering of a new personality is as difficult—and as hopeless—as a new creation of the world. Whatever we do, whatever we pretend to be, we reveal nothing but our insane desire to be changed, not to be Jews. All our activities are directed to attain this aim: we don't want to be refugees, since we don't want to be Jews; we pretend to be English-speaking people, since German-speaking immigrants of recent years are marked as Jews; we don't call ourselves stateless, since the majority of stateless people in the world are Jews; we are willing to become loyal Hottentots, only to hide the fact that we are Jews. We don't succeed and we can't succeed; under the cover of our "optimism" you can easily detect the hopeless sadness of assimilationists.

With us from Germany the word "assimilation" received a "deep" philosophical meaning. You can hardly realize how serious we were about it. Assimilation did not mean the necessary adjustment to the country where we happened to be born and to the people whose language we happened to speak. We adjust in principle to everything and everybody. This attitude became quite clear to me once by the words of one of my compatriots who, apparently, knew how to express his feelings. Having just arrived in France, he founded one of these societies of adjustment in which German Jews asserted to each other that they were already Frenchmen. In his first speech he said: "We have been good Germans in Germany and therefore we shall be good Frenchmen in France." The public applauded enthusiastically and nobody laughed; we were happy to have learned how to prove our loyalty.

If patriotism were a matter of routine or practice, we should be the most patriotic people in the world. Let us go back to our Mr. Cohn; he certainly has beaten all records. He is that ideal immigrant who always, and in every country into which a terrible fate has driven him, promptly sees and loves the native mountains. But since patriotism is not yet believed to be a matter of practice, it is hard to convince people of the sincerity of our repeated transformations. This struggle makes our own society so intolerant; we demand full affirmation without our own group because we are not in the position to obtain it from the natives. The natives, confronted with such strange beings as we are, become suspicious; from their point of view, as a rule, only a loyalty to our old countries is understandable. That makes life very bitter for us. We might overcome this suspicion if we would explain that, being Jews, our patriotism in our original countries had rather a peculiar aspect. Though it was indeed sincere and deep-rooted. We wrote big volumes to prove it; paid an entire bureaucracy to explore its antiquity and to explain it statistically. We had scholars write philosophical dissertations on the predestined harmony between Jews and Frenchmen, Jews and Germans, Jews and Hungarians, Jews and . . . Our so frequently suspected loyalty of today has a long history. It is the history of 150 years of assimilated Jewry who performed an unprecedented feat: though proving all the time their non-Jewishness, they succeeded in remaining Jews all the same.

The desperate confusion of these Ulysses-wanderers who, unlike their great prototype, don't know who they are is easily explained by their perfect mania for refusing to keep their identity. This mania is much older than the last ten years, which revealed the profound absurdity of our existence. We are like people with a fixed idea who can't help trying continually to disguise an imaginary stigma. Thus we are enthusiastically fond of every new possibility which, being new, seems able to work miracles. We are fascinated by every new nationality in the same way as a woman of tidy size is delighted with every new dress which promises to give her the desired waistline. But she likes the new dress only as long as she believes in its miraculous qualities, and she will throw it away as soon as she discovers that it does not change her stature—or, for that matter, her status.

One may be surprised that the apparent uselessness of all our odd disguises has not yet been able to discourage us. If it is true that men seldom learn from history, it is also true that they may learn from personal experiences which, as in our case, are repeated time and again. But before you cast the first stone at us, remember that being a Jew does not give any legal status in this world. If we should start telling the truth that we are nothing but Jews, it would mean that we expose ourselves to the fate of human beings who, unprotected by any specific law or political convention, are nothing but human beings. I can hardly imagine an attitude more dangerous, since we actually live in a world in which human beings as such have ceased to exist for quite a while; since society has discovered discrimination as the great social weapon by which one may kill men without any bloodshed; since passports or birth certificates, and sometimes even income tax receipts, are no longer formal papers but matters of social distinction. It is true that most of us depend entirely upon social standards; we lose confidence in ourselves if society does not approve us; we are—and always were—ready to pay any price in order to be accepted by society. But it is equally true that the very few among us who have tried to get along without all these tricks and jokes of adjustment and assimilation have paid a much higher price than they could afford: they jeopardized the few chances even outlaws are given in a topsy-turvy world.

The attitude of these few whom, following Bernard Lazare, one may call "conscious pariahs," can as little be explained by recent events alone as the attitude of our Mr. Cohn who tried by every means to become an upstart. Both are sons of the nineteenth century which, not knowing legal or political outlaws, knew only too well social pariahs and their counterpart, social parvenus. Modern Jewish history, having started with court Jews and continuing with Jewish millionaires and philanthropists, is apt to forget about this other thread of Jewish tradition—the tradition of Heine, Rahel Varnhagen, Sholom Aleichem, of Bernard Lazare, Franz Kafka, or even Charlie Chaplin. It is the tradition of a minority of Jews who have not wanted to become upstarts, who preferred the status of "conscious pariah." All vaunted Jewish qualities—the "Jewish heart," humanity, humor, disinterested intelligence—are pariah qualities. All Jewish shortcomings—tactlessness, political stupidity, inferiority complexes, and money-grubbing—are characteristic of upstarts. There have always been Jews who did not think it worthwhile to change their humane attitude and their natural insight into reality for the narrowness of caste spirit or the essential unreality of financial transactions.

History has forced the status of outlaws upon both, upon pariahs and parvenus alike. The latter have not yet accepted the great wisdom of Balzac's "On ne parvient pas deux fois"; thus they don't understand the wild dreams of the former and feel humiliated in sharing their fate. Those few refugees who insist upon telling the truth, even to the point of "indecency," get in exchange for their unpopularity one priceless advantage: history is no longer a closed book to them and politics is no longer the privilege of gentiles. They know that the outlawing of the Jewish people in Europe has been followed closely by the outlawing of most European nations. Refugees driven from country to country represent the vanguard of their peoples—if they keep their identity. For the first time Jewish history is not separate but tied up with that of all other nations. The comity of European peoples went to pieces when, and because, it allowed its weakest member to be excluded and persecuted.

1943

THE JEW AS PARIAH:
A HIDDEN TRADITION

When it comes to claiming its own in the field of European arts and letters, the attitude of the Jewish people may best be described as one of reckless magnanimity. With a grand gesture and without a murmur of protest it has calmly allowed the credit for its great writers and artists to go to other peoples, itself receiving in return (in punctiliously regular payments) the doubtful privilege of being acclaimed father of every notorious swindler and mountebank. True enough, there has been a tendency in recent years to compile long lists of European worthies who might conceivably claim Jewish descent, but such lists are more in the nature of mass graves for the forgotten than of enduring monuments to the remembered and cherished. Useful as they may be for purposes of propaganda (offensive as well as defensive), they have not succeeded in reclaiming for the Jews any single writer of note unless he happened to have written specifically in Hebrew or Yiddish. Those who really did most for the spiritual dignity of their people, who were great enough to transcend the bounds of nationality and to weave the strands of their Jewish genius into the general texture of European life, have been given short shrift and perfunctory recognition. With the growing tendency to conceive of the Jewish people as a series of separate territorial units and to resolve its history into so many regional chronicles and parochial records, its great figures have been left perforce to the tender mercies of assimilationist propagandists—to be exploited only in order to bolster selfish interests or furnish alleged illustrations of dubious ideologies.

No one fares worse from this process than those bold spirits who tried to make of the emancipation of the Jews that which it really should have been—an admission of Jews *as Jews* to the ranks of humanity, rather than a permit to ape the gentiles or an opportunity to play the parvenu. Realizing only too well that they did not enjoy political freedom nor full admission to the life of nations, but that, instead, they had been separated from their own people and lost contact with the simple natural life of the common man, these men yet achieved liberty and popularity by the sheer force of imagination. As individuals they started an emancipation of their own, of their own hearts and brains. Such a conception was, of course, a gross misconstruction of what emancipation had been intended to be; but it was also a vision, and out of the impassioned intensity with which it was evinced and expressed it provided the fostering soil on which Jewish creative genius could grow and contribute its products to the general spiritual life of the Western world.

That the status of the Jews in Europe has been not only that of an oppressed people but also of what Max Weber has called a "pariah people" is a fact most clearly appreciated by those who have had practical experience of just how ambiguous is the freedom which emancipation has ensured, and how treacherous the promise of equality which assimilation has held out. In their own position as social outcasts such men reflect the political status of their entire people. It is therefore not surprising that out of their personal experience Jewish poets, writers, and artists should have been able to evolve the concept of the pariah as a human type—a concept of supreme importance for the evaluation of mankind in our day and one which has exerted upon the gentile world an influence in strange contrast to the spiritual and political ineffectiveness which has been the fate of these men among their own brethren. Indeed, the concept of the pariah has become traditional, even though the tradition be but tacit and latent, and its continuance automatic and unconscious. Nor need we wonder why: for over a hundred years the same basic conditions have obtained and evoked the same basic reaction.

However slender the basis out of which the concept was created and out of which it was progressively developed, it has nevertheless loomed larger in the thinking of assimilated Jews than might be inferred from standard Jewish histories. It has endured, in fact, from Salomon Maimon in the eighteenth century to Franz Kafka in the early twentieth. But out of the variety of forms which it has assumed we shall here select four, in each of which it expresses an alternative portrayal of the Jewish people. Our first type will be Heinrich Heine's schlemiel and "lord of dreams" (*Traumweltherrscher*); our second, Bernard Lazare's "conscious pariah"; our third, Charlie Chaplin's grotesque portrayal of the suspect;[1] and our fourth, Franz Kafka's poetic vision of the fate of the man of goodwill. Between these four types there is a significant connection—a link which in fact unites all genuine concepts and sound ideas when once they achieve historical actuality.

I. *Heinrich Heine: The Schlemiel and Lord of Dreams*

In his poem "Princess Sabbath," the first of his *Hebrew Melodies,* Heinrich Heine depicts for us the national background from which he sprang and which inspired his verses. He portrays his people as a fairy prince turned by witchcraft into a dog. A figure of ridicule throughout the week, every Friday night he suddenly regains his mortal shape, and freed from the preoccupations of his canine existence (*von huendischen Gedanken*), goes forth like a prince to welcome the sabbath bride and to greet her with the traditional hymeneal, "Lecha Dodi."[2]

This poem, we are informed by Heine, was especially composed for the purpose by the people's poet—the poet who, by a stroke of fortune, escapes the grueling weekly transformation of his people and who continually leads the sabbathlike existence which is to Heine the only positive mark of Jewish life.

Poets are characterized in greater detail in Part IV of the poem, where Heine speaks of Yehudah Halevi. They are said to be descended from "Herr Schlemihl ben Zurishaddai"—a name taken from Shelumiel ben Zurishaddai, mentioned in the biblical Book of Numbers as the leader of the tribe of Simeon. Heine relates his name to the word "schlemiel" by the humorous supposition that by standing too close to his brother chieftain Zimri, he got himself killed accidentally when Zimri was beheaded by the priest Phinehas for dallying with a Midianite woman (Numbers 25: 6–15). But if they may claim Shelumiel as their ancestor, they must also claim Phinehas—the ruthless Phinehas whose

> . . . spear is with us,
> And above our heads unpausing
> We can hear its fatal whizzing
> And the noblest hearts it pierces.
> [Trans. Leland]

History preserves to us no "deeds heroic" of those "noblest hearts." All we know is that—they were schlemiels.

Innocence is the hallmark of the schlemiel. But it is of such innocence that a people's poets—its "lords of dreams"—are born. No heroes they and no stalwarts, they are content to seek their protection in the special tutelage of an ancient Greek deity. For did not Apollo, that "inerrable godhead of delight," proclaim himself once and for all the lord of schlemiels on the day when—as the legend has it—he pursued the beauteous Daphne only to receive for his pains a crown of laurels? To be sure, times have changed since then, and the transformation of the ancient Olympian has been described by Heine himself in his poem "The God Apollo." This tells of a nun who falls in love with that great divinity and gives herself up to the search for him who can play the lyre so beautifully and charm hearts so wondrously. In the end, however, after wandering far and wide, she discovers that the Apollo of her dreams exists in the world of reality as Rabbi Faibusch (a Yiddish distortion of Phoebus), cantor in a synagogue at Amsterdam, holder of the humblest office among the humblest of peoples. Nor this alone; the father is a mohel (ritual circumciser), and the mother peddles sour pickles and assortments of odd trousers; while the son is a good-for-nothing who makes the rounds of the annual fairs playing the clown and singing the Psalms of David to the accompaniment of a bevy of "Muses" consisting of nine buxom wenches from the Amsterdam casino.

Heine's portrayal of the Jewish people and of himself as their poet-king is, of course, poles apart from the conception entertained by the privileged wealthy Jews of the upper classes. Instead, in its gay, insouciant impudence it is characteristic of the common people. For the pariah, excluded from formal society and with no desire to be embraced within it, turns naturally to that which entertains and delights the common people. Sharing their social ostracism, he also shares their joys and sorrows, their pleasures and their tribulations. He turns, in fact, from the world of men and the fashion thereof to the open and unrestricted bounty of the earth. And this is precisely what Heine did. Stupid and undiscerning critics have called it materialism or atheism, but the truth is that there is only so much of the heathen in it that it seems irreconcilable with certain interpretations of the Christian doctrine of original sin and its consequent sense of perpetual guilt. It is, indeed, no more than that simple *joie de vivre* which one finds everywhere in children and in the common people—that passion which makes them revel in tales and romances, which finds its supreme literary expression in the ballad and which gives to the short love song its essentially popular character. Stemming as it does from the basic affinity of the pariah to the people, it is something which neither literary criticism nor antisemitism could ever abolish. Though they dub its author "unknown," the Nazis cannot eliminate the "Lorelei" from the repertoire of German song.

It is but natural that the pariah, who receives so little from the world of men that even fame (which the world has been known to bestow on even the most abandoned of her children) is accounted to him a mere sign of schlemieldom, should look with an air of innocent amusement, and smile to himself at the spectacle of human beings trying to compete with the divine realities of nature. The bare fact that the sun shines on all alike affords him daily proof that all men are essentially equal. In the presence of such universal things as the sun, music, trees, and children—things which Rahel Varnhagen called "the true realities" just because they are cherished most by those who have no place in the political and social world—the petty dispensations of men which create and maintain inequality must necessarily appear ridiculous. Confronted with the natural order of things, in which all is equally good, the fabricated order of society, with its manifold classes and ranks, must appear a comic, hopeless attempt of creation to throw down the gauntlet to its creator. It is no longer the outcast pariah who appears the schlemiel, but those who live in the ordered ranks of society and who have exchanged the generous gifts of nature for the idols of social privilege and prejudice. Especially is this true of the parvenu, who was not even born to the system, but chose it of his own free will, and who is called upon to pay the cost meticulously and exactly, whereas others can take things in their stride. But no less are they schlemiels who enjoy power and high station. It needs but a poet to compare their vaunted grandeur with the real majesty of the sun, shining on king and beggarman alike, in order to demonstrate that all their pomp and circumstance is but sounding brass and a tinkling cymbal. All of these truths are old as the hills. We know them from the songs of oppressed and despised peoples who—so long as man does not aspire to halt the course of the sun—will always seek refuge in nature, hoping that beside nature all the devices of men will reveal themselves as ephemeral trifles.

It is from this shifting of the accent, from this vehement protest on the part of the pariah, from this attitude of denying the reality of the social order and of confronting it, instead, with a higher reality, that Heine's spirit of mockery really stems. It is this too which makes his scorn so pointed. Because he gauges things so consistently by the criterion of what is really and manifestly natural, he is able at once to detect the weak spot in his opponent's armor, the vulnerable point in any particular stupidity which he happens to be exposing. And it is this aloofness of the pariah from all the works of man that Heine regards as the essence of freedom. It is this aloofness that accounts for the divine laughter and the absence of bitterness in his verses. He was the first Jew to whom freedom meant more than mere "liberation from the house of bondage" and in whom it was combined, in equal measure, with the traditional Jewish passion for justice. To Heine, freedom had little to do with liberation from a just or unjust yoke. A man is born free, and he can lose his freedom only by selling himself into bondage. In line with this idea, both in his political poems and in his prose writings Heine vents his anger not only on tyrants but equally on those who put up with them.

The concept of *natural* freedom (conceived, be it noted, by an outcast able to live beyond the struggle between bondage and tyranny) turns both slaves and tyrants into equally unnatural and therefore ludicrous figures of fun. The poet's cheerful insouciance could hardly be expected from the more respectable citizen, caught as he was in the toils of practical affairs and himself partly responsible for the order of things. Even Heine, when confronted with the only social reality from which his pariah existence had not detached him—the rich Jews of his family—loses his serenity and becomes bitter and sarcastic.

To be sure, when measured by the standard of political realities, Heine's attitude of amused indifference seems remote and unreal. When one comes down to earth, one has to admit that laughter does not kill and that neither slaves nor tyrants are extinguished by mere amusement. From this standpoint, however, the pariah is always remote and unreal; whether as schlemiel or as "lord of dreams" he stands outside the real world and attacks it from without. Indeed, the Jewish tendency toward utopianism—a propensity most clearly in evidence in the very countries of emancipation—stems, in the last analysis, from just this lack of social roots. The only thing which saved Heine from succumbing to it, and which made him transform the political nonexistence and unreality of the pariah into the effective basis of a world of art, was his creativity. Because he sought nothing more than to hold up a mirror to the political world, he was able to avoid becoming a doctrinaire and to keep his passion for freedom unhampered by fetters of dogma. Similarly, because he viewed life through a long-range telescope, and not through the prism of an ideology, he was able to see further and clearer than others, and takes his place today among the shrewdest political observers of his time. The basic philosophy of this "prodigal son" who, after "herding the Hegelian swine for many years," at last became even bold enough to embrace a personal god, could always have been epitomized in his own lines:

> Beat on the drum and blow the fife
> And kiss the *vivandière*, my boy.
> Fear nothing—that's the whole of life,
> Its deepest truth, its soundest joy.
> Beat reveille, and with a blast
> Arouse all men to valiant strife.
> Waken the world; and then, at last
> March on. . . . That is the whole of life.
>   [Trans. Untermeyer]

By fearlessness and divine impudence Heine finally achieved that for which his coreligionists had vainly striven with fear and trembling, now furtively and now ostentatiously, now by preening and vaunting, and now by obsequious sycophancy. Heine is the only German Jew who could truthfully describe himself as both a German and a Jew. He is the only outstanding example of a really happy assimilation in the entire history of that process. By seeing Phoebus Apollo in Rabbi Faibusch, by boldly introducing Yiddish expressions in the German language, he in fact put into practice that true blending of cultures of which others merely talked. One has only to remember how zealously assimilated Jews avoid the mention of a Hebrew word before gentiles, how strenuously they pretend not to understand it if they hear one, to appreciate the full measure of Heine's accomplishment when he wrote, as pure German verse, lines like the following, praising a distinctively Jewish dish:

> Schalet, ray of light immortal
> Schalet, daughter of Elysium!

So had Schiller's song resounded,
Had he ever tasted Schalet.
[Trans. Leland]

In these words, Heine places the fare of Princess Sabbath on the table of the gods, beside nectar and ambrosia.

While the privileged wealthy Jews appealed to the sublimities of the Hebrew Prophets in order to prove that they were indeed the descendants of an especially exalted people, or else—like Disraeli—sought to validate their people by endowing it with some extraordinary, mystic power, Heine dispensed with all such rarefied devices and turned to the homespun Judaism of everyday life, to that which really lay in the heart and on the lips of the average Jew; and through the medium of the German language he gave it a place in general European culture. Indeed, it was the very introduction of these homely Jewish notes that helped to make Heine's works so essentially popular and human.

Heine is perhaps the first German prose writer really to embody the heritage of Lessing. In a manner least expected, he confirmed the queer notion so widely entertained by the early Prussian liberals that once the Jew was emancipated he would become more human, more free and less prejudiced than other men. That this notion involved a gross exaggeration is obvious. In its political implications, too, it was so lacking in elementary understanding as to appeal only to those Jews who imagined—as do so many today—that Jews could exist as "pure human beings" outside the range of peoples and nations. Heine was not deceived by this nonsense of "world citizenship." He knew that separate peoples are needed to focus the genius of poets and artists; and he had no time for academic pipe dreams. Just because he refused to give up his allegiance to a people of pariahs and schlemiels, just because he remained consistently attached to them, he takes his place among the most uncompromising of Europe's fighters for freedom—of which, alas, Germany has produced so few. Of all the poets of his time Heine was the one with the most character. And just because German bourgeois society had none of its own, and feared the explosive force of his, it concocted the slanderous legend of his characterlessness. Those who spread this legend, and who hoped thereby to dismiss Heine from serious consideration, included many Jewish journalists. They were averse to adopting the line he had suggested; they did not want to become Germans and Jews in one, because they feared that they would thereby lose their positions in the social order of German Jewry. For Heine's attitude, if only as a poet, was that by achieving emancipation the Jewish people had achieved a genuine freedom. He simply ignored the condition which had characterized emancipation everywhere in Europe—namely, that the Jew might only become a man when he ceased to be a Jew. Because he held this position he was able to do what so few of his contemporaries could—to speak the language of a free man and sing the songs of a natural one.

II. *Bernard Lazare: The Conscious Pariah*

If it was Heine's achievement to recognize in the figure of the schlemiel the essential kinship of the pariah to the poet—both alike excluded from society and never quite at home in this world—and to illustrate by this analogy the position of the Jew in the world of European culture, it was the merit of Bernard Lazare to translate the same basic fact into terms of political significance. Living in the France of the Dreyfus affair, Lazare could appreciate at first hand the pariah quality of Jewish existence. But he knew where the solution lay: in contrast to his unemancipated brethren who accept their pariah status automatically and unconsciously, the emancipated Jew must awake to an awareness of his position and, conscious of it, become a rebel against it— the champion of an oppressed people. His fight for freedom is part and parcel of that which all the downtrodden of Europe must wage to achieve national and social liberation.

In this heroic effort to bring the Jewish question openly into the arena of politics, Lazare was to discover certain specific, Jewish factors which Heine had overlooked and could afford to ignore. If Heine could content himself with the bare observation that "Israel is ill-served, with false friends guarding her doors from without and Folly and Dread keeping watch within," Lazare took pains to investigate the political implications of this connection between Jewish folly and gentile duplicity. As the root of the mischief he recognized that "spurious doctrine" (*doctrine bâtarde*) of assimilation, which would have the Jews "abandon all their characteristics, individual and moral alike, and give up distinguishing themselves only by an outward mark of the flesh which served but to expose them to the hatred of other faiths." He saw that what was necessary was to rouse the Jewish pariah to a fight against the Jewish parvenu. There was no other way to save him from the latter's own fate—inevitable destruction. Not only, he contended, has the pariah nothing but suffering to expect from the domination of the parvenu, but it is he who is destined sooner or later to pay the price of the whole wretched system. "I want no longer," he says in a telling passage, "to have against me not only the wealthy of my people, who exploit me and sell me, but also the rich and poor of other peoples who oppress and torture me in the name of my rich." And in these words he puts his finger squarely on that phenomenon of Jewish life which the historian Jost had so aptly characterized as "double slavery"—dependence, on the one hand, upon the hostile elements of his environment and, on the other, on his own "highly placed brethren" who are somehow in league with them. Lazare was the first Jew to perceive the connection between these two elements, both equally disastrous to the pariah. His experience of French politics had taught him that whenever the enemy seeks control, he makes a point of using some oppressed element of the population as his lackeys and henchmen, rewarding them with special privileges, as a kind of sop. It was thus that he construed the mechanism which made the rich Jews seek protection behind the notorious general Jewish poverty, to which they referred whenever their own position was jeopardized. This, he divined, was the real basis of their precarious relationship with their poorer brethren—on whom they would be able, at any time it suited them, to turn their backs.

As soon as the pariah enters the arena of politics and translates his status into political terms, he becomes perforce a rebel. Lazare's idea was, therefore, that the Jew should come out openly as the representative of the pariah, "since it is the duty of every human being to resist oppression." He demanded, that is, that the pariah relinquish once and for all the prerogative of the schlemiel, cut loose from the world of fancy and illusion, renounce the comfortable protection of nature, and come to grips with the world of men and women. In other words, he wanted him to feel that he was himself responsible for what society had done to him. He wanted him to stop seeking release in an attitude of superior indifference or in lofty and rarefied cogitation about the nature of man per se. However much the Jewish pariah might be, from the historical viewpoint, the product of an unjust dispensation ("look what you have made of the people, ye Christians and ye princes of the Jews"), politically speaking, every pariah who refused to be a rebel was partly responsible for his own position and therewith for the blot on mankind which it represented. From such shame there was no escape, either in art or in nature. For insofar as a man is more than a mere creature of nature, more than a mere product of divine creativity, insofar will he be called to account for the things which men do to men in the world which they themselves condition.

Superficially, it might appear as though Lazare failed because of the organized opposition of the rich, privileged Jews, the nabobs and philanthropists whose leadership he had ventured to challenge and whose lust for power he had dared to denounce. Were this the case, it would be but the beginning of a tradition which might have outlived his own premature death and determined, if not the fate, at least the effective volition of the Jewish people. But it was not the case; and Lazare himself knew—to his own sorrow—the real cause of his failure. The decisive factor was not the parvenu; neither was it the existence of a ruling caste which—whatever complexion it might choose to assume—was still very much the same as that of any other people. Immeasurably more serious and decisive was the fact that the pariah simply refused to become a rebel. True to type, he preferred to "play the revolutionary in the society of others, but not in his own," or else to assume the role of *schnorrer* feeding on the crumbs from the rich man's table, like an ancient Roman commoner ready to be fobbed off with the merest trifle that the patrician might toss at him. In either case, he mortgaged himself to the parvenu, protecting the latter's position in society and in turn protected by him.

However bitterly they may have attacked him, it was not the hostility of the Jewish nabobs that ruined Lazare. It was the fact that when he tried to stop the pariah from being a schlemiel, when he sought to give him a political significance, he encountered only the *schnorrer*. And once the pariah becomes a *schnorrer*, he is worth nothing, not because he is poor and begs, but because he begs from those whom he ought to fight, and because he appraises his poverty by the standards of those who have caused it. Once he adopts the role of *schnorrer*, the pariah becomes automatically one of the props which hold up a social order from which he is himself excluded. For just as *he* cannot live without his benefactors, so *they* cannot live without him. Indeed, it is just by this system of organized charity and almsgiving that the parvenus of the Jewish people have contrived to secure control over it, to determine its destinies and set its standards. The parvenu who fears lest he becomes a pariah, and the pariah who aspires to become a parvenu, are brothers under the skin and appropriately aware of their kinship. Small wonder, in face of this fact, that of all Lazare's efforts—unique as they were—to forge the peculiar situation of his people into a vital and significant political factor, nothing now remains. Even his memory has faded.

III. *Charlie Chaplin: The Suspect*

While lack of political sense and persistence in the obsolete system of making charity the basis of national unity have prevented the Jewish people from taking a positive part in the political life of our day, these very qualities, translated into dramatic forms, have inspired one of the most singular products of modern art—the films of Charlie Chaplin. In Chaplin the most unpopular people in the world inspired what was long the most popular of contemporary figures—not because he was a modern Merry Andrew, but because he represented the revival of a quality long thought to have been killed by a century of class conflict, namely, the entrancing charm of the little people.

In his very first film, Chaplin portrayed the chronic plight of the little man who is incessantly harried and hectored by the guardians of law and order— the representatives of society. To be sure, he too is a schlemiel, but not of the old visionary type, not a secret fairy prince, a protégé of Phoebus Apollo. Chaplin's world is of the earth, grotesquely caricatured if you will, but nevertheless hard and real. It is a world from which neither nature nor art can provide escape and against whose slings and arrows the only armor is one's own wits or the kindness and humanity of casual acquaintances.

In the eyes of society, the type which Chaplin portrays is always fundamentally suspect. He may be at odds with the world in a thousand and one ways, and his conflicts with it may assume a manifold variety of forms, but always and everywhere he is under suspicion, so that it is no good arguing rights or wrongs. Long before the refugee was to become, in the guise of the "stateless," the living symbol of the pariah, long before men and women were to be forced in their thousands to depend for their bare existence on their own wits or the chance kindnesses of others, Chaplin's own childhood had taught him two things. On the one hand, it had taught him the traditional Jewish fear of the "cop"—that seeming incarnation of a hostile world; but on the other, it had taught him the time-honored Jewish truth that, other things being equal, the human ingenuity of a David can sometimes outmatch the animal strength of a Goliath.

Standing outside the pale, suspected by all the world, the pariah—as Chaplin portrays him—could not fail to arouse the sympathy of the common people, who recognized in him the image of what society had done to them. Small wonder, then, that Chaplin became the idol of the masses. If they laughed at the way he was forever falling in love at first sight, they realized at the same time that the kind of love he evinced was their kind of love—however rare it may be.

Chaplin's suspect is linked to Heine's schlemiel by the common element of innocence. What might have appeared incredible and untenable if presented as a matter of casuistic discussion, as the theme of high-flown talk about the persecution of the guiltless, becomes, in Chaplin's treatment, both warm and convincing. Chaplin's heroes are not paragons of virtue, but little men with a thousand and one little failings, forever clashing with the law. The only point that is made is that the punishment does not always fit the crime, and that for the man who is in any case suspect there is no relation between the offense he commits and the price he pays. He is always being "nabbed" for things he never did, yet somehow he can always slip through the toils of the law, where other men would be caught in them. The innocence of the suspect whom Chaplin so consistently portrays in his films is, however, no more a mere trait of character, as in Heine's schlemiel; rather is it an expression of the dangerous incompatibility of general laws with individual misdeeds. Although in itself tragic, this incompatibility reveals its comic aspects in the case of the suspect, where it becomes patent. There is obviously no connection at all between what Chaplin does or does not do and the punishment which overtakes him. Because he is suspect, he is called upon to bear the brunt of much that he has not done. Yet at the same time, because he is beyond the pale, unhampered by the trammels of society, he is able to get away with a great deal. Out of this ambivalent situation springs an attitude both of fear and of impudence, fear of the law as if it were an inexorable natural force, and familiar, ironic impudence in the face of its minions. One can cheerfully cock a snook at them, because one has learned to duck them, as men duck a shower by creeping into holes or under a shelter. And the smaller one is the easier it becomes. Basically, the impudence of Chaplin's suspect is of the same kind as charms us so much in Heine's schlemiel; but no longer is it carefree and unperturbed, no longer the divine effrontery of the poet who consorts with heavenly things and can therefore afford to thumb noses at earthly society. On the contrary, it is a worried, careworn impudence—the kind so familiar to generations of Jews, the effrontery of the poor "little Yid" who does not recognize the class order of the world because he sees in it neither order nor justice for himself.

It was in this "little Yid," poor in worldly goods but rich in human experience, that the little man of all peoples most clearly discerned his own image. After all, had he not too to grapple with the problem of circumventing a law which, in its sublime indifference, forbade "rich and poor to sleep under bridges or steal bread?" For a long time he could laugh good-humoredly at himself in the role of a schlemiel—laugh at his misfortunes and his comic, sly methods of escape. But then came unemployment, and the thing was not funny anymore. He knew he had been caught by a fate which no amount of cunning and smartness could evade. Then came the change. Chaplin's popularity began rapidly to wane, not because of any mounting antisemitism, but because his underlying humanity had lost its meaning. Men had stopped seeking release in laughter; the little man had decided to be a big one.

Today it is not Chaplin, but Superman. When, in *The Great Dictator*, the comedian tried, by the ingenious device of doubling his role, to point up the contrast between the "little man" and the "big shot," and to show the almost brutal character of the Superman ideal, he was barely understood. And when, at the end of that film, he stepped out of character, and sought, in his own name, to reaffirm and vindicate the simple wisdom and philosophy of the "little man," his moving and impassioned plea fell, for the most part, upon unresponsive audiences. This was not the idol of the thirties.

IV. *Franz Kafka: The Man of Goodwill*

Both Heine's schlemiel and Lazare's "conscious pariah" were conceived essentially as Jews, while even Chaplin's suspect betrays what are clearly

Jewish traits. Quite different, however, is the case of the last and most recent typification of the pariah—that represented in the work of Franz Kafka. He appears on two occasions, once in the poet's earliest story, "Description of a Fight," and again in one of his latest novels, entitled *The Castle*.

"Description of a Fight" is concerned, in a general way, with the problem of social interrelations, and advances the thesis that within the confines of society the effects of genuine or even friendly relations are invariably adverse. Society, we are told, is composed of "nobodies"—"I did wrong to nobody, nobody did wrong to me; but nobody will help me, nothing but nobodies"—and has therefore no real existence. Nevertheless, even the pariah, who is excluded from it, cannot account himself lucky, since society keeps up the pretense that it is somebody and he nobody, that it is "real" and he "unreal."[3] His conflict with it has therefore nothing to do with the question whether society treats him properly or not; the point at issue is simply whether it or he has real existence. And the greatest injury which society can and does inflict on him is to make him doubt the reality and validity of his own existence, to reduce him in his own eyes to a status of nonentity.

The reality of his existence thus assailed, the pariah of the nineteenth century had found escape in two ways, but neither could any longer commend itself to Kafka. The first way led to a society of pariahs, of people in the same situation and—so far as their opposition to society was concerned—of the same outlook. But to take this way was to end in utter detachment from reality—in a bohemian divorce from the actual world. The second way, chosen by many of the better Jews whom society had ostracized, led to an overwhelming preoccupation with the world of beauty, be it the world of nature in which all men were equal beneath an eternal sun, or the realm of art where everyone was welcome who could appreciate eternal genius. Nature and art had, in fact, long been regarded as departments of life which were proof against social or political assault; and the pariah therefore retreated to them as to a world where he might dwell unmolested. Old cities, reared in beauty and hallowed by tradition, began to attract him with their imposing buildings and spacious plazas. Projected, as it were, from the past into the present, aloof from contemporary rages and passions, they seemed in their timelessness to extend a universal welcome. The gates of the old palaces, built by kings for their own courts, seemed now to be flung open to all, and even unbelievers might pace the great cathedrals of Christ. In such a setting the despised pariah Jew, dismissed by contemporary society as a nobody, could at least share in the glories of the past, for which he often showed a more appreciative eye than the esteemed and full-fledged members of society.

But it is just this method of escape, this retreat into nature and art against which Kafka directs his shafts in "Description of a Fight." To his twentieth-century sense of reality, nature had lost its invulnerable superiority over man since man would not "leave it in peace." He denied, too, the living actuality of monuments which were merely inherited from the dead and abandoned to everybody—that same everybody whom contemporary society would call a "nobody." In his view, the beauties of art and nature when used as an escape mechanism by those to whom its right had been refused were merely products of society. It does no good, he says, to keep thinking of them; in time they die and lose their strength. For Kafka only those things are real whose strength is not impaired but confirmed by thinking. Neither the freedom of the schlemiel and poet nor the innocence of the suspect nor the escape into nature and art, but thinking is the new weapon—the only one with which, in Kafka's opinion, the pariah is endowed at birth in his vital struggle against society.

It is, indeed, the use of this contemplative faculty as an instrument of self-preservation that characterizes Kafka's conception of the pariah. Kafka's heroes face society with an attitude of outspoken aggression, poles apart from the ironic condescension and superiority of Heine's "lord of dreams" or the innocent cunning of Chaplin's perpetually harassed little man. The traditional traits of the Jewish pariah, the touching innocence and the enlivening schlemieldom, have alike no place in the picture. *The Castle,* the one novel in which Kafka discusses the Jewish problem, is the only one in which the hero is plainly a Jew; yet even there what characterizes him as such is not any typically Jewish trait, but the fact that he is involved in situations and perplexities distinctive of Jewish life.

K. (as the hero is called) is a stranger who can never be brought into line because he belongs neither to the common people nor to its rulers. ("You are not of the Castle and you are not of the village, you are nothing at all.") To be sure, it has something to do with the rulers that he ever came to the village in the first place, but he has no legal title to remain there. In the eyes of the minor bureaucratic officials his very existence was due merely to a bureaucratic "error," while his status as a citizen was a paper one, buried "in piles of documents forever rising and crashing" around him. He is charged continually with being superfluous, "unwanted and in everyone's way," with having, as a stranger, to depend on other people's bounty and with being tolerated only by reason of a mysterious act of grace.

K. himself is of the opinion that everything depends on his becoming "indistinguishable," and "that as soon as possible." He admits that the rulers will assuredly obstruct the process. What he seeks, namely, complete assimilation, is something which they are not prepared to recognize—even as an aspiration. In a letter from the castle he is told distinctly that he will have to make up his mind "whether he prefers to become a village worker with a distinctive but merely apparent connection with the Castle or an ostensible village worker whose real occupation is determined through the medium of Barnabas (the court messenger)."

No better analogy could have been found to illustrate the entire dilemma of the modern would-be assimilationist Jew. He, too, is faced with the same alternative, whether to belong ostensibly to the people, but really to the rulers—as their creature and tool—or utterly and forever to renounce their protection and seek his fortune with the masses. "Official" Jewry has preferred always to cling to the rulers, and its representatives are always only "ostensible villagers." But it is with the other sort of Jew that Kafka is concerned and whose fate he portrays. This is the Jew who chooses the alternative way—the way of goodwill, who construes the conventional parlance of assimilation literally. What Kafka depicts is the real drama of assimilation, not its distorted counterpart. He speaks for the average small-time Jew who really wants no more than his rights as a human being: home, work, family, and citizenship. He is portrayed as if he were alone on earth, the only Jew in the whole wide world—completely, desolately alone. Here, too, Kafka paints a picture true to reality and to the basic human problem which assimilation involves, if taken seriously. For insofar as the Jew seeks to become "indistinguishable" from his gentile neighbors he has to behave as if he were indeed utterly alone; he has to part company, once and for all, with all who are like him. The hero of Kafka's novel does, in fact, what the whole world wants the Jew to do. His lonely isolation merely reflects the constantly reiterated opinion that if only there were nothing but individual Jews, if only the Jews would not persist in banding together, assimilation would become a fairly simple process. Kafka makes his hero follow this "ideal" course in order to show clearly how the experiment in fact works out. To make a thorough success of it, it is, of course, necessary also that a man should renounce all distinctive Jewish traits. In Kafka's treatment, however, this renunciation assumes a significance for the whole problem of mankind, and not merely for the Jewish question. K., in his effort to become "indistinguishable," is interested only in universals, in things which are common to all mankind. His desires are directed only toward those things to which all men have a natural right. He is, in a word, the typical man of goodwill. He demands no more than that which constitutes every man's right, and he will be satisfied with no less. His entire ambition is to have "a home, a position, real work to do," to marry and "to become a member of the community." Because, as a stranger, he is not permitted to enjoy these obvious prerequisites of human existence, he cannot afford to be ambitious. He alone, he thinks (at least at the beginning of the story), must fight for the minimum—for simple human rights, as if it were something which embraced the sum total of all possible demands. And just because he seeks nothing more than his minimum human rights, he cannot consent to obtain his demands—as might otherwise have been possible—in the form of "an act of favor from the Castle." He must perforce stand on his rights.

As soon as the villagers discover that the stranger who has chanced to come into their midst really enjoys the protection of the castle, their original mood of contemptuous indifference turns to one of respectful hostility. From then on their one desire is to cast him back upon the castle as soon as possible; they want no truck with the "upper crust." And when K. refuses, on the grounds that he wants to be free, when he explains that he would rather be a simple but genuine villager than an ostensible one really living under the protection of the castle, their attitude changes in turn to one of suspicion mingled with anxiety—an attitude which, for all his efforts, haunts him continually. The villagers feel uneasy not because he is a stranger, but because he refuses to accept favors. They try constantly to persuade him that his attitude is "dumb," that he lacks acquaintance with conditions as they are. They tell him all kinds of tales concerning the relations of the castle to the villagers, and seek thereby to impart to him something of that knowledge of the world which he so obviously lacks. But all they succeed in doing is to show him, to his increasing alarm, that such things as human instinct, human rights, and plain normal life—things which he himself has taken for granted as the indisputed property of all normal human beings—have as little existence for the villagers as for the stranger.

What K. experiences in his efforts to become indistinguishable from the villagers is told in a series of grim and ghastly tales, all of them redolent of human perversity and the slow attrition of human instincts. There is the tale of the innkeeper's wife, who had the "honor" as a girl to be the short-lived mistress of some underling at the castle, and who so far never forgets it as to turn her marriage into the merest sham. Then there is K.'s own young fiancée, who had the same experience but who, though she is able to forget it long enough to fall genuinely in love with him, still cannot endure indefinitely a simple life without "high connections" and who absconds in the end with the aid of the "assistants"—two minor officials of the castle. Last but not least, there is the weird, uncanny story of the Barnabases living under a curse, treated as lepers till they feel themselves such, merely because one of their pretty daughters once dared to reject the indecent advances of an important courtier. The plain villagers, controlled to the last detail by the ruling class, and slaves even in their thoughts to the whims of their all-powerful officials, have long since come to realize that to be in the right or to be in the wrong is for them a matter of pure "fate" which they cannot alter. It is not, as K. naïvely assumes, the sender of an obscene letter who is exposed, but the recipient who becomes branded and tainted. This is what the villagers mean when they speak of their "fate." In K.'s view, "it's unjust and monstrous"; but he is "the only one in the village of that opinion."

It is the story of the Barnabases that finally makes K. see conditions as they really are. At long last he comes to understand that the realization of his designs, the achievement of basic human rights—the right to work, the right to be useful, the right to found a home and become a member of society—are in no way dependent on complete assimilation to one's milieu, on being "indistinguishable." The normal existence which he desires has become something exceptional, no longer to be realized by simple, natural methods. Everything natural and normal in life has been wrested out of men's hands by the prevalent regime of the village, to become a present endowed from without—or, as Kafka puts it, from "above." Whether as fate, as blessing, or as curse, it is something dark and mysterious, something which a man receives but does not create, and which he can therefore observe but never fathom. Accordingly K.'s aspiration, far from being commonplace and obvious, is, in fact, exceptional and magnificent. So long as the village remains under the control of the castle, its inhabitants can be nothing but the passive victims of their respective "fates"; there is no place in it for any man of goodwill who wishes to determine his own existence. The simplest inquiry into right and wrong is regarded as a querulous disputation; the character of the regime, the power of the castle, are things which may not be questioned. So, when K., thoroughly indignant and outraged, bursts out with the words, "So that's what the officials are like," the whole village trembles as if some vital secret, if not indeed the whole pattern of its life, had been suddenly betrayed.

Even when he loses the innocence of the pariah, K. does not give up the fight. But unlike the hero of Kafka's last novel, *Amerika,* he does not start dreaming of a new world and he does not end in a great "Nature Theatre" where "everyone is welcome," where "there is a place for everyone" in accordance with his talents, his bent, and his will. On the contrary, K.'s idea seems to be that much could be accomplished, if only one simple man could succeed in living his own life like a normal human being. Accordingly, he remains in the village and tries, in spite of everything, to establish himself under existent conditions. Only for a single brief moment does the old Jewish ideal stir his heart, and he dreams of the lofty freedom of the pariah—the "lord of dreams." But "nothing more senseless," he observes, "nothing more hopeless than this freedom, this waiting, this inviolability." All these things have no purpose and take no account of men's desire to achieve something in the here below, if it be only the sensible direction of their lives. Hence, in the end, he reconciles himself readily to the "tyranny of the teacher," takes on "the wretched post" of a school janitor, and "does his utmost to get an interview with Klamm"—in a word, he takes his share in the misery and distress of the villagers.

On the face of it, all is fruitless, since K. can and will not divorce himself from the distinction between right and wrong and since he refuses to regard his normal human rights as privileges bestowed by the "powers that be." Because of this, the stories which he hears from the villagers fail to rouse in him that sense of haunting fear with which they take pains to invest them and which endows them with that strange poetic quality so common in the folk-tales of enslaved peoples. And since he cannot share this feeling he can never really be one of them. How baseless a feeling it is, how groundless the fear which seems by some magic to possess the entire village, is clear from the fact that nothing whatever materializes of all the dreadful fate which the villagers predict for K. himself. Nothing more serious happens to him, in fact, than that the authorities at the castle, using a thousand and one excuses, keep holding up his application for legal title of residence.

The whole struggle remains undecided, and K. dies a perfectly natural death; he gets exhausted. What he strove to achieve was beyond the strength of any one man. But though his purpose remained unaccomplished, his life was far from being a complete failure. The very fight he has put up to obtain the few basic things which society owes to men has opened the eyes of the villagers, or at least of some of them. His story, his behavior, has taught them both that human rights are worth fighting for and that the rule of the castle is not divine law and, consequently, can be attacked. He has made them see, as they put it, that "men who suffered our kind of experiences, who are beset by our kind of fear . . . who tremble at every knock at the door, cannot see things straight." And they add: "How lucky are we that you came to us!"

In an epilogue to the novel, Max Brod relates with what enthusiasm Kafka once repeated to him the story of how Flaubert, returning from a visit to a simple, happy family of many children, had exclaimed spontaneously: *ils sont dans le vrai* ("Those folk are right"). A true human life cannot be led by people who feel themselves detached from the basic and simple laws of humanity nor by those who elect to live in a vacuum, even if they be led to do so by persecution. Men's lives must be normal, not exceptional.

It was the perception of this truth that made Kafka a Zionist. In Zionism he saw a means of abolishing the "abnormal" position of the Jews, an instrument whereby they might become "a people like other peoples." Perhaps the last of Europe's great poets, he could scarcely have wished to become a nationalist. Indeed, his whole genius, his whole expression of the modern spirit, lay precisely in the fact that what he sought was to be a human being, a normal member of human society. It was not his fault that this society had ceased to be human, and that, trapped within its meshes, those of its members who were really men of goodwill were forced to function within it as something exceptional and abnormal—saints or madmen. If Western Jewry of the nineteenth century had taken assimilation seriously, had really tried to resolve the anomaly of the Jewish people and the problem of the Jewish individual by becoming "indistinguishable" from their neighbors, if they had made equality with others their ultimate objective, they would only have found in the end that they were faced with inequality and that society was slowly but surely disintegrating into a vast complex of inhuman crosscurrents. They would have found, in short, the same kind of situation as Kafka portrayed in dealing with the relations of the stranger to the established patterns of village life.

So long as the Jews of Western Europe were pariahs only in a social sense, they could find salvation, to a large extent, by becoming parvenus. Insecure as their position may have been, they could nevertheless achieve a modus vivendi by combining what Ahad Haam described as "inner slavery" with "outward freedom." Moreover, those who deemed the price too high could still remain mere pariahs, calmly enjoying the freedom and untouchability of outcasts. Excluded from the world of political realities, they could still retreat into their quiet corners there to preserve the illusion of liberty and unchallenged humanity. The life of the pariah, though shorn of political significance, was by no means senseless.

But today it is. Today the bottom has dropped out of the old ideology. The pariah Jew and the parvenu Jew are in the same boat, rowing desperately in the same angry sea. Both are branded with the same mark; both alike are outlaws. Today the truth has come home: there is no protection in heaven or earth against bare murder, and a man can be driven at any moment from the streets and broad places once open to all. At long last, it has become clear that the "senseless freedom" of the individual merely paves the way for the senseless suffering of his entire people.

Social isolation is no longer possible. You cannot stand aloof from society, whether as a schlemiel or as a lord of dreams. The old escape mechanisms have broken down, and a man can no longer come to terms with a world in which the Jew cannot be a human being either as a parvenu using his elbows or as a pariah voluntarily spurning its gifts. Both the realism of the one and the idealism of the other are today utopian.

There is, however, a third course—the one that Kafka suggests, in which a man may forgo all claims to individual freedom and inviolability and modestly content himself with trying to lead a simple, decent life. But—as Kafka himself points out—this is impossible within the framework of contemporary society. For while the individual might still be allowed to make a career, he is no longer strong enough to fulfill the basic demands of human life. The man of goodwill is driven today into isolation, like the Jew-stranger at the castle. He gets lost—or dies from exhaustion. For only within the framework of a people can a man live as a man among men, without exhausting himself. And only when a people lives and functions in consort with other peoples can it contribute to the establishment upon earth of a commonly conditioned and commonly controlled humanity.

1944

Notes

1. Chaplin has recently declared that he is of Irish and Gypsy descent, but he has been selected for discussion because, even if not himself a Jew, he has epitomized in an artistic form a character born of the Jewish pariah mentality.

2. "Lecha Dodi": "Come, my beloved, to meet the bride; Let us greet the sabbath-tide"—a Hebrew song chanted in the synagogue on Friday night.

3. Yet of all who have dealt with this agelong conflict Kafka is the first to have started from the basic truth that "society is a nobody in a dress-suit." In a certain sense, he was fortunate to have been born in an epoch when it was already patent and manifest that the wearer of the dress-suit was indeed a nobody. Fifteen years later, when Marcel Proust wanted to characterize French society, he was obliged to use a far grimmer metaphor. He depicted it as a masquerade with a death's-head grinning behind every mask.

CREATING A CULTURAL
ATMOSPHERE

Culture, as we understand it today, made its appearance rather recently and grew out of the secularization of religion and the dissolution of traditional values. When we talk about the Christian culture of the Middle Ages, we are using the term loosely and in a sense that would have been almost incomprehensible to medieval man. The process of secularization may or may not have undermined the foundations of religious faith—I am inclined to think that this undermining has been less decisive than we sometimes assume; in any event secularization transformed religious concepts and the results of religious speculation in such a way that they received new meaning and new relevance independent of faith. This transformation marked the beginning of culture as we know it—that is, from then on religion became an important part of culture, but it no longer dominated all spiritual achievements.

Even more important for the establishment of culture than the mere dissolution of traditional values was that great fear of oblivion which followed close upon the eighteenth century's Enlightenment and which pervaded the whole nineteenth century. The danger of losing historical continuity as such, along with the treasures of the past, was obvious; the fear of being robbed of the specifically human background of a past, of becoming an abstract ghost like the man without a shadow, was the driving power behind that new passion for impartiality and for the collecting of historical curiosities that gave birth to our present historical and philological sciences as well as to the nineteenth century's monstrosities of taste. Just because the old traditions were no longer alive, culture was stimulated into being, with all its good and all its ridiculous aspects. The stylelessness of the last century in architecture, its insane attempts to imitate all styles of the past, was only one aspect of what was really a new phenomenon called culture.

. . .

Culture is by definition secular. It requires a kind of broadmindedness of which no religion will ever be capable. It can be thoroughly perverted through ideologies and weltanschauungs which share, though on a lower and more vulgar level, religion's contempt for tolerance and claim to "possess" the truth. Although culture is "hospitable," we should not forget that neither religion nor ideologies will, nor ever can, resign themselves to being only parts of a whole. The historian, though hardly ever the theologian, knows that secularization is not the ending of religion.

It so happened that the Jewish people not only did not share in the slow process of secularization that started in Western Europe with the Renaissance, and out of which modern culture was born, but that the Jews, when confronted with and attracted by Enlightenment and culture, had just emerged from a period in which their own secular learning had sunk to an all-time low. The consequences of this lack of spiritual links between Jews and non-Jewish civilization were as natural as they were unfortunate: Jews who wanted "culture" left Judaism at once, and completely, even though most of them remained conscious of their Jewish origin. Secularization and even secular learning became identified exclusively with non-Jewish culture, so that it never occurred to these Jews that they could have started a process of secularization with regard to their own heritage. Their abandonment of Judaism resulted in a situation within Judaism in which the Jewish spiritual heritage became more than ever before the monopoly of rabbis. The German *Wissenschaft des Judentums*, though it was aware of the danger of a complete loss of all the past's spiritual achievements, took refuge from the real problem in a rather dry scholarship concerned only with preservation, the results of which were at best a collection of museum objects.

While this sudden and radical escape by Jewish intellectuals from everything Jewish prevented the growth of a cultural atmosphere in the Jewish community, it was very favorable for the development of individual creativity. What had been done by the members of other nations as part and parcel of a more collective effort and in the span of several generations was achieved by individual Jews within the narrow and concentrated framework of a single human lifetime and by the sheer force of personal imagination. It was as individuals, strictly, that the Jews started their emancipation from tradition.

It is true that a unique and impassioned intensity possessed only the few and was paid for by the fact that a particularly high percentage of Jews occupied themselves as pseudocultural busybodies and succumbed to mass culture and the mere love of fame. But it still brought forth a remarkably great number of authentic Jewish writers, artists, and thinkers who did not break under the extraordinary effort required of them, and whom this sudden empty freedom of spirit did not debase but on the contrary made creative.

Since, however, their individual achievements did not find reception by a prepared and cultured Jewish audience, they could not found a specifically Jewish tradition in secular writing and thinking—though these Jewish writers, thinkers, and artists had more than one trait in common. Whatever tradition the historian may be able to detect remained tacit and latent, its continuance automatic and unconscious, springing as it did from the basically identical conditions that each of these individuals had to confront all over again for himself, and master by himself without help from his predecessors.

There is no doubt that no blueprint and no program will ever make sense in cultural matters. If there is such a thing as a cultural policy it can aim only at the creation of a cultural atmosphere—that is, in Elliot Cohen's words, a "culture for Jews," but not a Jewish culture. The emergence of talent or genius is independent of such an atmosphere, but whether we shall continue to lose Jewish talent to others, or whether we will become able to keep it within our own community to the same extent that the others do, will be decided by the existence or nonexistence of this atmosphere. It is this that seems to me to be the problem. One may give a few suggestions on how to approach it.

There is first of all that great religious and metaphysical postbiblical tradition which we will have to win back from the theologians and scholars—to both of whom we owe, however, a large debt of gratitude for having preserved it at all. But we shall have to discover and deal with this tradition anew in our own terms, for the sake of people to whom it no longer constitutes a holy past or an untouchable heritage.

There is on the other hand the much smaller body of Jewish secular writings—dating from all periods, but particularly from the nineteenth century in Eastern Europe; this writing grew out of secular folk life, and only the absence of a cultural atmosphere has prevented a portion of it from assuming the status of great literature; instead it was condemned to the doubtful category of folklore. The cultural value of every author or artist really begins to make itself felt when he transcends the boundaries of his own nationality, when he no longer remains significant only to his fellow Jews, fellow Frenchmen, or fellow Englishmen. The lack of Jewish culture and the prevalence of folklore in secular Jewish life has denied this transcendence to Jewish talent that did not simply desert the Jewish community. The rescue of the Yiddish writers of Eastern Europe is of great importance; otherwise they will remain lost to culture generally.

Last but not least, we shall have to make room for all those who either came, and come, into conflict with Jewish Orthodoxy or turned their backs on Judaism for the reasons mentioned above. These figures will be of special significance for the whole endeavor; they may even become the supreme test of its success or failure. Not only because creative talent has been especially frequent among them in recent times, but also because they, in their individual efforts towards secularization, offer the first models for that new amalgamation of older traditions with new impulses and awareness without which a specifically Jewish cultural atmosphere is hardly conceivable. These talents do not need us; they achieve culture on their own responsibility. We, on the other hand, do need them since they form the only basis, however small, of culture that we have got—a basis we shall have to extend gradually in both directions: the secularization of religious tradition and rescue from folklore of the great artists (mostly Yiddish) of secular folk life.

Whether such a development will be realized, nobody can possibly foretell. *Commentary** looks to me like a good beginning and it certainly is a novum in Jewish cultural life. The reason for some optimism, however, is in the last analysis a political one.

The *yishuv* in Palestine is the first Jewish achievement brought about by an entirely secular movement. There is no doubt that whatever may happen to Hebrew literature in the future, Hebrew writers and artists will not need to confine themselves to either folk life or religion in order to remain Jews. They are the first Jews who as Jews are free to start from more than a precultural level.

---

*A journal emphasizing Jewish political and cultural affairs. Arendt published a number of articles in it, including this one, from 1945 to 1960.

The Jewish people of America, on the other hand, live a reasonably safe and reasonably free life that permits them to do, relatively, what they please. The central and strongest part of Diaspora Jewry no longer exists under the conditions of a nation-state but in a country that would annul its own constitution if ever it demanded homogeneity of population and an ethnic foundation for its state. In America one does not have to pretend that Judaism is nothing but a denomination and resort to all those desperate and crippling disguises that were common among the rich and educated Jews of Europe.

The development of a Jewish culture, in other words, or the lack of it, will from now on not depend upon circumstances beyond the control of the Jewish people, but upon their own will.

1947

JEWISH HISTORY, REVISED

Jewish historians of the last century, consciously or not, used to ignore all those trends of the Jewish past which did not point to their own major thesis of Diaspora history, according to which the Jewish people did not have a political history of their own but were invariably the innocent victims of a hostile and sometimes brutal environment. Once this environment changed, Jewish history logically would cease to be history at all, as the Jewish people would cease to exist as a people. In sharp contrast to all other nations, the Jews were not history makers but history sufferers, preserving a kind of eternal identity of goodness whose monotony was disturbed only by the equally monotonous chronicle of persecutions and pogroms. Within this framework of prejudice and persecution, the historian could still somehow manage to record the main developments of the history of ideas. But Jewish mystical thought, leading as it did to political action in the Sabbatian movement, was so serious an obstacle to this interpretation that it could be overcome only through rash disparagement or complete disregard.

Scholem's new presentation and appreciation of Jewish mysticism[1] not only fills a gap, but actually changes the whole picture of Jewish history. One of the most important changes is his entirely new interpretation of the Reform movement and other modern developments that broke away from Orthodoxy. These used to be viewed as the consequences of the emancipation granted to sections of the Jewish people and as the necessary reactions of a new adjustment to the requirements of the gentile world. But Scholem, in the last chapter of his book, conclusively proves that the Reform movement, with its curiously mixed tendencies toward liquidating Judaism and yet preserving it, was not a mechanical assimilation to the ideas and demands of a foreign environment but the outgrowth of the debacle of the last great Jewish political activity, the Sabbatian movement, of the loss of messianic hope, and of the despair about the ultimate destiny of the people.

A similar collapse of religious standards, followed by a similar despair, was among the outstanding experiences of Europe after the French Revolution. But whereas Romantic pessimism despaired of the political capacities of man as a lawmaker and became resigned to considering him as capable only of obeying laws, whose ultimate legitimation was no longer in God but in history and tradition, Jewish nihilism grew out of the despair of the ability of man ever to discover the hidden law of God and to act accordingly.

Scholem's book, clarifying for the first time the role played by the Jews in the formation of modern man, contributes a good deal to more general, typically modern phenomena whose historical origins were never quite understood. In this respect, his discoveries are more likely to reconcile Jewish history with the history of Europe than all apologetic attempts which try to prove the impossible, that is, the identity between Jews and other nations, or which attempt to demonstrate something essentially inhuman, namely the passivity and thus the irresponsibility of the Jewish people as a whole.

> In [the Kabbalists'] interpretation of the religious commandments, these are not represented as allegories of more or less profound ideas, or as pedagogical measures [as in the interpretation of the philosophers] but rather as the performance of a secret rite . . . this transformation of Halakhah into a sacrament . . . raised the Halakhah to a position of incomparable importance for the mystic, and strengthened its hold over the people. Every mitzvah became an event of cosmic importance. . . . The religious Jew became a protagonist in the drama of the World; he manipulated the strings behind the scenes.

Kabbalah is a name that covers a great variety of doctrines, from early Gnostic speculations through all kinds of magical practices up to the great and genuine philosophical speculations of the Book of Zohar. The name expresses the power and the final victory of Rabbinism, which combats all antagonistic and heterodox tendencies of Jewish thought by lumping them under the same name, rather than naming them specifically and in consonance with the actual content of these thoughts. But the transformation of Halakhah into magical rite with its inherent influence upon popular imagination, referred to in the above quotation, seems to form the essential basis for all kinds of Jewish mystical conceptions. The new interpretation of Law was based on the new doctrine of the "hidden God" who, in sharp opposition to the God of the revelation, is impersonal, *"that* which is infinite"* (12), a force instead of a person, revealing itself only to the "chosen few" but concealed rather than revealed in the revelation of the Bible. With this concept of God as an impersonal, divine power is connected that main heterodox doctrine against which Jewish as well as Christian orthodoxy have fought their most embittered battles, the doctrine of the *emanation* of the universe as opposed to the *creation* of man and the world. In all emanation theories, the primal man is supposed to be a hidden power; the clear distinction between God and man as between creator and creature disappears, and man, conceived as a material part of the divine, becomes endowed with a material-mystical power to retrace the "hidden path" of emanation that led him away from the divine, to return into the lap of the substance from which he emanated and which is expressed by various paraphrases such as the *"En-sof,"* the "indifferent unity," and, most characteristically, the *Nothing.* The transformation of Halakhah into a secret rite sprang, like all other magical practices, from these speculations which asserted that the search for the hidden power may lead to the discovery of secret means by which man can regain divine power, and transform himself into a part of God.

All such doctrines concerned with the "hidden" seem to have an inherent paradoxical effect. Their adherents always insisted upon strictest secrecy, exclusiveness, and the esoteric character of their speculations, which could be revealed only to the "chosen few." Yet in spite of all these assertions, mystical ideas did not appeal only to the few, but exercised, on the contrary, an enormous popular influence. Mystical ideas appealed to the masses much more than did the teachings of the learned rabbis and philosophers, who maintained that their interpretations could be understood by everybody. This is especially true of the mystical trends in Jewish history, which apparently dominated popular thought and answered the most urgent needs of the common people.

It would be a serious error to think of this paradox as a problem of the past alone, for this religious past actually survives today in all the superstitious beliefs in "secret societies," in the "hands working behind the scenes" of popular politics, and even in the ideologies that insist on the exclusive power of economic or historical "laws" which, too, work hidden from the eyes of ordinary men. The speculations by which Jewish and Christian mystics transformed the Jewish God of creation into a secret force were the first form of an essentially materialistic concept, and all modern doctrines asserting that man is but a part of matter, subject to physical laws and without freedom of action, confront us with the old originally Gnostic belief in emanation. Whether the substance of which man is held to be a part is material or "divine" has little importance. What matters is that man is no longer an independent entity, an end in himself.

Today, as in the past, these speculations appeal to all who are actually excluded from action, prevented from altering a fate that appears to them unbearable and, feeling themselves helpless victims of incomprehensible forces, are naturally inclined to find some secret means for gaining power for participating in the "drama of the World." Therefore the secrecy of these speculations has a somewhat artificial character: they are held secret, like the discovery of the philosopher's stone, which is supposed to transform all metals into pure gold, which is desired by everybody and, precisely for this reason, is hidden by those who pretend they have discovered it.

More important than this ambiguous esotericism was the mystic's justification of action, even if they offer only a substitute for it. In this connection, it does not greatly matter whether Kabbalists were ordinary magicians (usually they were not) or whether they practiced only what Abulafia has admitted and what Scholem calls a "magic of inwardness." In both cases the believers could participate in the power which rules the world.

> The Kabbalists . . . are no friends of mystical autobiography. . . . They glory in objective description and are deeply averse to letting their own personalities intrude into the picture. . . . I am inclined to believe that this dislike of a too personal indulgence in self-expression may have been caused by the fact, among others, that the Jews retained a particularly vivid sense of the incongruity of mystical experience with that idea of God which stressed the aspects of Creator, King and Lawgiver.

The denial of creation and the doctrine of emanation, with the consequent concept of human participation in the drama of the world, was the most striking common feature of Jewish and Gnostic mysticism. The lack of autobiography, the dislike of self-expression, is the most striking contrast of Jewish to Christian mysticism. This restraint is all the more surprising because invariably the main mystical organon of cognition is experience, and never reason, or faith in revelation. This experience comes very close to the modern notion of an experiment: it has to be tested several times before its truth is admitted. (Describing an overwhelming mystical experience as the result of combining the letters of the name of God, a mystical author says: "Once more I took up the Name to do with it as before and, behold, it had exactly the same effect on me. Nevertheless I did not believe until I had tried it four or five times.")

The experimental character of the mystical experience contributed largely to its popularity. It seemed for centuries the only path to the real world, discarded by Rabbinical Judaism. Reality as experienced by the mystics may sometimes appear strange to us; compared with the logistic and legal arguments of Orthodoxy, it was as real as real could be, because it was discovered and tested by way of experience, and not by way of interpretation and logic. This approach frequently took the form of interest in one's own soul, because psychological experiences could be repeated and tested indefinitely, the material of the experiments always being at hand, and their results therefore appeared to be the most reliable. Descartes's axiom *Cogito, ergo sum* still bears a trace of this tradition: the inner experience of thinking becomes proof of the reality of being. Just as the modern scientific and technical approach toward nature derives from alchemy, so the modern concept of reality as something that can be tested by experiment, and is therefore trusted as permanent, has one of its origins in mystical experience. Mysticism in contrast to orthodox Judaism or Christianity, and modern science in contrast to Jewish or Christian philosophy, trust neither revelation nor pure reasoning but only experience, because they are both concerned not with the problem of truth but with the discovery of a working knowledge of reality.

To the vital concern of Christian mysticism with the problem of reality must be added its equally vital though not specifically mystical concern with the redemption of man. The subject of Jewish mysticism, on the contrary, "is never man, be he even a saint" (78). Even when Jewish mysticism, in its later phases, leaves the pure sphere of research into reality (as represented by Merkabah Kabbalism) and becomes more concerned with practical life, it merely wants man to become part of the higher reality and to act accordingly. The eternal question of Christian philosophy, formulated by Augustine as "quaestio mihi factus sum," stimulated Christian mystics more than anything else, but never penetrated into Kabbalah. (And this seems to me one of the reasons for the curious fact that Meister Eckehart, a true disciple of Augustine, was more strongly influenced by the philosopher Maimonides than any Jewish mystic. In this one respect, Jewish philosophy was much closer to Christian mystical thought than was Jewish mysticism.)

The lack of autobiography in Jewish mysticism and the conscious omission of biographical data seem to mean more than "a particularly vivid sense of the incongruity of mystical experience with [the] idea of God." Autobiographical data are worth retelling only if they are felt to be unique, to possess some unique unrepeatable value. Mystical experiences, on the contrary, were felt to have value only if and insofar as they were repeated, only if they had experimental character. The fact that Christian mystics, in spite of this inherent character of mystical experiences, related them in autobiographies seems to me based not on their being mystics, but on their general philosophical concern with the nature of man. For Jewish mystics, man's own self was not subject to salvation and therefore became interesting only as an instrument for supreme action, believed to be a better instrument than the Law. Christian mystics, although they shared with the Jewish mystics in the search for reality, were not primarily interested in action as such, because according to their faith, the supreme event, the salvation of world and man, had already taken place. It appears as though the same experience was undergone, or rather the same experiments made, by Jewish and Christian mystics alike, by the Jews in order to develop instruments for active participation in the destiny of mankind, but by the Christians as ends to themselves. This might also partly explain the fact that Christian mysticism has always been a matter for individuals and has hardly any continuous tradition of its own, whereas one of the most significant features of Jewish mysticism was that it founded a genuine tradition running parallel to the official tradition of Orthodox Judaism. Biographical data, because they stressed individual and unique features, not only appeared irrelevant as to the mystical content but were a real danger to this tradition, which taught man repeatable experiments and the handling of the supreme instrument that he himself is.

The doctrine of Tikkun (Lurianic Kabbalah) raised every Jew to the rank of a protagonist in the great process of restitution in a manner never heard of before.

Sabbatianism represents the first serious revolt in Judaism since the Middle Ages; it was the case of mystical ideas leading directly to the disintegration of the orthodox Judaism of the "believers."

It was the influence of these elements which had not openly cut themselves off from Rabbinical Judaism which, after the French Revolution, became important in fostering the movement towards reform liberalism and "enlightenment" in many Jewish circles.

Until the outbreak of the Sabbatian movement, Jewish mysticism had refrained from attacks on Orthodoxy and kept itself within the Law. Only after many centuries of rich development did strong antinomian tendencies come out into the open. This might be explained by the political function of the Law in the Diaspora as the only tie for the people. But in spite of cautious restraint and careful avoidance of all conflicts, mystical thought had always prepared its followers for action, thereby breaking with the mere interpretation of the Law and with the mere hope for the coming of the Messiah. In this direction, however, the school of Isaac Luria was bolder than all predecessors when it dared to give a new interpretation of the exile existence of the people: "Formerly [the Diaspora] had been regarded either as a punishment for Israel's sins or as a test of Israel's faith. Now it still is all this, but intrinsically it is a mission: its purpose is to uplift the fallen sparks from all their various locations." For the first time, the role of the "protagonist in the drama of the world" was defined in terms which applied to every Jew.

One remarkable aspect of this "Myth of Exile" is that it served two conflicting purposes: through its mystical interpretation of exile as action instead of suffering, it could rouse the people to hasten the coming of the Messiah and lead to "an explosive manifestation of all those forces to which it owed its rise and its success" in the Sabbatian movement. But after the decline of this movement, it served equally well the needs of the disillusioned people who, having lost the messianic hope, wanted a new, more general justification of exile, of their inactive existence and mere survival. In the latter form, Isaac Luria's theory has been adopted by assimilated Jewry—though its representatives would not have enjoyed Scholem's discovery that they are the heirs of Kabbalism. This survival of mystical thought in the self-interpretation of assimilated and even de-Judaized Jewry was no mere accident, as can be seen from the amazing influence of Hasidism, the other heir of Kabbalism, upon the same "de-Judaized" Jewry when they were initiated into Hasidism at the beginning of our century. A genuine enthusiasm for this last phase of Jewish mysticism spread through the younger generation, who generally were quite unconcerned with the intellectual life of their Eastern brethren, but felt themselves surprisingly close to this spiritual world and mentality. The "neutralization of the Messianic element" (that is, the neutralization of political attitudes), the outspoken antinomian tendencies, and the conservation of the Myth of Exile, these three main elements of Hasidism corresponded almost uncannily to the needs of assimilated Jewry. Both Reform Judaism and Hasidism had been concerned solely with Jewish survival, renounced all hope of the restoration of Zion, and accepted the Exile as the ultimate and unchangeable fate of the people. It seems as though the mere loss of messianic hope, followed by the decline of Rabbinical authority, had essentially identical consequences on the self-interpretation of all sections of the people, widely separated though they were by different social and political conditions. In the long struggle between Jewish orthodoxy and Jewish mysticism, the latter seems to have won the last battle. This victory is all the more surprising, because it was won through defeat.

From its very beginnings, Jewish mysticism had tended toward action and realization; but before ending in utter resignation it attained maximum development in the Sabbatian movement, which, in the new picture given by Scholem, appears as the turning point in Jewish history. It is true that the working power of mystical thought had proved its existence more than once during the Middle Ages in outbreaks of sectarian fanaticism; but never before had a huge popular movement and immediate political action been inspired, prepared, and directed by nothing more than the mobilization of mystical speculations. The hidden experiments of Jewish mystics through the centuries, their efforts to attain a higher reality which, in their opinions, was hidden rather than revealed in the tangible world of everyday life or in the traditional revelation of Mount Sinai, were repeated on a tremendous and absolutely unique scale, by and through the whole Jewish people. For the first time, mysticism showed not only its deep-seated hold on the soul of Man, but its enormous force of action through him. The search for a working knowledge of reality had resulted in a working psychology of the masses, and the powerful will for "realization at any price" had to pay, finally, the price of every tradition, of every established authority and even the price of human standards for truth, as shown by the early acceptance of an apostate Messiah.

Of all mystical trends of the past, Jewish mysticism seems unique in its exclusive concern with reality and action; hence, Jewish mysticism alone was able to bring about a great political movement and to translate itself directly into real popular action. The catastrophe of this victory of mystical thought was greater for the Jewish people than all other persecutions had been, if we are to measure it by the only available yardstick, its far-reaching influence upon the future of the people. From now on, the Jewish body politic was dead and the people retired from the public scene of history.

Perhaps one of the most exciting aspects of the story is the fact that mysticism could survive its own defeat, that its theory as represented in the Myth of Exile fitted equally well the needs of popular action and the needs of popular resignation. What survived was the old mystical conception of the actor behind the scenes—one of the favorite ideas of Benjamin Disraeli, for instance—and a general yearning for world redemption as apart from the definite hope of return to Zion, represented by the many "apostles of an unbound political apocalypse" after the outbreak of the French Revolution. With this last allusion, the three spiritual trends in modern Jewish history—Hasidism, the Reform movement, and "political apocalypse," that is, revolutionary utopianism—which one used to regard as independent if not contradictory tendencies, are found to stem from the same mighty source, from mysticism. The catastrophe of Shabbetai Tzevi, after closing one book of Jewish history, becomes the cradle of a new era.

1948

Notes

1. Gershom G. Scholem, *Major Trends in Jewish Mysticism*, rev. ed. (New York: Schocken Books, 1946).

THE MORAL OF HISTORY

Die naemlich, welche zu gleicher
Zeit Juden sein und Juden
nicht sein wollen . . .
                    —*H.E.G. Paulus* (1831)

Wilhelm von Humboldt, one of the rare genuine German democrats, who played a big part in the emancipation of Prussian Jewry in 1812 and a still bigger part in the intervention in behalf of the Jews at the Congress of Vienna, looked back in 1816 to the days of his public battle for Jewish rights and his many years of personal intercourse with Jews and said: "I love the Jew really only *en masse; en détail* I strictly avoid him."[1] This amazing and paradoxical utterance, standing as it does in extreme contrast to the personal history of Humboldt—he had many personal friends among Jews—is unique in the history of the arguments presented for Jewish emancipation. Since Lessing and Dohm in Prussia, since Mirabeau and the Abbé Grégoire in France, the advocates of the Jews always based their arguments on the "Jews *en détail*," on the notable exceptions among the Jewish people. Humboldt's humanism, in the best traditions of Jewish emancipation in France, aimed to liberate the people as a whole, without bestowing special privileges upon individuals. As such his viewpoint was appreciated very little by his contemporaries, and it had still less influence on the later history of emancipated Jewry.

More in keeping with the sentiments of the time were the views of H.E.G. Paulus, a liberal Protestant theologian and contemporary of Humboldt. Paulus protested against the idea of emancipating the Jews as a group. Instead he urged that individuals be granted the rights of man according to their personal merits.[2] A few decades later, Gabriel Riesser, the Jewish publicist, vented his irony upon the sort of official Jewish propaganda which based its appeal upon stories of "virtuous Jews" who saved Christians from drowning.³ The basic principle of granting special privileges to individuals and refusing civic rights to the Jewish people as a group had successfully asserted itself.

In the minds of the privileged Jews such measures taken by the state appeared to be the workings of a sort of heavenly tribunal, by whom the virtuous—who had more than a certain income—were rewarded with human rights, and the unworthy—living in mass concentration in the eastern provinces—were punished as pariahs. Since that time it has become a mark of assimilated Jews to be unable to distinguish between friend and enemy, between compliment and insult, and to feel flattered when an antisemite assures them that he does not mean them, that they are exceptions—exceptional Jews.

The events of recent years have proved that the "excepted Jew" is more the Jew than the exception; no Jew feels quite happy anymore about being assured that he is an exception. The extraordinary catastrophe has converted once again all those who fancied themselves extraordinarily favored beings into quite ordinary mortals. Were history a closed book, sealed after each epoch, we would not be much interested in the story of the privileged Jews. The vitality of a nation, however, is measured in terms of the living remembrance of its history. We Jews are inclined to have an inverted historical perspective; the more distantly removed events are from the present, the more sharply, clearly, and accurately they appear. Such an inversion of historical perspective means that in our political conscience we do not want to take the responsibility for the immediate past and that we, together with our historians, want to take refuge in periods of the past, which leave us secure in terms of political consequences.

Behind us lies a century of opportunist politics, a century in which an unusual concurrence of circumstances allowed our people to live from day to day. During the same period scholars and philologists have succeeded in estranging history from the people in the same manner as opportunist statesmen alienated them from politics. The sublime concept of human progress was robbed of its historic sense and perverted into a simple natural fact, according to which the son is always presented as better and wiser than his father, the grandson as more enlightened than his grandfather. Or it was degraded to an economic law, according to which the accumulated wealth of the forebears determines the well-being of the sons and grandsons, making each of them advance further in the unending career of the family. In the light of such developments, to forget has become a holy duty, inexperience a privilege, and ignorance a guarantee of success.

Since the circumstances under which we live are created by man, the deceased force themselves upon us and upon the institutions that govern us and refuse to disappear into the darkness into which we try to plunge them. The more we try to forget the more their influence dominates us. The succession of generations may be a natural guarantee for the continuity of history but it is certainly not a guarantee of progress. Because we are the sons of our fathers and the grandsons of our grandfathers their misdeeds may persecute us into the third and fourth generations. Inactive ourselves, we cannot even enjoy their deeds, for, like all human works, they have the fatal tendency to turn into dross, just as a room painted white always turns black if not repainted frequently.

History, in this sense, has its moral, and if our scholars, with their impartial objectivity, are unable to discover this moral in history, it means only that they are incapable of understanding the world we have created; just like the people who are unable to make use of the very institutions they have produced. History, unfortunately, does not know Hegel's *"List der Vernunft"*; rather does unreason begin to function automatically when reason has abdicated to it.

The automatism of events, reigning since the beginning of the nineteenth century in place of human reason, prepared with incomparable precision for the spiritual collapse of Europe before the bloody idol of race. It is no mere accident that the catastrophic defeats of the peoples of Europe began with the catastrophe of the Jewish people, a people in whose destiny all others thought they could remain uninterested because of the tenet that Jewish history obeys *"exceptional laws."* The defeat of the Jewish people started with the catastrophe of the German Jews, in whom European Jews were not interested because they suddenly discovered that German Jews constituted an exception. The collapse of German Jewry began with its splitting up into innumerable factions, each of which believed that special privileges could protect human rights—for example, the privilege of having been a veteran of the First World War, the child of a war veteran, or if such privileges were not recognized anymore, a crippled war veteran or the son of a father killed at the front. Jews *"en masse"* seemed to have disappeared from the earth; it was easy to dispose of Jews *"en détail."* The terrible and bloody annihilation of individual Jews was preceded by the bloodless destruction of the Jewish people.

The European background against which Jewish history appears is complicated and involved. Sometimes the Jewish thread is lost in the maze but most of the time it is easily recognizable. The general history of Europe, from the French Revolution to the beginning of the First World War, may be described in its most tragic aspect as the slow but steady transformation of the *citoyen* of the French Revolution into the *bourgeois* of the prewar period. The stages of the history of this period of nearly 150 years are manifold, and often present magnificent and very human aspects. The period of *enrichissez-vous* (get rich quick) was also that of the flowering of French painting; the period of German misery was also that of the great age of classic literature; and we cannot imagine the Victorian age without Dickens. At the end of the era, however, we are confronted by a strange dehumanized kind of humanity. The moral of the history of the nineteenth century is the fact that men who were not ready to assume a responsible role in public affairs in the end were turned into mere beasts who could be used for anything before being led to slaughter. Institutions, moreover, left to themselves without control and guidance by men, turned into monsters devouring nations and countries.

The Jewish phase of nineteenth-century history reveals similar manifestations. While reading Heine and Börne, who just because as Jews they insisted on being considered men and thus were incorporated into the universal history of mankind, we forgot all about the tedious speeches of the representatives of the special group of privileged Jews in Prussia at the same time. In the country which made Disraeli its prime minister, the Jew Karl Marx wrote *Das Kapital,* a book which in its fanatical zeal for justice, carried on the Jewish tradition much more efficaciously than all the success of the "chosen man of the chosen race."[4] Finally, who does not, in thinking of the great literary work of Marcel Proust and the powerful bill of indictment by Bernard Lazare, forget those French Jews who filled the aristocratic salons of the Faubourg St. Germain and who, unconsciously following the unseemly example of their Prussian predecessors of the beginning of the nineteenth century, endeavored to be "Jews yet at the same time not Jews"?[5]

This ambiguity became decisive for the social behavior of the assimilated and emancipated Jewry in Western Europe. They did not want to and could not belong to the Jewish people anymore, but they wanted to and had to remain Jews—exceptions among the Jewish people. They wanted to and could play their part in non-Jewish society, but they did not desire to and could not disappear among the non-Jewish peoples. Thus they became exceptions in the non-Jewish world. They maintained they were able to be "men like others on the street but Jews at home."[6] But they felt they were different from other men on the street as Jews, and different from other Jews at home in that they were superior to the masses of the Jewish people.

1946

Notes

1. *Wilhelm von Humboldt und Karoline von Humboldt in ihren Briefen* (Berlin, 1900), vol. 5, p. 236.

2. H.E.G. Paulus, *Beitraege von jüdischen und christlichen Gelehrten zur Verbesserung der Bekenner jüdischen Glaubens* (Frankfurt, 1817). "The separation of the Jews will only be encouraged if the governments continue to treat them as a whole, in a bad or good sense. If however every one of them is given individual treatment, with justice for every one, according to his behavior, this separation will be dissolved through action." The attack is directed particularly against Humboldt, who defended the cause of the Jews at the Congress of Vienna. Humboldt's argument for the liberation of the Jews *"en masse"* and against a slow method of amelioration, is clearly outlined in his "Expert Opinion" of 1809: "A gradual abolition confirms the separation which it intends to destroy. In all points which are not abolished, it draws attention—by the very fact of the new liberty—to all still existing restrictions and thereby acts against itself." Cited in Ismar Freund, *Die Emanzipation der Juden in Preussen* (Berlin, 1912), vol. 2, p. 270.

3. Gabriel Riesser, *Gesammelte Schriften* (Leipzig, 1867), vol. 4, p. 290.

4. Cf. Horace B. Samuel, *Modernities* (London, 1914), p. 50 ff.

5. H.E.G. Paulus, *Die jüdische Nationalabsonderung nach Ursprung, Folgen und Besserungsmitteln* (1831), pp. 6–7.

6. It is not without its irony that this excellent formula, which may serve as a motto for Western European assimilation as a whole, was propounded by a Russian Jew and first published in Hebrew. It comes from Judah Leib Gordon's Hebrew poem, *Hakitzah ammi* (1863).

STEFAN ZWEIG: JEWS IN
THE WORLD OF YESTERDAY

A hundred and thirty-five years ago Rahel Varnhagen jotted down the following dream: She had died and gone to heaven, together with her friends Bettina von Arnim and Caroline von Humboldt. To relieve themselves of the burdens they had acquired in their lives, the three friends assigned themselves the task of inquiring into the worst things they had experienced. Rahel thus asked: Did you know disappointed love? The other two women broke into tears, and all three thus relieved this burden from their hearts. Rahel asked further: Did you know disloyalty? Sickness? Worry? Anxiousness? Each time the women said yes, as they cried, and again all three were relieved of their burdens. Finally Rahel asked: Did you know disgrace? As soon as this word had been spoken, there was a hushed silence, and the two friends took their distance from Rahel and looked at her in a disturbed and strange manner. Then did Rahel know that she was entirely alone and that this burden could not be taken away from her heart. And then she awoke.

Disgrace and honor are political concepts, categories of public life. In the world of culture, cultural goings-on, and purely private existence, it is just as impossible to get a handle on these categories as in the life of business. Businessmen know only success or failure, and their disgrace is poverty. The literati know only fame or obscurity, and their disgrace is anonymity. Stefan Zweig was a man of letters, and in his last book* he describes the world of the literati—a world in which he had once acquired *Bildung* and fame. A friendly fate protected him from poverty, a favorable star from anonymity. Concerned only with his personal dignity, he had kept himself so completely aloof from politics that, in retrospect, the catastrophe of the last ten years seemed to him like a lightning bolt from the sky, as if it were a monstrous,

*The World of Yesterday: An Autobiography (New York: Viking Press, 1943).

inconceivable natural disaster. In the midst of this disaster, he tried to safe-guard his dignity and bearing as well and as long as he could. He considered it unbearably humiliating when the hitherto wealthy and respected citizens of Vienna had to go begging for visas to countries which only a few weeks before they would have been unable to find on a map. That he himself, only yesterday so famous and welcome a guest in foreign countries, should also belong to this miserable host of the homeless and suspect was simply hell on earth. But deeply as the events of 1933 had changed his personal existence, they had no effect on his basic attitude with respect to the world and to his own life. He continued to boast of his unpolitical point of view; it never occurred to him that, politically speaking, it might be an honor for him to stand outside the law when all men were no longer equal before it. What he sensed—and did not hide from himself—was that during the 1930s the better classes in Germany and elsewhere were steadily yielding to Nazi precepts and discriminating against those whom the Nazis proscribed and banned.

Not one of his reactions during all this period was the result of political convictions; they were all dictated by his hypersensitivity to social humilia-tion. Instead of hating the Nazis, he just wanted to annoy them. Instead of despising those of his coterie who had been *gleichgeschaltet*, he thanked Richard Strauss for continuing to accept his libretti.* Instead of fighting, he kept silent, happy that his books had not been immediately banned. And later, though comforted by the thought that his works were removed from German bookstores together with those of equally famous authors, this could not reconcile him to the fact that his name had been pilloried by the Nazis like that of a "criminal," and that the famous Stefan Zweig had become the Jew Zweig. Like so many of his less sensible, less talented, and less endangered colleagues, he failed to perceive that the dignified restraint which society had so long considered a criterion of true *Bildung* was under such circumstances tantamount to plain cowardice in public life. And he like-wise failed to perceive that the distinction that had so effectively and for so long protected him from all kinds of unpleasant and embarrassing events

---

*Arendt uses *gleichgeschaltet* in the English version of the essay. It refers to the Nazi policy of *Gleich-schaltung*, or "coordination," in which every aspect of life was to accord with the dictates and direction of the Nazi "movement." Richard Strauss (1864–1949), the German composer and conductor, was appointed by Goebbels to the presidency of the State Music Board, from which he was forced to resign in 1935 because he included Zweig's name on the playbill for an opera (as its librettist).

would suddenly give rise to an endless series of humiliations that really did turn his life into a hell.

Before Stefan Zweig took his own life, he recorded—with the pitiless accuracy that springs from the coldness of genuine despair—what the world had given him and then done to him. He records the pleasure of fame and the curse of humiliation. He tells of the paradise from which he had been banished—the paradise of cultured [*gebildeten*] enjoyment, of meetings with like-minded and equally famous people, of infinite interest in the dead geniuses of humanity; penetrating into their private lives and gathering their personal relics was the most enjoyable pursuit of an inactive existence. And then he tells of how he suddenly found himself facing a reality in which there was nothing left to enjoy, in which those as famous as himself either avoided him or pitied him, and in which cultured [*gebildete*] curiosity about the past was continuously and unbearably disturbed by the tumult of the present, the murderous thunder of bombardment, the infinite humiliations at the hands of the authorities.

Gone, destroyed forever, was that other world in which, "frühgereift und zart und traurig" [early ripe and tender and mournful] (Hofmannsthal), one had established oneself so comfortably; razed was the park of the living and the dead, in which the chosen few—those with taste, that is—idolized art; broken were the trellises that kept out the *profanum vulgus* of the uncultured more effectively than a Chinese wall. With that world had passed also its counterpart, the society of famous young men, among whom, astonishingly enough, one hoped to discover "real life": the bohemians. For the young son of a bourgeois household, craving escape from parental protection, the bohemians—from whom he was completely separated by essential things (the bohemians, after all, only rarely combed their hair and when they did, they weren't happy about it, and anyway they could never pay for their coffee)—became identified with men experienced in the adversities of life. For the arriviste, those "unarrived," who only dreamed of large editions of their works, became the symbol of unrecognized genius and the example of the dreadful fate that "real life" could prepare for hopeful young men.

Naturally, the world that Zweig depicts was anything but *the* world of yesterday; naturally, the author of this book did not actually live in *the* world, only on its rim. The gilded trellises of this peculiar sanctuary were very thick, depriving the inmates of every view and every insight that could disturb their enjoyment. Not once does Zweig mention the most ominous manifestations of the years after the First World War, which struck his native Austria more violently than any other European country: unemployment. But the rare value of his document is not diminished in the least by the fact that, for us today, the trellises behind which these people spent their lives and to which they owed their extraordinary feeling of security seem little different from the walls of a prison or a ghetto. It is astounding, even spooky, that there were still people living among us whose ignorance was so great and whose conscience was so pure that they could continue to look on the prewar period with the eyes of the nineteenth century, and could regard the impotent pacifism of Geneva and the treacherous lull before the storm, between 1924 and 1933, as a return to normalcy. But it is admirable and gratifying that at least one of these men had the courage to record it all in detail, without hiding or prettifying anything. Zweig finally realized what fools they all had been, even if he never gained insight into the connection between their misfortune and their folly.

The same period that Zweig calls the Golden Age of Security was described by his contemporary Charles Péguy (shortly before he fell in the First World War) as the era in which political forms, presumably outmoded, lived on with inexplicable monotony:* in Russia, anachronistic despotism; in Austria, the corrupt bureaucracy of the Habsburgs; in Germany, the militarist and stupid regime of the Junkers, hated by the liberal middle class and the workers alike; in France, the Third Republic, which was granted twenty-odd years more despite its chronic crises. The solution to the puzzle lay in the fact that Europe was much too busy expanding its economic radius for any social stratum or nation to take political questions seriously. For fifty years— before the opposing economic interests burst into national conflicts, sucking the political systems of all Europe into their vortex—political representation had become a kind of theatrical performance, sometimes an operetta, of varying quality. Simultaneously, in Austria and Russia, the theater became the focus of national life for the upper ten thousand.

During the Golden Age of Security a peculiar dislocation of the balance of power occurred. The enormous development of all industrial and economic potential produced the steady weakening of purely political factors,

---

*Charles Péguy (1874–1914) was a French writer, poet, and committed Dreyfusard.

while at the same time economic forces became dominant in the international play of power. Power became synonymous with economic potential, which could bring a government to its knees. This was the real reason why governments played ever-narrowing and empty representative roles, which grew more and more obviously theatrical and operettalike. The Jewish bourgeoisie, in sharp contrast to its German and Austrian equivalents, was uninterested in positions of power, even of the economic kind. It was content with its accumulated wealth, happy in the security and peace that its wealth seemed to guarantee. An increasing number of sons from well-to-do homes deserted commercial life, since the empty accumulation of wealth was senseless. The consequence of this situation was that within a few decades both Germany and Austria saw a great number of their cultural enterprises, such as newspapers, publishing houses, and the theater, fall into Jewish hands.

Had the Jews of Western and Central European countries displayed even a modicum of concern for the political realities of their times, they would have had reason enough not to feel secure. For, in Germany, the first antisemitic parties arose during the 1880s; Treitschke made antisemitism "fit for the salon."* The turn of the century brought the Lueger-Schoenerer agitation in Austria, ending with the election of Lueger as mayor of Vienna. And in France the Dreyfus affair dominated both internal and foreign policies for years.† Even as late as 1940 Zweig could admire Lueger as an "able leader" and a kindly person whose "official antisemitism never stopped him from being helpful and friendly to his former Jewish friends." Among the Jews of Vienna no one took antisemitism, in the amiable Austrian version Lueger represented, seriously—with the exception of the "crazy" feuilleton editor of the *Neue Freie Presse*, Theodor Herzl.

At least, so it would appear at first glance. Closer examination changes the picture. After Treitschke had made antisemitism fit for the salon, conversion ceased to be a ticket of admission to non-Jewish circles in Germany and Austria. Just how antisemitic "better society" had become could not be easily

---

*Heinrich von Treitschke (1834–96), German historian, became one of the major exponents of Prussian conservatism in the latter half of the nineteenth century. His anti-British and especially antisemitic opinions were highly influential among the educated elite of Wilhelmine Germany.
†Karl Lueger (1844–1910), an Austrian politician, was a major exponent of antisemitism. He served as the mayor of Vienna from 1897 until his death. Georg von Schoenerer (1841–1921), another antisemitic Austrian politician, was intent on creating a racist foreign policy.

ascertained by the Jewish businessmen of Austria, for they pursued only commercial interests and cared nothing about invitations to non-Jewish groups. But their children discovered soon enough that in order for a Jew to be fully accepted into society, there was one and only one thing to do: become famous.

There is no better document of the Jewish situation in this period than the opening chapters of Zweig's book. They provide the most impressive evidence of how fame and the will to fame motivated the youth of his generation. Their ideal was the genius that seemed incarnate in Goethe. Every Jewish youth able to rhyme passably played the young Goethe, as everyone able to draw a line was a future Rembrandt, and every musical child was a demonic Beethoven. The more cultured the parental homes, the more coddled were these imitative *Wunderkinder*. Nor did this stop with poetry and art; it dominated every detail of personal life. They felt as sublime as Goethe, imitated his "Olympian" aloofness from politics; they collected rags and gewgaws that had once belonged to famous people of other periods; and they strove to come into direct touch with every living period of renown, as if a tiny reflection of fame would thus fall upon them—or as if one could prepare oneself for fame by attending a school of celebrity.

Of course, the idolatry of genius was not restricted to the Jews. It was a gentile, Gerhardt Hauptmann, who, as was well known, carried this idolatry as far as to make himself look, if not like Goethe, at least like one of the many cheap busts of the master.* And if the parallel enthusiasm that the German petite bourgeoisie showed for Napoleonic splendor did not actually produce Hitler, it contributed mightily to the hysterical raptures with which this "great man" was greeted by many German and Austrian intellectuals.

Although deification of the "great man," without much consideration for what he actually achieved, was a general disease of the era, it assumed a special form among the Jews and their particular passion for the great men of culture. In any case, the school of fame that the Jewish youth of Vienna attended was the theater; the image of fame that they held before them was that of the actor.

---

*Gerhardt Hauptmann (1862–1946), a German writer and dramatist, won the Nobel Prize in 1912 and stayed in Germany throughout his life. The Nazis allowed his plays to be staged as a demonstration that famous members of the German cultural elite preferred to remain in Germany.

Again a qualification is in order. In no other European city did the theater ever acquire the same significance that it had in Vienna during the period of political dissolution. Zweig recounts how the death of a famous court actress made his family cook, who had never heard or seen her, burst into tears. Simultaneously, as political activity began to resemble theater or operetta, the theater itself developed into a kind of national institution, the actor into a national hero. Since the world had undeniably acquired a theatrical air, the theater could appear as the world of reality. It is hard for us today to believe that even Hugo von Hofmannsthal fell under the spell of this theater hysteria and for many years believed that behind the Viennese absorption in the theater lay something of the Athenian public spirit. He overlooked the fact that Athenians attended the theater for the sake of the play, its mythological content, and the grandeur of its language, through which they hoped to become masters of their passions and molders of their national destiny. The Viennese went to the theater exclusively for the actors; playwrights wrote for this or that performer; critics discussed only the actor or his parts; directors accepted or rejected plays purely on the basis of effective roles for their matinee idols. The star system, as the cinema later perfected it, was completely forecast in Vienna. What was in the making there was not a classical renaissance but Hollywood.

Whereas political conditions made this inversion of being and appearance possible, Jews put it into motion, supplied the public demand, and spread its fame. And since the European world, not unjustifiably, considered Austrian backstage culture representative of the whole period, Zweig is not wrong when he proudly asserts that "nine-tenths of what the world celebrated as Viennese culture in the nineteenth century was promoted, nourished, or even created by Viennese Jewry."

A culture built around an actor or virtuoso established standards that were as novel as they were dubious. "Posterity weaves no wreaths for the mime," and so the mime requires an incredible amount of present fame and applause. His well-known vanity is, as it were, an occupational disease. To the degree that every artist dreams of leaving his mark on future generations, of transporting his period into another, the artistic impulses of virtuosi and actors are forever frustrated and require hysterical outlets. Since the actor must renounce immortality, his criterion of greatness depends altogether on contemporary success. Contemporary success was also the only criterion that remained for the "geniuses in general," who were detached from their achievements and considered only in the light of "greatness in itself." In the field of letters this took the form of biographies describing no more than the appearance, the emotions, and the demeanor of great men. This approach not only satisfied vulgar curiosity about the kind of secrets a man's valet would know; it was prompted by the belief that such idiotic abstraction would clarify the essence of greatness. In their respect for "greatness in itself," Jews and gentiles stood side by side. That was why Jewish organizations of most cultural enterprises, and particularly of the theatrical culture of Vienna, could go on without restraint, and even become in a sense the epitome of European culture.

Stefan Zweig's thorough knowledge of history preserved him from adopting this yardstick without any qualms. Yet, despite his "connoisseurship," this knowledge could not prevent him from simply ignoring the greatest poets of the postwar period, Franz Kafka and Bertolt Brecht, neither of whom were ever great successes. Nor could it prevent him from confusing the historical significance of writers with the size of their editions: "Hofmannsthal, Arthur Schnitzler, Beer-Hofmann, and Peter Altenberg gave Viennese literature European standing such as it had not possessed under Grillparzer and Stifter."*

Precisely because Zweig was modest about himself, discreetly glossing over the uninteresting personal data in his autobiography, the repeated enumeration of famous people he met in his life or entertained at home is especially striking. It seems like exact proof that even the best of those cultured Jews could not escape the curse of their time—the worship of that great leveling idol, Success. Nothing does more harm to a highly differentiated sensibility than the comic vanity that, without any principle of selection and without any sense for differences, drops as many famous names as possible.

---

*Arthur Schnitzler (1862–1931) was an Austrian writer, dramatist, and physician whose frank representations of sexuality were sometimes considered scandalous. Richard Beer-Hofmann (1866–1945) was a Jewish-Austrian dramatist and poet who fled from Austria in 1939 and whose work was banned under the Nazis. Peter Altenberg, pseudonym of Richard Engländer (1859–1919), was a Jewish-Austrian writer who called his brief sketches "literary pencil drawings." Franz Grillparzer (1791–1872) was an Austrian writer and dramatist who also occupied administrative posts in the imperial bureaucracy, including that of finance minister. Adalbert Stifter (1805–68) was an Austrian writer whose major works include *Bunte Steine* (Colored Stones, 1853), *Der Nachsommer* (Indian Summer, 1857), and *Witiko* (1865–67).

In his guest book at Salzburg, Zweig gathered "eminent contemporaries" as passionately as he had collected the handwriting and relics of dead poets, musicians, and scientists. His own success, the benign renown of his own accomplishments, failed to sate the appetite of a vanity that could hardly have originated in his character. Presumably his character found it repulsive, but this vanity was solidly rooted in the depths of a conviction that formed its own weltanschauung—the conviction that began with the search for the "born genius" or "poet made flesh" and considers life worth living only insofar as it plays itself out in the midst of an atmosphere of fame among a chosen elite.

Incomplete satisfaction in one's own success, the attempt rather to transform fame into a social atmosphere, to create a caste of famous men like a caste of aristocrats, to organize a society of the renowned—these were the traits that distinguished the Jews of the period and differentiated their manner from the general genius-lunacy of the times. That was also why the world of art, literature, music, and the theater played, as it were, right into their hands. They alone were really more interested in those things than even in their own personal achievements or their own fame.

While the turn of the twentieth century brought economic security to the Jews and recognized their civic rights as a matter of course, at the same time it made their situation in society questionable, their social position insecure and ambiguous. Seen from the perspective of society, they were and remained pariahs as long as they failed to make themselves fit for the salon by some extraordinary means, such as fame. With regard to a famous Jew, society would forget its unwritten law. Zweig's "radiant power of fame" was a very real social force, in whose aura one could move freely and could even have antisemites as friends, such as Richard Strauss and Karl Haushofer.* Fame and success offered the means for the socially homeless to create a home and an environment for themselves. Since great success transcended national borders, famous people could easily become the representatives of a nebulous international society, where national prejudice appeared to be no longer valid. In any case, a famous Austrian Jew was more apt to be accepted

---

*Karl Ernst Haushofer (1869–1946) was a German general and theoretician of war who developed the "geopolitical" idea of *Lebensraum* (life space). A friend of Rudolf Hess, he probably contributed to the writing of Hitler's *Mein Kampf.*

as an Austrian in France than in Austria. The world citizenship of this generation, this remarkable nationality that its members claimed as soon as their Jewish origin was mentioned, somewhat resembles those modern passports that grant the bearer the right of sojourn in every country except the one that issued it.

This international society of famous people was punctured for the first time in 1914 and finally buried in 1933. It is all to Zweig's credit that he never allowed himself to be fooled into participating in the universal hysteria of the First World War. He remained loyal to his principles and kept his distance from politics; he never yielded to the temptation that afflicted so many literati—the temptation of using the war to establish a place in society outside of the circle of international intellectuals. It thus came about that, for him, the remnants of this prewar society preserved itself throughout the war. And it is well known that in the 1920s, which is to say, in the years to which Zweig owes his greatest success, the international society of fame once again functioned in Europe. But after 1938 Zweig learned some bitter lessons: that this international society, including the rights of its citizenry, depended on the possession of a very national passport, and that, for the stateless, there is no "international" anything.

The international society of the successful was the only one in which Jews enjoyed equal rights. Little wonder, then, that the most meager talents developed quite happily; still less that, for them, "the most beautiful odor on earth, sweeter than the rose of Schirach, [was] the smell of printers' ink." There was nothing in their lives more joyous than the printing of a book, the reviews, the complimentary copies, the translations into foreign languages. It was an ever-renewed ritual of placing oneself in relation to a world where one gets one's name into print so as to be admitted.

The fame that gave the social pariah something like the rights to a homeland in the international elite of the successful brought another privilege, which, according to Zweig's own judgment, was at least equally important— the suspension of anonymity, the possibility of being recognized by unknown people, of being admired by strangers. Even if one fell back into anonymity for a time, fame stood like a solid suit of armor that one could don again at any moment in order to protect oneself from the terrible effects of life. There is no question that Zweig feared nothing more than sinking back into an obscurity where, stripped of his fame, he would become again what he had been at the beginning of his life—except that now everything would be different and much worse: he would be no more than one of the many unfortunates who are confronted with the almost insuperable problem of conquering, bedazzling, and forcing oneself onto a strange, uncanny world—which is precisely how society must look to anyone who does not belong to it from birth and to all those against whom it discriminates.

Fate, in the form of a political catastrophe, eventually did almost thrust him into this very anonymity. Robbed of his fame, he knew—better than many of his colleagues—that the fame of a writer flickers out when he cannot write and publish in his own language. His collections were stolen from him, and with them his intimacy with the famous dead. His house in Salzburg was stolen, and with it his association with the famous among the living. Stolen, finally, was the invaluable passport, which had not only enabled him to represent his native land in other countries but had also helped him to evade the questionable character of his own civic existence within his native land.

And again, as during the First World War, it is to Zweig's credit that he was neither enflamed by the universal hysteria nor beguiled by his newly acquired British citizenship. He could hardly have represented England in other countries. Since, finally, the international society of the famous disappeared completely with the Second World War, this homeless man lost the only world in which he had once had the delusion of a home.

In a last article, "The Great Silence" (*ONA*, March 9, 1942), written shortly before his death—an article which seems to me to belong with the finest of Stephan Zweig's work—he tried to take a political stand for the first time in his life. The word "Jew" does not occur to him, for Zweig strove once again to represent Europe—more exactly, Central Europe—now that it was shocked into silence. Had he spoken about the terrible fate of his own people, he would have been closer to all the European peoples who are today, in the battle against their oppressor, struggling against the persecutor of the Jews. The European peoples know—better than did this self-appointed spokesman who had never in his whole lifetime concerned himself with their political destiny—that yesterday is not detached from today, "as if a man had been hurled down from a great height as the result of a violent blow." To them yesterday was in no way that "century whose progress, whose science, whose art, and whose magnificent inventions were the pride and the faith of us all."

Without the protective armor of fame, naked and disrobed, Stefan Zweig was confronted with the reality of the Jewish people. There had been various escapes from social pariahdom, including the ivory tower of fame. But only flight around the globe could offer salvation from political outlawry. Thus this Jewish bourgeois man of letters, who had never concerned himself with the affairs of his own people, became nevertheless a victim of their foes—and felt so disgraced that he could bear his life no longer. Since he had wanted all his life to live in peace with the political and social standards of his time, he was unable to fight against a world in whose eyes it was and is a disgrace to be a Jew. When finally the whole structure of his life, with its aloofness from civic struggle and politics, broke down, and he experienced disgrace, he was unable to discover what honor can mean to men.

For honor never will be won by the cult of success or fame, by cultivation of one's own self, nor even by personal dignity. From the "disgrace" of being a Jew there is but one escape—to fight for the honor of the Jewish people as a whole.

1943

THE CRISIS OF ZIONISM

It is a well-known fact, stressed time and again, that since the outbreak of this war and even before, a conspiracy of silence has covered the sufferings and losses of the Jewish people. This fact that so much upsets us is only the immediate consequence of another circumstance that in itself is disastrous: the Jews as a people have no share whatsoever in this war, though war had been declared upon them six years earlier than upon the Czechs, seven years earlier than upon Poland, France, and England, and almost nine years earlier than upon Russia and the United States. Unfortunately, during the years between 1933, the year in which Hitler came to power, and 1940, only a small fraction of the Jewish people could grasp the fact that they were at war, and this small fraction was without influence, formed of scattered individuals who more often than not did not even know one another.

Even German Jewry, the first victims of this ten years' war, needed more than five years and actual pogroms to be able to understand that they could no longer live in peace under a government composed of their enemies. Up to 1938, the bulk of German Jewry lived in the illusion of outliving their enemies, by accommodating themselves for the time being to certain restrictions. Neither the pogroms of fall 1938 nor the subsequent first years of the European war were sufficient to convince other parts of the Jewish people of the simple fact that war had been declared upon them. They simply did not react, or they answered the challenge by giving charitable gifts—a rather strange response. But it is also true that we behaved like any other people, and that our politicians tried to appease our enemies like the statesmen of all other nations—only with even less success. This appeasement policy started with the Jewish Agency's transfer arrangements with the German government in 1934. It was followed by the subsequent decisions of Jews of other countries not to use their influence upon their respective governments in their relations with Germany, to help German Jewry but not to speak about the events that made help necessary. Long before the period of appeasement found its natural end in total warfare, the boycott movement among the Jewish masses in America and in Poland had died down. The most honest expression of solidarity had ended in disillusionment and deception, and if our politicians, like the politicians of other countries, did not succeed in appeasing Hitler, they had a remarkable success in appeasing the Jewish people's rightful indignation and their instinctive attempts to fight back.

It would be a terrible understatement to speak of a crisis of Judaism; but it is certainly true whether we like it or not that the catastrophe of the last years was accompanied by a deep and dangerous crisis of Jewish politics, in other words of Zionism. Those among us who for many years closely followed the several developments of this crisis may almost feel relieved today, when the crisis is no longer to be concealed but has come into the open with all the complicated and involved problems of our political status in Palestine and abroad, with all the real conflicts and conflicting interests that we vainly tried to conceal.

The first symptom of the critical situation in which the Zionist movement found itself at the outbreak of this war was the entirely equivocal attitude of the British government in the face of a certain number of basic demands. Refugees who had barely escaped out of the hell of European countries occupied by the Germans tried vainly to enter Palestine: the Jewish homeland actually was less hospitable than other gentile countries; the names of the ships *Patria* and *Struma* are still in our memories, and you know that even those few who finally managed to land were sent to concentration camps on Mauritius. The Jewish Agency was incapable of dealing with the situation in a favorable way. And if these extremely sad facts mean little to you, since you live so far away and you know of these things only through the newspapers, I can assure you that they mean a very great deal to the Jews in the occupied countries, even if they did not try to escape. These happenings, which Nazi propaganda broadcast everywhere, drove the Jews to despair, and, believe me or not, these events dealt a considerable blow to the idea of a Jewish homeland that had so pathetically failed and an even bigger blow to the traditional confidence of Jews in British policies. Another kind of propaganda had tried to make us believe that all Jews in the concentration camps and ghettos, if they only remain alive, will automatically become ardent Zionists.

These propagandists had better bear these facts in mind; they will be remembered only too well in Europe—if there are still Jews to remember.

The second big failure of Zionist politics was the failure to raise a Jewish army. Nobody but the warmakers will be the peacemakers, and as things are going today there is very little hope left that Jews will be able to have their word at the peace table. This fact contrasts with the many plans Jews of all political parties are preparing for the postwar period; we know from experience that from a large amount of paper to the smallest deed is a very long way. From mass meetings in New York and other cities, we know that the idea of a Jewish army fighting under their own flag for their own freedom is the most popular idea that so far has roused the Jewish masses. And I stress the popularity of this idea because it is a consolation—more, a bright hope for the future of our people, who twice in the last ten years have shown so much more political insight and cleverness than most of our official politicians. The first time was when the Jewish masses almost instinctively started the boycott of German goods; the second time when they realized at once that during a war one must have an army and that against attack one has to defend and to counterattack—and this not under the flag of an empire and not in the regiments of a colonial army, but freely and openly, under one's own flag and under the orders of one's own officers.

The immediate results of these failures were serious enough, though we might expect far more serious ones in the future. Here in America a so-called Committee for a Jewish Army for Palestinian and Stateless Jews was set up and won in a very short period the support of great parts of the more progressive public opinion in this country. This committee, founded by the members of the Revisionist party but supported by many of our best friends among gentiles, could not but deal a very heavy blow to the authority of the Jewish Agency in this country and abroad and among Jews as well as among, for example, gentile officials in Washington. For even those gentiles who actually oppose creation of a Jewish army will take it for granted that Zionists must ask for an army in time of war when the creation of an army is the most important political issue for any people or nation. A committee with public support which stands for nothing but an army is serious competition for another group that, though pretending to be the only representative of the Jewish people, is, to say the least, not chiefly concerned with this issue.

A second result of the fact that Jews in their homeland lack the right to bear arms under their own flag is of equal importance. A great part of the Palestine *yishuv* is formed by recent refugees who have not yet obtained Palestinian citizenship. When the Jewish Agency started its recruiting campaign for the British colonial army, those refugees who happened to come from Czechoslovakia or even Poland could enlist in the legions of their former countries—and they did. For the advantages were obvious: in those legions, which today at least theoretically give equal rights to Jews, our boys had a far better position, legally and practically, than in the British army, in which they play the role of Palestinian natives. In the Czech legion, Jews have the same rights, the same advancement chances, and the promise of the Czech government in exile of full citizenship in the Czech state of tomorrow, which with the White Paper governing Palestine is much more than the British can guarantee.

Of course, we might argue with these boys. We might find that they are not idealistic enough or that the prospects of their being reintegrated into their former countries are not very bright. We might also argue with those Zionists and with those gentile friends of the Jewish and Zionist cause who see in the Committee for a Jewish Army a more important representative body than the Jewish Agency. And we certainly shall do so. But unfortunately politics are made not only with arguments but with facts. And the facts are: a Jewish army, the only guarantee we could have created during the war for our demands after the war, has been neglected by the Jewish Agency, has been entombed by Weizmann himself, who at the last Extraordinary Zionist Conference spoke about "the so-called Jewish army"; and all arguments we could use against the Jewish boys who even in Palestine prefer to serve under the flag of their former homeland become a little inconsistent in the face of the British policy in Palestine today. If the promises of governments in exile are problematic, the future protection of Jewish rights in Palestine is equally problematic.

During the last weeks, we had to add two other very critical signs of immediate political danger. Both came from Palestine. The first and the more important is the well-known Magnes declaration. The outstanding features of his proposal, centered as it is on the Arab question, are the following: in outspoken contradiction to the Zionist demands as they were formulated by the Jewish Agency and the Zionist Organization of this country, he asks for a binational state to be included in an Arab federation and for the Arab federation to be connected with a kind of Anglo-American alliance. There is no use hiding before ourselves the fact that Magnes is the spokesman for a considerable opposition not only in America but also in Palestine, where intellectuals like Buber and Ernst Simon and representatives of the farmers of Petach Tikhwah like Smilanski and so outstanding a personality as Henrietta Szold back his ideas. Even more significant, a recent war program of the Hashomer Haza'ir, a very important factor for labor in Palestine, also aims for a binational state. Though the Hashomer Haza'ir has nothing to do with the Magnes group, one can conclude from their demands how popular certain views of Magnes must be in Palestine. It is clear that Magnes's program and actions are a direct challenge to the authority of the Jewish Agency.

The second bad news from Palestine during the last weeks was the formation of a new party, the so-called Aliyah Hadashah, the party of new immigrants, which came out of their first elections second only to the Poale-Zion. The strength of this party, with only a very vague program, is due to the Central European *aliyah*—mostly from Germany—which for years had been discriminated against by the older elements and which obviously could not get adjusted or be melted in. These difficulties were a secret for nobody who happened to know Palestinian affairs, but it was a kind of unwritten law not to speak about them publicly. The result of this clever tactic is that for the first time the Zionist movement has produced a political party based upon those *sh'wath* differences, those tribal differences, which have split the unity of the Jewish people for more than 150 years. These differences became more and more inconsistent during the twentieth century, but since Hitler's rise to power they lost every political meaning: the fate of German or French Jewry is exactly the same as that of Polish Jewry. The lessons of the last ten years teach us that the fate of the Jewish people is one and indivisible. One of the internal political problems in Palestine is of course the overcoming of differences within the Jewish people themselves; the creation of a political party based upon such differences in Palestine is not less a danger for the *yishuv* than the creation of an Irish party would be for the unity of the United States.

I have enumerated the most outstanding signs of the crisis, each of which points in a similar direction: the weakening of the authority of the Jewish Agency, the growing discontent with the results of our political achievements, and the lack of trust in the conduct of our political affairs. The challenges to the authority of our supreme governing body come from very different quarters—the Magnes declaration and the Jewish Army Committee might be regarded as their most extreme poles. It is significant, however, that both break ranks with the official Zionist organization; both by different means try to address the Jewish people over the heads of Jewish officials, and neither tries to fight its battles within the established administration.

The true reasons for this state of affairs are not to be found—as some oppositional leaders of the Zionist organization would say—in red tape or a certain obsoleteness of our administrative body, in old-fashioned methods or a lack of new approaches. If tomorrow we had a brand-new team of men to run our politics it can only be doubted whether things would not go on in the same old way. Behind the whole picture lies a crisis of the very foundation of the whole movement, a crisis of every political means we used and of every political aim we sought during the last twenty years.

I will try very briefly to remind you of these few basic convictions, all of them dear to our heart, which in the political world of today have either lost their old meaning or in which we have—consciously or not—lost our ultimate confidence. There comes first the old belief that the Jewish question as a whole can be solved only by the reconstruction of Palestine, that the building up of the country will eradicate antisemitism and that more important than general political conditions (the famous charter of Herzl) is the so-called constructive approach, meaning the immediate practical tasks at hand. Let us consider this series of general convictions which pervade all of our propaganda and our public speeches one by one.

The Russian Revolution has dealt a blow to the first contention that the Jewish question can be solved only in Palestine and that antisemitism is only to be eradicated by the building up of Palestine, in other words by the exodus of Jews from their former homelands. There are many problems unsolved in Soviet Russia, and I for one do not believe that even the economic problems have been resolved there, let alone the most important of all questions, the question of political freedom; but one thing has to be admitted: the Russian Revolution found an entirely new and—as far as we can see today—an entirely just way to deal with nationality or minorities. The new historic fact is this: that for the first time in modern history, an identification of nation and state has not even been attempted. The government represents a federation of peoples and nationalities, all of them having their own, if very restricted, rights, none of them privileged and none of them dominated.

Nor seems this solution a purely Russian affair, without any bearing on other countries and continents. On the contrary, without any revolution, only by the natural course of events, the United States has come very close to the same conception. Jews know better than anyone else that they might be Americans and Jews at the same time, as Irishmen are Irish and American at the same time and Italians Italian and American. The president of the United States speaks to the "Jewish people of America"—in other words, the president expresses himself as if the government is not only a government of united states but of united peoples as well. The same holds true for other countries which up to now have not yet achieved their national freedom. Take for instance the Indian question. If the British say, let Indians first settle all their problems among themselves, or if Indian leaders refuse the partition of India on the ground that there is one unique Indian people, they both are wrong. The Indian subcontinent contains a multitude of peoples and rather than an old national state in the European sense, where one people, the majority of the inhabitants, holds the reins of government and rules over other inhabitants as minorities, you might expect that sooner or later these peoples will get together and form a government that unites all the nationalities of the Indian subcontinent.

It is not easy to speak about Europe; but it is probable that the talk of a federated Europe—or, if you like, the dream—will come true one day. All more progressive men, European or not, know that many problems could be solved with a federal government and with a constitution giving equal rights to each and every nationality on the continent.

But let us come back to Zionism and Palestine. If among the Zionist leaders many progressives know and talk about the end of small nations and the end of nationalism in the old narrow European sense, no official document or program expresses these ideas. On the contrary, if you remember the last conference of the Zionist Organization in New York, you certainly remember too how many speeches pointing in this direction you have heard, but that the resolutions only asked for a Jewish state in Palestine, as if we actually believe that this small land of ours—which is not even entirely ours—could live an autonomous political life. The reason for this shyness is the following: the foundations of Zionism were laid during a time when nobody could imagine any other solution of minority or nationality problems than the autonomous national state with a homogeneous population; Zionists are afraid that the whole building might crack if they abandon their old ideas. The contrary is true: the building will collapse if we don't adapt our minds and our ideas to new facts and new developments.

This general distrust against the old nationalist formulas is the backbone of the success of the Magnes declaration, whose inherent falseness and danger are hidden by the smoke screen created by the equivocal attitudes of our official policy. I. Newman, in the last conference, has rightly and vigorously pointed out that the Arab federation is nothing more than one of the tools and even inventions of British power politics. Magnes, in a certain sense, is only the successor and follower of Weizmann's politics, which in Weizmann's own words "always made the cooperation with the British Empire the cornerstone." It need not be proved that British policy in the Near East today is based upon cooperation with the Arabs at the expense of the Jews. Even the Magnes plan betrays the fact that it is built up entirely at our expense: a binational state protected by an Arab federation is nothing else than minority status within an Arab empire, and this empire is to be protected by an Anglo-American alliance which, to safeguard the way to India, has to deal with and to respect the majority—the Arabs—and not so tiny a minority as the Jews. Magnes, too, thinks along the old lines of national states, only he has given another name to the old baby; he calls it "federation." This use of the term "federation" kills its new and creative meaning in the germ; it kills the idea that a federation is—in contrast to a nation—made up of different peoples with equal rights. In other words, within a federation the old minority problem no longer exists. The Magnes proposal if realized would make out of Palestine one of our worst Galuth countries. The same idea of the Arab federation, but explained much more clearly, we can find in the declarations of British colonial officials, one of whom, Lord Moyne, even proposed a "resettlement of the Jews" after the war, their expulsion from Palestine; after this speech he received a special appointment to the Near East. People like Magnes, living on the spot and seeing clearly the immense danger to the Palestinian *yishuv* and our whole work in Palestine, hear no official word from our public institutions, not even a protest against these utterances by very responsible British officials. Instead, they read nothing but pathetic declarations about the sufferings of the Jewish people and hollow demands of "self-government" and "Jewish commonwealth"— hollow they are because no reality is behind them, because they are spoken as in an empty space without even noticing the hostile plans of Britain or the general trends of world politics. That these people try to take matters in their own hands is easily understood, even if we must deplore the way it is done.

FEBRUARY 1943

HERZL AND LAZARE

To Western Jewry, never really assimilated despite the recourse of some to the antisemitic salons, the Dreyfus case was scarcely of decisive consequence. But to the "modern, cultured Jew who had outgrown the ghetto and its haggling it was a thrust to the heart."[1] For him Herzl's naïve generalization was true: it had taken "the common enemy" to make him once more a member of a people.[2] These "prodigal sons" had learned a lot from their environment and when they returned to the ancestral hearth they found themselves possessed by that intense discontent which has always been the hallmark of true patriotism and of true devotion to one's people. Sadly and with a certain amazement they came to realize that the moment they proposed improvements in the age-old structure, it was at once decided to expel them from it. And all the time they saw the building in danger of collapse. Theodor Herzl arrived just in time to report the first Dreyfus trial for a Vienna paper. He heard the rabble cry "Death to the Jews!" and proceeded to write *The Jewish State*. Bernard Lazare had come from his hometown in the south of France some years before, in the midst of the antisemitic furor caused by the Panama scandal. Shortly before the Dreyfus case he had published a two-volume work on antisemitism, in which he had laid it down that this was due, among other things, to the unsocial behavior of the Jews.[3] At that time he believed that he had found in socialism the solution. Lazare likewise was an eyewitness of the Dreyfus trial and he determined not to wait for the world revolution. As he came face to face with the rising hatred of the mob, he realized at once that from now on he was an outcast[4] and accepted the challenge. Alone among the champions of Dreyfus he took his place as a conscious Jew, fighting for justice in general but for the Jewish people in particular.[5]

Both men were turned into Jews by antisemitism. Neither concealed the fact.[6] Both realized just because they were so "assimilated" that normal life was possible for them only on the condition that emancipation should not remain a dead letter, while they saw that in reality the Jew had become the pariah of the modern world.[7] Both stood outside the religious tradition of Judaism and neither wished to return to it. Both were removed, as intellectuals, from those narrow and parochial Jewish cliques which had somehow grown up within the framework of gentile society. Both were poles apart from that spiritual ghetto which had retained everything of the ghetto's life except its inwardness. Yet both were its natural products; it was from this that both had escaped. When they were drawn back Judaism could no longer mean to them a religion, yet to neither could it mean a halfhearted adherence to one of many cliques. For them their Jewish origin had a political and national significance. They could find no place for themselves in Jewry unless the Jewish people was a nation. In their subsequent careers both men came into serious conflict with the forces which then controlled Jewish politics, namely, the philanthropists. In these conflicts, which in the end exhausted them, both were to learn that the Jewish people was threatened not only by the antisemites from without but also by the influence of its own "benefactors" from within.[8]

But here the similarity ends and there begins that great difference which was to lead ultimately to a personal breach between the two men, when they were serving together on the executive committee of the Zionist Organization. Herzl's solution of the Jewish problem was, in the final analysis, escape or deliverance in a homeland. In the light of the Dreyfus case the whole of the gentile world seemed to him hostile; there were only Jews and antisemites.[9] He considered that he would have to deal with this hostile world and even with avowed antisemites. To him it was a matter of indifference just how hostile a gentile might be; indeed, thought he, the more antisemitic a man was the more he would appreciate the advantages of a Jewish exodus from Europe![10] To Lazare, on the other hand, the territorial question was secondary—a mere outcome of the primary demand that "the Jews should be emancipated as a people and in the form of a nation."[11] What he sought was not an escape from antisemitism but a mobilization of the people against its foes. This is shown clearly by his part in the Dreyfus case and by his later memorandum on the persecution of the Jews in Romania.[12] The consequence of this attitude was that he did not look around for more or less antisemitic protectors but for real comrades-in-arms, whom he hoped to find among all the oppressed groups of contemporary Europe.[13] He knew that antisemitism was neither an isolated nor a universal phenomenon and that the shameful complicity of the powers in the East European pogroms had been symptomatic of something far deeper, namely, the threatened collapse of all moral values under the pressure of imperialist politics.[14]

In the light of the Dreyfus case and of his own experience in fighting alongside Jews for one of their brethren,[15] Lazare came to realize that the real obstacle in the path of his people's emancipation was not antisemitism. It was "the demoralization of a people made up of the poor and downtrodden, who live on the alms of their wealthy brethren, a people revolted only by persecution from without but not by oppression from within, revolutionaries in the society of others but not in their own."[16] Ill would it serve the cause of freedom, thought he, if a man were to begin by abandoning his own. Fighters for freedom could be internationalists only if by that they meant that they were prepared to recognize the freedom of all nations; antinational they could never be.[17] Lazare's criticism of his people was at least as bitter as Herzl's but he never despised them and did not share Herzl's idea that politics must be conducted from above.[18] Faced with the alternative of remaining politically ineffective or of including himself among the elite group of saviors, he preferred to retreat into absolute isolation, where, if he could do naught else, he could at least remain one of the people.[19] For Lazare could find no supporters in France. The only element of Western Europe which might have responded to his message, the Jews who had outgrown the petty trader's haggling, the intellectuals in the liberal professions, were virtually nonexistent in the country. On the other hand, the impoverished masses, whom he had loved so deeply, and the Jewish oppressed, whom he had championed so devotedly,[20] were separated from him by thousands of miles as well as by a difference in language. In a certain sense, therefore, Herzl, with the support of German and Austrian Jewry, succeeded where Lazare failed. So utter, indeed, was his failure that he was passed over in silence by his Jewish contemporaries,[21] to be recovered to us by Catholic writers. Better than we those men knew that Lazare was a great Jewish patriot as well as a great writer.[22]

1942

Notes

1. Cf. the remarks of Theodor Herzl in his opening address of the first Zionist Congress (*Gesammelte Werke*, vol. 1, p. 176): "That sense of inner cohesion, with which we have so often and so virulently been charged, was in a state of utter dissolution when antisemitism fell upon us. We have, so to speak, come home. . . . But those of us who have returned like prodigal sons to the ancestral hearth find much that urgently requires improvement."

2. Cf. Herzl's statement before the British Aliens Commission: "A nation is an historic group of men united by clearly discernible ties, and held together by a common foe." *Gesammelte Werke*, vol. 1, p. 474.

3. Bernard Lazare, *L'antisémitisme: son histoire et ses causes* (Paris, 1894).

4. Cf. Lazare, *Le fumier de Iob* (Paris, 1928), p. 64: "Henceforth I am a pariah."

5. Cf. Péguy, *Notre jeunesse* pp. 68–69, 74: "The politicians, the rabbis, the official communities of Israel . . . were only too willing to sacrifice Dreyfus for the sake of an illusion. The great mass of the Jews . . . has never been led to its great, if sad, destiny except by force—that is, by a band of fanatics grouped around certain heads, or more precisely, around the prophets of Israel. In this great crisis for Israel and the world the prophet was Bernard Lazare."

6. Cf. Herzl's remark in a letter of the year 1895: "My Judaism was to me a matter of indifference. . . . However, just as antisemitism sent the feeble, cowardly and ambitious Jews into the ranks of Christendom, so it sent me back with renewed vigor to my Judaism." *Tagebücher*, vol. 1, pp. 120–21. Similar statements occur *passim* in his diaries. Bernard Lazare's declaration may be found in his *Fumier de Iob:* "I am a Jew, yet I ignore everything Jewish. . . . I must needs know who I am, why I am hated and what I might be."

7. Cf. the remark of Herzl at the "family council" of the Rothschilds: "You will never be recognized as full citizens, nay, nor even as second-class *(Staatsangehörige)*." *Tagebücher*, vol. 1, p. 187. Similarly in the memoranda for his interview with Baron Hirsch there occurs the observation: "You are pariahs. You have to live on tenterhooks lest anyone deprive you of your rights or property." *Gesammelte Werke*, vol. 6, p. 462. Cf. also Lazare's remark about the "unconscious pariah," i.e., the nonemancipated Jew and the "conscious pariah" of Western society, in *Le nationalisme juif* (Paris, 1898), p. 8.

8. In his interview with Lord Rothschild, Herzl described Jewish charity as "a mechanism for keeping the needy in subjection." *Tagebücher*, vol. 3, p. 218. He came into open conflict with the philanthropists when he established the Jewish Colonial Bank and the latter subsequently foundered, as the result of being boycotted by Jewish financial circles. The matter is discussed at length in his *Gesammelte Werke*, vol. 1, p. 406 ff., and there are frequent references to it in the diaries. Similarly Lazare came into conflict with the whole of French Jewry through his championship of Dreyfus. Cf. Baruch Hagani, *Bernard Lazare, 1865–1903* (Paris, 1919), p. 28 ff. That he got the worst of this conflict is shown fully by Péguy, *Notre jeunesse*, p. 75 ff. One example quoted by Péguy (p. 84) is significant: "When negotiations were started for founding a large-scale daily, the Jewish backers always made it a condition that Bernard Lazare should not write for it."

9. Cf. his remark in *Der Judenstaat* (*Gesammelte Werke*, vol. 1, p. 36): "The peoples among whom Jews live are one and all shamefully or shamelessly antisemitic."

10. Cf. the recurrent observation recorded in his *Tagebücher*, vol. 1, p. 93: "It is the antisemites who will be our staunchest friends, and the antisemitic countries which will be our allies." How he interpreted this notion in practice is revealed in a letter to Katznelson, written in connection with the Kishinev pogroms of 1903. In that letter he seeks to "derive some measure of advantage from the threatening calamity."

11. In *Le fumier de Iob.*

12. *Les juifs en Roumanie* (Paris, 1902).

13. Characteristic of this attitude is the following passage from his *Juifs en Roumanie*, p. 103: "It may well be that if it [the Romanian bourgeoisie] plunges the Jew into despair and pushes him to the limit, this very fact, despite his passivity and despite the advice of his wealthy faint-hearts, will forge a link between him and the agricultural laborer and aid both to throw off the yoke." In marked contrast is the attitude of Herzl, as revealed when, following his interview with the sultan, he received telegrams of protest from student meetings comprising persons of all kinds of oppressed nationalities. He was, he confessed, "pained and distressed," but the only political effect this had on him was to make him talk about using those telegrams in his conversations with the sultan! Cf. *Tagebücher,* vol. 3, p. 103.

14. Cf. his remark in *Les juifs en Roumanie,* p. 91: "Besides, what other nation dares open its mouth? England, who wiped out the Boers? Russia, who oppressed the Finns and Jews? France, who massacred the Annamites . . . and is now getting ready to butcher the Moors? Italy, who ravages in Eritrea today and in Tripoli tomorrow? Or Germany, the savage executioner of the negroes?"

An interesting insight into the connection between antisemitism's brutalization of peoples and the policies of imperialism is revealed by Fernand Labori, would-be counsel for Dreyfus, in his article "Le Mal politique et les partis," in *La Grande Revue* (October–December 1901), p. 276: "Similarly, the movement of colonial expansion provides . . . a characteristic trait of the present era. It is a commonplace to point out that this policy has cost humanity moral as well as material sacrifices."

15. Writing in *L'Echo Sioniste* (April 20, 1901), Lazare had the following to say about the French Jews, as he had learned to know them during the Dreyfus crisis: "Take our French Jews. I know that crowd and what they are capable of. It isn't enough for them to reject any solidarity with their foreign-born brethren; they have also to go charging them with all the evils which their own cowardice engenders. They are not content with being more jingoist than the native-born Frenchmen; like all emancipated Jews everywhere they have also, of their own volition, broken all ties of solidarity. Indeed, they go so far that for the three dozen or so men in France who are ready to defend one of their martyred brethren you can find some thousands ready to stand guard over Devil's Island, alongside the most rabid patriots of the country."

16. *Le fumier de Iob,* p. 151.

17. Péguy, *Notre jeunesse,* p. 130, stresses this contrast between the international and the antinational as illustrating Lazare's Jewish patriotism.

18. Cf. *Tagebücher,* vol. 1, p. 193.

19. On March 24, 1899, Lazare wrote to Herzl that he felt obliged to resign from the executive committee, which, he added, "tries to direct the Jewish masses as if they were an ignorant child. . . . That is a conception radically opposed to all my political and social opinions and I can therefore not assume responsibility for it." Quoted by Hagani, *Bernard Lazare,* p. 39.

20. Péguy, *Notre jeunesse,* p. 87, describes him as follows: "A heart which beat to all the echoes of the world, a man who could skim four, six, eight or a dozen pages of a newspaper to light, like a streak of lightning, on a single line containing the word Jew . . . a heart which bled in all the ghettos of the world . . . wherever the Jew was oppressed, that is, in a sense, everywhere."

21. *Ibid.,* p. 84: "Everything was set in motion to make him die quietly of hunger."

22. If it were not for Péguy's memoir, "Le portrait de Bernard Lazare," prefixed to the posthumous edition of *Le fumier de Iob,* we would know little about Lazare. Hagani's biography is based to a large extent on Péguy, while it was only with the latter's help that Lazare himself was able to publish his work on the Jews of Romania. The saddest part of this sad story is the fact, pointed out by Péguy, that the only man who really appreciated Lazare's greatness and love for Jewry, even though he regarded him as an enemy, was Edouard Drumont.

ZIONISM RECONSIDERED

The end result of fifty years of Zionist politics was embodied in the recent resolution of the largest and most influential section of the World Zionist Organization. American Zionists from left to right adopted unanimously, at their last annual convention held in Atlantic City in October 1944, the demand for a "free and democratic Jewish commonwealth . . . [which] shall embrace the whole of Palestine, undivided and undiminished." This is a turning point in Zionist history; for it means that the Revisionist program, so long bitterly repudiated, has proved finally victorious. The Atlantic City Resolution goes even a step further than the Biltmore Program (1942), in which the Jewish minority had granted minority rights to the Arab majority. This time the Arabs were simply not mentioned in the resolution, which obviously leaves them the choice between voluntary emigration or second-class citizenship. It seems to admit that only opportunist reasons had previously prevented the Zionist movement from stating its final aims. These aims now appear to be completely identical with those of the extremists as far as the future political constitution of Palestine is concerned.[1] It is a deadly blow to those Jewish parties in Palestine itself that have tirelessly preached the necessity of an understanding between the Arab and the Jewish peoples. On the other hand, it will considerably strengthen the majority under the leadership of Ben-Gurion, which, through the pressure of many injustices in Palestine and the terrible catastrophes in Europe, have turned more than ever nationalistic.

Why "general" Zionists should still quarrel officially with Revisionists is hard to understand, unless it be that the former do not quite believe in the fulfillment of their demands but think it wise to demand the maximum as a base for future compromises, while the latter are serious, honest, and intransigent in their nationalism. The general Zionists, furthermore, have set their hopes on the help of the big powers, while the Revisionists seem pretty much decided to take matters into their own hands. Foolish and unrealistic as this may be, it will bring to the Revisionists many new adherents from among the most honest and most idealistic elements of Jewry.

In any case, the significant development lies in the unanimous adherence of all Zionist parties to the ultimate aim, the very discussion of which was still taboo during the 1930s. By stating it with such bluntness in what seemed to them an appropriate moment, Zionists have forfeited for a long time to come any chance of *pourparlers* with Arabs; for whatever Zionists may offer, they will not be trusted. This, in turn, leaves the door wide open for an outside power to take over without asking the advice of either of the two parties most concerned. The Zionists have now indeed done their best to create that insoluble "tragic conflict" which can only be ended through cutting the Gordian knot.

It would certainly be very naïve to believe that such a cutting would invariably be to the Jewish advantage, nor is there any reason to assume that it would result in a lasting solution. To be more specific, the British government may tomorrow decide to partition the country and may sincerely believe it has found a working compromise between Jewish and Arab demands. This belief on the British part would be all the more natural since partition might indeed be an acceptable compromise between the pro-Arab anti-Jewish colonial administration and the rather pro-Jewish English public opinion: thus it would seem to solve an inner British disagreement over the Palestine question. But it is simply preposterous to believe that further partition of so small a territory whose present border lines are already the result of two previous partitions—the first from Syria and the second from Transjordan—could resolve the conflict of two peoples, especially in a period when similar conflicts are not territorially soluble on much larger areas.

Nationalism is bad enough when it trusts in nothing but the rude force of the nation. A nationalism that necessarily and admittedly depends upon the force of a foreign nation is certainly worse. This is the threatened fate of Jewish nationalism and of the proposed Jewish state, surrounded inevitably by Arab states and Arab peoples. Even a Jewish majority in Palestine— nay, even a transfer of all Palestine Arabs, which is openly demanded by Revisionists—would not substantially change a situation in which Jews must either ask protection from an outside power against their neighbors or come to a working agreement with their neighbors.

If such an agreement is not brought about, there is the imminent danger that, through their need and willingness to accept any power in the Mediterranean basin which might assure their existence, Jewish interests will clash with those of all other Mediterranean peoples; so that, instead of one "tragic conflict" we shall face tomorrow as many insoluble conflicts as there are Mediterranean nations. For these nations, bound to demand a *mare nostrum* shared only by those who have settled territories along its shores, must in the long run oppose any outside—that is, interfering—power creating or holding a sphere of interest. These outside powers, however powerful at the moment, certainly cannot afford to antagonize the Arabs, one of the most numerous peoples of the Mediterranean basin. If, in the present situation, the powers should be willing to help the establishment of a Jewish homestead, they could do so only on the basis of a broad understanding that takes into account the whole region and the needs of all its peoples. On the other hand, the Zionists, if they continue to ignore the Mediterranean peoples and watch out only for the big faraway powers, will appear only as their tools, the agents of foreign and hostile interests. Jews who know their own history should be aware that such a state of affairs will inevitably lead to a new wave of Jew-hatred; the antisemitism of tomorrow will assert that Jews not only profiteered from the presence of the foreign big powers in that region but had actually plotted it and hence are guilty of the consequences.

The big nations that can afford to play the game of power politics have found it easy to forsake King Arthur's Round Table for the poker table; but small powerless nations that venture their own stakes in that game, and try to mingle with the big, usually end by being sold down the river. The Jews, trying their hand "realistically" in the horse-trading politics of oil in the Near East, are uncomfortably like people who, with a passion for horse-trading but disposing of neither horse nor money, decide to make up for the lack of both by imitating the magnificent shouting that usually accompanies these gaudy transactions.

II

The Revisionist landslide in the Zionist Organization was brought on by the sharpening of political conflicts during the past ten years. None of these conflicts, however, is new; the new factor is the situation in which Zionism is forced to give an answer to questions which for at least twenty years had been held deliberately in suspense. Under Weizmann's leadership in foreign affairs, and partly because of the great achievements of Palestine Jewry, the Zionist Organization had developed a genius for not answering, or answering ambiguously, all questions of political consequence. Everybody was free to interpret Zionism as he pleased; stress was laid, especially in the European countries, on the purely "ideological" elements.

In the light of present decisions, this ideology must appear to any neutral and not too well-informed spectator like deliberately complicated talk designed to hide political intentions. But such an interpretation would not do justice to the majority of Zionists. The truth of the matter is that the Zionist ideology, in the Herzlian version, had a definite tendency toward what later was known as Revisionist attitudes, and could escape from them only through a willful blindness to the real political issues that were at stake.

The political issues on which the course of the whole movement depended were few in number and could be plainly recognized. Foremost among them was the question of which kind of a political body Palestine Jewry was to form. The Revisionist insistence on a national state, refusing to accept a mere "national homeland," has proven victorious. Almost as an afterthought of the first came the next question, namely, what relationship this body should have with the Jews of Diaspora countries.

Here enters the double-loyalty conflict, never clearly answered, which is an unavoidable problem of every national movement of a people living within the boundaries of other states and unwilling to resign their civil and political rights therein. For over twenty years the president of the World Zionist Organization and of the Jewish Agency for Palestine has been a British subject whose British patriotism and loyalty are certainly beyond doubt. The trouble is only that by the very nature of his passport he is forced into a theory of predestined harmony of Jewish and British interests in Palestine. Such harmony may or may not exist; but the situation reminds one very vividly of the similar theories of European assimilationists. Here, too, the Revisionists—at least their extreme wing in America, the "Hebrew Committee for National Liberation"—have given the answer which has great chances of being accepted by Zionism, because it corresponds so well with the ideology of most Zionists and fulfills expertly their present needs.

The answer is that in Palestine we have a Hebrew nation, in the Diaspora a Jewish people. This chimes in with the old theory that only the remnant will return, the remnant being the elite of the Jewish people upon whom Jewish survival exclusively depends. This furthermore has the tremendous advantage of fitting in beautifully with the need for a reformulation of Zionism for America. Here not even the pretense of a willingness to move to Palestine is upheld; so here the movement has lost its initial character as that of changing the life of Jews in the Diaspora. The differentiation between the "Jewish people" in America and the "Hebrew nation" in Palestine and Europe could indeed solve, in theory at least, the double-loyalty conflict of American Jews.

Of equal importance has been the question, always open, as to what Jews should do against antisemitism: what kind of fight or explanation the new national movement, which had after all been occasioned by the anti-Jewish agitation of the end of the century, could and would offer. The answer to this, since Herzl's time, has been an utter resignation, an open acceptance of antisemitism as a "fact," and therefore a "realistic" willingness not only to do business with the foes of the Jewish people but also to take propaganda advantage of anti-Jewish hostility. Here, too, the difference between Revisionists and general Zionists has been hard to detect. While the Revisionists were violently criticized by other Zionists for entering into negotiations with the antisemitic prewar Polish government for the evacuation of a million Polish Jews, in order to win Polish support for extreme Zionist demands before the League of Nations and thus exercise pressure on the British government, the general Zionists themselves were in constant contact with the Hitler government in Germany about the transfer business.

The last, and at the moment certainly most important, issue is the Jewish-Arab conflict in Palestine. The intransigent attitude of the Revisionists is well known. Always claiming the whole of Palestine and Transjordan, they were the first to advocate the transfer of Palestine Arabs to Iraq—a proposition which a few years ago was earnestly discussed in general Zionist circles as well. Since the latest resolution of the American Zionist Organization, from which neither the Jewish Agency nor the Palestine Vaad Leumi differs in principle, leaves practically no choice for the Arabs but minority status in Palestine or voluntary emigration, it is obvious that in this question, too, the Revisionist principle, if not yet the Revisionist methods, has won a decisive victory.

The only distinct difference between the Revisionists and the general Zionists today lies in their attitude toward England, and this is not a fundamental political issue. The Revisionists, decidedly anti-British, share this position, at least on sentimental grounds, with a great many Palestine Jews who have the experience of British colonial administration. Moreover, they enjoy in this respect the support of many American Zionists who are either influenced by the American distrust of British imperialism or hope that America and not Great Britain will be the future great power in the Near East. The last obstacle between them and victory in this field is Weizmann, who is backed by the British Zionist Organization and a small minority in Palestine.

III

In a rather summary way it may be asserted that the Zionist movement was fathered by two typical nineteenth-century European political ideologies—socialism and nationalism. The amalgam of these two seemingly contradictory doctrines was generally effected long before Zionism came into being: it was effected in all those national revolutionary movements of small European peoples whose situation was equally one of social as of national oppression. But within the Zionist movement such an amalgam has never been realized. Instead, the movement was split from the beginning between the social revolutionary forces which had sprung from the Eastern European masses and the aspiration for national emancipation as formulated by Herzl and his followers in the Central European countries. The paradox of this split was that, whereas the former was actually a people's movement, caused by national oppression, the latter, created by social discrimination, became the political creed of intellectuals.

For a long time the Eastern movement had so strong an affinity with socialism in the Tolstoyan form that its followers almost adopted it as their exclusive ideology. The Marxists among them believed Palestine to be the ideal place to "normalize" the social aspects of Jewish life, by establishing there appropriate conditions for Jewish participation in the all-important class struggle from which the ghetto existence had excluded the Jewish masses: this was to give them a "strategical base" for future participation in the world revolution and the coming classless and nationless society (Borochov). Those who adopted the more Eastern variation of the messianic dream went to Palestine for a kind of personal salvation through work within a collective (A. D. Gordon). Spared the ignominies of capitalist exploitation, they could realize at once and by themselves the ideals they preached, and build up the new social order that was only a far-off dream in the social revolutionary teachings of the West.

The national aim of the socialist Zionists was attained when they settled in Palestine. Beyond that they had no national aspirations. Absurd as it may sound today, they had not the slightest suspicion of any national conflict with the present inhabitants of the promised land; they did not even stop to think of the very existence of Arabs. Nothing could better prove the entirely unpolitical character of the new movement than this innocent obliviousness. True, those Jews were rebels; but they rebelled not so much against the oppressions of their people as against the crippling, stifling atmosphere of Jewish ghetto life, on the one hand, and the injustices of social life in general, on the other. From both they hoped to have escaped when once established in Palestine, whose very name was still holy as well as familiar to them, emancipated though they were from Jewish Orthodoxy. They escaped to Palestine as one might wish to escape to the moon, to a region beyond the wickedness of the world. True to their ideals, they established themselves on the moon; and with the extraordinary strength of their faith they were able to create small islands of perfection.

Out of these social ideals grew the *chalutz* and kibbutz movement. Its members, a small minority in their native lands, are a hardly larger minority in Palestine Jewry today. But they did succeed in creating a new type of Jew, even a new kind of aristocracy, with their newly established values: their genuine contempt for material wealth, exploitation, and bourgeois life; their unique combination of culture and labor; their rigorous realization of social justice within their small circle; and their loving pride in the fertile soil, the work of their hands, together with an utter and surprising lack of any wish for personal possessions.

Great as these achievements are, they have remained without any appreciable political influence. The pioneers were completely content within the small circle where they could realize their ideals for themselves; they were little interested in Jewish or Palestine politics, were in fact frequently wearied by it, unaware of the general destiny of their people. Like all true sectarians, they tried hard to convince people of their way of life, to win over to their convictions as many adherents as possible, even to educate the Jewish youth of the Diaspora to follow in their footsteps. But once in Palestine, and even before within the safe shelter of the various youth movements, these idealists became self-contented, concerned only with the personal realization of lofty ideals, as indifferent as their teachers had been to the world at large which had not accepted the salutary way of living in an agricultural collective. In a sense, indeed, they were too decent for politics, the best among them somehow afraid of soiling their hands with it; but they were also completely uninterested in any event in Jewish life outside Palestine which did not land thousands of Jews as new immigrants; and they were bored by any Jew who was not himself a prospective immigrant. Politics, therefore, they gladly left to the politicians—on condition they were helped with money, left alone with their own social organization, and guaranteed a certain influence upon education of the youth.

Not even the events of 1933 roused their political interest; they were naïve enough to see in them, above all, a God-sent opportunity for an undreamed-of wave of immigration to Palestine. When the Zionist Organization, against the natural impulses of the whole Jewish people, decided to do business with Hitler, to trade German goods against the wealth of German Jewry, to flood the Palestine market with German products and thus make a mockery of the boycott against German-made articles, they found little opposition in the Jewish national homeland, and least of all among its aristocracy, the so-called kibbutzniks. When accused of dealing with the enemy of Jewry and of labor, these Palestinians used to argue that the Soviet Union too had extended its trade agreements with Germany. Thereby once more these Palestinians underlined the fact that they were interested only in the existing and prospective *yishuv*, the Jewish settlement, and were quite unwilling to become the protagonists of a worldwide national movement.

This consent to the Nazi-Zionist transfer agreement is only one outstanding instance among many of the political failure of the aristocracy of Palestine Jewry. Much as, despite their small number, they influenced the social values in Palestine, so little did they exercise their force in Zionist politics.

Invariably they submitted to the Organization which, nonetheless, they held in contempt, as they held in contempt all men who were not producing and living from the work of their hands.

So it has come to pass that this new class of Jews, who possess such a rich new experience in social relationships, have not uttered a single fresh word, have not offered a single new slogan, in the wide field of Jewish politics. They took no differing stand on political antisemitism—content merely with repeating the old socialist or the new nationalist banalities, as though the whole affair did not concern them. Without a single fresh approach to the Arab-Jewish conflict (the "binational state" of Hashomer Haza'ir is no solution since it could be realized only as a result of a solution), they limited themselves to fighting either for or against the slogan of Jewish labor. Revolutionary as were their background and their ideology, they failed to level a single criticism at the Jewish bourgeoisie outside of Palestine, or to attack the role of Jewish finance in the political structure of Jewish life. They even adapted themselves to the charity methods of fund-raising, which they were taught by the Organization when sent to other countries on special missions. Amid the turmoil of conflicts in Palestine today, most of them have become loyal supporters of Ben-Gurion, who indeed, in contrast to Weizmann, comes from their own ranks; though many of them have, in the old tradition, simply refused to vote; and only a few of them have protested that under the leadership of Ben-Gurion, whose Revisionist leanings were still violently denounced by Palestine labor in 1935, the Zionist Organization has adopted the Revisionist Jewish state program.

Thus the social revolutionary Jewish national movement, which started half a century ago with ideals so lofty that it overlooked the particular realities of the Near East and the general wickedness of the world, has ended— as do most such movements—with the unequivocal support not only of national but of chauvinist claims—not against the foes of the Jewish people but against its possible friends and present neighbors.

IV

This voluntary and, in its consequences, tragic abdication of political leadership by the vanguard of the Jewish people left the course free to the devotees of the movement who may be truly called political Zionists. Their Zionism belongs to those nineteenth-century political movements that carried ideologies, weltanschauungs, keys to history, in their portmanteaus. Not less than its better-known contemporaries, such as socialism or nationalism, Zionism was once fed on the very lifeblood of genuine political passions; and it shares with them the sad fate of having outlived their political conditions only to stalk together like living ghosts amid the ruins of our times.

Socialism—which, despite all its materialist superstitions and naïve atheistic dogmatism, was once an inspiring source of the revolutionary labor movement—laid the heavy hand of "dialectical necessity" upon the heads and hearts of its adherents until they were willing to fit into almost any inhumane conditions. They were so willing because, on the one hand, their genuine political impulses for justice and freedom had grown fainter and fainter and, on the other hand, their fanatical belief in some superhuman, eternally progressive development had grown stronger and stronger. As for nationalism, it never was more evil or more fiercely defended than since it became apparent that this once great and revolutionary principle of the national organization of peoples could no longer either guarantee true sovereignty of the people within or establish a just relationship among different peoples beyond the national borders.

The pressure of this general European situation made itself felt in Jewish life through a new hostile philosophy, which centered its whole outlook around the role of the Jews in political and social life. In a sense, antisemitism was the father of both assimilationism and Zionism—to such a degree, indeed, that we can hardly understand a single word of the great war of arguments between them, which was to last for decades, without keeping in mind the standard contentions of antisemitism.

At that time antisemitism was still the expression of a typical conflict such as must inevitably occur within the framework of a national state whose fundamental identity between people and territory and state cannot but be disturbed by the presence of another nationality which, in whatever forms, wants to preserve its identity. Within the framework of a national state there are only two alternatives for the solution of nationality conflicts: either complete assimilation—that is, actual disappearance—or emigration. If, then, the assimilationists had simply preached national suicide for Jewry and the Zionists had simply challenged this in proposing means of national survival, we would have witnessed two factions of Jewry fighting each other on the ground of genuine and serious differences. Instead, each preferred to dodge the issue and to develop an "ideology." Most of the so-called assimilationists never wanted complete assimilation and national suicide: they imagined that by escaping from actual history into an imaginary history of mankind they had found an excellent method of survival. The Zionists likewise fled the field of actual conflicts into a doctrine of eternal antisemitism governing the relations of Jews and gentiles everywhere and always, and mainly responsible for the survival of the Jewish people. Thus both sides relieved themselves of the arduous task of fighting antisemitism on its own grounds, which were political, and even of the unpleasant task of analyzing its true causes. The assimilationists began their futile writing of a ponderous library of refutations which nobody ever read—except perhaps the Zionists. For they obviously accepted the validity of the utterly stupid reasoning, since they concluded from that kind of propaganda that all reasoning was entirely futile—a surprising conclusion if one considers the level of the "reasons."

But now the way was free for talking in general terms and developing the respective isms. It was a struggle in which political issues were touched on only when the Zionists charged that the solution of the Jewish problem through assimilation meant suicide. This was true enough; but it was something most of the assimilationists neither wished nor dared to refute. They were frightened by gentile critics all unaware that they too, the very assimilationists, wanted Jewish survival and were actually engaged in Jewish politics. On the other side, when the assimilationists talked about the danger of double loyalty and the impossibility of being German or French patriots and Zionists at the same time, they rudely raised a problem which for obvious reasons the Zionists did not care to talk of frankly.

V

Sad as it must be for every believer in government of the people, by the people, and for the people, the fact is that a political history of Zionism could easily pass over the genuine national revolutionary movement which sprang from the Jewish masses. The political history of Zionism must be concerned mainly with those elements that did not come of the people: it must be concerned with men who believed in government by the people as little as did Theodor Herzl, whom they followed—although it is true that they all emphatically wished to do something for the people. They had the advantage of a general European education and outlook, together with some knowledge of how to approach and deal with governments. They called themselves political Zionists, which indicated clearly their special and one-sided interest in foreign politics. They were confronted by the similarly one-sided concern with domestic politics on the part of the Eastern European adherents of the movement.

It was only after Herzl's death in 1904, and because of the failure of all of Herzl's ventures into high diplomacy, that they became converts to Weizmann's "practical" Zionism, which preached practical achievements in Palestine as the basis for political success. This approach, however, was to meet with as little actual success. In the absence of a political guarantee (Herzl's famous Charter) and in the presence of the hostile Turkish administration, very few Jews could be induced to settle in Palestine prior to the Balfour Declaration in 1917. This Declaration was not issued—nor was it ever pretended to have been issued—because of practical achievements in Palestine. The practical Zionists, therefore, became "general Zionists," this term designating their ideological creed as opposed to the philosophy of assimilation.

For the most part interested in the relationship between the movement and the great powers, and in the propaganda results among a few outstanding personalities, the general Zionists were sufficiently unprejudiced, despite their bourgeois origin, to leave to their Eastern brethren—those who actually did go to Palestine—a completely free hand with their experiments in social and economic life, insisting only on an equal chance for capitalist enterprise and investment. Both groups could work together rather smoothly just because of their entirely different outlooks. However, the result of this cooperation, in the actual upbuilding of Palestine, was a most paradoxical conglomerate of radical approach and revolutionary social reforms domestically, with outmoded and outright reactionary political lines in the field of foreign politics, that is, the relationship of the Jews to other nations and peoples.

The men who now assumed Zionist leadership were no less the moral aristocracy of Western Jewry than were the founders of the kibbutz and *chalutz* movement of Eastern Jewry. They constituted the best part of that new Jewish intelligentsia in Central Europe, whose worst representatives were to be found in the offices of Ullstein and Mosse in Berlin or the *Neue Freie Presse* in Vienna. It was not their fault they were not of the people, for in these Western and Central European countries a "Jewish people" simply did not exist. Nor can they be blamed for not believing in government by the people, since the Central European countries of their birth and upbringing had no political traditions of this kind. Those countries had left their Jewries in a social, if not economic, vacuum wherein they knew the gentiles of their environment as little as they knew their fellow Jews who lived far away, beyond the borders of their own native lands. It was their moral courage, their feeling for personal honor and cleanliness in life, which more than anything else served to propagate among them the new solution of the Jewish question. With their stressing of personal salvation from a life of hollow pretenses—something more important to them than the upbuilding of Palestine (where, after all, this type of European Jew appeared in numbers only after the catastrophe of 1933)—they resembled more than they could have known their Eastern brethern. Zionism was for the former what socialism had been for the latter, and in both cases Palestine functioned as an ideal place, out of the bleak world, where one might realize one's ideals and find a personal solution for political and social conflicts. It was, indeed, this very factor of personalizing political problems which led Western Zionism to an enthusiastic acceptance of the *chaluziuth* ideal of the East. With the difference, however, that this ideal did not actually play any considerable part in the West until the arrival of Hitler. True, it was preached in the Zionist youth movement; but that movement shared with the other German pre-Hitler youth movements the fate that its ideals became only a source of tender recollections in adult life.

Western Zionists, then, were a fraction of those sons of wealthy Jewish bourgeois families who could afford to see their children through the university. Simply by so doing, and without giving the matter much thought, the wealthy Jews, mainly of Germany and Austria-Hungary, created an entirely new class in Jewish life—modern intellectuals given to the liberal professions, to art and science, without either spiritual or ideological link to Judaism. They—"das moderne gebildete, dem ghetto entwachsene, des Schachers entwoehnte Judentum" (Herzl)—had to find both their daily bread and their self-respect outside of Jewish society—"ihr Brod und ihr bisschen Ehre ausserhalb des juedischen Schachers" (Herzl); and they alone were exposed without shelter and defense to the new Jew-hatred at the turn of the century. If they did not wish to sink to the moral and intellectual level of the Ullstein-Mosse clique, nor to establish themselves as "freischwebende Intellektuelle" (Karl Mannheim), they had perforce to go back to Jewish life and find a place for themselves in the midst of their own people.

This, however, quickly proved almost as difficult as complete assimilation with self-respect. For in "the house of their fathers" (Herzl) there was no place for them. The Jewish classes, like Jewish masses, clung together socially, linked by the never-ending chain of family and business connections. Those relationships were further solidified through the charity organization to which every member of the community, though he may never in his life have entered a synagogue, gave his appropriate share. Charity, this leftover of the once autonomous Jewish communities, had proved through two hundred years strong enough to prevent the destruction of the interrelationship of the Jewish people throughout the world. As family and business connections sufficed to keep the Jewry of each country a closely knit social body, Jewish charity had come very near to organize world Jewry into a curious sort of body politic.

However, the new Jewish intellectuals had not been provided for in this undirected but nevertheless efficiently functioning organization. True, if they were lawyers and doctors—the heart's desire of all Jewish parents— they still needed Jewish social connections for their living. But for those who chose the professions of writers and journalists, of artists or scientists, of teachers or state employees—as happened frequently—there was no need of Jewish social connections, and Jewish life had no need of those intellectuals. Socially, they were outside the pale. But if they did not fit locally into the social body of emancipated Jewry, still less did they fit into the body politic of charitable world Jewry. For in this great and truly international organization one had to be either on the receiving or on the giving end in order to be accounted for as a Jew. Now, since these intellectuals were too poor to be philanthropists and too rich to become *schnorrers*, charity took as little interest in them as they could take in charity. Thus were the intellectuals excluded from the only practical way in which Western Jewry proved its solidarity with the Jewish people. The intellectuals didn't belong, either socially or politically; there was no place for them in the house of their fathers. To remain Jews at all they had to build a new house.

Zionism, hence, was destined primarily, in Western and Central Europe, to offer a solution to these men who were more assimilated than any other class of Jewry and certainly more imbued with European education and cultural values than their opponents. Precisely because they were assimilated enough to understand the structure of the modern national state, they realized the political actuality of antisemitism even if they failed to analyze it, and they wanted the same body politic for the Jewish people. The hollow word struggles between Zionism and assimilationism have completely distorted the simple fact that the Zionists, in a sense, were the only ones who sincerely wanted assimilation, that is, "normalization" of the people ("to be a people like all other peoples"), whereas the assimilationists wanted the Jewish people to retain their unique position.

In sharp contrast to their Eastern comrades, these Western Zionists were no revolutionaries at all; they neither criticized nor rebelled against the social and political conditions of their time; on the contrary, they wanted only to establish the same set of conditions for their own people. Herzl dreamed of a kind of huge transfer enterprise by which "the people without a country" was to be transported into "the country without a people"; but the people themselves were to him poor, uneducated, and irresponsible masses (an "ignorant child," as Bernard Lazare put it in his critique of Herzl), which had to be led and governed from above. Of a real popular movement Herzl spoke but once—when he wanted to frighten the Rothschilds and other philanthropists into supporting him.

VI

During the decade after Herzl's death until the outbreak of the First World War, Zionism was without any major political success. In this period Zionism developed more and more into an expression of personal affirmation, so to speak—into a type of almost religious profession which helped a man go straight and keep his head high; Zionism lost more and more of what little political impetus it had had before Herzl's death. Instead, and mostly by means of an entirely academic and theoretical critique of Jewish opposition within, it unfolded all the "ideological" elements of Herzl's writings. For the time, during the long stagnation years of the movement, these tenets had but little actual practical significance; anyway they avoided every serious issue. But if ever a fundamentally unpolitical attitude had political consequences, this one had.

First, and for the personal problems of Jewish intellectuals most important of all, was the question of antisemitism. This phenomenon—though extensively described, especially in its rather harmless social aspects—was never analyzed on its political grounds and in context with the general political situation of the time. It was explained as the natural reaction of one people against another, as though they were two natural substances destined by some mysterious natural law to antagonize each other to eternity.

This appraisal of antisemitism—as an eternal phenomenon attending inevitably the course of Jewish history through all the Diaspora countries— sometimes took more rational forms, as when interpreted with the categories of the national state. Then antisemitism could appear as "a feeling of peripheral tension" comparable to "the tension between nations . . . at the national boundaries where the constant human contacts of national elements at variance with each other tend constantly to renew the international conflict" (Kurt Blumenfeld). But even this most advanced interpretation, in which at least one aspect of Jew-hatred is correctly attributed to the national organization of peoples, still presupposes the eternity of antisemitism in an eternal world of nations and, moreover, denies the Jewish part of responsibility for existing conditions. Thereby it not only cuts off Jewish history from European history and even from the rest of mankind; it ignores the role that European Jewry played in the construction and functioning of the national state; and thus it is reduced to the assumption, as arbitrary as it is absurd, that every gentile living with Jews must become a conscious or subconscious Jew-hater.

This Zionist attitude toward antisemitism—which was held to be sound precisely because it was irrational, and therefore explained something unexplainable and avoided explaining what could be explained—led to a very dangerous misappraisal of political conditions in each country. Antisemitic parties and movements were taken at their face value, were considered genuinely representative of the whole nation, and hence not worthwhile fighting against. And since the Jewish people, still in the manner of antique nations with their own ancient traditions, divided the whole of mankind between themselves and the foreigners, the Jews and the goyim—as the Greeks divided the world between Greeks and *barbaroi*—they were only too willing to accept an unpolitical and unhistorical explanation of the hostility against them. In their estimate of antisemitism Zionists could simply fall back upon this Jewish tradition; they found little serious opposition whether they expressed themselves in half-mystical or, following the fashions of the time, in half-scientific terms, as long as they appealed to this basic Jewish attitude. They fortified the dangerous, time-honored, deep-seated distrust of Jews for gentiles.

Not less dangerous and quite in accord with this general trend was the sole new piece of historical philosophy which the Zionists contributed out of their own new experiences; "A nation is a group of people . . . held together by a common enemy" (Herzl)—an absurd doctrine containing only this bit of truth: that many Zionists had, indeed, been convinced they were Jews by the enemies of the Jewish people. Thereupon these Zionists concluded that without antisemitism the Jewish people would not have survived in the countries of the Diaspora; and hence they were opposed to any attempt to liquidate antisemitism on a large scale. On the contrary, they declared that our foes, the antisemites, "will be our most reliable friends, the antisemitic countries our allies" (Herzl). The result could only be, of course, an utter confusion in which nobody could distinguish between friend and foe, in which the foe became the friend and the friend the hidden, and therefore all the more dangerous, enemy.

Even before the Zionist Organization descended into the shameful position of joining the part of Jewry that willingly treated with its enemy, this doctrine had several not unimportant consequences.

One immediate consequence was that it made superfluous a political understanding of the part Jewish plutocracy played within the framework of national states, and its effects on the life of the Jewish people. The new Zionist definition of a nation as a group of people held together by a common enemy strengthened the general Jewish feeling that "we are all in the same boat"—which simply did not correspond to the realities. Hence the merely sporadic Zionist attacks on the Jewish powers that be remained harmless, confined to a few bitter remarks about charity, which Herzl had called the "machinery to suppress the outcries." Even such tame criticisms were silenced after 1929, the year of the formation of the Jewish Agency, when the Zionist Organization traded the hope of a larger income (which was not to be realized) against the independence of the only large Jewish organization that had ever been beyond the control of Jewish plutocracy and had ever dared to criticize the Jewish notables. In that year the true revolutionary possibilities of Zionism for Jewish life were definitely sacrificed.

In the second place, the new doctrine of nationalism influenced very strongly the Zionists' attitude toward the Soviet attempt to liquidate antisemitism without liquidating the Jews. This, it was asserted, could in the long and even short run lead only to the disappearance of Russian Jewry. It is true that today little is left of their hostility, although it still plays a role, if only a subordinate one, in the minds of that minority who are wholly tied up with Weizmann and, consequently, hostile to any influence in the Near East besides the British. We witness, rather, a new sympathy for Soviet Russia among Zionists throughout the world. So far it has remained mostly sentimental, ready to admire everything Russian; but, out of disillusionment with Great Britain's promises, there has also arisen a widespread, though politically still inarticulate, hope to see the Soviet Union take an active part in the future of the Near East. The belief in an unalterable friendship of the USSR for the Jews would, of course, be no less naïve than the former belief in England. What every political and national movement in our times should give its utmost attention to with respect to Russia—namely, its entirely new and successful approach to nationality conflicts, its new form of organizing different peoples on the basis of national equality—has been neglected by friends and foes alike.

A third political consequence of a fundamentally unpolitical attitude was the place which Palestine itself was assigned in the philosophy of Zionism. Its clearest expression may be found in Weizmann's dictum during the thirties that "the upbuilding of Palestine is our answer to antisemitism"—the absurdity of which was to be shown only a few years later, when Rommel's army threatened Palestine Jewry with exactly the same fate as in European countries. Since antisemitism was taken to be a natural corollary of nationalism, it could not be fomented, it was supposed, against that part of world Jewry established as a nation. In other words, Palestine was conceived as the place, the only place, where Jews could escape from Jew-hatred. There, in

Palestine, they would be safe from their enemies; nay, their very enemies would miraculously change into their friends.

At the core of this hope which—were ideologies not stronger for some people than realities—should by now be blown to bits, we find the old mentality of enslaved peoples, the belief that it does not pay to fight back, that one must dodge and escape in order to survive. How deep-rooted is this conviction could be seen during the first years of the war, when only through the pressure of Jews throughout the world was the Zionist Organization driven to ask for a Jewish army—which, indeed, was the only important issue in a war against Hitler. Weizmann, however, always refused to make this a major political issue, spoke deprecatingly of a "so-called Jewish army," and, after five years of war, accepted the "Jewish Brigade," which another spokesman of the Jewish Agency hastened to diminish in importance. The whole matter apparently was, for them, a question of prestige for Palestine Jewry. That an early, distinct, and demonstrable participation of Jews *as Jews* in this war would have been the decisive way to prevent the antisemitic slogan which, even before victory was won, already represented Jews as its parasites, apparently never entered their heads.

Ideologically more important was the fact that, by their interpretation of Palestine in the future life of the Jewish people, the Zionists shut themselves off from the destiny of the Jews all over the world. Their doctrine of the inevitable decline of Jewish life in the Galuth, the Diaspora the world over, made it easy for the conscience of the *yishuv*, the settlement in Palestine, to develop its attitude of aloofness. Palestine Jewry, instead of making itself the political vanguard of the whole Jewish people, developed a spirit of self-centeredness, though its preoccupation with its own affairs was veiled by its readiness to welcome refugees who would help it become a stronger factor in Palestine. While the assimilated Jewries of the Western world had pretended to ignore the strong ties which had always connected Leningrad with Warsaw, and Warsaw with Berlin, and both with Paris and London, and all together with New York, and had presumed unique unrelated conditions for each country, Zionism followed suit by pretending special conditions for Palestine, unrelated to Jewish destinies elsewhere, while at the same time generalizing adverse conditions for Jews everywhere else in the world.

This pessimism for Jewish life in any other political form, and in any other territory of the earth, seems to be unaffected in the Zionist mind by the very size of Palestine, a small country that at best can give homestead to several millions of the Jewish people but never to all the millions of Jews still remaining throughout the world. Hence only two political solutions could be envisioned. Zionists used to argue that "only the remnant will return," the best, the only ones worth saving; let us establish ourselves as the elite of the Jewish people and we shall be the only surviving Jews in the end; all that matters is our survival; let charity take care of the pressing needs of the masses, we shall not interfere; we are interested in the future of a nation, not in the fate of individuals.

But in the face of the terrible catastrophe in Europe, there are few Zionists left who would stick to their former doctrine of the necessary perishing of Galuth Jewry. Therefore the alternative solution of the problem, once preached only by Revisionists, has won the day. Now they talk the language of all extreme nationalists. To the puzzling question of how Zionism can serve as an answer to antisemitism for the Jews who remain in the Diaspora they cheerfully assert, "Pansemitism is the best answer to antisemitism."

VII

It was during and after the First World War that the Zionist attitude toward the great powers took definite shape. There had already been, however, almost since the seizure of political leadership by the Western branch in the 1890s, significant signs indicating the way the new national movement was to choose for the realization of its aims. It is well known how Herzl himself started negotiations with governments, appealing invariably to their interest in getting rid of the Jewish question through the emigration of their Jews. It is known, too, how he invariably failed, and for a simple reason: he was the only one who took the anti-Jewish agitation at its face value. Precisely those governments that indulged most in Jew-baiting were the least prepared to take his proposal seriously; they could scarcely understand a man who insisted on the spontaneity of a movement which they themselves had stirred up.

Even more significant for the future were Herzl's negotiations with the Turkish government. The Turkish Empire was one of those nationality-states based on oppression which were already doomed and, indeed, disap-

peared during the First World War. Yet the Turkish Empire was to be interested in Jewish settlements on this premise: with the Jews a new and completely loyal factor would be introduced into the Near East; and a new loyal
element would certainly help to keep down the greatest of the menaces that
threatened the imperial government from all sides: the menace of an Arab
uprising. Therefore when Herzl, during these negotiations, received cables
from students of various oppressed nationalities protesting against agreements with a government which had just slaughtered hundreds of thousands
of Armenians, he only observed: "This will be useful for me with the Sultan."

It was in this same spirit, following what had already become a tradition,
that as late as 1913 the Zionist leaders, in their reawakened hope to sway the
sultan to their side, broke off negotiations with the Arabs. Whereupon one
of the Arab leaders shrewdly remarked: "Gardez-vous bien, Messieurs les
Sionistes, un gouvernement passe, mais un peuple reste." (For this and later
references to Arab-Jewish negotiations, see M. Perlmann's "Chapters of
Arab-Jewish Diplomacy, 1918–1922," in *Jewish Social Studies*, April 1944.)

Those who are dismayed at the spectacle of a national movement that,
starting out with such an idealistic élan, sold out at the very first moment to
the powers that be; that felt no solidarity with other oppressed peoples
whose cause, though historically otherwise conditioned, was essentially the
same; that endeavored even in the morning-dream of freedom and justice to
compromise with the most evil forces of our time by taking advantage of
imperialistic interests—those who are dismayed should in fairness consider
how exceptionally difficult the conditions were for the Jews who, in contrast
to other peoples, did not even possess the territory from which to start their
fight for freedom. The alternative to the road that Herzl marked out, and
Weizmann followed through to the bitter end, would have been to organize
the Jewish people in order to negotiate on the basis of a great revolutionary
movement. This would have meant an alliance with all progressive forces in
Europe; it would certainly have involved great risks. The only man within
the Zionist Organization known to have ever considered this way was the
great French Zionist Bernard Lazare, the friend of Charles Péguy—and he
had to resign from the Organization at the early date of 1899. From then on
no responsible Zionist trusted the Jewish people for the necessary political
strength of will to achieve freedom instead of being transported to freedom;

thus no official Zionist leader dared to side with the revolutionary forces in Europe.

Instead, the Zionists went on seeking the protection of the great powers, trying to trade it against possible services. They realized that what they could offer must conform to the interests of the governments. In the consequent subservience to British policy, which is associated with Weizmann's unswerving loyalty to the cause of the British Empire in the Near East, the Zionists were abetted by sheer ignorance of the new imperialist forces at work. Though these forces had been active ever since the 1880s, they had begun to show clearly in all their intricacies only at the beginning of the twentieth century. Since theirs was a national movement, the Zionists could think only in national terms, seemingly unaware of the fact that imperialism was a nation-destroying force, and therefore, for a small people, it was near-suicide to attempt to become its ally or its agent. Nor have they even yet realized that protection by these interests supports a people as the rope supports for hanging. When challenged by opponents, the Zionists would answer that British national interests and Jewish national interests happen to be identical and therefore this is a case not of protection but of alliance. It is rather hard to see what national, and not imperial, interest England could possibly have in the Near East—though it has never been hard to foretell that; till we achieve the bliss of messianic times, an alliance between a lion and a lamb can have disastrous consequences for the lamb.

Opposition from within the ranks of Zionists themselves never gained enough numerical strength to offset the official political line; moreover, any such opposition always showed itself hesitant in action, uneasy and weak in argument, as though it were insecure in thought as well as in conscience. Such leftist groups as Hashomer Haza'ir—which have a radical program for world politics, so radical that, at the beginning of this war, they even opposed it on the ground of its being an "imperialist war"—express themselves only by abstention when it comes to vital questions of Palestine foreign policy. In other words, they sometimes, in spite of the undoubted personal integrity of most of their members, give the all too familiar impression of leftist groups of other countries, that hide under official protests their secret relief at having the majority parties do the dirty work for them.

This uneasiness of conscience, widespread among other leftist groups and explainable by the general bankruptcy of socialism, is among Zionists older than the general conditions and points to other and more special reasons. Since the days of Borochov, whose adherents can still be found in the small sectarian group of Poale-Zion, the leftist Zionists never thought of developing any answer of their own to the national question: they simply added official Zionism to their socialism. This addition hasn't made for an amalgam, since it claims socialism for domestic and nationalist Zionism for foreign affairs. The result is the existing situation between Jews and Arabs.

In fact, the uneasiness of conscience dates from the days of the surprising discovery that within the very domestic field, in the upbuilding of Palestine, there were factors present of foreign policy—by the existence of "a foreign people." Since that time Jewish labor has fought against Arab labor under the pretense of class struggle against the Jewish planters, who certainly did employ Arabs for capitalist reasons. During this fight—which more than anything else, up to 1936, poisoned the Palestine atmosphere—no attention was paid to the economic conditions of the Arabs, who, through the introduction of Jewish capital and labor and the industrialization of the country, found themselves changed overnight into potential proletarians, without much chance of finding the corresponding work positions. Instead, Zionist labor repeated the true but wholly inadequate arguments regarding the feudal character of Arab society, the progressive character of capitalism, and the general rise of the Palestine standard of life shared in by the Arabs. How blind people can become if their real or supposed interests are at stake is shown by the preposterous slogan they used: although Jewish labor fought as much for its economic position as for its national aim, the cry was always for *Avodah Ivrith* (Jewish Labor); and one had to peer behind the scenes to detect that their chief menace was not simply Arab labor but, more actually, *avodah zolah* (cheap labor), represented, it is true, by the unorganized, backward Arab worker.

In the resulting pickets of Jewish workers against Arab workers the leftist groups, most important among them Hashomer Haza'ir, did not directly participate; but they did little else: they remained abstentionists. The consequent local troubles, the latent internal war which has been going on in Palestine since the early twenties, interrupted by more and more frequent outbreaks, in turn strengthened the attitude of official Zionism. The less able was Palestine Jewry to find allies among the neighbors, the more the Zionists had to look upon Great Britain as the great protecting power.

Outstanding among the reasons why labor and left-wing groups consented to this policy is again the general outlook of Zionism they had accepted. With an eye only for "the unique character" of Jewish history, insisting on the unparalleled nature of Jewish political conditions which were held to be unrelated to any other factors in European history and politics, the Zionists had ideologically placed the center of the Jewish people's existence outside the pale of European peoples and outside the destiny of the European continent.

Among all the misconceptions harbored by the Zionist movement because it had been influenced so strongly by antisemitism, this false notion of the non-European character of the Jews has had probably the most far-reaching and the worst consequences. Not only did the Zionists break the necessary solidarity of European peoples—necessary not only for the weak but for the strong as well—incredibly, they would even deprive the Jews of the only historical and cultural homestead they possibly can have; for Palestine together with the whole Mediterranean basin has always belonged to the European continent: geographically, historically, culturally, if not at all times politically. Thus the Zionists would deprive the Jewish people of its just share in the roots and development of what we generally call Western culture. Indeed, the attempts were numerous to interpret Jewish history as the history of an Asiatic people that had been driven by misfortune into a foreign comity of nations and culture wherein, regarded as an eternal stranger, it could never feel at home. (The absurdity of this kind of argumentation could be proved by citing the example of the Hungarian people alone: the Hungarians were of Asiatic origin, but had always been accepted as members of the European family since they were Christianized.) Yet no serious attempt was ever made to integrate the Jewish people into the pattern of Asiatic politics, for that could only mean an alliance with the national revolutionary peoples of Asia and participation in their struggle against imperialism. In the official Zionist conception, it seems, the Jewish people is uprooted from its European background and left somehow in the air, while Palestine is a place in the moon where such footless aloofness may be realized.

Only in its Zionist variant has such a crazy isolationism gone to the extreme of escape from Europe altogether. But its underlying national philosophy is far more general; indeed, it has been the ideology of most Central European national movements. It is nothing else than the uncritical acceptance of German-inspired nationalism. This holds a nation to be an eternal organic body, the product of inevitable natural growth of inherent qualities; and it explains peoples, not in terms of political organizations, but in terms of biological superhuman personalities. In this conception European history is split up into the stories of unrelated organic bodies, and the grand French idea of the sovereignty of the people is perverted into the nationalist claims to autarchical existence. Zionism, closely tied up with that tradition of nationalist thinking, never bothered much about sovereignty of the people, which is the prerequisite for the formation of a nation, but wanted from the beginning that utopian nationalist independence.

To such an independence, it was believed, the Jewish nation could arrive under the protecting wings of any great power strong enough to shelter its growth. Paradoxical as it may sound, it was precisely because of this nationalist misconception of the inherent independence of a nation that the Zionists ended by making the Jewish national emancipation entirely dependent upon the material interests of another nation.

The actual result was a return of the new movement to the traditional methods of *shtadlonus*, which the Zionists once had so bitterly despised and violently denounced. Now Zionists too knew no better place politically than the lobbies of the powerful, and no sounder basis for agreements than their good services as agents of foreign interests. It was in the interest of foreign powers that the so-called Weizmann-Feisal agreement was "allowed to pass into oblivion until 1936. It also stands to reason that British apprehension and compromise was behind the tacit abandonment. . . ." (Perlmann, "Chapters of Arab-Jewish Diplomacy"). When in 1922 new Arab-Jewish negotiations took place, the British ambassador in Rome was kept fully informed, with the result that the British asked a postponement until "the Mandate has been conferred"; the Jewish representative, Asher Saphir, held "little doubt that members of a certain political school took the view that it was not in the interest of the peaceful administration of Near and Middle Eastern territories that the two Semitic races . . . should cooperate again on the platform of the recognition of Jewish rights in Palestine" (Perlmann). From then onward Arab hostility has grown year by year; and Jewish dependence on British protection has become so desperate a need that one may well call it a curious case of voluntary unconditional surrender.

VIII

This, then, is the tradition to fall back upon in times of crisis and emergency like ours—these the political weapons with which to handle the new political situation of tomorrow, these the "ideological categories" to utilize the new experiences of the Jewish people. Up to now no new approaches, no new insights, no reformulation of Zionism or the demands of the Jewish people have been visible. And it is therefore only in the light of this past, with consideration of this present, that we can gauge the chances of the future.

One new factor, however, should be noted, although so far it has not brought about anything like a fundamental change. It is the tremendously increased importance of American Jewry and American Zionism within the World Zionist Organization. Never before has any Jewry of any country produced such a large number of members of the Zionist Organization, together an even larger number of sympathizers. Indeed, the platforms of both the Democratic and Republican parties last year, the declarations of both President Roosevelt and Governor Dewey at election time, would seem to prove that the great majority of voting Jews in America are regarded as pro-Palestinians and that, so far as there is "a Jewish vote," it is influenced by the program for Palestine to the same degree as the Polish vote is influenced by American foreign policy toward Poland and the Italian vote by events in Italy.

The Zionism of the American Jewish masses, however, differs remarkably from Zionism in the countries of the old continent. The men and women who are members of the Zionist Organization here would have been found in Europe in the so-called pro-Palestine committees. In those committees were organized the people who held Palestine to be a good solution for oppressed and poor Jews, the best of all philanthropic enterprises, but who never considered Palestine to be a solution for their own problems, the very existence of which they were rather inclined to deny. At the same time, most of those who here in America call themselves non-Zionists also have a pronounced tendency toward this pro-Palestine view; at any rate, they take a much more positive and constructive attitude toward the Palestine enterprise, and for the rights of the Jewish people as a people, than did the "assimilants" in Europe.

The reason is to be found in the political structure of the United States, which is not a national state in the European sense of the word. A vital interest in Palestine as the homeland of the Jewish people is only natural, needs no excuses, in a country where so many national splinter groups show loyalty to their mother countries. Indeed, a Jewish mother country might thus rather tend to "normalize" the situation of the Jews in America and be a good argument against political antisemitism.

However, this "normalization," inherent in pro-Palestinism, would instantly be thrown into reverse if Zionism in the official sense of the term were to get hold of American Jews. Then they would have to start a really national movement, at least preach if not actually practice *chaluziuth* (pioneering and self-realization); they would have to insist in principle on *aliyah* (immigration to Zion) for every Zionist. In fact, Weizmann has recently called on American Jews to come and settle in Palestine. The old question of double loyalty would emerge again, in a more violent form than in any other country, because of the multinational structure of the United States. Just because the American body politic can afford a far greater tolerance for community life of the numerous nationalities which all together form and determine the life of the American nation, this country could never permit one of these "splinter groups" to start a movement to take them away from the American continent. The argument once heard in European Zionist discussions that, after all, the European countries could get along very well without their Jews, whereas the Jewish people needs to reclaim its best sons, can never be valid here. On the contrary, it would set a dangerous precedent; it could easily serve to upset the balance of a community of peoples who need to get along with each other within the limits of the American constitution and on the territory of the American continent. It is for this reason—because of the acute menace of any outright national movement for the constitution of a nationality-state—that the Zionist movement has been so bitterly opposed in Soviet Russia.

Probably on account of this unique position of theirs in the World Zionist Organization, their vague if not explicit consciousness of it, American Zionists have not attempted to change the general ideological outlook. That is held to be good enough for European Jews, who, after all, are the principal ones concerned. Instead, American Zionists have simply taken the pragmatic stand of the Palestine maximalists, and hope—together with them, though for more complex reasons—that American interest and power will at least equal the British influence in the Near East. This would, of course, be the best way to solve all their problems. If Palestine Jewry could be charged with a share in the caretaking of American interests in that part of the world, the famous dictum of Justice Brandeis would indeed come true: you would have to be a Zionist in order to be a perfect American patriot. And why should this good fortune not come to pass? Has it not been for more than twenty-five years the foundation of British Zionism that one had to be a good Zionist to be a good British patriot—that by supporting the Balfour Declaration one supported the very government whose loyal subject one was? We should be prepared to see a similar, though government-inspired, "Zionism" among Russian Jewry, if and when Soviet Russia takes up her old claims to Near Eastern politics. Should this happen it will quickly enough become clear to what an extent Zionism has inherited the burden of assimilationist politics.

It must be admitted, however, that while the question of present and future power politics in the Near East is very much in the foreground today, the political realities and experiences of the Jewish people are very much in the background, and they have only too little connection with the main movements in the world. But the new experiences of Jewry are as numerous as the fundamental changes in the world are tremendous; and the chief question to be addressed to Zionism is how well it is prepared to take both into consideration and act accordingly.

IX

The most important new experience of the Jewish people is again concerned with antisemitism. It is a matter of record that the Zionist outlook for the future of emancipated Jewry has always been dark, and Zionists occasionally boast of their foresight. Compared with the earthquake that has shaken the world in our time, those predictions read like prophecies of a storm in a teacup. The fierce outburst of popular hatred which Zionism predicted, and which fitted well with its general distrust of the peoples and overconfidence in governments, did not take place. Rather, in a number of countries it was replaced by concerted government action, which proved infinitely more detrimental than any popular outburst of Jew-hatred had ever been.

The point is that antisemitism, in Europe at least, has been discovered as the best political, and not merely demagogic, weapon of imperialism. Wherever politics are centered around the race concept, the Jews will be in the center of hostility. It would lead us too far here to ask the reasons for this entirely new state of affairs. But one thing is certain. Inasmuch as imperialism—in sharp contrast to nationalism—does not think in terms of limited territories but, as the saying goes, "in continents," Jews will be secure from this new type of antisemitism nowhere in the world, and certainly not in Palestine, one of the crossroads of imperialist interests. The question to be asked of Zionists today would therefore be what political stand they propose to take in view of a hostility that is far less concerned with dispersed Jewish individuals than with the people as a whole, no matter where it happens to live.

Another question to be asked of Zionists concerns national organization. We have been seeing the catastrophic decline of the national-state system in our time. The new feeling that has grown among European peoples since the first war is that the national state is neither capable of protecting the existence of the nation nor able to guarantee the sovereignty of the people. The national border lines, once the very symbol of security against invasion as well as against an unwelcome overflow of foreigners, have proved to be no longer of any real avail. And while the old Western nations were threatened either by lack of manpower and the resulting lag in industrialization or by an influx of foreigners they could not assimilate, the Eastern countries gave the best possible examples that the national state cannot exist with a mixed population.

For Jews, however, there is only too little reason for rejoicing in the decline of the national state and of nationalism. We cannot foretell the next steps of human history, but the alternatives seem to be clear. The resurgent problem of how to organize politically will be solved by adopting either the form of empires or the form of federations. The latter would give the Jewish people, together with other small peoples, a reasonably fair chance for survival. The former may not be possible without arousing imperialist passions as a substitute for outdated nationalism, once the motor to set men into action. Heaven help us if that comes to pass.

X

It is within this general framework of realities and possibilities that the Zionists propose to solve the Jewish question by means of a national state. Yet the essential characteristic of a national state, sovereignty, is not even hoped for. Suppose the Zionists had succeeded twenty-five years ago in securing Palestine as a Jewish commonwealth: what would have happened? We should have seen the Arabs turn against the Jews as the Slovaks turned against the Czechs in Czechoslovakia, and the Croats against the Serbs in Yugoslavia. And though not a single Arab were left in Palestine, the lack of real sovereignty amid Arab states, or peoples hostile to the Jewish state, would have had exactly the same result.

In other words, the slogan of a Jewish commonwealth or Jewish state actually means that. Jews propose to establish themselves from the very beginning as a "sphere of interest" under the delusion of nationhood. Either a binational Palestine state or a Jewish commonwealth might conceivably have been the outcome of a working agreement with Arabs and other Mediterranean peoples. But to think that by putting the cart before the horse one can solve genuine conflicts between peoples is a fantastic assumption. The erection of a Jewish state within an imperial sphere of interest may look like a very nice solution to some Zionists, though to others as something desperate but unavoidable. In the long run, there is hardly any course imaginable that would be more dangerous, more in the style of an adventure. It is, indeed, very bad luck for a small people to be placed without any fault of its own in the territory of a "sphere of interest," though one can hardly see where else it could be placed in the economically and politically shrunken world of today. But only folly could dictate a policy which trusts a distant imperial power for protection, while alienating the goodwill of neighbors. What then, one is prompted to ask, will be the future policy of Zionism with respect to big powers, and what program have Zionists to offer for a solution of the Arab-Jewish conflict?

In this connection there is a further question. The most optimistic estimates hope for annual postwar emigration from Europe to Palestine of about 100,000 Jews, during at least ten years. Assuming this can be brought about, what is to happen to those who are not in the first groups of immigrants?

What status are they to have in Europe? What kind of social, economic, political life will they lead? Zionists apparently hope for restoration of the status quo ante. In that case, will the restored Jews be willing to go to Palestine after, say, a period of five years which, even under the darkest circumstances, would mean a period of normalization? For if European Jews are not at once claimed as the prospective citizens of the new Jewish commonwealth (to say nothing of the question of their admission), there will be the additional trouble of claiming majority rights in a country where Jews are very clearly a minority. Such a claim, on the other hand, if granted, would of course exclude a restoration of the status quo in Europe, and thus possibly create a not entirely harmless precedent. Even the most superficial restoration of the status quo in Europe would still make it well-nigh impossible to cloud the double loyalty issue with the same meaningless generalities as in the good old days of the past.

The last question, then, which Zionism has so far succeeded in not answering, solemnly protesting that an answer would be "beneath its dignity," is this old problem of the relationship between the proposed new state and the Diaspora. And this problem is by no means restricted to European Jewries.

It is a matter of record, ideologies notwithstanding, that up to now the *yishuv* had been not only an asylum for persecuted Jews from some Diaspora countries. It is also a community which has had to be supported by other Diaspora Jewries. Without the power and resources of American Jewry, above all, the catastrophe in Europe would have been a deadly blow to Palestine Jewry, politically as well as economically. If a Jewish commonwealth is obtained in the near future—with or without partition—it will be due to the political influence of American Jews. This would not need to affect their status of American citizenship if their "homeland," or "mother country," were a politically autonomous entity in a normal sense, or if their help were likely to be only temporary. But if the Jewish commonwealth is proclaimed against the will of the Arabs and without the support of the Mediterranean peoples, not only financial help but political support will be necessary for a long time to come. And that may turn out to be very troublesome indeed for Jews in this country, who after all have no power to direct the political destinies of the Near East. It may eventually be far more of a responsibility than today they imagine or tomorrow can make good.

These are some of the questions Zionism will face in the very near future. To answer them sincerely, with political sense and responsibility, Zionism will have to reconsider its whole obsolete set of doctrines. It will not be easy either to save the Jews or to save Palestine in the twentieth century; that it can be done with categories and methods of the nineteenth century seems at the very most highly improbable. If Zionists persevere in retaining their sectarian ideology and continue with their shortsighted "realism," they will have forfeited even the small chances that small peoples still have in this none too beautiful world of ours.

1944

Note

1. This program was confirmed by the World Zionist Conference held in London in August 1945.

THE JEWISH STATE:
Fifty Years After, Where Have Herzl's Politics Led?

Rereading Herzl's *The Jewish State* today is a peculiar experience. One becomes aware that those things in it that Herzl's own contemporaries would have called utopian now actually determine the ideology and policies of the Zionist movement; while those of Herzl's practical proposals for the building of a Jewish homeland which must have appeared quite realistic fifty years ago have had no influence whatsoever.

The last is all the more surprising because these practical proposals are far from antiquated even for our own age. Herzl proposed a "Jewish Company" that would build a state with "Relief by Labor"—that is, by paying a "good-for-nothing beggar" charity rates for forced full-time work—and by the "truck system" consisting of labor gangs "drafted from place to place like a body of troops" and paid in goods instead of wages. Herzl was also determined to suppress all "opposition" in case of lack of gratitude on the part of people to whom the land would be given. All this sounds only too familiar. And it is altogether to the honor of the Jewish people that nobody—as far as I know—ever discussed these "realistic" proposals seriously, and that Palestinian reality has turned out to be almost the opposite of what Herzl dreamed.

The above features of Herzl's program, though happily forgotten in the present political state of affairs in Palestine, are nevertheless significant. For all their innocence, they show to which category of politician in the framework of European history Herzl belonged. When he wrote *The Jewish State* Herzl was deeply convinced that he was under some sort of higher inspiration, yet at the same time he was earnestly afraid of making a fool of himself. This extreme self-esteem mixed with self-doubt is not a rare phenomenon; it is usually the sign of the "crackpot." And in a sense this Viennese, whose style, manner, and ideals hardly differed from those of his more obscure fellow journalists, was indeed a crackpot.

But even in Herzl's time—the time of the Dreyfus affair, when the crackpots were just embarking on their political careers in many movements, functioning outside the parliaments and the regular parties—even then they were already in closer touch with the subterranean currents of history and the deep desires of the folk than were all the sane leaders of affairs with their balanced outlooks and utterly uncomprehending mentalities. The crackpots were already beginning to be prominent everywhere—the antisemites Stoecker and Ahlwardt in Germany, Schoenerer and Lueger in Austria, and Drumont and Déroulède in France.

Herzl wrote *The Jewish State* under the direct and violent impact of these new political forces. And he was among the first to estimate correctly their chances of ultimate success. Even more important, however, than the correctness of his forecast was the fact that he was not altogether out of sympathy with the new movements. When he said, "I believe that I understand antisemitism," he meant that he not only understood historical causes and political constellations, but also that he understood—and to a certain extent, correctly—the man who hated Jews. It is true, his frequent appeals to "honest antisemites" to "subscribe small amounts" to the national fund for the establishment of a Jewish state were not very realistic; and he was equally unrealistic when he invited them "whilst preserving their independence [to] combine with our officials in controlling the transfer of our estates" from the Diaspora to the Jewish homeland; and he frequently asserted, in all innocence, that antisemites would be the Jews' best friends and antisemitic governments their best allies. But this faith in antisemites expressed very eloquently and even touchingly how close his own state of mind was to that of his hostile environment and how intimately he did belong to the "alien" world.

With the demagogic politicians of his own and more recent times, Herzl shared both a contempt for the masses and a very real affinity with them. And like these same politicians, he was more an incarnation than a representative of the strata of society to which he belonged. He did more than "love" or simply speak for the new and ever-increasing class of Jewish "intellects that we produce so super-abundantly and that are persecuted everywhere"; he did more than merely discern in these intellectuals the real *Luftmenschen* of

Western Jewry—that is, Jews who, though economically secure, had no place in either Jewish or gentile society and whose personal problems could be solved only by a reorientation of the Jewish people as a whole. Herzl actually incarnated these Jewish intellectuals in himself in the sense that everything he said or did was exactly what they would have, had they shown an equal amount of moral courage in revealing their inmost secret thoughts.

Another trait Herzl shared with the leaders of the new antisemitic movements by whose hostility he was so deeply impressed was the furious will to action at any price—action, however, that was to be conducted according to certain supposedly immutable and inevitable laws and inspired and supported by invincible natural forces. Herzl's conviction that he was in alliance with history and nature themselves saved him from the suspicion that he himself might have been insane. Antisemitism was an overwhelming force and the Jews would have either to make use of it or to be swallowed up by it. In his own words, antisemitism was the "propelling force" responsible for all Jewish suffering since the destruction of the Temple and it would continue to make the Jews suffer until they learned how to use it for their own advantage. In expert hands this "propelling force" would prove the most salutary factor in Jewish life: it would be used the same way that boiling water is used to produce steam power.

This mere will to action was something so startlingly new, so utterly revolutionary in Jewish life, that it spread with the speed of wildfire. Herzl's lasting greatness lay in his very desire to do something about the Jewish question, his desire to act and to solve the problem in political terms.

During the twenty centuries of their Diaspora the Jews have made only two attempts to change their condition by direct political action. The first was the Shabbetai Tzevi movement, the mystic-political movement for the salvation of Jewry which terminated the Jewish Middle Ages and brought about a catastrophe whose consequences determined Jewish attitudes and basic convictions for over two centuries thereafter. In preparing as they did to follow Shabbetai Tzevi, the self-appointed "Messiah," back to Palestine in the mid-1600s, the Jews assumed that their ultimate hope of a messianic millennium was about to be realized. Until Shabbetai Tzevi's time they had been able to conduct their communal affairs by means of a politics that existed in the realm of imagination alone—the memory of a far-off past and the hope of a far-off future. With the Shabbetai Tzevi movement these centuries-old memories and hopes culminated in a single exalted moment. Its catastrophical aftermath brought to a close—probably forever—the period in which religion alone could provide the Jews with a firm framework within which to satisfy their political, spiritual, and everyday needs. The attendant disillusionment was lasting insofar as from then on their religion no longer afforded the Jews an adequate means of evaluating and dealing with contemporary events, political or otherwise. Whether a Jew was pious or not, whether he kept the Law or lived outside its fence, he was henceforth to judge secular events on a secular basis and make secular decisions in secular terms.

Jewish secularization culminated at last in a second attempt to dissolve the Diaspora. This was the rise of the Zionist movement.

The mere fact that a catastrophe had thrown the Jews from the two extremes of the past and the future into the middle ground of the present does not signify that they had now become "realistic." To be confronted by reality does not automatically produce an understanding of reality or make one feel at home in it. On the contrary, the process of secularization made Jews even less "realistic"—that is, less capable than ever before of facing and understanding the real situation. In losing their faith in a divine beginning and ultimate culmination of history, the Jews lost their guide through the wilderness of bare facts; for when man is robbed of all means of interpreting events he is left with no sense whatsoever of reality. The present that confronted the Jews after the Shabbetai Tzevi debacle was the turmoil of a world whose course no longer made sense and in which, as a result, the Jews could no longer find a place.

The need for a guide or key to history was felt by all Jews alike. But by the nineteenth century it was a need that was not at all specific to the Jews alone. In this context Zionism can be included among the many "isms" of that period, each of which claimed to explain reality and predict the future in terms of irresistible laws and forces. Yet the case of the Jews was and still remains different. What they needed was not only a guide to reality, but reality itself; not simply a key to history, but the experience itself of history.

As I have just indicated, this need of reality had existed since the collapse of the Shabbetai Tzevi movement and the disappearance of messianic hope as a lively factor in the consciousness of the Jewish masses. But it became an effective force only at the end of the nineteenth century, mainly because of two entirely separate factors whose coincidence produced Zionism and formed Herzl's ideology.

The first of these factors had little to do, essentially, with Jewish history. It so happened that in the 1880s antisemitism sprang up as a political force simultaneously in Russia, Germany, Austria, and France. The pogroms of 1881 in Russia set in motion that huge migratory movement from East to West which remained the most characteristic single feature of modern Jewish history until 1933. Moreover, the emergence of political antisemitism at exactly the same moment in both Central and Western Europe and the support, if not leadership, given it by sizable sections of the European intelligentsia refuted beyond doubt the traditional liberal contention that Jew-hatred was only a remnant of the so-called Dark Ages.

But even more important for the political history of the Jewish people was the fact that the westward migration—despite the objections to the *"Ostju-den"* so loudly voiced by the emancipated Jews of the West—brought together the two main sections of Jewry, laid the foundation for a new feeling of solidarity—at least among the moral elite—and taught both Eastern and Western Jews to see their situation in identical terms. The Russian Jew who came to Germany in flight from persecution discovered that Enlightenment had not extinguished violent Jew-hatred, and the German Jew who saw the homelessness of his Eastern brother began to view his own situation in a different light.

The second factor responsible for the rise of Zionism was entirely Jewish—it was the emergence of a class entirely new to Jewish society, the intellectuals, of whom Herzl became the main spokesman and whom he himself termed the class of "average *(durchschnittliche)* intellects." These intellectuals resembled their brethren in the more traditional Jewish occupations insofar as they, too, were entirely de-Judaized in respect to culture and religion. What distinguished them was that they no longer lived in a cultural vacuum; they had actually become "assimilated": they were not only de-Judaized, they were also Westernized. This, however, did not make for their social adjustment. Although gentile society did not receive them on equal terms, they had no place in Jewish society either, because they did not fit into its atmosphere of business and family connections.

The psychological result of their situation was to make these Jewish intellectuals the first Jews in history capable of understanding antisemitism on its own political terms, and even to make them susceptible to the deeper and more basic political attitudes of which antisemitism was but one expression among others.

The two classic pamphlets of Zionist literature, Pinsker's *Auto-emancipation* and Herzl's *The Jewish State*, were written by members of this new Jewish class. For the first time Jews saw themselves as a people through the eyes of the nations: "To the living the Jew is a corpse, to the native a foreigner, to the homesteader a vagrant, to the proprietor a beggar, to the poor an exploiter and millionaire, to the patriot a man without a country, to all a hated rival"— this was the characteristically precise and sober way Pinsker put it. Both Herzl and Pinsker identified the Jewish question in all its aspects and connections with the fact of antisemitism, which both conceived of as the natural reaction of all peoples, always and everywhere, to the very existence of Jews. As Pinsker put it, and as both believed, the Jewish question could be solved only by "finding a means of reintegrating this exclusive element in the family of nations so that the basis of the Jewish question would be permanently removed."

What still is Zionism's advantage over assimilationism is that it placed the whole question on a political level from the very beginning and asked for this "readjustment" in political terms. The assimilationists sought readjustment no less desperately, but spent their energies in founding innumerable vocational training societies for Jews, without, however, having the least power to force Jews to change their occupations. The intellectual followers of assimilationism carefully avoided political issues and invented the "salt of the earth" theory, making it quite clear that they would prefer the crudest secularization of the Jewish religious concept of chosenness to any radical redefinition of the Jewish position in the world of nations.

In other words, the great advantage of the Zionists' approach lay in the fact that their will to convert the Jews into a "nation like all other nations" saved them from falling into that Jewish brand of chauvinism automatically produced by secularization, which somehow persuades the average de-Judaized Jew that, although he no longer believes in a God who chooses or rejects, he is still a superior being simply because he happened to be born a Jew—the salt of the earth, or the motor of history.

The Zionist will to action, to come to grips with reality, embodied a second advantage—this time over the internationalist and revolutionary approach to the Jewish question. This approach, no less than assimilationist chauvinism, was the consequence of the secularization of religious attitudes. But it was not initiated by average Jews, rather by an elite. Having lost their hope of a messianic millennium that would bring about the final reconciliation of all peoples, these Jews transferred their hopes to the progressive forces of history which would solve the Jewish question automatically, along with all other injustices. Revolutions in the social systems of other peoples would create a mankind without classes and nations; the Jews together with their problems would be dissolved in this new mankind—at the end of days somehow. What happened in the meantime did not count so much; Jews would have to suffer as a matter of course along with all other persecuted classes and peoples.

The Zionists' fight against this spurious selflessness—which could only arouse suspicion as to the ultimate aims and motives of a policy that expected one's own people to behave like saints and to make the chief sacrifices—has been of great importance because it tried to teach the Jews to solve their problems by their own efforts, not by those of others.

But this struggle hardly enters the picture of Herzl's Zionism. He had a blind hatred of all revolutionary movements as such and an equally blind faith in the goodness and stability of the society of his times. The aspect of Zionism here in question received its best expression in the writings of the great French Jewish writer, Bernard Lazare. Lazare wanted to be a revolutionary among his own people, not among others, and could find no place in Herzl's essentially reactionary movement.

Yet in considering Herzl's movement as a whole and in assessing his definite merits within the given historical situation, it is necessary to say that Zionism opposed a comparatively sound nationalism to the hidden chauvinism of assimilationism and a relatively sound realism to the obvious utopianism of Jewish radicals.

However, the more ideological and utopian elements expressed in *The Jewish State* had greater influence in the long run on the formulations and practice of Zionism than did the undeniable assets set forth above. Herzl's will to reality at any price rested on a view that held reality to be an unchanging and unchangeable structure, always identical with itself. In this reality he saw little else but eternally established nation-states arrayed compactly against the Jews on one side, and on the other side the Jews themselves, in dispersion and eternally persecuted. Nothing else mattered: differences in class structure, differences between political parties or movements, between various countries or various periods of history, did not exist for Herzl. All that did exist were unchanging bodies of people viewed as biological organisms mysteriously endowed with eternal life; these bodies breathed an unchanging hostility toward the Jews that was ready to take the form of pogroms or persecution at any moment. Any segment of reality that could not be defined by antisemitism was not taken into account and any group that could not be definitely classed as antisemitic was not taken seriously as a political force.

Jewish political action meant for Herzl finding a place within the unchanging structure of this reality, a place where Jews would be safe from hatred and eventual persecution. A people without a country would have to escape to a country without a people; there the Jews, unhampered by relations with other nations, would be able to develop their own isolated organism.

Herzl thought in terms of nationalism inspired from German sources—as opposed to the French variety, which could never quite repudiate its original relationship to the political ideas of the French Revolution. He did not realize that the country he dreamed of did not exist, that there was no place on earth where a people could live like the organic national body he had in mind, and that the real historical development of a nation does not take place inside the closed walls of a biological entity. And even if there had been a country without a people and even if questions of foreign policy had not arisen in Palestine itself, Herzl's brand of political philosophy would still have given rise to serious difficulties in the relations of the new Jewish state with other nations.

Even more unrealistic but just as influential was Herzl's belief that the establishment of a Jewish state would automatically wipe out antisemitism. This belief was based on his assumption of the essential honesty and sincerity of the antisemites, in whom he saw nothing but nationalists pure and simple. This point of view may have been appropriate before the end of the nineteenth century, when antisemitism did actually derive more or less from the feeling that Jews were strangers within any given homogeneous society. But by Herzl's own time antisemitism had become transformed into a political weapon of a new kind and was supported by the new sect of racists whose loyalties and hatreds did not stop at national boundaries.

The fault in Herzl's approach to antisemitism lay in the fact that the anti-semites he had in view were hardly extant anymore—or if they were, they no longer determined antisemitic politics. The real antisemites had become dishonest and wanted to preserve the availability of the Jews as a scapegoat in case of domestic difficulties; or else, if they were "honest," they wanted to exterminate the Jews wherever they happened to live. There was no escape from either variety of antisemite into a promised land "whose upbuilding"—in Weizmann's words—"would be the answer to antisemitism."

The building up of Palestine is indeed a great accomplishment and could be made an important and even decisive argument for Jewish claims in Palestine—at least a better and more convincing one than the current pleas that argue our desperate situation in Europe and the justifiability, therefore, of the "lesser injustice" that would be done to the Arabs. But the upbuilding of Palestine has little to do with answering the antisemites; at most it has "answered" the secret self-hatred and lack of self-confidence on the part of those Jews who have themselves consciously or unconsciously succumbed to some parts of antisemitic propaganda.

The third thesis of Herzl's political philosophy was the Jewish state. Though for Herzl himself this was certainly the most daring and attractive facet of the whole, the demand for a state seemed neither doctrinaire nor utopian at the time his book was first published. In Herzl's view reality could hardly express itself in any other form than that of the nation-state. In his period, indeed, the claim for national self-determination of peoples was almost self-evident justice as far as the oppressed peoples of Europe were concerned, and so there was nothing absurd or wrong in a demand made by Jews for the same kind of emancipation and freedom. And that the whole structure of sovereign national states, great and small, would crumble within another fifty years under imperialist expansion and in the face of a new power situation, was more than Herzl could have foreseen. His demand for a state has been made utopian only by more recent Zionist policy—which did not ask for a state at a time when it might have been granted by everybody, but did ask for one only when the whole concept of national sovereignty had become a mockery.

Justified as Herzl's demand for a Jewish state may have been in his own time, his way of advancing it showed the same unrealistic touch as elsewhere. The opportunism with which he carried on his negotiations to this end stemmed from a political concept that saw the destinies of the Jews as completely without connection with the destinies of other nations, and saw Jewish demands as unrelated to all other events and trends. Although the demand for a state could be understood in his period only in terms of national self-determination, Herzl was very careful not to tie the claims for Jewish liberation to the claims of other peoples. He was even ready to profit by the minority troubles of the Turkish Empire: he offered the rulers of that empire Jewish aid in coping with them. In this instance Herzl's was the classic example of a policy hard-boiled enough to seem "realistic," but in reality completely utopian because it failed to take into account either one's own or the other party's relative strength.

The constant miscalculations that were to become so characteristic of Zionist policy are not accidental. The universality with which Herzl applied his concept of antisemitism to all non-Jewish peoples made it impossible from the very beginning for the Zionists to seek truly loyal allies. His notion of reality as an eternal, unchanging hostile structure—all goyim everlastingly against all Jews—made the identification of hard-boiledness with realism plausible because it rendered any empirical analysis of actual political factors seemingly superfluous. All one had to do was use the "propelling force of antisemitism," which, like "the wave of the future," would bring the Jews into the promised land.

Today reality has become a nightmare. Looked at through the eyes of Herzl, who from the outside sought a place inside reality into which the Jews could fit and where at the same time they could isolate themselves from it—looked at in this way, reality is horrible beyond the scope of the human imagination and hopeless beyond the strength of human despair. Only when we come to feel ourselves part and parcel of a world in which we, like everybody else, are engaged in a struggle against great and sometimes overwhelming odds, and yet with a chance of victory, however small, and with allies, however few—only when we recognize the human background against which recent events have taken place, knowing that what was done was done by men and therefore can and must be prevented by men—only then will we be able to rid the world of its nightmarish quality. That quality taken in itself and viewed from the outside—by people who consider themselves as cut off from the nightmarish world in principle and who are thus ready to accept the course of that world "realistically"—can inhibit all action and exclude us altogether from the human community.

Herzl's picture of the Jewish people as surrounded and forced together by a world of enemies has in our day conquered the Zionist movement and become the common sentiment of the Jewish masses. Our failure to be surprised at this development does not make Herzl's picture any truer—it only makes it more dangerous. If we actually are faced with open or concealed enemies on every side, if the whole world is ultimately against us, then we are lost.

For Herzl's way out has been closed—his hope in an escape from the world and his naïve faith in appeasement through escape have been rendered illusory. *Altneuland* is no longer a dream. It has become a very real place where Jews live together with Arabs, and it has also become a central junction of world communications. Whatever else it may be, Palestine is not a place where Jews can live in isolation, nor is it a promised land where they would be safe from antisemitism. The simple truth is that Jews will have to fight antisemitism everywhere or else be exterminated everywhere. Though Zionists no longer regard antisemitism as an ally, they do seem to be more convinced than ever that struggle against it is hopeless—if only because we would have to fight the whole world.

The danger of the present situation—in which Herzl's Zionism is accepted as a matter of course as the determinant of Zionist policy—lies in the semblance to common sense that the recent experiences of the Jews in Europe have lent Herzl's philosophy. Beyond doubt, the center of Jewish politics today is constituted by the remnants of European Jewry now in the camps of Germany. Not only is all our political activity concentrated upon them—even more important is the fact that our whole political outlook springs of necessity from their experiences, from our solidarity with them.

Every one of these surviving Jews is the last survivor of a family, every one of them was saved only by a miracle, every one of them has had the basic experience of witnessing and feeling the complete breakdown of international solidarity. Among all those who were persecuted, only Jews were singled out for certain death. What the Nazis or the Germans did was not decisive in this connection; what was decisive was the experiences of the Jews with the majority of all the other nationalities and even with the political prisoners in the concentration camps. The question is not whether the non-Jewish antifascists could have done more than they actually did for their Jewish comrades—the essential point is that only the Jews were sent inevitably to the gas chambers; and this was enough to draw a line between them that, perhaps, no amount of goodwill could have erased. For the Jews who experienced this, all gentiles became alike. This is what lies at the bottom of their present strong desire to go to Palestine. It is not that they imagine they will be safe there—it is only that they want to live among Jews alone, come what may.

Another experience—also of great importance to the future of Jewish politics—was gained from the realization, not that six million Jews had been killed, but that they had been driven to death helplessly, like cattle. There are stories telling how Jews tried to obviate the indignity of this death by their attitude and bearing as they were marched to the gas chambers—they sang or they made defiant gestures indicating that they did not accept their fate as the last word upon them.

What the survivors now want above all else is the right to die with dignity—in case of attack, with weapons in their hands. Gone, probably forever, is that chief concern of the Jewish people for centuries: survival at any price. Instead, we find something essentially new among Jews, the desire for dignity at any price.

As great an asset as this new development would be to an essentially sane Jewish political movement, it nevertheless constitutes something of a danger within the present framework of Zionist attitudes. Herzl's doctrine, deprived as it now is of its original confidence in the helpful nature of antisemitism, can only encourage suicidal gestures for whose ends the natural heroism of people who have become accustomed to death can be easily exploited. Some of the Zionist leaders pretend to believe that the Jews can maintain themselves in Palestine against the whole world and that they themselves can persevere in claiming everything or nothing against everybody and everything. However, behind this spurious optimism lurks a despair of everything and a genuine readiness for suicide that can become extremely dangerous should they grow to be the mood and atmosphere of Palestinian politics.

There is nothing in Herzlian Zionism that could act as a check on this; on the contrary, the utopian and ideological elements with which he injected the new Jewish will to political action are only too likely to lead the Jews out of reality once more—and out of the sphere of political action. I do not know—nor do I even want to know—what would happen to Jews all over the world and to Jewish history in the future should we meet with a catastrophe in Palestine. But the parallels with the Shabbetai Tzevi episode have become terribly close.

1946

TO SAVE THE JEWISH HOMELAND

When, on November 29, 1947, the partition of Palestine and the establishment of a Jewish state were accepted by the United Nations, it was assumed that no outside force would be necessary to implement this decision.

It took the Arabs less than two months to destroy this illusion and it took the United States less than three months to reverse its stand on partition, withdraw its support in the United Nations, and propose a trusteeship for Palestine. Of all the member states of the United Nations, only Soviet Russia and her satellites made it unequivocally clear that they still favored partition and the immediate proclamation of a Jewish state.

Trusteeship was at once rejected by both the Jewish Agency and the Arab Higher Committee. The Jews claimed the moral right to adhere to the original United Nations decision; the Arabs claimed an equally moral right to adhere to the League of Nations principle of self-determination, according to which Palestine would be ruled by its present Arab majority and the Jews be granted minority rights. The Jewish Agency, on its part, announced the proclamation of a Jewish state for May 16, [1948,] regardless of any United Nations decision. It remains a fact, meanwhile, that trusteeship, like partition, would have to be enforced by an outside power.

A last-minute appeal for a truce, made to both parties under the auspices of the United States, broke down in two days. Upon this appeal had rested the last chance of avoiding foreign intervention, at least temporarily. As matters stand at this moment, not a single possible solution or proposition affecting the Palestinian conflict is in sight that could be realized without enforcement by external authority.

The past few weeks of guerrilla warfare should have shown both Arabs and Jews how costly and destructive the war upon which they have embarked promises to be. In recent days, the Jews have won a few initial successes that prove their relative superiority over present Arab forces in Palestine. The Arabs, however, instead of concluding at least local truce agreements, have decided to evacuate whole cities and towns rather than stay in Jewish-dominated territory. This behavior declares more effectively than all proclamations the Arab refusal of any compromise; it is obvious that they have decided to expend in time and numbers whatever it may take to win a decisive victory. The Jews, on the other hand, living on a small island in an Arab sea, might well be expected to jump at the chance to exploit their present advantage by offering a negotiated peace. Their military situation is such that time and numbers necessarily work against them. If one takes into account the objective vital interests of the Arab and the Jewish peoples, especially in terms of the present situation and future well-being of the Near East—where a full-fledged war will inevitably invite all kinds of international interventions—the present desire of both peoples to fight it out at any price is nothing less than sheer irrationality.

One of the reasons for this unnatural and, as far as the Jewish people are concerned, tragic development is a decisive change in Jewish public opinion that has accompanied the confusing political decisions of the great powers.

The fact is that Zionism has won its most significant victory among the Jewish people at the very moment when its achievements in Palestine are in gravest danger. This may not seem extraordinary to those who have always believed that the building of a Jewish homeland was the most important— perhaps the only real—achievement of Jews in our century, and that ultimately no individual who wanted to stay a Jew could remain aloof from events in Palestine. Nevertheless, Zionism had in actuality always been a partisan and controversial issue; the Jewish Agency, though claiming to speak for the Jewish people as a whole, was still well aware that it represented only a fraction of them. This situation has changed overnight. With the exception of a few anti-Zionist die-hards, whom nobody can take very seriously, there is now no organization and almost no individual Jew that doesn't privately or publicly support partition and the establishment of a Jewish state.

Jewish left-wing intellectuals who a relatively short time ago still looked down upon Zionism as an ideology for the feebleminded, and viewed the building of a Jewish homeland as a hopeless enterprise that they, in their great wisdom, had rejected before it was ever started; Jewish businessmen whose interest in Jewish politics had always been determined by the all-important question of how to keep Jews out of newspaper headlines; Jewish philanthropists who had resented Palestine as a terribly expensive charity, draining off funds from other "more worthy" purposes; the readers of the Yiddish press, who for decades had been sincerely, if naïvely, convinced that America was the promised land—all these, from the Bronx to Park Avenue down to Greenwich Village and over to Brooklyn, are united today in the firm conviction that a Jewish state is needed, that America has betrayed the Jewish people, that the reign of terror by the Irgun and the Stern groups is more or less justified, and that Rabbi Silver, David Ben-Gurion, and Moshe Shertok are the real, if somewhat too moderate, statesmen of the Jewish people.

Something very similar to this growing unanimity among American Jews has arisen in Palestine itself. Just as Zionism had been a partisan issue among American Jews, so the Arab question and the state issue had been controversial issues within the Zionist movement and in Palestine. Political opinion was sharply divided there between the chauvinism of the Revisionists, the middle-of-the-road nationalism of the majority party, and the vehemently antinationalist, antistate sentiments of a large part of the kibbutz movement, particularly the Hashomer Haza'ir. Very little is now left of these differences of opinion.

The Hashomer Haza'ir has formed one party with the Ahdut Avodah, sacrificing its age-old binational program to the "accomplished fact" of the United Nations decision—a body, by the way, for which they never had too much respect when it was still called the League of Nations. The small Aliyah Hadashah, mostly composed of recent immigrants from Central Europe, still retains some of its old moderation and its sympathies for England, and it would certainly prefer Weizmann to Ben-Gurion—but since Weizmann and most of its members have always been committed to partition, and, like everybody else, to the Biltmore Program, this opposition does not amount to much more than a difference over personalities.

The general mood of the country, moreover, has been such that terrorism and the growth of totalitarian methods are silently tolerated and secretly applauded; and the general, underlying public opinion with which anybody desiring to appeal to the *yishuv* has to reckon shows no notable divisions at all.

Even more surprising than the growing unanimity of opinion among Palestinian Jews on one hand and American Jews on the other is the fact that they are essentially in agreement on the following more or less roughly stated propositions: the moment has now come to get everything or nothing, victory or death; Arab and Jewish claims are irreconcilable and only a military decision can settle the issue; the Arabs—all Arabs—are our enemies and we accept this fact; only outmoded liberals believe in compromises, only philistines believe in justice, and only schlemiels prefer truth and negotiation to propaganda and machine guns; Jewish experience in the last decades—or over the last centuries, or over the last two thousand years—has finally awakened us and taught us to look out for ourselves; this alone is reality, everything else is stupid sentimentality; everybody is against us, Great Britain is antisemitic, the United States is imperialist—but Russia might be our ally for a certain period because her interests happen to coincide with ours; yet in the final analysis we count upon nobody except ourselves; in sum—we are ready to go down fighting, and we will consider anybody who stands in our way a traitor and anything done to hinder us a stab in the back.

It would be frivolous to deny the intimate connection between this mood on the part of Jews everywhere and the recent European catastrophe, with the subsequent fantastic injustice and callousness toward the surviving remnant that were thereby so ruthlessly transformed into displaced persons. The result has been an amazing and rapid change in what we call national character. After two thousand years of "Galuth mentality," the Jewish people have suddenly ceased to believe in survival as an ultimate good in itself and have gone over in a few years to the opposite extreme. Now Jews believe in fighting at any price and feel that "going down" is a sensible method of politics.

Unanimity of opinion is a very ominous phenomenon, and one characteristic of our modern mass age. It destroys social and personal life, which is based on the fact that we are different by nature and by conviction. To hold different opinions and to be aware that other people think differently on the same issue shields us from that Godlike certainty which stops all discussion and reduces social relationships to those of an ant heap. A unanimous public opinion tends to eliminate bodily those who differ, for mass unanimity is not the result of agreement, but an expression of fanaticism and hysteria. In contrast to agreement, unanimity does not stop at certain well-defined objects, but spreads like an infection into every related issue.

Thus Jewish unanimity on the Palestine issue has already prompted a somewhat vague and inarticulate shift of Jewish public opinion in the direction of pro-Soviet sympathies, a shift that even affects people who for more than twenty-five years have consistently denounced Bolshevik policies. Even more significant that such changes of mood and general attitude have been the attempts to establish an anti-Western and pro-Soviet orientation inside the Zionist movement. The resignation of Moshe Sneh, the organizer of illegal immigration and formerly prominent in the Haganah, is important in this respect; and occasional utterances by almost every one of the Palestinian delegates in America point even more strongly in this direction. The program, finally, of the new left-wing Palestinian party formed by the merger of the Hashomer Haza'ir and the Ahdut Avodah has put plainly on record as its chief reason for not joining the majority party the desire to have Zionist foreign policy rely on Russia more than on the Western democracies.

The mentality behind this unrealistic understanding of Russian policy and the consequences of subjecting oneself to it has a long tradition in Zionism. As is understandable enough among people without political experience, a childlike hope has always been present that some big brother would come along to befriend the Jewish people, solve their problems, protect them from the Arabs, and present them eventually with a beautiful Jewish state with all the trimmings. This role was filled in Jewish imagination by Great Britain—until the issuance of the White Paper; and because of this naïve trust, and an equally naïve underestimation of Arab forces, for decades Jewish leaders let slip one opportunity after another to come to an understanding with the Arabs. After the outbreak of the Second World War, and particularly since the Biltmore Program, the imaginary role of the big brother of the Jews fell to the United States. But it has very quickly become clear that America is no more in a position to fill the bill than the British, and so Soviet Russia is now left as the only power upon which foolish hopes can be pinned. It is remarkable, however, that Russia is the first big brother whom even Jews do not quite trust. For the first time a note of cynicism has entered Jewish hopes.

Unfortunately, this healthy distrust is not caused so much by a specific suspicion of Soviet policy as by another traditionally Zionist feeling that has by now seized all sections of the Jewish people: the cynical and deep-rooted conviction that all gentiles are antisemitic, and everybody and everything is against the Jews, that, in the words of Herzl, the world can be divided into *verschämte und unverschämte Antisemiten,* and that the "essential meaning of Zionism is the revolt of the Jews against their pointless and hapless mission— which has been to challenge the Gentiles to be crueler than they dare without forcing them to be as kind as they ought, [with the result that the Zionist revolt has ended in reproducing] in altered perspective the dynamic picture of Israel's mission" (Benjamin Halpern in the *New Leader,* December 1947). In other words, general gentile hostility, a phenomenon that Herzl thought was directed only at Galuth Jewry, and which would therefore disappear with the normalization of the Jewish people in Palestine, is now assumed by Zionists to be an unalterable, eternal fact of Jewish history that repeats itself under any circumstances, even in Palestine.

Obviously this attitude is plain racist chauvinism and it is equally obvious that this division between Jews and all other peoples—who are to be classed as enemies—does not differ from other master-race theories (even though the Jewish "master race" is pledged not to conquest but to suicide by its protagonists). It is also plain that any interpretation of politics oriented according to such "principles" is hopelessly out of touch with the realities of this world. Nevertheless it is a fact that such attitudes tacitly or explicitly permeate the general atmosphere of Jewry; and therefore Jewish leaders can threaten mass suicide to the applause of their audiences, and the terrible and irresponsible "or else we shall go down" creeps into all official Jewish statements, however radical or moderate their sources.

Every believer in a democratic government knows the importance of a loyal opposition. The tragedy of Jewish politics at this moment is that it is wholly determined by the Jewish Agency and that no opposition to it of any significance exists either in Palestine or America.

From the time of the Balfour Declaration the loyal opposition in Zionist politics was constituted by the non-Zionists (certainly this was the case after 1929, when the enlarged Jewish Agency elected half of the Executive from the non-Zionists). But for all practical purposes the non-Zionist opposition no longer exists today. This unfortunate development was encouraged, if not caused, by the fact that the United States and the United Nations finally endorsed an extremist Jewish demand that non-Zionists had always held to be totally unrealistic. With the support of a Jewish state by the great powers, the non-Zionists believed themselves refuted by reality itself. Their sudden loss of significance, and their helplessness in the face of what they felt justified in thinking an accomplished fact, were the results of an attitude that has always identified reality with the sum of those facts created by the powers that be—and by them only. They had believed in the Balfour Declaration rather than in the wish of the Jewish people to build its homeland; they had reckoned with the British or American governments rather than with the people living in the Near East. They had refused to go along with the Biltmore Program—but they accepted it once it was recognized by the United States and the United Nations.

Now, if the non-Zionists had wanted to act as genuine realists in Jewish politics, they should have insisted and continued to insist that the only permanent reality in the whole constellation was the presence of Arabs in Palestine, a reality no decision could alter—except perhaps the decision of a totalitarian state, implemented by its particular brand of ruthless force. Instead, they mistook decisions of great powers for the ultimate realities and lacked the courage to warn, not only their fellow Jews, but also their respective governments of the possible consequences of partition and the declaration of a Jewish state. It was ominous enough that no significant Zionist party was left to oppose the decision of November 29, the minority being committed to the Jewish state, and the others (the majority under Weizmann) to partition; but it was downright tragic that at this most crucial of all moments the loyal opposition of the non-Zionists simply disappeared.

In the face of the "despair and resoluteness" of the *yishuv* (as a Palestinian delegate recently put it) and the suicide threats of the Jewish leaders, it might be useful to remind the Jews and the world what it is that will "go down" if the final tragedy should come in Palestine.

Palestine and the building of a Jewish homeland constitute today the great hope and the great pride of Jews all over the world. What would happen to Jews, individually and collectively, if this hope and this pride were to be extinguished in another catastrophe is almost beyond imagining. But it is certain that this would become the central fact of Jewish history and it is possible that it might become the beginning of the self-dissolution of the Jewish people. There is no Jew in the world whose whole outlook on life and the world would not be radically changed by such a tragedy.

If the *yishuv* went down, it would drag along in its fall the collective settlements, the kibbutzim—which constitute perhaps the most promising of all social experiments made in the twentieth century, as well as the most magnificent part of the Jewish homeland.

Here, in complete freedom and unhampered by any government, a new form of ownership, a new type of farmer, a new way of family life and child education, and new approaches to the troublesome conflicts between city and country, between rural and industrial labor have been created.

The people of the kibbutzim have been too absorbed in their quiet and effective revolution to make their voices sufficiently heard in Zionist politics. If it is true that the members of the Irgun and the Stern group are not recruited from the kibbutzim, it is also true that the kibbutzim have offered no serious obstacle to terrorism.

It is this very abstention from politics, this enthusiastic concentration on immediate problems, that has enabled the kibbutz pioneers to go ahead with their work, undisturbed by the more noxious ideologies of our times, realizing new laws and new behavior patterns, establishing new customs and new values, and translating and integrating them in new institutions. The loss of the kibbutzim, the ruin of the new type of man they have produced, the destruction of their institutions and the oblivion that would swallow the fruit of their experiences—this would be one of the severest of blows to the hopes of all those, Jewish and non-Jewish, who have not and never will make their peace with present-day society and its standards. For this Jewish experiment in Palestine holds out hope of solutions that will be acceptable and applicable, not only in individual cases, but also for the large mass of men everywhere whose dignity and very humanity are in our time so seriously threatened by the pressures of modern life and its unsolved problems.

Still another precedent, or at least its possibility, would go down with the *yishuv*—that of close cooperation between two peoples, one embodying the most advanced ways of European civilization, the other an erstwhile victim of colonial oppression and backwardness. The idea of Arab-Jewish cooperation, though never realized on any scale and today seemingly farther off than ever, is not an idealistic daydream but a sober statement of the fact that without it the whole Jewish venture in Palestine is doomed. Jews and Arabs could be forced by circumstances to show the world that there are no differences between two peoples that cannot be bridged. Indeed, the working out of such a modus vivendi might in the end serve as a model of how to counteract the dangerous tendencies of formerly oppressed peoples to shut themselves off from the rest of the world and develop nationalist superiority complexes of their own.

Many opportunities for Jewish-Arab friendship have already been lost, but none of these failures can alter the basic fact that the existence of the Jews in Palestine depends on achieving it. Moreover, the Jews have one advantage in the fact that, excluded as they were from official history for centuries, they have no imperialist past to live down. They can still act as a vanguard in international relations on a small but valid scale—as in the kibbutzim they have already acted as a vanguard in social relations despite the relatively insignificant numbers of the people involved.

There is very little doubt about the final outcome of an all-out war between Arabs and Jews. One can win many battles without winning a war. And up to now, no real battle has yet taken place in Palestine.

And even if the Jews were to win the war, its end would find the unique possibilities and the unique achievements of Zionism in Palestine destroyed. The land that would come into being would be something quite other than the dream of world Jewry, Zionist and non-Zionist. The "victorious" Jews would live surrounded by an entirely hostile Arab population, secluded inside ever-threatened borders, absorbed with physical self-defense to a degree that would submerge all other interests and activities. The growth of a Jewish culture would cease to be the concern of the whole people; social experiments would have to be discarded as impractical luxuries; political thought would center around military strategy; economic development would be determined exclusively by the needs of war. And all this would be the fate of a nation that—no matter how many immigrants it could still absorb and how far it extended its boundaries (the whole of Palestine and

Transjordan is the insane Revisionist demand)—would still remain a very small people greatly outnumbered by hostile neighbors.

Under such circumstances (as Ernst Simon has pointed out) the Palestinian Jews would degenerate into one of those small warrior tribes about whose possibilities and importance history has amply informed us since the days of Sparta. Their relations with world Jewry would become problematical, since their defense interests might clash at any moment with those of other countries where large numbers of Jews lived. Palestine Jewry would eventually separate itself from the larger body of world Jewry and in its isolation develop into an entirely new people. Thus it becomes plain that at this moment and under present circumstances a Jewish state can only be erected at the price of the Jewish homeland.

Fortunately, there are still some Jews left who have shown in these bitter days that they have too much wisdom and too great a sense of responsibility to follow blindly where desperate, fanaticized masses would lead them. There are still, despite all appearances, a few Arabs who are unhappy about the increasingly fascist coloration of their national movements.

Until very recently, moreover, Palestinian Arabs were relatively unconcerned in the conflict with the Jews and the actual fighting against them is even now left to so-called volunteers from neighboring countries. But now even this situation has begun to change. The evacuations of Haifa and Tiberias by their Arab populations are the most ominous occurrences of the whole Arab-Jewish war so far. These evacuations could not have been carried out without careful preparation, and it is hardly likely that they are spontaneous. Nevertheless, it is very doubtful that Arab leadership, which by creating homelessness among Palestinian Arabs aims to arouse the Muslim world, would have succeeded in persuading tens of thousands of city dwellers to desert all their earthly possessions at a moment's notice, had not the massacre of Deir Yassin struck fear of the Jews into the Arab population. And another crime that played into the hands of the Arab leadership had been committed only a few months back in Haifa itself when the Irgun had thrown a bomb into a line of Arab workers outside the Haifa refinery, one of the few places where Jews and Arabs had for years worked side by side.

The political implications of these acts, neither of which had any military objective whatsoever, are all too clear in both instances: they were aimed at those places where neighborly relations between Arabs and Jews had not been completely destroyed; they were intended to arouse the wrath of the Arab people in order to cut off the Jewish leadership from all temptations to negotiate; they created that atmosphere of factual complicity which is always one of the main prerequisites for the rise to power of terrorist groups. And, indeed, no Jewish leadership did come forward to stop the Irgun from taking political matters into its own hands and declaring war on all Arabs in the name of the Jewish community. The lukewarm protests of the Jewish Agency and the Haganah, forever limping behind, were followed two days later by an announcement from Tel Aviv that Irgun and Haganah were about to conclude an agreement. The Irgun attack on Jaffa, first denounced by Haganah, was followed by an agreement for joint action and the dispatch of Haganah units to Jaffa. This shows to what extent political initiative is already in terrorist hands.

The present Executive of the Jewish Agency and the Vaad Leumi have by now amply demonstrated that they are either unwilling or incapable of preventing the terrorists from making political decisions for the whole *yishuv*. It is even questionable whether the Jewish Agency is still in a position to negotiate for a temporary truce, since its enforcement would largely depend upon the consent of the extremist groups. It is quite possible that this was one of the reasons why representatives of the Agency, though they must know the desperate needs of their people, allowed the recent negotiations for a truce to break down. They may have been reluctant to reveal to the whole world their lack of effective power and authority.

The United Nations and the United States have up to now simply accepted the elected delegates of the Jewish and the Arab peoples, which was of course the proper thing to do. After the breakdown of truce negotiations, however, it would seem that there are now only two alternatives left for the great powers: either to leave the country (with the possible exception of the holy places) to a war that not only may mean another extermination of Jews but may also develop into a large-scale international conflict; or else to occupy the country with foreign troops and rule it without giving much consideration to either Jews or Arabs. The second alternative is clearly an imperialist one and would very likely end in failure if not carried out by a totalitarian government with all the paraphernalia of police terror.

However, a way out of this predicament may be found if the United Nations could summon up the courage in this unprecedented situation to take an unprecedented step by going to those Jewish and Arab individuals who at present are isolated because of their records as sincere believers in Arab-Jewish cooperation, and asking them to negotiate a truce. On the Jewish side, the so-called Ihud group among the Zionists, as well as certain outstanding non-Zionists, are clearly the people most eligible for this purpose at the moment.

Such a truce, or better, such a preliminary understanding—even negotiated between nonaccredited parties—would show the Jews and the Arabs that it could be done. We know the proverbial fickleness of masses; there is a serious chance for a rapid and radical change of mood, which is the prerequisite for any real solution.

Such a move, however, could be effective only if concessions are made at once on both sides. The White Paper has been an enormous obstacle, in view of the terrible needs of Jewish DP's. Without the solution of their problem, no improvement in the mood of the Jewish people can be expected. Immediate admission of Jewish DP's to Palestine, though limited in terms of time and number, as well as immediate admission of Jewish and other DP's to the United States outside the quota system, are prerequisites for a sensible solution. On the other hand, the Palestinian Arabs should be guaranteed a well-defined share in the Jewish development of the country, which under any circumstances will still continue to be their common homeland. This would not be impossible if the huge amounts now expended in defense and rebuilding could be used instead for the realization of the Jordan Valley Authority project.

There can be no doubt that a trusteeship as proposed by President Truman and endorsed by Dr. Magnes is the best temporary solution. It would have the advantage of preventing the establishment of sovereignty whose only sovereign right would be to commit suicide. It would provide a cooling-off period. It could initiate the Jordan Valley Authority project as a government enterprise and it could establish for its realization local Arab-Jewish committees under the supervision and the auspices of an international authority. It could appoint members of the Jewish and the Arab intelligentsia to posts in local and municipal offices. Last but not least, trusteeship over the whole of Palestine would postpone and possibly prevent partition of the country.

It is true that many non-fanatical Jews of sincere goodwill have believed in partition as a possible means of solving the Arab-Jewish conflict. In the light of political, military, and geographic realities, however, this was always a piece of wishful thinking. The partition of so small a country could at best mean the petrifaction of the conflict, which would result in arrested development for both peoples; at worst it would signify a temporary stage during which both parties would prepare for further war. The alternative proposition of a federated state, also recently endorsed by Dr. Magnes, is much more realistic; despite the fact that it establishes a common government for two different peoples, it avoids the troublesome majority-minority constellation, which is insoluble by definition. A federated structure, moreover, would have to rest on Jewish-Arab community councils, which would mean that the Jewish-Arab conflict would be resolved on the lowest and most promising level of proximity and neighborliness. A federated state, finally, could be the natural stepping-stone for any later, greater federated structure in the Near East and the Mediterranean area.

A federated state, however, such as is proposed by the Morrison Plan, is outside the actual political possibilities of the day. As matters now stand, it would be almost as unwise to proclaim a federated state over the heads and against the opposition of both peoples as it has already been to proclaim partition. This is, certainly, no time for final solutions; every single possible and practicable step is today a tentative effort whose chief aim is pacification and nothing more.

Trusteeship is not an ideal and not an eternal solution. But politics seldom offers ideal or eternal solutions. A United Nations trusteeship could be effectively carried through only if the United States and Great Britain were ready to back it up, no matter what happened. This does not necessarily mean great military commitments. There is still a good chance of recruiting police forces on the spot if the present memberships of the Arab Higher Committee and the Jewish Agency were to be denied authority in the country. Small local units composed of Jews and Arabs under the command of higher officers from countries that are members of the United Nations could become an important school for future cooperative self-government.

. . .

Unfortunately, in a hysterical atmosphere such proposals are only too liable to be dismissed as "stabs in the back" or unrealistic.

They are neither; they are, on the contrary, the only way of saving the reality of the Jewish homeland.

No matter what the outcome of the present deadlock, the following objective factors should be axiomatic criteria for the good and the bad, the right and the wrong:

1) The real goal of the Jews in Palestine is the building up of a Jewish homeland. This goal must never be sacrificed to the pseudo-sovereignty of a Jewish state.

2) The independence of Palestine can be achieved only on a solid basis of Jewish-Arab cooperation. As long as Jewish and Arab leaders both claim that there is "no bridge" between Jews and Arabs (as Moshe Shertok has just put it), the territory cannot be left to the political wisdom of its own inhabitants.

3) Elimination of all terrorist groups (and not agreements with them) and swift punishment of all terrorist deeds (and not merely protests against them) will be the only valid proof that the Jewish people in Palestine has recovered its sense of political reality and that Zionist leadership is again responsible enough to be trusted with the destinies of the *yishuv*.

4) Immigration to Palestine, limited in numbers and in time, is the only "irreducible minimum" in Jewish politics.

5) Local self-government and mixed Jewish-Arab municipal and rural councils, on a small scale and as numerous as possible, are the only realistic political measures that can eventually lead to the political emancipation of Palestine.

It is still not too late.

1948

THE ASSETS OF PERSONALITY

A Review of Chaim Weizmann: Statesman, Scientist,
Builder of the Jewish Commonwealth*

Twenty-four of its pages give this book its high value—buried in a long
series of contributions of varying quality, mostly after-dinner speeches that
compete with each other for superlatives. The twenty-four pages are by
Weizmann himself, a reprint of a statement made before the Palestine Royal
Commission in 1936.

They open with a brief account of the Jewish problem, which is defined as
the "homelessness of a people." Carefully avoiding theoretical remarks, it
points directly to the pressing needs of some six million Jews in Eastern and
Central Europe. A brief allusion is made to certain "destructive tendencies in
Jewry" which Weizmann had fought "since his early youth," and a vague
impression is left that Zionism is coupled with the fight against revolutionary
tendencies—an old argument, already used and abused by Herzl. There follows an equally cautious reference to Jewish uneasiness in the Western
world.

The second part of the speech opens with a strong appeal to history. The
messianic movements—"a less rationalistic form of the modern Zionist
movement"—are related in a masterly way to three hundred years of British
history during which British "statesmen, divines advocated the return of
the Jews to Palestine." Thus the Balfour Declaration issued from a "semi-
religious, semi-romantic" feeling that might "have been mixed up with other
reasons." The analysis of the Balfour Declaration that Weizmann then proceeds to give is couched in very prudent terms, avoiding any reference to
Palestine *as* a national home, but referring to the national home *in* Palestine.
With the catchword that it should be "as Jewish as England is English," such

*Edited by Meyer W. Weisgal. Foreword by Felix Frankfurter (New York: Dial Press, 1944).

controversial issues as self-administration or the development of political independence are evaded. Only when alluding to a certain British opinion that reproached the Zionists with having brought "the scum of Europe to Palestine" does Weizmann—for the first and last time in his whole speech—abandon the calculated coolness and neutrality of his presentation: "If they deserve the definition of the scum of Europe, I should like to be counted among this scum."

A few paragraphs on the Arab problem mention Jewish-Arab cooperation during the Middle Ages and manage to skirt almost completely the contemporary Jewish-Arab conflict. On the other hand Weizmann becomes very up-to-date, precise, and detailed on the questions of land and labor in Palestine. He concludes with the polite rejection of a legislative council for Palestine (a British proposal that would automatically have given majority rights to the Arabs) and the equally polite wish that the commission find a way out of the present difficulties. He takes no initiative, offers no political proposition of his own.

No one acquainted with the circumstances of this statement can deny that it is a masterpiece of moderation, self-restraint, and dignity. Even with those circumstances discounted, it makes very impressive reading. It exhibits Weizmann's most typical traits as a politician, which are those of a negotiator and diplomat. These very qualities, however, hardly make for the lasting greatness so many of the contributors to this book attribute to the man—some because they are genuinely impressed and some because they are victims of the vulgar leader-worship of our times.

Yet this document breathes more than skill, diplomacy, and good form; it embodies in a most inconspicuous way the two main elements that have formed Weizmann's political convictions: an unshakable faith in England ("If I were no believer I could not be a Zionist. And . . . I believe in England") and an equally strong belief that all political questions are not only secondary to practical achievements but are actually solved in the very process of planting and building. He once even thought of forming a Jewish army in Palestine, in spite of political prohibitions, by recruiting it patiently "man after man." Recent political events have not shaken his confidence in either of these two principles—which is surprising only when the present situation in Palestine is considered realistically, but not if one realizes how well these principles complement each other.

Weizmann's success—probably the greatest achieved by a Jew in our time—is based less upon his rather commonplace political convictions than upon his social gifts, which are very rare. His extraordinary sense for atmosphere is the secret of his "Englishness," as Norman Angell calls it—in addition to fascination and wit. His political influence in England is firmly based on his position in high society, where he is received on equal terms. In this as in other respects, he can be likened only to Benjamin Disraeli, and it is certainly no accident that both men conquered society by exactly the same weapon: they presented their Jewishness as a sign of distinction and knew how to bear it as such—in an aristocratic society founded on distinction by birth.

It is obvious that this career makes a strong appeal to popular imagination. His universal success with Jews—friends and foes alike—can be explained almost by the titles Sholem Asch and Jacob Fishman have given their articles in this book: "He Shall Stand Before Kings" and ". . . Like the Rest of Us." Weizmann's great achievement in the Jewish world and elsewhere is to have assimilated his Russian Jewish origin to his actual social position in such a way that both are transparent in his general behavior at every moment.

The book at hand bores the reader with overlavish praise and hyperbole utterly alien to Weizmann's personality: he is compared with great men all the way from Abraham to Lenin. Careless editing has failed to eliminate the numerous repetitions of the same anecdotes. Even the better articles suffer from a general lack of reason or warmth. One wonders whether the contributors, chosen seemingly for their distinguished names rather than for comradeship-in-arms, are to blame, or whether the root does not lie at the curious personality of the man himself, whose greatest quality, fascination, is by its very nature transitory.

1945

SINGLE TRACK TO ZION

A Review of Trial and Error:
The Autobiography of Chaim Weizmann

The great charm of this personal account of fifty years of history lies in one of those fortunate coincidences where biography and history become one. Dr. Chaim Weizmann can tell of his childhood in Russia in terms of the Chibath Zion movement (the forerunner of Zionism), of his early manhood in Germany and Switzerland in terms of the early Zionist congresses in Basel, of his maturity in England in terms of the Balfour Declaration and the British Mandate in Palestine, and of this last year, when he sat down to tell the story of a lifelong pursuit of one single goal, in terms of its accomplishment—the state of Israel.

The whole narrative is permeated with a stubborn determination never to lose this identification, despite the fact that the establishment of a Jewish state came about through the defeat of Dr. Weizmann's most cherished principles: cooperation with Great Britain (the cornerstone of his foreign policy) and insistence on the slow and "hard way," on the primacy of practical pioneer work over political actions (the foundation of his internal policy). Perhaps nothing illustrates his great political skill better than the way he handles a situation that has been taken out of his hands by his old political opponents, whom he hardly mentions by name, yet manages to remind of his old warnings against "shortcuts" and the dangers of "seeking to live by a sort of continuous miracle." Dr. Weizmann makes it very clear that he does not consider his autobiography a last searching statement, rendered at the close of his life and written for eternity. It is, on the contrary, the story which a man, temporarily forced out of the political arena, chooses to tell at this particular moment and with certain political objectives.

The political purpose of the book is patent on and enlivens every page. It is only natural that it should also occasionally come into conflict with the historical truth. In fact the most consistently pro-British section of Zionism lost its significance when Great Britain was entrusted with the mandate. For reasons of expediency, Dr. Weizmann understates the role of Central European—specifically German and Austrian—Zionism, which had the queer misfortune to suffer defeat through the realization of its own goals and the fulfillment of its own prophecies (German Zionists, the most radical negators of the Jewish Diaspora, suffered as irreparable a loss of prestige in Palestine through Hitler's rise to power as German Jews in other countries of refuge). It is characteristic of Dr. Weizmann's kind of realism that he never thinks it his business to right this inevitable historical wrong, despite the fact that his own party in Palestine, the Progressive Zionists, is composed almost entirely of Central European immigrants.

The same tendency to rearrange facts for the sake of political argument is visible in the treatment of the Balfour Declaration. In order to justify, in a completely changed situation, his long, exclusively British orientation, he repeatedly stresses that "England felt she had no business in Palestine except as part of the plan for the creation of the Jewish Homeland" and that the only British opposition to the Balfour Declaration came from Mr. Montagu and other assimilated and influential Jews. Yet his presentation itself contains the refutation of both statements: negotiations were started for the case that "Palestine [should] fall within the British sphere of interest" and with the argument of "the importance of a Jewish Palestine in the British imperial scheme of things"; and the colonial administration is pictured as pro-Arab and anti-Jewish from the beginning of the mandate.

Such inconsistencies, however, are only the reverse side of Dr. Weizmann's great political gifts: his ability to adjust to circumstances, to find striking political slogans on the spur of the moment, his talent for quick repartee and for dealing with people of all classes and all countries. These explain the extraordinary career of this man, who succeeded in winning his place among the leading men of his time and, what was much more difficult, his place in British society as a complete outsider and with the help of no one—something which nobody, except Benjamin Disraeli, had ever accomplished before. Yet, as significant for the character of the man as his extreme adjustability and pliability is a hard core of unwavering purposefulness. Not only, as he says himself, have few things ever interested him except Zionism and chemistry, but everything and everyone he met in a long and rich life have been considered and, so to speak, classified according to this one purpose. For him science is not the eternal search for truth but the urge "to make something practical," an instrument for a well-defined task: the building of Palestine most of all, but also the possibility of that financial independence to which he owes so much of his political success, and, last not least, his unsurpassable entrance ticket to the international world.

What emerges therefore from the pages of this autobiography is not at all a life torn between political and scientific concerns, split painfully between the passions of scholar and statesman. It is rare, indeed, to witness so completely organic and integrated a life as that of Chaim Weizmann, whose main direction was fixed in early childhood and was never interrupted by the impact of personal experiences or historical events. The highlights of his private life—marriage, children, death of one son, the eye disease of his later years—are mentioned with a curious restraint, as though the one purpose of his life never left the man any time or leisure to apply his gift for formulations to his personal experience. Could it be that this is why this book, which makes such arresting and enjoyable reading, lacks so completely that dimension of depth which alone could have given it greatness? . . .

1949

THE FAILURE OF REASON

The Mission of Bernadotte

During the weeks which have passed since the assassination of the United Nations' mediator in Palestine, the situation has deteriorated steadily. The uneasy truce has come to an end, the authority of the United Nations has grown weaker, and the popular strength of the extremists on both sides has come more to the forefront. The murderers have not been caught and the members of the Stern gang, whom the Israeli government had rounded up during the first days after the *attentat,* took advantage of their sojourn in prison to demonstrate to the world that even the police of the state of Israel sympathized with the terrorists and was prepared to fraternize with them.

The attitude of the Israeli government up to now has been equivocal and confusing. The moderate statements by Foreign Minister Moshe Shertok, immediately after the murder, were followed by a declaration of Prime Minister Ben-Gurion to the Israeli State Council, according to which "the fate of Israel would be determined in Palestine either in battle or in peace negotiations between the Arabs and Israel, and not in the UN conference rooms in Paris."

When, however, under the shock of the assassination, the growing coordination of British and American policy in Palestine resulted in a common endorsement of Bernadotte's proposals to the United Nations, Shertok announced suddenly that his government might be willing to "consider a 'confederation' in which fully independent sovereign states worked together." That is something which nobody but Dr. Magnes and the Ihud group in Palestine had ever proposed, and whose concept coincided with the peace proposals which Bernadotte had outlined in his first report to the United Nations at the end of the first truce, but which he had been forced to abandon altogether, partly because of the entirely negative attitude of Mr. Shertok.

Shertok's most recent statement, on the other hand, is the only ray of hope in the present situation. A confederate Palestine is indeed the only alternative to international control, which the Western powers will be forced to impose because of their paramount interest in peace in the Near East. Nor is there much doubt that in this case imperialist interests will again dominate the destinies of both peoples. Only confederation, the political implementation and guarantee of permanent cooperation, and not national sovereignty, offers a solution in which the true national interests of both peoples might be safeguarded.

If the United Nations should agree with Count Bernadotte's final analysis of the situation and accept his conclusions, they would have to depart from their original decision of November 29, 1947, in one decisive point. The original decision had been based on the assumption that no external force would be necessary to establish a Jewish state in Palestine and that partition would definitely liquidate the mandate or any other kind of international supervision. Bernadotte, however, recommended a kind of United Nations trusteeship in the form of a "Palestine Conciliation Commission," which for a limited period would be given the rights and duties normally associated with the rights and duties of a trustee.

This would be the first time that an international body has undertaken to rule directly over a specific territory, and the success of such an experiment is very uncertain. For, the obvious advantage of direct international authority, greater neutrality, and lack of specific national interests may well be counterbalanced by permanent difficulties of implementation. If a British soldier with long imperialist traditions found it difficult to "die for Palestine," a member of an international police force will probably feel that it is outrageous, whereas the local populations have proved that they know how to die for their causes.

But if the United Nations should decide to assume this heavy responsibility, at least it has done everything possible to avoid the risk of serious loss of moral prestige that would accompany an international trusteeship. The mission of the UN mediator had no other objective than to reach a settlement which would avoid, by an internationally supported mediation of the conflict, any permanent international rule. If this attempt should prove futile, and if the UN should accept the establishment of a "Palestine Conciliation Commission," this may well serve as a sorry precedent and lead the UN into a reconsideration of the defunct League of Nations mandate system. The choice of Count Bernadotte for this mission, the way he approached and interpreted his task, placed the experiment, despite its unhappy end, on the very highest level. If the last word of this reasonable and indefatigable man was that reason and compromise are impracticable in the near future, it really looks as though the only alternative to the risks of a UN trusteeship would be (for the international community and especially for the Western powers) the greater risk of a Jewish-Arab war.

The political significance of Bernadotte's last report to the UN lies chiefly in its difference from his initial proposals for a settlement in Palestine, submitted at the end of the first truce. His earlier conviction of the existence of a "common denominator" between the two parties, namely of the realization that they both will ultimately have to live in peace, has given way to a description of how he "has striven ceaselessly to find a common basis," has "abundantly employed both reason and persuasion" and yet found nowhere any basis for discussion, let alone agreement. The earlier insistence on a spirit of mediation that excluded "imposition" and the "handing down of decisions" is being superseded by an appeal for "prompt action by the General Assembly" and the Security Council and the hope that "moral pressure" will force both parties to abide by the majority decision of the UN. The principles which the earlier proposals had laid down as a "reasonable frame of reference" for a negotiated peace—that boundaries should be negotiated and not imposed, that economic union should have some kind of political implementation, that immigration should be limited after two years—are abandoned. Tentative suggestions, however, which he had appended to the original report and termed purely optional, and which were more an enumeration of topics of discussion than actual suggestions, form now the very nucleus of his ultimate recommendations. It seems that Bernadotte took Mr. Shertok's reaction to his plan that he "reconsider [his] whole approach to the problem" very much to heart, even though in a way which Mr. Shertok may not have foreseen.

The reason Bernadotte changed his approach to the Palestinian question is not that his original suggestions were repudiated by both parties; this he had expected. He did not expect that either party would think it worthwhile to make any countersuggestions. On the contrary, both sides became even more stubbornly determined to ignore the other's point of view altogether. The Arabs continued to demand a unitary Arab state with vague provisions for a Jewish minority; the Jews said that they no longer considered themselves bound to either the UN borders or economic union, which "must now be left to the free and unfettered discretion of the Government of Israel."

The recommendations of the second report indeed grant the new state of Israel all the trimmings of sovereignty—under UN supervision. Boundaries would be imposed—the exchange of the Negev for Western Galilee (a heavy loss for the Jewish state, which needs areas for colonization, and for Palestine, whose deserts can be transformed into fertile land only by Jewish skill, labor, and capital); Haifa and Lydda would become free sea and air ports respectively; and Jerusalem, which Bernadotte first tentatively suggested should be Arab territory, will come under UN control and through its strategic and symbolic value for Palestine become the center of international control of the whole country. Economic union is considered as being already "outrun and irrevocably revised by the actual facts of recent Palestine history," that is, chiefly by the Arab determination not to cooperate and the Jewish handling of the Arab refugee problem. Free immigration will be granted because the United Nations is supposed "to undertake to provide special assurance that the boundaries between the Arab and Jewish territories shall be respected and maintained," that international control would restrict Jewish immigration automatically to the limitations of economic absorptive capacity.

The decisive difference between the spirit of the first and the second reports lies in the different answer to the political question of who is going to rule Palestine. Everything in the first report indicated Bernadotte's firm conviction that peace could be achieved only through bringing the two peoples closer together, through a compromise which would be virtually independent of any international or other third power. Everything in the second report points in the opposite direction: real self-government without international control will be disastrous and one of the chief tasks of international supervision of the two parties will be "their wide separation by creation of broad demilitarized zones under UN supervisions."

What Bernadotte actually proposed in his second report and its conclusions is a kind of dictatorship of reason. For while he finally and much against his will had come to the realization that one could not talk reason to either of the parties, he had not changed his appreciation of the "vital factors" involved in the situation. He had "left no stone unturned" to persuade Jews and Arabs of the reality in which they lived: he had told the Arabs that a Jewish state existed and had been recognized by most of the major powers and that there was no sound reason to assume that it would not continue to exist; he had stressed that partition of Palestine was based upon the fact that "the Jews have been all along and are now in fact a completely separate cultural and political community." He had told the Jews that theirs was "a small State precariously perched on a coastal shelf with its back to the sea and defiantly facing on three sides a hostile Arab world"; he had warned them that the "violent reaction of the Arab world . . . is also a vital factor in the equation" and that their development and even their survival "must very largely depend in the long run on the cultivation of peaceful and mutually trusting relations with the neighboring Arab States whose overwhelming numbers dwarf into insignificance any population total to which the Jewish State may aspire." These facts are indeed outstanding and form the vital factors of the situation for everybody except the two conflicting parties, who prefer to believe that there is a plot to thwart their ambitions rather than to recognize the simple fact that Palestine is being inhabited by two different peoples.

Bernadotte knew that "territorial, political, and economic unity would be highly desirable" and that "lacking such complete unity, some form of political and economic union would be a reasonable alternative." But he realized that "the present antagonism between the Arab and Jewish communities renders impractical . . . the application of any such arrangement." What he had learned in the three months following his first peace proposals, during his negotiations in Tel Aviv, Amman, Cairo, Damascus, and Beirut, was that the true denominator between the two communities was the firm conviction that only force and not reason would decide their conflict.

Bernadotte's chief concern was peace. A pacifist by conviction, he felt that the United Nations had asked him to stop a war in the Near East at any price. If force was admittedly the only argument to which Arabs and Jews would listen, then force should be exercised by the international community in order to prevent war. If force was the only accepted framework of reference then, in any event, one would not have to bother with "formal agreements" which though "highly desirable" were no longer considered by him "indispensable to a peaceful settlement." The United Nations, and especially the Western bloc, has hardly any other alternative but to overrule the reckless stubbornness of the two peoples, who either do not understand or do not heed the consequences of their actions within the larger framework of international politics.

Bernadotte has been denounced as a British agent by the Jews and as a Zionist agent by the Arabs. He was of course the agent of nobody, not even of the UN in any narrow sense, since he did not consider himself bound by the textual provisions of the UN decision of November 29, 1947. The point is that these denunciations, precisely because of their absurdity, show very clearly a certain state of mind which, in order to escape reality and truth, looks for ulterior motives and secret plots everywhere. What neither the Jews nor the Arabs could understand any longer was that there could exist in our world even one independent man without any prejudices and with no ax to grind, and yet passionately interested in the international state of affairs. Deafened by the incessant noise of their own propaganda, they could no longer distinguish the voice of integrity; and overheated by their own fanaticism, they had become insensitive to real warmth of heart. Bernadotte, the agent of nobody, died the death of a hero of peace when he was murdered by the agents of war.

1948

ABOUT "COLLABORATION"

The August issue of *Jewish Frontier* carried an article by Ben Halpern, "The Partisan in Israel," in which, together with Robert Weltsch and Ernst Simon, I was singled out for an attack on my political views and my personal motives. Since Mr. Halpern's attack on the latter was based on an unexplained and certainly unexpected insight into my "subconsciousness," I don't think it necessary to reply to it. However, some of the political points which his article raised seem to be pertinent enough to merit closer attention.

Mr. Halpern is correct in stating that there exists an opposition to present Zionist politics which is based on a long-term analysis of the Jewish position in the Near East on one hand, and on a moral and political distrust of all racial chauvinist attitudes on the other, and that this opposition will not be silenced or disproved through the changing constellations of the moment. He also is correct in stating that apprehensions voiced by some members of this opposition and especially by myself have most fortunately been unfounded for the time being.

I do not think that the time has come to discuss the very complicated and very dangerous political background of the military victories of the state of Israel. Even without such an analysis, no "metaphysical" interpretation should be needed in order to understand the difference in emphasis and importance between a few military successes in a small country against ill-armed, ill-trained soldiers and the solid threatening opposition of many millions of people from Morocco down to the Indian Ocean. This and similar constellations constitute the long-range reality, which certainly is not less "real" than what happens in Jerusalem or in the Galilee. The trouble with reality is that, without transcending into another world, it sometimes does not lie before our noses.

What Mr. Halpern, like many of our politically interested intellectuals, does not understand is that we deal in politics only with warnings and not with prophecies. If I were foolish and resigned enough to play the role of the prophet, I certainly should also be content to share his eternal fate, which is to be proved wrong time and again, except at the decisive moment, when it is too late.

Much more to the point than this controversy about "realism" are those paragraphs in Halpern's article which deal with the difference between the "type of the partisan" and the "type of the collaborationist." (Here Mr. Halpern uses Max Weber's method of constructing *Idealtypen* and thus proves how difficult it seems to be to avoid "a type of reasoning which [is] . . . in essence metaphysical.") The term "collaborationist" is, of course, a defamation: actually, however, Halpern restores it to its noncommittal and literal meaning. For it is perfectly true that all the people attacked by him have been concerned, in different ways, with the relationship between the *yishuv* and the outside world, and have been constantly on the lookout for countries, persons, and institutions with which one might collaborate. This has been notably the case with Dr. Magnes's outstanding effort to bring about a Jewish-Arab agreement as the basis for any solution to the Palestinian problem. Halpern dismisses the Ihud group, of course, as unpractical. Yet Dr. Magnes's recent proposal of a confederation of Palestine is in agreement with some of the basic ideas contained in Count Bernadotte's peace proposals of July 4. Does Mr. Halpern think that the mediator was a very unpractical man?

The central question in this controversy is really the question whether one wants or does not want to collaborate. And this question, again, is tied up with an older troublesome question of Zionist politics, that is, the problem of the distinction between friend and foe. When, in the 1930s, the Jewish Agency concluded a "Transfer Agreement" with Nazi Germany, the problem of this distinction was involved. Official Zionism thought the agreement a wise step because it made possible the transfer of part of Jewish property from Germany to Palestine in the form of German merchandise. The agreement was severely criticized by a large part of Jewry because, from a long-range political point of view, it seemed unwise for a Jewish political agency to do business with an antisemitic government. A similar error in judgment, though in an opposite sense, is one of the basic conflicts between official Zionism and its current "collaborationist" opposition, and it has misled Mr. Halpern into a complete misunderstanding of my analysis of the all-or-nothing attitude.

Indeed, if Great Britain were an enemy of the Jews, like Nazi Germany, the all-or-nothing attitude would be justified. The point is precisely that today a certain general hysteria imposes all-or-nothing policies upon a moderately friendly world. This is chauvinism; it tends to divide the world into two halves, one of which is one's own nation, which fate, or ill will, or history has pitted against a whole world of enemies.

Neither the Arabs nor the British are enemies against whom an all-or-nothing attitude could be justified. With both, we shall have to live in peace. The struggle in Palestine takes place within a broad international framework, and the right distinction between friend and foe will be a life-or-death matter for the state of Israel. Changing opportunities of the moment are now dangerously blurring such fundamental distinctions. The program of left-wing Labor in Israel with respect to Russia on the one hand, and to Britain on the other, is a case in point.

This is also one of the reasons why the "partisan" attitude cannot be generalized—no matter how tempting Halpern's enthusiastic description may sound. A closer analysis would easily show that the moment the "partisan" is backed by the machinery of state power, he changes into that type of "political soldier" whom we know only too well in totalitarian governments. What the new state of Israel will need most are responsible citizens (the "type of the *citoyen*," to speak in Mr. Halpern's language) who don't lose their pioneer qualities and who, after having lost their faith in internationalist ideologies, may acquire a new, more sober, and juster international outlook upon the world that still surrounds them.

1948

NEW PALESTINE PARTY

Visit of Menachem Begin and Aims of Political Movement Discussed *

Among the most disturbing political phenomena of our times is the emergence in the newly created state of Israel of the "Freedom Party" (Tnuat Haherut), a political party closely akin in its organization, methods, political philosophy, and social appeal to the Nazi and Fascist parties. It was formed out of the membership and following of the former Irgun Zvai Leumi, a terrorist, right-wing, chauvinist organization in Palestine.

The current visit of Menachem Begin, leader of this party, to the United States is obviously calculated to give the impression of American support for his party in the coming Israeli elections, and to cement political ties with conservative Zionist elements in the United States. Several Americans of national repute have lent their names to welcome his visit. It is inconceivable that those who oppose fascism throughout the world, if correctly informed as to Mr. Begin's political record and perspectives, could add their names and support to the movement he represents.

Before irreparable damage is done by way of financial contributions, public manifestations in Begin's behalf, and the creation in Palestine of the impression that a large segment of America supports fascist elements in Israel, the American public must be informed as to the record and objectives of Mr. Begin and his movement.

The public avowals of Begin's party are no guide whatever to its actual character. Today they speak of freedom, democracy and anti-imperialism, whereas until recently they openly preached the doctrine of the fascist state. It is in its actions that the terrorist party betrays its real character; from its past actions we can judge what it may be expected to do in the future.

*An open letter to the *New York Times,* December 4, 1948, drafted by Arendt and co-signed by her, Albert Einstein, Sidney Hook, and Seymour Melman, among others.—Ed.

Attack on Arab Village

A shocking example was their behavior in the Arab village of Deir Yassin. This village, off the main roads and surrounded by Jewish lands, had taken no part in the war, and had even fought off Arab bands who wanted to use the village as their base. On April 9 *The New York Times* reported that terrorist bands attacked this peaceful village, which was not a military objective in the fighting, killed most of its inhabitants—240 men, women, and children—and kept a few of them alive to parade as captives through the streets of Jerusalem. Most of the Jewish community was horrified at the deed, and the Jewish Agency sent a telegram of apology to King Abdullah of Transjordan. But the terrorists, far from being ashamed of their act, were proud of this massacre, publicized it widely, and invited all the foreign correspondents present in the country to view the heaped corpses and the general havoc at Deir Yassin.

The Deir Yassin incident exemplifies the character and actions of the Freedom Party.

Within the Jewish community they have preached an admixture of ultra-nationalism, religious mysticism, and racial superiority. Like other fascist parties they have been used to break strikes, and have themselves pressed for the destruction of free trade unions. In their stead they have proposed corporate unions on the Italian Fascist model.

During the last year of sporadic anti-British violence, the IZL and Stern groups inaugurated a reign of terror in the Palestine Jewish community. Teachers were beaten up for speaking against them, adults were shot for not letting their children join them. By gangster methods, beatings, window-smashing, and widespread robberies, the terrorists intimidated the population and exacted a heavy tribute.

The people of the Freedom Party have had no part in the constructive achievements in Palestine. They have reclaimed no land, built no settlements, and only detracted from Jewish defense activities. Their much-publicized immigration endeavors were minute, and devoted mainly to bringing in fascist compatriots.

Discrepancies Seen

The discrepancies between the bold claims now being made by Begin and his party, and their record of past performance in Palestine, bear the imprint of no ordinary political party. This is the unmistakable stamp of a fascist party for whom terrorism (against Jews, Arabs, and British alike), and misrepresentation are the means and a "Führer State" is the goal.

In the light of the foregoing considerations, it is imperative that the truth about Mr. Begin and his movement be made known in this country. It is all the more tragic that the top leadership of American Zionism has refused to campaign against Begin's efforts, or even to expose to its own constituents the dangers to Israel of supporting Begin.

The undersigned therefore take this means of publicly presenting a few salient facts concerning Begin and his party; and of urging all concerned not to support this latest manifestation of fascism.

1948

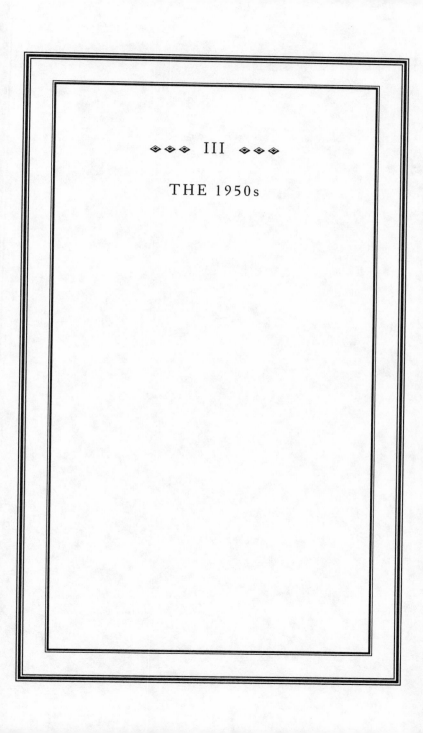

❖❖❖ III ❖❖❖

THE 1950s

PEACE OR ARMISTICE
IN THE NEAR EAST?

Peace in the Near East is essential to the state of Israel, to the Arab people, and to the Western world. Peace, as distinguished from an armistice, cannot be imposed from the outside; it can only be the result of negotiations, of mutual compromise and eventual agreement between Jews and Arabs.

The Jewish settlement in Palestine may become a very important factor in the development of the Near East, but it will always remain a comparatively small island in an Arab sea. Even in the event of maximum immigration over a long period of years, the reservoir of prospective citizens of Israel is limited to roughly two million, a figure that could be substantially increased only by catastrophic events in the United States or the Soviet Union. Since, however (apart from the improbability of such a turn of events), the state of Israel owes its very existence to these two world powers, and since failure to achieve a genuine Jewish-Arab understanding will necessarily make its survival even more dependent upon continued sympathy and support of one or the other, a Jewish catastrophe in the two great surviving centers of world Jewry would lead almost immediately to a catastrophe in Israel.

The Arabs have been hostile to the building of a Jewish homeland almost from the beginning. The uprising of 1921, the pogrom of 1929, the disturbances from 1936 to 1939 have been the outstanding landmarks in the history of Arab-Jewish relations under British rule. It was only logical that the evacuation of British troops coincided with the outbreak of a Jewish-Arab war; and it is remarkable how little the accomplished fact of a state of Israel and Jewish victories over Arab armies have influenced Arab politics. All hopes to the contrary notwithstanding, it seems as though the *one* argument the Arabs are incapable of understanding is force.

As far as Arab-Jewish relations are concerned, the war and the Israeli victories have not changed or solved anything. Any settlement short of genuine peace will give the Arabs time to grow stronger, to mend the rivalries between the Arab states, possibly to promote revolutionary changes, social, economic, and political. Probably such changes in the Arab world will come about in any event, but the question is whether they will be inspired by the thought of *revanche* and crystallize around a common hostility against Israel, or whether they will be prompted by an understanding of common interests and crystallize around close economic and political cooperation with the Jews, the most advanced and Westernized people of the region. Arab reluctance, on the one hand, to begin direct peace talks and the (implied) admission that they may prefer a peace imposed by an outside power, and Israeli handling of the Arab refugee problem on the other, argue in favor of the first possibility. But all considerations of the self-interest of both peoples speak for the second. To be sure, these reasons are weak in a century when political issues are no longer determined by common sense and when the representatives of great powers frequently behave more like gamblers than statesmen.

To such general considerations must be added the education in irresponsibility which was the concomitant of the mandate system. For twenty-five years, the peoples of Palestine could rely upon the British government to uphold adequate stability for general constructive purposes and feel free to indulge in all kinds of emotional, nationalistic, illusionary behavior. Occasional outbreaks, even if they enlisted almost unanimous popular support (as, for instance, the disturbances of 1936 to 1939, which were preceded by a successful Arab general strike, or the Jewish fight against Arab labor, 1934–36, which was supported by practically the whole Jewish population), led to nothing more serious than another inquiry commission or another turn in the complicated game of British imperialist policy.

It is only natural that in an atmosphere where nothing was quite serious both parties grew more and more reckless and were more and more inclined to consider only their own interests and to overlook the vital realities of the country as a whole. Thus the Arabs neglected to take into account the rapid growth of Jewish strength and the far-reaching consequences of economic development, while the Jews ignored the awakening of colonial peoples and the new nationalist solidarity in the Arab world from Iraq to French Morocco. In hope or in hate both peoples have focused their attention so exclusively upon the British that they practically ignored each other: the Jews forgot that the Arabs, not the English, were the permanent reality in

Near Eastern policies and the Arabs that Jewish settlers, and not British troops, intended to stay permanently in Palestine.

The British, on the other hand, were quite content with this state of affairs, because it prevented both a working agreement between Jews and Arabs, which might have resulted in a rebellion against British rule, and an open conflict between them, which might have endangered the peace of the country. No doubt, "if the British Government had really applied itself with energy and good will to the establishment of good relations between the Jews and the Arabs, such could have been accomplished" (Chaim Weizmann). Yet British interest in Arab-Jewish understanding awoke only when the British had decided to evacuate the country—a decision, by the way, which was caused neither by Jewish terrorism nor by the Arab League, but came as a consequence of the Labor government's liquidation of British rule in India. Since then the British have been genuinely interested in an Arab-Jewish settlement and in the prevention of the Balkanization of the region which may again attract a third power. But although the interests of the peoples of the Near East certainly coincide with British interests at this moment, the past record of British imperialism has made it impossible for her to negotiate a reasonable settlement.

But the choice between genuine peace and armistice is by no means only, or even primarily, an issue of foreign policy. The internal structure of the Arab states as well as of the Jewish state will depend upon it. A mere armistice would force the new Israeli state to organize the whole people for permanent potential mobilization; the permanent threat of armed intervention would necessarily influence the direction of all economic and social developments and possibly end in a military dictatorship. The cultural and political sterility of small, thoroughly militarized nations has been sufficiently demonstrated in history. The examples of Sparta and similar experiments are not likely to frighten a generation of European Jews who are trying to wipe out the humiliation of Hitler's slaughterhouses with the newly won dignity of battle and the triumph of victory. Nevertheless, even this generation should be able to realize that an independent Spartan existence will be possible only after the country has been built up and after the Jewish homeland has been definitely established, by no means the case now. Excessive expenditures on armaments and mobilization would not only mean the stifling of the young Jewish economy and the end of the country's social experiments, but lead to an increasing dependence of the whole population upon financial and other support from American Jewry.

A condition of no peace and no war will be far easier for the Arabs to bear, precisely because of the stagnation of their economic life and the backwardness of their social life. In the long run, however, the poverty-stricken, undeveloped, and unorganized Near East needs peace as badly as the Jews; it needs Jewish cooperation in order quickly to achieve the strength to prevent its remaining a power vacuum and to assure its independence. If the Arab states are not just pretending but really are afraid of Russian aggression, their only salvation lies in sincere collaboration with the state of Israel. The Arabs' argument that they can do without Jewish help and prefer to grow slowly and organically rather than be influenced by "foreign" Western methods and ideas may sound very attractive to a few romantics inside and outside the Arab world. The simple truth of the matter is that the world's political pace will not allow them enough time for "organic" development; the Arabs, though potentially stronger than the Jews, are not a great power either and hardly on the way to becoming one. The victories of the Israeli army are dangerous to them not so much because of possible Jewish domination as because of the demonstrated power vacuum. If they continue to be anti-Western, to spend their energies fighting the tiny Jewish state and indulging their sterile pride in keeping the national character intact, they are threatened with something far worse, and much more real, than the bogey of Jewish domination.

In terms of international politics, the danger of this little war between two small peoples is that it inevitably tempts and attracts the great powers to interfere, with the result that existing conflicts explode because they can be fought out by proxy. Until now, neither the Jewish charge of an *Anglo*-Arab invasion nor the Arab countercharge of a *Russian*-Jewish aggression has contained any truth at all. The reason, however, why both legends sound so plausible and are so frequently accepted is that such a situation can indeed develop.

Moreover, the last war showed all too clearly that no better pretext or greater help exists for would-be aggressors than petty national conflicts fought out in chauvinist violence. The peoples of the Near East who show such a disturbing resemblance in psychology and political mentality to the small nations of Central and Eastern Europe would do well to consider how easily these latter were conquered by Stalin as well as by Hitler, and to compare them with the more fortunate small nations, like the Scandinavian countries and Switzerland, who were not devoured by hate and not torn by chauvinistic passion.

The great good fortune of Jews as well as Arabs at this moment is that America and Great Britain not only have no interest in further hostilities, but, on the contrary, are genuinely eager to bring about an authentic pacification of the whole region. Mutual denunciations by Jews and Arabs to the effect that they are either British or Russian agents serve only to cloud the real issues: Jewish determination to keep and possibly extend national sovereignty without consideration for Arab interests, and Arab determination to expel the Jewish "invaders" from Palestine without consideration for Jewish achievements there. If this "independent and sovereign" behavior (Arab unwillingness during the war to take British advice, and the Jewish inclination to interpret as pressure any advice which America might offer, for instance, on the question of Arab refugees) goes on unabated, then all independence and sovereignty will be lost. Since a trusteeship under the United Nations has become impossible, continuance of this stubbornness leaves only three kinds of peace which the world may finally be willing to offer the Near East: a Pax Britannica, which is very unlikely at the moment; a Pax Americana, which is even more unlikely; or a Pax Moscovita, which, alas, is the only actual danger.

The Incompatibility of Claims

A good peace is usually the result of negotiation and compromise, not necessarily of a program. Good relationships between Jews and Arabs will depend upon a changed attitude toward each other, upon a change in the atmosphere in Palestine and the Near East, not necessarily upon a formula. Hardly any conflict in the history of the world has given rise to so many programs and formulae from the outside; yet none of them has ever been acceptable to either side. Each has been denounced as soon as it was published as pro-Jewish by the Arabs and pro-Arab by the Jews.

The reception of the two Bernadotte peace proposals is typical. The first report to the United Nations concluded with a series of recommendations, made in the spirit of the United Nations' decision of partition; they provided for political implementation of economic cooperation through a "coordinated foreign policy" and "measures of common defense," for negotiated boundaries and for a limited guarantee of Jewish immigration. The second report, on the contrary, recommended two completely sovereign and independent political entities, separated by neutralized zones, and temporarily supervised by a UN commission. Both reports were denounced equally by both sides. The differences between the two peace proposals were hardly recognized because they had one thing in common: the recognition of the existence of a state of Israel on one side, and the existence of an Arab population in Palestine and the Near East on the other.

Since no formula, however good and sensible, seems to be acceptable to either side while the present mood of the two peoples persists, it may well be that any plan, however rudimentary, will be a sufficient basis of negotiations as soon as this mood is changed.

The past two years will stand out in Jewish history for many decades, and perhaps for many centuries to come. Even if the establishment of a Jewish state and the outbreak of an Arab-Jewish war may turn out ultimately to be one of many ephemeral episodes in an unhappy history of a country that has known many changes of rulers and fortune, their place as a turning point in Jewish history has already been decided. The majority of the Jewish people feel that the happenings of the last years have a closer relation to the destruction of the Temple in A.D. 70 and the messianic yearnings of two thousand years of dispersion, than to the United Nations' decision of 1947, the Balfour Declaration of 1917, or even the fifty years of pioneering in Palestine. Jewish victories are not judged in the light of present realities in the Near East but in the light of a very distant past; the present war fills every Jew with "such satisfaction as we have not had for centuries, perhaps not since the days of the Maccabees" (Ben-Gurion).

This feeling of historical momentum, this determination to regard these recent events as a final verdict of history, is doubtless strengthened by success, but success is not its source. The Jews went into battle against the British occupation troops and the Arab armies with the "spirit of Masadah," inspired by the slogan "or else we shall go down," determined to refuse all compromise even at the price of national suicide. Today the Israeli government speaks of accomplished facts, of Might is Right, of military necessities, of the law of conquest, whereas two years ago, the same people in the Jewish Agency spoke of justice and the desperate needs of the Jewish people. Palestinian Jewry bet on one card—and won.

Against Jewish determination to regard the outcome as final stands the determination of the Arabs to view it as an interlude. Here, too, we are confronted with a decision which is neither deducible from events nor changed in the least by them. Defeats seem to confirm the Arabs' attitude as much as victories do that of the Jews. Arab policy in this respect is very simple and consists mainly in a diplomacy which discounts defeats and states and restates with undisturbed stubbornness the old claim to ownership of the country and refusal to recognize the state of Israel.

This mutual refusal to take each other seriously is perhaps the clearest sign of the seriousness of the situation. During the war, it expressed itself in the dangerous inclination to interpret the whole conflict as the result of a sinister behind-the-scenes conspiracy in which the Arabs were not confronted with 700,000 or 800,000 Palestinian Jews but with the overwhelming strength of American or Russian imperialism or both, while the Jews insisted that they fought not so much the members of the Arab League as the entire might of the British Empire. That the Arabs should attempt to find a plausible explanation for the fact that six Arab states could not win a single victory against the tiny forces of Palestinian Jewry, and that the Jews should shrink from the idea of being permanently surrounded by hostile neighbors who so hopelessly outnumber them, is understandable enough. The net result, however, of a propaganda (by itself hardly worthy of consideration) which treats the real opponent as a kind of ghost or tool is an atmosphere where negotiations are impossible: for what is the point of taking statements and claims seriously if you believe that they serve a conspiracy?

This utterly unreal situation is not new. For more than twenty-five years, Jews and Arabs have made perfectly incompatible claims on each other. The Arabs never gave up the idea of a unitary Arab state in Palestine, though they sometimes reluctantly conceded limited minority rights to Jewish inhabitants. The Jews, with the exception of the Revisionists, for many years refused to talk about their ultimate goals, partly because they knew only too well the uncompromising attitude of the Arabs and partly because they had unlimited confidence in British protection. The Biltmore Program of 1942 for the first time formulated Jewish political aims officially—a unitary Jewish state in

Palestine with the provision of certain minority rights for Palestinian Arabs who then still formed the majority of the Palestinian population. At the same time, the transfer of Palestinian Arabs to neighboring countries was contemplated and openly discussed in the Zionist movement.

Nor is this incompatibility only a matter of politics. The Jews are convinced, and have announced many times, that the world—or history or higher morality—owes them a righting of the wrongs of two thousand years and, more specifically, a compensation for the catastrophe of European Jewry which, in their opinion, was not simply a crime of Nazi Germany but of the whole civilized world. The Arabs, on the other hand, reply that two wrongs do not make a right and that "no code of morals can justify the persecution of one people in an attempt to relieve the persecution of the other." The point of this kind of argumentation is that it is unanswerable. Both claims are nationalistic because they make sense only in the closed framework of one's own people and history, and legalistic because they discount the concrete factors of the situation.

Social and Economic Separation

The complete incompatibility of claims which until now has frustrated every attempt to compromise and every effort to find a common denominator between two peoples whose common interests are patent to all except themselves is only the outward sign of a deeper, more real incompatibility. It is incredible and sad, but it is true, that more than three decades of intimate proximity have changed very little the initial feeling of complete strangeness between Arabs and Jews. The way the Arabs conducted this war has proved better than anything else how little they knew of Jewish strength and the will to fight. To the Jews, similarly, the Arabs they met for so many years in every city, village, and rural district, with whom they had constant dealings and conflicts, have remained phantoms, beings whom they have considered only on the irrelevant levels of folklore, nationalist generalizations, or idle idealistic dreams.

The Jewish and Arab failure to visualize a close neighbor as a concrete human being has many explanations. Outstanding among them is the economic structure of the country in which the Arab and Jewish sectors were separated by, so to speak, watertight walls. The few exceptions, such as common export organizations of Jewish and Arab orange growers or a few factories that employed both Jewish and Arab labor, only confirmed the rule. The building of the Jewish homeland, the most important economic factor in the recent history of the entire Near East, never depended on Jewish-Arab cooperation, but exclusively on the enterprise and pioneering spirit of Jewish labor and the financial support of world Jewry. The Jewish economy may eventually have to depend heavily if not exclusively on the Arab markets of the Near East. But this stage of mutual dependence is still far off and will be reached only after Palestine has been fully industrialized and the Arab countries have reached a level of civilization that could offer a market for high-quality merchandise, which only the Jewish economy will probably be able to produce profitably.

The struggle for political sovereignty, necessarily accompanied by heavy expenditure for armaments and even more decisive losses in work hours, has retarded considerably the development toward economic independence. As long as outside financial support on a large scale is assured, Jewish-Arab cooperation can hardly become an economic necessity for the new Israeli state. The same has been true in the past. The financial support of world Jewry, without which the whole experiment would have failed, signified economically that the Jewish settlement could assert itself without much thought of what was going on in the surrounding world, that it had no vital interest, except on humanitarian grounds, in raising the Arab standard of living, and that economic issues could be fought out as though the Jewish national home were completely isolated from its neighbors.

Naturally, economic and social isolation had its good and its bad aspects. Its advantage was that it made possible such experiments as the collective and cooperative settlements, and that an advanced and in many respects very promising economic structure could impose itself upon an environment of hopeless misery and sterility. Its economic disadvantage was that the experiment dangerously resembled a hothouse plant and that the social and political problems which arose from the presence of a native population could be handled without consideration of objective factors.

Organized Jewish labor fought and won a relentless battle against cheap Arab labor; the old-time Arab fellahin, even though they were not deprived of their soil by Jewish settlement, quickly became a kind of relic, unfit for and superfluous to the new modernized structure of the country. Under the leadership of Jewish labor, Palestine underwent the same industrial revolution, the same change from a more or less feudal to a more or less capitalist order, as European countries did 150 years ago. The decisive difference was only that the industrial revolution had created and employed its own fourth estate, a native proletariat, whereas in Palestine the same development involved the importation of workers and left the native population a potential proletariat with no prospect of employment as free laborers.

This unhappy potential Arab proletariat cannot be argued away by statistics about land sales, nor can it be counted in terms of the destitute. Figures do not show the psychological changes of the native population, their deep resentment against a state of affairs which seemingly left them untouched, and in reality demonstrated to them the possibility of a higher standard of living without ever fulfilling the implied promises. The Jews introduced something new into the country which, through sheer productivity, soon became the decisive factor. Compared to this new life, the primitive Arab economy assumed a ghostlike appearance, and its backwardness and inefficiency seemed to await a catastrophe to sweep it away.

It was, however, no accident that Zionist officials allowed this economic trend to take its course and that none of them ever made, in Judah L. Magnes's words, Jewish-Arab cooperation "the chief objective of major policy." Zionist ideology, which after all is at least thirty years older than the Balfour Declaration, started not from a consideration of the realities in Palestine but from the problem of Jewish homelessness. The thought that "the people without a country needed a country without a people" so occupied the minds of the Zionist leaders that they simply overlooked the native population. The Arab problem was always "the veiled issue of Zionist politics" (as Isaac Epstein called it as long ago as 1907), long before economic problems in Palestine forced Zionist leadership into an even more effective neglect.

The temptation to neglect the Arab problem was great indeed. It was no small matter, after all, to settle an urban population in a poor, desertlike country, to educate thousands of young potential tradesmen and intellectuals to the arduous life and ideas of pioneerdom. Arab labor was dangerous because it was cheap; there was the constant temptation for Jewish capital to employ Arabs instead of the more expensive and more rights-conscious Jewish workers. How easily could the whole Zionist venture have degenerated in those crucial years into a white man's colonial enterprise at the expense of, and based upon, the work of natives. Jewish class struggle in Palestine was for the most part a fight against Arab workers. To be anticapitalist in Palestine almost always meant to be practically anti-Arab.

The social aspect of Jewish-Arab relationships is decisive because it convinced the only section of the population that had not come to Palestine for nationalistic reasons that it was impossible to come to terms with the Arabs without committing national and social suicide. The crude nationalist demand of "a country without a people" seemed so indisputably right in the light of practical experience that even the most idealistic elements in the Jewish labor movements let themselves be tempted first into forgetfulness and neglect, and then into narrow and inconsiderate nationalistic attitudes.

British administration which, according to the terms of the mandate, was supposed to prepare "the development of self-governing institutions," did nothing to bring the two peoples together and very little to raise the Arab standard of living. In the twenties, this may have been a half-conscious policy of *divide et impera;* in the late thirties, it was open sabotage of the Jewish national home, which the colonial services had always held to be dangerous to imperialist interests and whose ultimate survival, as the British knew perhaps better than Zionist leadership, depended upon cooperation with the Arabs. Much worse, however, though much less tangible, was the romantic attitude of the colonial services; they adored all the charming qualities of Arab life, which definitely impeded social and economic progress. The urban Jewish middle class and especially the free professions in Jerusalem were for a certain time inclined to imitate the British society they met among the administrative personnel. Here they learned, at best, that it was fashionable to be interested in Arab folk life, to admire the noble gestures and customs of the Bedouins, to be charmed by the hospitality of an ancient civilization. What they overlooked was that Arabs were human beings like themselves and that it might be dangerous not to expect them to act and react in much the same way as Jews; in other words, that because of the presence of the Jews in the country, the Bedouins were likely to want even more urgently land to settle on (a revival of the "inherent tendency in nomad society to desert the weariness and hopelessness of pastoral occupations for the superior comforts of agriculture"—H. St. J. B. Philby), the fellahin to feel for the first time the need for machines with which one obtained better products with less toil, and the urban population to strive for a standard of living which they had hardly known before the arrival of the Jews.

The Arab masses awoke only gradually to a spirit of envy and frustrated competition. In their old disease-stricken poverty, they looked upon Jewish achievements and customs as though they were images from a fairy tale which would soon vanish as miraculously as they had appeared and interrupted their old way of life. This had nothing to do with neighborliness between Jewish and Arab villages, which was the rule rather than the exception for a long time, which survived the disturbances of 1936–39 and came to an end only under the impact of Jewish terrorism in 1947 and 1948. These relations, however, could be so easily destroyed without harming Jewish municipal and economic interests because they had always been without consequence, a simple, frequently touching expression of human neighborliness. With the exception of the Haifa municipality, not a single common institution, not a single common political body had been built up on this basis in all those years. It was as though, by tacit agreement, the neighbors had decided that their ways of life were different to the point of mutual indifference, that no common interests were possible except their human curiosity. No neighborliness could alter the fact that the Jews regarded the Arabs as an interesting example of folk life at best, and as a backward people who did not matter at worst, and that the Arabs considered the whole Jewish venture a strange interlude out of a fairy tale at best, and, at worst, an illegal enterprise which one day would be fair game for looting and robbery.

The Uniqueness of the Country

While the mood of the country was only too typical, quite like other small nations' fierce chauvinism and fanatic provincialism, the realities of Jewish achievement in Palestine were unique in many respects. What happened in Palestine was not easy to judge and evaluate: it was extraordinarily different from anything that had happened in the past.

The building of a Jewish national home was not a colonial enterprise in which Europeans came to exploit foreign riches with the help and at the expense of native labor. Palestine was and is a poor country and whatever riches it possesses are exclusively the product of Jewish labor which are not likely to survive if ever the Jews are expelled from the country. Exploitation or robbery, so characteristic of the "original accumulation" in all imperialist enterprises, were either completely absent or played an insignificant role. American and European capital that flooded the country came not as dividend-paying capital held by absentee shareholders but as "charity" money which the recipients were free to expend at will. It was used for the acquisition and nationalization of the soil, the establishment of collective settlements, long-term loans to farmers' and workers' cooperatives, social and health services, free and equal education, and generally for the building of an economy with a pronounced socialist physiognomy. Through these efforts, in thirty years the land was changed as completely as if it had been transplanted to another continent, and this without conquest and with no attempt at extermination of natives.

The Palestinian experiment has frequently been called artificial, and it is true that everything connected with the building of a Jewish national home—the Zionist movement as well as the realities in Palestine—has not been, as it were, in the nature of things, not according to the ways of the world. No economic necessities prompted the Jews to go to Palestine in the decisive years when immigration to America was the natural escape from misery and persecution; the land was no temptation for capital export, did not in itself offer opportunities for the solution of population problems. The collective rural settlements, the backbone of Palestinian society and the expression of pioneerdom, can certainly not be explained by utilitarian reasons. The development of the soil, the erection of a Hebrew University, the establishment of great health centers, were all "artificial" developments, supported from abroad and initiated by a spirit of enterprise which paid no heed to calculations of profit and loss.

A generation brought up in the blind faith in necessity—of history or economy or society or nature—found it difficult to understand that precisely this artificiality gave the Jewish achievements in Palestine their human significance. The trouble was that Zionists as well as anti-Zionists thought that the artificial character of the enterprise was to be reproached rather than praised.

Zionists, therefore, tried to explain the building of a Jewish national home as the only possible answer to a supposedly eternal antisemitism, the establishment of collective settlements as the only solution to the difficulties of Jewish agricultural labor, the foundation of health centers and the Hebrew University in terms of national interests. Each of these explanations contains part of the truth and each is somehow beside the point. The challenges were all there, but none of the responses was "natural." The point was that the responses were of much more permanent human and political value than the challenges, and that only ideological distortions made it appear that the challenges by themselves—antisemitism, poverty, national homelessness—had produced something.

Politically, Palestine was under a British mandate, that is, a form of government supposedly devised only for backward areas where primitive peoples have not yet learned the elementary rules of self-government. But under the not too sympathetic eye of the British trustee the Jews erected a kind of state within a nonexistent state, which in some respects was more modern than the most advanced governments of the Western world. This nonofficial Jewish government was represented only on the surface by the Jewish Agency, the recognized political body of world Zionism, or by the Vaad Leumi, the official representative of Palestinian Jewry. What actually ruled the Jewish sector of the country much more efficiently than either and became more decisive in everyday life than British administration was the Histadruth, the Palestinian trade unions, in which the overwhelming majority of Jewish labor, that is, the majority of the population, was organized. The trade unions stepped into all those areas which are usually regulated by municipal or national government as well as into a great number of activities which in other countries are the domain of free enterprise. All sorts of functions, such as administration, immigration, defense, education, health, social services, public works, communications, and so forth, were developed upon the initiative and under the leadership of the Histadruth, which, at the same time, grew into the largest single employer in the country. This explains the miraculous fact that a mere proclamation of Jewish self-government eventually sufficed to bring a state machine into being. The present government of Israel, though a coalition government in appearance, is actually the government of the Histadruth.

Although the Jewish workers and farmers had an emotional awareness of the uniqueness of their achievements, expressed in a new kind of dignity and pride, neither they nor their leaders realized articulately the chief features of the new experiment. Thus Zionist leadership could go on for decades talking about the natural coincidence between Jewish interests and British imperialism, showing how little they understood themselves. For while they were talking this way, they built up a country that was economically so independent of Great Britain that it fitted into neither the empire nor the Commonwealth; and they educated the people in such a way that it could not possibly fit into the political scheme of imperialism because it was neither a master nor a subject nation.

This would have been greatly to the credit of the Israeli state and even to its advantage today, if it had only been realized in time. But even now this is not the case. To defend their nationalist aggressiveness Israeli leadership today still insists on old truisms like "No people ever gets anything, least of all freedom, as a gift, but has to fight for it," thus proving that they do not understand that the whole Jewish venture in Palestine is an excellent indication that some changes have occurred in the world and one may conquer a country by transforming its deserts into flourishing land.

Ideological explanations are those which do not fit realities but serve some other ulterior interests or motives. This does not mean that ideologies are ineffective in politics; on the contrary, their very momentum and the fanaticism they inspire frequently overwhelm more realistic considerations. In this sense, almost from the beginning, the misfortune of the building of a Jewish national home has been that it was accompanied by a Central European ideology of nationalism and tribal thinking among the Jews, and by an Oxford-inspired colonial romanticism among the Arabs. For ideological reasons, the Jews overlooked the Arabs, who lived in what would have been an empty country, to fit their preconceived ideas of national emancipation. Because of romanticism or a complete inability to understand what was actually going on, the Arabs considered the Jews to be either old-fashioned invaders or newfangled tools of imperialism.

The British-inspired romanticization of poverty, of "the gospel of bareness" (T. E. Lawrence), blended only too well with the new Arab national consciousness and their old pride, according to which it is better to accept bribes than help. The new nationalist insistence on sovereignty, supported by an older desire to be left alone, served only to bolster exploitation by a few ruling families and prevent the development of the region. In their blind ideological hostility toward Western civilization, a hostility which, ironically enough, was largely inspired by Westerners, they could not see that this region would be modernized in any case and that it would be far wiser to form an alliance with the Jews, who naturally shared the general interests of the Near East, than with some big faraway power whose interests were alien and who would necessarily consider them a subject people.

The Nonnationalist Tradition

Against this background of ideological thinking the few protagonists of Jewish-Arab cooperation find their true stature. So few in number that they can hardly be called a real opposition force, so isolated from the masses and mass propaganda media that they were frequently ignored or suffocated by that peculiar praise which discredits a man as impractical by calling him an "idealist" or a "prophet," they nevertheless created, on the Jewish as well as the Arab side, an articulate tradition. At least their approach to the Palestinian problem begins in the objective realities of the situation.

Since it is usually asserted that goodwill toward the Jewish national home in Palestine was always completely lacking on the Arab side and that Jewish spokesmen for Arab-Jewish understanding never could produce a single Arab of any standing who was willing to cooperate with them, a few instances of Arab initiative in trying to bring about some kind of Jewish-Arab agreement may be mentioned. There was the meeting of Zionist and Arab leaders in Damascus in 1913, charged with preparing an Arab-Jewish conference in Lebanon. At that time the whole Near East was still under Turkish rule, and the Arabs felt that as an oppressed people they had much in common with the Eastern European sections of the Jewish people. There was the famous friendship treaty of 1919 between King Faisal of Syria and Chaim Weizmann, which both sides allowed to slip into oblivion. There was the Jewish-Arab conference of 1922 in Cairo, when the Arabs showed themselves willing to agree to Jewish immigration within the limitations of the economic capacity of Palestine.

There were negotiations carried on between Judah L. Magnes (with the subsequent knowledge of the Jewish Agency) and the Palestinian Arab Higher Committee at the end of 1936, immediately after the outbreak of the Arab disturbance. A few years later, tentative consultations were carried out between leading Egyptians and the Jews. "The Egyptians," reports Weizmann in his autobiography, "were acquainted and impressed by our progress and suggested that perhaps in the future they might serve to bridge the gulf between us and the Arabs of Palestine. They assumed that the White Paper . . . would be adopted by England, but its effects might be mitigated, perhaps even nullified, if the Jews of Palestine showed themselves ready to cooperate with Egypt."

And last but not least, as late as 1945, Azzam Bey, then secretary of the Arab League, stated that "the Arabs [were] prepared to make far-reaching concessions toward the gratification of the Jewish desire to see Palestine established as a spiritual and even a material home." To be sure, such Arabs had as little Arab mass support as their Jewish counterparts. But who knows what might have happened if their hesitating and tentative efforts had gotten a more sympathetic reception on the other side of the table? As it was, these Arabs were discredited among their own people when they discovered that the Jews either ignored them (as happened to Azzam Bey's statement) or broke off negotiations as soon as they hoped to find support from an outside ruling power (the Turkish government in 1913 and the British in 1922) and generally made the solution of the problem dependent upon the British, who naturally "found its difficulties insuperable" (Weizmann). In the same way Jewish spokesmen for Arab-Jewish understanding were discredited when their very fair and moderate demands were distorted and taken advantage of, as happened with the efforts of the Magnes group in 1936.

The necessity of Jewish-Arab understanding can be proved by objective factors; its possibility is almost entirely a matter of subjective political wisdom and personalities. Necessity, based on economic, military, and geographic considerations, will make itself felt in the long run only, or possibly, at a time when it is too late. Possibility is a matter of the immediate present, a question of whether there is enough statesmanship on both sides to anticipate the direction of long-range necessary trends and channel them into constructive political institutions.

It is one of the most hopeful signs for the actual possibility of a common Arab-Jewish policy that its essentials have only recently been formulated in very cogent terms by at least one outstanding Arab, Charles Malik, the representative of Lebanon to the United Nations, and one outstanding Palestinian Jew, Dr. Magnes, the late president of the Hebrew University and chairman of the Palestinian group of Ihud (Unity).

The speech Dr. Malik made on May 28, 1948, before the Security Council of the United Nations on the priority of Jewish-Arab agreement over all other solutions of the Palestinian problem is noteworthy for its calm and open insistence on peace and the realities of the Near East, and also because it found a "responsive echo" in the Jewish Agency's delegate, Maj. Aubrey Eban.

Dr. Malik, addressing the Security Council, warned the great powers against a policy of fait accompli. "The real task of world statesmanship," he said, was "to help the Jews and the Arabs not to be permanently alienated from one another." It would be a grave disservice to Jews to give a Jewish state a false sense of security as the result of successful manipulation of international machinery, for this would distract them from the fundamental task of establishing a "reasonable, workable, just, abiding understanding with the Arabs."

Dr. Malik's words sound like a late echo to Martin Buber's (the philosopher of the Hebrew University) earlier denunciation of the Zionist Biltmore Program as "admitting the aim of the minority to 'conquer' the country by means of international maneuvers." But Dr. Magnes's statement of the case and the conditions for Jewish-Arab cooperation before the Anglo-American Committee of Inquiry in 1946, when the White Paper's ban on Jewish immigration was still in force, read like an anticipated response from the Jewish side to the Arab challenge: "Our view is based on two assumptions, first that Jewish-Arab cooperation is not only essential, it is also possible. The alternative is war. . . ."

Dr. Magnes recognized that Palestine is a holy land for three monotheistic religions. To it the Arabs have a natural right and the Jews historical rights, both of equal validity. Thus, Palestine was already a binational state. This means political equality for the Arabs and justifies numerical equality for the Jews, that is, the right of immigration to Palestine. Dr. Magnes did not believe that all Jews would be satisfied with his proposal, but he thought that many would accept it, since they wanted the Jewish state mainly as a place to which to migrate. He urged the necessity of revising the whole concept of the state. To the Arabs he argued that sovereign independence in tiny Palestine was impossible. Indeed, he called for Palestinian participation in a

Middle Eastern regional federation as both a practical necessity and as a further assurance to the Arabs. "What a boon to mankind it would be if the Jews and Arabs of Palestine were to strive together in friendship and partnership to make this Holy Land into a thriving peaceful Switzerland in the heart of this ancient highway between East and West. This would have incalculable political and spiritual influence in all the Middle East and far beyond. A binational Palestine could become a beacon of peace in the world."

The Hebrew University and the Collective Settlements

If nationalism were nothing worse than a people's pride in outstanding or unique achievement, Jewish nationalism would have been nourished by two institutions in the Jewish national home: the Hebrew University and the collective settlements. Both are rooted in permanent nonnationalist trends in Jewish tradition—the universality and predominance of learning and the passion for justice. Here was a beginning of something true liberals of all countries and nationalities had hoped for when the Jewish people, with its peculiar tradition and historical experience, were given freedom and cultural autonomy. No one expressed this hope better than Woodrow Wilson, who called for "not merely the rebirth of the Jewish people, but the birth also of new ideals, of new ethical values, of new conceptions of social justice which shall spring as a blessing for all mankind from that land and that people whose lawgivers and prophets . . . spoke those truths which have come thundering down the ages" (quoted from Selig Adler, "The Palestine Question in the Wilson Era," in *Jewish Social Studies*, October 1948).

These two institutions, the kibbutzim (collective settlements) on one hand, the Hebrew University on the other, supported and inspired the nonnationalist, antichauvinist trend and opposition in Zionism. The university was supposed to represent the universalism of Judaism in the particular Jewish land. It was not conceived just as the university of Palestine, but as the university of the Jewish people.

It is highly significant that the most consistent and articulate spokesmen for Jewish-Arab understanding came from the Hebrew University. The two groups that made cooperation with the Arabs the cornerstone of their political philosophy, the Brith Shalom (Covenant of Peace) in the twenties and the Ihud (Unity) Association in the forties—both founded and inspired by Dr. Magnes, the cofounder and president of the Hebrew University since 1925—are not simply the expression of Western-educated intellectuals who find it difficult to swallow the crude slogans of a Balkanized nationalism. From the beginning Zionism contained two separate tendencies that met only in their agreement about the necessity of a Jewish homeland.

The victorious trend, the Herzlian tradition, took its chief impulse from the view of antisemitism as an "eternal" phenomenon in all countries of Jewish dispersion. It was strongly influenced by other nineteenth-century small national liberation movements and denied the possibility of Jewish survival in any country except Palestine, under any conditions except those of a full-fledged sovereign Jewish state. The other trend, dating back to Ahad Haam, saw in Palestine the Jewish cultural center which would inspire the spiritual development of all Jews in other countries, but would not need ethnic homogeneity and national sovereignty. As far back as the 1890s, Ahad Haam insisted on the presence in Palestine of an Arab native population and the necessity for peace. Those who followed him never aimed to make "Palestine as Jewish as England is English" (in the words of Weizmann), but thought that the establishment of a center of higher learning was more important for the new revival movement than the foundation of a state. The main achievement of the Herzlian tradition is the Jewish state; it came about (as Ahad Haam feared at the turn of the century and as Dr. Magnes warned for more than twenty-five years) at the price of an Arab-Jewish war. The main achievement of the Ahad Haam tradition is the Hebrew University.

Another part of the movement, influenced by though not connected with Ahad Haam's Zionism, grew out of Eastern European socialism, and ultimately led to the foundation of collective settlements. As a new form of agricultural economy, social living, and workers' cooperatives, it became the mainstay of the economic life of the Jewish homeland. The desire to build a new type of society in which there would be no exploitation of man by man did more to attract the best elements of Eastern European Jewry—that is, the powerful revolutionary ferment in Zionism without which not a single piece of land would have been tilled or a single road built—than the Herzlian analyses of Jewish assimilation, or Jabotinsky's propaganda for a Jewish state, or the cultural Zionists' appeal for a revival of the religious values of Judaism.

In the rural collective settlements, an age-old Jewish dream of a society based on justice, formed in complete equality, indifferent to all profit motives, was realized, even if on a small scale. Their greatest achievement was the creation of a new type of man and a new social elite, the birth of a new aristocracy which differed greatly from the Jewish masses in and outside of Palestine in habits, manners, values, and way of life, and whose claim to leadership in moral and social questions was clearly recognized by the population. Completely free and unhampered by any government, a new form of ownership, a new type of farmer, a new way of family life and child education, and new approaches to the troublesome conflicts between city and country, between rural and industrial labor, were created. Just as the very universalism of teaching and learning at the Hebrew University could be trusted to secure firm links between the Jewish national home, world Jewry, and the international world of scholarship, so could the collective settlements be trusted to keep Zionism within the highest tradition of Judaism, whose "principles call for the creation of a visible tangible society founded upon justice and mercy" (M. Buber). At the same time these experiments hold out hope for solutions that may one day become acceptable and applicable for the large mass of men everywhere whose dignity and humanity are today so seriously threatened by the standard of a competitive and acquisitive society.

The only larger groups who ever actively promoted and preached Jewish-Arab friendship came from this collective settlement movement. It was one of the greatest tragedies for the new state of Israel that these labor elements, notably the Hashomer Haza'ir, sacrificed their binational program to the fait accompli of the United Nations' partition decision.

The Results of the War

Uninfluenced by the voices raised in a spirit of understanding, compromise, and reason, events have been allowed to take their course. For more than twenty-five years, Dr. Magnes and the small group of his followers in Palestine and in Zionism had predicted that there would be either Jewish-Arab cooperation or war, and there has been war; that there could be either a binational Palestine or domination of one people by the other, and there has been the flight of more than 500,000 Arabs from Israeli-dominated territory; that the British White Paper policy and its ban on immigration in the years of the Jewish European catastrophe had to be immediately annulled or the Jews would risk everything to obtain a state if only for the sake of immigration, and, with no one on the British side willing to make any concessions, there is the fact that the Jews obtained a sovereign state.

Similarly, and despite the great impression which Dr. Malik's speech made on his colleagues in the Security Council of the United Nations, the whole policy not only of Israel but of the United Nations and the United States itself is a policy of fait accompli. True, on the surface it looks as though the armed forces of Israel had created the fait accompli of which Dr. Malik warned so eloquently. Yet who would doubt that no number of victories in themselves would have been sufficient to secure Israel's existence without the support of the United States and American Jewry?

The most realistic way to measure the cost to the peoples of the Near East of the events of the past year is not by casualties, economic losses, war destruction, or military victories, but by the political changes, the most outstanding of which has been the creation of a new category of homeless people, the Arab refugees. These not only form a dangerous potential irredenta dispersed in all Arab countries where they could easily become the visible uniting link; much worse, no matter how their exodus came about (as a consequence of Arab atrocity propaganda or real atrocities or a mixture of both), their flight from Palestine, prepared by Zionist plans of large-scale population transfers during the war and followed by the Israeli refusal to readmit the refugees to their old home, made the old Arab claim against Zionism finally come true: the Jews simply aimed at expelling the Arabs from their homes. What had been the pride of the Jewish homeland, that it had not been based upon exploitation, turned into a curse when the final test came: the flight of the Arabs would not have been possible and not have been welcomed by the Jews if they had lived in a common economy. The reactionary Arabs of the Near East and their British protectors were finally proved right: they had always considered "the Jews dangerous not because they exploit the fellaheen, but because they do not exploit them" (Weizmann).

Liberals in all countries were horrified at the callousness, the haughty dismissal of humanitarian considerations by a government whose representatives, only one year ago, had pleaded their own cause on purely humanitarian grounds, and were educated by a movement that, for more than fifty years, had based its claims exclusively on justice. Only one voice eventually was raised in protest to Israel's handling of the Arab refugee question, the voice of Dr. Magnes, who wrote a letter to the editor of *Commentary* (October 1948):

> It seems to me that any attempt to meet so vast a human situation except from the humane, the moral point of view will lead us into a morass. . . . If the Palestine Arabs left their homesteads "voluntarily" under the impact of Arab propaganda and in a veritable panic, one may not forget that the most potent argument in this propaganda was the fear of a repetition of the Irgun-Stern atrocities at Deir Yassin, where the Jewish authorities were unable or unwilling to prevent the act or punish the guilty. It is unfortunate that the very men who could point to the tragedy of Jewish DP's as the chief argument for mass immigration into Palestine should now be ready, as far as the world knows, to help create an additional category of DP's in the Holy Land.

Dr. Magnes, feeling the full significance of actions which forfeited the old proud claim of Zionist pioneerdom that theirs was the only colonizing venture in history not carried out with bloody hands, based his protest on purely humanitarian grounds—and laid himself wide open to the old accusations of quixotic morality in politics where supposedly only advantage and success count. The old Jewish legend about the thirty-six unknown righteous men who always exist and without whom the world would go to pieces says the last word about the necessity of such "quixotic" behavior in the ordinary course of events. In a world like ours, however, in which politics in some countries has long since outgrown sporadic sinfulness and entered a new stage of criminality, uncompromising morality has suddenly changed its old function of merely keeping the world together and has become the only medium through which true reality, as opposed to the distorted and essentially ephemeral factual situations created by crimes, can be perceived and planned. Only those who are still able to disregard the mountains of dust which emerge out of and disappear into the nothingness of sterile violence can be trusted with anything so serious as the permanent interests and political survival of a nation.

Federation or Balkanization?

The true objectives of a nonnationalist policy in the Near East and particularly in Palestine are few in number and simple in nature. Nationalist insistence on absolute sovereignty in such small countries as Palestine, Syria, Lebanon, Iraq, Transjordan, Saudi Arabia, and Egypt can lead only to the Balkanization of the whole region and its transformation into a battlefield for the conflicting interests of the great powers to the detriment of all authentic national interests.

In the long run, the only alternative to Balkanization is a regional federation, which Dr. Magnes (in an article in *Foreign Affairs*) proposed as long ago as 1943, and which more recently was proclaimed as a distant but desired goal by Major Eban, Israeli representative at the United Nations. While Dr. Magnes's original proposal comprised only those countries which the peace treaties of 1919 had dismembered but which had formed an integrated whole under Turkish government, that is, Palestine, Transjordan, Lebanon, and Syria, the concept of Aubrey Eban (as published in an article in *Commentary* in 1948) aimed at a "Near Eastern League, comprising all the diverse nationalities of the area, each free within its own area of independence and cooperating with others for the welfare of the region as a whole." A federation which according to Eban might possibly include "Turkey, Christian Lebanon, Israel and Iran as partners of the Arab world in a league of nonaggression, mutual defense and economic cooperation" has the great advantage that it would comprise more than the two peoples, Jews and Arabs, and thus eliminate Jewish fears of being outnumbered by the Arabs.

The best hope for bringing this federation nearer would still be a confederation of Palestine, as Dr. Magnes and Ihud proposed, after partition and a sovereign Jewish state had become an accomplished fact. The very term "confederation" indicates the existence of two independent political entities, as contrasted with a federal system, which is usually regarded "as a multiple government in a single state" (*Encyclopedia of Social Sciences*), and could well serve also as a model for the difficult relationships between Muslim Syria and Christian Lebanon. Once such small federated structures are established, Major Eban's League of Near Eastern countries will have a much better chance of realization. Just as the Benelux agreement was the first hopeful sign for an eventual federation of Europe, so the establishment of lasting agreement between two of the Near Eastern peoples on questions of defense, foreign policy, and economic development could serve as a model for the whole region.

One of the chief advantages of federal (or confederate) solutions of the Palestinian problem has been that the more moderate Arab statesmen (particularly from Lebanon) agreed to them. While the plan for a federal state was proposed only by a minority of the United Nations' Special Committee on Palestine in 1947, namely by the delegates of India, Iran, and Yugoslavia, there is no doubt that it could very well have served as a basis for a compromise between Jewish and Arab claims. The Ihud group at that time practically endorsed the minority report; it was in basic accordance with the principles set down and best expressed in the following sentence: "The federal state is the most constructive and dynamic solution in that it eschews an attitude of resignation towards the question of the ability of Arabs and Jews to cooperate in their common interest, in favor of a realistic and dynamic attitude, namely, that under changed conditions the will to cooperate can be cultivated." Mr. Camille Chamoun, representative of Lebanon, speaking before the United Nations' General Assembly on November 29, 1947, in a desperate effort to reach a compromise formula on the very day partition was decided, called once more for an independent state of Palestine to be "constituted on a federal basis and . . . [comprise] a federal government and cantonal governments of Jewish and Arab cantons." Like Dr. Magnes in his explanation of the plan for a confederation of Palestine, he invoked the constitution of the United States of America to serve as a model for the future constitution of the new state.

The plan for a confederate Palestine with Jerusalem as a common capital was nothing more or less than the only possible implementation of the UN partition decision, which made economic union a prerequisite. The purely economic approach of the United Nations would have met with difficulty under any circumstances, because, as Major Eban rightly stressed, "the economic interdependence of all Palestine was much overrated by the General Assembly." It would, moreover, have run into the same difficulties as the European Recovery Program, which also presupposed the possibility of economic cooperation without political implementation. These inherent difficulties of an economic approach became plain impossibility with the outbreak of the war, which first of all can be concluded only by political measures. Moreover, the war has destroyed all sectors of a combined Jewish-Arab economy and eliminated, with the expulsion of almost all Arabs from Israeli-held territories, the very small common economic basis upon which hopes for a future development of common economic interests had rested.

Indeed, an obvious shortcoming of our arguments for peace as against a precarious armistice and for confederation as against further Balkanization is that they can hardly be based upon anything like economic necessity. In order to arrive at a correct estimate of the impact of war on the Israeli economy, one cannot simply add up the staggering losses in working hours and destruction of property which Israel has suffered. Against them stands a very substantial increase in income from "charity" which never would have been given without the establishment of a state and the present tremendous immigration, both of which were the direct causes of the Jewish-Arab war. Since the Jewish economy in Palestine in any case depended largely upon investment through donation, it might even be possible that the gains obtained through emergency aid outweigh the losses suffered through war.

Pacification of the region might well attract more dividend-paying investment capital from American Jewry and even international loans. Yet it would also automatically diminish the Israeli income in non-dividend-paying money. At first glance, such a development might seem to lead to a sounder economy and greater political independence. Actually it might well mean greatly reduced resources and even increased interference from the outside, for the simple reason that the investing public is likely to be more businesslike and less idealistic than mere donors.

But even if we assume that American Jewry, after the European catastrophe, would not have needed the emergency of war and the stimulation of victories to mobilize support to the extent of $150 million a year, the economic advantages of the war probably outweigh its losses. There are first the clear gains resulting from the flight of the Arabs from Israeli-occupied territory. This evacuation of almost 50 percent of the country's population in no way disrupted the Jewish economy because it had been built in almost complete isolation from its surroundings. But more important than these gains, with their heavy moral and political mortgage, is the factor of immigration itself. The new immigrants, who are partly settled in the deserted homesteads of Arab refugees, were urgently needed for reconstruction purposes and to offset the great loss in manpower brought about by mobilization; they are not only an economic burden to the country, they constitute also its surest asset. The influx of American money, chiefly raised and used for the resettlement of DP's, combined with the influx of manpower, might stimulate the Israeli economy in much the same way, only on a much larger scale, as, ten years ago, the influx of American money together with the immigration of youngsters (Youth Aliyah) helped the enlargement and modernization of the collective settlements.

The same absence of economic necessity marks the argument for confederation. As things stand today, the Israeli state is not only a Jewish island in an Arab sea and not only a Westernized and industrialized outpost in the desert of a stagnant economy; it is also a producer of commodities for which no demand exists in its immediate neighborhood. Doubtless this situation will change some time in the future, but nobody knows how close or how distant this future may be. At the moment, at any rate, federation could hardly base itself on existing economic realities, on a functioning interdependence. It could become a working device only if—in the words of Dr. Magnes in 1947—"Jewish scientific ability, Jewish organizing power, perhaps finance, perhaps the experience of the West, which many of the countries of this part of the world have need of, [were] placed at their disposal for the good of the whole region."

Such an enterprise would call for great vision and even sacrifices, though the sacrifices might be less difficult to bear if the channeling of Jewish pioneering skill and capital into Arab countries were connected with some agreement about the resettlement of Arab DP's. Without such a modernization of the Near East, Israel will be left in economic isolation, without the prerequisites for a normal exchange of its products, even more dependent on outside help than now. It is not and never has been an argument against the great achievements of the Jewish national home that they were "artificial," that they did not follow economic laws and necessities but sprang from the political will of the Jewish people. But it would be a tragedy if, once this home or this state has been established, its people continued to depend upon "miracles" and were unable to accommodate themselves to objective necessities, even if these are of a long-range nature. Charity money can be mobilized in great quantities only in emergencies, such as in the recent catastrophe in Europe or in the Arab-Jewish war; if the Israeli government cannot win its economic independence from such money it will soon find itself in the unenviable position of being forced to create emergencies, that is, forced into a policy of aggressiveness and expansion. The extremists understand this situation very well when they propagate an artificial prolongation of the war, which, according to them, should never end before the whole of Palestine and Transjordan are conquered.

In other words, the alternative between federation and Balkanization is a political one. The trouble is not that rampant nationalism has disrupted a common economic structure, but that justified national aspirations could develop into rampant nationalism because they were not checked by economic interests. The task of a Near East federation would be to create a common economic structure, to bring about economic and political cooperation, and to integrate Jewish economic and social achievements. Balkanization would isolate even further the new Jewish pioneer and worker who have found a way to combine manual labor with a high standard of culture and to introduce a new human element into modern life. They, together with the heirs of the Hebrew University, would be the first victims of a long period of military insecurity and nationalistic aggressiveness.

But only the first victims. For without the cultural and social *hinterland* of Jerusalem and the collective settlements, Tel Aviv could become a Levantine city overnight. Chauvinism of the Balkan type could use the religious concept of the chosen people and allow its meaning to degenerate into hopeless vulgarity. The birth of a nation in the midst of our century may be a great event; it certainly is a dangerous event. National sovereignty, which so long had been the very symbol of free national development, has become the greatest danger to national survival for small nations. In view of the international situation and the geographical location of Palestine, it is not likely that the Jewish and Arab peoples will be exempt from this rule.

1950

Note

This paper was written in 1948 upon the suggestion of Judah L. Magnes, the late president of the Hebrew University in Jerusalem, who from the close of the First World War to the day of his death in October 1948 was the outstanding Jewish spokesman for Arab-Jewish understanding in Palestine. It is dedicated to his memory.

MAGNES, THE CONSCIENCE
OF THE JEWISH PEOPLE

One cannot speak about Magnes without speaking about Israel, which was his spiritual and physical home. And in Israel, nothing essential has changed in the years that have followed his death. He died a few months after the establishment of the Israeli state and the flight of the Arabs from their Palestine homeland, a few weeks after the murder of Bernadotte. The Palestinian Arabs are still homeless exiles and the murderers of Bernadotte have not yet been found. The Arab problem is what it always has been, namely the only real political and moral issue of Israeli politics. The victorious Israeli state has not been able to conclude a single peace treaty with its Arab neighbors.

The only change since Magnes's death is this death itself, which, as time goes on, has become more and more an authentic historical event. Who a man is, one does not know until he is dead. This is the truth of the Roman saying—*nemo ante mortem beatus dici potest*. The eternity into which we say that a man passes when he dies is also the eternal essence that he represented while he lived and which is never clearly revealed to the living before his death. *Magnes was the conscience of the Jewish people* and much of that conscience has died with him—at least for our time. Magnes's protest rose from the Zionist ranks themselves and its validity lay in this origin. He raised his voice primarily on moral grounds, and his authority was that he was a citizen of Jerusalem, that their fate was his fate, and that therefore nothing he said could ever be blamed on ulterior motives. He was a very practical and a very realistic man; it may be that he, like the rest of us, was also inspired by fear for coming generations of Jews, who may have to suffer for the wrongs committed in our time. But this was not his primary motive. He passionately wanted to do the right thing and had a healthy distrust of the wisdom of our *Realpolitiker;* and if fear did not really touch him, he was very sensitive to shame. *Being a Jew and being a Zionist, he was simply ashamed of what Jews and Zionists were doing.*

As it frequently happens with one's conscience, the Jewish people heard him and chose not to listen to him, and the few who did listen to him sometimes did it for the wrong reasons—or at least for reasons which were not his own. It has happened that the last years of his life coincided with a great change in the Jewish national character. A people that for two thousand years had made justice the cornerstone of its spiritual and communal existence has become emphatically hostile to all arguments of such a nature, as though these were necessarily the arguments of failure. We all know that this change has come about since Auschwitz, but that is little consolation. The fact is that nobody among the Jewish people could succeed Magnes. This is the measure of his greatness; it is, by the same token, the measure of our failure.

1952

THE HISTORY OF THE GREAT CRIME

A Review of Bréviaire de la haine: Le IIIᵉ Reich et les juifs
[Breviary of Hate: The Third Reich and the Jews] *by Léon Poliakov*

Leon Poliakov's excellent book on the Third Reich and the Jews is the first to describe the last phases of the Nazi regime on the basis, strictly, of primary source material. This consists chiefly of documents presented at the Nuremberg trials and published in several volumes by the American government under the title *Nazi Conspiracy and Aggression*. These volumes contain, in addition to captured Nazi archives, a considerable number of sworn reports and affidavits by former Nazi officials. Mr. Poliakov, with a reasoned obstinacy, tells the story as the documents themselves unfold it, thus avoiding the prejudices and preconceived judgments that mar almost all the other published accounts. He has an eye for the relevant, and possesses complete and intimate knowledge of Nazi Germany's complicated administrative machinery, of the fluctuating relations between the different services, as well as the ups and downs of the different cliques around Hitler.

The excellence of this book can be measured by the abundance of errors, misunderstandings, and misjudgments it corrects in every chapter. There are also many minor revisions. Nazis like Alfred Rosenberg, whose power has been generally exaggerated, are cut down to size; such little-known facts as the preponderant role in the organization of extermination played by Austrians are given their due importance. And without this resolute clearing away of the whole thicket of error and rash generalization the story could not have been properly told.

One of Mr. Poliakov's signal achievements is the reconstruction of the chronology of the extermination process. Though there may still be some room for speculation as to the exact time when the gas chambers were decided upon, we now know with certainty that Hitler—perhaps after discussion with Bormann and Goebbels—issued the order for organized mass murder either in the fall of 1940, when it had become evident that the war could not be ended shortly, or early in 1941, during the preparation of the attack on Russia. By this decision, he automatically discarded several more moderate "solutions." Among them was the Madagascar project, originally conceived by Himmler and adopted officially by the German Foreign Office before the outbreak of the war. Also proposed—it was a pet idea of Himmler's—was the mass sterilization by X-ray of all male Jews (along with the intellectual elite of other non-Germanic peoples); they would be told simply to line up before windows and fill out fake questionnaires, being kept in ignorance of what was to happen to them. It would have been more practicable, however, to exterminate the Jews by starvation in the ghettos—a course favored by such "moderate" Nazis as Poland's governor-general Hans Frank—or by working them to death, as Goebbels and Heydrich suggested. Hitler, as usual, dared to seize upon the most radical solution, and—again as usual—was right, *for his own purposes,* insofar as the gas chamber promised the surest results.

The Madagascar project had been a compromise between the Nazi brand of antisemitism and the older forms dear to German nationalism, which saw a "solution" of the Jewish question in Zionism; with the outbreak of the war, however, such compromises had been "outdated by events"—as Hitler liked to put it. Mass sterilization had proved to be impracticable; the machinery simply did not work effectively. Starvation was a slow process, full of unpredictable hazards, and likely to spread epidemics and cause needless and prolonged discussion among Germans themselves, as well as among subject peoples; all that could be stopped by drastic and irrevocable measures.

There was the intention, finally, of extracting the maximum of work from the Jews, who being doomed in any case, could be exploited without mercy—a course that appealed to the Nazis as much as it did to the Wehrmacht, whose manpower requirements were increasing constantly. But this plan suffered from an inherent contradiction: if a man is to work, he must have the necessities for a more or less normal process of life; otherwise he will die.

The first mass executions carried out by special troops, the so-called *Einsatzgruppen,* took place immediately after the invasion of Russia. In the fall of 1941, blueprints for gas chambers were ordered and soon afterward approved by Hitler himself. The first mobile gas trucks were ready by the spring of 1942, and the huge death factories at Auschwitz and Belzec by the fall of 1942. From then until the fall of 1944—that is, throughout the crucial years of the war—the trains carrying Jews from every corner of Europe to Poland had priority over all other rail traffic except troop movements. Contrary to present notions, it was Hitler whose orders set the systematic extermination process in motion, whereas Himmler seems to have obeyed rather reluctantly. And it was the latter who ordered the horror to be halted, in the fall of 1944, and the death factories dismantled and razed. Hitler himself never learned—apparently because nobody had the nerve to tell him—that what he considered one of his greatest "achievements" had been prematurely terminated.

The surviving Jews and other inmates of Auschwitz and the remaining death camps were herded westward before the Russian armies, dying on their way by the thousands, and put into "ordinary" concentration camps in Germany, where tens of thousands more starved to death before the Allied troops finally arrived. What met the liberating armies in these camps horrified them more than anything they had seen on the field of battle, and actually did more to arouse public opinion than anything that had leaked out about the death factories in Poland—which had by then disappeared without leaving much visible trace. Ironically, however, the corpses and survivors that the British and American soldiers saw at Buchenwald and elsewhere were the victims largely of the sole unpremeditated crime committed by the Nazis—unpremeditated insofar as it was the result of the chaos during the last months of the war rather than of deliberate design.

This chronicle, though correct, tells only part of the story, the Jewish part. Mr. Poliakov is the first to understand and stress the close connection between the mass murder of Jews and an earlier experiment of the Nazis, the "mercy" killings during the first year of the war of 70,000 deranged and feebleminded people in Germany. Not only did this precede the mass murder of other peoples; Hitler's order of September 1, 1939 (significantly enough, on the very first day of hostilities), to liquidate all "incurably sick persons" in the Third Reich set the stage for everything that followed. It was certainly no accident that this decree was not carried out literally and that none but mental cases were killed; it is also possible that what caused the killings to be suspended after a year and a half was, as Poliakov and others maintain, the protests of the victims' families and of other Germans. Nor is it likely that the fact that the beginning of the mass murder of Jews practically coincided with the termination of the "mercy" killings was due to accident either.

It looks as though Hitler, bent on realizing his race program by organized mass murder, followed at any given moment whatever line of least resistance promised the most immediate results. That he never abandoned his original intention of liquidating all "racially unfit" persons, regardless of nationality, can be seen from his plan to introduce a "national health bill" in Germany after the war, according to which the blood relatives of "sick persons, particularly those with lung and heart diseases," would "no longer be able to remain among the public and no longer be allowed to produce children. What [would] happen to these families [was to] be the subject of further orders."

By showing that the first day of the war was also the first day of organized mass murder, Mr. Poliakov throws new light on certain aspects of totalitarianism in general, and of Nazism in particular. Only Germany's war-enforced isolation from the Western world—which meant also from fascist fellow travelers in nontotalitarian countries—made possible the full development of the totalitarian tendencies inherent in the Nazi regime. Hitler more than once expressed his thankfulness that the war, regardless of all doubt and fear as to its outcome, had given him the opportunity to realize certain "ideas" that would have had to remain in abeyance otherwise.

The war in all probability conferred still another "blessing" upon Hitler. Pacifism, under the impact of the new experience of machine-made warfare, became after 1918 the first ideological movement to insist on equating war with sheer slaughter. The Nazi party during the 1920s developed side by side with German pacifism and through conflict with it. In distinction, however, from all purely nationalist propagandists for militarism, the Nazis never questioned the correctness of the pacifist equation; rather, they frankly approved of all forms of murder, and of war as one among them. In their opinion all notions of military honor or chivalry, with their implied respect for certain universal laws of humanity, were so much hypocrisy, and included in that hypocrisy was any conception of war that envisaged the defeat of the enemy without his utter destruction. For the Nazis, as for the pacifists, war was slaughter.

This seems to be why they waited until the actual outbreak of war before embarking on their "mercy killing" program, reasoning that with so many healthy young men being slaughtered at the front, Germans would not pay much attention now to the slaughtering of "worthless" people at home, and there would be no serious resistance to the execution of the program. For what difference was there between one kind of killing and any other? But subsequent experience taught the Nazis that the families of mentally sick persons are not prone to listen to "logic" when the life of one of their own is at stake; this may be the reason—or one of the reasons—why in his above-quoted draft of a "national health bill," which was probably outlined in 1943, two years after the suspension of the "mercy killings," Hitler proposed to murder the relatives of sick people too.

Whatever the true case was, the connection between mass extermination and "mercy killing" in Germany is one of Poliakov's most important insights, and he traces this in all its ramifications. The physicians, engineers, and others who perfected the techniques of euthanasia during the first year of the war for application to German mental cases were the same ones later put in charge of the installations at Auschwitz and Belzec. Even more conclusive as to the reality of this connection was the fact, inexplicable otherwise, that the same effort was made in Poland, as previously in the smaller death factories in Germany, to perfect the machinery of death and "attain the goal without torture and without agony." Cruelty and brutality, still prevalent among the soldiers and policemen selected at random for concentration-camp duties, were conspicuously absent among the death factory technicians. For them, as Himmler once put it, antisemitism was like "delousing," race problems were a question of "cleanliness," and the "solution of the problem of blood by action" meant elimination of "contaminating elements."

Another of Mr. Poliakov's major contributions is his deflation of the myth that the German officers' corps and the old pre-Hitler civil servants, particularly those in the Foreign Office and the diplomatic corps, either did not know what was going on or, when they did, protested. General Jodl himself had carefully weighed the pros and cons of extermination policy in terms of German morale and had concluded that its obvious liabilities were outweighed by one great psychological factor—the ordinary German soldier would fight better once he knew he had burnt all bridges behind him, and was involved in indissoluble complicity with the perpetrators of an enormous crime. Wehrmacht units, not SS troops, initiated the so-called *Heuaktion*, in which some 40,000 to 50,000 children were kidnapped from Eastern Europe and brought to Germany. And it was Undersecretary of State Luther who, together with the German military authorities, was responsible for the extermination of the Serbian Jews.

Some Germans, of course, did protest, both Nazi and non-Nazi. Mr. Poliakov quotes from a few of the protests that were set down in writing. Not quite fairly, perhaps, he is amazed at the arguments used, which stress military and economic disadvantages, the nervous strain on the executioners, and deplore the bad effect on the morale of the German troops and the conquered populations. It is unlikely that these protests could have been voiced at all had they invoked moral considerations. What is more remarkable is that few of them came from the German military and civil hierarchy, and that more were made, probably, by old Nazi party members and even SS leaders.

Up to now it has not been sufficiently recognized that the only country behind the Nazi lines that resolutely and effectively shielded the Jews was Germany's one important European ally, Italy. (The one other center of refuge for Jews appears to have been in the areas of Croatia where Tito's partisans were firmly established.) Mr. Poliakov discusses the Italian episode at length in connection with Vichy France's attitude toward Jews, of which he gives a complete and accurate account. Vichy's willingness to cooperate precisely on the score of antisemitism was such that one can well believe that Adolf Eichmann, the organizer of the deportations of Jews from all parts of Europe, did not miscalculate the psychology of the Vichy French when, at a particularly critical moment, he actually threatened them with the possibility of "excluding France as one of the countries of [Jewish] evacuation."

Nowhere does Mr. Poliakov's integrity and objectivity show to better advantage than in his account of the ghettos and the role of their *Judenräte*, or Jewish councils. He neither accuses nor excuses, but reports fully and faithfully what the sources tell him—the growing apathy of the victims as well as their occasional heroism, the terrible dilemma of the *Judenräte,* their despair as well as their confusion, their complicity and their sometimes pathetically ludicrous ambitions. In the famous and very influential *Reichsvertretung* of German Jews, which functioned smoothly until the last German Jew had been deported, he sees the forerunner of the *Judenräte* of the Polish ghettos; he makes it clear that the German Jews, in this respect too, served the Nazis as guinea pigs in their investigation of the problem of how to get people to help carry out their own death sentences, the last turn of the screw in the totalitarian scheme of total domination.

These are but a few samples taken from the extraordinary abundance of new factual material in this book. Anyone who wants to know "what really happened" and "how it really happened"—the "what" and the "how" being not only the most terrible experience of our generation, but probably the most significant too—cannot afford to overlook this study, and would perhaps do best to begin with it. (Unhappily, it has not yet interested any American publisher.) The close documentation of the book and its almost complete refusal to indulge in guesswork will serve as a solitary contrast to an alarming type of "neo-German" literature that has begun to appear lately in that country. For, under the pretext of giving the "what" and "how" of what really happened under Hitler, we are presented with a disgusting spectacle in which vanity, complacency, and ambition are displayed at their worst: the civil and military hierarchy, though denying their all too obvious complicity in Hitler's crimes, nevertheless try eagerly to show the world what very important and distinguished roles they once played under him— and, consequently, are capable of playing again in the future. (See Peter de Mendelssohn's "Germany's Generals Stage a Comeback," in *Commentary* of October 1951.) The doubtful value of these memoirs and autobiographies as source material has been pointed out again and again by competent authorities, but this has not diminished their popular appeal in Germany. Part of this is due to the German public's justified desire to get at the basic truth about a series of events whose horror was such that the real facts—it is assumed— were kept highly secret, and therefore can be told correctly only by actual participants. From this point of view, it seems natural that the more prominent a man was in the Nazi regime the more valuable his "confessions" ought to be.

The truth is, as I think Mr. Poliakov's book helps make clear, that the secrets of the Nazi regime were not so well kept by the Nazis themselves. They behaved according to a basic tenet of our time, which may be remembered in the future as the Age of Paper. Today no man in an official position can take the slightest action without immediately starting a stream of files, memos, reports, and publicity releases. The Nazis left behind them mountains of records that make it unnecessary to confide the slaking of our thirst for knowledge to the memories of people who were in the main untrustworthy to begin with. Nor could it have been otherwise. Hitler's great ambition was to found a millennial empire and his great fear, in case of defeat, was lest he and his fellows go unremembered in centuries to come. Red tape was not simply a necessity forced on the Nazis by the organizational methods of our time; it was also something they enthusiastically welcomed and multiplied, and so they left to history, and *for* history, typewritten records of each and every one of their crimes in at least ten copies.

There is a mystery about the Nazi regime, but it has nothing to do with secrets. It resides solely in a response, humanly unavoidable, that makes us go on asking, Why—but why? long after all the facts are reported, all stages of the process known, all conceivable motives considered. Apart from a few not too relevant remarks on the German national character, Mr. Poliakov's book neither poses nor attempts to answer this question. Yet it does not suppress it either; the author is too scrupulous and has too much intellectual integrity to content himself with those glib sociological and psychological rationalizations that have become modern man's standard refuge from reality. It is this point, precisely—this determination to refuse easy explanations—that, in my opinion, should be made the decisive criterion by which to judge any and all attempts to describe and explain these recent and unprecedented events.

Only if the reader continues, after everything about the exterminations has been made tangible and plausible, to feel his first reaction of outraged disbelief, only then will he be in the position to begin to understand that totalitarianism, unlike all other known modes of tyranny and oppression, has brought into the world a *radical* evil characterized by its divorce from all humanly comprehensible motives of wickedness.

It would be the greatest error to assume that these horrors are a thing of the past. Concentration and extermination camps are the most novel and most significant devices of all totalitarian forms of domination. Reports on the Soviet Russian system, whose "forced labor camps" are extermination camps in disguise, are numerous enough and trustworthy enough to permit comparison with the Nazi system. The differences between the two are real, but not radical; both systems result in the destruction of people selected as "superfluous." The development of this notion of "superfluity" is one of the central calamities of our century, and has produced its most horrible "solution." Research into Nazism, therefore, so frequently minimized today as "mere" history, is indispensable for our understanding of the problems of the present and the immediate future.

1952

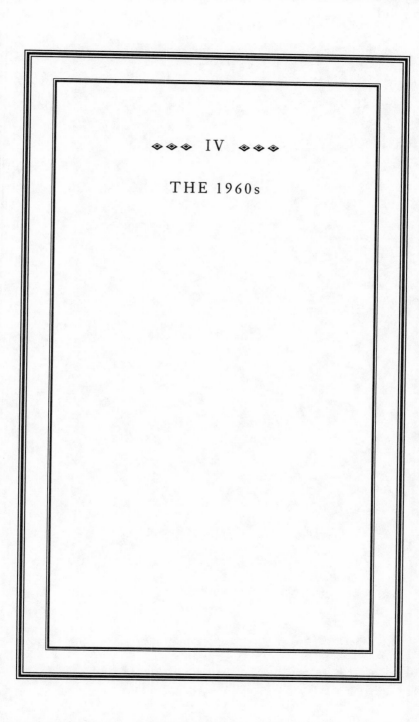

❖❖❖ IV ❖❖❖

THE 1960s

THE EICHMANN CONTROVERSY
A Letter to Gershom Scholem

The long and bitter controversy caused by Arendt's Eichmann in Jerusalem: A Report on the Banality of Evil *is discussed in both the Preface and the Introduction to the present volume. Gershom (or Gerhard) Scholem—see "Jewish History, Revised"—and Arendt were well acquainted, one tie being their friendship with Walter Benjamin. Scholem contributed, somewhat more temperately than most, to the controversy when he wrote to Arendt on June 23, 1963. In his letter he questions her German intellectual-political background, and her Jewish identity, suggesting that she lacks "love of the Jewish people." He questions her right to judge events at which she was not present, and especially the conduct of the Judenräte ("Nor do I presume to judge. I was not there"). He accuses her of making a "mockery" of Zionism, and of employing no more than a "catchword" or "slogan" for her "thesis" on the banality of evil. Arendt answers these charges, and enlarges upon them, in her response to Scholem.*

New York City, July 24, 1963

Dear Gerhard,

I found your letter when I got back home a week ago. You know what it's like when one has been away for five months. I'm writing now in the first quiet moment I have; hence my reply may not be as elaborate as perhaps it should be.

There are certain statements in your letter which are not open to controversy, because they are simply false. Let me deal with them first so that we can proceed to matters which merit discussion.

I am not one of the "intellectuals who come from the German Left." You could not have known this, since we did not know each other when we were young. It is a fact of which I am in no way particularly proud and which I am somewhat reluctant to emphasize—especially since the McCarthy era in this country. I came late to an understanding of Marx's importance because I was interested neither in history nor in politics when I was young. If can be said to "have come from anywhere," it is from the tradition of German philosophy.

As to another statement of yours, I am unfortunately not able to say that you could not have known the facts. I found it puzzling that you should write "I regard you wholly as a daughter of our people, and in no other way." The truth is I have never pretended to be anything else or to be in any way other than I am, and I have never even felt tempted in that direction. It would have been like saying that I was a man and not a woman—that is to say, kind of insane. I know, of course, that there is a "Jewish problem" even on this level, but it has never been my problem—not even in my childhood. To be a Jew belongs for me to the indisputable facts of my life, and I have never had the wish to change or disclaim facts of this kind. There is such a thing as a basic gratitude for everything that is as it is; for what has been *given* and not *made;* for what is *physei* and not *nomō.* To be sure, such an attitude is prepolitical, but in exceptional circumstances—such as the circumstances of Jewish politics—it is bound to have also political consequences, though, as it were, in a negative way. This attitude makes certain types of behavior impossible—indeed precisely those which you chose to read into my considerations. (To give another example: In his obituary of Kurt Blumenfeld, Ben-Gurion expressed his regret that Blumenfeld had not seen fit to change his name when he came to live in Israel. Isn't it obvious that Blumenfeld did not do so for exactly the same reasons that had led him in his youth to become a Zionist?) My stand in these matters must surely have been known to you, and it is incomprehensible to me why you should wish to stick a label on me which never fitted in the past and does not fit now.

To come to the point: let me begin, going on from what I have just stated, with what you call "love of the Jewish people" or *Ahabath Israel.* (Incidentally, I would be very grateful if you could tell me since when this concept has played a role in Judaism, when it was first used in Hebrew language and literature, etc.) You are quite right—I am not moved by any "love" of this sort, and for two reasons: I have never in my life "loved" any people or collective—neither the German people, nor the French, nor the American, nor the working class or anything of that sort. I indeed love "only" my friends and the only kind of love I know of and believe in is the love of persons. Secondly, this "love of the Jews" would appear to me, since I am myself Jewish, as something rather suspect. I cannot love myself or anything which I know is part and parcel of my own person. To clarify this, let me tell you of a conversation I had in Israel with a prominent political personality* who was defending the—in my opinion disastrous—nonseparation of religion and state in Israel. What he said—I am not sure of the exact words anymore— ran something like this: "You will understand that, as a Socialist, I, of course, do not believe in God; I believe in the Jewish people." I found this a shocking statement and, being too shocked, I did not reply at the time. But I could have answered: The greatness of this people was once that it believed in God, and believed in Him in such a way that its trust and love toward Him was greater than its fear. And now this people believes only in itself? What good can come out of that?—Well, in this sense I do not "love" the Jews, nor do I "believe" in them; I merely belong to them as a matter of course, beyond dispute or argument.

We could discuss the same issue in political terms; and we should then be driven to a consideration of patriotism. That there can be no patriotism without permanent opposition and criticism is no doubt common ground between us. But I can admit to you something beyond that, namely, that wrong done by my own people naturally grieves me more than wrong done by other peoples. This grief, however, in my opinion is not for display, even if it should be the innermost motive for certain actions or attitudes. Generally speaking, the role of the "heart" in politics seems to me altogether questionable. You know as well as I how often those who merely report certain unpleasant facts are accused of lack of soul, lack of heart, or lack of what you call *Herzenstakt*. We both know, in other words, how often these emotions are used in order to conceal factual truth. I cannot discuss here what happens when emotions are displayed in public and become a factor in political affairs; but it is an important subject, and I have attempted to describe

---

*This "personality" was Golda Meir, then foreign minister and later prime minister of Israel. At Scholem's urging, Arendt deleted her name and changed the feminine pronoun when the letters were first published. —Ed.

the disastrous results in my book *On Revolution* in discussing the role of compassion in the formation of the revolutionary character.

It is a pity that you did not read the book before the present campaign of misrepresentation against it got under way from the side of the Jewish "establishment" in Israel and America. There are, unfortunately, very few people who are able to withstand the influence of such campaigns. It seems to me highly unlikely that without being influenced you could possibly have misunderstood certain statements. Public opinion, especially when it has been carefully manipulated, as in this case, is a very powerful thing. Thus, I never made Eichmann out to be a "Zionist." If you missed the irony of the sentence—which was plainly in *oratio obliqua*, reporting Eichmann's own words—I really can't help it. I can only assure you that none of dozens of readers who read the book before publication had ever any doubt about the matter. Further, I never asked why the Jews "let themselves be killed." On the contrary, I accused Hausner of having posed this question to witness after witness. There was no people and no group in Europe which reacted differently under the immediate pressure of terror. The question I raised was that of the cooperation of Jewish functionaries during the "Final Solution," and this question is so very uncomfortable because one cannot claim that they were traitors. (There were traitors too, but that is irrelevant.) In other words, until 1939 and even until 1941, whatever Jewish functionaries did or did not do is understandable and excusable. Only later does it become highly problematic. This issue came up during the trial and it was of course my duty to report it. This constitutes our part of the so-called unmastered past, and although you may be right that it is too early for a "balanced judgment" (though I doubt this), I do believe that we shall only come to terms with this past if we begin to judge and to be frank about it.

I have made my own position plain, and yet it is obvious that you did not understand it. I said that there was no possibility of resistance, but there existed the possibility of *doing nothing*. And in order to do nothing, one did not need to be a saint, one needed only to say: "I am just a simple Jew, and I have no desire to play any other role." Whether these people, or some of them, as you indicate, deserved to be hanged is an altogether different question. What needs to be discussed are not the people so much as the arguments with which they justified themselves in their own eyes and in those of others.

Concerning these arguments we are entitled to pass judgment. Moreover, we should not forget that we are dealing here with conditions which were terrible and desperate enough, but which were not the conditions of concentration camps. These decisions were made in an atmosphere of terror but not under the immediate pressure and impact of terror. These are important differences in degree, which every student of totalitarianism must know and take into account. These people had still a certain, limited freedom of decision and of action. Just as the SS murderers also possessed, as we now know, a limited choice of alternatives. They could say: "I wish to be relieved of my murderous duties," and nothing would happen to them. Since we are dealing in politics with men, and not with heroes or saints, it is this possibility of *"nonparticipation"* (Kirchheimer) that is decisive if we begin to judge, not the system, but the individual, his choices, and his arguments.

And the Eichmann trial was concerned with an individual. In my report I have only spoken of things which came up during the trial itself. It is for this reason that I could not mention the "saints" about whom you speak. Instead I had to limit myself to the resistance fighters, whose behavior, as I said, was the more admirable because it occurred under circumstances in which resistance had really ceased to be possible. There were no saints among the witnesses for the prosecution, but there was one utterly pure human being, old Grynszpan, whose testimony I therefore reported at some length. On the German side, after all, one could also have mentioned more than the single case of Sergeant Schmidt.* But since his was the only case mentioned in the trial, I had to restrict myself to it.

That the distinction between victims and persecutors was blurred in the concentration camps, deliberately and with calculation, is well known, and I as well as others have insisted on this aspect of totalitarian methods. But to repeat: this is not what I mean by a Jewish share in the guilt, or by the totality of the collapse of all standards. This was part of the system and had indeed nothing to do with Jews.

How you could believe that my book was "a mockery of Zionism" would be a complete mystery to me, if I did not know that many people in Zionist

*Arendt refers to Anton Schmidt who, while serving in the German army in Poland, helped Jewish partisans. His story is movingly told in chapter 14 of *Eichmann in Jerusalem.* —Ed.

circles have become incapable of listening to opinions or arguments which are off the beaten track and not consonant with their ideology. There are exceptions, and a Zionist friend of mine remarked in all innocence that the book, the last chapter in particular (recognition of the competence of the court, the justification of the kidnapping), is very pro-Israel—as indeed it is. What confuses you is that my arguments and my approach are different from what you are used to; in other words, the trouble is that I am independent. By this I mean, on the one hand, that I do not belong to any organization and always speak only for myself, and on the other hand, that I have great confidence in Lessing's *selbstdenken,* for which, I think, no ideology, no public opinion, and no "convictions" can ever be a substitute. Whatever objections you may have to the results, you won't understand them unless you realize that they are really my own and nobody else's.

I regret that you did not argue your case against the carrying out of the death sentence. For I believe that in discussing this question we might have made some progress in finding out where our most fundamental differences are located. You say that it was "historically false;" and I feel very uncomfortable seeing the specter of History raised in this context. In my opinion, it was *politically* and *juridically* (and the last is actually all that mattered) not only correct—it would have been utterly impossible not to have carried out the sentence. The only way of avoiding it would have been to accept Karl Jaspers's suggestion and to hand Eichmann over to the United Nations. Nobody wanted that, and it was probably not feasible; hence there was no alternative left but to hang him. Mercy was out of the question, not on juridical grounds—pardon is anyhow not a prerogative of the juridical system—but because mercy is applicable to the person rather than to the deed; the act of mercy does not forgive murder but pardons the murderer insofar as he, as a person, may be more than anything he ever did. This was not true of Eichmann. And to spare his life without pardoning him was impossible on juridical grounds.

In conclusion, let me come to the only matter where you have not misunderstood me, and where indeed I am glad that you have raised the point. You are quite right: I changed my mind and do no longer speak of "radical evil." It is a long time since we last met, or we would perhaps have spoken about the subject before. (Incidentally, I don't see why you call my term "banality of evil" a catchword or slogan. As far as I know no one has used the term before me; but that is unimportant.) It is indeed my opinion now that evil is never "radical," that it is only extreme, and that it possesses neither depth nor any demonic dimension. It can overgrow and lay waste the whole world precisely because it spreads like a fungus on the surface. It is "thought-defying," as I said, because thought tries to reach some depth, to go to the roots, and the moment it concerns itself with evil, it is frustrated because there is nothing. That is its "banality." Only the good has depth and can be radical. But this is not the place to go into these matters seriously; I intend to elaborate them further in a different context. Eichmann may very well remain the concrete model of what I have to say.

You propose to publish your letter and you ask if I have any objection. My advice would be not to recast the letter in the third person. The value of this controversy consists in its epistolary character, namely in the fact that it is informed by personal friendship. Hence, if you are prepared to publish my answer simultaneously with your letter, I have, of course, no objection.

Hannah Arendt

ANSWERS TO QUESTIONS
SUBMITTED BY SAMUEL GRAFTON

On September 19, 1963, Hannah Arendt received a letter from Samuel Grafton, who wrote that Look magazine had commissioned him "to do a study of the immensely interesting reaction caused by your book, Eichmann in Jerusalem." He went on to say that he hoped she would "be kind enough to entertain written questions from me, with the thought that these might lead to an interview with you," adding that she ought not to consider his questions "in any way an inquisition." As far as is known there was no interview, and no article ever appeared in Look. But the next day, September 20, Arendt wrote Grafton saying, "I thank you for your letter and I am perfectly willing to answer all your questions—including the amusing canard about my 'conversion to Catholicism.'"

I am a writer, like yourself, seeking the truth. It seems to me that the reaction to your book is an important political phenomenon in itself, deserving of analysis. In that spirit I have set down the following questions:

1. Do you feel that the reactions to your book throw any new light on the tensions in Jewish life and politics today? If so, what has been revealed?

2. What would you say are the real causes of the violent reaction to your book on the part of those who have attacked it?

3. Would you, in the light of that reaction, want to change anything if you were starting to write the book now? I don't mean in order to conciliate the opposition—I mean, rather, has the reaction indicated to you a sensitivity on the part of some Jews which has surprised you, and which you would want now to take into account?

4. Do you consider it possible that the word "banality" may have offended some readers, or rubbed them the wrong way, by making them jump to the conclusion that perhaps you considered their sufferings to be "banal"?

5. The word "banal" means, essentially, "commonplace." Do you feel it is possible that the subtitle had too general and sweeping a sound? Admittedly, evil was commonplace under the Nazis. But did your use of the word "banality" seem to some readers, at least, to imply that evil was banal and commonplace everywhere? I know what you meant the word to mean, and you know what you meant the word to mean—but what about the impression created before one had read the book?

6. Would you admit as permissible the thought that Hausner, acting, after all, as a prosecutor, was under no obligation to behave with full judicial balance? Was not his duty, like that of any prosecutor, limited to winning his case? Or do you think he went beyond allowable limits into a too one-sided presentation?

7. What do you consider that the Jews in Europe might have done, in the way of a stronger resistance? You have probably read Oscar Handlin's "Jewish Resistance to the Nazis," in *Commentary* for November 1962. Do you reject the case he makes? (Interestingly, he wrote his article before your book appeared, and he seems to have been quite prescient in feeling that this issue would arise.)

8. If, as you say, the Nazis concealed the purpose of the death-camp transports, even to disguising a killing center as a railroad station, were not the Jews victims of deception rather than of betrayal of their leaders? At what moment should their community leaders have said to them: "Cooperate no longer, but fight!"?

9. Have not Jewish leaders worked with their gentile overlords throughout the Diaspora, cajoling, cooperating, pleading, maneuvering? Was not the method frequently successful? If the old methods had become obsolete were not Jewish leaders then guilty, at most, of an historical misinterpretation? Could they have been expected to realize that Nazism was not the final development of antisemitism, but the first manifestation of a new evil, complete totalitarianism linked with genocide?

10. Could not Eichmann, even in the limited role you describe him as having, have caused transport delays and confusion, under war conditions, if he had been minded to save at least a few lives? Does not the obvious answer, that he was not so minded, make him enough of a monster to fit under any definition of the word? Your book, of course, says he was guilty, and I understand the point you are making, that even clerks can carry out unimaginable

evil under totalitarianism, but was there not something more here, in Eichmann's devotion and dedication to his task? I am trying to comprehend why
Musmanno took off like a rocket against your description of Eichmann, and
why others have been upset. I found that I accepted your explanation intellectually, and then became ruffled every time you minimized Eichmann's
importance. Then I calmed down as you explained more, and became upset
all over again when you downgraded Eichmann later. Is it possible that your
thesis has come on the scene a little too early—that the reaction would be
quite different, say twenty-five years from now? Is timing, in other words, at
the bottom of the controversy, in your view?

11. Do you consider that the Jews, as a whole, have learned anything from
the Hitler experience?

12. Have any Jewish leaders supported the book, and, if so, who are they?

13. This last is not a question, as I do not ask such questions. Purely as a
point of information, I will tell you that one of the comments concerning
you now going around in Jewish circles is that you have been "converted to
Catholicism." As I do not probe into anyone's religious beliefs, I do not ask
you to comment on this. Should you care to do so, your remarks would be
welcomed, but no conclusions will be drawn by me from any refusal on your
part to say anything about this matter.

Hannah Arendt's responses to the thirteen questions:

Let me begin by answering a question you did not raise: Why did I, a writer
and teacher of political philosophy who had never done a reporter's job,*
want to go to Jerusalem for the Eichmann trial? Apart from an obvious
answer, which I indicated in the book when I included myself in the audience, not of reporters and journalists, but of "survivors" ("immigrants from
Europe like myself, who knew by heart all there was to know"), I had three
reasons:

First, I wanted to see one of the chief culprits with my own eyes as he
appeared in the flesh. When, many years ago, I described the totalitarian sys-

---

*Arendt had written articles for newspapers before—the *Aufbau* pieces included in this volume, for
example—but this was the first time she had been given an assignment (by *The New Yorker*) to cover a
specific event. —Ed.

tem and analyzed the totalitarian mentality, it was always a "type," rather than individuals, I had to deal with, and if you look at the system as a whole, every individual person becomes indeed "a cog small or big," in the machinery of terror. It is the great advantage of court procedure that it inevitably confronts you with the person and personal guilt, with individual motivation and decisions, with particulars, which in another context, the context of theory, are not relevant. In other words, I wanted to know: Who was Eichmann? What were his deeds, not insofar as his crimes were part and parcel of the Nazi system, but insofar as he was a free agent? This is essentially the same question a court of justice must answer when it renders judgment. And it is for this reason that the whole small-cog theory (the theory of the defense) is quite irrelevant in this context.

Second, there exists a widespread theory, to which I also contributed, that these crimes defy the possibility of human judgment and explode the framework of our legal institutions. And this argument is frequently connected with the more common notions of the uncertainties of "political justice," with the difficulties of judging crimes committed by a sovereign state, or with the "difficult position" of a soldier who may be "liable to be shot by a court-martial if he disobeys an order, and to be hanged by a judge and jury if he obeys it" (Dicey, *Law of the Constitution*). There is finally the legally most important question: To what an extent did the accused know he was doing wrong when he committed his acts? This question, as you may know, has played a decisive role in many trials of war criminals in Germany. In short, the facts of the case were such that there was no "ordinary crime" and no "common criminal," but that this "could not conceivably mean that he who had murdered millions should for this very reason escape punishment." What I wanted to find out was: What are the possibilities of rendering justice through our legal system and institutions when confronted with this new type of crime and criminal?

Third, I have been thinking for many years, or to be specific thirty years, about the nature of evil. And the wish to expose myself—not to the deeds, which, after all, were well known, but to the evildoer himself—probably was the most powerful motive in my decision to go to Jerusalem.

Let me now come to your questions. I certainly agree with you that the reaction to my book "is an important political phenomenon in itself," but I hope you will understand that, apart from the inconveniences this reaction has caused me, it is of decidedly secondary importance to me.

1. I have no final answer to your first question—Do these reactions throw new light on Jewish life and politics, and what has been revealed? My feeling is that I have inadvertently touched upon the Jewish part of what the Germans call their "unmastered past" (*die unbewältigte Vergangenheit*). It looks to me now as though this question was bound to come up anyhow and that my report crystallized it in the eyes of those who do not read big books (Hilberg's, for instance*) and perhaps also accelerated its coming up for *public* discussion. This feeling is supported by a letter dated March 7, 1963, from Dr. Siegfried Moses, former state comptroller of Israel, president of the Leo Baeck Institute, and also, I think, of the Council of Jews from Germany. He writes: "I came to New York with the draft of a statement which was to be published by the Council of Jews from Germany. It was to attack the presentation given in Hilberg's book and in articles published by Bettelheim. Now [i.e., after the publication of my articles in *The New Yorker*], the defense of the council must oppose primarily your articles." (The letter is written in German; I translated. You can of course see the original. Upon receipt of the letter I had a long talk with Dr. Moses in Basel. If you wish, I can tell you about it; it does not seem relevant in the context of your questions.)

2. I indicated one of the real causes of the violent reaction to my book. Another important cause seems that people are under the impression that I attacked the Jewish establishment because I not only brought out the role of the Jewish councils during the Final Solution, but indicated (as Hilberg had done before) that the members of these councils were not simply "traitors." In other words, since the trial had touched upon the role of the Jewish leadership during the Final Solution, and I had reported these incidents, all present Jewish organizations and their leaders thought they were under attack. What then happened, in my opinion, was a concerted and organized effort at creating an "image" and at substituting this image for the book I had written. Something very similar seems to have happened in response to Hochhuth's play *The Deputy* (*Der Stellvertreter*), which questions Vatican policy with

---

*Raul Hilberg, *The Destruction of the European Jews* (Chicago, 1961), frequently cited by Arendt in *Eichmann in Jerusalem*. —Ed.

respect to the Nazi system. The question Hochhuth raises is very simple: Why did Pacelli never protest publicly, first against the persecutions and finally the mass murder of Jews? Nobody ever contested the fact that the pope knew all the details. Thereupon the *Osservatore Romano* wrote as follows: "If Hochhuth's thesis is right it follows that neither Hitler himself, nor Eichmann, nor the SS were responsible for Auschwitz, Dachau, Buchenwald, Mauthausen, and all the other crimes. . . , but Pope Pius." This, of course, was sheer nonsense, and Hochhuth never said anything of the sort. But it served an important purpose: an "image" was created at the expense of the real issue; the *image* is now discussed widely, and Hochhuth is in the absurd position of having to defend himself against things he never said. Such willful distortions and outright falsifications can be effective if they are organized and massive. The author under attack can do little more than say with Anatole France: "If I am accused of having stolen the towers of Notre Dame, I leave the country." (Source for the Hochhuth issue: *Mercur*, no. 186, August 1963, p. 812 ff.)

3. I was not surprised by the "sensitivity of some Jews," and since I am a Jew myself, I think I had every reason not to be alarmed by it; I believe it is against the honor of our profession—"a writer . . . seeking the truth"—to take such things into account. However, the violence and, especially, the unanimity of public opinion among organized Jews (there are very few exceptions) has surprised me indeed. I conclude that I hurt not merely "sensitivities" but vested interests, and this I did not know before.

But there is another side to this matter, and in order to discuss it I must refer you to my book *On Revolution* (something I hate to do but it can't be helped). On p. 227 ff. (and in other places as well) I speak of the political significance of public opinion, which, in my view, stands in opposition to authentic public spirit. I report there the opinions of the Founding Fathers and say: "Democracy . . . was abhorred because public opinion was held to rule where public spirit ought to prevail, and the sign of this perversion was the unanimity of the citizenry: for 'when men exert their reason coolly and freely on a variety of distinct questions, they inevitably fall into different opinions on some of them. When they are governed by a common passion, their opinions, if they are so to be called, will be the same' (James Madison, *The Federalist Papers*, no. 50)."

There is, I say, a "decisive incompatibility between the rule of a unanimously held 'public opinion' and freedom of opinion," for "the rule of public opinion endangers even the opinion of those few who may have the strength not to share it. . . . This is the reason why the Founding Fathers tended to equate rule based on public opinion with tyranny. . . ." The point is that "opinions never belong to groups but exclusively to individuals, who 'exert their reason coolly and freely,' and no multitude, be it the multitude of a part or of the whole of society, will ever be capable of forming an opinion." Pseudo-opinions are those of interest groups, and if such groups, for whatever reasons, right or wrong ones, feel threatened, they will try to rule out of their community "independent" people, who belong to no organization, in order to be able to say: these people, far from being independent, speak only in the name of other interests. The many canards now being spread in Jewish circles—that I am on the point of converting to Catholicism (your question 13), or that I am now a member of the American Council for Judaism, or that I am a "self-hating antisemite," and so on—are well-known devices in such political campaigns.

Hence, your third question seems to me slightly wrong. I can only ask myself: Would I, in the light of this political campaign, change anything? The answer is: My only alternative would have been to remain silent altogether; once I wrote, I was bound to tell the truth as I saw it. I was not aware of the dangers. Would I have dodged the issues if I had known? This question is a very real one to me. I am not in politics, and I am neither willing nor able to deal with the situation that has arisen; it interferes very seriously with my work, and the publicity connected with it is for me and my way of life a first-rate nuisance. Still, because of the nature of my work and the task I have set for myself—What is the nature of evil?—I suppose I would have done it anyway and reported the trial on the factual level. The alternative would have been to incorporate whatever I learned there into my theoretical work, which of course is entirely without danger, because those who oppose me would never have read it.

4. and 5. Why readers who read "banality of evil" should jump to the conclusion that "their sufferings are banal" is beyond me. It can be answered only by another question: Why can't Johnny read?

I hope you don't mind the joke. Since I had never written for mass audiences I didn't know what could happen. You equate "banal" with "commonplace," and I am afraid you have the dictionaries on your side. For me, there is a very important difference: commonplace is what frequently, commonly happens, but something can be banal even if it is not common. Moreover, as the phrase now stands—"banality of evil"—it is contrasted with "radical evil" (Kant) and, more popularly, with the widely held opinion that there is something demonic, grandiose, in great evil, that there is even such a thing as the power of evil to bring forth something good. Mephisto in *Faust* is the *Geist der stets das Böse will und stets das Gute schafft;* the devil seen as a fallen angel (Lucifer) suggests that the best are most likely to become the worst; Hegel's whole philosophy rests on the "power of negation," of necessity, for instance, to bring about "the realm of freedom," and so on. The question came up in the trial through Servatius [Eichmann's defense attorney] on the most vulgar level of course. But the trouble is that European Zionism (as distinguished from views held by American Zionists!) has often thought and said that the evil of antisemitism was necessary for the good of the Jewish people. In the words of a well-known Zionist in a letter to me discussing "the original Zionist argumentation: The antisemites want to get rid of the Jews, the Jewish State wants to receive them, a perfect match." The notion that we can use our enemies for our own salvation has always been to me the "original sin" of Zionism. Add to this what an even more prominent Zionist leader once told me in the tone of stating an innermost belief: "Every *goy* is an antisemite," the implication being, "and it is good so, for how else could we get Jews to come to Israel?," and you will understand why I believe that certain elements of the Zionist ideology are very dangerous and should be discarded for the sake of Israel.

But to return to your question. It is of course true that evil was commonplace in Nazi Germany and that "there were many Eichmanns," as the title of a German book about Eichmann reads. But I did not mean this. I meant that evil is not *radical,* going to the roots (*radix*), that it has no depth, and that for this very reason it is so terribly difficult to think about, since thinking, by definition, wants to reach the roots. Evil is a surface phenomenon, and instead of being radical, it is merely extreme. We resist evil by not being swept away by the surface of things, by stopping ourselves and beginning to think—that is, by reaching another dimension than the horizon of everyday life. In other words, the more superficial someone is, the more likely he will be to yield to evil. An indication of such superficiality is the use of clichés, and Eichmann,

God knows, was a perfect example. Each time he was tempted to think for himself, he said: Who am I to judge if all around me—that is, the atmosphere in which we unthinkingly live—think it is right to murder innocent people? Or to put it slightly differently: Each time Eichmann tried to think, he thought immediately of his career, which up to the end was the thing uppermost in his mind.

I am afraid I still have not answered your main question: "what about the impression created before one had read the book?" Perhaps you are right. I am not in the habit of thinking about the "impression" created by what I write, at least not in the sense you mean it here. I am content when I have found the word or the sentence which appears to me objectively adequate and appropriate. But do you really believe it would have mattered the slightest bit if the subtitle had not been there? I think that is an illusion.

6. Not only would I "admit as permissible the thought that Hausner [the prosecuting attorney] was under no obligation to behave with full judicial balance," I myself said so: "Obviously, the Attorney General is not obliged to make available evidence that does not support the case for the prosecution." But it turns out that we both may be wrong, at least for the Jerusalem trial whose formal procedure is still governed by British law. For I received the following correction from a Canadian lawyer: "That proposition is neither obvious nor a correct statement of the duties of a prosecutor to conduct a fair trial under Canadian law." He then goes on to quote a Canadian Supreme Court decision which states *inter alia* that it is "the duty of the prosecutor to bring forward evidence of every material fact known to the prosecution whether favorable to the accused or otherwise."

However, there seems to be more involved: it is one thing not "to behave with full judicial balance" and quite another to drag into the proceedings an enormous amount of material that has nothing whatsoever to do with the crimes of the accused. During the trial, it was the presiding judge who most strenuously objected to "picture painting" by the prosecution, so that this time there was not the usual tug of war between prosecution and defense, but between prosecutor and judge. Many correspondents who covered the trial were painfully aware of this.

7. and 8. The question of resistance: I nowhere raised this question, and what I said before about the "image" which has been created about the book

applies here. This question was raised by Hausner. I spoke about it twice, in the first chapter, where I called it "silly and cruel," and later where I said that Hausner's question "served as a smoke screen for the question that was not asked": Why did Jewish functionaries cooperate? The distinction between these two questions seems to me almost too obvious for comment. There never was a moment when "the community leaders" could have said, "Cooperate no longer, but fight!" as you phrase it. Resistance, which existed but played a very small role, meant only: We don't want that kind of death, we want to die with honor. But the question of cooperation is indeed bothersome. There certainly was a moment when the Jewish leaders could have said: We shall no longer cooperate, we shall try to disappear. This moment might have come when they, already fully informed of what deportation meant, were asked by the Nazis to prepare the lists for deportation. The Nazis themselves gave them the number and the categories of those to be shipped to the killing centers, but who then went and who was given a chance to survive was decided by the Jewish authorities. In other words, those who cooperated were at that particular moment masters over life and death. Can you imagine what that meant in practice? Take the example of Theresienstadt, where every detail of daily life was in the hands of the Jewish elders, and think what would have happened to an inmate if he ever dared to question the "wisdom" of any decision taken by the elders.

As for the justifications of this policy, there are many, the most important ones in the Kastner report, which appeared in Germany. It was common enough to think: (*a*) If some of us have to die, it is better that we decide than the Nazis. I disagree. It would have been infinitely better to let the Nazis do their own murderous business. (*b*) With a hundred victims we shall save a thousand. This sounds to me like the last version of human sacrifice: pick seven virgins, sacrifice them to placate the wrath of the gods. Well, this is not my religious belief, and most certainly it is not the faith of Judaism. Finally, the theory of the lesser evil: Let us serve in order to prevent worse men from taking these positions; let us do bad things in order to prevent the worst. (There are analogies with "good people" serving the Nazis in Germany.)

The question of what was known and what was not known is often difficult to decide, but in quite a number of instances it is clear that the Jewish *leaders* knew what the Jewish people at large did not know. This is especially true for Theresienstadt and for Hungary. Kastner wrote in his report: We knew more than enough. It is here, as in other respects, of paramount importance to keep in mind the distinction between the Jewish leaders, who had constant dealings with Nazis and were generally rather well informed, and the Jewish people, who ordinarily were in contact only with the Jewish authorities. The decision in Theresienstadt, for instance, not to tell people what transports meant, resulted in people volunteering for deportation!

I have answered your questions with respect to this point, but I should like to point out that it was never my intention to bring this part of our "unmastered past" to the attention of the public. It so happened that the *Judenräte* came up at the trial and I had to report on this, as I reported on everything else. Within the context of my report, this plays no prominent role either in space or in emphasis. It has been blown up out of all reasonable proportions.

9. Your thesis here is somewhat similar to the thesis of Hilberg. I have no theory of my own; in order to make a proposition, I'd have to go deeply into Jewish history, something I do not intend to do. On the spur of the moment, I would say, however, that even if your thesis is correct, it can apply only to the initial states of the Nazi regime; it cannot possibly explain the role of the *Judenräte* in sending people to their death.

10. I do not believe that Eichmann could have sabotaged his orders even if he had wanted to. (He did something of the sort once, as I reported.) But he could have resigned, and nothing would have happened to him except a stop to his career. Of course he did his best, as I say several times, to do as he was told. If his devotion to the task is sufficient proof to call him a monster, you must conclude that a large majority of the German people under Hitler were "monsters." I do not quite understand why you were so upset "every time [I] minimized Eichmann's importance": I do not think I minimized anything, I just told what he could and what he could not do, what his competences were and so on. The prosecution, later followed by the judgment of the Supreme Court (as sharply distinct from that of the District Court), acted as though not Eichmann, but Heydrich or even Hitler were in the dock. This was absurd. I did not "downgrade Eichmann," the evidence did. When I decided to go to Jerusalem, I myself had been under the impression that he had been much more important than he actually was. One of the reasons for this misconception was that he had always been in charge of negotiations with Jews,

and hence played in our imagination a larger role than he possessed within the Nazi hierarchy.

No doubt, we all hope that the reaction to my report will "be quite different . . . twenty-five years from now." But does that mean that it is too early to write and judge now? After all, eighteen years is a considerable time, and judging from other such episodes, the danger is that we shall soon be flooded with the kind of literature which is interest-inspired and tries to whitewash everything. This, for instance, is the case in Germany with respect to the people of July 20, 1944, who attempted to assassinate Hitler. But let me repeat once more: If such is the case, and if my book plus a few others, which try at least to tell the truth without any other considerations, should result in the production of more lies than otherwise would have seen the light of day, I certainly shall not take part in the research and the history writing that is to follow. I did not write a "book on Jews," and if I had wanted to write about the Jewish Holocaust, I certainly would never have dreamed of taking off from the Eichmann trial.

11. This question is difficult to answer because you relate it to the "Jews as a whole." No doubt the Hitler experience has had the deepest impact upon Jews all over the world, that is, upon every single one of us. I spoke about the immediate reaction in the book, and have sometimes thought that we are witnessing a profound change of "national character"—that is, to the extent that such a thing is possible. But I am not sure; and while I think it is high time to tell the facts of the matter, I would feel that for such a sweeping statement the time indeed has not yet come. Let us leave that for coming generations.

12. I received many letters from Jews supporting my book. As to Jewish leaders—a few rabbis and the Council for Judaism. By and large the Jews who support my book are like me—Jews with no strong connections to the Jewish community, for whom, however, the fact of their Jewishness is not a matter of indifference. Before the campaign started, the reaction was different. There was, for instance, a Yiddish critic, I think by the name of Glattstein, who wrote a favorable review. Four weeks later, as though he never had said anything of the sort, he wrote about an evil book by an evil person—or something to that effect. More interesting: The first report in the *Jerusalem Post* about *The New Yorker* articles was quite favorable. And the

important Hebrew daily *Haaretz* asked for serial rights (they printed, indeed, two large installments without any derogatory remarks by the editors) and for an option for the Hebrew rights for the Schocken publishing house, Gustav Schocken being the editor and owner of *Haaretz*. Again, a sudden change of mind took place.

13. I answered the question before. There is no truth in it whatsoever. I suppose the rumor has been started in the old hope—*semper aliquid adhaeret*.

THE EICHMANN CASE
AND THE GERMANS
A Conversation with Thilo Koch

KOCH: What are the theses of your controversial book about Eichmann?

ARENDT: The book really has no theses. It's a report that gives voice to all the facts that were dealt with at the trial in Jerusalem. During those proceedings both the prosecution and the defense presented certain theses that I reported about, but that people then claimed were my theses—for instance, that Eichmann was just a "cog" or that the Jews could have offered some resistance. As for the second, I have expressly argued against it, and as far as the cog theory goes, all I did was report that Eichmann didn't share his lawyer's opinion.

Unfortunately the controversy about the book is mostly about facts and not theses or opinions, about facts that are then rigged into theories to rob them of their factual character. The book and the trial share the same focal point, the defendant himself. What came to light during the proceedings establishing his guilt was the totality of a moral collapse in the heart of Europe, in all its horrible factuality. One can dodge that factuality in various ways—by denying it, by responding with pathos-laden admissions of guilt that carry no obligations and smother anything specific, by talking about the German people's collective guilt, or by asserting that what happened at Auschwitz was merely the consequence of an ancient hatred of Jews—the greatest pogrom of all times.

KOCH: So that what has been called the "unmastered past of the Jews" is only a small part of your thoughts in the context of the Jerusalem trial?

ARENDT: Since you're asking about my thoughts, I can only say that at the start the "unmastered past of the Jews" played no role in them whatever. That only emerged during the trial and I reported about it. Eichmann's actions took place within an environment and not in a vacuum. Jewish functionaries were part of that environment. During his police interrogation in Jerusalem—and even before that in an interview that he gave to the Dutch Nazi journalist Sassen in Argentina—he himself spoke at great length about his "cooperation" with Jewish functionaries.

People have concluded that because I talk about these facts that I was trying to offer some sort of description of the destruction of European Jewry, in which indeed the actions of Jewish councils would have to have their place. But that was never my intention. My book is a report *about the trial,* not a presentation of that history. Anyone wanting to write a history of that time would surely not choose the Eichmann trial as his point of departure.

But to return to the Jewish part of the "unmastered past," I must say it took the incredible propaganda directed against me, along with consequences extending far beyond the Jewish world, to first make it clear to me what a difficult problem this "unmastered past" evidently is, not so much in the minds of people in general but in the minds of the ranks of Jewish functionaries, who have rightly been called the "Jewish establishment."

KOCH: How did such a misunderstanding come about, the notion that your book, your report on the Eichmann trial, indirectly excuses or trivializes Nazi crimes?

ARENDT: It seems to me there are two things at work here. The first is a malicious distortion, the second a genuine misunderstanding. No one who has read my book can claim that I have "made excuses" for the crimes of the Nazi period. Something similar happened with Hochhuth's book.* Because Hochhuth criticized Pacelli's position at the time of the Final Solution, it was claimed that he had thereby excused Hitler and the SS and presented Pius XII as the real guilty party. And then the attempt is made to center the discussion on nonsense that no one has claimed and that is easily refuted. It's the same with some of the controversy surrounding my Eichmann book. People claim I have "made excuses" for Eichmann and then they prove him guilty—and mostly with quotes that come from my book. As is well known, the manipulation of opinion in the modern world is done primarily by way of "image making"—that is, one sends out into the world certain "images" that not only have nothing to do with reality

*Arendt refers to Rolf Hochhuth's play *The Deputy* (1963). —Ed.

but are also often merely intended to disguise unpleasant realities. They have had considerable success at this in the case of my Eichmann book. There can be no reply to a good part of the discussion—both here in America and in Europe—that you're familiar with, because it all deals with a book that no one wrote. As far as the misunderstanding goes, the subtitle, *On the Banality of Evil,* really has frequently been misinterpreted. Nothing could be further from my mind than to trivialize the greatest catastrophe of our century. Something banal is not therefore either trivial or all that common an occurrence. I can regard a thought or a feeling as banal even if no one has ever uttered such a thing before and its consequences lead to disaster. That's how Tocqueville, for example, responded in the middle of the last century to what at the time were the original, if also at the same time both pernicious and superficial, racial theories of Gobineau. It was mischief loaded with consequences. But did that make it *loaded with meaning* as well? As you know, there have been many attempts to trace National Socialism into the depths of Germany's, and even Europe's, intellectual past. I consider such attempts mistaken and even pernicious because they argue away the phenomenon's most conspicuous hallmark: that is, its utter shallowness. That something can be born in the gutter and despite its lack of depth can at the same time gain power over almost everyone—that is what makes the phenomenon so frightening.

KOCH: And is that why you think it is so important to remove Eichmann and the Eichmann case from the realm of the demonic?

ARENDT: In my opinion I haven't done that with Eichmann, he took care of that himself, and so fundamentally that it bordered on the truly comical. I merely wanted to point out what being "demonic" is all about when you get a close look at it. I learned a good many things myself from all this, and in fact I think it might be important if others were to learn from it as well. For instance, the idea that evil is demonic, which, moreover, sees its precedence in the tale of the fallen angel Lucifer, is extraordinarily appealing to people. (Perhaps you recall the lines from Stefan George's poem "The Culprit": "Who never has measured the spot where the dagger should pierce, how paltry his life, how frail the train of his thought.") Precisely because these criminals were not driven by the evil and murderous motives that we're familiar with—they murdered not to murder, but simply as a part of their career—it seemed only too obvious to us all that we needed to demonize the catastrophe in order to find some historical meaning in it. And I admit, it is easier to bear the thought that the victim is the victim of the devil in human disguise—or as the prosecutor in the Eichmann trial put it, of a historical principle stretching from Pharaoh to Haman*—the victim of a metaphysical principle, rather than the victim of some average man on the street who is not even crazy or particularly evil. What all of us cannot cope with about the recent past is not the number of victims, but the shabbiness of these mass murderers lacking any sense of guilt and the mindless shoddiness of their so-called ideals. "Our idealism was abused" is a statement one hears not infrequently from former Nazis who have now had second thoughts. Yes, indeed, but what a shoddy affair that idealism had always been.

KOCH: What contribution can your book, now that it has been recently published in Germany, make to help us Germans in 1964 deal with the Nazi past of 1933 to 1945?

ARENDT: I'm afraid I don't have the answer to that. But I might at least mention something that has bothered me for a long time, actually ever since 1949 when I returned to Germany the first time. It's been my experience that all those Germans who've never done the least harm in all their lives constantly insist on talking about how guilty they feel, whereas if you run into an ex-Nazi you're confronted with the clearest conscience in the world—even if he doesn't lie to you outright and use his clear conscience as camouflage. In the early postwar years I told myself that this wholesale confession of guilt should be understood in terms of Jaspers's grand statement right after Germany's collapse: "We're guilty of being alive." In the meantime, however, especially in view of the fact that until Eichmann was captured, people in Germany had grown astonishingly blasé about the idea that "there are murderers among us"—they never put them on trial and in many cases even made it possible for them to continue their careers, without the murder and mayhem of course, as if nothing or almost nothing had happened—I mean, given what has come to light in the last few years, I've begun to have my doubts about the innocent confessing their guilt. Such statements have often served to cover up the

---

*In the Bible Haman decreed "to destroy, to slay, and to cause [the Jews] to perish." —Ed.

guilty—when everyone shouts "we're guilty," one can no longer discover what real crimes were actually committed. Whether someone participated in the murder of hundreds of thousands or just kept silent and lived in seclusion then becomes a question where the degree of difference is irrelevant. And that, I think, is intolerable.

As I see it, that same category of intolerability includes the recent palaver about the "Eichmann within us"—as if everyone, simply because he is human, inevitably has an Eichmann inside of him. Or the latest objections to trying Nazis for their crimes—which you could already hear applied to the Eichmann trial—about how all this will simply lead to finding scapegoats, which would then allow the German people to feel collectively innocent again. Politically the German people have to accept the responsibility for crimes committed in their name and by members of their nation—something that only a more or less insignificant minority does not believe nowadays. But that has nothing whatever to do with the personal feelings of individuals. Politically, it seems to me, the German people will be quite justified in declaring that they have mastered this horrible past once they have convicted the murderers still living quietly among them and have removed all those truly accountable from their positions in the public sphere—by which I do not mean private or commercial life. If that does not happen, the past will remain unmastered despite all the talk—or we shall have to wait until we are all dead.

1964

THE DESTRUCTION OF SIX MILLION

A Jewish World *Symposium*

In September 1964, the Jewish World published the responses to two questions it had posed to Hannah Arendt, Nahum Goldmann, Arnold Toynbee, André Maurois, and Yaacov Herzog. The two questions were:

A. *Hitler slaughtered and the world kept silent. Does the continuous silence and the reappearance of neo-Nazism imply that the Nazi barbarism may have its roots in European humanism?*

B. *Are the sources of the helplessness of the Jewish masses, as displayed when they were driven to their slaughter, as well as the helplessness displayed by the Jewish leadership both in Palestine and in the Diaspora, before and during the catastrophe—of an objective or of a subjective nature?*

Arendt's answers follow.

A. *The world did not keep silent; but* apart from not keeping silent, the world did nothing.

In 1938, years before the slaughter began, the world, for example England and America, almost unanimously reacted with "horror and indignation" (Alan Bullock) to the November pogroms. But these verbal denunciations were contradicted by administrative measures in the immigration policy of all European and a great number of overseas countries; this policy confirmed in fact, though only rarely in words, Nazi antisemitism. Those whom the Nazis had declared to be outlaws in their own territory became outlaws everywhere. Antisemitism was neither the only nor the decisive reason for this development; the political structure of the European nation-state was unable to assimilate large groups of foreigners, and its legal system was unable to cope with statelessness. However, the simple fact that all refugees from Nazi territories had been "undesirable" by definition was of considerable importance as a psychological preparation for the Holocaust.

The slaughter took place in the midst of a war whose outcome for years was, to put it mildly, uncertain. It is understandable that the reaction was slow to come; it came in 1943, when victory had become a certainty, with the Moscow Declaration, where for the first time "monstrous crimes" are officially mentioned. At about the same time, the first preparations for the trials of "war criminals" were made, and the peace aims, laid down in 1941 in the Atlantic Charter, were changed into "unconditional surrender." These were matters of policy, considerably more than verbal denunciations; since deliberate extermination of a whole people was unprecedented since the days of antiquity, it is difficult to compare the world's reaction to the slaughter of the Jewish people with its reaction to similar atrocities in time of war. The nearest analogy is the Armenian massacre in the First World War, when 600,000 people were slaughtered by the Turks—a very high figure if one considers the difference in technique—and there is hardly any doubt that "the world's" reaction both in word and deed was stronger in our case. Still, the truth is that, apart from planning for the coming victory, the Allies did nothing to stop the slaughter: they did not bomb the death centers or the communication lines leading to them; and the neutral powers, with very few exceptions, did less than nothing: they did their best in closing their borders hermetically against all those who might try to escape.

Before we jump to any general conclusions about "European humanism," let us consider some of these facts. *First,* the denunciations were wrong and remained ineffective because they did not mention the Jews by name, although everybody knew that Jews were killed regardless of nationality and denomination. The reason was that not only those in power but public opinion in general—large parts of Jewish public opinion not excluded—labored under the fantastic illusion that to call a Jew a Jew and a spade a spade would be a concession to Hitler. This was a failure, not of European humanism, but of European liberalism (socialism not excluded)—its unwillingness to face realities and its tendency to escape into some fool's paradise of firmly held ideological convictions when confronted with facts.

Second, while we don't yet know the reason for the failure of the Allies to act on the military level, there is no doubt that a fatal misunderstanding was among the contributing factors: since the slaughter took place in time of war and was perpetrated by people in uniform, it was considered as part of the war, a "war crime" in the authentic sense of the word, that is, an excess transgressing the rules in the pursuit of victory. The best way to stop the excesses of war, thus the argument ran, was to stop the war. That these massacres had not the slightest connection with military operations was obvious even then, but it was not understood, and the fact that first the Nuremberg trials and then all other postwar trials have counted these killing operations among "war crimes"—the new concept of "crime against humanity" notwithstanding—shows how plausible this argument must have sounded during the war. It seems that the world has needed two decades to realize what actually happened in those few years and how disastrously almost all those concerned, and certainly all men in high position, failed to understand it even when they were in possession of all the factual data.

The last sentence implies that I don't agree with you about the "continuous silence." A study of the literature published during the last decade, even a mere glance at the best-seller lists of the last few years—Grass and Hochhuth in Germany, Schwartz-Bart in France, Shirer in America, the Anne Frank Diary everywhere—prove, on the contrary, that few matters are so much in the center of the world's interest and attention as that "Hitler slaughtered" and *the world did nothing*. Moreover, public denunciations on the governmental level have by now become a routine performance in most countries outside the Arab world. And still, there is an ominous continuity with the past and its catastrophic failures in the continuing disparity between word and deed. Millions of words have been written and spoken about the "crime against humanity," and yet there is no sign that we have come any nearer to the establishment of an international tribunal where mankind, the plaintiff, could bring suit against those who have offended humanity. Or take Germany, where people continue to assure us of how guilty they "feel" and where nevertheless surprisingly lenient sentences are handed down in almost all cases of convicted Nazi murderers, while prominent former Nazis are being kept in high public positions. Recent public opinion polls show that about 40 percent of the German population are against all these trials and another 40 percent prefer to know nothing about them. This failure to act is dangerous enough, but I don't believe that it is due to a "reappearance of neo-Nazism," of which I can hardly see any serious signs in either Europe or America (I presume you are thinking Nasser's Egypt).

What then is the connection between "Nazi barbarism" and "European humanism"? The Nazis, alas, were no "barbarians," and I even suspect that your question was prompted by those Holderlin-reading mass murderers with academic titles who were so very prominent in the Nazi bureaucracy. But is it really an argument against Holderlin or Beethoven to be read and listened to, perhaps even appreciated, by the commanders of the *Einsatzgruppen*? What does it prove for or against Greek culture when a well-known professor of Greek in Germany was able to translate the "Horst-Wessel-Lied" into classical Greek verse in order to prove how reliably he would serve the new regime?

Still, I don't deny the significance of the extraordinary ease with which almost the whole intelligentsia in Germany, and a large part of it in other countries, could be made into Nazi fellow travelers and sometimes into fellow criminals. But this is hardly to be blamed upon the contents of "European humanism," however one may define it; it speaks against no ideas or notions or even ideologies so much as it does against this new class of intellectuals who, as literati and bureaucrats, as scholars and scientists, no less than as critics and providers of entertainment, are so urgently needed by modern society that they are about to become its "ruling class." Here we have indeed every reason to be worried, for they have proved more than once in recent times that they are more susceptible to whatever happens to be "public opinion" and less capable of judging for themselves than almost any other social group.

There is, finally, another aspect to your question which you don't mention and upon which I touch only because it seems to me rather important. European humanism, far from being the "root of Nazism," was so little prepared for it or any other form of totalitarianism that, in understanding and trying to come to terms with this phenomenon, we can rely neither on its conceptual language nor on the traditional metaphors. And while the ensuing and necessary reappraisal of our mental habits is truly agonizing, this situation certainly contains also a threat to "humanism" in all its forms—it is in the danger of becoming *irrelevant*.

B. *The Jewish masses inside Nazi-occupied Europe were objectively helpless.*

Once they were caught and driven to their death, they behaved like all other groups in the same circumstances. Many reports from the concentration camps as well as the death centers, where of course not only Jews were massacred, stress the horror of watching "these processions of human beings going like dummies to their deaths." (I quote intentionally from David Rousset's report on Buchenwald, where no Jews were involved.)

There are several factors which may help to explain this apathy. *Foremost* among them is the simple and often forgotten fact that there are many things considerably worse than death, that there is a great difference between dying a slow and agonizing death and dying the relatively quick and easy death before the firing squad or in the gas chambers. There is, *second,* what Tadeusz Borowski, the Polish poet, had to say in his report on his own stay in Auschwitz: "Never before was hope stronger than man, and never before did hope result in so much evil as in this camp. We were taught not to give up hope. That is why we die in the gas oven." *Hope stronger than man*—that means hope destructive of the very humanity of man. And even more destructive perhaps of this humanity was the very innocence of those who were trapped in this whole monstrosity, namely, that they were innocent even from the viewpoint of their persecutors. Their apathy was to a very large extent the almost physical, automatic response to the challenge of *absolute meaninglessness.*

The Jewish leadership inside Europe was objectively hardly less helpless than the Jewish masses. And nothing more needed to be said about them if they had recognized this helplessness and relinquished their positions. Objectively speaking, there were hardly more than three alternatives: to admit their impotence and to tell the people all is lost, *sauve qui peut;* or to accompany their charges on the voyage to the East and suffer the same fate; or, as was notably done in France, to use the Nazi-controlled Jewish council as a cover for underground work in which one tried to help Jews to escape. Wherever Jews, either because of their numbers or because of their geographical location, could not be killed on the spot—that is, everywhere except in Soviet Russia—the Jewish leadership, instead of being merely helpless, became in fact an important factor in the bureaucracy of destruction. To quote but one of the many extant documents—from the Nazis or from survivors—"with the aid of the Jewish council, the deportations from [Dutch] provinces proceeded without a hitch."

And now, finally, the Jewish leadership both in Palestine and in the Diaspora: it has often been argued that these leaders failed to dramatize the plight of European Jewry, that they were not insistent or not imaginative or not courageous enough in their dealings with the Allies, and I have no wish to deny this. Still, I believed then, and I am inclined to believe today, that under the circumstances nothing would have helped but a "normalization" of the Jewish position, that is, a real declaration of war, the establishment of a Jewish army, composed of Palestinian and stateless Jews all over the world, and the recognition of the Jewish people as belligerents. (It is well known that Jews who enjoyed the status of belligerents were saved—American and British Jews in civilian internment camps, Jewish prisoners of war from all Allied armies, even from the defeated French army. The only exception was the Red Army. Russia had never signed the Geneva Convention.)

Whether or not this was a pipe dream, no one can tell who has not studied the archives of the Jewish Agency for Palestine and those of Britain and America, which are not yet open to the public.

1964

"THE FORMIDABLE DR. ROBINSON"

A Reply by Hannah Arendt

"Miss Arendt," said Mr. Laqueur in his review of Jacob Robinson's book *And the Crooked Shall Be Made Straight* (*New York Review of Books,* November 1965), "had stumbled on what seemed a hornets' nest but is in fact a very intricate and painful problem." This sentence would be true if it read: "She stumbled on what in fact was a hornets' nest because she had touched upon what seemed an intricate problem and is indeed a painful one."

Reviewing Robinson's "full-scale attempt to refute" my report of the Eichmann trial, Mr. Laqueur was so overwhelmed by his author's "eminent authority" that he thought it superfluous to acquaint himself with the subject under attack. He accepts Mr. Robinson's basic distortion, contained in the subtitle of his book, "The Jewish Catastrophe and Hannah Arendt's Narrative," which implies that I recounted part of "Jewish contemporary history," while in fact I have criticized the prosecution for taking the Eichmann trial as a pretext for doing just that. (Needless to say, I would never have gone to Jerusalem if I had wanted to write a book on "contemporary Jewish history.") Mr. Laqueur believes that *I* asked "why was there not more active resistance" among the Jews, while it was the prosecution that had brought up this question; I had reported this incident and dismissed the question twice as "silly and cruel, since it testified to a fatal ignorance of the conditions of the time" (pp. 11 and 283 of the second edition). He claims that I have been unaware of the "particular vulnerability" of the Jewish communities in the face of organized persecution, whereas I actually have enumerated these vulnerabilities—no territory, no government, no army, no government in exile, no weapons, no youth with military training (p. 125). He insists that I "argue that justice was not done in Jerusalem," while I actually argue that *despite* a number of carefully enumerated irregularities, the very opposite of "countless" ones, justice was done insofar as the trial's "main purpose—to prosecute and to defend, to judge and to punish Adolf Eichmann—was achieved," a passage even quoted in Robinson's book.

Nowhere did I say, as Mr. Laqueur claims, that "Eichmann was hanged . . . by the wrong court and for the wrong reasons," or that "irreparable harm was done to the rule of law." On the contrary, I justified the competence of the court and the kidnapping of the accused (pp. 259–65) and stated that the trial in Jerusalem was "no more, but also no less, than the last of the numerous Successor Trials which followed the Nuremberg Trials." Finally, Mr. Laqueur—knowing neither my book nor the trial in Jerusalem—believes that I attacked the court proceedings as a whole, whereas what I attacked was the prosecution. (The conflict between bench and prosecution ran like a red thread through the proceedings. I reported it, and sided in nearly all cases with the bench—which was rather common among the members of the press.) Had Mr. Laqueur been at all familiar with the subject matter, he would not have been so naïve as to identify "betrayal and collaboration," for the whole point of the matter is that the members of the Jewish councils as a rule were *not* traitors or Gestapo agents, and *still* they became the tools of the Nazis. (The distinction was made by the witnesses for the prosecution; if the members of the Jewish councils had been scoundrels, there would be no "problem," let alone a "painful and intricate" one.)

After misinforming the reader about the subject matter of my book, Mr. Laqueur proceeds to enumerate my opponent's "formidable credentials." He deplores that Mr. Robinson's name is not well known among "students of political science," which is true, and not "one to conjure with in literary circles," which is untrue: since the appearance of my book, Mr. Robinson's name has become famous, particularly in New York's literary circles, and especially among writers for *Partisan Review* and *Dissent.* Paralleling the publisher's blurb, Mr. Laqueur draws attention to this "eminent authority on international law" and assures us that "his standing is high among students of contemporary Jewish history" (something of a letdown, for the publisher has claimed eminence for this field as well). He rounds out the picture with praise of "unrivaled mastery of the sources," "great erudition," and "awe-inspiring," "almost obsessive" scholarship. Finally, he tells us what Mr. Robinson's present position is: he "coordinates research between the various institutes devoted to the study of the Jewish catastrophe" ("throughout the world," as the publisher has it), but he does not tell us what these institutes are. Are they too numerous to be enumerated? Hardly. They are the YIVO (the Yiddish Scientific Institute) in New York, the Wiener Library in London, the Centre de Documentation Juive in Paris, and Yad Vashem in Jerusalem. There are reasons not to be too specific in these matters. Mr. Laqueur himself, the reviewer of Mr. Robinson's book, is director of research in one of the coordinated research centers, the Wiener Library.

In view of the recent vintage of Mr. Robinson's "eminent authority," Mr. Laqueur's information is deplorably vague. Let us see whether we can help the reader. Since Mr. Laqueur so closely follows publishers' blurbs, we may note that in 1960, when Mr. Robinson's last book was published, the jacket did not yet know that he was either "eminent" or an "authority." Then, in the summer of 1963, a couple of months after the publication of *Eichmann in Jerusalem*, he wrote a propaganda pamphlet for the (B'nai B'rith's) Anti-Defamation League, called *Facts*, directed against my book. The change in his worldly fortunes was sudden and radical. While on earlier publishers' jackets he was mentioned as "special consultant on *Jewish Affairs*" at the Nuremberg trial, he was now described as "special consultant" *tout court*— obviously a much greater distinction for an "authority" on international law, especially if one is aware of the minor role the crime against the Jewish people had played at Nuremberg. These still rather modest beginnings— compared to his present status—show already that, while Mr. Robinson recently acquired a number of startlingly new qualities, he also lost a few which up to then had been his very own. Nowhere are we any longer told that Mr. Robinson's specialty is "Minority Problems," that he founded the Institute of Jewish Affairs, sponsored by the American and World Jewish Congress, where, with the exception of an article on the United Nations, all of Mr. Robinson's contributions since 1940 appeared, and, most surprisingly, nowhere in Mr. Laqueur's review is there any mention at all of Mr. Robinson's very important role in Jerusalem. In the ADL pamphlet, the reader is still told of his having been "a special consultant to the prosecution of the Eichmann trial," on the jacket of the present book he merely "advised the Israelis on questions of documentation and law"—no special connection with the prosecution any longer—whereas in fact, and according to the Israeli press handouts, giving "brief biographies" of the team of prosecutors, "Dr. Jacob Robinson" ranked directly after Gideon Hausner, the attorney general, and was then followed by two deputy state attorneys; hence, Mr. Robinson was second in importance for the prosecution only to the attorney general himself. From which one may conclude that Mr. Robinson had a personal interest in "prosecuting" me for a change, and in defending the case for the prosecution. *It was, in fact, his own case.*

Since Mr. Laqueur believes that the core of the conflict between Mr. Robinson and myself consists of the antagonism of "professional historians" and "amateurs . . . eager to write a *roman à thèse*," he may be surprised to learn that prior to 1963 Mr. Robinson was not a historian—the Israeli trial authorities correctly mention his training as a lawyer—and that the present book, published in cooperation with the Jewish Publication Society, is in fact his first venture into the field of Jewish history. The best way to settle this difficult question of who is the amateur and who the professional is perhaps to consult the *Guide to Jewish History Under Nazi Impact*, a bibliography covering all languages, including Hebrew and Yiddish, published under the coauthorship of the late Philip Friedman and Jacob Robinson by the YIVO and Yad Vashem in 1960. There, Mr. Robinson appears with two entries: a short preface to a book by Boris Shub (1943) and a five-page study on "Palestine and the United Nations" (1947), a subject totally unrelated to the question that came up during the Eichmann trial. But most surprising of all, at that time Mr. Robinson must have thought that I was much more a "professional" than he himself, for I appear there with four items, one of them a book more substantial and relevant to modern Jewish history and to the period in question than anything by the two authors.

II

Shortly after the appearance of my book, Mr. Robinson said he had found "hundreds of factual errors"—four hundred, to be exact, a figure which he later upped to six hundred. However, upon closer inspection it turned out that these were miscalculations; the number of mistakes can be counted only by the number of words I used. This would make it rather difficult to reply under all circumstances but is actually the least of the difficulties. Mr. Laqueur is vaguely aware of certain shortcomings in Mr. Robinson's book;

he ascribes them to a refusal to think, to "pause for reflection between foot-notes," and it is indeed true that the greatest difficulty in dealing meaning-fully with this book is its complete lack of consistent argument or point of view. To be sure, Mr. Robinson has one overriding interest, namely, to con-tradict me line by line, and one overriding ambition, namely, to display his "erudition." But while the former led him more often than not into a kind of super-quibbling the like of which I never saw in black and white (when I say: "According to international law, it was the privilege of the sovereign Ger-man nation to declare a national minority of whatever part of its population it saw fit," he replies: no, not at all, except that "there is no prohibition . . . in international law to declare part of a population a national minority," p. 73), the latter tempted him into filling countless pages with complete irrelevan-cies—as for instance a four-page excursion into Hungarian history, complete with "basic sources," though all his facts could be found in a one-volume *Encyclopedia of World History*. This is no proof of scholarship but of its very opposite.

In addition to these difficulties, the book displays in all innocence a total unawareness of the most common distinctions in the historical sciences. Such questions as: How many Jews lived in Rome in 1943? (Mr. Robinson's figure, taken from the year 1925, is certainly too high.) When did the Hitler regime become fully totalitarian? (Mr. Robinson actually believes that this can be found out by consulting a *Zeittafel*, a chronological enumeration of events.) Are there connections between the Final Solution and the earlier euthanasia program? (Gerald Reitlinger, as I stated, has proved these con-nections "with documentary evidence that leaves no doubt"; Mr. Robinson prefers to ignore my statement as well as Reitlinger's evidence, simply ascribing the discovery of these connections to me and claiming that they do not exist.) All these and many more questions are treated on exactly the same level, or rather they are reduced to the level of the first question, an isolated fact which, to be established, needs neither the context of a story nor the sup-port of interpretation nor the judgment of the reporter.

Clearly, the number of "mistakes" one can discover in any book with the help of Mr. Robinson's extraordinary methods is staggering. And we have by no means exhausted them yet. Mr. Robinson belongs among the happy few who are psychologically color blind; they see only black and white. Hence, when I described Eichmann as not at all stupid and yet entirely thoughtless, or point out that on the basis of the evidence he was not an inveterate liar and yet lied occasionally, and then proceed to give some instances where he actually lied, Mr. Robinson is firmly convinced that these are "contradictions," "hopping back and forth," in his inimitable jargon. Needless to say, my "contradictions" are almost as countless as my "mistakes." All these methodological difficulties, however, which perhaps can be excused in a book written by a lawyer and meant to restate a prosecutor's case, are overshadowed by a truly dazzling display of sheer inability to read.

In his Preface, Robinson charges me with "misreading" documents and books, and on page 2 of his book he starts to pile up examples of what he understands by reading and misreading, until at the end one finds oneself overwhelmed by a unique *embarras de richesse*. There are first the endlessly repeated instances in which Eichmann's words, often given by me in indirect discourse and sometimes even in quotation marks, are misread for direct discourse of the author. Thus, quoting from a passage which is introduced in the original by *"According to the version [Eichmann] gave* at the police examination" and is liberally sprinkled with clear indications of indirect discourse ("as he saw it," etc.), Mr. Robinson writes: *"According to Miss Arendt,* the story of Adolf Eichmann is a 'bad luck story if there ever was one.'" But even when I quote verbatim from the police examination, in which Eichmann had described his visit to Auschwitz to meet Mr. Storfer and said: "'We had a normal human encounter,'" and conclude the episode by saying, "Six weeks after this normal human encounter, Storfer was dead," Mr. Robinson thinks that *I* "considered it a 'normal human encounter.'" And since he apparently wrote his book without consulting the "primary sources," namely the trial proceedings, he can write, *"In the face of what she says [Eichmann] referred to* 'a cross-examination that lasted longer than any known before,'" completely unaware of the fact that Eichmann (in the 106th session) had said literally: "Above all I wish that . . . my sons can say . . . 'Please, he was in the longest cross-examination that ever was known. . . .'"

Another difficulty with Mr. Robinson's strange reading habits comes to light whenever he accuses me of not offering "explanation" or "support" for my statements. In all these instances he would have had to turn the page, and in some instances a couple of pages, to find lengthy explanations, and while he may find this too complicated because he seems incapable of remembering what he read only a few short sentences before, it is, unfortunately, indispensable for reading books or documents. Thus he can for instance quote me correctly on one page: "*To a Jew* this role of the Jewish leaders in the destruction of their own people is undoubtedly the darkest chapter of the whole dark story," and then on the very next page reply: "The destruction of six million Jews—not 'the role of the Jewish leaders'—is the 'darkest chapter' of Jewish history," as though he never read the qualifying clause. The difference between what I say and what Mr. Robinson makes me say is the difference between "patriotism"—"that wrong done by my own people naturally grieves me more than wrong done by other peoples," as I put it in my reply to Gershom Scholem (*Encounter*, January 1964)—and a monstrous lie. And the alternative to assuming Mr. Robinson's inability to read would be to charge him with character assassination. However, the alternative of bad faith is difficult to entertain in view of the fact that Mr. Robinson's difficulties with sentence structure occasionally work against his own interest. Thus he begins his treatment of "Behavior of the Victims" (p. 187 ff.) by ascribing to me a description which was taken, word for word, from the attorney general's examination of witnesses during the twenty-second session and was quoted by me for the deliberate purpose of denouncing Mr. Hausner's attack on these survivors. Since Mr. Robinson honestly believes he denounces me and not his colleague, he finds now what he failed to discover when he advised him, that this "picture contrasts radically with reality," which, of course, was my whole point to begin with.

Mr. Laqueur found in Mr. Robinson's book a few inconsequential mistakes and believes that more could be found by "a team of researchers." Actually, the book abounds in monumental errors, of which I can give here only two representative examples. The first concerns the Nazi legal system, a clear understanding of which was of course of the greatest importance for the Jerusalem trial. The second deals with the widespread antisemitism in Europe prior to Nazi occupation, because this was an important contributing factor to the success of the Final Solution.

(1) The discussion of the Nazi legal system occurs on pp. 274–76 of Robinson's book, and only after having read these pages did it dawn upon me that the case for the prosecution had been presented in honest ignorance of it. That this legal system was actually criminal did not make it any less "legal" for those who lived in the country. Robinson obviously never heard of the famous Nazi slogan *Führerworte haben Gesetzes Kraft*, "the Führer's

words have the force of law," because he does not recognize it in the English paraphrase. Hence, he does not know that the Führer's orders, whether given orally or in writing, "canceled all *written* law" (Hans Buchheim). He therefore believes that the sections in the German Criminal Code dealing with murder made Hitler's order "illegal," and is in doubt "whether [the order for the Final Solution] emanated from Hitler or Himmler (p. 371). Only a "specialist," as Mr. Laqueur would put it, can judge how fantastic this doubt is. That many of these orders were secret is a matter of course, but this by no means prevented them from being legally binding, because, contrary to what Mr. Robinson thinks, promulgation was not "the very essence of the binding force of law" in Nazi Germany; he simply does not know that there exist five fat volumes of *Verfügungen, Anordnungen, Bekanntgaben* (Decrees, Ordinances, Notices) which regulated very important areas in the life of the German people and still were classified as "top secret." (Four of these volumes, published by the *Parteikanzlei,* are available in the archives of the Hoover Library.) In short, the order for the Final Solution was binding law in Nazi Germany because Germany had become a criminal state, and nothing could be more preposterous than to assert that it "constituted nothing but an illegal secret promise of the Führer of immunity from prosecution."

(2) In my discussion of the situation in the Netherlands, I stated that "the prewar Dutch government had officially declared [Jewish refugees] to be 'undesirable.'" Mr. Robinson declares categorically as usual: "This never happened," because he never heard of the circular letter, issued by the Dutch government on May 7, 1938, in which refugees are declared to be "undesirable aliens." I would not mention this if it were merely a factual error, but the point of the matter is that the attitude of the Dutch government was only more outspoken than that of other European countries. Refugees, and especially Jewish refugees, were "undesirable" all over Europe, and Mr. Robinson tries in all instances to present the situation of Jews in Europe prior to the Nazi occupation in rosy colors. (His only exception to the rule is Italy, where antisemitic legislation actually was enacted, in 1938, only under pressure from Berlin—the evidence is too well known to be quoted. For reasons best known to Mr. Robinson, I suddenly stand accused of "whitewashing Mussolini.") The rampant Jew-hatred in Eastern Europe and the rapidly growing antisemitism in Western Europe can be interpreted and explained in many different ways, but there is no doubt about the extent to which it later

facilitated Hitler's Final Solution. This attempt to deny the historical truth is especially noticeable in Mr. Robinson's discussion of Romania. The drift of his argument is to accuse me of "minimizing German influence in Romania's *Judenpolitik*," and to deny, in the face of all evidence, that Romania, in the words of Reitlinger, was the "nation which began its deportations to Russia before Hitler had even given the signal, but which was constrained . . . through jealousy of the Germans." Mr. Robinson, because of his mistaken notions about scholarship, despises standard works (which explains, incidentally, why he is at a loss to find out how I "know" that Hitler thought Antonescu to be more "radical" than the Nazis [p. 362]; I cited a famous remark of Hitler to Goebbels, well known to all "professionals"); he prefers to base his presentation on an admittedly highly "selective" (*lückenhafte*) collection of documents, prepared for the trial by the United Restitution Organization, a group established to press Jewish claims against Germany; it includes a research department whose raison d'être is of course to "prove" that all initiative during this period came from Berlin, and therefore to "minimize" indigenous antisemitism.

III

A major part of Mr. Robinson's book is devoted to "Jewish Behavior in the Face of Disaster," which in my book played a minor role. Even the admiring Mr. Laqueur thinks that this chapter is the most disappointing of Robinson's book. And it is true that much of its space is wasted on proving what nobody ever doubted—namely, that the Jewish councils were established by the Nazis—as well as on what no one at all familiar with concentration and extermination camps will ever believe—namely, that there was no deliberate and infernal blurring of the line between victims and executioners. In the center of these sections are the Jewish councils, and Robinson's two main theses are expressed in two sentences: first, "Legally and morally, the members of the Jewish Councils can no more be judged accomplices of their Nazi rulers than can a store owner be judged an accomplice of an armed robber to whom he surrenders *his store* at gunpoint" (p. 159, italics added). The worst reproach one could level at the Jewish councils would indeed be to accuse them of disposing of Jewish lives and properties as though they *owned* them, and no one to my knowledge has ever dared to go that far until Mr. Robinson, with his inability "to pause for reflection," appeared on the scene. And since he cannot remember what he wrote on p. 159 when he comes to p. 223 we hear, second, that whoever "accepted appointment to a Council . . . did so as a rule out of feeling of responsibility," hence was by no means forced at gunpoint.

Mr. Robinson's second thesis has become common property among writers for the Jewish establishment. The first thesis had a certain success in New York's literary circles, partly, to be sure, because they knew absolutely nothing of the whole issue, but partly also, I am afraid, because of a moral obtuseness which Mary McCarthy very pointedly exposed in *Partisan Review*.* (No one, of course, ever combined the two before for obvious reasons.)

This moral obtuseness (like tone deafness) is actually the most alarming aspect of the whole book. Mr. Robinson quotes endlessly from announcements and deliberations of the *Judenräte*, one more terrible than the next, and then mentions—as though this was no more than one among many legitimate opinions—an instance in which the rabbinate intervened and told the *Judenrat* in Vilna "that he had no right to select Jews and deliver them to the Germans," in accordance with the old prescription. If the gentiles should tell you, " 'give us one of yours and we shall kill him, otherwise we shall kill all of you,' they should all be killed and not a single Jewish soul should be delivered."

At this point, not knowing what he is doing, Mr. Robinson raises one of the most disturbing "problems" of the whole issue, a problem I had been careful not to raise because it was not raised at the trial and therefore was not my business: the conduct of the European rabbinate during the catastrophe. It seems there was not one rabbi who did what Dompropst Bernhard Lichtenberg, a Catholic priest, or Propst Heinrich Grüber, a Protestant minister, had tried to do—to volunteer for deportation.

These are serious and even terrible questions, and neither the present unanimity of Jewish official opinion nor any "coordination" of research will be able to prevent independent scholars from asking them and trying to find an answer. The greatest weakness of this unanimity is that it is of so very recent origin. History textbooks used in Israeli schools abound in the most extreme

---

*Cf. H. Arendt, *Responsibility and Judgment*, ed. J. Kohn (New York: Schocken Books, 2003), p. 18.—Ed.

opinions on Jewish behavior; generally they are as unable to distinguish between the behavior of the victims and the conduct of the Jewish leadership as Mr. Hausner was when he questioned his witnesses. He complained about the lack of Jewish resistance in general terms because this was "a popular view among many Israeli writers," who held that "Hitler was helped in exterminating all European Jews by the appeasement tactics of Jewish leaders," and because "Jews went to their death like sheep to slaughter." (See Mark M. Krug's "Young Israelis and Jews Abroad—A Study of Selected History Textbooks," in *Comparative Education Review,* October 1963.)

Naturally, I know much more about this issue today than when I wrote my book and could only be marginally concerned with it. My insufficient knowledge of the intricacies of the problem came out in many letters from survivors, and the most knowledgeable and interesting one came from a colleague of mine who was in Hungary under the Nazi occupation and in Israel during the Kastner trial. (Rudolf Kastner had been the most prominent member of the Hungarian *Judenrat.*) He said that I was in error when I wrote "that Kastner was murdered by Hungarian survivors," that "during the trial it came out that out of the four or five accused . . . there was only one who was not at one time or another in the service of the Israeli Security Service," though "none of them was actually in the Service at the time of the murder." And he told me what I had not known, that "the Government did everything in its power to support Kastner. The reason for this, apart from the dirty-linen argument, was that there was and is a strong link between the Establishment in Israel and the leadership which was in charge in Europe during the war." (Kastner was of course a case in point; at the time of his trial he was a high public official in Israel, although his role in Hungary was known to everybody.) This, and nothing else, makes the problem "intricate" in addition to "painful," for it won't be possible to elucidate it until the archives of the respective Jewish organizations have been opened.

IV

To anyone willing and able to read, the result of Mr. Robinson's long labors will look like a prime example of a nonbook. But this is not to deny that its author is "formidable" and "awe inspiring." It *is* formidable that the book found two respectable publishers and was reviewed in respected magazines; and it *is* awe-inspiring that for years now, simply on his having said so, the news has echoed around the globe that my book contained "hundreds of factual errors" and that I had not written a trial report but "scrutinized the data concerned with the Nazi extermination of European Jewry"—as a student paper recently put it, without, of course, meaning any harm. Even apart from these spectacular successes, how could anybody deny the formidableness of a man who represented the government of Israel, and thus can count upon its unflinching support, together with its consulates, embassies, and missions throughout the world, is backed by both the American and the World Jewish Congress, by B'nai B'rith, with its powerful Anti-Defamation League and student organizations on all campuses, and who has four coordinated research institutes at his beck and call?

And these are merely the organizations in whose name Mr. Robinson has the right to speak. To them we must add his allies, also international in scope, though perhaps a shade less powerful. They are best represented by Dr. Siegfried Moses—state comptroller of Israel, now in retirement, president of the Leo Baeck Institute, with headquarters in Jerusalem, New York, and London, and on the board of the Council of Jews from Germany, with branches in the United States, Israel, Europe, and South America—who wrote me (in a letter in German, dated March 3, 1963) that he had come to New York with a draft statement against Raul Hilberg's book, to be published by the Council of Jews from Germany, but that now he had to send *me* "a declaration of war" instead. (The Council did indeed publish a protest on March 12 against Hilberg and me, and it was considerably less than an act of war: it defended the activities of the Nazi-established *Reichsvereinigung* by citing the work done by its predecessor, the independent *Reichsvertretung,* which was not under attack; admitted that Jewish "leaders and officials" had given "technical assistance in the execution" of Nazi orders; claimed "secret resistance" for which "no documentary evidence existed"; and finally mentioned a single known case where "Nazi orders had not been *fully* carried out" [italics added]—all of which of course tended to prove my point.)

I do not know to what extent Moses, a high Israeli government official, was instrumental in measures taken by the Israeli government; the first reaction of the Israeli press to my book had been sympathetic: the *Jerusalem Post* printed a friendly report from its correspondent; *Haaretz* published long excerpts; and the Schocken publishing house asked for, and then canceled, an option on the Hebrew edition. I was informed by reliable Israeli sources that Ben-Gurion himself had intervened to change this atmosphere. However, I am reasonably sure that Dr. Moses's "war" consisted not in the harmless declaration of the council but in organizing attacks by former functionaries of German-Jewish organizations who are now dispersed all over the world.

The "war" in America, at any rate, preceded by no friendly declaration, began on March 11, 1963, when the Anti-Defamation League sent out its first memorandum—from Arnold Forster to all regional offices, national commissions, and national committees—informing them of the article series in *The New Yorker,* and stating its fear that my "concept about Jewish participation in the Nazi holocaust . . . *may plague Jews for years to come*" (italics added). This was followed two weeks later by another memorandum, which summed up the articles in five sentences and recommended this summary to "book reviewers and others when the volume appears." The points to be attacked were as follows:

(1) "That Eichmann was, as he himself claimed, only a small cog in the extermination machine." (Not even Eichmann, let alone I, had ever claimed this. It was the thesis of the defense.)

(2) "That the trial did not fulfill an original Israeli Government hope—enlarging international law to include the crime of racial and religious genocide." (Just plain nonsense; no one had accused the Israeli government of not fulfilling a nonexistent promise.)

(3) "That the Eichmann trial was little more than a legal circus." (I never thought or said so, but this was indeed a widespread opinion, shared incidentally by quite a number of old and trusted Zionists: Martin Buber told me in Jerusalem that the trial was part of "Ben-Gurion's policies of *panis et circenses,*" and a well-known Jewish journalist wrote me in August 1963: "No one can seriously question that the trial was a political and not a juridical act"—firmly believing, incidentally, that this was my opinion too!)

(4) "That the Jewish victims of the Holocaust in Nazi Europe failed, by and large, to resist the *final solution,*" which was, as I said before, the point insisted upon by the prosecutor.

(5) "That Europe's Jewish organizations, in the main, played a 'disastrous role' by cooperating with the Nazi extermination machine. As a result, the Jews, themselves, bear a large share of the blame for the murder of mil-

lions of their kinsmen killed by the Nazis." (In other words, as everybody soon knew and repeated, my "thesis" was that the Jews had murdered themselves.)

This summary was then once more summed up for the press by Gideon Hausner himself: according to the New York *Daily News* (May 20, 1963), he "flew here to answer Hannah Arendt's bizarre defense of Eichmann in her book *Eichmann in Jerusalem*. The author would have you believe that Eichmann really wasn't a Nazi, that the Gestapo aided Jews, that Eichmann was actually unaware of Hitler's evil plans. The record, to the contrary, shows that Eichmann shipped 434,351 Jews to the Auschwitz gas chamber." (One really would like to know how Mr. Hausner arrived at this figure.)

Those who are familiar with the ensuing "controversy" will know that four of the ADL's five sentences were used from then on by almost every reviewer, just as if, in Mary McCarthy's telling phrase, they came out of a "mimeographing machine." Which in fact they had, although it must be admitted that, apart from his colleague Robinson, only Michael Musmanno, in the *New York Times*, reflected fully Hausner's line. (With the result that the Jewish Center Lecture Bureau of the National Jewish Welfare Board recommended him to Jewish communities all over the country.)

Mr. Robinson's present book is only the last, the most elaborate, and the least competent variation of this "image" of a posthumous defense of Eichmann, a book that no one ever wrote but of whose reality even people who had read my book became convinced, having quickly changed their minds under this stupendous barrage. It is in the nature of such campaigns that they gain in momentum and viciousness as they proceed. (ADL's first communication still stressed that mine was an "otherwise masterful report," that "Dr. Arendt is a recognized scholar," "a person of eminent respectability"—characterizations which must make them shudder today if ever they consult their old files.) This is due to the fact that the more successful the image makers are the more likely they are to fall victim not only to their own fabrication but to its inherent logic. The image they had created was that of an "evil book"; now they had to prove that it was written by an "evil person." When this happened there were still quite a few Jewish functionaries who thought that things had gone too far. Thus, I received a letter from an officer of the United Restitution Organization—on whose help Mr. Robinson so heavily relied—telling me that he could only "shake his head in uneasiness" when he read the "very vicious [*gehässige*] discussion, especially in the whole Jewish press" (mentioning, incidentally, the "*New York Times* and the London *Observer*"), and he singled out the articles "of Syrkin, Steiner, Nehemiah Robinson, Jacob Robinson, etc." This was in July 1963; a few months later, this communication would have been impossible.

No one will doubt the effectiveness of modern image making, and no one acquainted with Jewish organizations and their countless channels of communication outside their immediate range will underestimate their possibilities in influencing public opinion. For greater than their direct power of control is the voluntary outside help upon which they can draw from Jews who, though they may not be at all interested in Jewish affairs, will flock home, as it were, out of age-old fears (no longer justified, let us hope, but still very much alive) when their people or its leaders are criticized. What I had done according to their lights was the crime of crimes: I had told "the truth in a hostile environment," as an Israeli official told me, and what the ADL and all the other organizations did was to hoist the danger signal. At this moment, all those among us who still think "their honor precarious, their liberty provisional . . . their position unstable" feared that "the days of funereal disaster when the majority rally round the victim as the Jews rallied round Dreyfus" (in Proust's great description of Jewish and homosexual society) were drawing to a close. It was of course a farce, but it was effective.

Or was it? After all, the denunciation of book and author, with which they achieved great, though by no means total, success, was not their goal. It was only the *means* with which to prevent the discussion of an issue "which may plague Jews for years to come." And as far as this goal was concerned, they achieved the precise opposite. If they had left well enough alone, this issue, which I had touched upon only marginally, would not have been trumpeted all over the world. In their efforts to prevent people from reading what I had written, or, in case such misfortune had already happened, to provide the necessary reading glasses, they blew it up out of all proportion, not only with reference to my book but with reference to what had actually happened. They forgot that they were mass organizations, using all the means of mass communication, so that every issue they touched at all, pro or contra, was liable to attract the attention of masses whom they then no longer could control. So what happened after a while in these meaningless and mindless debates was that people began to think that all the nonsense the image makers had made me say was the actual historical truth.

Thus, with the unerring precision with which a bicyclist on his first ride will collide with the obstacle he is most afraid of, Mr. Robinson's formidable supporters have put their whole power at the service of propagating what they were most anxious to avoid. So that now, as a result of their folly, literally everybody feels the need for a "major work" on Jewish conduct in the face of catastrophe. I doubt that such a book is as "badly needed" as Mr. Laqueur thinks, but Mr. Robinson, in any case, is most unlikely to produce it. The methods used in the pursuit of historical truth are not the methods of the prosecutor, and the men who stand guard over facts are not the officers of interest groups—*no matter how legitimate their claims*—but the reporters, the historians, and finally the poets.

1966

AFTERWORD
"Big Hannah"—My Aunt

Edna Brocke

> There is radical evil, but not radical good. Radical
> evil always appears when a radical good is desired.
> *Hannah Arendt,* Denktagebuch *1950–73, p. 341*

A photograph taken on April 5, 1925, in Rauschen, near Königsberg, shows two girls and three boys. Together with her good friend from Berlin Kaete Lewin, five years younger and still a schoolgirl at this point, Hannah Arendt (reclining in the foreground) had arrived for a short family visit. With her cousin Ernst Fuerst (the first on the left), whom she particularly liked, they had all undertaken a short bicycle excursion. The brothers Konrad and Heinz Jacoby (on the right in the picture) had joined them. Thus a triangle took shape that would last a lifetime. Although each of the three would pursue different studies at different universities, they remained close. Hannah Arendt immigrated via Paris to the United States, her cousin Ernest and her good friend Kaete—who had become in the meantime Mrs. Kaete Fuerst— moved to what was at that time the British mandate territory of Palestine.

As a sign of their profound connection, Ernest and Kaete named their first daughter, born in Jerusalem, Hannah. In time she came to be known as "little Hannah," to distinguish her from her distant New York cousin, "Big Hannah."

As the younger sister of Little Hannah, I expected a giant woman as I awaited Big Hannah at the Lod Airport in Tel Aviv in 1955 at the start of her second visit to Israel. How surprised was I, barely twelve years old, when a rather delicate woman with a hearty laugh and a hoarse voice appeared, smoking one cigarette after another, a woman with lively eyes full of vitality

that displayed a curiosity unimpaired by age, a woman who exuded a rare combination of self-confidence and hesitancy. Her throaty, unmistakable voice made its most lasting impression on me when she would recite long poems in German, without pause or searching for words, with an intonation almost suitable for the stage. And it was the same with the numerous classical texts that she quoted by heart in Greek, as if she was engaged in a perpetual inner dialogue with these texts. Her face, marked by a high brow, was partly hidden by hair combed against its natural direction, a nonhairdo that fit very well with her hoarse voice. The repeated lip movements attempting to hide her beautiful, white, prominent teeth, together with a particular gesture that brought her cigarette to her mouth with long, delicate fingers, also made a great impression.

The occasion for her visit in 1955 was the thirteenth birthday of my cousin, a nephew of Hannah's, who was not celebrating a bar mitzvah but was nonetheless observing the birthday as a special one. One of the family's gifts to him was a dark-green padded sleeping bag that he had wanted. I climbed into the sleeping bag before we drove to Jerusalem to present the gift. When Hannah saw me in it, she merely remarked: "Now you are as green as a frog." And so I acquired the nickname "Fröschlein" (Froglette), to which almost all her letters to me were addressed even after I had long since become a married woman.

This first encounter had a long-lasting effect. She immediately took me under her wing, providing me with many books (most of them written in English), giving me a gramophone—at this time in Israel a great luxury—and worrying unduly about the cost of my education. She placed great confidence in my driving ability and on her repeated visits to Israel entrusted me with the responsibility of chauffeuring her around the country.

When she visited Israel after the 1963 publication of her book on the Eichmann trial, so vehement were the emotions in the Jewish world in general, and Israel in particular, over this "report on the banality of evil," she remained incognito. During the trial itself I had accompanied her many times to the Menorah Club in Jerusalem to discuss with her a host of issues raised by the trial. Of particular significance was the Israeli Independence Day, which fell during the trial and which we spent together in Jerusalem. At the time this holiday was celebrated with considerable enthusiasm, since statehood was still a relatively new experience for Jews. It was impossible not to sense Hannah's ambivalent relation to this ceremony. It awoke in her an earlier identification with the Zionist idea, while at the same time returning her to the contradiction that she had adopted as her own. On another occasion, I was privileged to be present during her meeting with Uri, an old friend from her "Zionist phase." As a seventeen-year-old Israeli girl I was very aware of the inner conflict the meeting provoked in her.

When my relationship to a German gentile student whom I had met at the university in Jerusalem grew closer and seemed to point toward an eventual marriage, Hannah urged my skeptical parents to support the connection. She invited me and my parents to meet her friend Karl Jaspers in Basel. The large, impressive, thoughtful, slow-speaking philosophy professor held an "audience" with each of us and tried to figure out Hannah's motivation for bringing the three of us to this meeting. We were left with the impression that she had done it out of gratitude toward Jaspers, who as a non-Jew had stood by his Jewish wife through the dark times of the European twentieth century. Perhaps this was meant to suggest to my parents that they could trust their daughter to their future son-in-law . . . On this visit to Basel I met Heinrich Blücher, Hannah's second husband, for the first time. It seemed to us "poor country relatives" that he exercised a strong influence on his wife, and he maintained a noticeable distance from us as a Jewish family. His communist background prevented him from coming to terms either with us Jews or with the state of Israel. Although he sometimes joined his wife on her journeys, he never accompanied her to Israel. He always waited for her in Athens. At the same time I was aware of how much he encouraged and promoted—one could even say disciplined—Hannah.

Once I moved to the Federal Republic of Germany in December 1968, I was able to see Hannah regularly each year, either in Munich (where she met her publisher) or in Regensburg, where she visited us, but most frequently in Tegna, a tiny village in Tessin near Locarno (Switzerland), where every year she stayed for three months in the same very idiosyncratically run boarding-house. My husband and I would visit her there regularly, each year meeting different friends of hers who were visiting her at the same time, and we were able to have long, extensive debates about Rudolf Bultmann and other theologians, about Zionism and the state of Israel, about German poetry and its significance in the postwar era. In the course of these discussions I frequently found myself in the role of mediator between Hannah and my parents. She often repeated the criticisms of Israel current among many leftists in Europe and the United States, which were usually based on scant knowledge of the real situation, and this caused tensions that needed to be overcome, because they had been so close to one another since childhood.

We also visited her in 1974 in New York. Naturally it was a significant meeting, since it took place in her new home. The view of the Hudson River from her work desk, an ornate and elegant, narrow, classically European table, was inspiring in itself. The study next door, with its entirely book-lined walls and a picture of her friend Heidenreich directly above the door, was obviously her refuge from the world.

Our last meeting took place in 1975. She arrived in Marbach to examine and systematize the papers of Karl Jaspers in the German Literary Archive. We visited her and listened to her on the last evening as if a Prophet of the Hebrew Bible were speaking to us. Only afterward did we understand that her intensive summary of the most diverse experiences and perceptions had been a drawing up of accounts. On the morning of July 5 we brought her to the train station. She was leaving for a meeting with Heidegger. As we took our leave from her on the platform, I whispered a question to her: "Do you have to?" The answer rings in my ear to this day: "Fröschlein, some things are stronger than a human being."

Like a great many Jews, she was very conscious of being a Jew without being Jewish in the religious sense. This was apparent on the one hand in her very close relationship to her small family in Israel, and on the other in her circle of friends in New York, which consisted for the most part of Jewish emigrants. This deeply rooted Jewish awareness conditioned her political and historical observations of the reality of her times, as well. She herself described this sensation in a letter to Karl Jaspers: "As far as the Jews are concerned: You are historically correct in everything you say. Nonetheless it is a fact that many Jews are like me entirely independent from Judaism in a religious sense and at the same time Jews. Perhaps that will bring about the end of this people, there's nothing to be done about it. What one can do is only to strive for political conditions that will not make their survival impossible."[1]

Many people, including her gentile friends in New York as well as many of her readers in Europe, were never able really to understand this central aspect of her identity. "I was sitting together with a couple of American friends a few days ago—a history professor, two famous journalists and a woman novelist; all non-Jews with many Jewish friends. They were drawing up an imaginary list of people who could be relied upon in the struggle for civil liberties; suddenly one of them said: Isn't it funny, only Hannah of all those Jews [is] with us."[2]

It is no accident that she first found employment exclusively with Jewish enterprises. From 1941 to 1944 she worked for *Aufbau*—the only German-language Jewish weekly newspaper in the United States, which closed in 2004. In addition to her regular column she also published numerous articles there. From 1944 to 1946 she was the leader of a research team for the Conference on Jewish Relations.[3] From 1946 to 1949 she served as an editorial director at Schocken Press. Later, after many visiting professorships and lecture series at various academic institutions, she was given a full professorship at the University of Chicago in 1963.

Her Relationship to Zionism

After 1933, Paris became the place in which she made lasting contact with many other Jewish emigrants, above all with Walter Benjamin, who remained a friend until his suicide in June 1940. Many refugees from non-French-speaking countries felt themselves generously welcomed in Paris. On account of her Parisian sojourn Arendt confronted her Jewish identity in unprecedented ways. During her time in Paris, she moved from mere theorizing to political action. Looking back during her 1964 television interview with the well-known German journalist Günter Gaus, a talk that has since become famous, she described herself in the following terms: "But now, belonging to Judaism had become my own problem, and my own problem was political. Purely political! I wanted to go into practical work, exclusively and only Jewish work."[4]

In exile in Paris she was active in the Zionist Organization. She understood Zionism as a concrete way of combating rising National Socialism, that is, as a possibility for rescuing Jews and above all children and young people from Europe by sending them to Palestine. In this capacity she accompanied a group of Jewish youths to Jerusalem in 1935 and considered that to be her active contribution to the defense of the Jewish people.

Her relation to Zionism first became ambivalent after she emigrated to the United States. There she came in contact with a large and diverse Jewish community whose Zionist organizations were structured differently from the Zionist groups she had encountered in Germany and France. Looking at the world from New York, Arendt wrote about Europe in 1954:

In the instant in which a war could even conceivably threaten the survival of human beings on earth, the alternative between freedom and death loses its old plausibility. As long as Europe remains divided, it can enjoy the luxury of avoiding the agitated problems of the modern world. It can continue to behave as if the threat to our civilization came from without, as if Europe were menaced by two foreign powers, America and Russia, each of them just as alien to it. Both tendencies, anti-Americanism and neutrality, are in a certain way indications that Europe is not at the moment prepared to confront the consequences

and problems of its own history. . . . If Europe were united, . . . this
escape route would automatically be closed.[5]

Already Arendt was able to write about Europe as if she were anticipating
the enormous political, cultural, economic, technological, and religious
transformations that only began after 1989. In any case, she "thought them
through ahead of time":

> One hundred twenty years ago Europe's image of America was the
> image of Democracy. . . . Today the image of America is called
> Modernity. . . . The central problems of the world today are the polit-
> ical organization of mass society and the political integration of techni-
> cal power. Because of the destructive potential inhabiting these
> problems, Europe is no longer confident that it can find its way in the
> modern world. And so, with the excuse of separating itself from Amer-
> ica, Europe is trying to evade the consequences of its own history. The
> image of America that exists in Europe today may not tell us much
> about the real situation in America or the everyday lives of American
> citizens, but if we are prepared to learn, then it can tell us something
> about the justified anxiety that troubles European spiritual identity and
> the even more profound fears that concern its physical survival.[6]

This sharp analysis earned Arendt great acclaim. But it also provoked
deep emotions, above all fear, which is why her pathbreaking book *The Origins of Totalitarianism* was rejected by the European left (Western as well as
the Eastern) without ever having properly been read. The extent to which
the European left was hampered by its own ideological prejudices has been
remarked upon by Daniel Cohn-Bendit: "Hannah Arendt has been not only
misrecognized, she is also the most ignored political theorist in the Federal
Republic of Germany. This is true above all for the German left. As a political thinker, Hannah Arendt embodies everything the German left did and
does not want to hear."[7]

Eichmann

Not only the book itself, but its provoking subtitle in particular aroused
vehement criticism among Jews. The ambiguity of the expression "the ba-

nality of evil" can easily be misunderstood in the context of the Shoah—
even if Eichmann as a person did make a "banal" impression.

In 1963 Karl Jaspers wrote to Arendt that he had heard from a mutual
friend that "Heinrich [Blücher, Hannah's second husband] had invented the
phrase 'banality of evil' and now regretted that you have to take the heat for
his invention."[8] Ursula Ludz, the German editor of Arendt's writings, drew
my attention to a contribution to this discussion by Elisabeth Young-Bruehl,
author of the well-known first biography of Hannah Arendt in 1982. Young-
Bruehl claims that Arendt wrote a reply to Jaspers on December 29, 1963,
which has not survived but from which she was able to copy extracts. In this
letter Arendt is supposed to have written: "Heinrich did not come up with
the subtitle; he once remarked years ago: Evil is a superficial phenomenon—
and I remembered that in Jerusalem; and that eventually led to the title."[9]

The worldwide controversy unleashed by this book, and in particular the
arguments within the Jewish community about some of its theses, led to the
long silence about her book in Israel. Hannah Arendt and Israel stand in a most
complicated relationship. Even if she was by no means the only one who cast a
critical eye on the political motivations behind the trial of Eichmann, she bore
the brunt of anger. "As a Jew, Hannah Arendt seemed dangerous and problematic because she criticized from within," the historian Steven Aschheim from
the Hebrew University in Jerusalem wrote. He recalled a letter from Gershom
Scholem from 1936, when he still could praise his friend Arendt as a "great
Zionist and extraordinary woman." Aschheim enthusiastically notes that the
taboo around Arendt has now become almost a cult. This 180-degree turn was
related in some way to the change in generations: "Today in Israel Hannah
Arendt is debated with as much subtlety as she herself desired in the foreword
to the Eichmann book. There she considers some of the shortcomings of the
report, writing cautiously about the 'possible banality of evil' and anticipates a
'genuine conflict about the subtitle.' . . . Hannah Arendt is no longer taboo
largely because of the growing pluralism in the interpretation of history."

A full five years after the historians Mosche Zimmermann and Oded Heil-
bronner from the University of Jerusalem had published a Hebrew translation of Hitler's *Mein Kampf* (1995), Hannah Arendt's *Eichmann in Jerusalem*
appeared for the first time in Hebrew (from the Babel Publishing House), but
only on account of private funding.

. . .

It is of crucial—and it seems to me thoroughly relevant—significance that Hannah Arendt's lucid analyses (both political and philosophical) and her diverse observations cannot be reduced to a "theory" or "doctrine." In this she was following—no doubt unconsciously—the Jewish principle of multiplicity, the principle of both/and as opposed to the Western principle of either/or. Unlike most of her colleagues she was of the opinion that an intellectual or a scientific analysis of political systems must always remain open, because political systems, like political regimes, must always be reevaluated in terms of a constantly changing reality. Her clear view of the realities and her shocking courage in adopting even uncomfortable positions is the source of her continuing relevance. Her judgments of most of the political themes of her day were what one would call prophetic, not predictive.

The obverse of this spiritual posture is obvious: openness to constantly changing conditions is inherently contradictory. If neither ideology nor a closed system of thought can provide the framework, then judgments of comparable phenomena can be contradictory at different times. To many of her readers this seemed to be inconsistency. It seems to me rather the ethically inspired framework that the millennia-old Jewish art of survival gave rise to.

So I am grateful to my aunt, Big Hannah, for her guidance toward an openness of thinking that continually attempts to pursue a changing reality. This gratitude I share, so it seems to me, with many of her admirers around the world.

On December 4, 1975, just having turned sixty-nine, Hannah Arendt suffered a second heart attack in New York. The words she once wrote about Rahel Varnhagen, "a German Jewish Woman in the Romantic Age," fit her as well: "[She] remained a Jewish woman and a pariah. Only because she clung to both identities was she able to find a place in the history of European humanity."[10]

Notes

1. Hannah Arendt to Karl Jaspers, September 4, 1947.

2. Hannah Arendt to Kurt Blumenfeld, February 2, 1953.

3. The Conference on Jewish Relations was founded in the mid-1930s by Salo W. Baron and others to combat the antisemitism of the Nazis.

4. "Was bleibt? Es bleibt die Muttersprache. Ein Gespräch mit Günter Gaus," in Adelbert Reif, ed., *Gespräche mit Hannah Arendt*, Serie Piper 1938 (Munich: 1976), pp. 9–34, quotation on p. 22. Recently published in English as "'What Remains? The Language Remains': A Conversation with Günther Gaus," in Jerome Kohn, ed., *Essays in Understanding*, 1930–1954 (New York: 1993), pp. 1–23, quotation on p. 12.

5. Hannah Arendt, "Europa und Amerika," first published in 1954 in English, quoted here from the German translation: *In der Gegenwart, Übungen im politischen Denken II* (Munich, 2000), p. 252. See Karl H. Klein-Rusteberg, "Today's Totalitarian Temptation—The Golden Age, Hannah Arendt and Islamistic Fundamentalism," in Alte Synagoge, ed., *Donnerstagshefte—Über Politik, Kultur, Gesellschaft*, vol. 7, July 2004, pp. 19–32.

6. Arendt, "Europe und Amerika," p. 257. Otto Kallscheuer, "Hannah Arendt eine Linke?" in Alte Synagoge, ed., *Treue als Zeichen der Wahrheit* (Essen: 1997), pp. 121–38.

7. Daniel Cohn-Bendit, Lecture at the 1994 Hannah Arendt Conference in Oldenburg.

8. Karl Jaspers to Hannah Arendt, December 13, 1963.

9. E. Young-Bruehl, "An Unpublished Letter from Hannah Arendt to Karl Jaspers," in *Hannah Arendt Newsletter*, no. 1, April 1999, pp. 51–55.

10. Hannah Arendt, *Rahel Varnhagen. Lebensgeschichte einer deutschen Jüdin aus der Romantik* (Frankfurt: 1974), p. 212.

ACKNOWLEDGMENTS

The first and largest debt of gratitude this volume owes is to Lotte Kohler, who is both Hannah Arendt's closest living friend and the only person I know who can always be relied upon to decipher Arendt's elegant but often bewildering handwriting. The manuscripts of the previously unpublished texts included here, especially those written in Germany and France in the 1930s, are replete with significant and sometimes crucial handwritten annotations and qualifications which, except for Mrs. Kohler, would never have seen the light of day. Under the most difficult circumstances, Lotte Kohler's sheer generosity of spirit and time is unparalleled in my experience, and I want to add that our friendship over many years has been among the greatest privileges of my life.

Edna Brocke, perhaps Hannah Arendt's favorite relative, has given unconditional moral and considerable financial support to the realization of this volume. Dr. Brocke, who is the director of the Alte Synagogue in Essen—no longer a place of worship but one of Germany's most distinguished Jewish cultural institutions—has also contributed an afterword to *The Jewish Writings*. There she charmingly and movingly recalls her famous aunt, from the time she first met her as a child in Israel until shortly before her death, and offers a personal perspective on Arendt's life and thought as a Jew. It is a pleasure to take this opportunity to thank Edna Brocke, whom I have known and admired for more than thirty years.

Dore Ashton, Antonia Grunenberg, Ursula Ludz, and Elisabeth Young-Bruehl—who are also old and cherished friends—have taken time from their pressing teaching, writing, and other commitments to discuss a variety of historical, political, and philosophic issues arising from these Jewish writings. Speaking together with each of them has cast light on the dark and troubled times these writings represent, and my gratitude to them for somehow having accomplished this is unbounded. A number of scholars have written on Hannah Arendt from a specifically Jewish point of view. Among them I want to single out four whose books have influenced and informed my own understanding of Arendt's Jewish experience: Dagmar Barnouw (*Visible Spaces: Hannah Arendt and the German-Jewish Experience*); Richard J. Bernstein (*Hannah Arendt and the Jewish Question*); Martine Leibovici (*Hannah Arendt, une Juive: Expérience, politique et histoire* and *Hannah Arendt et la tradition juive: Le judaïsme à l'épreuve de la sécularisation*); and Idith Zertal (*Israel's Holocaust and the Politics of Nationhood*).

The fine work of the translators of many pages in this volume—principally John Woods, but also James McFarland, who came to the rescue when help was most needed, and in one case Susanna Young-ah Gottlieb, all of whom transformed Arendt's splendidly complex German into sterling English prose; and Catherine Temerson, who undertook the unusual task of translating Arendt's French—is gratefully acknowledged. The articles in French, as well as the one in German on the Gustloff trial, all from the 1930s, are not to be found in Arendt's papers in the Library of Congress. They were found in archives in France, and I thank Michelle de Brudny for her gracious help in searching them out, and also Katrin Tenenbaum. My thanks go to Jessica Reifer for her thoughtful and diligent assistance throughout the preparation of *The Jewish Writings*. Finally, I find myself once again filled with respect for Daniel Frank, the editorial director of Pantheon Books, whose judgment, encouragement, and patience have guided this long, toilsome, but ultimately satisfying work from beginning to end; and I thank Dan's assistant, Fran Bigman, for her consistent helpfulness.   —JK

Numerous teachers, colleagues, and friends made key contributions to my study of Hannah Arendt over the years. I first learned of Arendt while studying Jewish history and the Holocaust from Steven Aschheim and Zeev Mankowitz, now of the Hebrew University. My friend Larry Fenster suggested Arendt as a subject for my senior thesis at the University of California at Santa Cruz. J. Peter Euben and David Biale, my thesis advisers, supported my research into Arendt's Jewish interests, and David continued to guide me through my Ph.D. in Jewish history and culture. In addition to mentoring my writing and teaching in Jewish studies, Murray Baumgarten quickly recognized the importance of Arendt's Jewish writings and encouraged my efforts to republish them once *The Jew as Pariah* was out of print. My coeditor,

Jerome Kohn, and our editor, Dan Frank of Pantheon Books, are due a special acknowledgment for their dedication to this project, which has taken many years to come to fruition. Most of all, I hope that my daughter Kalia (now a freshman at Bard College—serendipitously, the final resting place of Hannah Arendt and Heinrich Blücher, and the location of Arendt's library) and others of her generation find the contents of this volume to be not only a testimony about the past but a source of inspiration for the future.   —RF

INDEX

Index

aristocracy (*cont.*)

"God given" hereditary privileges of, xx–xxi, 99

Jews and, 88–90, 92–93, 97–111

Aristotle, xxvi

Armenian massacre, 491

Armenians, 130

Arnheim (banking house), 82

Arnim, Achim von, 46, 97

Arnim, Bettina von, 317

Arnstein, Baron, 24

Aryans, 69, 214, 217

Asch, Sholem, 404

"Assets of Personality: A Review of *Chaim Weizmann: Statesman, Scientist, Builder of the Jewish Commonwealth*" (Arendt), 402–4

Associated Press (AP), 217

Atlantic Charter, 491

Atlantic City Resolution, 343

Atlit, 159

Aufbau:

HA's articles in, xxii–xxiii, xxxiv, 134–240, 474*n*

"Jewish World" insert in, 149–85, 490–95

"This Means You" column in, xxiii, 149–85

Augustine, Saint, 307–8

forms of love distinguished by, xiii

HA's dissertation on, x, xii–xiii

Auschwitz, 452, 455, 478, 485, 494, 501, 509

Australia, 207, 208

Austria, 77, 82, 139

Hitler's invasion of, 267

Jews in, 78, 79, 81, 84, 267, 317–28

Lueger-Schoener agitation in, 321

theatrical performance in, 320, 322–24

Austria-Hungary, 355

Austrian Edict of Toleration, 83, 117*n.14*

auto-emancipation, 57–58

"Auto-emancipation" (Pinsker), 57–58

Avodah Ivrith (Jewish Labor), 365

Babylonian exile, xlvii

Balfour, Arthur James, Lord, 180, 205

Balfour Declaration, xviii, 58, 125, 136, 180, 183, 204–5, 236, 238, 354, 370, 393, 394, 402, 405, 406, 428, 432

"Balfour Declaration and the Palestine Mandate, The" (Arendt), 204–6

Balzac, Honoré de, 141, 274

bankruptcy, 83

baptism, 9, 22, 23, 28, 69, 94, 110, 131

barbarism, 17*n.8*, 44, 61, 66–67

medieval, xx, 50, 66

worldlessness and, li

Bar-Kochba unit, 223

Bauer, Bruno, 70

Bavaria, 79, 114*n.1*, 116*n.5*

Bedouins, 433

Beer-Hofmann, Richard, 324

Beethoven, Ludwig van, 322, 493

Begin, Menachem, 417, 419

Beirut, 412

Belgium, 234, 260

Belzec, 455

Ben-Ami, Y., 148

Benda, Julien, 187

Ben-Gurion, David, 228, 231, 232, 343, 351, 390, 408, 428, 466, 508

Benjamin, Walter, xliii, 465, 517

Berek-Yeselevitch unit, 223

Bergon group, 208*n*, 209–10

Berlin, 170

Adass Jisroel Congregation in, 21

Brandenburg Gate, 168

HA in, xvii

Jewish schools in, 21

Jews in, 21, 83–84, 90, 91, 97, 162, 163, 175

Karstadt's department store in, 269

Berliner Zeitung, 40

Bermuda Conference, 212

Bernadotte, Folke, xxv–xxvi, xxxiv, 408–13, 415, 427–28

assassination of, 408, 413

Bernanos, Georges, 188–89

Index

Index

Index